CHRYSLER FULL-SIZE VANS 1989-98 REPAIR MANUAL

CHILTON'S™

CEO	Rick Van Dalen
President	Dean F. Morgantini, S.A.E.
Vice President–Finance	Barry L. Beck
Vice President–Sales	Glenn D. Potere
Executive Editor	Kevin M. G. Maher, A.S.E.
Manager–Consumer Automotive	Richard Schwartz, A.S.E.
Manager–Professional Automotive	Richard J. Rivele
Manager–Marine/Recreation	James R. Marotta, A.S.E.
Production Specialists	Brian Hollingsworth, Melinda Possinger
Project Managers	Thomas A. Mellon, A.S.E., S.A.E., Eric Michael Mihalyi, A.S.E., S.T.S., S.A.E., Christine L. Sheeky, S.A.E., Richard T. Smith, Ron Webb
Schematics Editors	Christopher G. Ritchie, A.S.E., S.A.E., S.T.S., Stephanie A. Spunt
Editor	James R. Marotta, A.S.E., S.T.S. Eric Michael Mihalyi, A.S.E., S.A.E., S.T.S.

CHILTON™ Automotive Books

PUBLISHED BY **W. G. NICHOLS, INC.**

Manufactured in USA
© 1998 W. G. Nichols, Inc.
1025 Andrew Drive
West Chester, PA 19380
ISBN 0-8019-8966-3
Library of Congress Catalog Card No. 98-71357
3456789012 9876543210

Contents

Contents

DRIVE TRAIN   **7**

SUSPENSION AND STEERING   **8**

BRAKES   **9**

BODY AND TRIM   **10**

GLOSSARY

MASTER INDEX

See last page for information on additional titles

SAFETY NOTICE

Proper service and repair procedures are vital to the safe, reliable operation of all motor vehicles, as well as the personal safety of those performing repairs. This manual outlines procedures for servicing and repairing vehicles using safe, effective methods. The procedures contain ma NOTES, CAUTIONS and WARNINGS which should be followed, along with standard procedures to eliminate the possibility of personal injury o improper service which could damage the vehicle or compromise its safety.

It is important to note that repair procedures and techniques, tools and parts for servicing motor vehicles, as well as the skill and experience the individual performing the work vary widely. It is not possible to anticipate all of the conceivable ways or conditions under which vehicles ma be serviced, or to provide cautions as to all possible hazards that may result. Standard and accepted safety precautions and equipment should b used when handling toxic or flammable fluids, and safety goggles or other protection should be used during cutting, grinding, chiseling, prying or any other process that can cause material removal or projectiles.

Some procedures require the use of tools specially designed for a specific purpose. Before substituting another tool or procedure, you must completely satisfied that neither your personal safety, nor the performance of the vehicle will be endangered.

Although information in this manual is based on industry sources and is complete as possible at the time of publication, the possibility exist that some car manufacturers made later changes which could not be included here. While striving for total accuracy, Nichols Publishing cannot assume responsibility for any errors, changes or omissions that may occur in the compilation of this data.

PART NUMBERS

Part numbers listed in this reference are not recommendations by Nichols Publishing for any product brand name. They are references that ca be used with interchange manuals and aftermarket supplier catalogs to locate each brand supplier's discrete part number.

SPECIAL TOOLS

Special tools are recommended by the vehicle manufacturer to perform their specific job. Use has been kept to a minimum, but where absolutely necessary, they are referred to in the text by the part number of the tool manufacturer. These tools can be purchased, under the appropriate part number, from your local dealer or regional distributor, or an equivalent tool can be purchased locally from a tool supplier or parts out let. Before substituting any tool for the one recommended, read the SAFETY NOTICE at the top of this page.

ACKNOWLEDGMENTS

Nichols Publishing expresses appreciation to Chrysler Corporation for their generous assistance.

Nichols Publishing would like to express thanks to all of the fine companies who participate in the production of our books:
- Hand tools supplied by Craftsman are used during all phases of our vehicle teardown and photography.
- Many of the fine specialty tools used in our procedures were provided courtesy of Lisle Corporation.
- Lincoln Automotive Products (1 Lincoln Way, St. Louis, MO 63120) has provided their industrial shop equipment, including jacks (engine transmission and floor), engine stands, fluid and lubrication tools, as well as shop presses.
- Rotary Lifts (1-800-640-5438 or www.Rotary-Lift.com), the largest automobile lift manufacturer in the world, offering the biggest variety o surface and in-ground lifts available, has fulfilled our shop's lift needs.
- Much of our shop's electronic testing equipment was supplied by Universal Enterprises Inc. (UEI).
- Safety-Kleen Systems Inc. has provided parts cleaning stations and assistance with environmentally sound disposal of residual wastes.
- United Gilsonite Laboratories (UGL), manufacturer of Drylok® concrete floor paint, has provided materials and expertise for the coating an protection of our shop floor.

1

GENERAL INFORMATION AND MAINTENANCE

HOW TO USE THIS BOOK

Chilton's Total Car Care manual for the 1989–98 Chrysler Full Size Vans is intended to help you learn more about the inner workings of your vehicle while saving you money on its upkeep and operation.

The beginning of the book will likely be referred to the most, since that is where you will find information for maintenance and tune-up. The other sections deal with the more complex systems of your vehicle. Operating systems from engine through brakes are covered to the extent that the average do-it-yourselfer becomes mechanically involved. This book will not explain such things as rebuilding a differential for the simple reason that the expertise required and the investment in special tools make this task uneconomical. It will, however, give you detailed instructions to help you change your own brake pads and shoes, replace spark plugs, and perform many more jobs that can save you money, give you personal satisfaction and help you avoid expensive problems.

A secondary purpose of this book is a reference for owners who want to understand their vehicle and/or their mechanics better. In this case, no tools at all are required.

Where to Begin

Before removing any bolts, read through the entire procedure. This will give you the overall view of what tools and supplies will be required. There is nothing more frustrating than having to walk to the bus stop on Monday morning because you were short one bolt on Sunday afternoon. So read ahead and plan ahead. Each operation should be approached logically and all procedures thoroughly understood before attempting any work.

All sections contain adjustments, maintenance, removal and installation procedures, and in some cases, repair or overhaul procedures. When repair is not considered practical, we tell you how to remove the part and then how to install the new or rebuilt replacement. In this way, you at least save the labor costs. Backyard repair of some components is just not practical.

Avoiding Trouble

Many procedures in this book require you to "label and disconnect . . ." a group of lines, hoses or wires. Don't be lulled into thinking you can remember where everything goes—you won't. If you hook up vacuum or fuel lines incorrectly, the vehicle will run poorly, if at all. If you hook up electrical wiring incorrectly, you may instantly learn a very expensive lesson.

You don't need to know the official or engineering name for each hose or line. A piece of masking tape on the hose and a piece on its fitting will allow you to assign your own label such as the letter A or a short name. As long as you remember your own code, the lines can be reconnected by matching similar letters or names. Do remember that tape will dissolve in gasoline or other fluids; if a component is to be washed or cleaned, use another method of identification. A permanent felt-tipped marker can be very handy for marking metal parts. Remove any tape or paper labels after assembly.

Maintenance or Repair?

It's necessary to mention the difference between maintenance and repair. Maintenance includes routine inspections, adjustments, and replacement of parts which show signs of normal wear. Maintenance compensates for wear or deterioration. Repair implies that something has broken or is not working. A need for repair is often caused by lack of maintenance. Example: draining and refilling the automatic transmission fluid is maintenance recommended by the manufacturer at specific mileage intervals. Failure to do this can ruin the transmission, requiring very expensive repairs. While no maintenance program can prevent items from breaking or wearing out, a general rule can be stated: MAINTENANCE IS CHEAPER THAN REPAIR.

Two basic mechanic's rules should be mentioned here. First, whenever the left side of the vehicle or engine is referred to, it is meant to specify the driver's side. Conversely, the right side of the vehicle means the passenger's side. Second, most screws and bolts are removed by turning counterclockwise, and tightened by turning clockwise.

Safety is always the most important rule. Constantly be aware of the dangers involved in working on an automobile and take the proper precautions. See the information in this section regarding SERVICING YOUR VEHICLE SAFELY and the SAFETY NOTICE on the acknowledgment page.

Avoiding the Most Common Mistakes

Pay attention to the instructions provided. There are 3 common mistakes in mechanical work:

1. Incorrect order of assembly, disassembly or adjustment. When taking something apart or putting it together, performing steps in the wrong order usually just costs you extra time; however, it CAN break something. Read the entire procedure before beginning disassembly. Perform everything in the order in which the instructions say you should, even if you can't immediately see a reason for it. When you're taking apart something that is very intricate, you might want to draw a picture of how it looks when assembled at one point in order to make sure you get everything back in its proper position. We will supply exploded views whenever possible. When making adjustments, perform them in the proper order; often, one adjustment affects another, and you cannot expect even satisfactory results unless each adjustment is made only when it cannot be changed by any other.

2. Overtorquing (or undertorquing). While it is more common for overtorquing to cause damage, undertorquing may allow a fastener to vibrate loose causing serious damage. Especially when dealing with aluminum parts, pay attention to torque specifications and utilize a torque wrench in assembly. If a torque figure is not available, remember that if you are using the right tool to perform the job, you will probably not have to strain yourself to get a fastener tight enough. The pitch of most threads is so slight that the tension you put on the wrench will be multiplied many times in actual force on what you are tightening. A good example of how critical torque is can be seen in the case of spark plug installation, especially where you are putting the plug into an aluminum cylinder head. Too little torque can fail to crush the gasket, causing leakage of combustion gases and consequent overheating of the plug and engine parts. Too much torque can damage the threads or distort the plug, changing the spark gap.

There are many commercial products available for ensuring that fasteners won't come loose, even if they are not torqued just right (a very common brand is Loctite®). If you're worried about getting something together tight enough to hold, but loose enough to avoid mechanical damage during assembly, one of these products might offer substantial insurance. Before choosing a threadlocking compound, read the label on the package and make sure the product is compatible with the materials, fluids, etc. involved.

3. Crossthreading. This occurs when a part such as a bolt is screwed into a nut or casting at the wrong angle and forced. Crossthreading is more likely to occur if access is difficult. It helps to clean and lubricate fasteners, then to start threading with the part to be installed positioned straight in. Then, start the bolt, spark plug, etc. with your fingers. If you encounter resistance, unscrew the part and start over again at a different angle until it can be inserted and turned several times without much effort. Keep in mind that many parts, especially spark plugs, have tapered threads, so that gentle turning will automatically bring the part you're threading to the proper angle, but only if you don't force it or resist a change in angle. Don't put a wrench on the part until it's been tightened a couple of turns by hand. If you suddenly encounter resistance, and the part has not seated fully, don't force it. Pull it back out to make sure it's clean and threading properly.

Always take your time and be patient; once you have some experience, working on your vehicle may well become an enjoyable hobby.

TOOLS AND EQUIPMENT

▶ **See Figures 1 thru 15**

Naturally, without the proper tools and equipment it is impossible to properly service your vehicle. It would also be virtually impossible to catalog every tool that you would need to perform all of the operations in this book. Of course, It would be unwise for the amateur to rush out and buy an expensive set of tools on the theory that he/she may need one or more of them at some time.

The best approach is to proceed slowly, gathering a good quality set of those tools that are used most frequently. Don't be misled by the low cost of bargain tools. It is far better to spend a little more for better quality. Forged wrenches, 6 or 12-point sockets and fine tooth ratchets are by far preferable to their less expensive counterparts. As any good mechanic can tell you, there are few worse experiences than trying to work on a vehicle with bad tools. Your monetary savings will be far outweighed by frustration and mangled knuckles.

Begin accumulating those tools that are used most frequently: those associated with routine maintenance and tune-up. In addition to the normal assortment of screwdrivers and pliers, you should have the following tools:

- Wrenches/sockets and combination open end/box end wrenches in sizes from ⅛–¾ in. or 3mm–19mm (depending on whether your vehicle uses standard or metric fasteners) and a ¹³⁄₁₆ in. or ⅝ in. spark plug socket (depending on plug type).

➡**If possible, buy various length socket drive extensions. Universal-joint and wobble extensions can be extremely useful, but be careful when using them, as they can change the amount of torque applied to the socket.**

- Jackstands for support.
- Oil filter wrench.
- Spout or funnel for pouring fluids.
- Grease gun for chassis lubrication (unless your vehicle is not equipped with any grease fittings—for details, please refer to information on Fluids and Lubricants, later in this section).
- Hydrometer for checking the battery (unless equipped with a sealed, maintenance-free battery).
- A container for draining oil and other fluids.

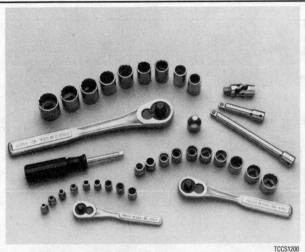

TCCS1200

Fig. 1 All but the most basic procedures will require an assortment of ratchets and sockets

TCCS1202

Fig. 3 A hydraulic floor jack and a set of jackstands are essential for lifting and supporting the vehicle

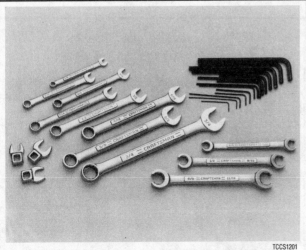

TCCS1201

Fig. 2 In addition to ratchets, a good set of wrenches and hex keys will be necessary

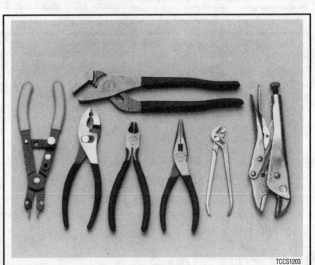

TCCS1203

Fig. 4 An assortment of pliers, grippers and cutters will be handy for old rusted parts and stripped bolt heads

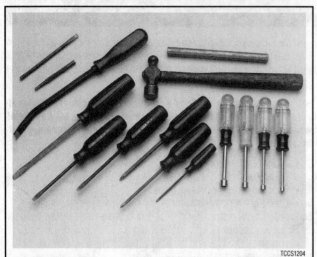

Fig. 5 Various drivers, chisels and prybars are great tools to have in your toolbox

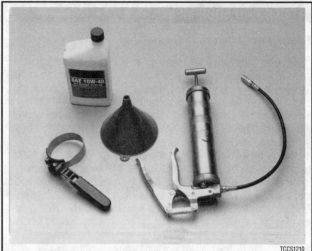

Fig. 8 A few inexpensive lubrication tools will make maintenance easier

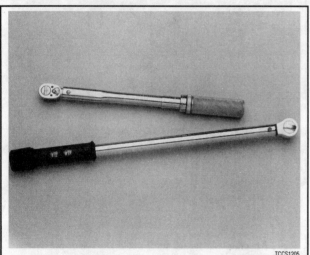

Fig. 6 Many repairs will require the use of a torque wrench to assure the components are properly fastened

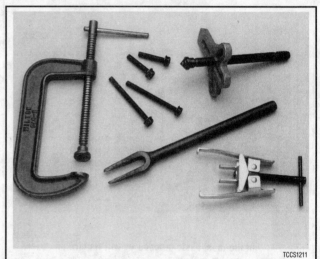

Fig. 9 Various pullers, clamps and separator tools are needed for many larger, more complicated repairs

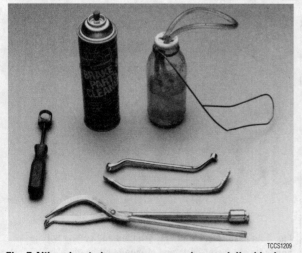

Fig. 7 Although not always necessary, using specialized brake tools will save time

Fig. 10 A variety of tools and gauges should be used for spark plug gapping and installation

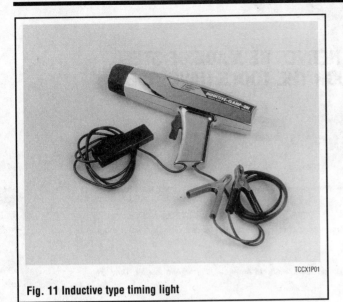

Fig. 11 Inductive type timing light

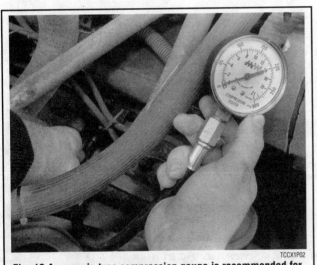

Fig. 12 A screw-in type compression gauge is recommended for compression testing

Fig. 13 A vacuum/pressure tester is necessary for many testing procedures

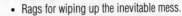

- Rags for wiping up the inevitable mess.

In addition to the above items there are several others that are not absolutely necessary, but handy to have around. These include Oil Dry® (or an equivalent oil absorbent gravel—such as cat litter) and the usual supply of lubricants, antifreeze and fluids, although these can be purchased as needed. This is a basic list for routine maintenance, but only your personal needs and desire can accurately determine your list of tools.

After performing a few projects on the vehicle, you'll be amazed at the other tools and non-tools on your workbench. Some useful household items are: a large turkey baster or siphon, empty coffee cans and ice trays (to store parts), ball of twine, electrical tape for wiring, small rolls of colored tape for

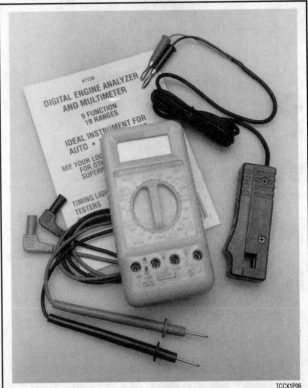

Fig. 14 Most modern automotive multimeters incorporate many helpful features

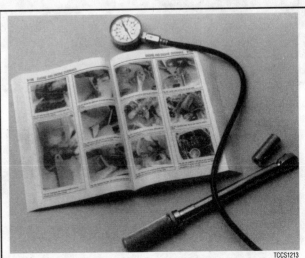

Fig. 15 Proper information is vital, so always have a Chilton Total Car Care manual handy

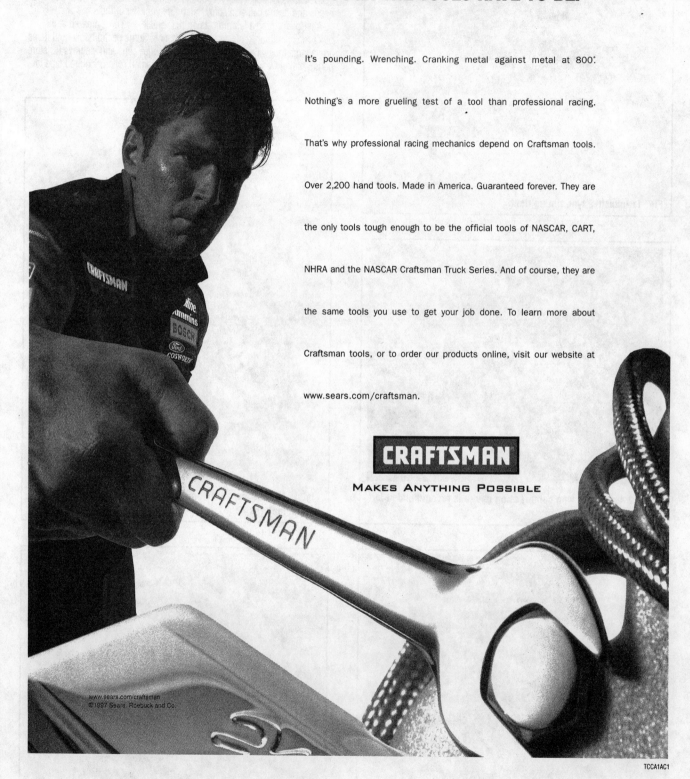

tagging lines or hoses, markers and pens, a note pad, golf tees (for plugging vacuum lines), metal coat hangers or a roll of mechanic's wire (to hold things out of the way), dental pick or similar long, pointed probe, a strong magnet, and a small mirror (to see into recesses and under manifolds).

A more advanced set of tools, suitable for tune-up work, can be drawn up easily. While the tools are slightly more sophisticated, they need not be outrageously expensive. There are several inexpensive tach/dwell meters on the market that are every bit as good for the average mechanic as a professional model. Just be sure that it goes to a least 1200–1500 rpm on the tach scale and that it works on 4, 6 and 8-cylinder engines. (If you have one or more vehicles with a diesel engine, a special tachometer is required since diesels don't use spark plug ignition systems). The key to these purchases is to make them with an eye towards adaptability and wide range. A basic list of tune-up tools could include:

- Tach/dwell meter.
- Spark plug wrench and gapping tool.
- Feeler gauges for valve or point adjustment. (Even if your vehicle does not use points or require valve adjustments, a feeler gauge is helpful for many repair/overhaul procedures).

A tachometer/dwell meter will ensure accurate tune-up work on vehicles without electronic ignition. The choice of a timing light should be made carefully. A light which works on the DC current supplied by the vehicle's battery is the best choice; it should have a xenon tube for brightness. On any vehicle with an electronic ignition system, a timing light with an inductive pickup that clamps around the No. 1 spark plug cable is preferred.

In addition to these basic tools, there are several other tools and gauges you may find useful. These include:

- Compression gauge. The screw-in type is slower to use, but eliminates the possibility of a faulty reading due to escaping pressure.
- Manifold vacuum gauge.
- 12V test light.
- A combination volt/ohmmeter
- Induction Ammeter. This is used for determining whether or not there is current in a wire. These are handy for use if a wire is broken somewhere in a wiring harness.

As a final note, you will probably find a torque wrench necessary for all but the most basic work. The beam type models are perfectly adequate, although the newer click types (breakaway) are easier to use. The click type torque wrenches tend to be more expensive. Also keep in mind that all types of torque wrenches should be periodically checked and/or recalibrated. You will have to decide for yourself which better fits your purpose.

Special Tools

Normally, the use of special factory tools is avoided for repair procedures, since these are not readily available for the do-it-yourself mechanic. When it is possible to perform the job with more commonly available tools, it will be pointed out, but occasionally, a special tool was designed to perform a specific function and should be used. Before substituting another tool, you should be convinced that neither your safety nor the performance of the vehicle will be compromised.

Special tools can usually be purchased from an automotive parts store or from your dealer. In some cases special tools may be available directly from the tool manufacturer.

SERVICING YOUR VEHICLE SAFELY

▶ **See Figures 16, 17, 18 and 19**

It is virtually impossible to anticipate all of the hazards involved with automotive maintenance and service, but care and common sense will prevent most accidents.

The rules of safety for mechanics range from "don't smoke around gasoline," to "use the proper tool(s) for the job." The trick to avoiding injuries is to develop safe work habits and to take every possible precaution.

Do's

- Do keep a fire extinguisher and first aid kit handy.
- Do wear safety glasses or goggles when cutting, drilling, grinding or prying, even if you have 20–20 vision. If you wear glasses for the sake of vision, wear safety goggles over your regular glasses.

- Do shield your eyes whenever you work around the battery. Batteries contain sulfuric acid. In case of contact with the eyes or skin, flush the area with water or a mixture of water and baking soda, then seek immediate medical attention.
- Do use safety stands (jackstands) for any undervehicle service. Jacks are for raising vehicles; jackstands are for making sure the vehicle stays raised until you want it to come down. Whenever the vehicle is raised, block the wheels remaining on the ground and set the parking brake.
- Do use adequate ventilation when working with any chemicals or hazardous materials. Like carbon monoxide, the asbestos dust resulting from some brake lining wear can be hazardous in sufficient quantities.
- Do disconnect the negative battery cable when working on the electrical system. The secondary ignition system contains EXTREMELY HIGH VOLTAGE. In some cases, it can even exceed 50,000 volts.

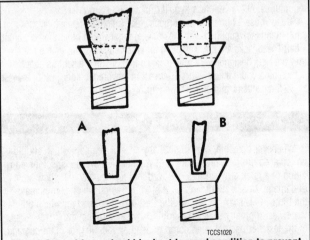

TCCS1020

Fig. 16 Screwdrivers should be kept in good condition to prevent injury or damage which could result if the blade slips from the screw

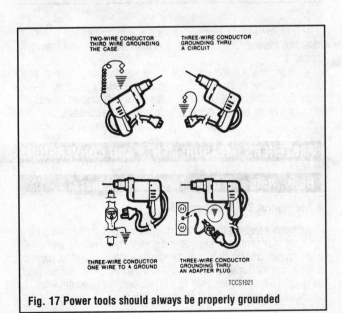

TCCS1021

Fig. 17 Power tools should always be properly grounded

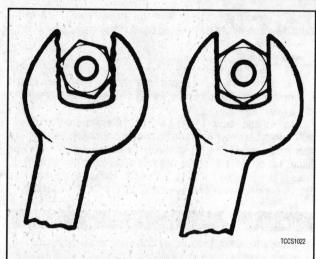

Fig. 18 Using the correct size wrench will help prevent the possibility of rounding off a nut

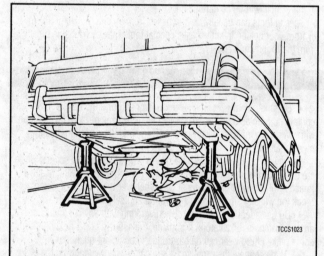

Fig. 19 NEVER work under a vehicle unless it is supported using safety stands (jackstands)

• Do follow manufacturer's directions whenever working with potentially hazardous materials. Most chemicals and fluids are poisonous if taken internally.

• Do properly maintain your tools. Loose hammerheads, mushroomed punches and chisels, frayed or poorly grounded electrical cords, excessively worn screwdrivers, spread wrenches (open end), cracked sockets, slipping ratchets, or faulty droplight sockets can cause accidents.

• Likewise, keep your tools clean; a greasy wrench can slip off a bolt head, ruining the bolt and often harming your knuckles in the process.

• Do use the proper size and type of tool for the job at hand. Do select a wrench or socket that fits the nut or bolt. The wrench or socket should sit straight, not cocked.

• Do, when possible, pull on a wrench handle rather than push on it, and adjust your stance to prevent a fall.

• Do be sure that adjustable wrenches are tightly closed on the nut or bolt and pulled so that the force is on the side of the fixed jaw.

• Do strike squarely with a hammer; avoid glancing blows.

• Do set the parking brake and block the drive wheels if the work requires a running engine.

Don'ts

• Don't run the engine in a garage or anywhere else without proper ventilation—EVER! Carbon monoxide is poisonous; it takes a long time to leave the human body and you can build up a deadly supply of it in your system by simply breathing in a little every day. You may not realize you are slowly poisoning yourself. Always use power vents, windows, fans and/or open the garage door.

• Don't work around moving parts while wearing loose clothing. Short sleeves are much safer than long, loose sleeves. Hard-toed shoes with neoprene soles protect your toes and give a better grip on slippery surfaces. Jewelry such as watches, fancy belt buckles, beads or body adornment of any kind is not safe working around a vehicle. Long hair should be tied back under a hat or cap.

• Don't use pockets for toolboxes. A fall or bump can drive a screwdriver deep into your body. Even a rag hanging from your back pocket can wrap around a spinning shaft or fan.

• Don't smoke when working around gasoline, cleaning solvent or other flammable material.

• Don't smoke when working around the battery. When the battery is being charged, it gives off explosive hydrogen gas.

• Don't use gasoline to wash your hands; there are excellent soaps available. Gasoline contains dangerous additives which can enter the body through a cut or through your pores. Gasoline also removes all the natural oils from the skin so that bone dry hands will suck up oil and grease.

• Don't service the air conditioning system unless you are equipped with the necessary tools and training. When liquid or compressed gas refrigerant is released to atmospheric pressure it will absorb heat from whatever it contacts. This will chill or freeze anything it touches. Although refrigerant is normally non-toxic, R-12 becomes a deadly poisonous gas in the presence of an open flame. One good whiff of the vapors from burning refrigerant can be fatal.

• Don't use screwdrivers for anything other than driving screws! A screwdriver used as an prying tool can snap when you least expect it, causing injuries. At the very least, you'll ruin a good screwdriver.

• Don't use a bumper or emergency jack (that little ratchet, scissors, or pantograph jack supplied with the vehicle) for anything other than changing a flat! These jacks are only intended for emergency use out on the road; they are NOT designed as a maintenance tool. If you are serious about maintaining your vehicle yourself, invest in a hydraulic floor jack of at least a 1½ ton capacity, and at least two sturdy jackstands.

FASTENERS, MEASUREMENTS AND CONVERSIONS

Bolts, Nuts and Other Threaded Retainers

▶ **See Figures 20, 21, 22 and 23**

Although there are a great variety of fasteners found in the modern car or truck, the most commonly used retainer is the threaded fastener (nuts, bolts, screws, studs, etc). Most threaded retainers may be reused, provided that they are not damaged in use or during the repair. Some retainers (such as stretch bolts or torque prevailing nuts) are designed to deform when tightened or in use and should not be reinstalled.

Whenever possible, we will note any special retainers which should be replaced during a procedure. But you should always inspect the condition of a retainer when it is removed and replace any that show signs of damage. Check all threads for rust or corrosion which can increase the torque necessary to achieve the desired clamp load for which that fastener was originally selected. Additionally, be sure that the driver surface of the fastener has not been compromised by rounding or other damage. In some cases a driver surface may become only partially rounded, allowing the driver to catch in only one direction. In many of these occurrences, a fastener may be installed and tightened, but the driver would

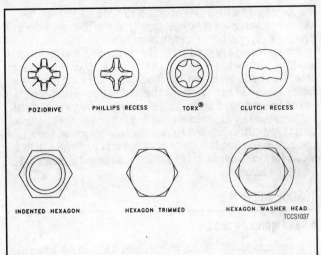

Fig. 20 Here are a few of the most common screw/bolt driver styles

not be able to grip and loosen the fastener again. (This could lead to frustration down the line should that component ever need to be disassembled again).

If you must replace a fastener, whether due to design or damage, you must ALWAYS be sure to use the proper replacement. In all cases, a retainer of the same design, material and strength should be used. Markings on the heads of most bolts will help determine the proper strength of the fastener. The same material, thread and pitch must be selected to assure proper installation and safe operation of the vehicle afterwards.

Thread gauges are available to help measure a bolt or stud's thread. Most automotive and hardware stores keep gauges available to help you select the proper size. In a pinch, you can use another nut or bolt for a thread gauge. If the bolt you are replacing is not too badly damaged, you can select a match by finding another bolt which will thread in its place. If you find a nut which threads properly onto the damaged bolt, then use that nut to help select the replacement bolt. If however, the bolt you are replacing is so badly damaged (broken or drilled out) that its threads cannot be used as a gauge, you might start by looking for another bolt (from the same assembly or a similar location on your vehicle) which will thread into the damaged bolt's mounting. If so, the other bolt can be used to select a nut; the nut can then be used to select the replacement bolt.

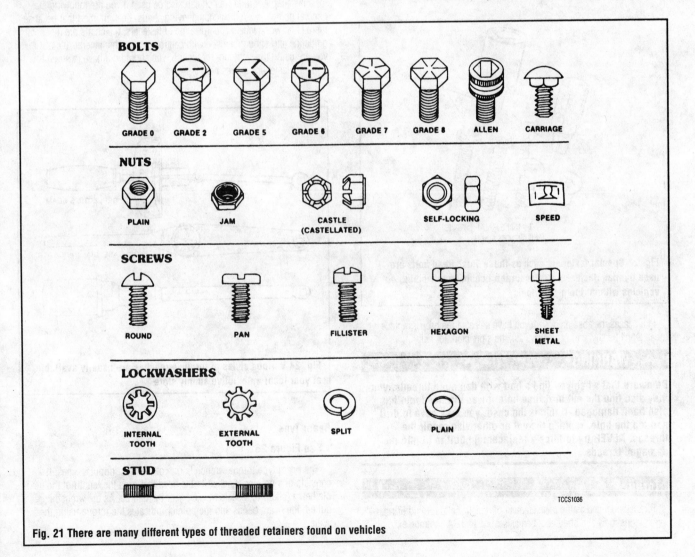

Fig. 21 There are many different types of threaded retainers found on vehicles

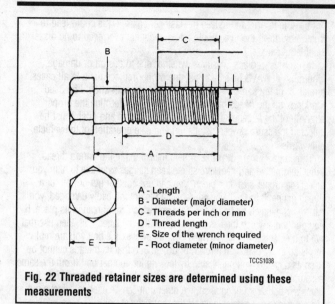

A - Length
B - Diameter (major diameter)
C - Threads per inch or mm
D - Thread length
E - Size of the wrench required
F - Root diameter (minor diameter)

TCCS1038

Fig. 22 Threaded retainer sizes are determined using these measurements

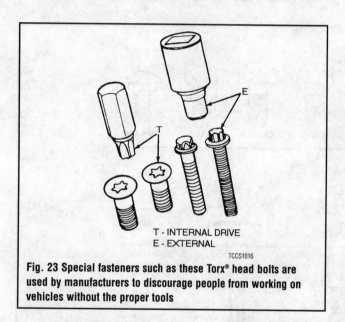

T - INTERNAL DRIVE
E - EXTERNAL

TCCS1016

Fig. 23 Special fasteners such as these Torx® head bolts are used by manufacturers to discourage people from working on vehicles without the proper tools

In all cases, be absolutely sure you have selected the proper replacement. Don't be shy, you can always ask the store clerk for help.

❊❊ WARNING

Be aware that when you find a bolt with damaged threads, you may also find the nut or drilled hole it was threaded into has also been damaged. If this is the case, you may have to drill and tap the hole, replace the nut or otherwise repair the threads. NEVER try to force a replacement bolt to fit into the damaged threads.

Torque

Torque is defined as the measurement of resistance to turning or rotating. It tends to twist a body about an axis of rotation. A common example of

this would be tightening a threaded retainer such as a nut, bolt or screw. Measuring torque is one of the most common ways to help assure that a threaded retainer has been properly fastened.

When tightening a threaded fastener, torque is applied in three distinct areas, the head, the bearing surface and the clamp load. About 50 percent of the measured torque is used in overcoming bearing friction. This is the friction between the bearing surface of the bolt head, screw head or nut face and the base material or washer (the surface on which the fastener is rotating). Approximately 40 percent of the applied torque is used in overcoming thread friction. This leaves only about 10 percent of the applied torque to develop a useful clamp load (the force which holds a joint together). This means that friction can account for as much as 90 percent of the applied torque on a fastener.

TORQUE WRENCHES

♦ See Figures 24 and 25

In most applications, a torque wrench can be used to assure proper installation of a fastener. Torque wrenches come in various designs and most automotive supply stores will carry a variety to suit your needs. A torque wrench should be used any time we supply a specific torque value for a fastener. A torque wrench can also be used if you are following the general guidelines in the accompanying charts. Keep in mind that because there is no worldwide standardization of fasteners, the charts are a general guideline and should be used with caution. Again, the general rule of "if you are using the right tool for the job, you should not have to strain to tighten a fastener" applies here.

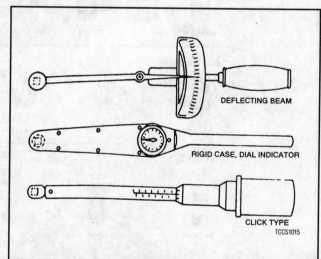

DEFLECTING BEAM

RIGID CASE, DIAL INDICATOR

CLICK TYPE

TCCS1015

Fig. 24 Various styles of torque wrenches are usually available at your local automotive supply store

Beam Type

♦ See Figure 26

The beam type torque wrench is one of the most popular types. It consists of a pointer attached to the head that runs the length of the flexible beam (shaft) to a scale located near the handle. As the wrench is pulled, the beam bends and the pointer indicates the torque using the scale.

Standard Torque Specifications and Fastener Markings

In the absence of specific torques, the following chart can be used as a guide to the maximum safe torque of a particular size/grade of fastener.

- There is no torque difference for fine or coarse threads.
- Torque values are based on clean, dry threads. Reduce the value by 10% if threads are oiled prior to assembly.
- The torque required for aluminum components or fasteners is considerably less.

U.S. Bolts

SAE Grade Number	1 or 2			5			6 or 7		
Number of lines always 2 less than the grade number.	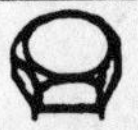			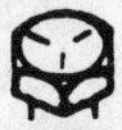			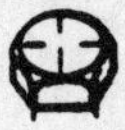		
Bolt Size (Inches)—(Thread)	Ft./Lbs.	Kgm	Nm	Ft./Lbs.	Kgm	Nm	Ft./Lbs.	Kgm	Nm
¼—20	5	0.7	6.8	8	1.1	10.8	10	1.4	13.5
—28	6	0.8	8.1	10	1.4	13.6			
5⁄16—18	11	1.5	14.9	17	2.3	23.0	19	2.6	25.8
—24	13	1.8	17.6	19	2.6	25.7			
3⁄8—16	18	2.5	24.4	31	4.3	42.0	34	4.7	46.0
—24	20	2.75	27.1	35	4.8	47.5			
7⁄16—14	28	3.8	37.0	49	6.8	66.4	55	7.6	74.5
—20	30	4.2	40.7	55	7.6	74.5			
½—13	39	5.4	52.8	75	10.4	101.7	85	11.75	115.2
—20	41	5.7	55.6	85	11.7	115.2			
9⁄16—12	51	7.0	69.2	110	15.2	149.1	120	16.6	162.7
—18	55	7.6	74.5	120	16.6	162.7			
5⁄8—11	83	11.5	112.5	150	20.7	203.3	167	23.0	226.5
—18	95	13.1	128.8	170	23.5	230.5			
¾—10	105	14.5	142.3	270	37.3	366.0	280	38.7	379.6
—16	115	15.9	155.9	295	40.8	400.0			
7⁄8—9	160	22.1	216.9	395	54.6	535.5	440	60.9	596.5
—14	175	24.2	237.2	435	60.1	589.7			
1—8	236	32.5	318.6	590	81.6	799.9	660	91.3	894.8
—14	250	34.6	338.9	660	91.3	849.8			

Metric Bolts

Relative Strength Marking	4.6, 4.8			8.8		
Bolt Markings	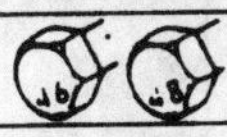			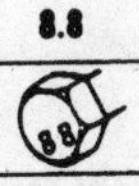		
Bolt Size Thread Size x Pitch (mm)	Ft./Lbs.	Kgm	Nm	Ft./Lbs.	Kgm	Nm
6 x 1.0	2–3	.2–.4	3–4	3–6	4–.8	5–8
8 x 1.25	6–8	.8–1	8–12	9–14	1.2–1.9	13–19
10 x 1.25	12–17	1.5–2.3	16–23	20–29	2.7–4.0	27–39
12 x 1.25	21–32	2.9–4.4	29–43	35–53	4.8–7.3	47–72
14 x 1.5	35–52	4.8–7.1	48–70	57–85	7.8–11.7	77–110
16 x 1.5	51–77	7.0–10.6	67–100	90–120	12.4–16.5	130–160
18 x 1.5	74–110	10.2–15.1	100–150	130–170	17.9–23.4	180–230
20 x 1.5	110–140	15.1–19.3	150–190	190–240	26.2–46.9	160–320
22 x 1.5	150–190	22.0–26.2	200–260	250–320	34.5–44.1	340–430
24 x 1.5	190–240	26.2–46.9	260–320	310–410	42.7–56.5	420–550

TCCS1098

Fig. 25 Standard and metric bolt torque specifications based on bolt strengths

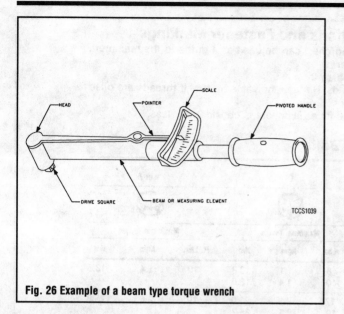

Fig. 26 Example of a beam type torque wrench

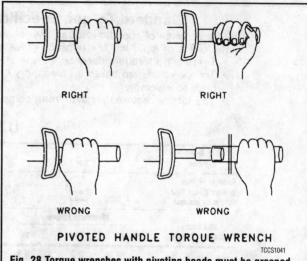

Fig. 28 Torque wrenches with pivoting heads must be grasped and used properly to prevent an incorrect reading

Click (Breakaway) Type

▶ See Figure 27

Another popular design of torque wrench is the click type. To use the click type wrench you pre-adjust it to a torque setting. Once the torque is reached, the wrench has a reflex signaling feature that causes a momentary breakaway of the torque wrench body, sending an impulse to the operator's hand.

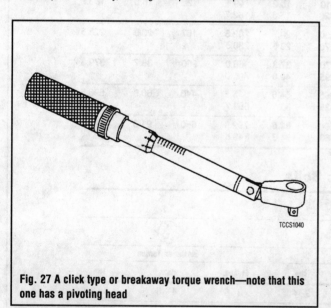

Fig. 27 A click type or breakaway torque wrench—note that this one has a pivoting head

Pivot Head Type

▶ See Figures 27 and 28

Some torque wrenches (usually of the click type) may be equipped with a pivot head which can allow it to be used in areas of limited access. BUT, it must be used properly. To hold a pivot head wrench, grasp the handle lightly, and as you pull on the handle, it should be floated on the pivot point. If the handle comes in contact with the yoke extension during the process of pulling, there is a very good chance the torque readings will be inaccurate because this could alter the wrench loading point. The design of the handle is usually such as to make it inconvenient to deliberately misuse the wrench.

➥ It should be mentioned that the use of any U-joint, wobble or extension will have an effect on the torque readings, no matter what

type of wrench you are using. For the most accurate readings, install the socket directly on the wrench driver. If necessary, straight extensions (which hold a socket directly under the wrench driver) will have the least effect on the torque reading. Avoid any extension that alters the length of the wrench from the handle to the head/driving point (such as a crow's foot). U-joint or wobble extensions can greatly affect the readings; avoid their use at all times.

Rigid Case (Direct Reading)

▶ See Figure 29

A rigid case or direct reading torque wrench is equipped with a dial indicator to show torque values. One advantage of these wrenches is that they can be held at any position on the wrench without affecting accuracy. These wrenches are often preferred because they tend to be compact, easy to read and have a great degree of accuracy.

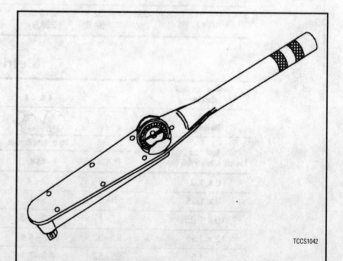

Fig. 29 The rigid case (direct reading) torque wrench uses a dial indicator to show torque

TORQUE ANGLE METERS

▶ See Figure 30

Because the frictional characteristics of each fastener or threaded hole will vary, clamp loads which are based strictly on torque will vary as well. In most applications, this variance is not significant enough to cause worry. But, in certain applications, a manufacturer's engineers may determine that more precise clamp loads are necessary (such is the case with many aluminum cylinder heads). In these cases, a torque angle method of installation would be specified. When installing fasteners which are torque angle tightened, a predetermined seating torque and standard torque wrench are usually used first to remove any compliance from the joint. The fastener is then tightened the specified additional portion of a turn measured in degrees. A torque angle gauge (mechanical protractor) is used for these applications.

Standard and Metric Measurements

♦ See Figure 31

Throughout this manual, specifications are given to help you determine the condition of various components on your vehicle, or to assist you in their installation. Some of the most common measurements include length (in. or cm/mm), torque (ft. lbs., inch lbs. or Nm) and pressure (psi, in. Hg, kPa or mm Hg). In most cases, we strive to provide the proper measurement as determined by the manufacturer's engineers.

Though, in some cases, that value may not be conveniently measured with what is available in your toolbox. Luckily, many of the measuring

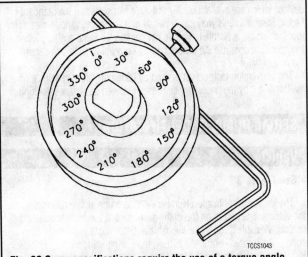

TCCS1043

Fig. 30 Some specifications require the use of a torque angle meter (mechanical protractor)

CONVERSION FACTORS

LENGTH–DISTANCE

Inches (in.)	x 25.4	= Millimeters (mm)	x .0394	= Inches
Feet (ft.)	x .305	= Meters (m)	x 3.281	= Feet
Miles	x 1.609	= Kilometers (km)	x .0621	= Miles

VOLUME

Cubic Inches (in3)	x 16.387	= Cubic Centimeters	x .061	= in3
IMP Pints (IMP pt.)	x .568	= Liters (L)	x 1.76	= IMP pt.
IMP Quarts (IMP qt.)	x 1.137	= Liters (L)	x .88	= IMP qt.
IMP Gallons (IMP gal.)	x 4.546	= Liters (L)	x .22	= IMP gal.
IMP Quarts (IMP qt.)	x 1.201	= US Quarts (US qt.)	x .833	= IMP qt.
IMP Gallons (IMP gal.)	x 1.201	= US Gallons (US gal.)	x .833	= IMP gal.
Fl. Ounces	x 29.573	= Milliliters	x .034	= Ounces
US Pints (US pt.)	x .473	= Liters (L)	x 2.113	= Pints
US Quarts (US qt.)	x .946	= Liters (L)	x 1.057	= Quarts
US Gallons (US gal.)	x 3.785	= Liters (L)	x .264	= Gallons

MASS–WEIGHT

Ounces (oz.)	x 28.35	= Grams (g)	x .035	= Ounces
Pounds (lb.)	x .454	= Kilograms (kg)	x 2.205	= Pounds

PRESSURE

Pounds Per Sq. In. (psi)	x 6.895	= Kilopascals (kPa)	x .145	= psi
Inches of Mercury (Hg)	x .4912	= psi	x 2.036	= Hg
Inches of Mercury (Hg)	x 3.377	= Kilopascals (kPa)	x .2961	= Hg
Inches of Water (H_2O)	x .07355	= Inches of Mercury	x 13.783	= H_2O
Inches of Water (H_2O)	x .03613	= psi	x 27.684	= H_2O
Inches of Water (H_2O)	x .248	= Kilopascals (kPa)	x 4.026	= H_2O

TORQUE

Pounds–Force Inches (in–lb)	x .113	= Newton Meters (N·m)	x 8.85	= in–lb
Pounds–Force Feet (ft–lb)	x 1.356	= Newton Meters (N·m)	x .738	= ft–lb

VELOCITY

Miles Per Hour (MPH)	x 1.609	= Kilometers Per Hour (KPH)	x .621	= MPH

POWER

Horsepower (Hp)	x .745	= Kilowatts	x 1.34	= Horsepower

FUEL CONSUMPTION*

Miles Per Gallon IMP (MPG)	x .354	= Kilometers Per Liter (Km/L)	
Kilometers Per Liter (Km/L)	x 2.352	= IMP MPG	
Miles Per Gallon US (MPG)	x .425	= Kilometers Per Liter (Km/L)	
Kilometers Per Liter (Km/L)	x 2.352	= US MPG	

*It is common to covert from miles per gallon (mpg) to liters/100 kilometers (1/100 km), where mpg (IMP) x 1/100 km = 282 and mpg (US) x 1/100 km = 235.

TEMPERATURE

Degree Fahrenheit (°F)	= (°C x 1.8) + 32
Degree Celsius (°C)	= (°F – 32) x .56

TCCS1044

Fig. 31 Standard and metric conversion factors chart

devices which are available today will have two scales so the Standard or Metric measurements may easily be taken. If any of the various measuring tools which are available to you do not contain the same scale as listed in the specifications, use the accompanying conversion factors to determine the proper value.

The conversion factor chart is used by taking the given specification and multiplying it by the necessary conversion factor. For instance, looking at

the first line, if you have a measurement in inches such as "free-play should be 2 in." but your ruler reads only in millimeters, multiply 2 in. by the conversion factor of 25.4 to get the metric equivalent of 50.8mm. Likewise, if the specification was given only in a Metric measurement, for example in Newton Meters (Nm), then look at the center column first. If the measurement is 100 Nm, multiply it by the conversion factor of 0.738 to get 73.8 ft. lbs.

SERIAL NUMBER IDENTIFICATION

Vehicle

▶ **See Figure 32**

The Vehicle Identification Number (VIN) is found at several locations on the vehicle. The first is on top of the dashboard at the driver's side of the vehicle, viewable through the windshield. Other spots include the body code plate, located behind the battery, the equipment identification plate, located at the left front of the inner hood panel, and the vehicle safety certification label, usually located on the door pillar.

The seventeen-digit vehicle number is composed of an identification number and a six-digit vehicle serial number.

The two most important digits are the eighth and tenth. The eighth digit identifies the engine type. This will be used later in the book to identify the

engines in the specification charts. The tenth digit identifies the model year.

Engine

▶ **See Figures 33, 34 and 35**

On most engines, the engine serial number is stamped into a machined pad located on the left front corner of the cylinder block. On some early model engines, the serial number is stamped into a machined pad located on the right side of the cylinder block, near the oil pan rail.

➡ **It is imperative that the engine type and serial number be used when ordering parts or making inquiries about the engine.**

Fig. 32 The Vehicle Identification Number (VIN) plate is located on the driver's side front corner of the dashboard

89661P10

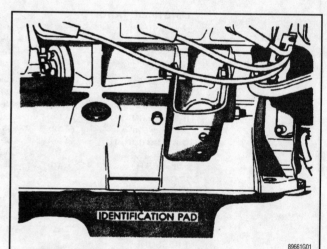

Fig. 33 Some early model engines have the serial number stamped into a machined pad on the right side of the engine, near the oil pan rail

89661G01

VEHICLE IDENTIFICATION CHART

Engine Code						Model Year	
Code	Liters	Cu. In. (cc)	Cyl.	Fuel Sys.	Eng. Mfg.	Code	Year
A	5.9	360 (5899)	V8	MFI	Chrysler	K	1989
W	5.9	360 (5899)	V8	TBI	Chrysler	L	1990
X	3.9	238 (3916)	V6	TBI/MFI	Chrysler	M	1991
Y	5.2	318 (5211)	V8	TBI/MFI	Chrysler	N	1992
Z	5.9	360 (5899)	V8	TBI/MFI	Chrysler	P	1993
						R	1994
						S	1995
						T	1996
						V	1997
						W	1998

MFI - Multi-port fuel injection

TBI - Throttle body fuel injection

89661C01

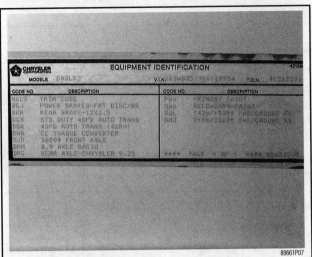

Fig. 34 An equipment identification label is located under the hood, and contains a listing of factory option codes

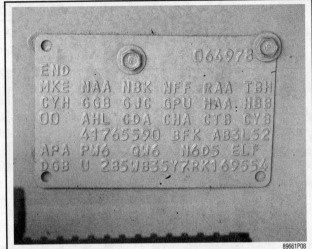

Fig. 35 A build plate, located on the firewall, was used by assembly line workers to determine which equipment to install

GENERAL ENGINE SPECIFICATIONS

Year	Engine ID/VIN	Engine Displacement Liters (cc)	Fuel System Type	Net Horsepower @ rpm	Net Torque @ rpm (ft. lbs.)	Bore x Stroke (in.)	Compression Ratio	Oil Pressure @ rpm
1989	X	3.9 (3916)	TBI	125@4000	195@2000	3.91x3.31	9.0:1	30-80@3000
	Y	5.2 (5211)	TBI	170@4000	260@2000	3.91x3.31	9.0:1	30-80@3000
	W	5.9 (5899)	TBI	185@4000	283@1600	4.00x3.58	8.1:1	30-80@3000
1990	X	3.9 (3916)	TBI	125@4000	195@2000	3.91x3.31	9.0:1	30-80@3000
	Y	5.2 (5211)	TBI	170@4000	260@2000	3.91x3.31	9.0:1	30-80@3000
	W	5.9 (5899)	TBI	185@4000	283@1600	4.00x3.58	8.1:1	30-80@3000
1991	X	3.9 (3916)	TBI	125@4000	195@2000	3.91x3.31	9.1:1	30-80@3000
	Y	5.2 (5211)	TBI	170@4000	260@2000	3.91x3.31	9.2:1	30-80@3000
	W	5.9 (5899)	TBI	190@4000	292@2400	4.00x3.58	8.1:1	30-80@3000
1992	X	3.9 (3916)	MFI	175@4800	220@3200	3.91x3.31	9.1:1	30-80@3000
	Y	5.2 (5211)	MFI	170@4000	260@2000	3.91x3.31	9.2:1	30-80@3000
	Z	5.9 (5899)	TBI	193@4000	292@2500	4.00x3.58	8.1:1	30-80@3000
1993	X	3.9 (3916)	MFI	175@4800	220@3200	3.91x3.31	9.1:1	30-80@3000
	Y	5.2 (5211)	MFI	230@4800	280@3200	3.91x3.31	9.1:1	30-80@3000
	Z	5.9 (5899)	MFI	230@4000	325@2500	4.00x3.58	8.9:1	30-80@3000
1994	A	5.9 (5899)	MFI	230@4000	330@3200	4.00x3.58	8.9:1	30-80@3000
	X	3.9 (3916)	MFI	175@4800	220@3200	3.91x3.31	9.1:1	30-80@3000
	Y	5.2 (5211)	MFI	220@4400	300@3200	3.91x3.31	9.1:1	30-80@3000
1995	X	3.9 (3916)	MFI	175@4800	220@3200	3.91x3.31	9.1:1	30-80@3000
	Y	5.2 (5211)	MFI	220@4400	300@3200	3.91x3.31	9.1:1	30-80@3000
	Z	5.9 (5899)	MFI	230@4000	330@3200	4.00x3.58	8.9:1	30-80@3000
1996	X	3.9 (3916)	MFI	175@4800	220@3200	3.91x3.31	9.1:1	30-80@3000
	Y	5.2 (5211)	MFI	220@4400	300@3200	3.91x3.31	9.1:1	30-80@3000
	Z	5.9 (5899)	MFI	230@4000	330@3250	4.00x3.58	9.1:1	30-80@3000
1997	X	3.9 (3916)	MFI	175@4800	220@3200	3.91x3.31	9.1:1	30-80@3000
	Y	5.2 (5211)	MFI	220@4400	300@3200	3.91x3.31	9.1:1	30-80@3000
	Z	5.9 (5899)	MFI	230@4000	330@3250	4.00x3.58	9.1:1	30-80@3000
1998	X	3.9 (3916)	MFI	175@4800	220@3200	3.91x3.31	9.1:1	30-80@3000
	Y	5.2 (5211)	MFI	220@4400	300@3200	3.91x3.31	9.1:1	30-80@3000
	Z	5.9 (5899)	MFI	230@4000	330@3250	4.00x3.58	9.1:1	30-80@3000

TBI - Throttle body fuel injection
MFI - Multi-port fuel injection

ENGINE IDENTIFICATION

Year	Model	Engine Displacement Liters (cc)	Engine Series (ID/VIN)	Fuel System	No. of Cylinders	Engine Type
1989	B150 Van	3.9 (3916)	X	TBI	6	OHV
	B150 Van	5.2 (5211)	Y	TBI	8	OHV
	B250 Van	3.9 (3916)	X	TBI	6	OHV
	B250 Van	5.2 (5211)	Y	TBI	8	OHV
	B250 Van	5.9 (5899)	W	TBI	8	OHV
	B350 Van	5.2 (5211)	Y	TBI	8	OHV
	B350 Van	5.9 (5899)	W	TBI	8	OHV
1990	B150 Van	3.9 (3916)	X	TBI	6	OHV
	B150 Van	5.2 (5211)	Y	TBI	8	OHV
	B250 Van	3.9 (3916)	X	TBI	6	OHV
	B250 Van	5.2 (5211)	Y	TBI	8	OHV
	B250 Van	5.9 (5899)	W	TBI	8	OHV
	B350 Van	5.2 (5211)	Y	TBI	8	OHV
	B350 Van	5.9 (5899)	W	TBI	8	OHV
1991	B150 Van	3.9 (3916)	X	TBI	6	OHV
	B150 Van	5.2 (5211)	Y	TBI	8	OHV
	B250 Van	3.9 (3916)	X	TBI	6	OHV
	B250 Van	5.2 (5211)	Y	TBI	8	OHV
	B250 Van	5.9 (5899)	W	TBI	8	OHV
	B350 Van	5.2 (5211)	Y	TBI	8	OHV
	B350 Van	5.9 (5899)	W	TBI	8	OHV
1992	B150 Van	3.9 (3916)	X	MFI	6	OHV
	B150 Van	5.2 (5211)	Y	MFI	8	OHV
	B250 Van	3.9 (3916)	X	MFI	6	OHV
	B250 Van	5.2 (5211)	Y	MFI	8	OHV
	B250 Van	5.9 (5899)	Z	TBI	8	OHV
	B350 Van	5.2 (5211)	Y	MFI	8	OHV
	B350 Van	5.9 (5899)	Z	TBI	8	OHV
1993	B150 Van	3.9 (3916)	X	MFI	6	OHV
	B150 Van	5.2 (5211)	Y	MFI	8	OHV
	B250 Van	3.9 (3916)	X	MFI	6	OHV
	B250 Van	5.2 (5211)	Y	MFI	8	OHV
	B250 Van	5.9 (5899)	Z	MFI	8	OHV
	B350 Van	5.2 (5211)	Y	MFI	8	OHV
	B350 Van	5.9 (5899)	Z	MFI	8	OHV
1994	B150 Van	3.9 (3916)	X	MFI	6	OHV
	B150 Van	5.2 (5211)	Y	MFI	8	OHV
	B250 Van	3.9 (3916)	X	MFI	6	OHV
	B250 Van	5.2 (5211)	Y	MFI	8	OHV
	B250 Van	5.9 (5899)	A	MFI	8	OHV
	B350 Van	5.2 (5211)	Y	MFI	8	OHV
	B350 Van	5.9 (5899)	A	MFI	8	OHV
1995	B150 Van	3.9 (3916)	X	MFI	6	OHV
	B150 Van	5.2 (5211)	Y	MFI	8	OHV
	B250 Van	3.9 (3916)	X	MFI	6	OHV
	B250 Van	5.2 (5211)	Y	MFI	8	OHV

ENGINE IDENTIFICATION

Year	Model	Engine Displacement Liters (cc)	Engine Series (ID/VIN)	Fuel System	No. of Cylinders	Engine Type
1995	B250 Van	5.9 (5899)	Z	MFI	8	OHV
	B350 Van	5.2 (5211)	Y	MFI	8	OHV
	B350 Van	5.9 (5899)	Z	MFI	8	OHV
1996	B1500 Van	3.9 (3916)	X	MFI	6	OHV
	B1500 Van	5.2 (5211)	Y	MFI	8	OHV
	B2500 Van	3.9 (3916)	X	MFI	6	OHV
	B2500 Van	5.2 (5211)	Y	MFI	8	OHV
	B2500 Van	5.9 (5899)	Z	MFI	8	OHV
	B3500 Van	5.2 (5211)	Y	MFI	8	OHV
	B3500 Van	5.9 (5899)	Z	MFI	8	OHV
1997	B1500 Van	3.9 (3916)	X	MFI	6	OHV
	B1500 Van	5.2 (5211)	Y	MFI	8	OHV
	B2500 Van	3.9 (3916)	X	MFI	6	OHV
	B2500 Van	5.2 (5211)	Y	MFI	8	OHV
	B2500 Van	5.9 (5899)	Z	MFI	8	OHV
	B3500 Van	5.2 (5211)	Y	MFI	8	OHV
	B3500 Van	5.9 (5899)	Z	MFI	8	OHV
1998	B1500 Van	3.9 (3916)	X	MFI	6	OHV
	B1500 Van	5.2 (5211)	Y	MFI	8	OHV
	B2500 Van	3.9 (3916)	X	MFI	6	OHV
	B2500 Van	5.2 (5211)	Y	MFI	8	OHV
	B2500 Van	5.9 (5899)	Z	MFI	8	OHV
	B3500 Van	5.2 (5211)	Y	MFI	8	OHV
	B3500 Van	5.9 (5899)	Z	MFI	8	OHV

TBI - Throttle body fuel injection
MFI - Multi-port fuel injection
OHV - Overhead valve

89661C03

Transmission

▶ **See Figures 36, 37 and 38**

The automatic transmission identification number is stamped into a pad located on the driver's side of the transmission, just above the oil pan rail. The number includes a ten-digit part number, a four-digit build date and a four-digit serial number.

The NP-2500 manual transmission identification plate is attached to the driver's side of the transmission case.

The AX-15 manual transmission identification number is stamped into a pad located on the bottom surface of the gear case. The number starts with a three-digit build, while the remainder of the digits are the serial number.

➡**It is imperative that the transmission serial number be used when ordering parts or making inquiries about the transmission.**

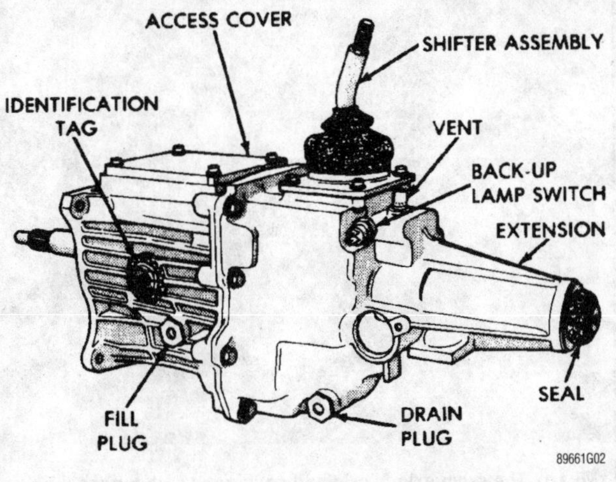

Fig. 36 The NP-2500 manual transmission identification plate is attached to the driver's side of the transmission case

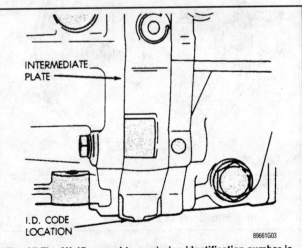

Fig. 37 The AX-15 manual transmission identification number is stamped into a pad located on the bottom surface of the gear case

Fig. 38 Automatic transmission identification number located on the side of the transmission pan rail

Fig. 40 Differential cover for 9¼ inch axle

Drive Axle

▶ **See Figures 39, 40, 41 and 42**

Drive axles are traditionally identified by the shape and number of bolts attaching the rear cover. The drive axle is originally equipped with a gear ratio identification tag attached to the rear cover by one of the cover bolts. However, this tag is easily misplaced and may no longer be attached to the cover.

To identify the rear axle ratio, simply count the number of teeth on the ring gear and divide that number by the number of teeth on the pinion gear.

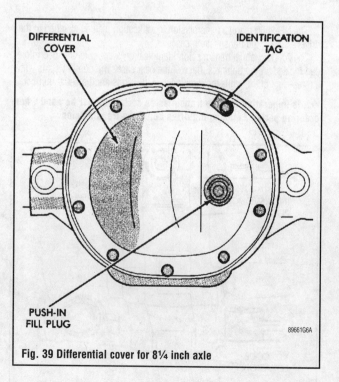

Fig. 39 Differential cover for 8¼ inch axle

Fig. 41 On some gears, the number of teeth on the ring gear and pinion gear are marked

Fig. 42 The drive axle is originally equipped with a gear ratio identification tag attached to the rear cover by one of the cover bolts

UNDERHOOD MAINTENANCE COMPONENT LOCATIONS

1. Oil fill tube
2. Oil dipstick
3. Radiator cap
4. Transmission fluid dipstick
5. Radiator reserve tank
6. Windshield washer solvent
   bottle
7. Brake master cylinder
8. Battery
9. Power steering fluid reservoir

ENGINE COMPARTMENT MAINTENANCE COMPONENT LOCATIONS

1. Air cleaner assembly
2. PCV valve
3. Breather element
4. Spark plug wires
5. Distributor cap
   (rotor underneath)

PASSENGER SIDE OF ENGINE COMPARTMENT COMPONENT LOCATIONS

1. Spark plugs
2. PCV valve
3. Spark plug wires

DRIVER'S SIDE OF ENGINE COMPARTMENT COMPONENT LOCATIONS

1. Spark plug
2. Spark plug wires
3. Oil fill tube
4. Breather element
   port and grommet

Proper maintenance and tune-up is the key to long and trouble-free vehicle life, and the work can yield its own rewards. Studies have shown that a properly tuned and maintained vehicle can achieve better gas mileage than an out-of-tune vehicle. As a conscientious owner and driver, set aside a Saturday morning, say once a month, to check or replace items which could cause major problems later. Keep your own personal log to jot down which services you performed, how much the parts cost you, the date, and the exact odometer reading at the time. Keep all receipts for such items as engine oil and filters, so that they may be referred to in case of related problems or to determine operating expenses. As a do-it-yourselfer, these receipts are the only proof you have that the required maintenance was performed. In the event of a warranty problem, these receipts will be invaluable.

The literature provided with your vehicle when it was originally delivered includes the factory recommended maintenance schedule. If you no longer have this literature, replacement copies are usually available from the dealer. A maintenance schedule is provided later in this section, in case you do not have the factory literature.

Air Cleaner (Element)

REMOVAL & INSTALLATION

▶ See Figures 43, 44 and 45

The air cleaner contains a dry paper element that keeps most dirt and dust from entering the engine. The paper element should be replaced every 30,000 miles (48,000 km).

1. Remove the air intake hose air duct.
2. Unfasten the air cleaner filter cover wing nut and remove the cover.
3. Remove the old filter element.
4. Clean the air box with a dry rag and insert a new filter element.
5. Install the air cleaner filter cover and fasten with the wing nut.
6. Install the air intake hose air duct.

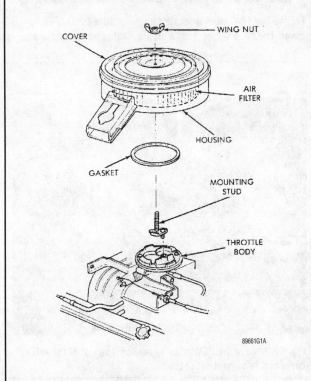

Fig. 43 Typical air cleaner components

Fig. 44 After the air cleaner lid is removed, simply lift the element out of the housing

Fig. 45 This is an example of an extremely neglected air cleaner element. Notice the debris and the dirty filter element

Fuel Filter

The fuel filter is an inline canister type filter secured to the frame rail of the vehicle. On some models, it is connected by special fittings that must be disconnected properly to avoid leaks. See Section 5 for more information.

Although the manufacturer does not recommend a specific replacement interval for the early model fuel filter, we at Chilton recommend that the filter be replaced every 30,000 miles (48,000 km).

The late model fuel filter should only be replaced when the filter becomes clogged and causes a drop in fuel pressure, or when the pressure regulator is faulty.

REMOVAL & INSTALLATION

▶ See Figures 46 and 47

The fuel filter on early model vehicles is located on the frame rail under the vehicle. On late model vehicles, the fuel filter is an integral part of the fuel pressure regulator assembly and cannot be serviced separately.

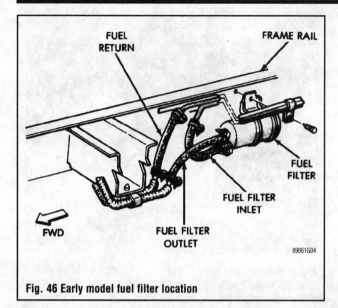

Fig. 46 Early model fuel filter location

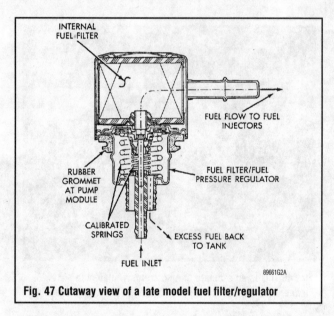

Fig. 47 Cutaway view of a late model fuel filter/regulator

➡This procedure covers the servicing of early model fuel filters only. For late model fuel filters, refer to the Fuel Pressure Regulator procedure in Section 5.

1. Properly relieve the fuel system pressure, as described in Section 5.
2. Disconnect the negative battery cable.
3. Raise and safely support the vehicle on jackstands.
4. Place a pan under the fuel filter to catch any residual fuel that may leak out when the filter is removed.
5. Remove the inlet and outlet connections while holding the fuel lines stationary.
6. Loosen the fuel filter clamp bolt.
7. Remove the filter.
8. Place the new fuel filter into the mounting bracket.
9. Tighten the fuel filter clamp bolt.
10. Connect the fuel inlet and outlet lines to the filter.
11. Connect the negative battery cable.
12. Start the engine and check the filter connections for leaks by running the tip of your finger around each fitting.

PCV Valve

A Positive Crankcase Ventilation (PCV) system is used to prevent pollutants (blow-by gases) from being released into the atmosphere. The PCV system supplies fresh air to the crankcase through the air cleaner. The fresh air mixes with the gases and is passed through the PCV valve to the intake manifold. The gases are then reburned in the combustion process. The PCV system should be inspected every 60,000 miles (96,000 km).

➡For more information on the Positive Crankcase Ventilation (PCV) system, please refer to Section 4 of this manual.

REMOVAL & INSTALLATION

▸ See Figures 48 and 49

1. Disconnect the ventilation hose from the PCV valve.
2. Remove the valve from the valve cover.
3. Inspect the valve cover grommet and replace as necessary.

Fig. 48 The PCV valve is located on the passenger side valve cover. The hose comes from a nipple located on the intake manifold

Fig. 49 Remove the PCV valve by pulling it up out of the valve cover and twisting it out of the hose

4. Install the PCV valve in the valve cover.
5. Connect the ventilation hose to the valve.

Evaporative Canister

The evaporative emission system stores gasoline vapors which rise from the sealed fuel system. The system prevents these unburned hydrocarbons from polluting the atmosphere. It consists of a charcoal vapor storage canister, valves and interconnecting lines. The system should be inspected every 60,000 miles (96,000 km).

➥**For more information on the evaporative emission system, please refer to Section 4 of this manual.**

SERVICING

▶ **See Figure 50**

1. Visually inspect the fuel vapor and vacuum lines for loose connections, sharp bends, distortion, cracks or fuel leakage.
2. Inspect the canister for cracks or damage.
3. Replace components as necessary.

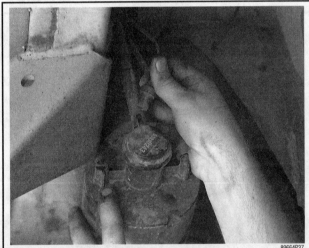

Fig. 50 The evaporative emissions canister is located in the fender well

Battery

PRECAUTIONS

Always use caution when working on or near the battery. Never allow a tool to bridge the gap between the negative and positive battery terminals. Also, be careful not to allow a tool to provide a ground between the positive cable/terminal and any metal component on the vehicle. Either of these conditions will cause a short circuit, leading to sparks and possible personal injury.

Do not smoke, have an open flame or create sparks near a battery; the gases contained in the battery are very explosive and, if ignited, could cause severe injury or death.

All batteries, regardless of type, should be carefully secured by a battery hold-down device. If this is not done, the battery terminals or casing may crack from stress applied to the battery during vehicle operation. A battery which is not secured may allow acid to leak out, making it discharge faster; such leaking corrosive acid can also eat away at components under the hood.

Always visually inspect the battery case for cracks, leakage and corrosion. A white corrosive substance on the battery case or on nearby components would indicate a leaking or cracked battery. If the battery is cracked, it should be replaced immediately.

GENERAL MAINTENANCE

▶ **See Figure 51**

A battery that is not sealed must be checked periodically for electrolyte level. You cannot add water to a sealed maintenance-free battery (though not all maintenance-free batteries are sealed); however, a sealed battery must also be checked for proper electrolyte level, as indicated by the color of the built-in hydrometer "eye."

Always keep the battery cables and terminals free of corrosion. Check these components about once a year. Refer to the removal, installation and cleaning procedures outlined in this section.

Keep the top of the battery clean, as a film of dirt can help completely discharge a battery that is not used for long periods. A solution of baking soda and water may be used for cleaning, but be careful to flush this off with clear water. DO NOT let any of the solution into the filler holes. Baking soda neutralizes battery acid and will de-activate a battery cell.

Batteries in vehicles which are not operated on a regular basis can fall victim to parasitic loads (small current drains which are constantly drawing current from the battery). Normal parasitic loads may drain a battery on a vehicle that is in storage and not used for 6–8 weeks. Vehicles that have additional accessories such as a cellular phone, an alarm system or other devices that increase parasitic load may discharge a battery sooner. If the vehicle is to be stored for 6–8 weeks in a secure area and the alarm system, if present, is not necessary, the negative battery cable should be disconnected at the onset of storage to protect the battery charge.

Remember that constantly discharging and recharging will shorten battery life. Take care not to allow a battery to be needlessly discharged.

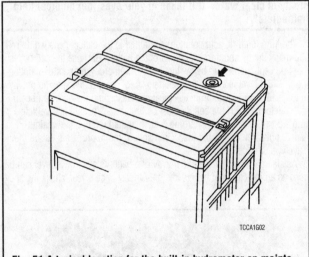

Fig. 51 A typical location for the built-in hydrometer on maintenance-free batteries

BATTERY FLUID

Check the battery electrolyte level at least once a month, or more often in hot weather or during periods of extended vehicle operation. On non-sealed batteries, the level can be checked either through the case on translucent batteries or by removing the cell caps on opaque-cased types. The electrolyte level in each cell should be kept filled to the split ring inside each cell, or the line marked on the outside of the case.

If the level is low, add only distilled water through the opening until the level is correct. Each cell is separate from the others, so each must be checked and filled individually. Distilled water should be used, because the chemicals and minerals found in most drinking water are harmful to the battery and could significantly shorten its life.

If water is added in freezing weather, the vehicle should be driven several miles to allow the water to mix with the electrolyte. Otherwise, the battery could freeze.

Although some maintenance-free batteries have removable cell caps for access to the electrolyte, the electrolyte condition and level on all sealed maintenance-free batteries must be checked using the built-in hydrometer "eye." The exact type of eye varies between battery manufacturers, but most apply a sticker to the battery itself explaining the possible readings. When in doubt, refer to the battery manufacturer's instructions to interpret battery condition using the built-in hydrometer.

➡**Although the readings from built-in hydrometers found in sealed batteries may vary, a green eye usually indicates a properly charged battery with sufficient fluid level. A dark eye is normally an indicator of a battery with sufficient fluid, but one which may be low in charge. And a light or yellow eye is usually an indication that electrolyte supply has dropped below the necessary level for battery (and hydrometer) operation. In this last case, sealed batteries with an insufficient electrolyte level must usually be discarded.**

Checking the Specific Gravity

▶ **See Figures 52, 53 and 54**

A hydrometer is required to check the specific gravity on all batteries that are not maintenance-free. On batteries that are maintenance-free, the specific gravity is checked by observing the built-in hydrometer "eye" on the top of the battery case. Check with your battery's manufacturer for proper interpretation of its built-in hydrometer readings.

✳✳ CAUTION

Battery electrolyte contains sulfuric acid. If you should splash any on your skin or in your eyes, flush the affected area with plenty of clear water. If it lands in your eyes, get medical help immediately.

The fluid (sulfuric acid solution) contained in the battery cells will tell you many things about the condition of the battery. Because the cell plates must be kept submerged below the fluid level in order to operate, maintaining the fluid level is extremely important. And, because the specific gravity of the acid is an indication of electrical charge, testing the fluid can be an aid in determining if the battery must be replaced. A battery in a vehicle with a properly operating charging system should require little maintenance, but careful, periodic inspection should reveal problems before they leave you stranded.

As stated earlier, the specific gravity of a battery's electrolyte level can be used as an indication of battery charge. At least once a year, check the spe-

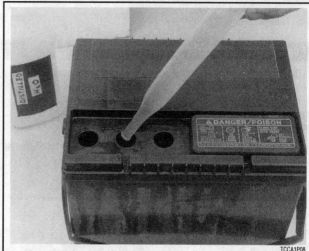
Fig. 53 If the fluid level is low, add only distilled water through the opening until the level is correct

Fig. 54 Check the specific gravity of the battery's electrolyte with a hydrometer

cific gravity of the battery. It should be between 1.20 and 1.26 on the gravity scale. Most auto supply stores carry a variety of inexpensive battery testing hydrometers. These can be used on any non-sealed battery to test the specific gravity in each cell.

The battery testing hydrometer has a squeeze bulb at one end and a nozzle at the other. Battery electrolyte is sucked into the hydrometer until the float is lifted from its seat. The specific gravity is then read by noting the position of the float. If gravity is low in one or more cells, the battery should be slowly charged and checked again to see if the gravity has come up. Generally, if after charging, the specific gravity between any two cells varies more than 50 points (0.50), the battery should be replaced, as it can no longer produce sufficient voltage to guarantee proper operation.

CABLES

▶ **See Figures 55, 56, 57, 58 and 59**

Once a year (or as necessary), the battery terminals and the cable clamps should be cleaned. Loosen the clamps and remove the cables, negative cable first. On batteries with posts on top, the use of a puller specially

Fig. 52 On non-maintenance-free batteries, the fluid level can be checked through the case on translucent models; the cell caps must be removed on other models

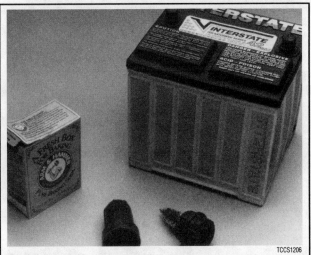

Fig. 55 Maintenance is performed with household items and with special tools like this post cleaner

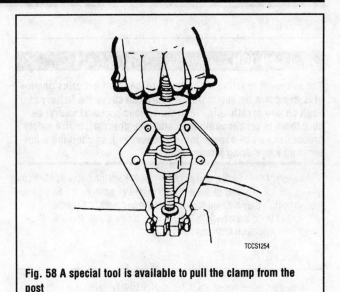

Fig. 58 A special tool is available to pull the clamp from the post

Fig. 56 The underside of this special battery tool has a wire brush to clean post terminals

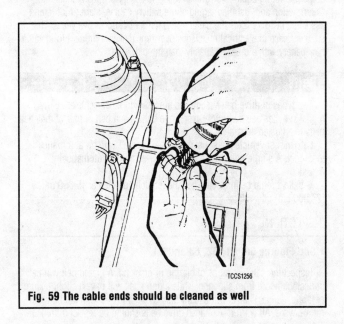

Fig. 59 The cable ends should be cleaned as well

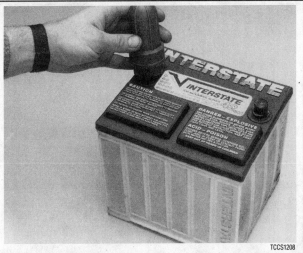

Fig. 57 Place the tool over the battery posts and twist to clean until the metal is shiny

made for this purpose is recommended. These are inexpensive and available in most auto parts stores. Side terminal battery cables are secured with a small bolt.

Clean the cable clamps and the battery terminal with a wire brush, until all corrosion, grease, etc., is removed and the metal is shiny. It is especially important to clean the inside of the clamp thoroughly (an old knife is useful here), since a small deposit of foreign material or oxidation there will prevent a sound electrical connection and inhibit either starting or charging. Special tools are available for cleaning these parts, one type for conventional top post batteries and another type for side terminal batteries. It is also a good idea to apply some dielectric grease to the terminal, as this will aid in the prevention of corrosion.

After the clamps and terminals are clean, reinstall the cables, negative cable last; DO NOT hammer the clamps onto battery posts. Tighten the clamps securely, but do not distort them. Give the clamps and terminals a thin external coating of grease after installation, to retard corrosion.

Check the cables at the same time that the terminals are cleaned. If the cable insulation is cracked or broken, or if the ends are frayed, the cable should be replaced with a new cable of the same length and gauge.

CHARGING

> ⁂ **CAUTION**
>
> **The chemical reaction which takes place in all batteries generates explosive hydrogen gas. A spark can cause the battery to explode and splash acid. To avoid serious personal injury, be sure there is proper ventilation and take appropriate fire safety precautions when connecting, disconnecting, or charging a battery and when using jumper cables.**

A battery should be charged at a slow rate to keep the plates inside from getting too hot. However, if some maintenance-free batteries are allowed to discharge until they are almost "dead," they may have to be charged at a high rate to bring them back to "life." Always follow the charger manufacturer's instructions on charging the battery.

REPLACEMENT

When it becomes necessary to replace the battery, select one with an amperage rating equal to or greater than the battery originally installed. Deterioration and just plain aging of the battery cables, starter motor, and associated wires makes the battery's job harder in successive years. The slow increase in electrical resistance over time makes it prudent to install a new battery with a greater capacity than the old.

Belts

Two types of drive belt assemblies are used on these vehicles. Early model vehicles use multiple V-type drive belts. Each belt or pair of matched belts is adjusted separately.

Late model vehicles use a serpentine drive belt with an automatic tensioner. A single belt drives all accessories and is automatically adjusted.

V-belts should be inspected and the tension adjusted at 15,000 mile (24,000 km) intervals.

INSPECTION

▶ **See Figures 60, 61, 62, 63 and 64**

Inspect the belts for signs of glazing or cracking. A glazed belt will be perfectly smooth from slippage, while a good belt will have a slight texture of fabric visible. Cracks will usually start at the inner edge of the belt and run outward. All worn or damaged drive belts should be replaced immedi-

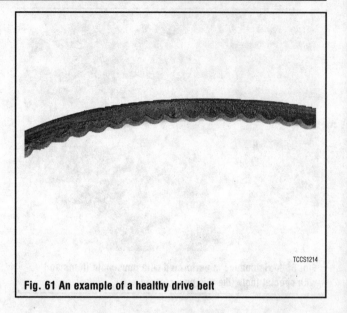
Fig. 61 An example of a healthy drive belt

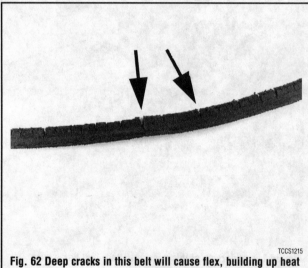
Fig. 62 Deep cracks in this belt will cause flex, building up heat that will eventually lead to belt failure

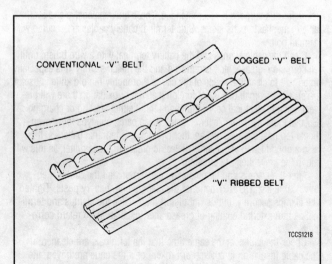
Fig. 60 There are typically 3 types of accessory drive belts found on vehicles today

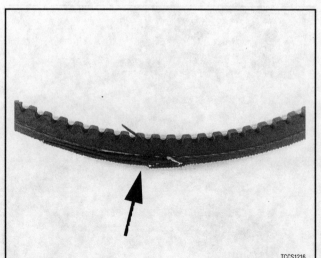
Fig. 63 The cover of this belt is worn, exposing the critical reinforcing cords to excessive wear

Fig. 64 Installing too wide a belt can result in serious belt wear and/or breakage

ately. It is best to replace all drive belts at one time, as a preventive maintenance measure, during this service operation.

REMOVAL & INSTALLATION

➡When installing the serpentine accessory drive belt, the belt must be routed correctly. Engine overheating may occur due to water pump rotating in the wrong direction if the belt is not routed properly.

V-Belts

▶ See Figures 65 and 66

Some vehicles use matched V-belt sets. These matched sets can be identified by looking for two belts of equal length and routing. When replacing matched V-belts, it is important to replace both belts simultaneously with a correct matched set.

➡It may be necessary to remove more than one belt in order to access the desired belt. Always note belt routing for reference upon installation.

1. Loosen the belt tension, as illustrated.
2. Remove belt from engine.
3. Inspect pulleys for damage or wear and replace as necessary.

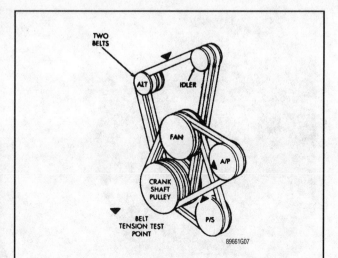

Fig. 65 Belt routing and tensioning guide for vehicles without air conditioning

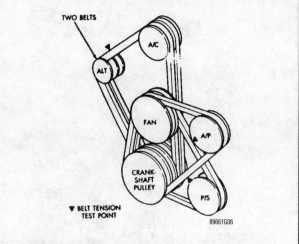

Fig. 66 Belt routing and tensioning guide for vehicles with air conditioning

4. Install belt, routing as illustrated.
5. Ensure that the belt is properly positioned on all pulleys.
6. Adjust belt tension to the proper specification (as measured on a belt tension gauge):
- Adjust new belts to 140 lbs.
- Adjust used belts to 80 lbs.

➡Any belt that has been operating for a minimum of 10 minutes is considered a used belt. In the first 10 minutes, the belt should stretch to its maximum extent. After 10 minutes, stop the engine and recheck the belt tension.

7. If a belt tension gauge is not available, tension may be set by using the following procedure:
  a. Position a ruler perpendicular to the drive belt at its longest straight run.
  b. Test the tightness of the belt by pressing it firmly with your thumb. The deflection should not exceed ¼ in.
  c. If the deflection exceeds ¼ in., loosen the mounting bolts and tighten the adjustment.
  d. When the belt is properly tensioned, tighten the mounting bolts to specification.

Serpentine Belts

▶ See Figures 67 and 68

Serpentine belts use an automatic belt tensioner assembly. Periodic belt tension adjustments are not necessary.

1. Using an appropriately sized wrench, rotate the belt tensioner clockwise to release the tension.
2. Remove the drive belt from the pulleys.
3. When installing the new drive belt, ensure that it is routed correctly and that it is properly installed on each pulley.

Hoses

INSPECTION

▶ See Figures 69, 70, 71 and 72

Upper and lower radiator hoses along with the heater hoses should be checked for deterioration, leaks and loose hose clamps at least every 7,500 miles (12,000 km). It is also wise to check the hoses periodically in early spring and at the beginning of the fall or winter when you are performing other maintenance. A quick visual inspection could discover a weakened hose which might have left you stranded if it had remained unrepaired.

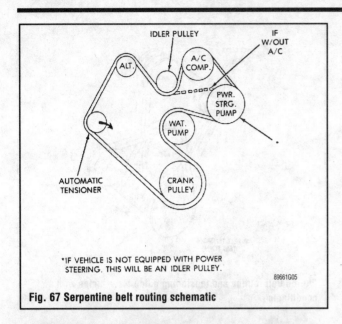

*IF VEHICLE IS NOT EQUIPPED WITH POWER STEERING. THIS WILL BE AN IDLER PULLEY.

Fig. 67 Serpentine belt routing schematic

Fig. 70 A hose clamp that is too tight can cause older hoses to separate and tear on either side of the clamp

Fig. 68 Rotate the tensioner to release the pressure on the belt for removal

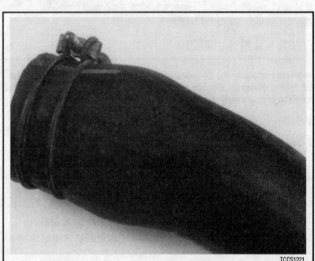

Fig. 71 A soft spongy hose (identifiable by the swollen section) will eventually burst and should be replaced

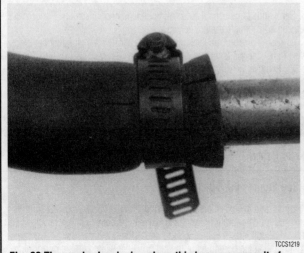

Fig. 69 The cracks developing along this hose are a result of age-related hardening

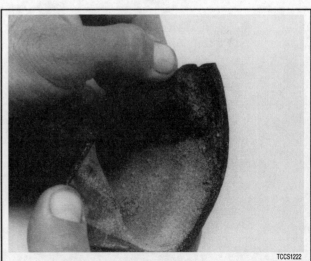

Fig. 72 Hoses are likely to deteriorate from the inside if the cooling system is not periodically flushed

Whenever you are checking the hoses, make sure the engine and cooling system are cold. Visually inspect for cracking, rotting or collapsed hoses, and replace as necessary. Run your hand along the length of the hose. If a weak or swollen spot is noted when squeezing the hose wall, the hose should be replaced.

REMOVAL & INSTALLATION

1. Remove the radiator pressure cap.

※※ CAUTION

Never remove the pressure cap while the engine is running, or personal injury from scalding hot coolant or steam may result. If possible, wait until the engine has cooled to remove the pressure cap. If this is not possible, wrap a thick cloth around the pressure cap and turn it slowly to the stop. Step back while the pressure is released from the cooling system. When you are sure all the pressure has been released, use the cloth to turn and remove the cap.

2. Position a clean container under the radiator and/or engine drain-cock or plug, then open the drain and allow the cooling system to drain to an appropriate level. For some upper hoses, only a little coolant must be drained. To remove hoses positioned lower on the engine, such as a lower radiator hose, the entire cooling system must be emptied.

※※ CAUTION

When draining coolant, keep in mind that cats and dogs are attracted by ethylene glycol antifreeze, and are quite likely to drink any that is left in an uncovered container or in puddles on the ground. This will prove fatal in sufficient quantity. Always drain coolant into a sealable container. Coolant may be reused unless it is contaminated or several years old.

3. Loosen the hose clamps at each end of the hose requiring replacement. Clamps are usually either of the spring tension type (which require pliers to squeeze the tabs and loosen) or of the screw tension type (which require screw or hex drivers to loosen). Pull the clamps back on the hose away from the connection.

4. Twist, pull and slide the hose off the fitting, taking care not to damage the neck of the component from which the hose is being removed.

➡If the hose is stuck at the connection, do not try to insert a screwdriver or other sharp tool under the hose end in an effort to free it, as the connection and/or hose may become damaged. Heater connections especially may be easily damaged by such a procedure. If the hose is to be replaced, use a single-edged razor blade to make a slice along the portion of the hose which is stuck on the connection, perpendicular to the end of the hose. Do not cut deep, so as to prevent damaging the connection. The hose can then be peeled from the connection and discarded.

5. Clean both hose mounting connections. Inspect the condition of the hose clamps and replace them, if necessary.

To install:

6. Dip the ends of the new hose into clean engine coolant to ease installation.

7. Slide the clamps over the replacement hose, then slide the hose ends over the connections into position.

8. Position and secure the clamps at least ¼ in. (6.35mm) from the ends of the hose. Make sure they are located beyond the raised bead of the connector.

9. Close the radiator or engine drains and properly refill the cooling system with the clean drained engine coolant or a suitable mixture of ethylene glycol (or other suitable) coolant and water.

10. If available, install a pressure tester and check for leaks. If a pressure tester is not available, run the engine until normal operating temperature is reached (allowing the system to naturally pressurize), then check for leaks.

※※ CAUTION

If you are checking for leaks with the system at normal operating temperature, BE EXTREMELY CAREFUL not to touch any moving or hot engine parts. Once temperature has been reached, shut the engine OFF, and check for leaks around the hose fittings and connections which were removed earlier.

Spark Plugs

▶ **See Figure 73**

A typical spark plug consists of a metal shell surrounding a ceramic insulator. A metal electrode extends downward through the center of the insulator and protrudes a small distance. Located at the end of the plug and attached to the side of the outer metal shell is the side electrode. The side electrode bends in at a 90° angle so that its tip is just past and parallel to the tip of the center electrode. The distance between these two electrodes (measured in thousandths of an inch or hundredths of a millimeter) is called the spark plug gap.

The spark plug does not produce a spark but instead provides a gap across which the current can arc. The coil produces anywhere from 20,000 to 50,000 volts (depending on the type and application) which travels through the wires to the spark plugs. The current passes along the center electrode and jumps the gap to the side electrode, and in doing so, ignites the air/fuel mixture in the combustion chamber.

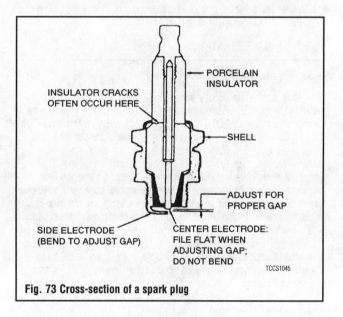

Fig. 73 Cross-section of a spark plug

SPARK PLUG HEAT RANGE

▶ **See Figure 74**

Spark plug heat range is the ability of the plug to dissipate heat. The longer the insulator (or the farther it extends into the engine), the hotter the plug will operate; the shorter the insulator (the closer the electrode is to the block's cooling passages) the cooler it will operate. A plug that absorbs little heat and remains too cool will quickly accumulate deposits of oil and carbon since it is not hot enough to burn them off. This leads to plug fouling and consequently to misfiring. A plug that absorbs too much heat will have no deposits but, due to the excessive heat, the electrodes will burn away quickly and might possibly lead to preignition or other ignition problems. Preignition takes place when plug tips get so hot that they glow sufficiently to ignite the air/fuel mixture before the actual spark occurs. This early ignition will usually cause a pinging during low speeds and heavy loads.

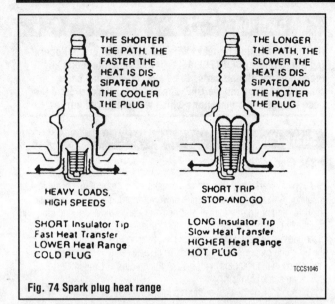

THE SHORTER THE PATH, THE FASTER THE HEAT IS DISSIPATED AND THE COOLER THE PLUG

THE LONGER THE PATH, THE SLOWER THE HEAT IS DISSIPATED AND THE HOTTER THE PLUG

HEAVY LOADS, HIGH SPEEDS

SHORT TRIP STOP-AND-GO

SHORT Insulator Tip
Fast Heat Transfer
LOWER Heat Range
COLD PLUG

LONG Insulator Tip
Slow Heat Transfer
HIGHER Heat Range
HOT PLUG

TCCS1046

Fig. 74 Spark plug heat range

The general rule of thumb for choosing the correct heat range when picking a spark plug is: if most of your driving is long distance, high speed travel, use a colder plug; if most of your driving is stop and go, use a hotter plug. Original equipment plugs are generally a good compromise between the 2 styles and most people never have the need to change their plugs from the factory-recommended heat range.

REMOVAL & INSTALLATION

♦ **See Figures 75, 76, 77 and 78**

A set of spark plugs usually requires replacement after about 30,000 miles (48,000 km), depending on your style of driving. In normal operation plug gap increases about 0.001 in. (0.025mm) for every 2500 miles (4000 km). As the gap increases, the plug's voltage requirement also increases. It requires a greater voltage to jump the wider gap and about two to three times as much voltage to fire the plug at high speeds than at idle. The improved air/fuel ratio control of modern fuel injection combined with the higher voltage output of modern ignition systems will often allow an engine to run significantly longer on a set of standard spark plugs, but keep in mind that efficiency will drop as the gap widens (along with fuel economy and power).

When you're removing spark plugs, work on one at a time. Don't start by removing the plug wires all at once, because, unless you number them, they may become mixed up. Take a minute before you begin and number the wires with tape.

1. Disconnect the negative battery cable, and if the vehicle has been run recently, allow the engine to thoroughly cool.

2. Carefully twist the spark plug wire boot to loosen it, then pull upward and remove the boot from the plug. Be sure to pull on the boot and not on the wire, otherwise the connector located inside the boot may become separated.

3. Using compressed air, blow any water or debris from the spark plug well to assure that no harmful contaminants are allowed to enter the combustion chamber when the spark plug is removed. If compressed air is not available, use a rag or a brush to clean the area.

➡ **Remove the spark plugs when the engine is cold, if possible, to prevent damage to the threads. If removal of the plugs is difficult, apply a few drops of penetrating oil or silicone spray to the area around the base of the plug, and allow it a few minutes to work.**

4. Using a spark plug socket that is equipped with a rubber insert to properly hold the plug, turn the spark plug counterclockwise to loosen and remove the spark plug from the bore.

✳✳ **WARNING**

Be sure not to use a flexible extension on the socket. Use of a flexible extension may allow a shear force to be applied to the plug. A shear force could break the plug off in the cylinder head, leading to costly and frustrating repairs.

To install:

5. Inspect the spark plug boot for tears or damage. If a damaged boot is found, the spark plug wire must be replaced.

6. Using a wire feeler gauge, check and adjust the spark plug gap. When using a gauge, the proper size should pass between the electrodes with a slight drag. The next larger size should not be able to pass while the next smaller size should pass freely.

7. Carefully thread the plug into the bore by hand. If resistance is felt before the plug is almost completely threaded, back the plug out and begin threading again. In small, hard to reach areas, an old spark plug wire and boot could be used as a threading tool. The boot will hold the plug while you twist the end of the wire, and the wire is supple enough to twist before it would allow the plug to crossthread.

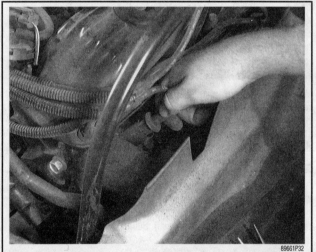

89661P32

Fig. 75 To remove a spark plug wire, simply twist the boot and carefully pull so that the boot comes off of the spark plug

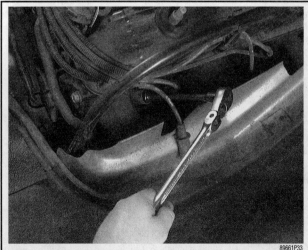

89661P33

Fig. 76 To remove spark plugs, you must use the proper tools; otherwise, the spark plug can break off in the cylinder head

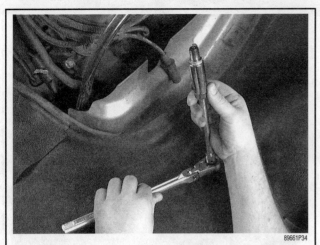

Fig. 77 Make sure the plug comes out smoothly when unscrewing from the head; if not, a cleaning or repair of threads may be necessary

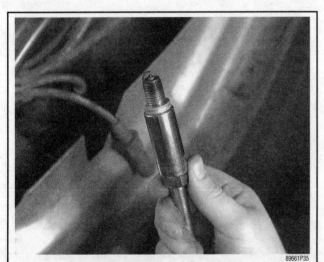

Fig. 78 After the plug is removed, inspect it for damage and condition using the chart in this section

✳✳ WARNING

Do not use the spark plug socket to thread the plugs. Always carefully thread the plug by hand or by using an old plug wire to prevent the possibility of crossthreading and damaging the cylinder head bore.

8. Carefully tighten the spark plug. If the plug you are installing is equipped with a crush washer, seat the plug, then tighten about ¼ turn to crush the washer. If you are installing a tapered seat plug, tighten the plug to specifications provided by the vehicle or plug manufacturer.

9. Apply a small amount of silicone dielectric compound to the end of the spark plug lead or inside the spark plug boot to prevent sticking, then install the boot to the spark plug and push until it clicks into place. The click may be felt or heard, then gently pull back on the boot to assure proper contact.

INSPECTION & GAPPING

▶ See Figures 79 thru 89

Check the plugs for deposits and wear. If they are not going to be replaced, clean the plugs thoroughly. Remember that any kind of deposit

Fig. 79 A normally worn spark plug should have light tan or gray deposits on the firing tip

Fig. 80 A carbon fouled plug, identified by soft, sooty, black deposits, may indicate an improperly tuned vehicle. Check the air cleaner, ignition components and engine control system

TCCS1212

Fig. 81 A variety of tools and gauges are needed for spark plug service

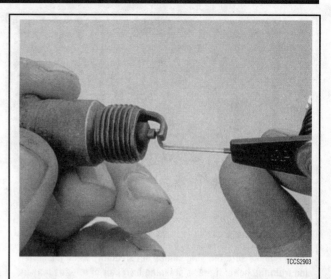

TCCS2903

Fig. 83 Checking the spark plug gap with a feeler gauge

TCCS2137

Fig. 82 A physically damaged spark plug may be evidence of severe detonation in that cylinder. Watch that cylinder carefully between services, as a continued detonation will not only damage the plug, but could also damage the engine

TCCS2138

Fig. 84 An oil fouled spark plug indicates an engine with worn piston rings and/or bad valve seals allowing excessive oil to enter the chamber

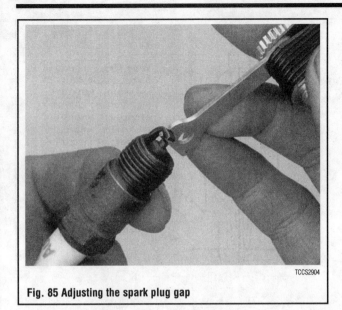

Fig. 85 Adjusting the spark plug gap

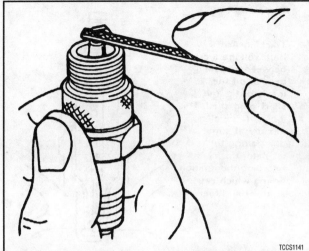

Fig. 87 If the standard plug is in good condition, the electrode may be filed flat—WARNING: do not file platinum plugs

Fig. 86 This spark plug has been left in the engine too long, as evidenced by the extreme gap—Plugs with such an extreme gap can cause misfiring and stumbling accompanied by a noticeable lack of power

Fig. 88 A bridged or almost bridged spark plug, identified by a build-up between the electrodes, and caused by excessive carbon or oil build-up on the plug

Tracking Arc
High voltage arcs between a fouling deposit on the insulator tip and spark plug shell. This ignites the fuel/air mixture at some point along the insulator tip, retarding the ignition timing which causes a power and fuel loss.

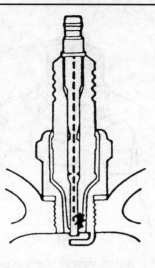

Wide Gap
Spark plug electrodes are worn so that the high voltage charge cannot arc across the electrodes. Improper gapping of electrodes on new or "cleaned" spark plugs could cause a similar condition. Fuel remains unburned and a power loss results.

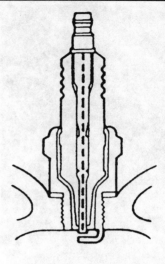

Flashover
A damaged spark plug boot, along with dirt and moisture, could permit the high voltage charge to short over the insulator to the spark plug shell or the engine. A buttress insulator design helps prevent high voltage flashover.

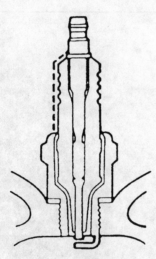

Fouled Spark Plug
Deposits that have formed on the insulator tip may become conductive and provide a "shunt" path to the shell. This prevents the high voltage from arcing between the electrodes. A power and fuel loss is the result.

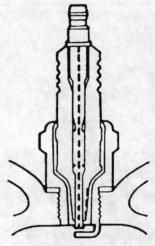

Bridged Electrodes
Fouling deposits between the electrodes "ground out" the high voltage needed to fire the spark plug. The arc between the electrodes does not occur and the fuel air mixture is not ignited. This causes a power loss and exhausting of raw fuel.

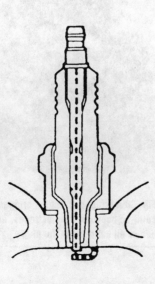

Cracked Insulator
A crack in the spark plug insulator could cause the high voltage charge to "ground out." Here, the spark does not jump the electrode gap and the fuel air mixture is not ignited. This causes a power loss and raw fuel is exhausted.

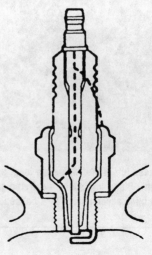

TCCS201A

Fig. 89 Used spark plugs which show damage may indicate engine problems

will decrease the efficiency of the plug. Plugs can be cleaned on a spark plug cleaning machine, which can sometimes be found in service stations, or you can do an acceptable job of cleaning with a stiff brush. If the plugs are cleaned, the electrodes must be filed flat. Use an ignition points file, not an emery board or the like, which will leave deposits. The electrodes must be filed perfectly flat with sharp edges; rounded edges reduce the spark plug voltage by as much as 50%.

Check spark plug gap before installation. The ground electrode (the L-shaped one connected to the body of the plug) must be parallel to the center electrode and the specified size wire gauge (please refer to the Tune-Up Specifications chart for details) must pass between the electrodes with a slight drag.

➡**NEVER adjust the gap on a used platinum type spark plug.**

Always check the gap on new plugs as they are not always set correctly at the factory. Do not use a flat feeler gauge when measuring the gap on a used plug, because the reading may be inaccurate. A round-wire type gapping tool is the best way to check the gap. The correct gauge should pass through the electrode gap with a slight drag. If you're in doubt, try one size smaller and one larger. The smaller gauge should go through easily, while the larger one shouldn't go through at all. Wire gapping tools usually have a bending tool attached. Use that to adjust the side electrode until the proper distance is obtained. Absolutely never attempt to bend the center electrode. Also, be careful not to bend the side electrode too far or too often as it may weaken and break off within the engine, requiring removal of the cylinder head to retrieve it.

Spark Plug Wires

TESTING

▶ **See Figure 90**

At every tune-up/inspection, visually check the spark plug cables for burns cuts, or breaks in the insulation. Check the boots and the nipples on the distributor cap and/or coil. Replace any damaged wiring.

Every 60,000 miles (96,000 km), the resistance of the wires should be checked with an ohmmeter.

➡**Wires with excessive resistance will cause misfiring, and may make the engine difficult to start in damp weather.**

1. Disconnect the spark plug wire at the spark plug and the distributor.
2. Measure and note the length of the spark plug wire.
3. Using an ohmmeter, measure the resistance between the spark plug wire terminals.
4. Resistance should be less than 7000 ohms per foot of spark plug wire.

Fig. 90 Checking individual plug wire resistance with a digital ohmmeter

➡**If one spark plug wire is found to be out of specification, it is a good idea to replace the entire set.**

5. If resistance is excessive, the spark plug wire is faulty.

REMOVAL & INSTALLATION

▶ **See Figure 91**

1. Label each spark plug wire and make a note of its routing.

➡**Don't rely on wiring diagrams or sketches for spark plug wire routing. Improper arrangement of spark plug wires will induce voltage between wires, causing misfiring and surging. Be careful to arrange spark plug wires properly.**

2. Starting with the longest wire, disconnect the spark plug wire from the spark plug and then from the distributor.
3. Remove the spark plug wire from the engine.

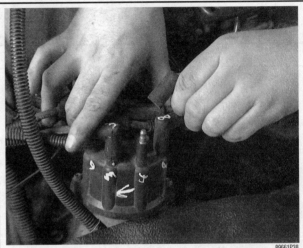

Fig. 91 To remove spark plug wires from the distributor cap, pull each wire's boot upward to remove from the cap tower

To install:

4. If replacing the spark plug wires, match the old wire with an appropriately sized wire in the new set.
5. Lubricate the boots and terminals with dielectric grease and install the wire on the distributor.
6. Route the wire in the exact path as the original and connect the wire to the spark plug.
7. Repeat the process for each remaining wire, working from the longest wire to the shortest.
8. When all wires are installed, check for proper routing and ensure that all terminals are securely connected.
9. Start the engine and check for proper performance.

Distributor Cap and Rotor

REMOVAL & INSTALLATION

▶ **See Figures 92, 93, 94, 95 and 96**

1. Disconnect the negative battery cable.
2. Label and disconnect the spark plug wires from the distributor cap.

➡**Depending on the reason for removing the distributor cap, it may make more sense to leave the spark plug wires attached. This is handy if you are testing spark plug wires, or if removal is necessary to access other components, and wire length allows you to reposition the cap out of the way.**

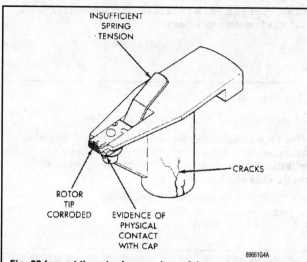

Fig. 92 Inspect the rotor for any signs of damage, and replace if defective

Fig. 95 Inspect the distributor cap for cracks, corroded or eroded terminals, a damaged button or broken towers

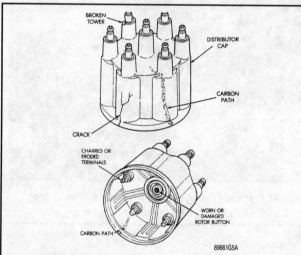

Fig. 93 Inspect the distributor cap for any signs of damage, and replace if defective

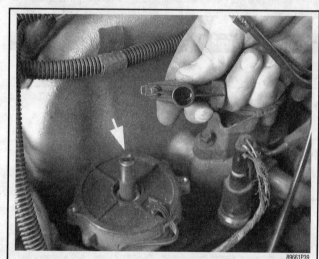

Fig. 96 When removing the rotor from the distributor, pay attention to the position, and note the slot onto which the rotor slides

3. Remove the two attaching screws (or disconnect the two spring clips) that secure the cap to the distributor.
4. Remove the cap from the distributor.

➡ **The rotor is press fit onto the distributor shaft.**

5. Pull the rotor straight up to remove.
To install:
6. Align the rotor on the distributor shaft and install by pressing into place.
7. Align the distributor cap on the distributor and secure using the screws (or spring clips).
8. Connect the spark plug wires to their proper terminals.
9. Connect the negative battery cable.

INSPECTION

1. Carefully check all surfaces of the rotor and distributor cap for cracks, carbon tracks, burns or other physical damage.
2. Make sure the rotor button is free of damage.
3. Check the distributor cap terminals for dirt or corrosion.
4. Check the rotor blade and spring closely for damage.
5. Replace components as necessary.

Fig. 94 Remove the retaining screws from the distributor cap. When inspecting the cap, it is not necessary to remove the wires

Ignition Timing

GENERAL INFORMATION

Ignition timing is the measurement, in degrees of crankshaft rotation, of the point at which the spark plugs fire in each of the cylinders. It is measured in degrees before or after Top Dead Center (TDC) of the compression stroke.

Ideally, the air/fuel mixture in the cylinder will be ignited by the spark plug just as the piston passes TDC of the compression stroke. If this happens, the piston will be at the beginning the power stroke just as the compressed and ignited air/fuel mixture forces the piston down and turns the crankshaft. Because it takes a fraction of a second for the spark plug to ignite the mixture in the cylinder, the spark plug must fire a little before the piston reaches TDC. Otherwise, the mixture will not be completely ignited as the piston passes TDC and the full power of the explosion will not be used by the engine.

The timing measurement is given in degrees of crankshaft rotation before the piston reaches TDC (BTDC). If the setting for the ignition timing is 5 BTDC, each spark plug must fire 5 degrees before each piston reaches TDC. This only holds true, however, when the engine is at idle speed.

As the engine speed increases, the pistons go faster. The spark plugs have to ignite the fuel even sooner if it is to be completely ignited when the piston reaches TDC. On all engines covered in this manual, spark timing changes are accomplished electronically by the Electronic Control Module (ECM) based on input from engine sensors.

If the ignition is set too far advanced (BTDC), the ignition and expansion of the fuel in the cylinder will occur too soon and tend to force the piston down while it is still traveling up. This causes engine ping. If the ignition spark is set too far retarded after TDC (ATDC), the piston will have already started on its way down when the fuel is ignited. The piston will be forced down for only a portion of its travel, resulting in poor engine performance and lack of power.

Timing marks or scales can be found on the rim of the crankshaft pulley and the timing cover. The marks on the pulley correspond to the position of the piston in the No. 1 cylinder. A stroboscopic (dynamic) timing light is hooked onto the No. 1 cylinder spark plug wire. Every time the spark plug fires, the timing light flashes. By aiming the light at the timing marks while the engine is running, the exact position of the piston within the cylinder can be easily read (the flash of light makes the mark on the pulley appear to be standing still). Proper timing is indicated when the mark and scale are in specified alignment.

✳✳ CAUTION

When making timing adjustments with the engine running, take care not to get the timing light wires tangled in the fan blades and/or drive belts.

INSPECTION & ADJUSTMENT

▶ **See Figure 97**

➡**No periodic adjustment of the ignition timing is possible on MFI engines covered in this manual. However, the ignition timing on TBI engines can be set using the following procedure.**

1. Set the gearshift selector in Park or Neutral and apply the parking brake firmly. All lights and accessories should be OFF.
2. Insert the pickup probe of a magnetic timing light into the tube near the timing marks on V6 and V8 engines. If a magnetic timing light is not

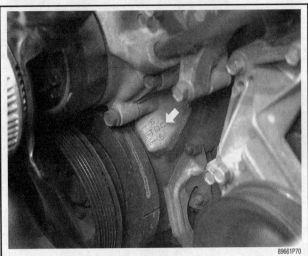

Fig. 97 The timing marks are located on the driver's side of the crankshaft, right under the water pump

available, use a conventional power timing light connected to the No. 1 spark plug wire.

➡**DO NOT puncture spark plug wires, boots or nipples with test probes. Always use proper adapters. Puncturing the spark plug cables with probes will damage them. Breaking the rubber insulator may permit a secondary current arc which can ruin the coil.**

3. Connect a tachometer to the engine and turn the selector to the proper cylinder position.
4. Start the engine and run it until operating temperature is reached.
5. Check engine for proper idle and adjust to specification.
6. Detach the coolant temperature sensor connector. The instrument panel warning lights should illuminate.
7. Aim the timing light at the timing marks on the front of the engine or read the magnetic timing unit.
8. Loosen the distributor hold-down bolt and adjust timing to specification. Tighten the hold-down bolt securely.
9. Turn the engine OFF.
10. Reconnect the coolant temperature sensor.
11. Disconnect the negative battery cable to clear stored fault codes.
12. Connect the negative battery cable.

Valve Lash

All engines covered in this manual use hydraulic lifters. No adjustment is necessary.

Idle Speed and Mixture Adjustments

Idle speed and mixture adjustments on all engines covered in this manual are controlled by the Powertrain Control Module (PCM). No adjustments are necessary.

If idle speed is not within specification, inspect the engine for:
• Proper idle speed control actuator functioning
• Engine or EGR vacuum leaks
• Proper ignition timing
• Proper coolant temperature sensor function

If engine functions are normal, perform the idle speed control actuator adjustment, as described in Section 4.

GASOLINE ENGINE TUNE-UP SPECIFICATIONS

Year	Engine ID/VIN	Engine Displacement Liters (cc)	Spark Plugs Gap (in.)	Ignition Timing (deg.) MT	AT	Fuel Pump (psi)	Idle Speed (rpm) MT	AT	Valve Clearance In.	Ex.
1989	X	3.9 (3916)	0.035	10B	10B	13-16	750	750	HYD	HYD
	Y	5.2 (5211)	0.035	10B	10B	13-16	700	700	HYD	HYD
	W	5.9 (5899)	0.035	10B	10B	13-16	700	700	HYD	HYD
1990	X	3.9 (3916)	0.035	10B	10B	13-16	750	750	HYD	HYD
	Y	5.2 (5211)	0.035	10B	10B	13-16	700	700	HYD	HYD
	W	5.9 (5899)	0.035	10B	10B	13-16	700	700	HYD	HYD
1991	X	3.9 (3916)	0.035	10B	10B	13-16	750	750	HYD	HYD
	Y	5.2 (5211)	0.035	10B	10B	13-16	700	700	HYD	HYD
	W	5.9 (5899)	0.035	10B	10B	13-16	700	700	HYD	HYD
1992	X	3.9 (3916)	0.035	①	①	37-41	750	750	HYD	HYD
	Y	5.2 (5211)	0.035	①	①	37-41	700	700	HYD	HYD
	Z	5.9 (5899)	0.035	10B	10B	35-45	700	700	HYD	HYD
1993	X	3.9 (3916)	0.035	①	①	37-41	750	750	HYD	HYD
	Y	5.2 (5211)	0.035	①	①	37-41	700	700	HYD	HYD
	Z	5.9 (5899)	0.035	10B	10B	35-45	700	700	HYD	HYD
1994	A	5.9 (5899)	0.035	①	①	35-45	②	②	HYD	HYD
	Y	5.2 (5211)	0.035	①	①	35-45	②	②	HYD	HYD
	Z	5.9 (5899)	0.035	①	①	35-45	②	②	HYD	HYD
1995	X	3.9 (3916)	0.030	①	①	35-45	②	②	HYD	HYD
	Y	5.2 (5211)	0.030	①	①	35-45	②	②	HYD	HYD
	Z	5.9 (5899)	0.030	①	①	35-45	②	②	HYD	HYD
1996	X	3.9 (3916)	0.035	①	①	49.2	②	②	HYD	HYD
	Y	5.2 (5211)	0.035	①	①	49.2	②	②	HYD	HYD
	Z	5.9 (5899)	0.035	①	①	49.2	②	②	HYD	HYD
1997	X	3.9 (3916)	0.035	①	①	49.2	②	②	HYD	HYD
	Y	5.2 (5211)	0.035	①	①	49.2	②	②	HYD	HYD
	Z	5.9 (5899)	0.035	①	①	49.2	②	②	HYD	HYD
1998	X	3.9 (3916)	0.035	①	①	49.2	②	②	HYD	HYD
	Y	5.2 (5211)	0.035	①	①	49.2	②	②	HYD	HYD
	Z	5.9 (5899)	0.035	①	①	49.2	②	②	HYD	HYD

NOTE: The Vehicle Emission Control Information label often reflects specification changes made during production. The label figures must be used if they differ from those in this chart.

B - Before top dead center

HYD - Hydraulic

① Ignition timing cannot be adjusted. Base engine timing is set at TDC during assembly

② Refer to the Vehicle Emission Control Information (VECI) label for correct specification

89661C05

Air Conditioning System

SYSTEM SERVICE & REPAIR

▶ See Figure 98

➡ It is recommended that the A/C system be serviced by an EPA Section 609 certified automotive technician utilizing a refrigerant recovery/recycling machine.

The do-it-yourselfer should not service his/her own vehicle's A/C system for many reasons, including legal concerns, personal injury, environmental damage and cost. The following are some of the reasons why you may decide not to service your own vehicle's A/C system.

According to the U.S. Clean Air Act, it is a federal crime to service or repair (involving the refrigerant) a Motor Vehicle Air Conditioning (MVAC) system for money without being EPA certified. It is also illegal to vent R-12 and R-134a refrigerants into the atmosphere. Selling or distributing A/C system refrigerant (in a container which contains less than 20 pounds of refrigerant) to any person who is not EPA 609 certified is also not allowed by law.

State and/or local laws may be more strict than the federal regulations, so be sure to check with your state and/or local authorities for further information. For further federal information on the legality of servicing your A/C system, call the EPA Stratospheric Ozone Hotline.

➡ Federal law dictates that a fine of up to $25,000 may be levied on people convicted of venting refrigerant into the atmosphere. Additionally, the EPA may pay up to $10,000 for information or services leading to a criminal conviction of the violation of these laws.

When servicing an A/C system you run the risk of handling or coming in contact with refrigerant, which may result in skin or eye irritation or frostbite. Although low in toxicity (due to chemical stability), inhalation of concentrated refrigerant fumes is dangerous and can result in death; cases of fatal cardiac arrhythmia have been reported in people accidentally subjected to high levels of refrigerant. Some early symptoms include loss of concentration and drowsiness.

➡ Generally, the limit for exposure is lower for R-134a than it is for R-12. Exceptional care must be practiced when handling R-134a.

Also, refrigerants can decompose at high temperatures (near gas heaters or open flame), which may result in hydrofluoric acid, hydrochloric acid and phosgene (a fatal nerve gas).

R-12 refrigerant can damage the environment because it is a Chlorofluorocarbon (CFC), which has been proven to add to ozone layer depletion, leading to increasing levels of UV radiation. UV radiation has been linked with an increase in skin cancer, suppression of the human immune system, an increase in cataracts, damage to crops, damage to aquatic organisms, an increase in ground-level ozone, and increased global warming.

R-134a refrigerant is a greenhouse gas which, if allowed to vent into the atmosphere, will contribute to global warming (the Greenhouse Effect).

It is usually more economically feasible to have a certified MVAC automotive technician perform A/C system service on your vehicle. Some possible reasons for this are as follows:

• While it is illegal to service an A/C system without the proper equipment, the home mechanic would have to purchase an expensive refrigerant

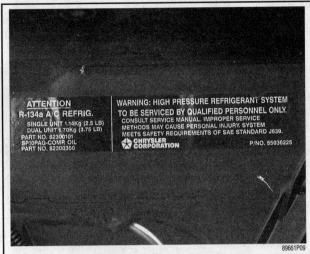

Fig. 98 The A/C certification label states the refrigerant capacity of the A/C system, as well as the proper oil

Fig. 99 A coolant tester can be used to determine the freezing and boiling levels of the coolant in your vehicle

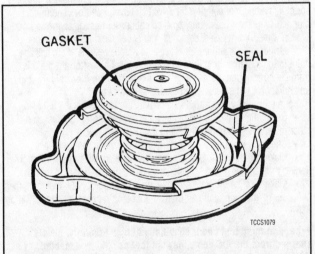

Fig. 100 To ensure efficient cooling system operation, inspect the radiator cap gasket and seal

recovery/recycling machine to service his/her own vehicle.
• Since only a certified person may purchase refrigerant—according to the Clean Air Act, there are specific restrictions on selling or distributing A/C system refrigerant—it is legally impossible (unless certified) for the home mechanic to service his/her own vehicle. Procuring refrigerant in an illegal fashion exposes one to the risk of paying a $25,000 fine to the EPA.

R-12 Refrigerant Conversion

If your vehicle still uses R-12 refrigerant, one way to save A/C system costs down the road is to investigate the possibility of having your system converted to R-134a. The older R-12 systems can be easily converted to R-134a refrigerant by a certified automotive technician by installing a few new components and changing the system oil.

The cost of R-12 is steadily rising and will continue to increase, because it is no longer imported or manufactured in the United States. Therefore, it is often possible to have an R-12 system converted to R-134a and recharged for less than it would cost to just charge the system with R-12.

If you are interested in having your system converted, contact local automotive service stations for more details and information.

PREVENTIVE MAINTENANCE

♦ See Figures 99 and 100

Although the A/C system should not be serviced by the do-it-yourselfer, preventive maintenance can be practiced and A/C system inspections can be performed to help maintain the efficiency of the vehicle's A/C system. For preventive maintenance, perform the following:
• The easiest and most important preventive maintenance for your A/C system is to be sure that it is used on a regular basis. Running the system for five minutes each month (no matter what the season) will help ensure that the seals and all internal components remain lubricated.

➡Some newer vehicles automatically operate the A/C system compressor whenever the windshield defroster is activated. When running, the compressor lubricates the A/C system components; therefore, the A/C system would not need to be operated each month.

• In order to prevent heater core freeze-up during A/C operation, it is necessary to maintain proper antifreeze protection. Use a hand-held coolant tester (hydrometer) to periodically check the condition of the antifreeze in your engine's cooling system.

➡Antifreeze should not be used longer than the manufacturer specifies.

• For efficient operation of an air conditioned vehicle's cooling system, the radiator cap should have a holding pressure which meets manufac-

turer's specifications. A cap which fails to hold these pressures should be replaced.
• Any obstruction of or damage to the condenser configuration will restrict air flow which is essential to its efficient operation. It is, therefore, a good rule to keep this unit clean and in proper physical shape.

➡Bug screens which are mounted in front of the condenser (unless they are original equipment) are regarded as obstructions.

• The condensation drain tube expels any water which accumulates on the bottom of the evaporator housing into the engine compartment. If this tube is obstructed, the air conditioning performance can be restricted and condensation buildup can spill over onto the vehicle's floor.

SYSTEM INSPECTION

♦ See Figure 101

Although the A/C system should not be serviced by the do-it-yourselfer, preventive maintenance can be practiced and A/C system inspections can be performed to help maintain the efficiency of the vehicle's A/C system. For A/C system inspection, perform the following:

The easiest and often most important check for the air conditioning system consists of a visual inspection of the system components. Visually

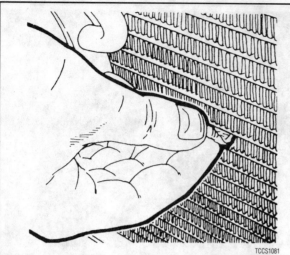

Fig. 101 Periodically remove any debris from the condenser and radiator fins

inspect the air conditioning system for refrigerant leaks, damaged compressor clutch, abnormal compressor drive belt tension and/or condition, plugged evaporator drain tube, blocked condenser fins, disconnected or broken wires, blown fuses, corroded connections and poor insulation.

A refrigerant leak will usually appear as an oily residue at the leakage point in the system. The oily residue soon picks up dust or dirt particles from the surrounding air and appears greasy. Through time, this will build up and appear to be a heavy dirt impregnated grease.

For a thorough visual and operational inspection, check the following:
• Check the surface of the radiator and condenser for dirt, leaves or other material which might block air flow.
• Check for kinks in hoses and lines. Check the system for leaks.
• Make sure the drive belt is properly tensioned. When the air conditioning is operating, make sure the drive belt is free of noise or slippage.
• Make sure the blower motor operates at all appropriate positions, then check for distribution of the air from all outlets with the blower on **HIGH** or **MAX**.

➡**Keep in mind that under conditions of high humidity, air discharged from the A/C vents may not feel as cold as expected, even if the system is working properly. This is because vaporized moisture in humid air retains heat more effectively than dry air, thereby making humid air more difficult to cool.**

• Make sure the air passage selection lever is operating correctly. Start the engine and warm it to normal operating temperature, then make sure the temperature selection lever is operating correctly.

Windshield Wiper (Elements)

ELEMENT (REFILL) CARE & REPLACEMENT

▶ **See Figures 102 thru 111**

For maximum effectiveness and longest element life, the windshield and wiper blades should be kept clean. Dirt, tree sap, road tar and so on will cause streaking, smearing and blade deterioration if left on the glass. It is advisable to wash the windshield carefully with a commercial glass cleaner at least once a month. Wipe off the rubber blades with the wet rag afterwards. Do not attempt to move wipers across the windshield by hand; damage to the motor and drive mechanism will result.

To inspect and/or replace the wiper blade elements, place the wiper switch in the **LOW** speed position and the ignition switch in the **ACC** position. When the wiper blades are approximately vertical on the windshield, turn the ignition switch to **OFF**.

Examine the wiper blade elements. If they are found to be cracked, bro-

ken or torn, they should be replaced immediately. Replacement intervals will vary with usage, although ozone deterioration usually limits element life to about one year. If the wiper pattern is smeared or streaked, or if the blade chatters across the glass, the elements should be replaced. It is easiest and most sensible to replace the elements in pairs.

If your vehicle is equipped with aftermarket blades, there are several different types of refills and your vehicle might have any kind. Aftermarket blades and arms rarely use the exact same type blade or refill as the original equipment. Here are some typical aftermarket blades; not all may be available for your vehicle:

The Anco® type uses a release button that is pushed down to allow the refill to slide out of the yoke jaws. The new refill slides back into the frame and locks in place.

Some Trico® refills are removed by locating where the metal backing strip or the refill is wider. Insert a small screwdriver blade between the frame and metal backing strip. Press down to release the refill from the retaining tab.

Other types of Trico® refills have two metal tabs which are unlocked by squeezing them together. The rubber filler can then be withdrawn from the frame jaws. A new refill is installed by inserting the refill into the front frame jaws and sliding it rearward to engage the remaining frame jaws. There are usually four jaws; be certain when installing that the refill is engaged in all of them. At the end of its travel, the tabs will lock into place on the front jaws of the wiper blade frame.

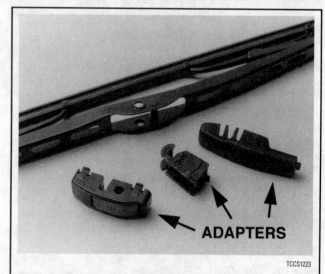

Fig. 102 Bosch® wiper blade and fit kit

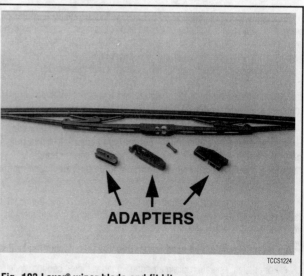

Fig. 103 Lexor® wiper blade and fit kit

Fig. 104 Pylon® wiper blade and adapter

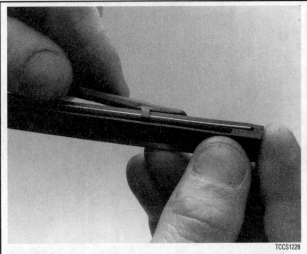

Fig. 107 To remove and install a Lexor® wiper blade refill, slip out the old insert and slide in a new one

Fig. 105 Trico® wiper blade and fit kit

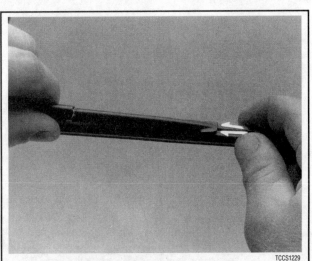

Fig. 108 On Pylon® inserts, the clip at the end has to be removed prior to sliding the insert off

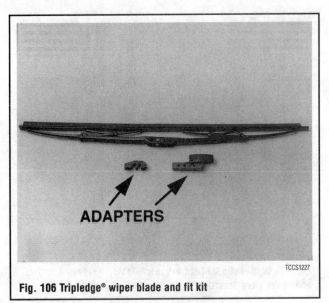

ADAPTERS

Fig. 106 Tripledge® wiper blade and fit kit

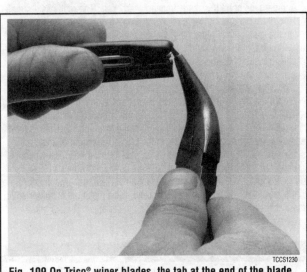

Fig. 109 On Trico® wiper blades, the tab at the end of the blade must be turned up . . .

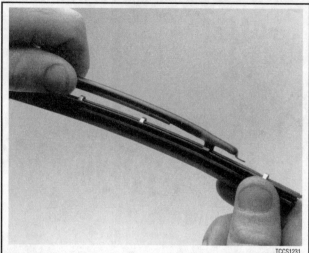

Fig. 110 . . . then the insert can be removed. After installing the replacement insert, bend the tab back

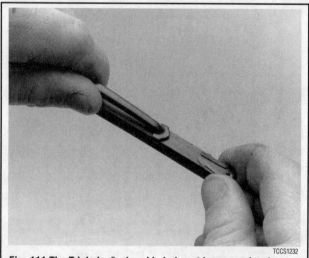

Fig. 111 The Tripledge® wiper blade insert is removed and installed using a securing clip

Another type of refill is made from polycarbonate. The refill has a simple locking device at one end which flexes downward out of the groove into which the jaws of the holder fit, allowing easy release. By sliding the new refill through all the jaws and pushing through the slight resistance when it reaches the end of its travel, the refill will lock into position.

To replace the Tridon® refill, it is necessary to remove the wiper blade. This refill has a plastic backing strip with a notch about 1 in. (25mm) from the end. Hold the blade (frame) on a hard surface so that the frame is tightly bowed. Grip the tip of the backing strip and pull up while twisting counter-clockwise. The backing strip will snap out of the retaining tab. Do this for the remaining tabs until the refill is free of the blade. The length of these refills is molded into the end and they should be replaced with identical types.

Regardless of the type of refill used, be sure to follow the part manufacturer's instructions closely. Make sure that all of the frame jaws are engaged as the refill is pushed into place and locked. If the metal blade holder and frame are allowed to touch the glass during wiper operation, the glass will be scratched.

Tires and Wheels

Common sense and good driving habits will afford maximum tire life. Fast starts, sudden stops and hard cornering are hard on tires and will shorten their useful life span. Make sure that you don't overload the vehicle or run with incorrect pressure in the tires. Both of these practices will increase tread wear.

➡**For optimum tire life, keep the tires properly inflated, rotate them often and have the wheel alignment checked periodically.**

Inspect your tires frequently. Be especially careful to watch for bubbles in the tread or sidewall, deep cuts or underinflation. Replace any tires with bubbles in the sidewall. If cuts are so deep that they penetrate to the cords, discard the tire. Any cut in the sidewall of a radial tire renders it unsafe. Also look for uneven tread wear patterns that may indicate the front end is out of alignment or that the tires are out of balance.

TIRE ROTATION

▶ **See Figures 112 and 113**

Tires must be rotated periodically to equalize wear patterns that vary with a tire's position on the vehicle. Tires will also wear in an uneven way as the front steering/suspension system wears to the point where the alignment should be reset.

Rotating the tires will ensure maximum life for the tires as a set, so you will not have to discard a tire early due to wear on only part of the tread. Regular rotation is required to equalize wear.

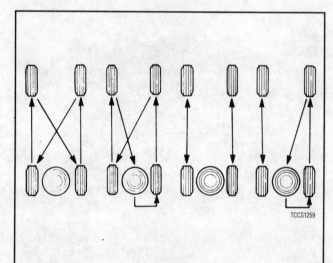

Fig. 112 Common tire rotation patterns for 4 and 5-wheel rotations

Fig. 113 Unidirectional tires are identifiable by sidewall arrows and/or the word "rotation"

When rotating "unidirectional tires," make sure that they always roll in the same direction. This means that a tire used on the left side of the vehicle must not be switched to the right side and vice-versa. Such tires should only be rotated front-to-rear or rear-to-front, while always remaining on the same side of the vehicle. These tires are marked on the sidewall as to the direction of rotation; observe the marks when reinstalling the tire(s).

Some styled or "mag" wheels may have different offsets front to rear. In these cases, the rear wheels must not be used up front and vice-versa. Furthermore, if these wheels are equipped with unidirectional tires, they cannot be rotated unless the tire is remounted for the proper direction of rotation.

➡️**The compact or space-saver spare is strictly for emergency use. It must never be included in the tire rotation or placed on the vehicle for everyday use.**

TIRE DESIGN

▶ **See Figure 114**

For maximum satisfaction, tires should be used in sets of four. Mixing of different types (radial, bias-belted, fiberglass belted) must be avoided. In most cases, the vehicle manufacturer has designated a type of tire on which the vehicle will perform best. Your first choice when replacing tires should be to use the same type of tire that the manufacturer recommends.

When radial tires are used, tire sizes and wheel diameters should be selected to maintain ground clearance and tire load capacity equivalent to the original specified tire. Radial tires should always be used in sets of four.

✳️ CAUTION

Radial tires should never be used on only the front axle.

When selecting tires, pay attention to the original size as marked on the tire. Most tires are described using an industry size code sometimes referred to as P-Metric. This allows the exact identification of the tire specifications, regardless of the manufacturer. If selecting a different tire size or brand, remember to check the installed tire for any sign of interference with the body or suspension while the vehicle is stopping, turning sharply or heavily loaded.

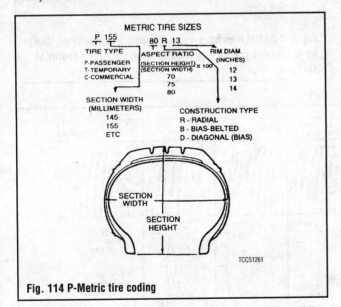

Fig. 114 P-Metric tire coding

Snow Tires

Good radial tires can produce a big advantage in slippery weather, but in snow, a street radial tire does not have sufficient tread to provide traction and control. The small grooves of a street tire quickly pack with snow and

the tire behaves like a billiard ball on a marble floor. The more open, chunky tread of a snow tire will self-clean as the tire turns, providing much better grip on snowy surfaces.

To satisfy municipalities requiring snow tires during weather emergencies, most snow tires carry either an M + S designation after the tire size stamped on the sidewall, or the designation "all-season." In general, no change in tire size is necessary when buying snow tires.

Most manufacturers strongly recommend the use of 4 snow tires on their vehicles for reasons of stability. If snow tires are fitted only to the drive wheels, the opposite end of the vehicle may become very unstable when braking or turning on slippery surfaces. This instability can lead to unpleasant endings if the driver can't counteract the slide in time.

Note that snow tires, whether 2 or 4, will affect vehicle handling in all non-snow situations. The stiffer, heavier snow tires will noticeably change the turning and braking characteristics of the vehicle. Once the snow tires are installed, you must re-learn the behavior of the vehicle and drive accordingly.

➡️**Consider buying extra wheels on which to mount the snow tires. Once done, the "snow wheels" can be installed and removed as needed. This eliminates the potential damage to tires or wheels from seasonal removal and installation. Even if your vehicle has styled wheels, see if inexpensive steel wheels are available. Although the look of the vehicle will change, the expensive wheels will be protected from salt, curb hits and pothole damage.**

TIRE STORAGE

If they are mounted on wheels, store the tires at proper inflation pressure. All tires should be kept in a cool, dry place. If they are stored in the garage or basement, do not let them stand on a concrete floor; set them on strips of wood, a mat or a large stack of newspaper. Keeping them away from direct moisture is of paramount importance. Tires should not be stored upright, but in a flat position.

INFLATION & INSPECTION

▶ **See Figures 115 thru 122**

The importance of proper tire inflation cannot be overemphasized. A tire employs air as part of its structure. It is designed around the supporting strength of the air at a specified pressure. For this reason, improper inflation drastically reduces the tire's ability to perform as intended. A tire will lose some air in day-to-day use; having to add a few pounds of air periodically is not necessarily a sign of a leaking tire.

Two items should be a permanent fixture in every glove compartment: an accurate tire pressure gauge and a tread depth gauge. Check the tire pressure (including the spare) regularly with a pocket type gauge. Too often, the gauge on the end of the air hose at your corner garage is not accurate because it suffers too much abuse. Always check tire pressure when the tires are cold, as pressure increases with temperature. If you must move the vehicle to check the tire inflation, do not drive more than a mile before checking. A cold tire is generally one that has not been driven for more than three hours.

A plate or sticker is normally provided somewhere in the vehicle (door post or hood) which shows the proper pressure for the tires. Never counteract excessive pressure build-up by bleeding off air pressure (letting some air out). This will cause the tire to run hotter and wear quicker.

✳️ CAUTION

Never exceed the maximum tire pressure embossed on the tire! This is the pressure to be used when the tire is at maximum loading, but it is rarely the correct pressure for everyday driving. Consult the owner's manual or the tire pressure sticker for the correct tire pressure.

Once you've maintained the correct tire pressures for several weeks, you'll be familiar with the vehicle's braking and handling personality. Slight

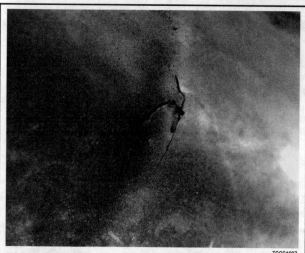

Fig. 115 Tires should be checked frequently for any sign of puncture or damage

TCCS1097

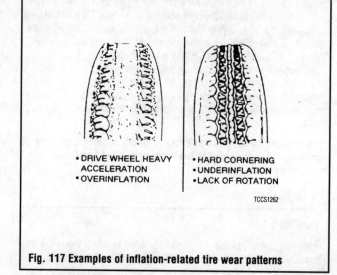

- DRIVE WHEEL HEAVY ACCELERATION
- OVERINFLATION

- HARD CORNERING
- UNDERINFLATION
- LACK OF ROTATION

TCCS1262

Fig. 117 Examples of inflation-related tire wear patterns

Fig. 116 Tires with deep cuts, or cuts which bulge, should be replaced immediately

TCCS1095

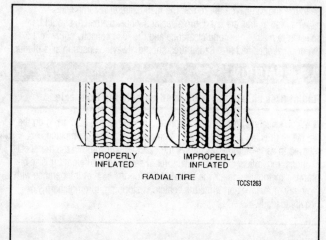

PROPERLY INFLATED   IMPROPERLY INFLATED

RADIAL TIRE

TCCS1263

Fig. 118 Radial tires have a characteristic sidewall bulge; don't try to measure pressure by looking at the tire. Use a quality air pressure gauge

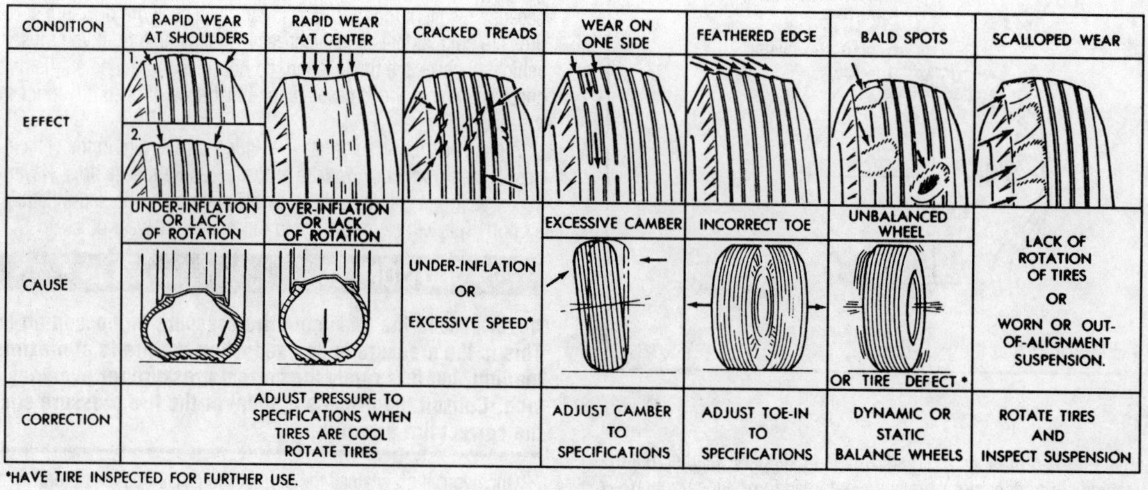

CONDITION	RAPID WEAR AT SHOULDERS	RAPID WEAR AT CENTER	CRACKED TREADS	WEAR ON ONE SIDE	FEATHERED EDGE	BALD SPOTS	SCALLOPED WEAR
EFFECT							
CAUSE	UNDER-INFLATION OR LACK OF ROTATION	OVER-INFLATION OR LACK OF ROTATION	UNDER-INFLATION OR EXCESSIVE SPEED*	EXCESSIVE CAMBER	INCORRECT TOE	UNBALANCED WHEEL _OR TIRE DEFECT *_	LACK OF ROTATION OF TIRES OR WORN OR OUT-OF-ALIGNMENT SUSPENSION.
CORRECTION	ADJUST PRESSURE TO SPECIFICATIONS WHEN TIRES ARE COOL ROTATE TIRES			ADJUST CAMBER TO SPECIFICATIONS	ADJUST TOE-IN TO SPECIFICATIONS	DYNAMIC OR STATIC BALANCE WHEELS	ROTATE TIRES AND INSPECT SUSPENSION

*HAVE TIRE INSPECTED FOR FURTHER USE.

Fig. 119 Common tire wear patterns and causes

TCCS1267

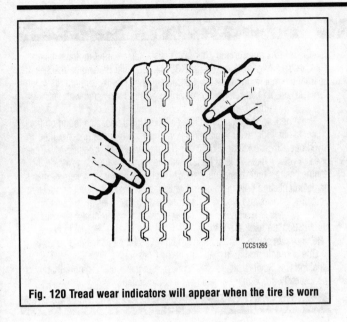

Fig. 120 Tread wear indicators will appear when the tire is worn

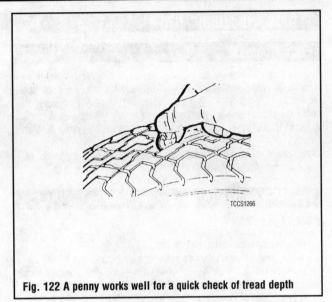

Fig. 122 A penny works well for a quick check of tread depth

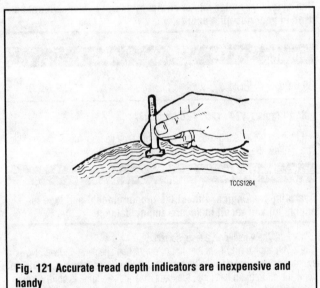

Fig. 121 Accurate tread depth indicators are inexpensive and handy

adjustments in tire pressures can fine-tune these characteristics, but never change the cold pressure specification by more than 2 psi. A slightly softer tire pressure will give a softer ride but also yield lower fuel mileage. A slightly harder tire will give crisper dry road handling but can cause skidding on wet surfaces. Unless you're fully attuned to the vehicle, stick to the recommended inflation pressures.

All tires made since 1968 have built-in tread wear indicator bars that show up as ½ in. (13mm) wide smooth bands across the tire when ⅟₁₆ in. (1.5mm) of tread remains. The appearance of tread wear indicators means that the tires should be replaced. In fact, many states have laws prohibiting the use of tires with less than this amount of tread.

You can check your own tread depth with an inexpensive gauge or by using a Lincoln head penny. Slip the Lincoln penny (with Lincoln's head upside-down) into several tread grooves. If you can see the top of Lincoln's head in 2 adjacent grooves, the tire has less than ⅟₁₆ in. (1.5mm) tread left and should be replaced. You can measure snow tires in the same manner by using the "tails" side of the Lincoln penny. If you can see the top of the Lincoln memorial, it's time to replace the snow tire(s).

CARE OF SPECIAL WHEELS

If you have invested money in magnesium, aluminum alloy or sport wheels, special precautions should be taken to make sure your investment is not wasted and that your special wheels look good for the life of the vehicle.

Special wheels are easily damaged and/or scratched. Occasionally check the rims for cracking, impact damage or air leaks. If any of these are found, replace the wheel. But in order to prevent this type of damage and the costly replacement of a special wheel, observe the following precautions:

• Use extra care not to damage the wheels during removal, installation, balancing, etc. After removal of the wheels from the vehicle, place them on a mat or other protective surface. If they are to be stored for any length of time, support them on strips of wood. Never store tires and wheels upright; the tread may develop flat spots.

• When driving, watch for hazards; it doesn't take much to crack a wheel.

• When washing, use a mild soap or non-abrasive dish detergent (keeping in mind that detergent tends to remove wax). Avoid cleansers with abrasives or the use of hard brushes. There are many cleaners and polishes for special wheels.

• If possible, remove the wheels during the winter. Salt and sand used for snow removal can severely damage the finish of a wheel.

• Make certain the recommended lug nut torque is never exceeded or the wheel may crack. Never use snow chains on special wheels; severe scratching will occur.

Maintenance Lights

An Emission Maintenance Reminder (EMR) lamp is used on most 1989–93 vehicles. The lamp illuminates to remind the driver that certain critical emissions maintenance procedures must be performed. The lamp will stay illuminated until reset.

RESETTING

1. A Chrysler Digital Read Out Box II (DRB-II) or equivalent scan tool is necessary to perform this procedure.

2. Connect the scan tool to the vehicle's diagnostic connector.

3. Follow the scan tool manufacturer's instructions regarding EMR lamp reset procedures.

4. These procedures reset the EMR timing in the computer and will turn off the reminder light.

FLUIDS AND LUBRICANTS

Fluid Disposal

Used fluids such as engine oil, transmission fluid, antifreeze and brake fluid are hazardous wastes and must be disposed of properly. Before draining any fluids, consult with your local authorities; in many areas waste oil, antifreeze, etc. is being accepted as a part of recycling programs. A number of service stations and auto parts stores are also accepting waste fluids for recycling.

Be sure of the recycling center's policies before draining any fluids, as many will not accept different fluids that have been mixed together.

Fuel and Engine Oil Recommendations

▶ See Figure 123

Unleaded gasoline having a minimum octane rating of 87 (R+M)/2 should be used. Engines may respond differently to gasolines having the same octane rating. Should the engine in your vehicle develop spark knock (ping), trying purchasing your gasoline from a different source or try a different brand. Use gasolines containing a high level of detergent additives. The use of a detergent type gasoline will reduce fuel injector and intake system deposit build-up and help maintain an excellent degree of vehicle driveability.

The recommended oil viscosities for sustained temperatures ranging from below 0°F (18°C) to above 32°F (0°C) are listed in this section. Multi-viscosity oils are recommended because of their wider range of acceptable temperatures and driving conditions. When adding oil to the crankcase or changing the oil or filter, it is important that oil of an equal quality to original equipment be used in your vehicle. The use of inferior oils may void the warranty, damage your engine, or both.

The Society of Automotive Engineers (SAE) grade of oil indicates the viscosity of the oil (its ability to lubricate at a given temperature). The lower the SAE number, the lighter the oil; the lower the viscosity, the easier it is to crank the engine in cold weather but the less the oil will lubricate and protect the engine in high temperatures. This number is marked on every oil container.

Oil viscosities should be chosen from those oils recommended for the lowest anticipated temperatures during the oil change interval. Due to the need for an oil that embodies both good lubrication at high temperatures and easy cranking in cold weather, multigrade oils have been developed. Basically, a multigrade oil is thinner at low temperatures and thicker at high temperatures. For example, a 10W-30 oil (the W stands for winter) exhibits the characteristics of a 10 weight (SAE 10) oil when the vehicle is first started and the oil is cold. Its lighter weight allows it to travel to the lubri-

cating surfaces quicker and offer less resistance to starter motor cranking than, say, a straight 30 weight (SAE 30) oil. But after the engine reaches operating temperature, the 10W-30 oil begins acting like straight 30 weight (SAE 30) oil, its heavier weight providing greater lubrication with less chance of foaming than a straight 30 weight oil.

The American Petroleum Institute (API) designations, also found on the oil container, indicates the classification of engine oil used under certain given operating conditions. Only oils designated as SH or better should be used in your vehicle. Oils of the SH type perform may functions inside the engine besides their basic lubrication. Through a balanced system of metallic detergents and polymeric dispersants, the oil prevents high and low temperature deposits and also keeps sludge and dirt particles in suspension. Acids, particularly sulphuric acid, as well as other by-products of engine combustion are neutralized by the oil. If these acids are allowed to concentrate, they can cause corrosion and rapid wear of the internal engine parts.

Oils currently available marked Energy Conserving, Fuel Saving, Fuel Efficient, Gas Saving, etc. on the lower part of the container logo, that meet the viscosity grade requirements are recommended.

✳✳ WARNING

Non-detergent motor oils or straight mineral oils should not be used in your gasoline engine.

Engine

OIL LEVEL CHECK

▶ See Figures 124, 125, 126 and 127

Engine oil level should be checked every time you put fuel in the vehicle or are under the hood performing other maintenance.

✳✳ WARNING

Operating the engine without the proper amount and type of engine oil will result in severe engine damage.

1. Park the vehicle on a level surface.
2. The engine may be either hot or cold when checking oil level. However, if it is hot, wait a few minutes after the engine has been turned **OFF** to allow the oil to drain back into the crankcase. If the engine is cold, do not start it before checking the oil level.

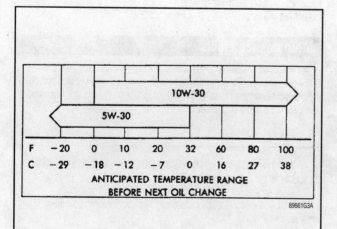

F	-20	0	10	20	32	60	80	100
C	-29	-18	-12	-7	0	16	27	38

ANTICIPATED TEMPERATURE RANGE
BEFORE NEXT OIL CHANGE

89661G3A

Fig. 123 Always choose an oil with the proper viscosity for the anticipated temperature

89661P15

Fig. 124 The engine oil dipstick is located in the front center of the engine compartment, right behind the radiator cap

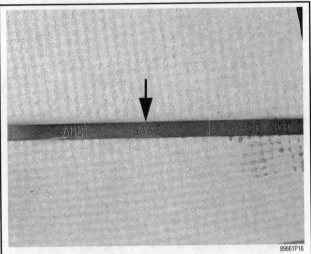

Fig. 125 The oil level is in the safe range when it is between the ADD and FULL marks, as in this photo

3. Open the hood and locate the engine oil dipstick. Pull the dipstick from its tube, wipe it clean, and reinsert it. Make sure the dipstick is fully inserted.

4. Pull the dipstick from its tube again. Holding it horizontally, read the oil level. The oil should be in the crosshatched area, above the **ADD** mark and below the **FULL** mark. If the oil is below the **ADD** mark, add oil of the proper viscosity through the capped opening on the valve cover.

5. Replace the dipstick, and check the level again after adding any oil. Approximately one quart of oil will raise the level from the **ADD** mark to the **FULL** mark.

➡Be careful not to overfill the crankcase. Excess oil will cause oil aeration and loss of oil pressure. This could severely damage the engine.

OIL & FILTER CHANGE

▶ See Figures 128 thru 136

The engine oil and filter should be changed every 7,500 miles (12,000 km). It is a good idea to warm the engine oil first so it will flow better. This can be accomplished by 15–20 miles (24–32 km) of highway driving. Fluid which is warmed to normal operating temperature will flow faster, drain more completely and remove more contaminants from the engine.

Fig. 126 The oil filler cap is located in the center of the engine compartment, on top of the oil filler tube

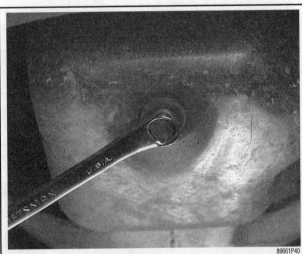

Fig. 128 Use the appropriate size wrench to loosen the engine oil drain plug

Fig. 127 Using a funnel to reduce spillage, add oil to the engine through the fill tube

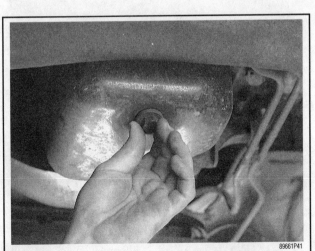

Fig. 129 When loosened sufficiently, remove the engine oil drain plug by hand. Keep pressure on the plug until it is fully unscrewed

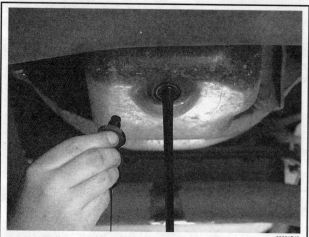

Fig. 130 When the drain plug is ready to come out, pull it away from the oil pan to reduce oil splashing on you or all over the ground

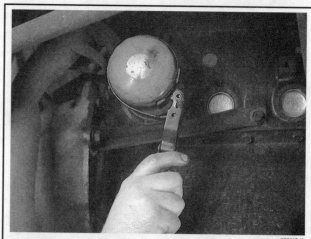

Fig. 133 Use an appropriate wrench to loosen the oil filter, then turn the filter slowly by hand until oil starts to drain out the bottom

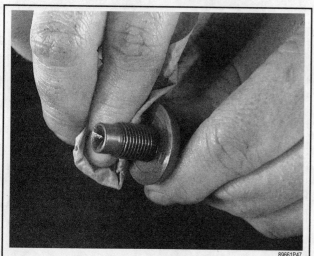

Fig. 131 Make sure you clean and inspect the threads on the drain plug before reinstalling it in the oil pan

Fig. 134 When removing the oil filter, keep it in an upright position. The filter is not completely drained and oil may spill out

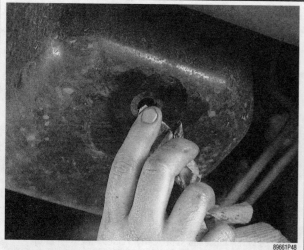

Fig. 132 Clean the oil pan to avoid getting dirt inside the drain plug hole, then inspect the hole's threads

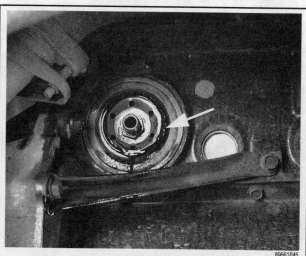

Fig. 135 When the filter is removed, make sure the gasket does not stick to the filter mounting boss, as in this photo

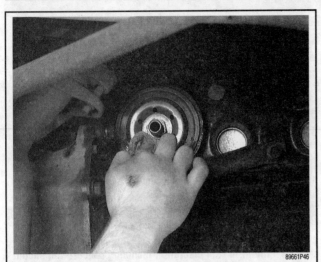

Fig. 136 Be sure to clean the mounting boss' gasket surface of any oil residue left before installing the new filter

The EPA warns that prolonged contact with used engine oil may cause a number of skin disorders, including cancer! You should make every effort to minimize your exposure to used engine oil. Protective gloves should be worn when changing the oil. Wash your hands and any other exposed skin areas as soon as possible after exposure to used engine oil. Soap and water, or waterless hand cleaner, should be used.

➡The engine oil and oil filter should be changed at the recommended intervals. Though some manufacturers have at times recommended changing the filter every other oil change, we at Chilton recommend that you should always change the filter with the oil. The benefit of fresh oil is quickly lost if the old filter is clogged and unable to do its job. Also, leaving the old filter in place leaves a significant amount of dirty oil in the system.

1. Raise and support the vehicle safely.
2. Make sure the oil drain plug is at the lowest point on the oil pan. If not, you may have to raise the vehicle slightly higher on one jackstand (side) than the other.
3. Before you crawl under the vehicle, take a look at where you will be working and gather all the necessary tools, such as a few wrenches or a strip of sockets, the drain pan and some clean rags. If the oil filter is more accessible from underneath the vehicle, you will also want to grab a bottle of oil, the new filter and a filter wrench at this time.
4. Position the drain pan beneath the oil pan drain plug. Keep in mind that the fast flowing oil, which will spill out as you pull the plug from the pan, will flow with enough force that it could miss the pan. Position the drain pan accordingly and be ready to move the pan more directly beneath the plug as the oil flow lessens to a trickle.
5. Loosen the drain plug with a wrench (or socket and driver), then carefully unscrew the plug with your fingers. Use a rag to shield your fingers from the heat. Push in on the plug as you unscrew it so you can feel when all of the screw threads are out of the hole, (and so you will keep the oil from seeping past the threads until you are ready to remove the plug). You can then remove the plug quickly to avoid having hot oil run down your arm. This will also help assure that you have the plug in your hand, not in the bottom of a pan of hot oil.

※ CAUTION

Be careful of the oil; when at operating temperature, it is hot enough to cause a severe burn.

6. Allow the oil to drain until nothing but a few drops come out of the drain hole. Check the drain plug to make sure the threads and sealing surface are not damaged. Carefully thread the plug into position and tighten it with a torque wrench to 25 ft. lbs. (34 Nm). If a torque wrench is not available, snug the drain plug and give a slight additional turn. You don't want the plug to fall out (as you would quickly become stranded), but the pan threads are EASILY stripped from overtightening (and this can be time consuming and/or costly to fix).
7. To remove the filter, you will need an oil filter wrench, since the filter may have been fitted too tightly and/or the heat from the engine may have made it even tighter. A filter wrench can be obtained at an auto parts store and is well worth the investment.
8. Loosen the filter with the filter wrench. With a rag wrapped around the filter, unscrew the filter from the boss on the engine. Be careful of the hot oil that will run down the side of the filter. Make sure that your drain pan is under the filter before you start to remove it from the engine; should some of the hot oil happen to get on you, there will be a place to dump the filter in a hurry and the filter will usually spill a good bit of dirty oil as it is removed.
9. Wipe the base of the mounting boss with a clean, dry cloth. As applicable, partially fill the filter with fresh engine oil. This will prevent the engine from running out of oil when started. When you install the new filter, smear a small amount of fresh oil on the gasket with your finger, just enough to coat the entire contact surface. When you tighten the filter, rotate it approximately ¾ turn beyond the point where it makes contact (or follow any instructions which are provided on the filter or parts box).

※ WARNING

Never operate the engine without engine oil, otherwise severe engine damage will result.

10. Remove the jackstands and carefully lower the vehicle, then immediately refill the engine crankcase with the proper amount of oil.
11. Refill the engine crankcase slowly, checking the level often. You may notice that it usually takes less than the amount of oil listed in the capacity chart to refill the crankcase. But, that is only until the engine is run and the oil filter is completely filled with oil. To make sure the proper level is obtained, run the engine to normal operating temperature, shut the engine OFF, allow the oil to drain back into the oil pan, and recheck the level. Top off the oil at this time to the FULL mark.

➡If the vehicle is not resting on level ground, the oil level reading on the dipstick may be slightly off. Be sure to check the level only when the vehicle is sitting level.

12. Empty your used oil into a suitable container for recycling.

Manual Transmission

The manual transmission oil should be replaced at 37,500 miles (60,000 km) intervals.

FLUID RECOMMENDATIONS

The use of 10W-30 weight engine oil meeting API service specification SH is recommended for use in all manual transmissions.

➡Dexron®II or equivalent automatic transmission fluid can be used as a substitute for the transmission's engine oil if high shift effort is experienced during warm-up in cold weather.

LEVEL CHECK

◆ See Figures 137 and 138

1. Park the vehicle on a level surface, turn the engine OFF, firmly apply the parking brake and block the drive wheels.

➡Ground clearance may make access to the transmission filler plug impossible without raising and supporting the vehicle. If the vehicle must be raised, it must be supported at four corners and level. If only the front or rear is supported, an improper fluid level will be indicated.

2. Remove the filler plug from the side of the transmission. The fluid level should be even with the bottom of the filler hole.

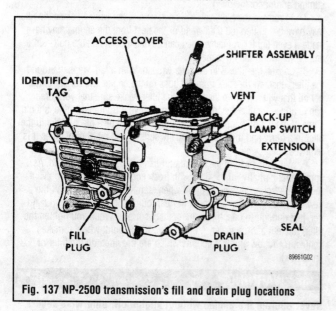

Fig. 137 NP-2500 transmission's fill and drain plug locations

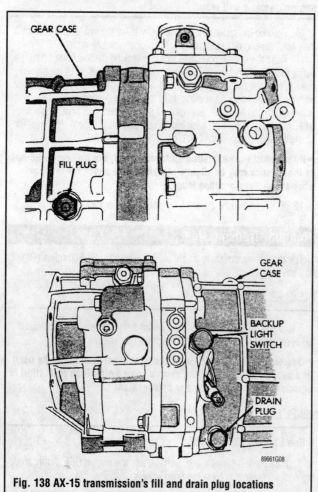

Fig. 138 AX-15 transmission's fill and drain plug locations

3. If additional fluid is necessary, add it through the filler hole using a siphon pump or squeeze bottle.

4. Carefully install the filler plug and tighten to 27 ft. lbs. (37 Nm).

➡DO NOT overtighten the filler plug, as this can damage the transmission.

5. Lower the vehicle.

DRAIN & REFILL

➡It is a good idea to warm the oil first so it will flow better. This can be accomplished by 15–20 miles (24–32 km) of highway driving. Oil which is warmed to normal operating temperature will flow faster, drain more completely and remove more contaminants from the transmission.

❊❊ CAUTION

The EPA warns that prolonged contact with used gear oil may cause a number of skin disorders, including cancer! You should make every effort to minimize your exposure to used gear oil. Protective gloves should be worn when changing the oil. Wash your hands and any other exposed skin areas as soon as possible after exposure to used gear oil. Soap and water, or waterless hand cleaner, should be used.

1. Raise and support the vehicle safely. Remember that the vehicle must be supported level (at four points) so the proper oil level can be determined.

2. Before you crawl under the vehicle, take a look at where you will be working and gather all the necessary tools, such as a few wrenches or a strip of sockets, the drain pan and some clean rags.

3. Position the drain pan beneath the transmission drain plug. Keep in mind that the fast flowing oil, which will spill out as you pull the plug from the transmission, will flow with enough force that it could miss the pan. Position the drain pan accordingly and be ready to move the pan more directly beneath the plug as the oil flow lessens to a trickle.

4. Loosen the filler plug with a wrench (or socket and driver), then carefully unscrew the plug with your fingers. This step is performed first to ensure the transmission can be filled with fresh oil after the used oil is drained.

5. Loosen the drain plug with a wrench (or socket and driver), then carefully unscrew the plug with your fingers. Use a rag to shield your fingers from the heat. Push in on the plug as you unscrew it so you can feel when all of the screw threads are out of the hole, (and so you will keep the oil from seeping past the threads until you are ready to remove the plug). You can then remove the plug quickly to avoid having hot oil run down your arm. This will also help assure that you have the plug in your hand, not in the bottom of a pan of hot oil.

❊❊ CAUTION

Be careful of the oil; when at operating temperature, it is hot enough to cause a severe burn.

6. Allow the oil to drain until nothing but a few drops come out of the drain hole. Check the drain plug to make sure the threads and sealing surface are not damaged. Carefully thread the plug into position and tighten it with a torque wrench to 27 ft. lbs. (37 Nm). If a torque wrench is not available, snug the drain plug and give it a slight additional turn. You don't want the plug to fall out (as you would quickly become stranded), but the threads are easily stripped from overtightening (and this can be time consuming and/or costly to fix).

❊❊ WARNING

Never operate the transmission without oil, otherwise severe damage will result.

7. Refill the transmission slowly, checking the level often with your finger, as illustrated. Due to the positioning of the filler hole, it is very difficult to see the level of oil in the transmission. This makes overfilling and

spilling the gear oil a good possibility. When the gear oil level reaches the bottom of the filler hole, the gear oil is at the proper level.

8. Check the filler plug to make sure the threads and sealing surface are not damaged. Carefully thread the plug into position and tighten it with a torque wrench to 27 ft. lbs. (37 Nm).

9. Remove the jackstands and carefully lower the vehicle.

10. Empty your used oil into a suitable container for recycling.

Automatic Transmission

The automatic transmission fluid and filter should be replaced every 37,500 miles (60,000 km).

FLUID RECOMMENDATIONS

The manufacturer recommends the use of genuine Mopar ATF Plus (Mopar ATF Type 7176) automatic transmission fluid. An equivalent Dexron®II ATF should be used only if the recommended fluid is not available.

LEVEL CHECK

▶ **See Figures 139, 140 and 141**

It is very important to maintain the proper fluid level in an automatic transmission. If the level is either too high or too low, poor shifting and/or internal damage are likely to occur. For this reason, a regular check of the transmission fluid level is essential.

➡ **Most manufacturers specify that the transmission fluid should be checked at normal operating temperature. Drive the vehicle for 15–20 miles (24–32 km) of highway driving, allowing the transmission to reach operating temperature. If the vehicle is driven at extended highway speeds, is driven in city traffic in hot weather, or is being used to pull a trailer, fluid temperatures will likely exceed normal operating and checking ranges. In these circumstances, give the fluid time to cool (about 30 minutes) before checking the level.**

1. Park the vehicle on a level surface, apply the parking brake and leave the engine idling. Shift the transmission and engage each gear, then place the selector in **P**.

2. Open the hood and locate the transmission dipstick. Wipe away any dirt in the area of the dipstick to prevent it from falling into the filler tube. Remove the dipstick, wipe it clean using a lint-free rag and reinsert it until it seats fully on the filler tube.

3. Remove the dipstick and hold it horizontally while noting the fluid level. The fluid level should be in the crosshatched area on the dipstick.

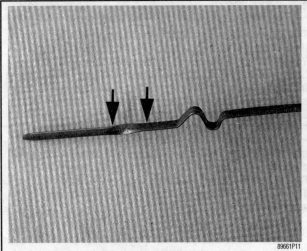
Fig. 140 The transmission fluid level is in the safe range when it falls in the crosshatched area

Fig. 141 Using a funnel to reduce spillage, add transmission fluid directly into the dipstick tube

4. If the level is below the crosshatched area, use a funnel and add fluid in small quantities through the dipstick filler tube. Keep the engine running while adding fluid and check the level after each small amount. Do not overfill.

➡ **Since the transmission fluid is added through the dipstick tube, if you check the fluid level too soon after adding fluid, an incorrect reading may occur. After adding fluid, wait a few minutes to allow it to fully drain into the transmission.**

5. The fluid on the dipstick should be a bright red color. If it is discolored (brown or black), or smells burnt, serious transmission troubles, probably due to overheating, should be suspected. The transmission should be inspected to locate the cause of the burnt fluid.

6. Replace the dipstick and make sure it is fully seated.

FLUID & FILTER SERVICE

▶ **See Figures 142 thru 155**

It is a good idea to warm the transmission fluid first so it will flow better. This can be accomplished by 15–20 miles (24–32 km) of highway driving. Fluid which is warmed to normal operating temperature will flow faster, drain more completely and remove more contaminants from the engine.

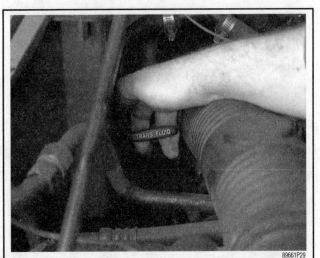
Fig. 139 The transmission dipstick is located on the passenger side of the engine compartment, adjacent to the evaporator case

✴✴ CAUTION

The EPA warns that prolonged contact with used transmission fluid may cause a number of skin disorders, including cancer! You should make every effort to minimize your exposure to used transmission fluid. Protective gloves should be worn when changing the fluid. Wash your hands and any other exposed skin areas as soon as possible after exposure to used transmission fluid. Soap and water, or waterless hand cleaner, should be used.

➡The transmission fluid and filter should be changed at the recommended intervals. Though some manufacturers have at times recommended changing the filter every other fluid change, we at Chilton recommend that you always change the filter with the fluid. The benefit of fresh fluid is quickly lost if the old filter is clogged and unable to do its job.

1. Raise and support the vehicle safely.
2. Make sure the transmission drain plug is at the lowest point on the pan.
3. Before you crawl under the vehicle, take a look at where you will be working and gather all the necessary tools, such as a few wrenches or a strip of sockets, an extra large (but shallow) drain pan and some clean rags.

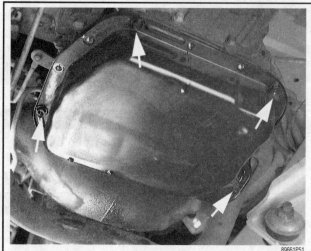

Fig. 144 Leave a bolt at each corner of the transmission fluid pan to keep the pan from bending and the fluid from spilling

Fig. 142 There are 14 bolts which retain the transmission fluid pan

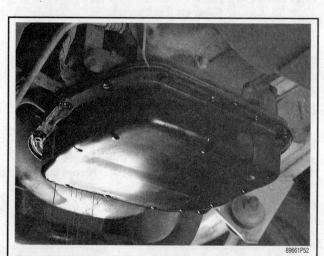

Fig. 145 As the four corner bolts are slowly loosened, the fluid will begin to drain; it may be necessary to gently pry or pull on the pan to unseat it

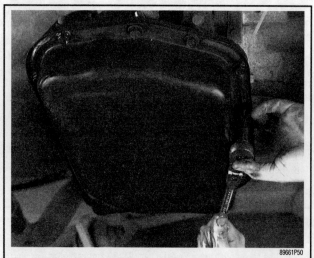

Fig. 143 Loosen and remove the transmission fluid pan bolts, except for those at the four corners

Fig. 146 When the fluid stops flowing, support the bottom of the pan before removing the remaining bolts to reduce spillage

Fig. 147 As you lower the pan, fluid will drip from the transmission, so make sure you are to the side

Fig. 150 Remove the bolts completely, and lower the filter to drain the remaining fluid

Fig. 148 Loosen the three bolts that retain the transmission filter, but do not remove them, so that fluid can drain out

Fig. 151 Note the positions of the filter bolt holes in the transmission's valve body (filter removed)

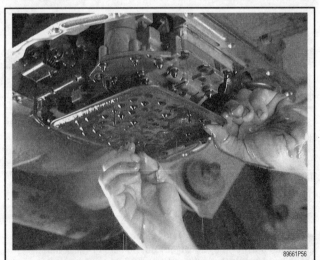

Fig. 149 Wait until the fluid stops draining out before you remove the bolts completely

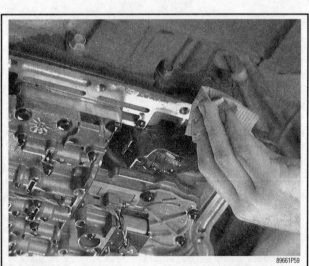

Fig. 152 Remove any gasket material left on the transmission case, and wipe it clean before installing the pan with a new gasket

Fig. 153 Be sure to also remove the gasket and other material left on the pan

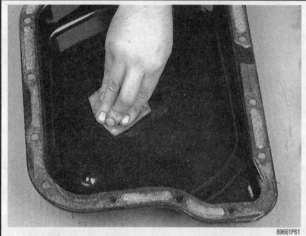

Fig. 154 Wipe out the inside of the pan, including the magnet(s); check for sediment in the pan or metal shavings on the magnet(s)

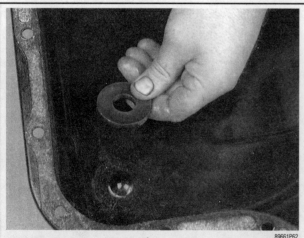

Fig. 155 Make sure the magnet(s) are clean and that you place them back inside the pan before installing it on the transmission case

4. Position the large, shallow drain pan beneath the fluid pan. Keep in mind that the fast flowing fluid, which will spill out as you lower the fluid pan, will flow with enough force that it could miss the pan. Position the drain pan accordingly and be ready to move the pan more directly beneath the transmission pan as the fluid flow lessens to a trickle.

5. Loosen, but do not remove, all of the fluid pan attaching bolts.

6. Remove all but the four corner bolts.

7. While supporting the pan with one hand, carefully remove two adjacent corner bolts and drain the fluid by allowing the pan to tip down on one side.

➡This procedure most often creates a messy situation. Have plenty of rags available to clean up the spilled fluid.

✳✳ CAUTION

Be careful of the fluid; when at operating temperature, it is hot enough to cause a severe burn.

8. Allow the fluid to drain until nothing but a few drops flow from the pan.

9. Remove the two remaining corner bolts and lower the fluid pan from the transmission.

10. Loosen the filter attaching bolts. The filter tube is usually held into the transmission with an O-ring. Make sure the O-ring comes out of the transmission when the filter is removed. Carefully remove the transmission filter.

11. Wipe the base of the filter mounting boss with a clean, dry cloth. When you install the new filter, smear a small amount of petroleum jelly on the O-ring with your finger, just enough to coat the entire contact surface. This will lubricate the O-ring and prevent it from getting damaged during installation of the filter.

12. Push the filter tube into the boss on the transmission and make sure it is fully seated. Install the transmission filter attaching bolts and tighten to 35 inch lbs. (4 Nm).

13. Clean all the sediment out of the transmission pan with solvent. Remove the magnet(s) from the pan and clean them thoroughly, then return them to the pan. The magnets are used to trap any metallic particles floating in the transmission fluid.

➡Most transmission pans and cases are made of aluminum and can be easily damaged. When removing old gasket material, take care not to gouge the aluminum.

14. Clean the transmission pan and transmission gasket mating surfaces of all old gasket material. After scraping all the old material off, wipe the area with a lint-free rag moistened with solvent. Allow it to dry completely.

15. Lay the new gasket on the transmission pan and check for proper alignment. Remove the gasket, place a few dabs of adhesive on the pan and place the gasket down again. Make sure the gasket is aligned before the adhesive is dry.

16. Position the pan on the transmission and install the pan bolts. Tighten the bolts in a crisscross pattern to 150 inch lbs. (17 Nm).

✳✳ WARNING

Never operate the transmission without fluid, otherwise severe damage will result.

17. Remove the jackstands and carefully lower the vehicle, then immediately refill the transmission with the proper amount and type of fluid.

18. Refill the transmission slowly, checking the level often. You may notice that it usually takes less than the amount of fluid listed in the Capacities chart to refill the transmission. This is due to the torque converter being partially filled with fluid. To make sure the proper level is obtained, start the engine and shift the transmission, engaging each gear. Then place the selector in **P**. Adjust the fluid to the proper level.

➡If the vehicle is not resting on level ground, the fluid level reading on the dipstick may be slightly off. Be sure to check the level only when the vehicle is sitting level.

19. Empty the used fluid into a suitable container for recycling.

Drive Axle

The manufacturer states that scheduled drive axle lubricant replacement is not necessary. However, we at Chilton recommend checking the level and condition every 30,000 miles (48,000 km), and replacing the lubricant as necessary.

FLUID RECOMMENDATIONS

The manufacturer recommends the use of a 80W-90 weight lubricant meeting API specification GL-5.

LEVEL CHECK

▶ See Figures 156, 157 and 158

1. Raise and support the vehicle safely.
2. With the vehicle level, remove the filler plug from the back side of the differential.

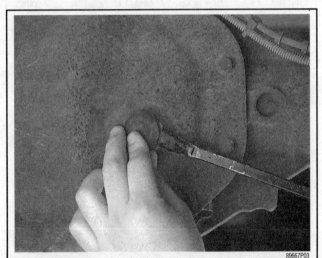

Fig. 156 The rear axle fluid is checked via a plug in the rear cover

Fig. 157 When checking gear oil level, stick your finger inside the check hole

Fig. 158 The gear oil level should be ⅜ in. (10mm) below the bottom of the filler hole

3. Drive axle lubricant is at the proper level if it is ⅜ in. (10mm) below the bottom of the filler hole. If the oil level is low, carefully insert your finger (watch out for sharp threads) into the hole and check that the oil level is within specification.
4. If not, add oil through the hole until the proper level is obtained. Most gear oils come in a plastic squeeze bottle with a nozzle that making addition simple. You can also use a common kitchen baster. Use only the specified lubricant.
5. Replace the filler plug and check for leaks.
6. Lower the vehicle.

DRAIN & REFILL

▶ See Figures 159 thru 169

➡It is a good idea to warm the gear oil first so it will flow better. This can be accomplished by 15–20 miles (24–32 km) of highway driving. Oil which is warmed to normal operating temperature will flow faster, drain more completely and remove more contaminants from the axle.

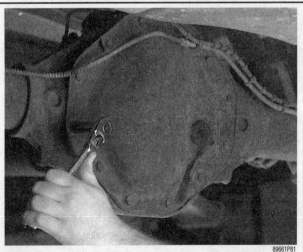

Fig. 159 Loosen all cover bolts and remove all bolts except two at the top and two at the bottom

Fig. 160 Use a prybar to carefully pry the cover from the axle housing

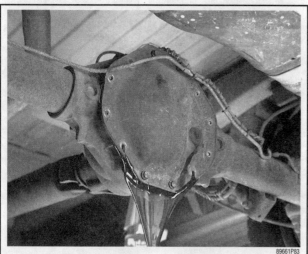

Fig. 161 The gear fluid should flow into the drain pan without causing a mess

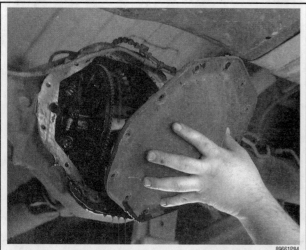

Fig. 162 Once the gear oil drains, remove the remaining bolts, then remove the axle housing cover

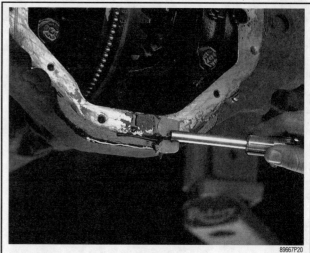

Fig. 163 Use a scraper to remove gasket material from the axle housing . . .

Fig. 164 . . . and the axle housing cover

Fig. 165 Wipe the cover clean, as sealer will not adhere to an oily surface

Fig. 166 Apply sealer in a continuous bead around the cover

Fig. 167 When installing the axle cover, always replace the metal identification tag. This tag provides the only means of externally identifying the axle ratio

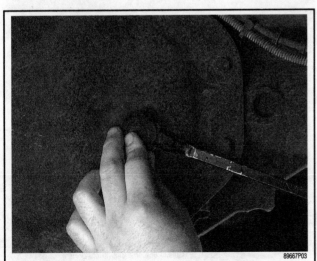

Fig. 168 Remove the plug in the axle housing cover to fill and check the rear axle fluid

Fig. 169 Fill the axle housing through the filler hole with the proper type and amount of gear oil

❋❋ CAUTION

The EPA warns that prolonged contact with used gear oil may cause a number of skin disorders, including cancer! You should make every effort to minimize your exposure to used gear oil. Protective gloves should be worn when changing the oil. Wash your hands and any other exposed skin areas as soon as possible after exposure to used gear oil. Soap and water, or waterless hand cleaner, should be used.

1. Raise and support the vehicle safely.
2. Before you crawl under the vehicle, take a look at where you will be working and gather all the necessary tools, such as a few wrenches or a strip of sockets, the drain pan and some clean rags.
3. Position the drain pan beneath the drive axle. Keep in mind that the fast flowing oil, which will spill out as you loosen the rear cover, will flow with enough force that it could miss the pan. Position the drain pan accordingly and be ready to move the pan more directly beneath the drive axle as the oil flow lessens to a trickle.
4. Loosen the rear cover bolts with a wrench (or socket and driver), then carefully unscrew all but the top bolt with your fingers.

❋❋ CAUTION

Be careful of the oil; when at operating temperature, it is hot enough to cause a severe burn.

5. Gently pry the cover loose from the drive axle.
6. Allow the oil to drain until nothing but a few drops come out of the drive axle.
7. Thoroughly clean all gasket mating surfaces and install a new gasket on the drive axle cover.

❋❋ WARNING

Never operate the drive axle without oil, otherwise severe damage will result.

8. Remove the plug from the axle housing cover.
9. Refill the drive axle slowly, checking the level with your finger. Due to the positioning of the filler hole, it is very difficult to see the level of oil in the drive axle. This makes overfilling and spilling the gear oil a good possibility.
10. Install the filler plug.
11. Remove the jackstands and carefully lower the vehicle.
12. Empty your used oil into a suitable container for recycling.

Cooling System

▶ **See Figures 170, 171, 172 and 173**

The cooling system level should be visually inspected each time the hood is opened. Antifreeze should be replaced at 52,500 miles (84,000 km) and then every 30,000 miles (48,000 km).

If necessary, hose clamps should be checked and soft or cracked hoses replaced. Damp spots or accumulations of rust or dye near hoses, the water pump or other areas indicate areas of possible leakage.

Check the surge tank cap for a worn or cracked gasket. If the cap doesn't seal properly, fluid will be lost and the engine will overheat. A worn cap should be replaced with a new one. The surge tank should be free of rust and the coolant should be free from oil. If oil is found in the coolant, the engine thermostat will not function correctly; in this case, the system must be flushed and filled with fresh coolant.

Periodically clean any debris such as leaves, paper, insects, etc. from the radiator fins. Pick the large pieces off by hand. The smaller pieces can be washed away with water pressure from a hose.

Carefully straighten any bent radiator fins with a pair of needlenose pliers. Be careful—the fins are very soft. Don't wiggle the fins back and forth too much. Straighten them once and try not to move them again.

FLUID RECOMMENDATIONS

The use of a good quality ethylene glycol based or other aluminum compatible antifreeze is recommended. It is best to add a 50/50 mix of antifreeze and water to avoid diluting the coolant in the system.

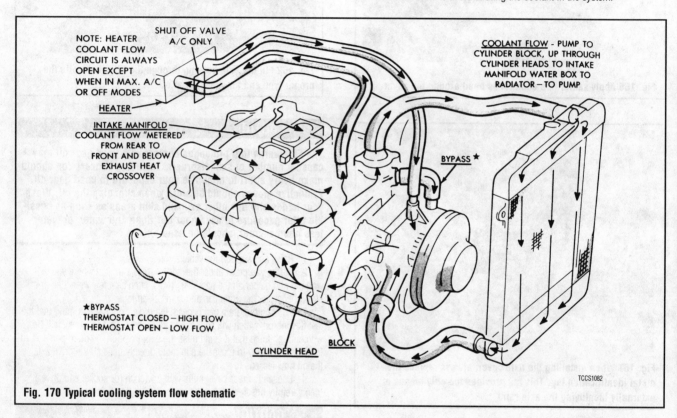

Fig. 170 Typical cooling system flow schematic

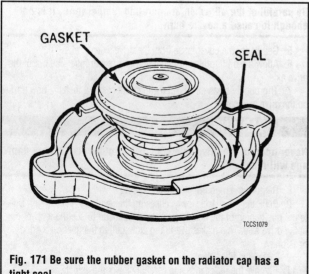

Fig. 171 Be sure the rubber gasket on the radiator cap has a tight seal

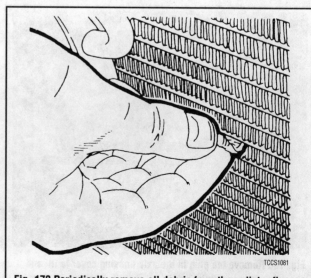

Fig. 172 Periodically remove all debris from the radiator fins

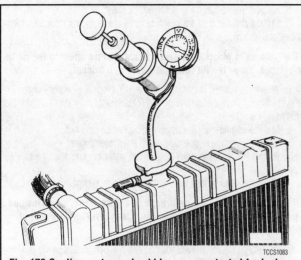

Fig. 173 Cooling systems should be pressure tested for leaks periodically

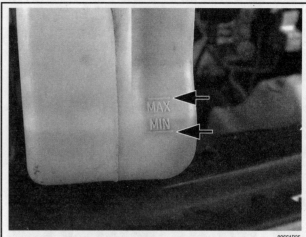

Fig. 175 The coolant level should be between these two lines when checking or adding the coolant mixture into the overflow bottle

LEVEL CHECK

▶ See Figures 174 and 175

1. Check the fluid level in the reserve tank to make sure the system is properly filled. Top off the cooling system using the recovery tank markings as a guideline. If you top off the system, make a note to check it again soon.

→Never overfill the reserve tank.

2. A coolant level that consistently drops is usually a sign of a small, hard to detect leak, although, in the worst case, it could be a sign of an internal engine leak (check the engine oil for milky white contamination). In most cases, you will be able to trace the leak to a loose fitting or damaged hose.

→Evaporating ethylene glycol antifreeze will leave small, white (salt-like) deposits, which can be helpful in tracing a leak.

DRAIN, FLUSH & REFILL

▶ See Figures 176, 177, 178 and 179

✳✳ CAUTION

When draining coolant, keep in mind that cats and dogs are attracted to ethylene glycol antifreeze, and are likely to drink any that is left in an uncovered container or in puddles on the ground. This will prove fatal in sufficient quantity. Always drain coolant into a sealable container. Coolant may be reused unless it is contaminated or several years old.

→Ensure that the engine is completely cool prior to starting this service.

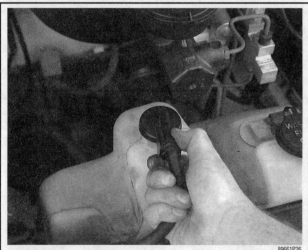

Fig. 174 The coolant overflow bottle is located in the left front of the engine compartment, adjacent to the washer solvent bottle

Fig. 176 The radiator drain is located at the bottom of the radiator, on the driver's side

Fig. 177 Loosen the drain plug and let the fluid drain; if drainage is slow, make sure that the radiator cap is off

Fig. 178 Inspect the radiator cap for damage to the seals (arrows), and check that the pressure relief spring is functional

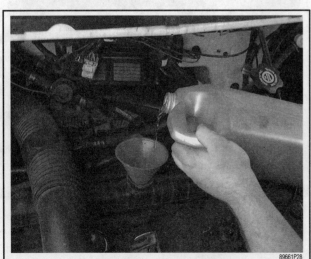

Fig. 179 Pour the coolant mixture directly into the radiator; a funnel can be used to avoid spillage

1. Remove the radiator and reserve tank caps.
2. Place a drain pan of sufficient capacity under the radiator and open the petcock (drain).

➡ **The petcock is plastic and easily binds. Before opening the radiator petcock, spray it with some penetrating lubricant.**

3. When the system is completely drained, close the petcock and fill the system with a radiator cleaning fluid (clean water may also be used, but is not as efficient).
4. Idle the engine until the upper radiator hose gets hot.
5. Allow the engine to cool and drain the system again.
6. Repeat this process until the drained water is clear and free of scale.
7. Flush the reserve tank with water and leave it empty.

➡ **If you decide to add the antifreeze and water separately (instead of pre-mixing them), be sure that you add a sufficient amount of antifreeze, before topping off with water.**

8. Determine the capacity of the coolant system, then properly refill the cooling system with a 50/50 mixture of fresh coolant (antifreeze and water), as follows:
   a. Fill the radiator with coolant until it reaches the radiator filler neck seat.
   b. Start the engine and allow it to idle until the thermostat opens (the upper radiator hose will become hot).
   c. Turn the engine **OFF** and refill the radiator until the coolant level is at the filler neck seat.
   d. Fill the engine coolant overflow tank with coolant to the proper mark, then install the radiator cap.
9. If available, install a pressure tester and check for leaks. If a pressure tester is not available, run the engine until normal operating temperature is reached (allowing the system to naturally pressurize), then check for leaks.
10. Check the level of protection with an antifreeze/coolant hydrometer.

Windshield Washer Reservoir

▶ **See Figure 180**

The windshield washer solvent bottle is located adjacent to the coolant reserve tank. Remove the cap on the bottle and check the fluid by looking down into the bottle; if it is not full, pour the proper mixture of washer solvent into the bottle. Washer solvent comes in a concentrated formula. Check the directions on the bottle you are using to determine the proper solvent and water mixture.

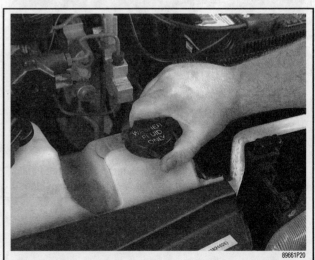

Fig. 180 The washer solvent reservoir is located in the front driver's side of the engine compartment, adjacent to the radiator

Brake Master Cylinder

FLUID RECOMMENDATIONS

The use of fresh, uncontaminated brake fluid meeting or exceeding DOT 3 standards, or equivalent, is recommended.

LEVEL CHECK

▶ See Figures 181, 182, 183 and 184

1. Check the level of fluid in the brake master cylinder reservoir. The fluid should be maintained between the markings on the reservoir.

➡ Any sudden decrease in fluid level indicates a probable leak in the system and should be inspected immediately.

2. Clean around the reservoir cap with a shop rag to prevent contaminating the fluid with dirt.
3. Remove the cap and add the required amount of fluid to the system.

Fig. 183 There are two caps for the master cylinder reservoir; be sure to open both and check the fluid level in both

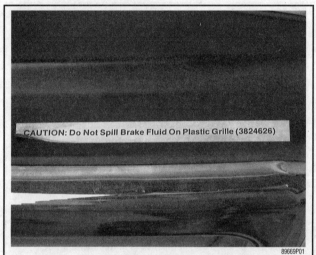

Fig. 181 Brake fluid will permanently damage the front grille, so avoid spilling brake fluid on the grille during servicing

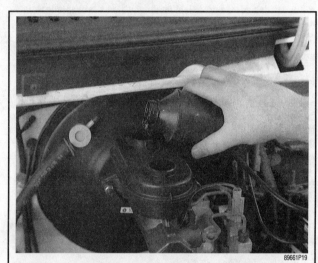

Fig. 184 Take care when adding brake fluid; it is corrosive and can damage surfaces of other components, especially paint

➡ When making additions of fluid, use only fresh, uncontaminated brake fluid meeting or exceeding DOT 3 standards. Be careful not to spill any brake fluid on painted surfaces, because it will damage the paint. Do not allow the fluid container or brake fluid reservoir to remain open any longer than necessary; brake fluid absorbs moisture from the air, reducing its effectiveness and causing brake line corrosion.

4. Install the reservoir cap.

Clutch Master Cylinder

FLUID RECOMMENDATIONS

The use of fresh, uncontaminated brake fluid meeting or exceeding DOT 3 standards or equivalent is recommended.

LEVEL CHECK

▶ See Figure 185

1. Check the level of fluid in the clutch master cylinder reservoir. The fluid should be maintained between the markings on the reservoir.

Fig. 182 Wipe off the top of the brake master cylinder before removing the cap, to avoid contaminating the fluid with dirt

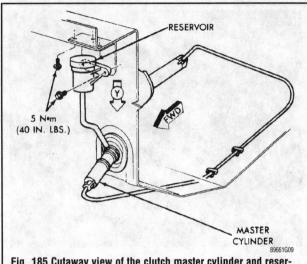

Fig. 185 Cutaway view of the clutch master cylinder and reservoir location

➡Any sudden decrease in fluid level indicates a probable leak in the system and should be inspected immediately.

2. Clean around the reservoir cap with a shop rag to prevent contaminating the fluid with dirt.

3. Remove the cap and add the required amount of fluid to the system.

➡When making additions of fluid, use only fresh, uncontaminated brake fluid meeting or exceeding DOT 3 standards. Be careful not to spill any brake fluid on painted surfaces, because it will damage the paint. Do not allow the fluid container or clutch reservoir to remain open any longer than necessary; brake fluid absorbs moisture from the air, reducing its effectiveness and causing brake line corrosion.

4. Install the reservoir cap.

Power Steering Pump

FLUID RECOMMENDATIONS

The manufacturer recommends the use of Mopar power steering fluid or equivalent.

LEVEL CHECK

▶ See Figures 186, 187, 188 and 189

☀ WARNING

Operating the engine without the proper amount and type of power steering fluid will result in decreased steering ability and severe damage to the pump.

1. Park the vehicle on a level surface.

2. Open the hood and locate the power steering fluid reservoir. Remove the combination cap/dipstick from the reservoir, wipe it clean, and reinsert it. Make sure the cap/dipstick is fully seated.

3. Pull the cap/dipstick from the reservoir again. Holding it horizontally, read the fluid level. The fluid should be in the crosshatched area, above the **ADD** mark and below the **FULL** mark.. If the fluid is below the **ADD** mark, add the required amount of the appropriate fluid to the reservoir.

4. Replace the dipstick, and check the level again after adding any fluid.

Fig. 186 The power steering pump is located on the driver's side front of the engine, and is driven by the serpentine belt

Fig. 187 The power steering dipstick is marked with a FULL COLD line. If low, fill the fluid to this level when the vehicle is cold

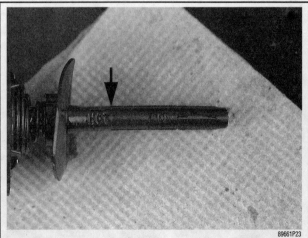

Fig. 188 The power steering dipstick is also marked FULL HOT. If necessary, fill the fluid to this level after the vehicle is warmed up

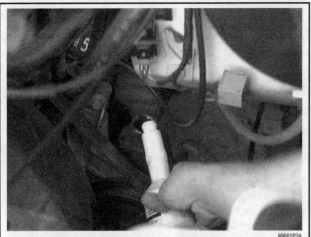

Fig. 189 Add power steering fluid directly to the reservoir. A funnel can be used, but be sure you can see the level while pouring

Fig. 191 View of the grease fittings for the front end on the left side; the right side is similar

Chassis Greasing

LUBRICATION

▶ See Figures 190, 191, 192 and 193

Some components are permanently lubricated during manufacture and do not need periodic maintenance. These components can be identified by the lack of a grease fitting.

Inspect each component to be lubricated. Replace components with

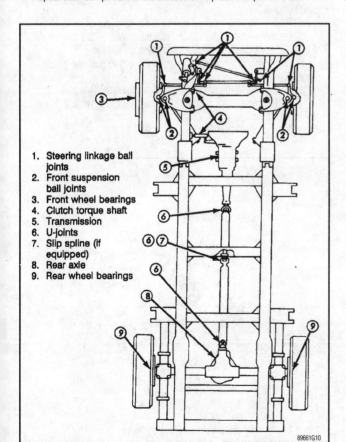

1. Steering linkage ball joints
2. Front suspension ball joints
3. Front wheel bearings
4. Clutch torque shaft
5. Transmission
6. U-joints
7. Slip spline (if equipped)
8. Rear axle
9. Rear wheel bearings

Fig. 190 Common chassis lubrication points

Fig. 192 Make sure the grease fittings are clean before applying grease to them

Fig. 193 Make sure you have the grease gun completely seated on the grease fitting before you pump grease into it

torn/ruptured ball joint seals. Damaged seals will eventually leak grease or allow contaminates to enter.

Body Lubrication and Maintenance

LUBRICATION

To lubricate lock cylinders, apply graphite lubricant sparingly through the key slot. Insert the key and operate the lock several times to be sure that the lubricant is worked into the lock cylinder.

At least once a year, use a multi-purpose grease to lubricate the body door hinges, including the hood and fuel door hinges and latches. The glove box, console doors and folding seat hardware should also be lightly lubricated. Open and close the door several times to be sure that the lubricant is evenly and thoroughly distributed.

MAINTENANCE

Door and window weatherstripping should be lubricated with silicone lubricant. Flush the underbody using plain water to remove any corrosive materials picked up from the road and used for ice, snow or dust control. Make sure you thoroughly clean areas where mud and dirt may collect. If necessary, loosen sediment packed in closed areas before flushing. Clean leaves from vent and cowl areas.

To preserve the appearance of your car, it should be washed periodically with a mild soap or detergent and water solution. A detergent specifically designed for automotive use should be used to loosen dirt or grease from the vehicle. Dishwashing detergent contains degreasers which will strip the vehicles surface of wax. Only wash the vehicle when the metal feels cool and the vehicle is in the shade. Rinse the entire vehicle with water, then wash and rinse one panel at a time, beginning with the roof and upper areas. After washing is complete, rinse the vehicle one final time and dry with a soft cloth or chamois. Air drying a vehicle, by driving at highway speeds for a few miles, may quickly and easily dry a vehicle without the need for excessive elbow grease.

Periodic polishing and waxing will remove harmful deposits from the vehicle's surface and protect the finish. If the finish has dulled due to age or neglect, non-abrasive cleaner may be necessary to restore the original gloss.

There are many specialized products available at your local auto parts store to care for the appearance of painted metal surfaces, plastic, chrome, wheels and tires, as well as the interior upholstery and carpeting. Be sure to follow the manufacturers' instructions before using them.

Wheel Bearings

REPACKING

▶ See Figure 194

➡Sodium based grease is not compatible with lithium based grease. Read the package labels and be careful not to mix the two types. If there is any doubt as to the type of grease used, completely clean the old grease from the bearing and hub before replacing.

Before handling the bearings, there are a few things that you should remember to do and not to do.

DO the following:
- Remove all outside dirt from the housing before exposing the bearing.
- Treat a used bearing as gently as you would a new one.
- Work with clean tools in clean surroundings.
- Use clean, dry gloves, or at least clean, dry hands.
- Clean solvents and flushing fluids are a must.
- Use clean paper when laying out the bearings to dry.

- Protect disassembled bearings from rust and dirt. Cover them up.
- Use clean, lint-free rags to wipe the bearings.
- Keep the bearings in oil-proof paper when they are to be stored or are not in use.
- Clean the inside of the housing before replacing the bearing.

Do NOT do the following:
- Do not work in dirty surroundings.
- Do not use dirty, chipped or damaged tools.
- Do not work on wooden work benches or use wooden mallets.
- Do not handle bearings with dirty or moist hands.
- Do not use gasoline for cleaning. Use a safe solvent.
- Do not spin dry bearings with compressed air. They will be damaged.
- Do not use cotton waste or dirty cloths to wipe bearings.
- Do not scratch or nick bearing surfaces.
- Do not allow the bearing to come in contact with dirt or rust at any time.

The front wheel bearings require periodic maintenance. A premium high melting point grease meeting NLGI Grade GC or GC–LB or equivalent must be used. Long fiber type greases must not be used. This service is recommended every 22,500 miles (36,000 km).

➡**For information on Wheel Bearing removal and installation, refer to Section 8 of this manual.**

1. Remove the wheel bearing.
2. Clean all parts in a non-flammable solvent and let them air dry.

➡**Only use lint-free rags to dry the bearings. Never spin-dry a bearing with compressed air, as this will damage the rollers.**

3. Check for excessive wear and damage. Replace the bearing as necessary.

➡**Packing wheel bearings with grease is best accomplished by using a wheel bearing packer (available at most automotive parts stores).**

4. If a wheel bearing packer is not available, the bearings may be packed by hand.
   a. Place a "healthy" glob of grease in the palm of one hand.
   b. Force the edge of the bearing into the grease so that the grease fills the space between the rollers and the bearing cage.
   c. Keep rotating the bearing while continuing to push the grease through.
   d. Continue until the grease is forced out the other side of the bearing.
5. Place the packed bearing on a clean surface and cover it until it is time for installation.
6. Install the wheel bearing.

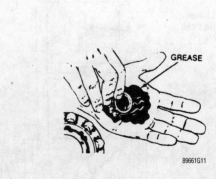

Fig. 194 Packing the wheel bearing by hand

TRAILER TOWING

General Recommendations

Your vehicle was primarily designed to carry passengers and cargo. It is important to remember that towing a trailer will place additional loads on your vehicle's engine, drive train, steering, braking and other systems. However, if you decide to tow a trailer, using the prior equipment is a must.

Local laws may require specific equipment such as trailer brakes or fender mounted mirrors. Check your local laws.

Trailer Weight

The weight of the trailer is the most important factor. A good weight-to-horsepower ratio is about 35:1, 35 lbs. of Gross Combined Weight (GCW) for every horsepower your engine develops. Multiply the engine's rated horsepower by 35 and subtract the weight of the vehicle, passengers and luggage. The number remaining is the approximate ideal maximum weight you should tow, although a numerically higher axle ratio can help compensate for heavier weight.

Hitch (Tongue) Weight

▶ **See Figure 195**

Calculate the hitch weight in order to select a proper hitch. The weight of the hitch is usually 9–11% of the trailer gross weight and should be measured with the trailer loaded. Hitches fall into various categories: those that mount on the frame and rear bumper, the bolt-on type, or the weld-on distribution type used for larger trailers. Axle mounted or clamp-on bumper hitches should never be used.

Check the gross weight rating of your trailer. Tongue weight is usually figured as 10% of gross trailer weight. Therefore, a trailer with a maximum gross weight of 2000 lbs. will have a maximum tongue weight of 200 lbs. Class I trailers fall into this category. Class II trailers are those with a gross weight rating of 2000–3000 lbs., while Class III trailers fall into the 3500–6000 lbs. category. Class IV trailers are those over 6000 lbs. and are for use with fifth wheel trucks, only.

When you've determined the hitch that you'll need, follow the manufacturer's installation instructions, exactly, especially when it comes to fastener torques. The hitch will subjected to a lot of stress and good hitches come with hardened bolts. Never substitute an inferior bolt for a hardened bolt.

Engine

One of the most common, if not THE most common, problems associated with trailer towing is engine overheating. If you have a cooling system without an expansion tank, you'll definitely need to get an aftermarket expansion tank kit, preferably one with at least a 2 quart capacity. These kits are easily installed on the radiator's overflow hose, and come with a pressure cap designed for expansion tanks.

Aftermarket engine oil coolers are helpful for prolonging engine oil life and reducing overall engine temperatures. Both of these factors increase engine life. While not absolutely necessary in towing Class I and some Class II trailers, they are recommended for heavier Class II and all Class III towing. Engine oil cooler systems usually consist of an adapter, screwed on in place of the oil filter, a remote filter mounting and a multi-tube, finned heat exchanger, which is mounted in front of the radiator or air conditioning condenser.

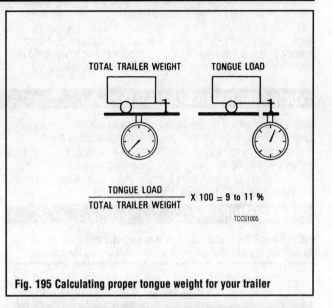

Fig. 195 Calculating proper tongue weight for your trailer

Transmission

An automatic transmission is usually recommended for trailer towing. Modern automatics have proven reliable and, of course, easy to operate, in trailer towing. The increased load of a trailer, however, causes an increase in the temperature of the automatic transmission fluid. Heat is the worst enemy of an automatic transmission. As the temperature of the fluid increases, the life of the fluid decreases.

It is essential, therefore, that you install an automatic transmission cooler. The cooler, which consists of a multi-tube, finned heat exchanger, is usually installed in front of the radiator or air conditioning compressor, and hooked in-line with the transmission cooler tank inlet line. Follow the cooler manufacturer's installation instructions.

Select a cooler of at least adequate capacity, based upon the combined gross weights of the vehicle and trailer.

Cooler manufacturers recommend that you use an aftermarket cooler in addition to, and not instead of, the present cooling tank in your radiator. If you do want to use it in place of the radiator cooling tank, get a cooler at least two sizes larger than normally necessary.

➡**A transmission cooler can, sometimes, cause slow or harsh shifting in the transmission during cold weather, until the fluid has a chance to come up to normal operating temperature. Some coolers can be purchased with or retrofitted with a temperature bypass valve which will allow fluid flow through the cooler only when the fluid has reached above a certain operating temperature.**

Handling a Trailer

Towing a trailer with ease and safety requires a certain amount of experience. It's a good idea to learn the feel of a trailer by practicing turning, stopping and backing in an open area such as an empty parking lot.

TOWING THE VEHICLE

Preferred Method—Flatbed

For maximum safety to the components of your drive train and chassis, it is most desirable to have your vehicle towed on a flatbed or whole car trailer. The only way to properly place the vehicle on a flatbed is to have it pulled on from the front.

Alternate Method—T-hook

If a flatbed is unavailable, your vehicle can be towed using a T-hook wrecker. In this case, it is best to tow from the rear, with the front wheels on or off the ground. Tow vehicle speed should not exceed 35 mph (56 km/h) when using this method.

When necessary, you can tow using the T-hook in the front. It is strongly recommended that the rear wheels be off the ground. If the vehicle must be towed from the front with the rear wheels on the ground, first disconnect and secure the driveshaft, if possible. If, however, the vehicle must be towed from the front with the rear wheels on the ground and the driveshaft connected, the total distance towed should NOT EXCEED 50 miles (80 km); otherwise, transmission damage may occur.

JUMP STARTING A DEAD BATTERY

Whenever a vehicle is jump started, precautions must be followed in order to prevent the possibility of personal injury. Remember that batteries contain a small amount of explosive hydrogen gas which is a by-product of battery charging. Sparks should always be avoided when working around batteries, especially when attaching jumper cables. To minimize the possibility of accidental sparks, follow the procedure carefully.

✳✳ CAUTION

NEVER hook the batteries up in a series circuit or the entire electrical system will go up in smoke, including the starter!

Vehicles equipped with a diesel engine may utilize two 12 volt batteries. If so, the batteries are connected in a parallel circuit (positive terminal to positive terminal, negative terminal to negative terminal). Hooking the batteries up in parallel circuit increases battery cranking power without increasing total battery voltage output. Output remains at 12 volts. On the other hand, hooking two 12 volt batteries up in a series circuit (positive terminal to negative terminal, positive terminal to negative terminal) increases total battery output to 24 volts (12 volts plus 12 volts).

Jump Starting Precautions

• Be sure that both batteries are of the same voltage. Vehicles covered by this manual and most vehicles on the road today utilize a 12 volt charging system.
• Be sure that both batteries are of the same polarity (have the same terminal, in most cases NEGATIVE grounded).
• Be sure that the vehicles are not touching or a short could occur.
• On serviceable batteries, be sure the vent cap holes are not obstructed.
• Do not smoke or allow sparks anywhere near the batteries.
• In cold weather, make sure the battery electrolyte is not frozen. This can occur more readily in a battery that has been in a state of discharge.
• Do not allow electrolyte to contact your skin or clothing.

Jump Starting Procedure

SINGLE BATTERY GASOLINE ENGINE MODELS

▶ **See Figure 196**

1. Make sure that the voltages of the 2 batteries are the same. Most batteries and charging systems are of the 12 volt variety.
2. Pull the jumping vehicle (with the good battery) into a position so the jumper cables can reach the dead battery and that vehicle's engine. Make sure that the vehicles do NOT touch.
3. Place the transmissions of both vehicles in **Neutral** (MT) or **P** (AT), as applicable, then firmly set their parking brakes.

➡**If necessary for safety reasons, the hazard lights on both vehicles may be operated throughout the entire procedure without significantly increasing the difficulty of jumping the dead battery.**

4. Turn all lights and accessories OFF on both vehicles. Make sure the ignition switches on both vehicles are turned to the **OFF** position.
5. Cover the battery cell caps with a rag, but do not cover the terminals.
6. Make sure the terminals on both batteries are clean and free of corrosion or proper electrical connection will be impeded. If necessary, clean the battery terminals before proceeding.

Last Chance Method—Dolly

If absolutely necessary, you can tow your vehicle with either the front or rear wheels on a dolly. Again, the preferred method would be to leave the front wheels on the ground and the rear on the dolly, so the drive train is not turning. All conditions which apply to the T-hook method also apply for the dolly method.

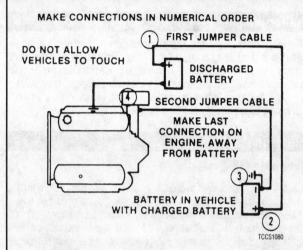

Fig. 196 Connect the jumper cables to the batteries and engine in the order shown

7. Identify the positive (+) and negative (-) terminals on both batteries.
8. Connect the first jumper cable to the positive (+) terminal of the dead battery, then connect the other end of that cable to the positive (+) terminal of the booster (good) battery.
9. Connect one end of the other jumper cable to the negative (-) terminal on the booster battery and the final cable clamp to an engine bolt head, alternator bracket or other solid, metallic point on the engine with the dead battery. Try to pick a ground on the engine that is positioned away from the battery in order to minimize the possibility of the 2 clamps touching should one loosen during the procedure. DO NOT connect this clamp to the negative (-) terminal of the bad battery.

✳✳ CAUTION

Be very careful to keep the jumper cables away from moving parts (cooling fan, belts, etc.) on both engines.

10. Check to make sure that the cables are routed away from any moving parts, then start the donor vehicle's engine. Run the engine at moderate speed for several minutes to allow the dead battery a chance to receive some initial charge.
11. With the donor vehicle's engine still running slightly above idle, try to start the vehicle with the dead battery. Crank the engine for no more than 10 seconds at a time and let the starter cool for at least 20 seconds between tries. If the vehicle does not start in 3 tries, it is likely that something else is also wrong or that the battery needs additional time to charge.
12. Once the vehicle is started, allow it to run at idle for a few seconds to make sure that it is operating properly.
13. Turn ON the headlights, heater blower and, if equipped, the rear defroster of both vehicles in order to reduce the severity of voltage spikes and subsequent risk of damage to the vehicles' electrical systems when the cables are disconnected. This step is especially important to any vehicle equipped with computer control modules.
14. Carefully disconnect the cables in the reverse order of connection.

Start with the negative cable that is attached to the engine ground, then the negative cable on the donor battery. Disconnect the positive cable from the donor battery and finally, disconnect the positive cable from the formerly dead battery. Be careful when disconnecting the cables from the positive terminals not to allow the alligator clips to touch any metal on either vehicle or a short and sparks will occur.

DUAL BATTERY DIESEL MODELS

▶ See Figure 197

Some diesel model vehicles utilize two 12 volt batteries, one on either side of the engine compartment. The batteries are connected in a parallel circuit (positive terminal to positive terminal and negative terminal to negative terminal). Hooking the batteries up in a parallel circuit increases battery cranking power without increasing total battery voltage output. The output will remain at 12 volts. On the other hand, hooking two 12 volt batteries in a series circuit (positive terminal to negative terminal and negative terminal to positive terminal) increases the total battery output to 24 volts (12 volts plus 12 volts).

※※ WARNING

Never hook the batteries up in a series circuit or the entire electrical system will be damaged, including the starter motor.

In the event that a dual battery vehicle needs to be jump started, use the following procedure:

1. Turn the heater blower motor **ON** to help protect the electrical system from voltage surges when the jumper cables are connected and disconnected.
2. Turn all lights and other switches **OFF**.

➡The battery cables connected to one of the diesel vehicle's batteries may be thicker than those connected to its other battery. (The passenger side battery often has thicker cables.) This set-up allows relatively high jump starting current to pass without damage. If so, be sure to connect the positive jumper cable to the appropriate battery in the disabled vehicle. If there is no difference in cable thickness, connect the jumper cable to either battery's positive terminal. Similarly, if the donor vehicle also utilizes two batteries, the jumper cable connections should be made to the battery with the thicker cables; if there is no difference in thickness, the connections can be made to either donor battery.

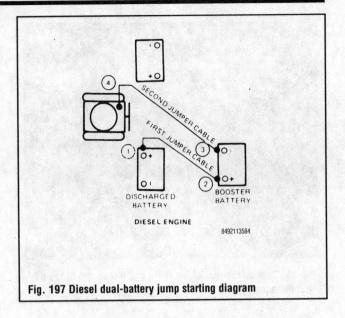

Fig. 197 Diesel dual-battery jump starting diagram

3. Connect the end of a jumper cable to one of the disabled diesel's positive (+) battery terminals, then connect the clamp at the other end of the same cable to the positive terminal (+) on the jumper battery.
4. Connect one end of the other jumper cable to the negative battery terminal (-) on the jumper battery, then connect the other cable clamp to an engine bolt head, alternator bracket or other solid, metallic point on the disabled vehicle's engine. DO NOT connect this clamp to the negative terminal (-) of the disabled vehicle's battery.

※※ CAUTION

Be careful to keep the jumper cables away from moving parts (cooling fan, belts, etc.) on both engines.

5. Start the engine on the vehicle with the good battery and run it at a moderate speed.
6. Start the engine of the vehicle with the discharged battery.
7. When the engine starts on the vehicle with the discharged battery, remove the cable from the engine block before disconnecting the cable from the positive terminal.

JACKING

Your vehicle was supplied with a jack for emergency road repairs. This jack is fine for changing a flat tire or other short term procedures not requiring you to go beneath the vehicle. If it is used in an emergency situation, carefully follow the instructions provided either with the jack or in your owner's manual. Do not attempt to use the jack on any portions of the vehicle other than specified by the vehicle manufacturer. Always block the diagonally opposite wheel when using a jack.

Never place the jack under the radiator, engine or transmission components. Severe and expensive damage will result when the jack is raised. Additionally, never jack under the floorpan or bodywork; the metal will deform.

Whenever you plan to work under the vehicle, you must support it on jackstands or ramps. Never use cinder blocks or stacks of wood to support the vehicle, even if you're only going to be under it for a few minutes. Never crawl under the vehicle when it is supported only by the tire-changing jack or other floor jack.

➡**Always position a block of wood or small rubber pad on top of the jack or jackstand to protect the lifting point's finish when lifting or supporting the vehicle.**

Small hydraulic, screw, or scissors jacks are satisfactory for raising the vehicle. Drive-on trestles or ramps are also a handy and safe way to both raise and safely support the vehicle on jackstands. Be careful though, some ramps may be too steep to drive your vehicle onto without scraping the front bottom panels. Never support the vehicle on any suspension member (unless specifically instructed to do so by a repair manual) or by an underbody panel.

Jacking Precautions

▶ See Figures 198, 199, 200 and 201

The following safety points cannot be overemphasized:
• Always block the opposite wheel or wheels to keep the vehicle from rolling off the jack.
• When raising the front of the vehicle, firmly apply the parking brake.
• When the drive wheels are to remain on the ground, leave the vehicle in gear to help prevent it from rolling.
• Always use jackstands to support the vehicle when you are working underneath. Place the stands beneath the vehicle's jacking brackets. Before climbing underneath, rock the vehicle a bit to make sure it is firmly supported.

Fig. 198 Jack up the rear of the vehicle by the bottom of the differential housing

Fig. 200 Jack up the front of the vehicle beneath the front crossmember. Try to get the jack as close to the center as possible

Fig. 199 After jacking, support the rear of the vehicle by placing jackstands at the ends of the axle housing

Fig. 201 After raising the front of the vehicle, place jackstands beneath the front lower control arms

MANUFACTURER RECOMMENDED MAINTENANCE INTERVALS
(1989-93 MODELS)

Inspection and service is also necessary anytime a malfunction is observed or suspected.

Where both time and mileage are shown, follow the interval which occurs first.	Miles (Thousand)	6	12	18	24	30	36	42	48	54	60	66	72	78	82½	84	90	96	102	108
	Kilometers (Thousand)	9.6	19	29	38	48	58	67	77	85	96	106	116	125	132	135	145	154	164	174
Coolant Condition, Coolant Hoses/Clamps		X	X	X	X	X	X	X	X	X	X	X	X	X		X	X	X	X	X
Exhaust System — Check		X	X	X	X	X	X	X	X	X	X	X	X	X		X	X	X	X	X
Oil — Change (6 Months)		X	X	X	X	X	X	X	X	X	X	X	X	X		X	X	X	X	X
Oil Filter — Change (2nd Oil Change)			X		X		X		X		X		X			X		X		X
Drive Belt Tension — Inspect & Adjust			X[1]				X			X[1]			X				X[1]			X
Drive Belts (V-Type) — Replace											X									
Air Filter/Air Pump Air Filter — Replace					X					X			X				X			
Crankcase Inlet Air Filter (6 & 8 Cyl. Eng. Only) — Clean					X					X			X					X		
Spark Plug — Replace						X					X						X			
Fuel Filter — Replace as necessary																				
Coolant — Flush/Replace (36 months) & 24 months/48 000 km (30,000 miles) thereafter																				
EGR Valve & Tube — Replace											X[2]									
EGR Tube — Clean Passengers											X[2]									
PCV Valve — Replace											X[2]									
Vacuum Emission Components — Replace											X									
Ignition Timing — Adjust to Specs, as necessary											X									
Ignition Cables, Distributor Cap & Rotor — Replace											X									
Manifold Heat Control Valve — Lubricate											X									
Battery — Replace											X									
Oxygen Sensor — Replace															X[2]					

[1] For California vehicles, this maintenance is recommended by Chrysler Motors to the owner but, is not required to maintain the warranty on the air pump drive belt.

[2] Requires Emission Maintenance Reminder Light. If so equipped, these parts are to be replaced at the indicated mileage, or when the emissions maintenance reminded light remains on continuously with the key in the "on" position, whichever occurs first.

89661C06

MANUFACTURER RECOMMENDED MAINTENANCE INTERVALS
(1994-98 MODELS—NORMAL SERVICE)

TO BE SERVICED		TYPE OF SERVICE	VEHICLE MILEAGE INTERVAL (x1000)													
			7.5	15	22.5	30	37.5	45	52.5	60	67.5	75	82.5	90	97.5	miles
			12	24	36	48	60	72	84	96	108	120	132	144	156	km
			6	12	18	24	30	36	42	48	54	60	66	72	78	months
Engine oil		D/R	✓	✓	✓	✓	✓	✓	✓	✓	✓	✓	✓	✓	✓	
Engine oil filter	(1)	R		✓		✓		✓		✓		✓		✓		
Front wheel bearings	(2)	S/I			✓			✓			✓			✓		
Brake linings		S/I			✓			✓			✓			✓		
Air cleaner element	(3)	R				✓				✓				✓		
Spark plugs	(3)	R				✓				✓				✓		
ATF / Replace filter, adjust bands		D/R					✓					✓				
Engine Coolant	(4)	R/F					✓									
Distributor cap and rotor	(3)	R								✓						
Ignition wires	(3)	R								✓						
PCV valve. Replace if nec.	(3)	S/I								✓						
Crankcase inlet air filter		C/L								✓						

R - Replace
S/I - Service or Inspect
R/F - Replace and flush system
D/R - Drain and refill
C/L - Clean and lubricate

1 - If your total distance is less than 7500 mi. (12,000 km) yearly, replace the engine oil filter at each oil change.
2 - Clean and repack if required
3 - Emission Control System Maintenance is listed in bold type. Service must be performed on-schedule to assure continued proper functioning of the system.
4 - Flush and refill at 36 mos. regardless of miles, then every 24 mos./30,000 mi. (48,000 km) thereafter

AT EACH OIL CHANGE

Inspect the exhaust system.
Inspect the brake hoses.
Rotate the tires.
Check engine coolant level, hoses and clamps.
Lubricate steering linkage.
If applicable, lubricate the driveshaft universal joints and slip spline at each oil change.

89661C07

MANUFACTURER RECOMMENDED MAINTENANCE INTERVALS
(1994-96 MODELS —SEVERE SERVICE)

TO BE SERVICED		TYPE OF SERVICE	VEHICLE MILEAGE INTERVAL (x1000)													
			3	6	9	12	15	18	21	24	27	30	33	36	39	miles ⑥
			5	10	14	19	24	29	34	39	43	48	53	58	63	km
Engine oil		D/R	✓	✓	✓	✓	✓	✓	✓	✓	✓	✓	✓	✓	✓	
Engine oil filter	①	R		✓		✓		✓		✓		✓		✓		
Front wheel bearings	②	S/I			✓			✓			✓			✓		
Brake linings		S/I				✓				✓				✓		
Air cleaner element	③	R										✓		✓		
Spark plugs	③	R										✓		✓		
ATF / Replace filter, adjust bands		D/R				✓ ④				✓ ④				✓ ④		
Rear axle fluid		R				✓				✓						
Engine Coolant	⑤	R/F														

R - Replace
S/I - Service or Inspect
R/F - Replace and flush system
D/R - Drain and refill

1 - If your distance travelled is less than 7500 mi. (12,000 km) yearly, replace the engine oil filter at each oil change.
2 - Clean and repack if required.
3 - Emission Control System Maintenance is listed in bold type. Service must be performed on-schedule to assure continued proper functioning of the system.
4 - Off-the-highway operation, trailer towing, snow plowing, prolonged operation with heavy loading, especially in hot weather require more frequent transmission service.
5 - Flush and refill at 36 mos. regardless of miles, then every 24 mos./30,000 m. (48,000 km) thereafter.
6 - Observe the same maintenance intervals for mileage beyond that which appears on this chart.

AT EACH OIL CHANGE

Inspect the exhaust system.
Inspect the brake hoses.
Check engine coolant level, hoses and clamps.
Lubricate steering linkage.
If applicable, lubricate the driveshaft universal joints and slip spline at each oil change.

AT EVERY OTHER OIL CHANGE

Rotate the tires.

89661C08

CAPACITIES

Year	Model	Engine ID/VIN	Engine Displacement Liters (cc)	Engine Oil with Filter (qts.)	Transmission (pts.) 4-Spd	5-Spd	Auto.	Transfer Case (pts.)	Drive Axle Front (pts.)	Rear (pts.)	Fuel Tank (gal.)	Cooling System (qts.)
1989	B150 Van	X	3.9 (3916)	4.5	7.0	6.8	①	-	-	③	22.0 ⑤	14.6 ⑥
	B150 Van	Y	5.2 (5211)	4.5	7.0	6.8	①	-	-	③	22.0 ⑤	16.5 ⑥
	B250 Van	X	3.9 (3916)	4.5	7.0	-	①	-	-	③	22.0 ⑤	14.6 ⑥
	B250 Van	Y	5.2 (5211)	4.5	7.0	-	①	-	-	③	22.0 ⑤	16.5 ⑥
	B250 Van	Z	5.9 (5899)	4.5	7.0	-	①	-	-	③	35.0	15.0 ⑥
	B350 Van	Y	5.2 (5211)	4.5	7.0	-	①	-	-	③	22.0 ⑤	11.5 ⑥
	B350 Van	Z	5.9 (5899)	4.5	7.0	-	①	-	-	③	35.0	15.0 ⑥
1990	B150 Van	X	3.9 (3916)	4.5	7.0	6.8	①	-	-	③	22.0 ⑤	14.6 ⑥
	B150 Van	Y	5.2 (5211)	4.5	7.0	6.8	①	-	-	③	22.0 ⑤	16.5 ⑥
	B250 Van	X	3.9 (3916)	4.5	7.0	-	①	-	-	③	22.0 ⑤	14.6 ⑥
	B250 Van	Y	5.2 (5211)	4.5	7.0	-	①	-	-	③	22.0 ⑤	16.5 ⑥
	B250 Van	Z	5.9 (5899)	4.5	7.0	-	①	-	-	③	35.0	15.0 ⑥
	B350 Van	Y	5.2 (5211)	4.5	7.0	-	①	-	-	③	22.0 ⑤	11.5 ⑥
	B350 Van	Z	5.9 (5899)	4.5	7.0	-	①	-	-	③	35.0	15.0 ⑥
1991	B150 Van	X	3.9 (3916)	4.5	7.0	6.8	①	-	-	③	22.0 ⑤	14.6 ⑥
	B150 Van	Y	5.2 (5211)	4.5	7.0	6.8	①	-	-	③	22.0 ⑤	16.5 ⑥
	B250 Van	X	3.9 (3916)	4.5	7.0	-	①	-	-	③	22.0 ⑤	14.6 ⑥
	B250 Van	Y	5.2 (5211)	4.5	7.0	-	①	-	-	③	22.0 ⑤	16.5 ⑥
	B250 Van	Z	5.9 (5899)	4.5	7.0	-	①	-	-	③	35.0	15.0 ⑥
	B350 Van	Y	5.2 (5211)	4.5	7.0	-	①	-	-	③	22.0 ⑤	11.5 ⑥
	B350 Van	Z	5.9 (5899)	4.5	7.0	-	①	-	-	③	35.0	15.0 ⑥
1992	B150 Van	X	3.9 (3916)	4.5	-	6.8	①	-	-	③	22.0 ⑤	14.6 ⑥
	B150 Van	Y	5.2 (5211)	4.5	-	6.8	①	-	-	③	22.0 ⑤	16.5 ⑥
	B250 Van	X	3.9 (3916)	4.5	-	6.8	①	-	-	③	22.0 ⑤	14.6 ⑥
	B250 Van	Y	5.2 (5211)	4.5	-	6.8	①	-	-	③	22.0 ⑤	16.5 ⑥
	B250 Van	Z	5.9 (5899)	4.5	-	6.8	①	-	-	③	35.0	15.0 ⑥
	B350 Van	Y	5.2 (5211)	4.5	-	-	①	-	-	③	22.0 ⑤	11.5 ⑥
	B350 Van	Z	5.9 (5899)	4.5	-	-	①	-	-	③	35.0	15.0 ⑥
1993	B150 Van	X	3.9 (3916)	4.5	-	6.8	①	-	-	③	22.0 ⑤	14.6 ⑥
	B150 Van	Y	5.2 (5211)	4.5	-	6.8	①	-	-	③	22.0 ⑤	16.5 ⑥
	B250 Van	X	3.9 (3916)	4.5	-	6.8	①	-	-	③	22.0 ⑤	14.6 ⑥
	B250 Van	Y	5.2 (5211)	4.5	-	6.8	①	-	-	③	22.0 ⑤	16.5 ⑥
	B250 Van	Z	5.9 (5899)	4.5	-	6.8	①	-	-	③	35.0	15.0 ⑥
	B350 Van	Y	5.2 (5211)	4.5	-	-	①	-	-	③	22.0 ⑤	11.5 ⑥
	B350 Van	Z	5.9 (5899)	4.5	-	-	①	-	-	③	35.0	15.0 ⑥
1994	B150 Van	X	3.9 (3916)	4.0	-	-	①	-	-	④	22.0 ⑤	14.6
	B150 Van	Y	5.2 (5211)	4.5	-	-	①	-	-	④	22.0 ⑤	16.5
	B250 Van	X	3.9 (3916)	4.5	-	-	①	-	-	④	22.0 ⑤	14.6
	B250 Van	Y	5.2 (5211)	4.5	-	-	①	-	-	④	22.0 ⑤	16.5
	B250 Van	A	5.9 (5899)	4.5	-	-	①	-	-	④	35.0	15.0 ⑦
	B350 Van	Y	5.2 (5211)	4.5	-	-	①	-	-	④	22.0 ⑤	16.5
	B350 Van	A	5.9 (5899)	4.5	-	-	①	-	-	④	35.0	15.0 ⑦
1995	B150 Van	X	3.9 (3916)	4.0	-	-	②	-	-	④	22.0 ⑤	14.6
	B150 Van	Y	5.2 (5211)	5.0	-	-	②	-	-	④	22.0 ⑤	16.5
	B250 Van	X	3.9 (3916)	4.0	-	-	②	-	-	④	22.0 ⑤	14.6

89661C09

CAPACITIES

Year	Model	Engine ID/VIN	Engine Displacement Liters (cc)	Engine Oil with Filter (qts.)	Transmission (pts.) 4-Spd	5-Spd	Auto.	Transfer Case (pts.)	Drive Axle Front (pts.)	Rear (pts.)	Fuel Tank (gal.)		Cooling System (qts.)	
1995	B250 Van	Y	5.2 (5211)	5.0	-	-	②	-	-	④	22.0	⑤	16.5	
	B250 Van	Z	5.9 (5899)	5.0	-	-	②	-	-	④	35.0		15.0	⑦
	B350 Van	Y	5.2 (5211)	5.0	-	-	②	-	-	④	22.0	⑤	16.5	
	B350 Van	Z	5.9 (5899)	5.0	-	-	②	-	-	④	35.0		15.0	⑦
1996	B1500 Van	X	3.9 (3916)	4.0	-	-	②	-	-	④	22.0	⑤	14.6	
	B1500 Van	Y	5.2 (5211)	5.0	-	-	②	-	-	④	22.0	⑤	16.5	
	B2500 Van	X	3.9 (3916)	4.0	-	-	②	-	-	④	22.0	⑤	14.6	
	B2500 Van	Y	5.2 (5211)	5.0	-	-	②	-	-	④	22.0	⑤	16.5	
	B2500 Van	Z	5.9 (5899)	5.0	-	-	②	-	-	④	35.0		15.0	⑦
	B3500 Van	Y	5.2 (5211)	5.0	-	-	②	-	-	④	22.0	⑤	16.5	
	B3500 Van	Z	5.9 (5899)	5.0	-	-	②	-	-	④	35.0		15.0	⑦
1997	B1500 Van	X	3.9 (3916)	4.0	-	-	②	-	-	④	22.0	⑤	14.6	
	B1500 Van	Y	5.2 (5211)	5.0	-	-	②	-	-	④	22.0	⑤	16.5	
	B2500 Van	X	3.9 (3916)	4.0	-	-	②	-	-	④	22.0	⑤	14.6	
	B2500 Van	Y	5.2 (5211)	5.0	-	-	②	-	-	④	22.0	⑤	16.5	
	B2500 Van	Z	5.9 (5899)	5.0	-	-	②	-	-	④	35.0		15.0	⑦
	B3500 Van	Y	5.2 (5211)	5.0	-	-	②	-	-	④	22.0	⑤	16.5	
	B3500 Van	Z	5.9 (5899)	5.0	-	-	②	-	-	④	35.0		15.0	⑦
1998	B1500 Van	X	3.9 (3916)	4.0	-	-	②	-	-	④	22.0	⑤	14.6	
	B1500 Van	Y	5.2 (5211)	5.0	-	-	②	-	-	④	22.0	⑤	16.5	
	B2500 Van	X	3.9 (3916)	4.0	-	-	②	-	-	④	22.0	⑤	14.6	
	B2500 Van	Y	5.2 (5211)	5.0	-	-	②	-	-	④	22.0	⑤	16.5	
	B2500 Van	Z	5.9 (5899)	5.0	-	-	②	-	-	④	35.0		15.0	⑦
	B3500 Van	Y	5.2 (5211)	5.0	-	-	②	-	-	④	22.0	⑤	16.5	
	B3500 Van	Z	5.9 (5899)	5.0	-	-	②	-	-	④	35.0		15.0	⑦

① A998/A999 and A727: 17.2 pts.
  A500: 20.4 pts.
  A518: 21.4 pts.
② 32RH: 17.0 pts.
  36RH: 16.6 pts.
  42RH: 20.2 pts.
  32RH: 17.0 pts.
  36RH: 16.6 pts.
  42RH: 20.2 pts.

③ Chrysler: 4.25 pts.
  Dana 60: 6.25 pts.
④ Chrysler 8.25 in.: 4.4 pts.
  Chrysler 9.25 in.: 4.8 pts.
⑤ Optional fuel tank: 35 gals.
⑥ With HD cooling or A/C, add one quart
⑦ With rear heater: 16.0 qts.

89661C10

ENGLISH TO METRIC CONVERSION: MASS (WEIGHT)

Current **mass** measurement is expressed in pounds and ounces (lbs. & ozs.). The metric unit of mass (or weight) is the kilogram (kg). Even although this table does not show conversion of masses (weights) larger than 15 lbs, it is easy to calculate larger units by following the data immediately below.

To convert ounces (oz.) to grams (g): multiply th number of ozs. by 28
To convert grams (g) to ounces (oz.): multiply the number of grams by .035

To convert pounds (lbs.) to kilograms (kg): multiply the number of lbs. by .45
To convert kilograms (kg) to pounds (lbs.): multiply the number of kilograms by 2.2

lbs	kg	lbs	kg	oz	kg	oz	kg
0.1	0.04	0.9	0.41	0.1	0.003	0.9	0.024
0.2	0.09	1	0.4	0.2	0.005	1	0.03
0.3	0.14	2	0.9	0.3	0.008	2	0.06
0.4	0.18	3	1.4	0.4	0.011	3	0.08
0.5	0.23	4	1.8	0.5	0.014	4	0.11
0.6	0.27	5	2.3	0.6	0.017	5	0.14
0.7	0.32	10	4.5	0.7	0.020	10	0.28
0.8	0.36	15	6.8	0.8	0.023	15	0.42

ENGLISH TO METRIC CONVERSION: TEMPERATURE

To convert Fahrenheit (F) to Celsius (°C): take number of °F and subtract 32; multiply result by 5; divide result by 9

To convert Celsius (°C) to Fahrenheit (°F): take number of °C and multiply by 9; divide result by 5; add 32 to total

Fahrenheit (F)		Celsius (C)		Fahrenheit (F)		Celsius (C)		Fahrenheit (F)		Celsius (C)	
°F	°C	°C	°F	°F	°C	°C	°F	°F	°C	°C	°F
−40	−40	−38	−36.4	80	26.7	18	64.4	215	101.7	80	176
−35	−37.2	−36	−32.8	85	29.4	20	68	220	104.4	85	185
−30	−34.4	−34	−29.2	90	32.2	22	71.6	225	107.2	90	194
−25	−31.7	−32	−25.6	95	35.0	24	75.2	230	110.0	95	202
−20	−28.9	−30	−22	100	37.8	26	78.8	235	112.8	100	212
−15	−26.1	−28	−18.4	105	40.6	28	82.4	240	115.6	105	221
−10	−23.3	−26	−14.8	110	43.3	30	86	245	118.3	110	230
−5	−20.6	−24	−11.2	115	46.1	32	89.6	250	121.1	115	239
0	−17.8	−22	−7.6	120	48.9	34	93.2	255	123.9	120	248
1	−17.2	−20	−4	125	51.7	36	96.8	260	126.6	125	257
2	−16.7	−18	−0.4	130	54.4	38	100.4	265	129.4	130	266
3	−16.1	−16	3.2	135	57.2	40	104	270	132.2	135	275
4	−15.6	−14	6.8	140	60.0	42	107.6	275	135.0	140	284
5	−15.0	−12	10.4	145	62.8	44	112.2	280	137.8	145	293
10	−12.2	−10	14	150	65.6	46	114.8	285	140.6	150	302
15	−9.4	−8	17.6	155	68.3	48	118.4	290	143.3	155	311
20	−6.7	−6	21.2	160	71.1	50	122	295	146.1	160	320
25	−3.9	−4	24.8	165	73.9	52	125.6	300	148.9	165	329
30	−1.1	−2	28.4	170	76.7	54	129.2	305	151.7	170	338
35	1.7	0	32	175	79.4	56	132.8	310	154.4	175	347
40	4.4	2	35.6	180	82.2	58	136.4	315	157.2	180	356
45	7.2	4	39.2	185	85.0	60	140	320	160.0	185	365
50	10.0	6	42.8	190	87.8	62	143.6	325	162.8	190	374
55	12.8	8	46.4	195	90.6	64	147.2	330	165.6	195	383
60	15.6	10	50	200	93.3	66	150.8	335	168.3	200	392
65	18.3	12	53.6	205	96.1	68	154.4	340	171.1	205	401
70	21.1	14	57.2	210	98.9	70	158	345	173.9	210	410
75	23.9	16	60.8	212	100.0	75	167	350	176.7	215	414

TCCS1C01

ENGLISH TO METRIC CONVERSION: LENGTH

To convert inches (ins.) to millimeters (mm): multiply number of inches by 25.4

To convert millimeters (mm) to inches (ins.): multiply number of millimeters by .04

Inches		Decimals	Milli-meters	Inches to millimeters		Inches		Decimals	Milli-meters	Inches to millimeters	
				inches	mm					inches	mm
	1/64	0.051625	0.3969	0.0001	0.00254		33/64	0.515625	13.0969	0.6	15.24
1/32		0.03125	0.7937	0.0002	0.00508	17/32		0.53125	13.4937	0.7	17.78
	3/64	0.046875	1.1906	0.0003	0.00762		35/64	0.546875	13.8906	0.8	20.32
1/16		0.0625	1.5875	0.0004	0.01016	9/16		0.5625	14.2875	0.9	22.86
	5/64	0.078125	1.9844	0.0005	0.01270		37/64	0.578125	14.6844	1	25.4
3/32		0.09375	2.3812	0.0006	0.01524	19/32		0.59375	15.0812	2	50.8
	7/64	0.109375	2.7781	0.0007	0.01778		39/64	0.609375	15.4781	3	76.2
1/8		0.125	3.1750	0.0008	0.02032	5/8		0.625	15.8750	4	101.6
	9/64	0.140625	3.5719	0.0009	0.02286		41/64	0.640625	16.2719	5	127.0
5/32		0.15625	3.9687	0.001	0.0254	21/32		0.65625	16.6687	6	152.4
	11/64	0.171875	4.3656	0.002	0.0508		43/64	0.671875	17.0656	7	177.8
3/16		0.1875	4.7625	0.003	0.0762	11/16		0.6875	17.4625	8	203.2
	13/64	0.203125	5.1594	0.004	0.1016		45/64	0.703125	17.8594	9	228.6
7/32		0.21875	5.5562	0.005	0.1270	23/32		0.71875	18.2562	10	254.0
	15/64	0.234375	5.9531	0.006	0.1524		47/64	0.734375	18.6531	11	279.4
1/4		0.25	6.3500	0.007	0.1778	3/4		0.75	19.0500	12	304.8
	17/64	0.265625	6.7469	0.008	0.2032		49/64	0.765625	19.4469	13	330.2
9/32		0.28125	7.1437	0.009	0.2286	25/32		0.78125	19.8437	14	355.6
	19/64	0.296875	7.5406	0.01	0.254		51/64	0.796875	20.2406	15	381.0
5/16		0.3125	7.9375	0.02	0.508	13/16		0.8125	20.6375	16	406.4
	21/64	0.328125	8.3344	0.03	0.762		53/64	0.828125	21.0344	17	431.8
11/32		0.34375	8.7312	0.04	1.016	27/32		0.84375	21.4312	18	457.2
	23/64	0.359375	9.1281	0.05	1.270		55/64	0.859375	21.8281	19	482.6
3/8		0.375	9.5250	0.06	1.524	7/8		0.875	22.2250	20	508.0
	25/64	0.390625	9.9219	0.07	1.778		57/64	0.890625	22.6219	21	533.4
13/32		0.40625	10.3187	0.08	2.032	29/32		0.90625	23.0187	22	558.8
	27/64	0.421875	10.7156	0.09	2.286		59/64	0.921875	23.4156	23	584.2
7/16		0.4375	11.1125	0.1	2.54	15/16		0.9375	23.8125	24	609.6
	29/64	0.453125	11.5094	0.2	5.08		61/64	0.953125	24.2094	25	635.0
15/32		0.46875	11.9062	0.3	7.62	31/32		0.96875	24.6062	26	660.4
	31/64	0.484375	12.3031	0.4	10.16		63/64	0.984375	25.0031	27	690.6
1/2		0.5	12.7000	0.5	12.70						

ENGLISH TO METRIC CONVERSION: TORQUE

To convert foot-pounds (ft. lbs.) to Newton-meters: multiply the number of ft. lbs. by 1.3

To convert inch-pounds (in. lbs.) to Newton-meters: multiply the number of in. lbs. by .11

in lbs	N-m	in lbs	N-m	in lbs	N-m	in lbs	N-m	in lbs	N-m
0.1	0.01	1	0.11	10	1.13	19	2.15	28	3.16
0.2	0.02	2	0.23	11	1.24	20	2.26	29	3.28
0.3	0.03	3	0.34	12	1.36	21	2.37	30	3.39
0.4	0.04	4	0.45	13	1.47	22	2.49	31	3.50
0.5	0.06	5	0.56	14	1.58	23	2.60	32	3.62
0.6	0.07	6	0.68	15	1.70	24	2.71	33	3.73
0.7	0.08	7	0.78	16	1.81	25	2.82	34	3.84
0.8	0.09	8	0.90	17	1.92	26	2.94	35	3.95
0.9	0.10	9	1.02	18	2.03	27	3.05	36	4.0

ENGLISH TO METRIC CONVERSION: TORQUE

Torque is now expressed as either foot-pounds (ft./lbs.) or inch-pounds (in./lbs.). The metric measurement unit for torque is the Newton-meter (Nm). This unit—the Nm—will be used for all SI metric torque references, both the present ft./lbs. and in./lbs.

ft lbs	N-m	ft lbs	N-m	ft lbs	N-m	ft lbs	N-m
0.1	0.1	33	44.7	74	100.3	115	155.9
0.2	0.3	34	46.1	75	101.7	116	157.3
0.3	0.4	35	47.4	76	103.0	117	158.6
0.4	0.5	36	48.8	77	104.4	118	160.0
0.5	0.7	37	50.7	78	105.8	119	161.3
0.6	0.8	38	51.5	79	107.1	120	162.7
0.7	1.0	39	52.9	80	108.5	121	164.0
0.8	1.1	40	54.2	81	109.8	122	165.4
0.9	1.2	41	55.6	82	111.2	123	166.8
1	1.3	42	56.9	83	112.5	124	168.1
2	2.7	43	58.3	84	113.9	125	169.5
3	4.1	44	59.7	85	115.2	126	170.8
4	5.4	45	61.0	86	116.6	127	172.2
5	6.8	46	62.4	87	118.0	128	173.5
6	8.1	47	63.7	88	119.3	129	174.9
7	9.5	48	65.1	89	120.7	130	176.2
8	10.8	49	66.4	90	122.0	131	177.6
9	12.2	50	67.8	91	123.4	132	179.0
10	13.6	51	69.2	92	124.7	133	180.3
11	14.9	52	70.5	93	126.1	134	181.7
12	16.3	53	71.9	94	127.4	135	183.0
13	17.6	54	73.2	95	128.8	136	184.4
14	18.9	55	74.6	96	130.2	137	185.7
15	20.3	56	75.9	97	131.5	138	187.1
16	21.7	57	77.3	98	132.9	139	188.5
17	23.0	58	78.6	99	134.2	140	189.8
18	24.4	59	80.0	100	135.6	141	191.2
19	25.8	60	81.4	101	136.9	142	192.5
20	27.1	61	82.7	102	138.3	143	193.9
21	28.5	62	84.1	103	139.6	144	195.2
22	29.8	63	85.4	104	141.0	145	196.6
23	31.2	64	86.8	105	142.4	146	198.0
24	32.5	65	88.1	106	143.7	147	199.3
25	33.9	66	89.5	107	145.1	148	200.7
26	35.2	67	90.8	108	146.4	149	202.0
27	36.6	68	92.2	109	147.8	150	203.4
28	38.0	69	93.6	110	149.1	151	204.7
29	39.3	70	94.9	111	150.5	152	206.1
30	40.7	71	96.3	112	151.8	153	207.4
31	42.0	72	97.6	113	153.2	154	208.8
32	43.4	73	99.0	114	154.6	155	210.2

TCCS1C03

ENGLISH TO METRIC CONVERSION: LIQUID CAPACITY

Liquid or fluid capacity is presently expressed as pints, quarts or gallons, or a combination of all of these. In the metric system the liter (l) will become the basic unit. Fractions of a liter would be expressed as deciliters, centiliters, or most frequently (and commonly) as milliliters.

To convert pints (pts.) to liters (l): multiply the number of pints by .47
To convert liters (l) to pints (pts.): multiply the number of liters by 2.1
To convert quarts (qts.) to liters (l): multiply the number of quarts by .95

To convert liters (l) to quarts (qts.): multiply the number of liters by 1.06
To convert gallons (gals.) to liters (l): multiply the number of gallons by 3.8
To convert liters (l) to gallons (gals.): multiply the number of liters by .26

gals	liters	qts	liters	pts	liters
0.1	0.38	0.1	0.10	0.1	0.05
0.2	0.76	0.2	0.19	0.2	0.10
0.3	1.1	0.3	0.28	0.3	0.14
0.4	1.5	0.4	0.38	0.4	0.19
0.5	1.9	0.5	0.47	0.5	0.24
0.6	2.3	0.6	0.57	0.6	0.28
0.7	2.6	0.7	0.66	0.7	0.33
0.8	3.0	0.8	0.76	0.8	0.38
0.9	3.4	0.9	0.85	0.9	0.43
1	3.8	1	1.0	1	0.5
2	7.6	2	1.9	2	1.0
3	11.4	3	2.8	3	1.4
4	15.1	4	3.8	4	1.9
5	18.9	5	4.7	5	2.4
6	22.7	6	5.7	6	2.8
7	26.5	7	6.6	7	3.3
8	30.3	8	7.6	8	3.8
9	34.1	9	8.5	9	4.3
10	37.8	10	9.5	10	4.7
11	41.6	11	10.4	11	5.2
12	45.4	12	11.4	12	5.7
13	49.2	13	12.3	13	6.2
14	53.0	14	13.2	14	6.6
15	56.8	15	14.2	15	7.1
16	60.6	16	15.1	16	7.6
17	64.3	17	16.1	17	8.0
18	68.1	18	17.0	18	8.5
19	71.9	19	18.0	19	9.0
20	75.7	20	18.9	20	9.5
21	79.5	21	19.9	21	9.9
22	83.2	22	20.8	22	10.4
23	87.0	23	21.8	23	10.9
24	90.8	24	22.7	24	11.4
25	94.6	25	23.6	25	11.8
26	98.4	26	24.6	26	12.3
27	102.2	27	25.5	27	12.8
28	106.0	28	26.5	28	13.2
29	110.0	29	27.4	29	13.7
30	113.5	30	28.4	30	14.2

TCCS1C05

ENGLISH TO METRIC CONVERSION: FORCE

Force is presently measured in pounds (lbs.). This type of measurement is used to measure spring pressure, specifically how many pounds it takes to compress a spring. Our present force unit (the pound) will be replaced in SI metric measurements by the Newton (N). This term will eventually see use in specifications for electric motor brush spring pressures, valve spring pressures, etc.

To convert pounds (lbs.) to Newton (N): multiply the number of lbs. by 4.45

lbs	N	lbs	N	lbs	N	oz	N
0.01	0.04	21	93.4	59	262.4	1	0.3
0.02	0.09	22	97.9	60	266.9	2	0.6
0.03	0.13	23	102.3	61	271.3	3	0.8
0.04	0.18	24	106.8	62	275.8	4	1.1
0.05	0.22	25	111.2	63	280.2	5	1.4
0.06	0.27	26	115.6	64	284.6	6	1.7
0.07	0.31	27	120.1	65	289.1	7	2.0
0.08	0.36	28	124.6	66	293.6	8	2.2
0.09	0.40	29	129.0	67	298.0	9	2.5
0.1	0.4	30	133.4	68	302.5	10	2.8
0.2	0.9	31	137.9	69	306.9	11	3.1
0.3	1.3	32	142.3	70	311.4	12	3.3
0.4	1.8	33	146.8	71	315.8	13	3.6
0.5	2.2	34	151.2	72	320.3	14	3.9
0.6	2.7	35	155.7	73	324.7	15	4.2
0.7	3.1	36	160.1	74	329.2	16	4.4
0.8	3.6	37	164.6	75	333.6	17	4.7
0.9	4.0	38	169.0	76	338.1	18	5.0
1	4.4	39	173.5	77	342.5	19	5.3
2	8.9	40	177.9	78	347.0	20	5.6
3	13.4	41	182.4	79	351.4	21	5.8
4	17.8	42	186.8	80	355.9	22	6.1
5	22.2	43	191.3	81	360.3	23	6.4
6	26.7	44	195.7	82	364.8	24	6.7
7	31.1	45	200.2	83	369.2	25	7.0
8	35.6	46	204.6	84	373.6	26	7.2
9	40.0	47	209.1	85	378.1	27	7.5
10	44.5	48	213.5	86	382.6	28	7.8
11	48.9	49	218.0	87	387.0	29	8.1
12	53.4	50	224.4	88	391.4	30	8.3
13	57.8	51	226.9	89	395.9	31	8.6
14	62.3	52	231.3	90	400.3	32	8.9
15	66.7	53	235.8	91	404.8	33	9.2
16	71.2	54	240.2	92	409.2	34	9.4
17	75.6	55	244.6	93	413.7	35	9.7
18	80.1	56	249.1	94	418.1	36	10.0
19	84.5	57	253.6	95	422.6	37	10.3
20	89.0	58	258.0	96	427.0	38	10.6

TCCS1C04

ENGLISH TO METRIC CONVERSION: PRESSURE

The basic unit of pressure measurement used today is expressed as pounds per square inch (psi). The metric unit for psi will be the kilopascal (kPa). This will apply to either fluid pressure or air pressure, and will be frequently seen in tire pressure readings, oil pressure specifications, fuel pump pressure, etc.

To convert pounds per square inch (psi) to kilopascals (kPa): multiply the number of psi by 6.89

Psi	kPa	Psi	kPa	Psi	kPa	Psi	kPa
0.1	0.7	37	255.1	82	565.4	127	875.6
0.2	1.4	38	262.0	83	572.3	128	882.5
0.3	2.1	39	268.9	84	579.2	129	889.4
0.4	2.8	40	275.8	85	586.0	130	896.3
0.5	3.4	41	282.7	86	592.9	131	903.2
0.6	4.1	42	289.6	87	599.8	132	910.1
0.7	4.8	43	296.5	88	606.7	133	917.0
0.8	5.5	44	303.4	89	613.6	134	923.9
0.9	6.2	45	310.3	90	620.5	135	930.8
1	6.9	46	317.2	91	627.4	136	937.7
2	13.8	47	324.0	92	634.3	137	944.6
3	20.7	48	331.0	93	641.2	138	951.5
4	27.6	49	337.8	94	648.1	139	958.4
5	34.5	50	344.7	95	655.0	140	965.2
6	41.4	51	351.6	96	661.9	141	972.2
7	48.3	52	358.5	97	668.8	142	979.0
8	55.2	53	365.4	98	675.7	143	985.9
9	62.1	54	372.3	99	682.6	144	992.8
10	69.0	55	379.2	100	689.5	145	999.7
11	75.8	56	386.1	101	696.4	146	1006.6
12	82.7	57	393.0	102	703.3	147	1013.5
13	89.6	58	399.9	103	710.2	148	1020.4
14	96.5	59	406.8	104	717.0	149	1027.3
15	103.4	60	413.7	105	723.9	150	1034.2
16	110.3	61	420.6	106	730.8	151	1041.1
17	117.2	62	427.5	107	737.7	152	1048.0
18	124.1	63	434.4	108	744.6	153	1054.9
19	131.0	64	441.3	109	751.5	154	1061.8
20	137.9	65	448.2	110	758.4	155	1068.7
21	144.8	66	455.0	111	765.3	156	1075.6
22	151.7	67	461.9	112	772.2	157	1082.5
23	158.6	68	468.8	113	779.1	158	1089.4
24	165.5	69	475.7	114	786.0	159	1096.3
25	172.4	70	482.6	115	792.9	160	1103.2
26	179.3	71	489.5	116	799.8	161	1110.0
27	186.2	72	496.4	117	806.7	162	1116.9
28	193.0	73	503.3	118	813.6	163	1123.8
29	200.0	74	510.2	119	820.5	164	1130.7
30	206.8	75	517.1	120	827.4	165	1137.6
31	213.7	76	524.0	121	834.3	166	1144.5
32	220.6	77	530.9	122	841.2	167	1151.4
33	227.5	78	537.8	123	848.0	168	1158.3
34	234.4	79	544.7	124	854.9	169	1165.2
35	241.3	80	551.6	125	861.8	170	1172.1
36	248.2	81	558.5	126	868.7	171	1179.0

TCCS1C06

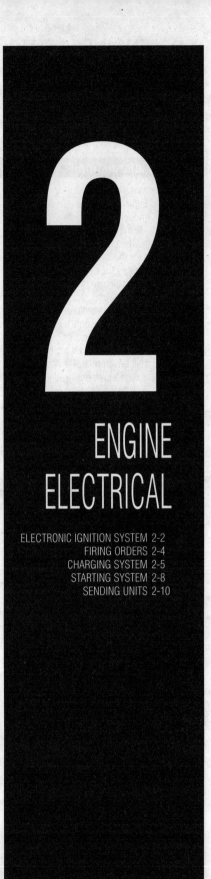

2

ENGINE ELECTRICAL

ELECTRONIC IGNITION SYSTEM

➡For information on understanding electricity and troubleshooting electrical circuits, please refer to Section 6 of this manual.

General Information

The Powertrain Control Module (PCM) or, as it was formerly known, Single Board Engine Controller (SBEC), is the on-board computer which controls the ignition and fuel systems. The PCM automatically regulates the spark advance to fire the spark plugs according to input from various engine sensors. The input signals are then used to compute the optimum ignition timing for the lowest exhaust emissions and best driveability during operation. During the crank-start period, ignition timing advance is set to ensure quick and efficient starting.

The amount of electronic spark advance provided is determined by four input factors: coolant temperature, engine rpm, throttle position and available manifold vacuum. On some late model systems, intake manifold temperature is also used.

All engines are equipped with a camshaft driven mechanical distributor containing a shaft driven rotor. The distributor is equipped with a camshaft position sensor which provides fuel injection synchronization and cylinder identification. The distributor does not have a built-in advance mechanism. Base ignition timing and all advance functions are controlled by the PCM and are not adjustable.

Battery voltage is supplied to the ignition coil from the Automatic Shut Down (ASD) relay. The PCM opens and closes the ignition coil ground circuit to operate the coil.

Diagnosis and Testing

SECONDARY SPARK TEST

♦ See Figure 1

The best way to perform this procedure is to use a spark tester (available at most automotive parts stores). Two types of spark testers are commonly available:

• A neon bulb type tester is connected to the spark plug wire, and flashes with each ignition pulse.

• An air gap type tester must be adjusted to the individual spark plug gap specified for the engine. This type of tester allows the user to not only detect the presence of spark, but also the intensity (orange/yellow is weak, blue is strong).

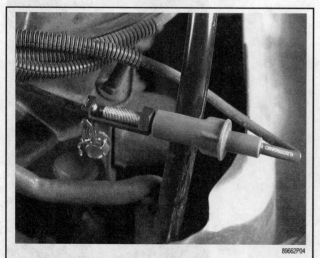

89662P04

Fig. 1 Be sure to have a proper ground when testing for spark with a spark tester

➡If a secondary spark tester is not available, a regular spark plug may be used.

1. Disconnect a spark plug wire at its spark plug.
2. Connect the plug wire to the spark tester and ground the tester to an appropriate location on the engine.
3. Crank the engine and check for spark at the tester.
4. If spark exists at the tester, the ignition system is functioning properly.
5. If spark does not exist at the spark plug wire, remove the distributor cap and check that the rotor is turning when the engine is cranked.
6. If the rotor is not turning, a problem exists in the engine, either in the engine itself or in the distributor.
7. If the rotor is turning, perform the spark test again using the ignition coil wire.
8. If spark does not exist at the ignition coil wire, test the ignition coil, power transistor and related wiring. Repair or replace components as necessary.

Adjustments

All adjustments in the ignition system are controlled by the PCM for optimum performance. No adjustments are possible.

Ignition Coil

TESTING

➡Prior to testing the coil, perform a secondary spark test. If spark occurs at the spark plug, the coil is functioning properly.

1. Turn the ignition **OFF**.
2. Disconnect the negative battery cable.
3. Perform a visual inspection of the coil. If the coil is cracked or damaged, the coil is faulty.
4. Label and disconnect the electrical harness from the ignition coil.
5. Inspect the harness connector and ignition coil terminals for dirt, corrosion or damage. Repair as necessary.
6. Using an ohmmeter, measure coil primary resistance between the ignition coil terminals. Resistance should be 1.34–1.55 ohms @ 68°F (20°C) on 1989–91 models, or 0.95–1.20 ohms @ 68°F (20°C) on 1992–98 models.
7. Measure coil secondary resistance between the ignition coil terminals and the distributor cap high tension lead terminals. Resistance on 1989–91 models should be 9.0–12.0 kilohms for the Chrysler coil and 15.0–19.0 kilohms for the Diamond coil. Resistance on 1992–98 models should be 11.3–15.3 kilohms @ 68°F (20°C).

➡If measured resistance is near the extreme high or low end of the scale, the coil is probably faulty and should be replaced.

8. If resistance is not within specifications, the coil may be faulty.

REMOVAL & INSTALLATION

Square Coil

♦ See Figures 2 and 3

Square coils are mounted to the front of the right cylinder head.
1. Disconnect the negative battery cable.
2. Disconnect the ignition coil high tension wire.
3. Label and disconnect the coil electrical harness.
4. Remove the coil mounting bolts.
5. Carefully remove the coil.
To install:
6. Position the coil and tighten the mounting bolts securely.

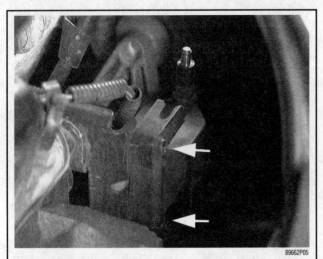

Fig. 2 The late model square coil is held in place by two screws and a bracket

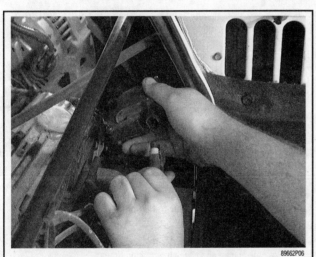

Fig. 3 It is easiest to remove the connector on the underside of the ignition coil after you remove the retaining screws

7. Connect the coil electrical harness.
8. Connect the coil high tension wire.
9. Connect the negative battery cable.

Round Coil

▶ See Figure 4

Round coils are mounted either to the rear of the right cylinder head or to the intake manifold.
1. Disconnect the negative battery cable.
2. Disconnect the ignition coil high tension wire.
3. Label and disconnect the coil electrical harness.
4. Loosen the coil retaining bracket.
5. Carefully remove the coil from the mounting bracket.
To install:
6. Carefully install the coil into the mounting bracket.
7. Tighten the coil mounting bracket bolt securely.
8. Connect the coil electrical harness.
9. Connect the coil high tension wire.
10. Connect the negative battery cable.

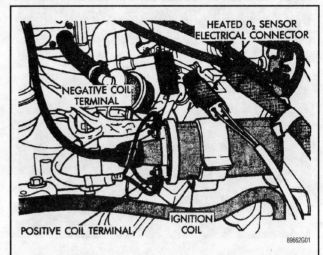

Fig. 4 The early model round coil is usually located on the intake manifold

Distributor

REMOVAL & INSTALLATION

▶ See Figures 5, 6 and 7

1. Disconnect the negative battery cable.
2. Label and disconnect the distributor electrical harness.

➡On some engines, it may be necessary to label and remove the distributor wires and cap in order to gain clearance to remove the distributor.

3. Remove the distributor cap and position it aside with the ignition wires still attached.
4. Matchmark the position of the rotor to the distributor housing and the distributor housing to the engine.
5. Remove the distributor hold-down bolt and clamp.
6. Remove the distributor from the engine.

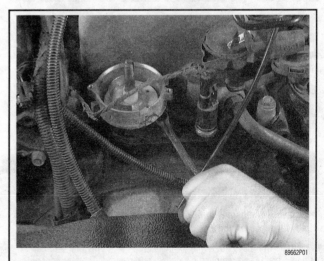

Fig. 5 Use an appropriate size wrench to remove the distributor hold-down bolt

Fig. 6 Pull the distributor straight upward to remove it from the engine block

Fig. 7 Be sure to carefully inspect the distributor seal for damage after removal

To install:

→Before installation, inspect the distributor O-ring and drive gear for wear and/or damage. Rotate the distributor shaft to make sure it moves freely, without binding.

Engine Not Disturbed

1. Install the distributor, aligning the distributor housing and rotor with the matchmarks made during removal.

2. Install the distributor hold-down bolt and clamp. Only snug the bolt at this time.
3. Connect the distributor electrical harness.
4. Install the distributor cap and wires.

→**Make sure the ignition wires are securely connected to the distributor cap and spark plugs.**

5. Connect the negative battery cable.
6. Start the engine and adjust the ignition timing. Refer to Section 1.
7. Tighten the distributor hold-down bolt securely.
8. Recheck the initial timing and re-adjust if necessary.

Engine Disturbed

Use this procedure if the engine position is disturbed after the distributor is removed.

1. Disconnect the ignition wire from the No. 1 cylinder spark plug and remove the spark plug.
2. Place a finger over the spark plug hole. Rotate the engine clockwise until compression is felt at the spark plug hole.
3. Install the No. 1 cylinder spark plug.
4. Align the timing pointer with the 0 degree (TDC) mark on the crankshaft damper.
5. Clean the distributor mounting at the engine and distributor base. Lightly oil the rubber O-ring seal on the distributor housing.
6. Hold the distributor over the mounting pad on the cylinder block so that the distributor body flange coincides with the mounting pad and the rotor points to the No. 1 cylinder firing position.
7. Install the distributor while holding the rotor in position, allowing it to move only enough to engage the slot in the drive gear.
8. Install the distributor hold-down bolt and clamp. Tighten to 17 ft. lbs. (22.5 Nm).

→**Ensure that the ignition wires are securely connected to the distributor cap and spark plugs.**

9. Install the distributor cap and wires.

→**Ensure that the rotor tip is pointing to the distributor cap's No. 1 spark plug tower position, prior to fastening the distributor cap in place.**

10. Connect the negative battery cable.
11. Start the engine and check the ignition timing.

Crankshaft Position Sensor

Refer to Electronic Engine Controls in Section 4 for information on servicing the crankshaft position sensor.

Camshaft Position Sensor

Refer to Electronic Engine Controls in Section 4 for information on servicing the camshaft position sensor.

FIRING ORDERS

♦ **See Figures 8 and 9**

→**To avoid confusion, remove and tag the spark plug wires one at a time, for replacement.**

If a distributor is not keyed for installation with only one orientation, it could have been removed previously and rewired. The resultant wiring would hold the correct firing order, but could change the relative placement of the plug towers in relation to the engine. For this reason, it is imperative that you label all wires before disconnecting any of them. Also, before removal, compare the current wiring with the accompanying illustrations. If the current wiring does not match, make notes in your book to reflect how your engine is wired.

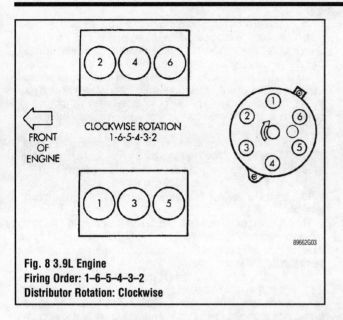

Fig. 8 3.9L Engine
Firing Order: 1–6–5–4–3–2
Distributor Rotation: Clockwise

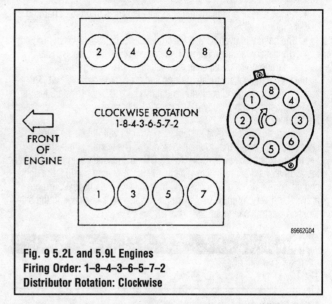

Fig. 9 5.2L and 5.9L Engines
Firing Order: 1–8–4–3–6–5–7–2
Distributor Rotation: Clockwise

CHARGING SYSTEM

A typical charging system contains an alternator (generator), drive belt, battery, voltage regulator and the associated wiring. The charging system, like the starting system, is a series circuit with the battery wired in parallel. After the engine is started and running, the alternator takes over as the source of power and the battery then becomes part of the load on the charging system.

Some vehicle manufacturers use the term generator instead of alternator. Many years ago there used to be a difference, but now the two terms are often used interchangeably. The alternator, which is driven by the belt, consists of a rotating coil of laminated wire called the rotor. Surrounding the rotor are more coils of laminated wire that remain stationary just inside the alternator case. This is how we get the name stator. When current is passed through the rotor via the slip rings and brushes, the rotor becomes a rotating magnet with, of course, a magnetic field. When a magnetic field passes through a conductor (the stator), alternating current (A/C) is generated. This A/C current is rectified, or turned into direct current (D/C), by the diodes located within the alternator.

The voltage regulator controls the alternator's field voltage by grounding one end of the field windings very rapidly. The frequency varies according to current demand. The more the field is grounded, the more voltage and current the alternator produces. Voltage is maintained at about 13.5–15 volts. During high engine speeds and low current demands, the regulator will adjust the voltage of the alternator field to lower the alternator output voltage. Conversely, when the vehicle is idling and the current demands may be high, the regulator will increase the field voltage, increasing the output of the alternator. Some vehicles actually turn the alternator off during periods of no load and/or wide open throttle. This was designed to reduce fuel consumption and increase power. Depending on the manufacturer, voltage regulators can be found in different locations, including inside or on the alternator, on the fender or firewall, and even inside the PCM.

Drive belts are often overlooked when diagnosing a charging system failure. Check the belt tension on the alternator pulley and replace/adjust the belt. A loose belt will result in an undercharged battery and a no-start condition. This is especially true in wet weather conditions when moisture causes the belt to become more slippery.

PRECAUTIONS

To prevent damage to the on-board computer, alternator and regulator, the following precautionary measures must be taken when working with the electrical system.
- Wear safety glasses when working on or near the battery.

- Don't wear a watch with a metal band when servicing the battery. Serious burns can result if the band completes the circuit between the positive battery terminal and ground.
- Be absolutely sure of the polarity of a booster battery before making connections. Connect the cables positive to positive, and negative to negative. Connect positive cables first and then make the last connection to ground on the body of the booster vehicle, so that arcing cannot ignite hydrogen gas that may have accumulated near the battery. Even momentary connection of a booster battery with the polarity reversed will damage alternator diodes.
- Disconnect both vehicle battery cables before attempting to charge a battery.
- Never ground the alternator or generator output or battery terminal. Be cautious when using metal tools around a battery to avoid creating a short circuit between the terminals.
- Never ground the field circuit between the alternator and regulator.
- Never run an alternator or generator without load unless the field circuit is disconnected.
- Never attempt to polarize an alternator.
- When installing a battery, make sure that the positive and negative cables are not reversed.
- When jump-starting the car, be sure that like terminals are connected. This also applies to using a battery charger. Reversed polarity will burn out the alternator and regulator in a matter of seconds.
- Never operate the alternator with the battery disconnected or on an otherwise uncontrolled open circuit.
- Do not short across or ground any alternator or regulator terminals.
- Do not try to polarize the alternator.
- Do not apply full battery voltage to the field (brown) connector.
- Always disconnect the battery ground cable before disconnecting the alternator lead.
- Always disconnect the battery (negative cable first) when charging it.
- Never subject the alternator to excessive heat or dampness. If you are steam cleaning the engine, cover the alternator.
- Never use arc-welding equipment on the car with the alternator connected.

SYSTEM TESTING

The charging system should be inspected if:
- A Diagnostic Trouble Code (DTC) is set relating to the charging system
- The charging system warning light is illuminated

• The voltmeter on the instrument panel indicates improper charging (either high or low)
• The battery is overcharged (electrolyte level is low and/or boiling out)
• The battery is undercharged (insufficient power to crank the starter)

The starting point for all charging system problems begins with the inspection of the battery, related wiring and the alternator drive belt. The battery must be in good condition and fully charged before system testing. If a Diagnostic Trouble Code (DTC) is set, diagnose and repair the cause of the trouble code first.

If equipped, the charging system warning light will illuminate if the charging voltage is either too high or too low. The warning light should illuminate when the key is turned to the **ON** position as a bulb check. When the alternator starts producing voltage due to the engine starting, the light should go out. A good sign of overly high voltage is lights that burn out and/or burn very brightly. Overcharging can also cause damage to the battery and electronic circuits.

Alternator

TESTING

▶ See Figure 10

➡Before testing, make sure all connections and mounting bolts are clean and tight. Many charging system problems are related to loose and corroded terminals or bad grounds. Don't overlook the engine ground connection to the body and the alternator drive belt. On some vehicles, it is beneficial to add an additional ground between the engine and the chassis. This may solve many intermittent problems.

Fig. 10 Regulator field connections (1 and 2), regulator ground connection (3), and battery positive cable (4)

Voltage Drop Test

➡Before proceeding, make sure the battery is in good condition and fully charged.

Perform a voltage drop test of the positive side of the circuit as follows:

1. Start the engine and allow it to reach normal operating temperature.
2. Turn the headlamps, heater blower motor and interior lights on.
3. Bring the engine to about 2,500 rpm and hold it there.
4. Connect the negative voltmeter lead directly to the battery positive terminal.

5. Touch the positive voltmeter lead directly to the alternator B+ output stud, not the nut. The meter should read no higher than about 0.5 volts. If it does, there is higher than normal resistance between the positive side of the battery and the B+ output at the alternator.
6. Move the positive meter lead to the nut and see if the voltage reading drops substantially. If it does, there is resistance between the stud and the nut. The theory is to keep moving closer to the battery terminal, one connection at a time, in order to find the area of high resistance (bad connection).

Perform a voltage drop test of the negative side of the circuit as follows:

7. Start the engine and allow it to reach normal operating temperature.
8. Turn the headlamps, heater blower motor and interior lights on.
9. Bring the engine to about 2,500 rpm and hold it there.
10. Connect the negative voltmeter lead directly to the negative battery terminal.
11. Touch the positive voltmeter lead directly to the alternator case or ground connection. The meter should read no higher than about 0.3 volts. If it does, there is higher than normal resistance between the battery ground terminal and the alternator ground.
12. Move the positive meter lead to the alternator mounting bracket. If the voltage reading drops substantially, you know that there is a bad electrical connection between the alternator and mounting bracket. The theory is to keep moving closer to the battery terminal, one connection at a time, in order to find the area of high resistance (bad connection).

Current Output Test

➡The current output test requires the use of a volt/amp tester with battery load control and an inductive amperage pick-up. Follow the manufacturer's instructions on the use of the equipment.

1. Start the engine and allow it to reach normal operating temperature.
2. Apply the parking brake and turn off all electrical accessories.
3. Connect the tester to the battery terminals and cable according to the instructions.
4. Bring the engine to about 2,500 rpm and hold it there.
5. Apply a load to charging system with the rheostat on the tester. Do not let the voltage drop below 12 volts.
6. The alternator should deliver to within 10% of the rated output. If the amperage is not within 10% and all other components test okay, replace the alternator.

Alternator Isolation Test

On some models, it is possible to isolate the alternator from the regulator by grounding the field terminal. Grounding the field terminal removes the regulator from the circuit and forces full alternator output. On alternators equipped with internal regulators, we recommend replacing the complete assembly if either the alternator or regulator is defective.

➡Chrysler models have two field terminals, one positive and one negative. The positive terminal will have battery voltage present and the negative terminal will have 3–5 volts less.

✴✴ WARNING

Do not let the voltage get higher than 18 volts. Damage to electrical circuits may occur.

1. Connect a voltmeter across the battery terminals so the voltage can be monitored.
2. Start the engine and let it reach normal operating temperature.
3. Connect a jumper lead to a good ground.
4. Locate the field terminal (negative) on the back of the alternator.
5. Momentarily connect the grounded jumper to the field terminal. If the alternator is okay, the voltage will climb rapidly. Disconnect the jumper before the output reaches 18 volts. If the voltage does not rise, replace the alternator. If the voltage rises, the regulator is bad.

REMOVAL & INSTALLATION

▶ **See Figures 11, 12, 13, 14 and 15**

1. Disconnect the negative battery cable.
2. Remove the accessory drive belt.
3. Label and disconnect the alternator's electrical harness.
4. Remove the alternator mounting bolts.
5. Carefully remove the alternator from the engine.

To install:

6. Position the alternator on the engine.
7. Install the alternator mounting bolts and, on serpentine belt equipped vehicles, tighten to 30 ft. lbs. (41 Nm).

➡**On V-belt equipped vehicles, do not yet tighten the alternator mounting bolts.**

8. Connect the electrical harness.
9. Install and properly tension the accessory drive belt. On V-belt equipped vehicles, now tighten the mounting bolts to 30 ft. lbs. (41 Nm).
10. Connect the negative battery cable.
11. Check the alternator for proper operation.

Fig. 13 This alternator is attached with the bolts shown here

Fig. 11 On this style of alternator, the battery cable is held in place by a nut

Fig. 14 Unfasten the attaching bolts and remove the alternator from the bracket

Fig. 12 On this style of alternator, the regulator is held in place by two small nuts, and the larger one is for the ground

Fig. 15 Take care when removing the alternator not to drop it or ground the connections on the back

STARTING SYSTEM

General Information

The starting system includes the battery, starter motor, solenoid, ignition switch and, in some cases, a starter relay. An inhibitor switch (neutral safety) is included in the starting system circuit to prevent the vehicle from being started while in gear.

When the ignition key is turned to the **START** position, current flows and energizes the starter's solenoid coil. The energized coil becomes a magnet which pulls the plunger into the coil, and the plunger closes a set of contacts which allow high current to reach the starter motor. On models where the solenoid is mounted on the starter, the plunger also serves to push the starter pinion into the teeth on the flywheel/flexplate.

To prevent damage to the starter motor when the engine starts, the pinion gear incorporates an over-running (one-way) clutch which is splined to the starter armature shaft. The rotation of the running engine may speed the rotation of the pinion, but not the starter motor itself.

Some starting systems employ a starter relay in addition to the solenoid. This relay may be located under the dashboard, in the kick panel, or in the fuse/relay center under the hood. This relay is used to reduce the amount of current which the ignition switch must carry.

PRECAUTIONS

Always disconnect the negative battery cable before servicing the starter. Battery voltage is always present at the large (B) terminal on the solenoid. When removing the starter motor, be prepared to support its weight after the last bolt is removed, because the starter motor is a fairly heavy component.

Never operate the starter for more than 30 seconds at a time. Too much cranking will cause the starter motor to overheat, causing permanent damage. Allow the starter to cool for at least two minutes between starting attempts.

SYSTEM TESTING

➡**A good quality digital multimeter with at least 10 megohms/volt impedance should be used when testing modern automotive circuits. These meters can accurately detect very small amounts of voltage, current and resistance. This type of meter also has a low internal resistance that will not load the circuit being tested. Loading the circuit gives inaccurate readings and may cause damage to sensitive computer circuits. Although we are not testing computer circuits in this section, accuracy is very important.**

1. Check the battery and clean the connections as follows:
   a. If the battery cells have removable caps, check the water level. Add distilled water if low. Load test the battery and charge if necessary. Refer to Section 1 for further information.
   b. Remove the cables and clean them with a wire brush. Reconnect the cables.
2. Check the starter motor ground circuit with a voltage drop test as follows:
   a. Set the meter to read DC voltage on the lowest possible scale.
   b. Connect the negative lead of your multimeter to the negative terminal of the battery.
   c. Connect the positive lead to the body of the starter. Make sure the starter mounting bolts are tight. The meter should read 0.2 volts or less. If the voltage reading is greater, remove and clean the negative battery connection on the engine block. The voltage reading should now be within specification; if not, replace the negative battery cable.
3. Check the motor feed circuit with a voltage drop test as follows:
   a. Disconnect the coil wire or the fuel injector harness to prevent the engine from possible starting.
   b. Using the same voltage scale as above, connect the positive lead of your meter to the positive terminal of the battery.
   c. Connect the negative meter lead to the motor feed terminal. This is the terminal closest to the starter motor on the solenoid.

d. Turn the ignition key to the **START** position. The meter should read 0.2 volts or less. If the voltage reading is greater, remove and clean the positive battery connection on the starter solenoid. The voltage reading should now be within specification; if not, replace the positive battery cable.
   e. Connect the coil wire or fuel injector harness.
4. Check for battery voltage at the S terminal on the starter solenoid as follows:
   a. Disconnect the coil wire or the fuel injector harness to prevent the engine from possible starting.
   b. Set the meter to read battery voltage. Move it to next higher range if set on the 2 volt scale.
   c. Connect the positive lead to the S terminal on the starter solenoid and the negative lead to a good ground.
   d. Turn the ignition key to the **START** position and crank the engine. The meter should read battery voltage. If battery voltage is not present, check the neutral safety switch, fuse(s) and wiring between the ignition switch and starter solenoid. If battery voltage is present at the S terminal on the solenoid and the starter does not operate, replace the starter and solenoid assembly.
   e. Connect the coil wire or fuel injector harness.

REMOVAL & INSTALLATION

▶ **See Figures 16, 17, 18, 19 and 20**

1. Disconnect the negative battery cable.
2. Raise and safely support the vehicle on jackstands.
3. Remove all components necessary to gain access to the starter motor (such as exhaust pipes, air intake ducts, hoses, brackets and heat shields.)
4. Label and disconnect the electrical harness from the starter.

➡**In some cases, the wiring may be more accessible after removing the mounting bolts and moving the starter.**

5. Remove the starter mounting bolts.
6. Remove the starter assembly from the vehicle. In some cases, the starter will have to be turned to a different angle to clear obstructions.

➡**Retain any shims that may fall out from between the starter and the mounting boss; they will need to be returned to their original position when replacing the starter. The shims are used to adjust the clearance between the starter pinion and flywheel/flexplate teeth.**

Fig. 16 There are two retaining bolts for the starter. Be sure to support the starter by hand before fully removing them

89662P07

Fig. 17 Remove the starter by pulling straight back after the bolts are fully removed; the cable terminals are on top

Fig. 18 It is not a good idea to let the starter dangle by its cables, so be sure to support it while unfastening terminal connections

Fig. 19 When removed from the vehicle, inspect the starter drive gear for damage

Fig. 20 Inspect the teeth on the flywheel or flexplate for damage before reinstalling the starter

To install:
  7. Position the starter on the engine.
  8. If necessary, measure and adjust the pinion-to-ring gear clearance.
  9. Position the shim(s) and the starter motor on the mounting boss. Tighten the mounting bolts to 50 ft. lbs. (65 Nm).
  10. Connect the electrical harness.
  11. Install any components that were removed to gain access to the starter.
  12. Connect the negative battery cable.

PINION DEPTH ADJUSTMENT

Generally, add shims if the starter whines after the engine starts, and remove shims if the starter whines only during cranking.

➡ **This procedure is used to diagnose starter noise caused by incorrect clearance between the starter pinion and flywheel while the starter is engaged.**

  1. Raise and safely support the vehicle on jackstands.
  2. Remove the flywheel cover.
  3. Inspect the flywheel teeth for chipped or missing teeth, abnormal wear, cracks and a possibly warped flywheel. Replace any damaged components and continue with the procedure.
  4. Make sure the vehicle is in Park or Neutral. Apply the parking brake and start the engine.

❊❊ CAUTION

Keep your fingers out of the way and be extremely careful when performing the next step.

  5. Carefully touch the outside edge of the rotating flywheel with a marker to highlight the high spot of the ring gear.
  6. Turn the engine **OFF**.
  7. Disconnect the negative battery cable.
  8. Turn the high spot of the flywheel to the area of the starter drive pinion.
  9. Using a wire gauge, measure the clearance between the tip of the ring gear tooth and bottom of the pinion gear teeth. Clearance should generally be 0.02–0.06 in. (0.5–1.5mm).
  10. Add or remove shims to adjust the clearance if needed.
  11. Install the flywheel cover.
  12. Lower the vehicle to the floor.
  13. Connect the negative battery cable.

SENDING UNITS

➡ **This section describes the operating principles of sending units, warning lights and gauges. Sensors which provide information to the Powertrain Control Module (PCM) are covered in Section 4 of this manual.**

Instrument panels contain a number of indicating devices (gauges and warning lights). These devices are composed of two separate components. One is the sending unit, mounted on the engine or other remote part of the vehicle, and the other is the actual gauge or light in the instrument panel.

Several types of sending units exist, however most can be characterized as being either a pressure type or a resistance type. Pressure type sending units convert liquid pressure into an electrical signal which is sent to the gauge. Resistance type sending units are most often used to measure temperature and use variable resistance to control the current flow back to the indicating device. Both types of sending units are connected in series by a wire to the battery (through the ignition switch). When the ignition is turned **ON**, current flows from the battery through the indicating device and on to the sending unit.

Coolant Temperature Sender

TESTING

▶ **See Figure 21**

A quick way to determine if the gauge, the so-called "idiot" light, or the sending unit is faulty, is to disconnect the sending unit electrical harness and ground it (if two-terminal, jumper between the terminals) with the ignition **ON**. If the gauge responds or the light illuminates, the sending unit may be faulty. Proceed with the following sending unit test.

1. Disconnect the sending unit electrical harness.
2. Remove the radiator cap and place a mechanic's thermometer in the coolant.
3. Using an ohmmeter, check the resistance between the sending unit terminals.
4. Resistance should be high with the engine coolant cold and low with the engine coolant hot.

➡ **It is best to check resistance with the engine cool, then start the engine and watch the resistance change as the engine warms.**

5. If resistance does not drop as engine temperature rises, the sending unit is faulty.

REMOVAL & INSTALLATION

1. Locate the coolant temperature sending unit on the engine.
2. Disconnect the sending unit electrical harness.
3. Drain the engine coolant below the level of the switch.
4. Unfasten and remove the sending unit from the engine.

To install:

5. Coat the new sending unit with Teflon® tape or electrically conductive sealer.
6. Install the sending unit and tighten to 11–15 ft. lbs. (15–20 Nm).
7. Attach the sending unit's electrical connector.
8. Replenish the necessary amount of coolant.
9. Start the engine, allow it to reach operating temperature and check for leaks.
10. Check for proper sending unit operation.

Oil Pressure Sender

TESTING

A quick way to determine if the gauge, the so-called "idiot" light, or the sending unit is faulty, is to disconnect the sending unit electrical harness and ground it (if two-terminal, jumper between the terminals) with the ignition **ON**. If the gauge responds or the light illuminates, the sending unit may be faulty. Proceed with the following sending unit test.

1. Disconnect the sending unit electrical harness.
2. Using an ohmmeter, check continuity between the sending unit terminals.
3. With the engine stopped, continuity should exist.

➡ **The switch inside the oil pressure sending unit closes at 10 psi or less of pressure.**

4. With the engine running, continuity should not exist.
5. If continuity does or does not exist as stated, the sending unit is faulty.

REMOVAL & INSTALLATION

▶ **See Figure 22**

1. Locate the oil pressure sending unit on the engine.
2. Disconnect the sending unit electrical harness.
3. Unfasten and remove the sending unit from the engine.

Fig. 21 The temperature sender is located at the front of the engine, adjacent to the thermostat

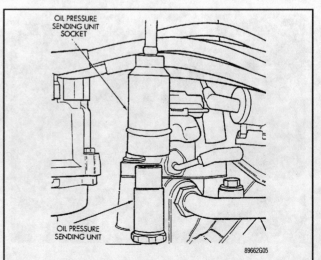

Fig. 22 The oil pressure sending unit is located near the distributor, at the rear of the engine

To install:

4. Coat the threads of the new sending unit with Teflon® tape or electrically conductive sealer.

5. Install the sending unit and tighten to 11–15 ft. lbs. (15–20 Nm).

6. Attach the sending unit's electrical connector.

7. Start the engine, allow it to reach operating temperature and check for leaks.

8. Check for proper sending unit operation.

Troubleshooting Basic Starting System Problems

Problem	Cause	Solution
Starter motor rotates engine slowly	• Battery charge low or battery defective • Defective circuit between battery and starter motor • Low load current • High load current	• Charge or replace battery • Clean and tighten, or replace cables • Bench-test starter motor. Inspect for worn brushes and weak brush springs. • Bench-test starter motor. Check engine for friction, drag or coolant in cylinders. Check ring gear-to-pinion gear clearance.
Starter motor will not rotate engine	• Battery charge low or battery defective • Faulty solenoid • Damaged drive pinion gear or ring gear • Starter motor engagement weak • Starter motor rotates slowly with high load current • Engine seized	• Charge or replace battery • Check solenoid ground. Repair or replace as necessary. • Replace damaged gear(s) • Bench-test starter motor • Inspect drive yoke pull-down and point gap, check for worn end bushings, check ring gear clearance • Repair engine
Starter motor drive will not engage (solenoid known to be good)	• Defective contact point assembly • Inadequate contact point assembly ground • Defective hold-in coil	• Repair or replace contact point assembly • Repair connection at ground screw • Replace field winding assembly
Starter motor drive will not disengage	• Starter motor loose on flywheel housing • Worn drive end busing • Damaged ring gear teeth • Drive yoke return spring broken or missing	• Tighten mounting bolts • Replace bushing • Replace ring gear or driveplate • Replace spring
Starter motor drive disengages prematurely	• Weak drive assembly thrust spring • Hold-in coil defective	• Replace drive mechanism • Replace field winding assembly
Low load current	• Worn brushes • Weak brush springs	• Replace brushes • Replace springs

TCCS2C01

Troubleshooting Basic Charging System Problems

Problem	Cause	Solution
Noisy alternator	• Loose mountings • Loose drive pulley • Worn bearings • Brush noise • Internal circuits shorted (High pitched whine)	• Tighten mounting bolts • Tighten pulley • Replace alternator • Replace alternator • Replace alternator
Squeal when starting engine or accelerating	• Glazed or loose belt	• Replace or adjust belt
Indicator light remains on or ammeter indicates discharge (engine running)	• Broken belt • Broken or disconnected wires • Internal alternator problems • Defective voltage regulator	• Install belt • Repair or connect wiring • Replace alternator • Replace voltage regulator/alternator
Car light bulbs continually burn out— battery needs water continually	• Alternator/regulator overcharging	• Replace voltage regulator/alternator
Car lights flare on acceleration	• Battery low • Internal alternator/regulator problems	• Charge or replace battery • Replace alternator/regulator
Low voltage output (alternator light flickers continually or ammeter needle wanders)	• Loose or worn belt • Dirty or corroded connections • Internal alternator/regulator problems	• Replace or adjust belt • Clean or replace connections • Replace alternator/regulator

TCCS2C02

3

ENGINE AND ENGINE OVERHAUL

ENGINE MECHANICAL

3.9L (3916cc) ENGINE MECHANICAL SPECIFICATIONS

Description	English Specifications	Metric Specifications
General Information		
Engine Type	90 degree V-6 OHV	
Bore & Stroke	3.91 x 3.31 in.	99.3 x 84.0mm
Displacement	238 c.i.	3.9 L
Compression Ratio	9.1:1	
Firing Order	1-6-5-4-3-2	
Lubrication	Pressure Feed - Full Flow Filtration	
Cooling System	Liquid Cooled - Forced Circulation	
Cylinder Block	Cast Iron	
Cylinder Head	Cast Iron	
Crankshaft	Modular Iron	
Camshaft	Modular Cast Iron	
Combustion Chambers	"Fast Burn" Design	
Pistons	Aluminum Alloy w/Strut	
Connecting Rods	Forged Steel	
Cylinder Compression Pressure (Min.)	100 psi	689.5 kPa
Camshaft		
Bearing Diameter (Inside)		
No. 1	2.000 - 2.001 in.	50.800 - 50.825mm
No. 2	1.984 - 1.985 in.	50.394 - 50.419mm
No. 3	1.953 - 1.954 in.	49.606 - 49.632mm
No. 4	1.5265 - 1.5635 in.	39.688 - 39.713mm
Journal Diameter		
No. 1	1.998 - 1.999 in.	50.749 - 50.775mm
No. 2		
1998 - 92	1.982 - 1.983 in.	50.343 - 50.368mm
1991 - 90	1.967 - 1.968 in.	49.962 - 49.987mm
No. 3	1.951 - 1.952 in.	49.555 - 49.581mm
No. 4	1.5605 - 1.5615 in.	39.637 - 39.662mm
Bearing-To-Journal Clearance		
Standard	0.001 - 0.003 in.	0.0254 - 0.0762mm
Max. Allowable	0.005 in.	0.127mm
Camshaft End-Play		
End-Play	0.002 - 0.010 in.	0.051 - 0.254mm
Connecting Rods		
Piston Pin Bore Diameter	0.9819 - 0.9834 in.	24.940 - 24.978mm
Side Clearance (Two Rods)	0.006 - 0.014 in.	0.152 - 0.356mm
Total Weight	25.61 oz.	726 grams
Bearing Clearance		
1995 - 90	0.0005 - 0.0022 in.	0.013 - 0.056mm
Max. Allowable		
1995 - 90	0.003 in.	0.08mm
Crankshaft		
Rod Journal		
Diameter	2.124 - 2.125 in.	53.950 - 53.975mm
Out Of Round (Max.)	0.001 in.	0.0254mm
Taper (Max.)	0.001 in.	0.0254mm
Bearing Clearance	0.0005 - 0.0022 in.	0.013 - 0.056mm
Service Limit	0.003 in.	0.08mm

89663C01

3.9L (3916cc) ENGINE MECHANICAL SPECIFICATIONS

Description	English Specifications	Metric Specifications
Main Journal		
Diameter	2.4995 - 2.5005 in.	63.487 - 63.513mm
Out Of Round (Max.)	0.001 in.	0.0254mm
Taper (Max.)	0.001 in.	0.0254mm
Bearing Clearance (#1)	0.0005 - 0.0015 in.	0.013 - 0.038mm
Service Limit	0.0025 in.	0.064mm
Bearing Clearance (#2 - 4)	0.0005 - 0.0020 in.	0.013 - 0.051mm
Service Limit	0.0025 in.	0.064mm
Crankshaft End-Play		
End-Play	0.002 - 0.007 in.	0.051 - 0.178mm
Service Limit	0.010 in.	0.254mm
Cylinder Block		
Cylinder Bore		
Diameter	3.910 - 3.912 in.	99.314 - 99.365mm
Out Of Round (Max.)	0.005 in.	0.127mm
Taper (Max.)	0.010 in.	0.254mm
Over Size Limit	0.040 in.	1.016mm
Lifter Bore		
Diameter	0.9501 - 0.9059 in.	22.99 - 23.01mm
Distributor Drive Bushing (Press Fit)		
Bushing-to-Bore Interference	0.0005 - 0.0140 in.	0.0127 - 0.3556mm
Shaft-to-Bushing Clearance	0.0007 - 0.0027 in.	0.0178 - 0.0686mm
Cylinder Head And Valves		
Compression Pressure		
1995- 90	100 psi	689 kPa
Gasket Thickness		
1995- 91	0.0475 - 1.2065 in.	1.2065mm
1990	0.033 in.	0.8382mm
Valve Seat		
Angle		
1998 - 91	44.25 - 44.75 degrees	
1990	45.0 - 45.5 degrees	
Run-out (Max.)	0.003 in.	0.0762mm
Width (Finish) - Intake		
1998 - 91	0.040 - 0.060 in.	1.016 - 1.542mm
1990	0.065 - 0.085 in.	1.651 - 2.159mm
Width (Finish) - Exhaust		
1998 - 91	0.060 - 0.080 in.	1.524 - 2.032mm
1990	0.080 - 0.100 in.	2.032 - 2.540mm
Valves		
Face Angle		
1998 - 91	43.25 - 43.75 degrees	
1990	44.5 - 45.0 degrees	
Head Diameter - Intake		
1998 - 92	1.916 in.	48.666mm
1991	1.88 in.	47.752mm
1990	1.780 in.	45.212mm

89663C02

3.9L (3916cc) ENGINE MECHANICAL SPECIFICATIONS

Description	English Specifications	Metric Specifications
Head Diameter - Exhaust		
1998 - 92	1.624 in.	41.250mm
1991	1.60 in.	40.640mm
1990	1.517 in.	38.532mm
Length (Overall) - Intake		
1998 - 92	4.893 - 4.918 in.	124.28 - 125.92mm
1991 - 90	4.962 - 4.987 in.	126.03 - 126.67mm
Length (Overall) - Exhaust		
1998 - 92	4.907 - 4.932 in.	124.64 - 125.27mm
1991 - 90	4.977 - 5.012 in.	126.42 - 127.30mm
Angle	44.25 - 44.75 degrees	
Lift (@ zero lash) - Intake/Exhaust		
1998 - 92	0.432 in.	10.973mm
Lift (@ zero lash) - Intake		
1991 - 90	0.373 in.	9.474mm
Lift (@ zero lash) - Exhaust		
1991 - 90	0.400 in.	10.160mm
Stem Diameter - Intake/Exhaust		
1998 - 92	0.311 - 0.312 in.	7.899 - 7.925mm
1991	0.3125 in.	7.9375mm
Stem Diameter - Intake		
1990	0.372 - 0.373 in.	9.449 - 9.474mm
Stem Diameter - Exhaust		
1990	0.371 - 0.372 in.	9.423 - 9.449mm
Guide Bore Diameter		
1998 - 92	0.313 - 0.314 in.	7.950 - 7.976mm
1991 - 90		
Stem-to-Guide Clearance - Intake/Exhaust		
1998 - 92	0.001 - 0.003 in.	0.0254 - 0.0762mm
Stem-to-Guide Clearance - Intake		
1991 - 90	0.001 - 0.003 in.	0.0254 - 0.0762mm
Stem-to-Guide Clearance -Exhaust		
1991 - 90	0.002 - 0.004 in.	0.5080 - 0.1015mm
Service Limit (Rocking Method)	0.017 in.	0.4318mm
Valve Spring		
Free Length - Intake/Exhaust		
1998 - 92	1.967 in.	49.962mm
Free Length - Intake		
1991 - 90	2.00 in.	50.8mm
Free Length - Exhaust		
1991 - 90	1.81 in.	45.974mm
Spring Tension (valve closed) - Intake/Exhaust		
1998 - 92	85 lbs. @ 1.64 in.	378 N @ 41.66mm
Spring Tension (valve closed) - Intake		
1991 - 90	78 - 88 lbs. @ 1.69 in.	347 - 391 N @ 42.86mm
Spring Tension (valve closed) - Exhaust		
1991 - 90	80 - 90 lbs. @ 1.203 in.	356 - 400 N @ 37.70mm
Spring Tension (valve open) - Intake/Exhaust		
1998 - 92	200 lbs. @ 1.212 in.	890 N @ 30.98mm

89663C03

3.9L (3916cc) ENGINE MECHANICAL SPECIFICATIONS

Description	English Specifications	Metric Specifications
Spring Tension (valve open) - Intake		
1991 - 90	170 - 819 lbs. @ 1.313 in.	756 - 819 N @ 33.34mm
Spring Tension (valve open) - Exhaust		
1991 - 90	180 - 194 lbs. @ 1.063 in.	810 - 863 N @ 27.38mm
Number of Coils - Intake/Exhaust		
1998 - 92		6.8
Number of Coils - Intake		
1991 - 90		6.4
Number of Coils - Exhaust		
1991 - 90		5.8
Installed Height - Intake/Exhaust		
1998 - 92	1.64 in.	41.66mm
Intake (Spring Seat-To-Retainer) - Intake		
1991 - 90	1.63 - 1.69 in.	41.275 - 42.863mm
Exhaust (Spring Seat-To-Retainer) -Exhaust		
1991 - 90	1.45 - 1.52 in.	39.909 - 38.497mm
Wire Diameter - Intake/Exhaust		
1998 - 92	0.177 in.	4.50mm
Wire Diameter - Intake		
1991 - 90	0.192 in.	4.877mm
Wire Diameter - Exhaust		
1991 - 90	0.185 in.	4.699mm
Hydraulic Tappets		
Body Diameter	0.9035 - 0.9040 in.	22.949 - 22.962mm
Clearance in Block	0.0011 - 0.0024 in.	0.0279 - 0.0610mm
Dry Lash	0.060 - 0.210 in.	1.524 - 5.334mm
Pushrod Length		
1998 - 95	6.915 - 6.935 in.	175.64 - 176.15mm
1994	6.794 - 6.814 in.	172.57 - 173.08mm
Oil Pressure		
@ Curb Idle (min.)*	6 psi	41.4 kPa
*CAUTION: if oil pressure is ZERO at curb idle, DO NOT run engine @ 3000 rpm.		
@ 3000 rpm	30 - 80 psi	207 - 552 kPa
Bypass Valve Setting	9 - 15 psi	62 - 103 kPa
Switch Actuating Pressure	5 - 7 psi	34.5 - 48.3 kPa
Oil Pump		
Clearance Over Rotors (Max.)	0.004 in.	0.1016mm
Cover Out of Flat (Max.)	0.0015 in.	0.0381mm
Inner Rotor Thickness (Min.)	0.825 in.	20.955mm
Outer Rotor Clearance (Max.)	0.014 in.	0.3556mm
Outer Rotor Diameter (Min.)	2.469 in.	62.7126mm
Outer Rotor Thickness (Min.)	0.825 in.	20.955mm
Tip Clearance Between Rotors (Max.)	0.008 in.	0.2032mm
Pistons		
Clearance at Top of Skirt	0.0005 - 0.0015 in.	0.0127 - 0.0381mm
Land Clearance (Diam.)		
1998 - 92	0.025 - 0.040 in.	0.635 - 1.016mm
1991- 90	0.019 - 0.024 in.	0.4826 - 0.6096mm
Piston Length	3.40 in.	86.360mm

89663C04

3.9L (3916cc) ENGINE MECHANICAL SPECIFICATIONS

Description	English Specifications	Metric Specifications
Ring Groove Depth (#1 & 2)		
1998-91	0.180 - 0.190 in.	4.572 - 4.826mm
1990	0.205 in.	5.207mm
Ring Groove Depth (#3)		
1998-91	0.150 - 0.160 in.	3.810 - 4.054mm
1990	0.194 in.	4.928mm
Weight	20.90 - 21.04 oz.	592.6 - 596.6 grams
Piston Pins		
Clearance in Piston		
1998-91	0.00025 - 0.00075 in.	0.0064 - 0.0191mm
1990	0.0000 - 0.0005 in.	0.0000 - 0.0127mm
Clearance in Rod (Interference)	0.0007 - 0.0014 in.	0.0178 - 0.0356mm
Diameter	0.9841 - 0.9843 in.	24.996 - 25.001mm
End-Play	NONE	
Length	2.990 - 3.010 in.	75.946 - 76.454mm
1990	2.990 - 3.020 in.	75.946 - 76.708mm
Piston Rings		
Ring Gap		
Compression Rings - Nos. 1 & 2		
1998 - 90, except 1991	0.010 - 0.020 in.	0.254 - 0.508mm
Compression Rings - No. 1		
1991	0.010 - 0.020 in.	0.254 - 0.508mm
Compression Rings - No. 2		
1991	0.020 - 0.030 in.	0.508 - 0.762mm
Oil Control (Steel Rails)		
1998 - 92	0.010 - 0.050 in.	0.254 - 1.270mm
1991- 90	0.015 - 0.055 in.	0.381 - 1.397mm
Ring Side Clearance		
Compression Rings	0.0015 - 0.0030 in.	0.038 - 0.076mm
Oil Control (Steel Rails)		
1998 - 90, except 1991	0.0002 - 0.0080 in.	0.005 - 0.203mm
1991	0.002 - 0.008 in.	0.06 - 0.21mm
Ring Width	0.0002 - 0.0050 in.	0.005 - 0.127mm
Compression Rings		
1990	0.0776 - 0.0783 in.	1.971 - 1.989mm
1991	0.0770 - 0.0780 in.	0.005 - 0.127mm
Oil Control (Steel Rails)	0.1515 - 0.1565 in.	3.848 - 3.975mm
1990	0.0252 in.	0.640mm
Valve Timing		
Exhaust Valve		
Closes (ATDC)		16 degrees
Opens (BBDC)		52 degrees
Duration		248 degrees
Intake Valve		
Closes (ABDC)		50 degrees
Opens (BTDC)		10 degrees
Duration		240 degrees
Valve Overlap		26 degrees

89663C05

5.2L (5211cc) ENGINE MECHANICAL SPECIFICATIONS

Description	English Specifications	Metric Specifications
General Information		
Engine Type		90 degree V8 OHV
Bore & Stroke	3.91 x 3.31 in.	99.3 x 84.0mm
Displacement	318 c.i.	5.2 L
Compression Ratio		9.1:1
Firing Order		1-8-4-3-6-5-7-2
Lubrication		Pressure Feed - Full Flow Filtration
Cooling System		Liquid Cooled - Forced Circulation
Cylinder Block		Cast Iron
Crankshaft		Nodular Iron
Cylinder Head		Cast Iron
Combustion Chambers		Wedge-High Swirl Valve Shrouding
Camshaft		Nodular Cast Iron
Pistons		Aluminum Alloy w/Strut
Connecting Rods		Forged Steel
Cylinder Compression Pressure (Min.)	100 psi	689.5 kPa
Camshaft		
Bearing Diameter (Inside)		
No. 1	2.000 - 2.001 in.	50.800 - 50.825mm
No. 2	1.984 - 1.985 in.	50.394 - 50.419mm
No. 3	1.969 - 1.970 in.	50.013 - 50.038mm
No. 4	1.953 - 1.954 in.	49.606 - 49.632mm
No. 5	1.5265 - 1.5635 in.	39.688 - 39.713mm
Journal Diameter		
No. 1	1.998 - 1.999 in.	50.749 - 50.775mm
No. 2	1.982 - 1.983 in.	50.343 - 50.368mm
No. 3	1.967 - 1.968 in.	49.962 - 49.987mm
No. 4	1.951 - 1.952 in.	49.555 - 49.581mm
No. 5	1.5605 - 1.5615 in.	39.637 - 39.662mm
Bearing-to-Journal Clearance		
Standard	0.001 - 0.003 in.	0.0254 - 0.0762mm
Max. Allowable	0.005 in.	0.127mm
Camshaft End-play		
End-play	0.002 - 0.010 in.	0.051 - 0.254mm
Connecting Rods		
Piston Pin Bore Diameter	0.9829 - 0.9834 in.	24.966 - 24.978mm
Side Clearance	0.006 - 0.014 in.	0.152 - 0.356mm
Crankshaft		
Rod Journal		
Diameter	2.124 - 2.125 in.	53.950 - 53.975mm
Out Of Round (Max.)	0.001 in.	0.0254mm
Taper (Max.)	0.001 in.	0.0254mm
Bearing Clearance	0.0005 - 0.0022 in.	0.013 - 0.056mm
Service Limit		
1998 - 91	0.003 in.	0.0762mm
1990	0.0022 in.	0.0559mm
Main Bearing Journal		
Diameter	2.4995 - 2.5005 in.	63.487 - 63.513mm
Out Of Round (Max.)		
1998 - 96	0.001 in.	0.127mm
1995 - 90	0.001 in.	0.0254mm

89663C06

5.2L (5211cc) ENGINE MECHANICAL SPECIFICATIONS

Description	English Specifications	Metric Specifications
Taper (Max.)	0.001 in.	0.0254mm
Bearing Clearance (#1 Journal)	0.0005 - 0.0015 in.	0.013 - 0.038mm
Service Limit (#1 Journal)	0.0018 in	0.0381mm
Bearing Clearance (#2 - 5 Journals)	0.0005 - 0.0020 in.	0.013 - 0.051mm
Service Limit (#2 - 5 Journals)	0.0025 in.	0.064mm
Crankshaft End-play		
End-play	0.002 - 0.007 in.	0.051 - 0.178mm
Service Limit	0.010 in.	0.254mm
Cylinder Block		
Cylinder Bore		
Diameter	3.910 - 3.912 in.	99.314 - 99.365mm
Out Of Round (Max.)	0.005 in.	0.127mm
Taper (Max.)	0.010 in.	0.254mm
Over Size Limit	0.040 in.	1.016mm
Lifter Bore		
Diameter	0.9501 - 0.9059 in.	22.99 - 23.01mm
Distributor Drive Bushing (Press Fit)		
Bushing-to-Bore Interference	0.0005 - 0.0140 in.	0.0127 - 0.3556mm
Shaft-to-Bushing Clearance	0.0007 - 0.0027 in.	0.0178 - 0.0686mm
Cylinder Head And Valves		
Compression Pressure		
1995 - 91	100 psi	689 kPa
Gasket Thickness (Compressed)		
1995 - 92	0.0475 in.	1.2065mm
1991 - 90	0.033 in.	0.8382mm
Valve Seat		
Angle		
1998 - 91	44.25 - 44.75 degrees	
1990	45 - 45.5 degrees	
Run-out (Max.)	0.003 in.	0.0762mm
Width (Finish) - Intake		
1998 - 91	0.040 - 0.060 in.	1.016 - 1.542mm
1990	0.065 - 0.085 in.	1.651 - 2.159mm
Width (Finish) - Exhaust		
1998 - 91	0.060 - 0.080 in.	1.524 - 2.032mm
1990	0.080 - 0.100 in.	2.032 - 2.540mm
Valves		
Face Angle		
1998-91	43.25 - 43.75 degrees	
1990	44.5 - 45 degrees	
Head Diameter - Intake		
1998 - 92	1.916 in.	48.666mm
1991	1.88 in.	47.752mm
1990	1.780 in.	45.212mm
Head Diameter - Exhaust		
1998 - 92	1.624 in.	41.250mm
1991	1.60 in.	40.640mm
1990	1.517 in.	38.532mm

89663C07

5.2L (5211cc) ENGINE MECHANICAL SPECIFICATIONS

Description	English Specifications	Metric Specifications
Length (Overall) - Intake		
1998 - 92	4.893 - 4.918 in.	124.28 - 125.92mm
1991 - 90	4.962 - 4.987 in.	126.03 - 126.67mm
Length (Overall) - Exhaust		
1998 - 92	4.907 - 4.932 in.	124.64 - 125.27mm
1991 - 90	4.977 - 5.012 in.	126.42 - 126.30mm
Lift (@ zero lash) - Intake/Exhaust		
1998 - 92	0.432 in.	10.973mm
Lift (@ zero lash) - Intake		
1991 - 90	0.373 in.	9.474mm
Lift (@ zero lash) - Exhaust		
1991 - 90	0.400 in.	10.160mm
Stem Diameter - Intake/Exhaust		
1998 - 92	0.311 - 0.312 in.	7.899 - 7.925mm
1991	0.3125 in.	7.9375mm
Stem Diameter - Intake		
1990	0.372 - 0.373 in.	9.449 - 9.474mm
Stem Diameter - Exhaust		
1990	0.371 - 0.372 in.	9.423 - 9.449mm
Guide Bore Diameter		
1998 - 91	0.313 - 0.314 in.	7.950 - 7.976mm
1990	0.374 - 0.375 in.	9.500 - 9.525mm
Stem-to-Guide Clearance - Intake/Exhaust		
1998 - 92	0.001 - 0.003 in.	0.0254 - 0.0762mm
Stem-to-Guide Clearance - Intake		
1991	0.001 - 0.003 in.	0.0254 - 0.0762mm
Stem-to-Guide Clearance - Exhaust		
1991	0.002 - 0.004 in.	0.0508 - 0.1016mm
Service Limit (Rocking Method)	0.017 in.	0.4318mm
Valve Spring		
Free Length		
1998 - 92	1.967 in.	49.962mm
Free Length - Intake		
1991 - 90	2.00 in.	50.800mm
Free Length - Exhaust		
1991 - 90	1.81 in.	45.974mm
Spring Tension (valve closed)		
1998 - 92	85 lbs. @ 1.64 in.	378 N @ 41.66mm
Spring Tension (valve closed) - Intake		
1991 - 90	78 - 88 lbs. @ 1.6875 in.	347 - 391 N @ 42.68mm
Spring Tension (valve closed) - Exhaust		
1991 - 90	80 - 90 lbs. @ 1.4844 in.	356 - 400 N @ 37.70mm
Spring Tension (valve open)		
1998 - 92	200 lbs.. @ 1.212 in.	890 N @ 30.89mm
Spring Tension (valve open) - Intake		
1991 - 90	170 - 184 lbs. @ 1.3125 in.	756 - 819 N @ 33.34mm
Spring Tension (valve open) - Exhaust		
1991 - 90	180 - 194 lbs. @ 1.0625 in.	801 - 863 N @ 27.38mm
Number of Coils		
1998 - 92	6.8	

89663C08

5.2L (5211cc) ENGINE MECHANICAL SPECIFICATIONS

Description	English Specifications	Metric Specifications
Number of Coils - Intake		
1991 - 90	6.4	
Number of Coils - Exhaust		
1991 - 90	5.8	
Installed Height		
1998 - 92	1.64 in.	41.66mm
Installed Height - Intake		
1991 - 90	1.63 - 1.69 in.	41.275 - 42.863mm
Installed Height - Exhaust		
1991 - 90	1.45 - 1.52 in.	36.909 - 38.497mm
Wire Diameter		
1998 - 92	0.177 in.	4.50mm
Wire Diameter - Intake		
1991 - 90	0.192 in.	4.877mm
Wire Diameter - Exhaust		
1991 - 90	0.185 in.	4.699mm
Hydraulic Tappets		
Body Diameter	0.9035 - 0.9040 in.	22.949 - 22.962mm
Clearance in Block	0.0011 - 0.0024 in.	0.0279 - 0.0610mm
Dry Lash	0.060 - 0.210 in.	1.524 - 5.334mm
Pushrod Length		
1998 - 95	6.915 - 6.935 in.	175.64 - 176.15mm
1994 - 90	6.794 - 6.814 in.	172.57 - 173.08mm
Oil Pressure		
@ Curb Idle (min.)*	6 psi	41.4 kPa
@ 3000 rpm	30 - 80 psi	207 - 552 kPa
Oil Pressure Bypass Valve Setting	9 - 15 psi	62 - 103 kPa
Switch Actuating Pressure	5 - 7 psi	34.5 - 48.3 kPa

*CAUTION: if oil pressure is ZERO at curb idle, DO NOT run engine @ 3000 rpm.

Description	English Specifications	Metric Specifications
Oil Pump		
Clearance Over Rotors (Max.)	0.004 in.	0.1016mm
Cover Out of Flat (Max.)	0.0015 in.	0.0381mm
Inner Rotor Thickness (Min.)	0.825 in.	20.955mm
Outer Rotor Clearance (Max.)	0.014 in.	0.3556mm
Outer Rotor Diameter (Min.)	2.469 in.	62.7126mm
Outer Rotor Thickness (Min.)	0.825 in.	20.955mm
Tip Clearance Between Rotors (Max.)	0.008 in.	0.2032mm
Pistons		
Clearance at Top of Skirt	0.0005 - 0.0015 in.	0.013 - 0.038mm
Land Clearance (Diam.)		
1998 - 92	0.025 - 0.040 in.	0.635 - 1.016mm
1991 - 90	0.019 - 0.024 in.	0.4826 - 0.6096mm
Piston Length	3.40 in.	86.360mm
Ring Groove Depth (#1 & 2)		
1998 - 91	0.180 - 0.190 in.	4.572 - 4.826mm
1990	0.205 in.	5.207mm
Ring Groove Depth (#3)		
1998 - 91	0.150 - 0.160 in.	3.810 - 4.064mm
1990	0.194 in.	4.928mm
Weight	20.90 - 21.04 oz.	592.6 - 596.6 grams

89663C09

5.2L (5211cc) ENGINE MECHANICAL SPECIFICATIONS

Description	English Specifications	Metric Specifications
Piston Pins		
Clearance in Piston	0.00025 - 0.00075 in.	0.00635 - 0.01905mm
Diameter	0.9841 - 0.9843 in.	24.996 - 25.001mm
End-play	NONE	
Length	2.990 - 3.010 in.	75.946 - 76.454mm
Piston Rings		
Ring Gap		
Compression Rings (Nos. 1 & 2)		
1998 - 90, except 1991	0.010 - 0.020 in.	0.254 - 0.508mm
Compression Rings (No. 1)		
1991	0.010 - 0.020 in.	0.254 - 0.508mm
Compression Rings (No. 2)		
1991	0.020 - 0.030 in.	0.508 - 0.762mm
Oil Control (Steel Rails)		
1998 - 92	0.010 - 0.050 in.	0.254 - 1.270mm
1991 - 90	0.015 - 0.055 in.	0.381 - 1.397mm
Ring Side Clearance		
Compression Rings	0.0015 - 0.0030 in.	0.038 - 0.076mm
Oil Control (Steel Rails)		
1998 - 92	0.002 - 0.008 in.	0.05 - 0.203mm
1991	0.002 - 0.008 in.	0.005 - 0.203mm
1990	0.002 - 0.005 in.	0.005 - 0.127mm
Ring Width		
Compression Rings		
1998 - 91	0.0776 - 0.0783 in.	1.971 - 1.989mm
1990	0.077 - 0.078 in.	1.9558 - 1.9812mm
Oil Control (Steel Rails)		
1998 - 91	0.1515 - 0.1565 in.	3.848 - 3.975mm
1990	0.0252 in.	0.640mm
Valve Timing		
Exhaust Valve		
Closes (ATDC)		
1998 - 96		21 degrees
1995 - 90		16 degrees
Opens (BBDC)		
1998 - 96		60 degrees
1995 - 90		52 degrees
Duration		
1998 - 96		264 degrees
1995 - 90		248 degrees
Intake Valve		
Closes (ABDC)		
1998 - 96		61 degrees
1995 - 90		50 degrees
Opens (BTDC)		
1998 - 90		10 degrees
Duration		
1998 - 96		250 degrees
1995 - 90		240 degrees
Valve Overlap		
1998 - 96		31 degrees
1995 - 90		26 degrees

89663C10

5.9L (5899cc) ENGINE MECHANICAL SPECIFICATIONS

Description	English Specifications	Metric Specifications
General Information		
Engine Type	90 degree V8 OHV	
Bore & Stroke	4.00 x 3.58 in.	99.3 x 84.0mm
Displacement	360 c.i.	5.9 L
Compression Ratio	9.1:1	
Firing Order	1-8-4-3-6-5-7-2	
Lubrication	Pressure Feed - Full Flow Filtration	
Cooling System	Liquid Cooled - Forced Circulation	
Cylinder Block	Cast Iron	
Crankshaft	Nodular Iron	
Cylinder Head	Cast Iron	
Combustion Chambers	Wedge-High Swirl Valve shrouding	
Camshaft	Nodular Cast Iron	
Pistons	Aluminum Alloy w/strut	
Connecting Rods	Forced Steel	
Cylinder Compression Pressure (Min.)	100 psi	689.5 kPa
Camshaft		
Bearing Diameter (Inside)		
No. 1	2.000 - 2.001 in.	50.800 - 50.825mm
No. 2	1.984 - 1.985 in.	50.394 - 50.419mm
No. 3	1.969 - 1.970 in.	50.013 - 50.038mm
No. 4	1.953 - 1.954 in.	49.606 - 49.632mm
No. 5	1.5265 - 1.5635 in.	39.688 - 39.713mm
Journal Diameter		
No. 1	1.998 - 1.999 in.	50.749 - 50.775mm
No. 2	1.982 - 1.983 in.	50.343 - 50.368mm
No. 3	1.967 - 1.968 in.	49.962 - 49.987mm
No. 4	1.951 - 1.952 in.	49.555 - 49.581mm
No. 5	1.5605 - 1.5615 in.	39.637 - 39.662mm
Bearing-to-Journal Clearance		
Standard	0.001 - 0.003 in.	0.0254 - 0.0762mm
Max. Allowable	0.005 in.	0.127mm
Camshaft End-Play		
End-Play	0.002 - 0.010 in.	0.051 - 0.254mm
Connecting Rods		
Piston Pin Bore Diameter	0.9829 - 0.9834 in.	24.966 - 24.978mm
Side Clearance	0.006 - 0.014 in.	0.152 - 0.356mm
Crankshaft		
Rod Journal		
Diameter	2.124 - 2.125 in.	53.950 - 53.975mm
Out Of Round (Max.)	0.001 in.	0.0254mm
Taper (Max.)	0.001 in.	0.0254mm
Bearing Clearance	0.0005 - 0.0022 in.	0.013 - 0.056mm
Service Limit		
1998 - 91	0.003 in.	0.0762mm
1990	0.005 in.	0.0929mm
Main Bearing Journal		
Diameter	2.8095 - 2.8105 in.	71.361 - 71.387mm

89663C11

5.9L (5899cc) ENGINE MECHANICAL SPECIFICATIONS

Description	English Specifications	Metric Specifications
Out Of Round (Max.)		
1998 - 96	0.001 in.	0.0254mm
1995 - 90	0.001 in.	0.0254mm
Taper (Max.)	0.001 in.	0.0254mm
Bearing Clearance (#1 Journal)	0.0005 - 0.0015 in.	0.013 - 0.038mm
Service Limit (#1 Journal)	0.0015 in	0.0381mm
Bearing Clearance (#2 - 5 Journals)	0.0005 - 0.0020 in.	0.013 - 0.051mm
Service Limit (#2 - 5 Journals)	0.0025 in.	0.064mm
Crankshaft End-Play		
End-Play	0.002 - 0.007 in.	0.051 - 0.178mm
Service Limit	0.010 in.	0.254mm
Cylinder Block		
Cylinder Bore		
Diameter	4.000 - 4.002 in.	101.60 - 101.65mm
Out Of Round (Max.)	0.005 in.	0.127mm
Taper (Max.)	0.010 in.	0.254mm
Lifter Bore		
Diameter	0.9501 - 0.9059 in.	22.99 - 23.01mm
Distributor Drive Bushing (Press Fit)		
Bushing-to-Bore Interference	0.0005 - 0.0140 in.	0.0127 - 0.3556mm
Shaft to Bushing Clearance	0.0007 - 0.0027 in.	0.0178 - 0.0686mm
Cylinder Head And Valves		
Compression Pressure	100 psi	689 Kpa
Gasket Thickness (Compressed)		
1995 - 92	0.0475 in.	1.2065mm
1991 - 90	0.033 in.	0.8382mm
Valve Seat		
Angle		
1998 - 92	44.25 - 44.75 degrees	
1991	45 - 45 degrees	
1990	45 - 45.5 degrees	
Run-out (Max.)	0.003 in.	0.0762mm
Width (Finish) - Intake		
1998 - 92	0.040 - 0.060 in.	1.016 - 1.542mm
1991 - 90	0.065 - 0.085 in.	1.651 - 2.159mm
Width (Finish) - Exhaust		
1998 - 92	0.060 - 0.080 in.	1.524 - 2.032mm
1991 - 90	0.080 - .0100 in.	2.032 - 2.540mm
Valves		
Face Angle		
1998 - 92	43.25 - 43.75 degrees	
1991 - 90	44.5 - 45 degrees	
Head Diameter - Intake	1.88 in.	47.752mm
Head Diameter - Exhaust	1.617 in.	41.072mm
Length (Overall) - Intake	4.969 - 4.994 in.	126.21 - 126.85mm
Length (Overall) - Exhaust	4.978 - 5.012 in.	126.44 - 127.30mm
Lift (@ zero lash) - Intake/Exhaust	0.410 in.	10.414mm
Stem Diameter - Intake	0.372 - 0.373 in.	9.449 - 9.474mm
Stem Diameter - Exhaust	0.371 - 0.372 in.	9.423 - 9.449mm

89663C12

5.9L (5899cc) ENGINE MECHANICAL SPECIFICATIONS

Description	English Specifications	Metric Specifications
Guide Bore Diameter	0.374 - 0.375 in.	9.500 - 9.525mm
Stem to Guide Clearance - Intake	0.001 - 0.003 in.	0.0254 - 0.0762mm
Stem to Guide Clearance - Exhaust	0.002 - 0.004 in.	0.0508 - 0.1016mm
Service Limit	0.017 in.	0.4318mm
Valve Spring		
Free Length		
1998 - 92	1.967 in.	49.962mm
Free Length - Intake		
1991 - 90	2.00 in.	50.800mm
Free Length - Exhaust		
1991 - 90	1.967 in.	45.974mm
Spring Tension (valve closed)		
1998 - 92	85 lbs.. @ 1.64 in.	378 N @ 41.66mm
Spring Tension (valve closed) - Intake		
1991- 90	78 - 88 lbs. @ 1.6875 in.	347 - 391 N @ 42.86mm
Spring Tension (valve closed) - Exhaust		
1991 - 90	80 - 90 lbs. @ 1.4844 in.	356 - 400 N @ 37.70mm
Spring Tension (valve open)		
1998 - 92	200 lbs.. @ 1.212 in.	890 N @ 30.89mm
Spring Tension (valve open) - Intake		
1991 - 90	170 - 184 lbs. @ 1.3125 in.	756 - 819 N @ 33.34mm
Spring Tension (valve open) - Exhaust		
1991 - 90	181- 197 lbs. @ 1.0625 in.	805 - 876 N @ 26.99mm
Number of Coils		
1998 - 92	6.8	
Number of Coils - Intake		
1991 - 90	6.4	
Number of Coils - Exhaust		
1991 - 90	5.6	
Installed Height		
1998 - 92	1.64 in.	41.66mm
Installed Height - Intake		
1991 - 90	1.63 - 1.69 in.	41.275 - 42.863mm
Installed Height - Exhaust		
1991 - 90	1.45 - 1.52 in.	36.909 - 38.497mm
Wire Diameter		
1998 - 92	0.177 in.	4.50mm
Wire Diameter - Intake/Exhaust		
1991 - 90	0.192 in.	4.877mm
Hydraulic Tappets		
Body Diameter	0.9035 - 0.9040 in.	22.949 - 22.962mm
Clearance in Block	0.0011 - 0.0024 in.	0.0279 - 0.0610mm
Dry Lash	0.060 - 0.210 in.	1.524 - 5.334mm
Pushrod Length		
1998 - 95	6.915 - 6.935 in.	175.64 - 176.15mm
1994 - 90	7.505 - 7.525 in.	190.63 - 191.14mm

89663C13

5.9L (5899cc) ENGINE MECHANICAL SPECIFICATIONS

Description	English Specifications	Metric Specifications
Oil Pressure		
@ Curb Idle (min.)*	6 psi	41.4 kPa
*CAUTION: if oil pressure is ZERO at curb idle, DO NOT run engine @ 3000 rpm.		
@ 3000 rpm	30 - 80 psi	207 - 552 kPa
Oil Pressure Bypass Valve Setting	9 - 15 psi	62 - 103 kPa
Switch Actuating Pressure	5 - 7 psi	34.5 - 48.3 kPa
Oil Pump		
Clearance over Rotors (Max.)	0.004 in.	0.1016mm
Cover Out of Flat (Max.)	0.0015 in.	0.0381mm
Inner Rotor Thickness (Min.)	0.825 in.	20.955mm
Outer Rotor Clearance (Max.)	0.014 in.	0.3556mm
Outer Rotor Diameter (Min.)	2.469 in.	62.7126mm
Outer Rotor Thickness (Min.)	0.825 in.	20.955mm
Tip Clearance between Rotors (Max.)	0.008 in.	0.2032mm
Pistons		
Clearance at Top of Skirt	0.0005 - 0.0015 in.	0.013 - 0.038mm
Land Clearance (Diam.)	0.020 - 0.026 in.	0.508 - 0.660mm
Piston Length	3.19 in.	81.03mm
Ring Groove Depth (#1 & 2)		
1998 - 92	0.187 - 0.193 in.	4.761 - 4.912mm
1991 - 90	0.210 in.	5.334mm
Ring Groove Depth (#3)		
1998 - 92	0.157 - 0.164 in.	3.996 - 4.177mm
1991 - 90	0.199 in.	5.055mm
Weight	20.53 - 20.67 oz.	582 - 586 grams
Piston Pins		
Clearance in Piston		
1998 - 92	0.00035 - 0.00074 in.	0.006 - 0.019mm
1991 - 90	0.00025 - 0.00075 in.	0.0064 - 0.0191mm
Diameter		
1998 - 92	0.9845 - 0.9848 in.	25.007 - 25.015mm
1991 - 90	0.9841 - 0.9843 in.	24.996 - 25.001mm
End-Play	NONE	
Length		
1998 - 92	2.67 - 2.69 in.	67.8 - 68.3mm
1991 -90	2.990 - 3.020 in.	75.946 - 76.708mm
Piston Rings		
Ring Gap		
Compression Ring (Top)		
1998 - 92	0.012 - 0.022 in.	0.30 - 0.55mm
1991 - 90	0.010 - 0.020 in.	0.254 - 0.508mm
Compression Rings (Second)	0.022 - 0.031 in.	0.55 - 0.80mm
Oil Control (Steel Rails)	0.015 - 0.055 in.	0.381 - 1.397mm
Ring Side Clearance		
Compression Rings		
1998 - 92	0.0016 - 0.0033 in.	0.040 - 0.085mm
1991 - 90	0.0015 - 0.0030 in.	0.038 - 0.076mm

89663C14

5.9L (5899cc) ENGINE MECHANICAL SPECIFICATIONS

Description	English Specifications	Metric Specifications
Oil Control (Steel Rails)		
1998 - 92	0.002 - 0.008 in.	0.05 - 0.21mm
1991 - 90	0.0002 - 0.0050 in.	0.005 - 0.127mm
Ring Width		
Compression Rings		
1998 - 92	0.060 - 0.061 in.	1.530 - 1.555mm
1991 - 90	0.0770 - 0.0780 in.	1.9558 - 1.9812mm
Oil Control (Steel Rails) -Max.		
1998 - 92	0.018 - 0.019 in.	0.447 - 0.473mm
1991 - 90	0.0252 in.	0.640mm
Valve Timing		
Exhaust Valve		
Closes (ATDC)		
1998 - 96		33 degrees
1995		23 degrees
1994 - 90, except 1991		16 degrees
1991		15 degrees
Opens (BBDC)		
1998 - 96		56 degrees
1995		61 degrees
1994 - 90, except 1991		52 degrees
1991		57 degrees
Duration		
1998 - 96		269 degrees
1995		264 degrees
1994 - 90, except 1991		248 degrees
1991		252 degrees
Intake Valve		
Closes (ABDC)		
1998 - 96		62 degrees
1995		80 degrees
1994 - 90, except 1991		50 degrees
1991		54 degrees
Opens (BTDC)		
1998 - 96		7 degrees
1995		13 degrees
1994 - 90, except 1991		10 degrees
1991		18 degrees
Duration		
1998 - 96		249 degrees
1995		274 degrees
1994 - 90, except 1991		240 degrees
1991		252 degrees
Valve Overlap		
1998 - 96		41 degrees
1995		36.5 degrees
1994 - 90, except 1991		26 degrees
1991		33 degrees

89663C15

Engine

REMOVAL & INSTALLATION

▶ **See Figures 1 thru 9**

In the process of removing the engine, you will come across a number of steps which call for the removal of a separate component or system, such as "disconnect the exhaust system" or "remove the radiator." In most instances, a detailed removal procedure can be found elsewhere in this manual.

It is virtually impossible to list each individual wire and hose which must be disconnected, simply because so many different model and engine combinations have been manufactured. Careful observation and common sense are the best possible approaches to any repair procedure.

Removal and installation of the engine can be made easier if you follow these basic points:

• If you have to drain any of the fluids, use a suitable container for each.

• Always label any wires or hoses and, if possible, the components they came from before disconnecting them.

• Because there are so many bolts and fasteners involved, store and label the retainers from components separately in muffin pans, jars or coffee cans. This will prevent confusion during installation.

• After unbolting the transmission, always make sure it is properly supported.

• If it is necessary to disconnect the air conditioning system, have this service performed by a qualified MVAC technician using a recovery/recycling station. If the system does not have to be disconnected, unbolt the compressor and set it aside.

• When unbolting the engine mounts, always make sure the engine is properly supported. When removing the engine, make sure that any lifting devices are properly attached to the engine. It is recommended that if your engine is supplied with lifting hooks, your lifting apparatus be attached to them.

• Lift the engine from its compartment slowly, checking that no hoses, wires or other components are still connected.

• After the engine is clear of the compartment, place it on an engine stand or workbench.

• After the engine has been removed, you can perform a partial or full teardown of the engine using the procedures outlined in this manual.

1. Properly relieve the fuel system pressure, as described in Section 5.
2. Disconnect the negative battery cable.
3. Drain and recycle the engine coolant.

❋❋ CAUTION

Never open, service or drain the radiator or cooling system when hot; serious burns can occur from the steam and hot coolant. Also, when draining engine coolant, keep in mind that cats and dogs are attracted to ethylene glycol antifreeze and could drink any that is left in an uncovered container or in puddles on the ground. This will prove fatal in sufficient quantities. Always drain coolant into a sealable container. Coolant should be reused unless it is contaminated or is several years old.

4. Remove the engine cover.
5. Remove the air cleaner assembly.
6. Remove the oil dipstick tube.
7. Remove the front bumper.
8. Remove the grille and support brace.
9. Remove the cowl plenum-to-upper radiator supports.
10. Remove the coolant recovery and washer solvent bottles from the radiator support.
11. Remove the fan shroud.
12. Remove the fan, pulley and drive belts.
13. Disconnect the upper radiator hose.

14. Disconnect the lower radiator hose.
15. Label, disconnect, and plug the transmission cooler lines (if equipped).
16. Label and disconnect the heater hoses.
17. If so equipped, have the air conditioning system discharged by an MVAC certified automotive technician.
18. Disconnect the refrigerant lines at the condenser. Cap all openings at once to prevent contamination of the system.
19. Remove the radiator and condenser (if equipped) as an assembly.
20. Remove the air conditioning compressor (if equipped).
21. Remove the power steering pump from its bracket and position it out of the way. It is not necessary to remove the lines.
22. Label and disconnect the alternator wiring harness.
23. Remove the alternator.
24. Label and disconnect the hoses and remove the air pump (if equipped).
25. Label and disconnect all vacuum lines at the engine.
26. Disconnect and label the necessary engine electrical connectors.
27. Remove the throttle body assembly.
28. Disconnect the fuel line(s).
29. Check for any other lines, vacuum hoses, or wiring harnesses that must be disconnected. Label and disconnect them.
30. Raise and support the vehicle.
31. Drain and recycle the engine oil.

❋❋ CAUTION

The EPA warns that prolonged contact with used engine oil may cause a number of skin disorders, including cancer! You should make every effort to minimize your exposure to used engine oil. Protective gloves should be worn when changing the oil. Wash your hands and any other exposed skin areas as soon as possible after exposure to used engine oil. Soap and water, or waterless hand cleaner should be used.

32. Remove the engine oil filter.
33. Remove the engine-to-transmission struts.
34. Remove the oil pan.
35. Remove the oil pump and pickup tube assembly.
36. Remove the starter.
37. Disconnect the O2 sensor.
38. Remove the exhaust crossover pipe.
39. Remove the inspection plate or converter cover plate from the bell housing (automatic transmission). Remove the converter-to-flexplate bolts/nuts (automatic transmission).

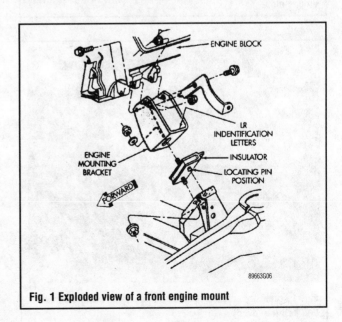

89663G06

Fig. 1 Exploded view of a front engine mount

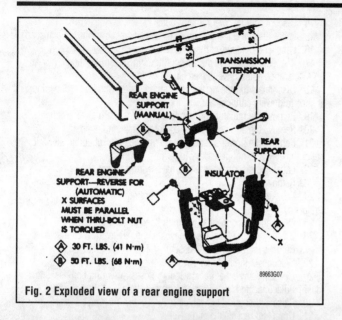

Fig. 2 Exploded view of a rear engine support

Fig. 5 One retaining bolt on the accessory bracket is hidden by the idler pulley; remove the pulley to access the bolt

Fig. 3 The engine block should be drained if you plan on removing it for overhaul. There are drain plugs on either side of the engine block

Fig. 6 The accessory bracket and bolts after removal from the engine. Note the location of each bolt, as they are different lengths

Fig. 4 Accessory bracket mounted on an engine using a serpentine belt (removed)

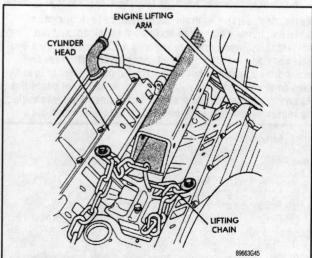

Fig. 7 Attach the lifting device directly to the crane arm to remove the engine assembly

Fig. 8 The A/C compressor, as mounted on the front of the engine

Fig. 9 Remove the A/C compressor from its mount and support it; detaching the refrigerant lines is not necessary

40. Support the transmission on a floor jack or equivalent.
41. Remove the transmission-to-bell housing bolts, or the converter housing-to-engine bolts.
42. Install an engine lifting fixture.
43. Attach an engine crane and take up the weight of the engine.
44. Remove the nuts and washers from the engine mounts.
45. Remove the left exhaust manifold.
46. Loosen the engine-to-transmission junction.
47. Raise the engine and maneuver it through the front of the van. It may be necessary to raise the van slightly to keep the crane arm horizontal.

To install:
48. Installation is the reverse of removal.
49. Please note the following torque specifications:
- Engine mount nuts—75 ft. lbs. (102 Nm)
- Torque converter-to-drive plate—23 ft. lbs. (31 Nm)
- Converter Y-pipe-to-exhaust manifold—25 ft. lbs. (34 Nm)
- Starter motor-to-block—50 ft. lbs. (68 Nm)
- Exhaust manifold-to-head—25 ft. lbs. (34 Nm)
- Throttle body-to-intake manifold—200 inch lbs. (23 Nm)

Rocker Arm (Valve) Cover

REMOVAL & INSTALLATION

▶ See Figures 10 thru 16

1. Disconnect the negative battery cable.
2. Remove the engine cover.
3. Remove the air cleaner assembly.
4. Remove the ignition wire separators from the studs on the valve cover.
5. To remove the passenger's side valve cover:
   a. Remove the PCV valve and hose from the valve cover.
6. To remove the driver's side valve cover:
   a. Remove the bracket on the cowl-to-radiator support brace that retains the oil fill tube.
   b. Remove the oil fill tube by twisting upward.

➡Note the bolt and stud locations prior to removing the valve cover.

Fig. 10 The ignition wire separators just slide off the valve cover studs

Fig. 11 Remove the wire harness from the inner valve cover studs

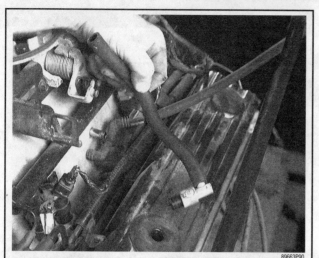

Fig. 12 The PCV valve is removable from the valve cover with a twist

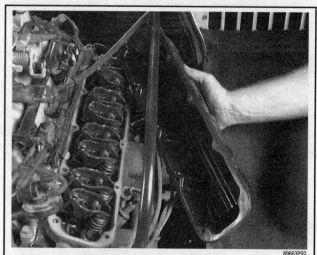

Fig. 15 When loosened, lift the valve cover up to clear the rocker arms and remove it

Fig. 13 The oil fill tube is removed from the front of the vehicle

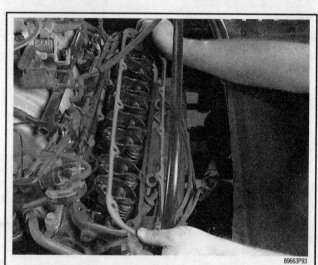

Fig. 16 Make sure that the valve cover and cylinder head are clean before installing with a new gasket

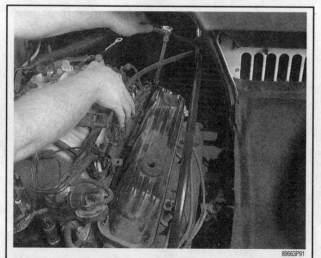

Fig. 14 Loosen the bolts and studs that retain the valve cover, and note their locations for reassembly

7. Remove the retaining bolts and studs from the valve cover. It may be necessary to tap the valve cover slightly with a soft mallet to loosen; do not pry on the valve cover.

8. Remove the valve cover from the cylinder head.

To install:

9. Clean all gasket mating surfaces thoroughly.

10. Lubricate all bolt and stud threads prior to installation.

11. Install a new valve cover gasket on the cylinder head and align the fastener holes.

12. Install the valve cover on the cylinder head.

➡Although the manufacturer does not specify a torque sequence, it is recommended that you start from the center and work your way outward, alternating sides of the valve cover. Remember to tighten evenly to prevent valve cover distortion.

13. Install the retaining bolts and studs, and tighten to 95 inch lbs. (11 Nm).

14. Install the ignition wire separators on the valve cover retaining studs.

15. To install the driver's side valve cover:
    a. Install the oil fill tube back into the valve cover.

b. Install the bracket on the cowl-to-radiator support brace for the oil fill tube.
16. To install the passenger's side valve cover:
   a. Install the PCV hose and valve into the valve cover.
17. Install the air cleaner assembly.
18. Connect the negative battery cable.
19. Check the engine oil level.

✳✳ WARNING

Operating the engine without the proper amount and type of engine oil will result in severe engine damage.

20. Start the engine and check for leaks.
21. Install the engine cover.

Rocker Arm/Shafts

REMOVAL & INSTALLATION

▸ **See Figures 17 thru 22**

1. Disconnect the negative battery cable.
2. Remove the engine cover.
3. Remove the valve cover(s).

➡ **Note the location of the rocker arms and shaft (if equipped, typically engines prior to 1992) before removing them; after removal, place them in order for reinstallation.**

4. On earlier engines:
   a. Remove the rocker shaft bolts and retainers, then remove the shaft and rocker arms as an assembly. If the rocker arms need to be removed , keep them in order for reinstallation.
5. On later engines:
   a. Remove the rocker arm retaining bolts and pivot plates, then remove the rocker arms from the cylinder head.
6. To remove the pushrods (if necessary), pull them straight up and off of the lifters, and note their position for reinstallation.

To install:

7. Install the pushrods, if removed, by placing them in their original positions. Place them through the cylinder head and on the top of the lifter.
8. On earlier engines:
   a. Install the rocker shaft and rocker arms on the cylinder head.

Fig. 18 The rocker arms for each cylinder sit on a pivot plate—later model engines

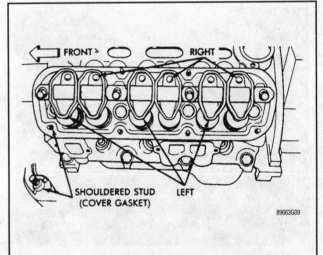
Fig. 19 Early model engines had their rocker arms attached to the cylinder head by a shaft

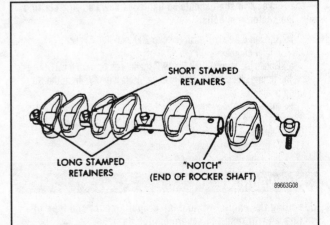
Fig. 20 If you remove the rocker arms from the shaft, note their positions for reassembly

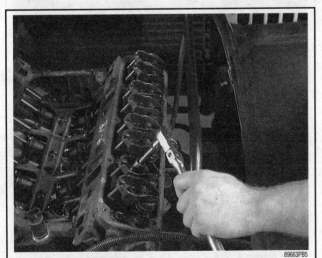
Fig. 17 Use a socket and extension to unfasten the rocker arm retaining bolts

Fig. 21 View of the cylinder head with its rocker arms and pushrods removed

Fig. 22 If applicable, be sure to return the pushrods to their original locations

➡The rocker arm shaft should be tightened down slowly, starting with the centermost bolts.

   b. Tighten the rocker shaft bolts to 200 inch lbs. (23 Nm).
  9. On later engines:
   a. Rotate the engine until the "V8" mark lines up with the TDC mark on the timing chain cover. This mark is located at 147° from the No. 1 firing position.
   b. Install the rocker arm and pivot on the correct cylinder.
   c. Tighten each rocker arm retaining bolt to 21 ft. lbs. (28 Nm).
  10. Install the valve cover(s).
  11. Connect the negative battery cable.
  12. Check the engine oil level.

✳✳ WARNING

Operating the engine without the proper amount and type of engine oil will result in severe engine damage.

  13. Start the engine and check for leaks.
  14. Install the engine cover.

Thermostat

REMOVAL & INSTALLATION

▸ See Figures 23 thru 29

✳✳ CAUTION

Never open, service or drain the radiator or cooling system when hot; serious burns can occur from the steam and hot coolant. Also, when draining engine coolant, keep in mind that cats and dogs are attracted to ethylene glycol antifreeze and could drink any that is left in an uncovered container or in puddles on the ground. This will prove fatal in sufficient quantities. Always drain coolant into a sealable container. Coolant should be reused unless it is contaminated or is several years old.

  1. Disconnect the negative battery cable.
  2. Drain and recycle the engine coolant.
  3. If equipped with air conditioning:
   a. Remove the engine cover.
   b. Remove the drive belt.
   c. Remove the alternator.
  4. Remove the upper radiator hose.
  5. Remove the upper radiator hose from the thermostat housing.
  6. Remove the retaining bolts from the thermostat housing.
  7. Remove the thermostat housing, thermostat, and gasket from the intake manifold.

To install:
  8. Clean the gasket mating surfaces.

➡**If a new thermostat is being installed, make sure the replacement is the specified part for the vehicle.**

  9. If the gasket goes beneath the thermostat flange, be sure to first install a new gasket. Install the thermostat spring side down into the intake manifold.
  10. If the gasket goes on top of the thermostat flange, install a new thermostat gasket above the thermostat.

➡**The thermostat housing may have the word FRONT on it; this goes towards the front of the vehicle.**

  11. Install the thermostat housing onto the intake manifold.

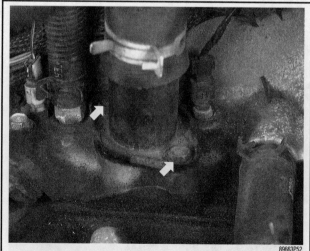

Fig. 23 The thermostat housing is located at the front of the intake manifold, and is attached by two retaining bolts

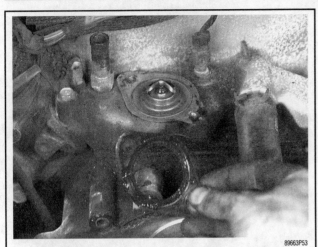

Fig. 24 The gasket usually sits atop the thermostat, as in this case. However, on some engines, the gasket is underneath the thermostat flange

Fig. 27 Place the new thermostat and gasket on the intake manifold before attaching the thermostat housing

Fig. 25 Remove the thermostat from the manifold by lifting it straight up

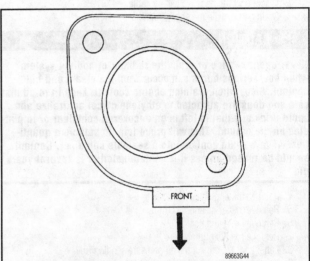

Fig. 28 The word FRONT is usually stamped on the thermostat housing. This goes toward the front of the vehicle for installation

Fig. 26 Take care when cleaning the surfaces for the new gasket; it is necessary to remove any residue to allow the gasket to adhere

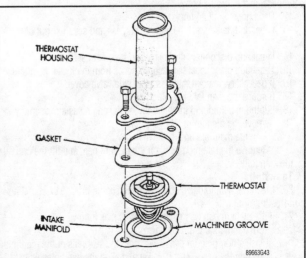

Fig. 29 This exploded view shows the typical order of installation of the thermostat

12. Tighten the housing bolts to 200 inch lbs. (23 Nm).
13. Reinstall the upper radiator hose onto the housing.
14. If the vehicle has air conditioning:
    a. Reinstall the alternator.
    b. Reinstall the drive belt.
    c. Reinstall the engine cover.

→Ensure that you have retightened the radiator drain before refilling with coolant.

15. Refill the radiator with a proper coolant mixture.
16. Connect the negative battery cable.
17. Start the engine and bleed the cooling system.
18. Ensure that the thermostat is operational (by checking the upper radiator hose for warmth), and that there are no leaks.

Intake Manifold

REMOVAL & INSTALLATION

▶ **See Figures 30 thru 41**

1. Properly relieve the fuel system pressure, as described in Section 5.
2. Disconnect the negative battery cable.
3. Drain and recycle the engine coolant.

☀☀ CAUTION

Never open, service or drain the radiator or cooling system when hot; serious burns can occur from the steam and hot coolant. Also, when draining engine coolant, keep in mind that cats and dogs are attracted to ethylene glycol antifreeze and could drink any that is left in an uncovered container or in puddles on the ground. This will prove fatal in sufficient quantities. Always drain coolant into a sealable container. Coolant should be reused unless it is contaminated or is several years old.

4. Remove the engine cover.
5. Remove the air cleaner assembly.
6. Remove the alternator.
7. Remove the distributor.
8. Label and disconnect the oil pressure sending unit.
9. Label and disconnect the intake air temperature sensor.
10. Disconnect the accelerator linkage, speed control cable (if equipped), and transmission kickdown cable (if equipped).
11. Label and disconnect the MAP sensor, IAC motor, and TP sensor (if equipped) on the throttle body.
12. Disconnect the fuel line(s).
13. Label and disconnect the injector harness and secure it out of the way.
14. Label and disconnect the heater and bypass hoses.
15. Label and disconnect the vacuum hoses from the intake manifold.
16. If necessary, remove the passenger side valve cover.
17. Remove the manifold retaining bolts.
18. Lift the manifold and throttle body off the engine as an assembly.
19. Remove the plenum pan (if necessary) as follows:
    a. Turn the manifold upside down.
    b. Remove the retaining bolts on the plenum pan, and lift the pan off the manifold.
To install:
20. Clean the manifold, cylinder head and engine block gasket mating surfaces thoroughly.
21. If the plenum pan was removed, install it as follows:
    a. Turn the manifold upside down.
    b. Place a new plenum pan gasket onto the seal rails of the manifold.
    c. Position the pan over the gasket and align the pan holes with those on the manifold.
    d. Hand-start the bolts.

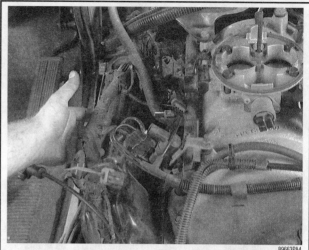

Fig. 30 Label and disconnect any components and harnesses necessary to remove the intake manifold

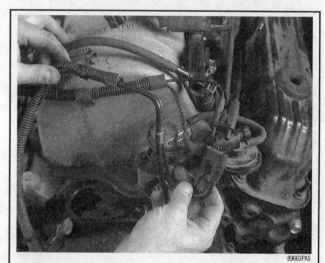

Fig. 31 Remove and label any vacuum lines necessary for intake manifold removal

Fig. 32 Loosen the intake manifold retaining bolts

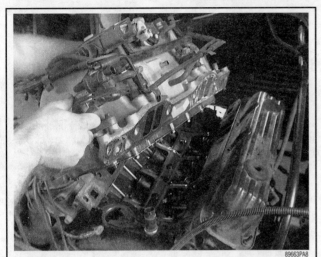

Fig. 33 Lift the intake manifold off the cylinder heads and engine block

Fig. 36 The intake manifold can be removed from the vehicle as an assembly

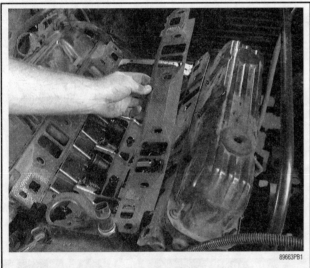

Fig. 34 Remove the old flange gaskets . . .

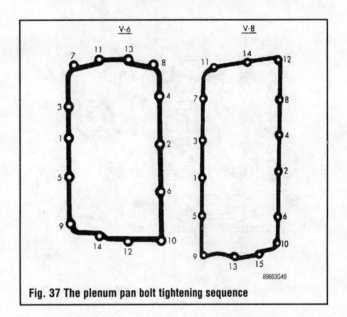

Fig. 37 The plenum pan bolt tightening sequence

Fig. 35 . . . and the old end seals

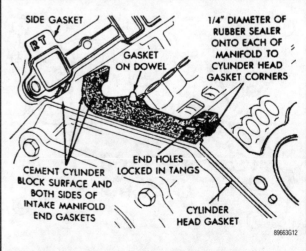

Fig. 38 When applying the intake manifold end seals, line up their holes with the dowels and tangs

Fig. 39 Apply a small bead of sealant to the corners of the end seals

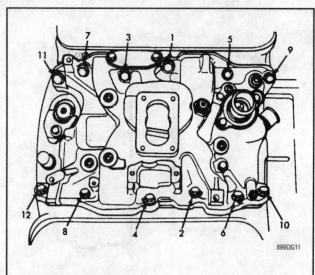

Fig. 40 Proper tightening sequence for the V6 intake manifold

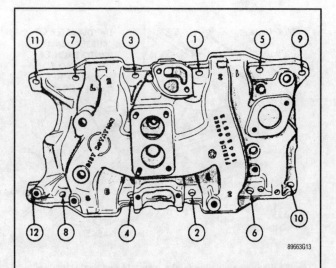

Fig. 41 Proper tightening sequence for the V8 intake manifold

e. Tighten the bolts in the proper sequence as follows:
- Tighten the bolts to—24 inch lbs. (2.7 Nm).
- Tighten the bolts to—48 inch lbs. (5.4 Nm).
- Tighten the bolts to—84 inch lbs. (9.5 Nm).
22. Place the plastic locator dowels (if supplied) in the engine block.
23. Apply RTV sealant to the four corner joints.
24. Install the new front and rear crossover gaskets over the dowels.
25. Install the new flange gaskets on the cylinder heads.

➡️**Ensure that the vertical port alignment tab is resting on the deck face of the block and that the horizontal alignment tabs are in position with the mating cylinder head gasket tabs. The words MANIFOLD SIDE should be visible on the center of each flange gasket.**

26. Place the manifold into position on the engine block and cylinder heads.
27. Ensure that the gaskets have not shifted after the manifold is in place.
28. Install the intake manifold bolts and tighten as follows:

V6 Engine
- Tighten bolts 1 and 2 to 72 inch lbs. (8 Nm), in alternating steps, 12 inch lbs. (1.4 Nm) at a time.
- Tighten bolts 3 through 12, in sequence, to 72 inch lbs. (8 Nm).
- Tighten all bolts, in sequence, to 12 ft. lbs. (16 Nm).

V8 Engines
- Tighten bolts 1 through 4, in sequence, to 72 inch lbs. (8 Nm), in alternating steps, 12 inch lbs. (1.4 Nm) at a time.
- Tighten bolts 5 through 12, in sequence, to 72 inch lbs. (8 Nm).
- Tighten all bolts, in sequence to 12 ft. lbs. (16 Nm).

29. Install the passenger side valve cover (if removed).
30. Install the vacuum hoses in their proper locations.
31. Install the heater and bypass hoses.
32. Install the injector harness.
33. Install the fuel line(s).
34. Reconnect the MAP sensor, IAC motor, and TP sensor.
35. Reconnect the accelerator linkage, speed control cable (if equipped), and transmission kickdown cable (if equipped).
36. Reconnect the intake air temperature sensor.
37. Reconnect the oil pressure sending unit.
38. Install the distributor.
39. Install the alternator.
40. Install the air cleaner assembly.
41. Connect the negative battery cable.
42. Check the engine oil level.

❊❊ **WARNING**

Operating the engine without the proper amount and type of engine oil will result in severe engine damage.

43. Fill and bleed the cooling system.
44. Check for leaks.
45. Install the engine cover.

Exhaust Manifold

REMOVAL & INSTALLATION

▶ **See Figures 42 thru 59**

1. Disconnect the negative battery cable.
2. Raise and safely support the vehicle.
3. From underneath the vehicle, remove the bolts and nuts attaching the exhaust pipe to the exhaust manifold.
4. Lower the vehicle.
5. Remove the heat shield(s).
6. Remove the engine cover.

➡️**It is a good idea to coat the manifold retaining bolts and studs with a suitable rust penetrant before attempting to loosen them.**

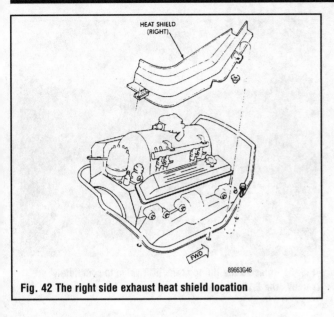

Fig. 42 The right side exhaust heat shield location

Fig. 45 Remove the heat shield after the bolts are loosened to gain access to the exhaust manifold retaining bolts and nuts

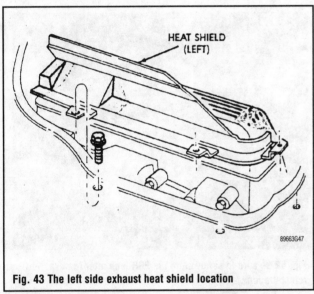

Fig. 43 The left side exhaust heat shield location

Fig. 46 The flanges at the exhaust manifold-to-Y-pipe have to be removed to facilitate manifold removal. Note the highlighted bolt locations

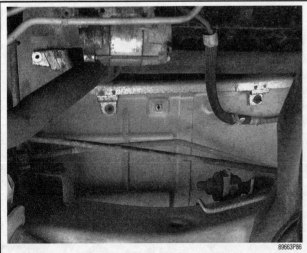

Fig. 44 The exhaust heat shields are held on by bolts and nuts located underneath the vehicle

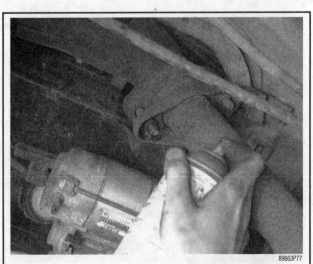

Fig. 47 Spray the flange bolts with a rust penetrant prior to loosening them. This may prevent them from breaking upon removal

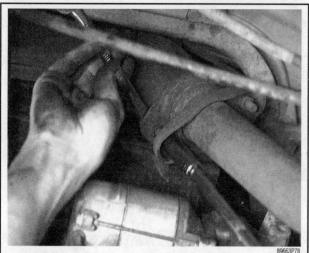

Fig. 48 Use a wrench or suitable tool to hold the nut at the top of the flange when removing the retaining bolt

Fig. 49 When the bolts are removed, pull the flange back to allow enough room for the manifold to come out

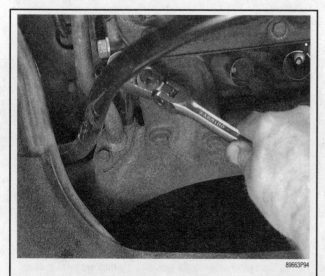

Fig. 50 Remove the EGR tube retaining nuts

Fig. 51 Unfasten the fitting at the EGR valve to completely remove the EGR tube

Fig. 52 Be sure to safely store the EGR tube after removal until reinstallation

Fig. 53 Remember to pull the old EGR tube gasket off of the exhaust manifold, and replace it before installation

Fig. 54 Remove the retaining bolts and nuts from the exhaust manifold(s)

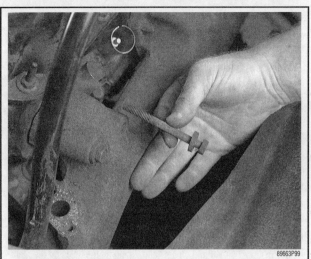

Fig. 57 Some of the exhaust manifold retaining hardware are bolts . . .

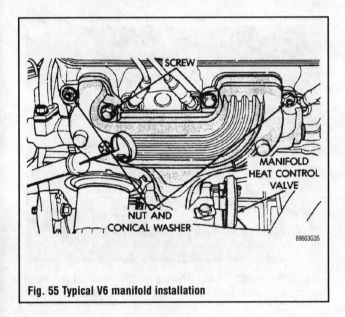

Fig. 55 Typical V6 manifold installation

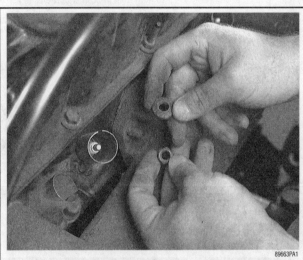

Fig. 58 . . . and some of them are nuts. It is important to note their locations at removal to ease installation

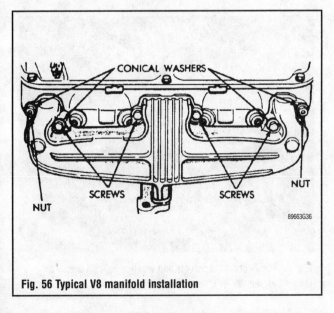

Fig. 56 Typical V8 manifold installation

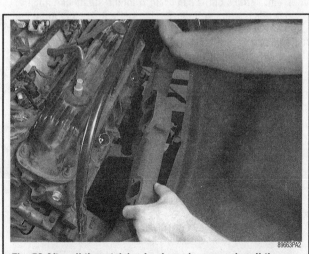

Fig. 59 After all the retaining hardware is removed, pull the exhaust manifold off the cylinder head and remove it from the engine

7. Remove the retaining bolts and studs on the exhaust manifold.

➡**Do not pry on the manifold, as this could cause the manifold to crack. If stuck, tap with a soft faced hammer to loosen.**

8. Remove the manifold from the cylinder block.

To install:

9. Thoroughly clean the manifold and the cylinder head mating surfaces; no gasket is used.

10. Inspect the manifold for cracks before installation.

11. With a straightedge or suitable tool, inspect the manifold and the cylinder head mating surfaces for flatness.

12. On some models, inspect the heat valve located in the passenger side manifold for proper operation by checking to make sure that it turns freely.

13. Clean the threads in the cylinder head before installing the bolts.

➡**If the manifold studs came out with the nuts, replace the studs, applying sealant to the coarse ends.**

14. Position the manifold on the head, lining up the holes on the manifold with the studs. Install the nuts and conical washers on the studs.

15. Install two bolts with conical washers at the inner ends, and two bolts without washers on the center arm of the manifold.

16. Tighten the bolts and nuts, working from the center outward, to 25 ft. lbs. (34 Nm).

17. Install the heat shield(s) and tighten the screws to 55 inch lbs. (6 Nm).

18. Raise and safely support the vehicle.

19. Install the flange at the exhaust pipe and the manifold junction. Tighten the bolts to 19 ft. lbs. (26 Nm).

20. Lower the vehicle.

21. Connect the negative battery cable.

22. Start the engine and check for exhaust leaks.

23. Install the engine cover.

Radiator

REMOVAL & INSTALLATION

◆ **See Figures 60 thru 76**

1. Disconnect the negative battery cable.
2. Drain and recycle the engine coolant.

✳✳ CAUTION

Never open, service or drain the radiator or cooling system when hot; serious burns can occur from the steam and hot coolant. Also, when draining engine coolant, keep in mind that cats and dogs are attracted to ethylene glycol antifreeze and could drink any that is left in an uncovered container or in puddles on the ground. This will prove fatal in sufficient quantities. Always drain coolant into a sealable container. Coolant should be reused unless it is contaminated or is several years old.

3. Remove the upper radiator hose from the outlet on the radiator.
4. Disconnect the coolant reservoir hose from the radiator.
5. Remove the fan shrouds from the vehicle.
6. Remove the lower radiator hose from the radiator outlet.
7. Label, disconnect, and cap the transmission cooler lines and the cooler openings to prevent contamination.
8. Remove the radiator top mounting bolts.
9. If equipped with air conditioning, remove the grille and remove the condenser mounting bolts.
10. Remove the lower radiator mounting bolts.
11. Remove the cowl-to-radiator support braces (if equipped).

➡**On some vehicles, it may be necessary to remove the hood release cable to remove the radiator from the top.**

12. Remove the radiator by lifting it out the top.

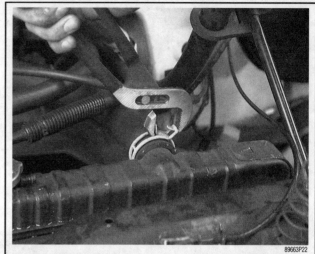

Fig. 60 The original equipment clamps can be released using a pair of pliers or equivalent to release the tension

Fig. 61 Remove the clamp, if equipped, then twist and pull the overflow reservoir hose from the nipple on the radiator neck

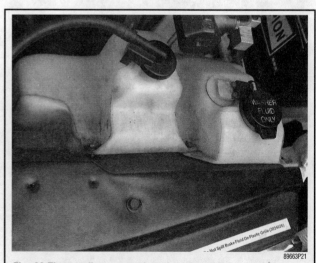

Fig. 62 The overflow reservoir and washer solvent bottle are located on the driver's side of the radiator

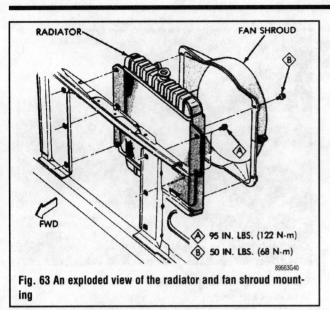

A 95 IN. LBS. (122 N·m)
B 50 IN. LBS. (68 N·m)

Fig. 63 An exploded view of the radiator and fan shroud mounting

Fig. 66 Location of the passenger side lower fan shroud retaining bolt

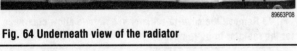

Fig. 64 Underneath view of the radiator

Fig. 67 Release the lower radiator hose clamp in the same manner as the upper hose clamp

Fig. 65 Location of the driver side lower fan shroud retaining bolt

Fig. 68 Use a suitable tool to release the clip in the transmission cooler line connections

Fig. 69 When the clip is released, remove and store it to reduce the chance of it getting lost

Fig. 72 The air cleaner intake tube will need to be removed on some vehicles

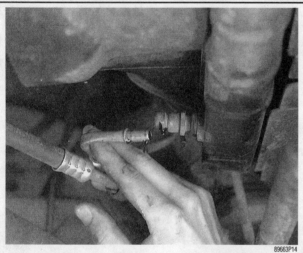

Fig. 70 When the line is released, fluid will likely come out, so place a container beneath it and be prepared to cap or plug the line

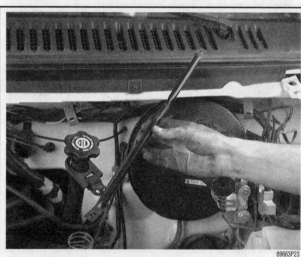

Fig. 73 Remove the cowl-to-radiator supports to allow clearance for the radiator to be removed

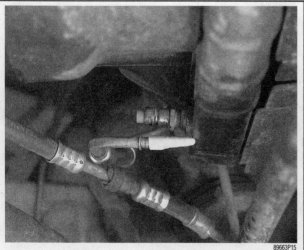

Fig. 71 Use a suitable cap to close off the line; also, don't forget to seal the radiator opening to prevent cooler contamination

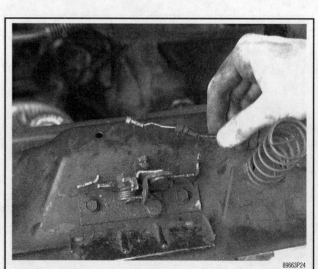

Fig. 74 It may be necessary to detach the hood release cable to remove the radiator

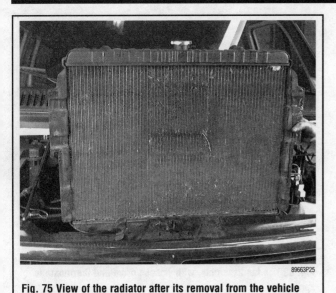

Fig. 75 View of the radiator after its removal from the vehicle

Fig. 76 After removal, check the radiator for damage and signs of leaks

➥Although the manufacturer states to remove the radiator from beneath, we at Chilton found it easier to remove it from above.

To install:
13. Carefully lower the radiator into place.
14. Install and tighten the mounting bolts to 95 inch lbs. (11 Nm).
15. Install the condenser mounting bolts (if equipped).
16. Install the grille (if necessary).
17. Install the lower radiator hose.
18. Connect the transmission cooler lines.
19. Install the fan shrouds. Tighten the mounting nuts to 95 inch lbs. (11 Nm).
20. Install the upper radiator hose.
21. Install the coolant reservoir hose.
22. Install the cowl-to-radiator support braces (if necessary).
23. Connect the negative battery cable.
24. Refill and bleed the cooling system.
25. Start the vehicle and run it until it reaches normal operating temperature.
26. Check the transmission fluid level.
27. Check the vehicle for leaks.

Engine Fan

REMOVAL & INSTALLATION

▶ **See Figures 77 thru 82**

1. Disconnect the negative battery cable.
2. On some vehicles, it may be necessary to remove the air cleaner intake tube.
3. Remove the upper fan shroud.
4. On vehicles with V-belts:
   a. Remove the water pump hub bolts.
   b. Remove the fan and viscous fan drive assembly from the vehicle.
5. On vehicles with a serpentine drive belt:

➥**The viscous fan drive's hub shaft has RIGHT HAND threads. Turn counterclockwise to loosen.**

   a. Using a 36mm fan wrench or suitable tool, loosen the shaft on the viscous fan drive assembly while holding the water pump pulley bolts with a prybar or suitable tool to keep it from turning.

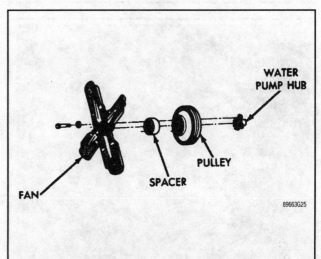

Fig. 77 Typical engine fan mounting on a vehicle with V-belts, but without A/C and maximum cooling

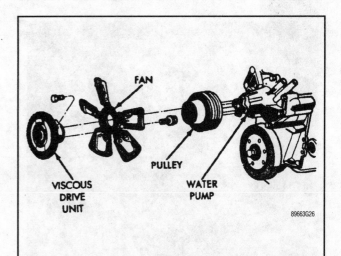

Fig. 78 Typical engine fan mounting on a vehicle with V-belts, A/C and maximum cooling

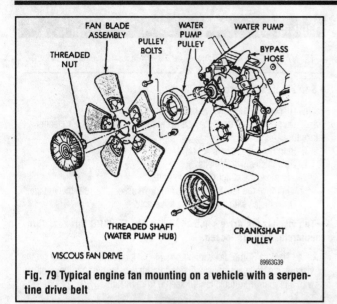

Fig. 79 Typical engine fan mounting on a vehicle with a serpentine drive belt

Fig. 80 The engine fan with its shrouds removed

Fig. 81 Use the appropriate size wrench to loosen the hub nut on the fan. Remember that the threads are RIGHT HAND

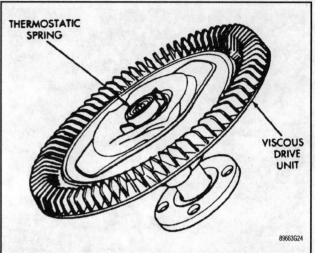

Fig. 82 The fan assembly, with viscous drive and thermostatic spring

  b. Remove the fan and the viscous fan drive assembly from the vehicle.

❊❊ WARNING

Do not place the viscous fan drive assembly in a horizontal position. If placed horizontally, the silicone fluid in the viscous drive could drain into its bearing assembly and contaminate the bearing lubricant.

6. If replacing the fan blade assembly or viscous fan drive, remove the bolts attaching them. Install the new part and tighten the bolts to 17 ft. lbs. (23 Nm).
  To install:
7. Install the viscous fan drive assembly on the vehicle.
8. Install the upper fan shroud.
9. Install the air cleaner intake tube (if necessary).
10. Connect the negative battery cable.

Water Pump

REMOVAL & INSTALLATION

♦ See Figures 83 thru 92

1. Disconnect the negative battery cable.
2. Drain and recycle the engine coolant.

❊❊ CAUTION

Never open, service or drain the radiator or cooling system when hot; serious burns can occur from the steam and hot coolant. Also, when draining engine coolant, keep in mind that cats and dogs are attracted to ethylene glycol antifreeze and could drink any that is left in an uncovered container or in puddles on the ground. This will prove fatal in sufficient quantities. Always drain coolant into a sealable container. Coolant should be reused unless it is contaminated or is several years old.

3. Remove the air cleaner intake tube (if necessary).
4. Remove the upper radiator hose.
5. Remove the fan shrouds.
6. Remove the engine fan.

✳✳ WARNING

Do not place the viscous fan drive assembly in the horizontal position. If placed horizontally, the silicone fluid in the viscous drive could drain into its bearing assembly and contaminate the bearing lubricant.

7. Remove the drive belt(s).
8. If the vehicle has V-belts:
   a. Remove the alternator.
   b. Remove the bracket that supports the alternator, compressor or idler pulley (without A/C). The compressor will be supported by a rear mounting bracket.
   c. Remove the air pump.
   d. Remove the power steering pump front mounting bracket (if equipped). It is not necessary to remove the hoses. Support the power steering pump with mechanic's wire or equivalent.
9. If the vehicle has a serpentine belt:
   a. Remove the water pump pulley bolts.
10. Disconnect the lower radiator hose from the water pump.

Fig. 85 The water pump mounting bolts are accessible after the pulley is removed

Fig. 83 Use a prybar to keep the water pump from rotating while removing its pulley bolts

Fig. 86 The lower radiator hose attaches to the water pump on the lower passenger side

Fig. 84 After the bolts are removed from the pulley, pull it off the water pump shaft

Fig. 87 Remove the bypass hose clamp in the same manner as the radiator hose clamps

Fig. 88 It is easier to slide the clamp up the bypass hose and remove the hose after the water pump is loose

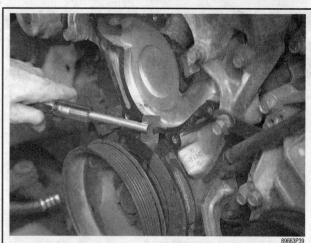

Fig. 91 Make sure all old gasket material is removed and the block surface is clean before installing the pump with a new gasket

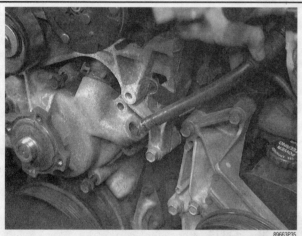

Fig. 89 The heater hose tube (if equipped) is held into the water pump by an O-ring, which can be released by gently twisting the tube

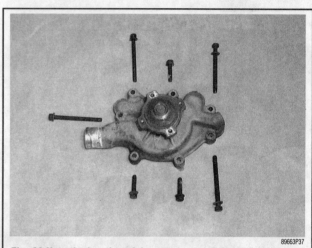

Fig. 92 Note the location of the water pump bolts when removing; they have different lengths and must be placed in their original locations

Fig. 90 After removing the retaining bolts, pull the water pump off the engine block, and place it in a safe location

11. Label and disconnect the heater and bypass hoses from the water pump. On later models, to ease installation, remove the pump before you remove the bypass hose.

➡On some later models, it may be necessary to remove the heater hose tube; this is done by removing the bracket and twisting the tube to release. Discard the old O-ring and replace with a new one for reassembly.

12. Remove the water pump retaining bolts, noting their location.

To install:

13. Clean the gasket surfaces thoroughly.

14. Install a new gasket and position the water pump on the engine block. If necessary, guide the bypass hose on at this time.

15. Install the bolts, in their original locations, and tighten in a criss-cross pattern to 30 ft. lbs. (40 Nm).

16. Install the heater hoses, and bypass tube, if necessary. Tighten the clamp on the heater hose placed on the pump before the bolts are tightened.

➡On the models where the tube had to be removed, install the tube into the water pump with a new O-ring, and tighten the bracket.

17. Install the lower radiator hose.
18. On models with V-belts:
   a. Install the power steering pump and bracket.
   b. Install the air pump.
   c. Install the bracket to the alternator and the air conditioning compressor (if equipped).
   d. Install the alternator.
19. On models with a serpentine belt:
   a. Install the water pump pulley bolts, and tighten to 20 ft. lbs. (27 Nm).
20. Install the drive belt(s).
21. Install the viscous fan assembly.
22. Install the fan shrouds.
23. Install the upper radiator hose.
24. If necessary, install the air cleaner intake tube.
25. Connect the negative battery cable.
26. Fill and bleed the cooling system.
27. Check the cooling system for leaks.

Cylinder Head

REMOVAL & INSTALLATION

▶ See Figures 93 thru 101

1. Properly relieve the fuel system pressure.
2. Disconnect the negative battery cable.

✳✳ CAUTION

Never open, service or drain the radiator or cooling system when hot; serious burns can occur from the steam and hot coolant. Also, when draining engine coolant, keep in mind that cats and dogs are attracted to ethylene glycol antifreeze and could drink any that is left in an uncovered container or in puddles on the ground. This will prove fatal in sufficient quantities. Always drain coolant into a sealable container. Coolant should be reused unless it is contaminated or is several years old.

3. Remove the engine cover.
4. Remove the air cleaner assembly.
5. Remove the alternator.
6. Remove the distributor cap and ignition wires and label them.
7. Remove the heat shields.
8. Disconnect the fuel line(s).

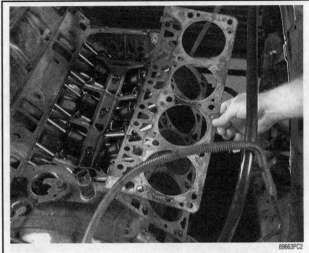

Fig. 94 Remove the old head gasket after the cylinder head is off the engine block

Fig. 95 Clean the cylinder head before inspecting for cracks, wear and damage

Fig. 93 After the retaining bolts have been removed, lift the cylinder head straight up off the block

Fig. 96 Don't forget to clean the ports for the intake and exhaust manifolds

Fig. 97 Also clean and inspect the engine block before assembly

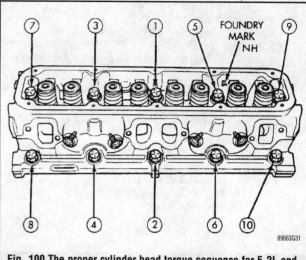

Fig. 100 The proper cylinder head torque sequence for 5.2L and 5.9L engines

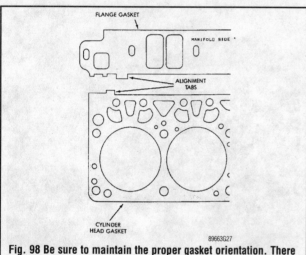

Fig. 98 Be sure to maintain the proper gasket orientation. There may be component identification markings on the gaskets to ease installation

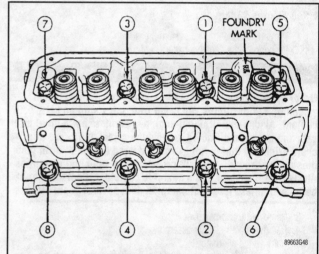

Fig. 101 The proper cylinder head torque sequence for 3.9L engines

Fig. 99 There are different lengths of cylinder head bolts, so be sure to note each bolt's location during disassembly

9. Disconnect the accelerator cable, speed control cable (if equipped), and transmission kickdown cable (if equipped).

10. Label and disconnect the coolant temperature sending unit.

11. Label and disconnect the heater and bypass hoses.

12. Label and remove all the necessary vacuum lines.

13. Make sure all necessary electrical connectors and vacuum lines are removed and labeled.

14. Remove the valve covers.

15. Remove the intake manifold, with the throttle body attached.

16. Mark and remove the rocker shaft assembly (if equipped), or the rocker arms and pivots.

17. Remove the exhaust manifold(s).

18. Remove the head bolts.

19. Lift the cylinder head(s) off of the engine block.

To install:

20. Refer to cylinder head cleaning and inspecting before installing.

21. Position the new cylinder head gasket(s) on the engine block.

22. Place the cylinder head(s) onto the gasket(s) and engine block.

23. Tighten, in sequence, all the head bolts to 50 ft. lbs. (68 Nm). Repeat procedure, tightening the bolts in sequence to 105 ft. lbs. (143 Nm).

24. Install the pushrods and rocker arm shafts or rockers and pivots in their correct positions. Tighten rocker shafts (if equipped) to 200 inch lbs. (23 Nm). Tighten rocker arms (if equipped) to 21 ft lbs. (28 Nm).
25. Install the intake manifold.
26. Install the valve covers.
27. Replace the vacuum hoses to their correct locations.
28. Replace all electrical connectors in their correct locations.
29. Install the heater and the bypass hoses.
30. Connect the accelerator cable, speed control cable (if equipped), and transmission kickdown cable(if equipped).
31. Connect the fuel line(s).
32. Install the heat shields.
33. Install the distributor cap and ignition wires.
34. Install the alternator.
35. Install the air cleaner assembly.
36. Connect the negative battery cable.
37. Refill with the proper coolant mixture, and bleed the cooling system.
38. Check for leaks.
39. Install the engine cover.

Oil Pan

REMOVAL & INSTALLATION

▶ See Figures 102 thru 107

1. Disconnect the negative battery cable.
2. Remove the engine oil dipstick.
3. Remove the air cleaner intake tube.
4. Unbolt the engine controller from the cowl. DO NOT DISCONNECT.
5. Raise and support the vehicle.
6. Drain the engine oil.

✳✳ CAUTION

The EPA warns that prolonged contact with used engine oil may cause a number of skin disorders, including cancer! You should make every effort to minimize your exposure to used engine oil. Protective gloves should be worn when changing the oil. Wash your hands and any other exposed skin areas as soon as possible after exposure to used engine oil. Soap and water, or waterless hand cleaner should be used.

7. Remove the transmission cooler lines from the oil pan mounting clips.

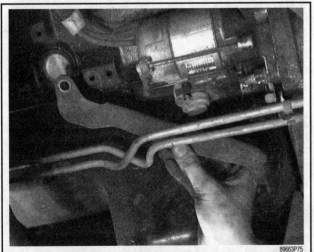
Fig. 102 The engine-to-transmission braces are bolted to the engine block and the bell housing

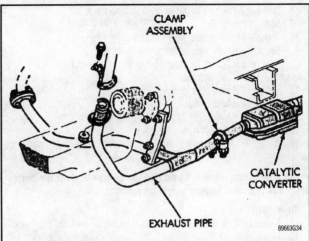
Fig. 103 The exhaust system's Y-pipe, which runs from the manifolds to the catalytic converter, must be removed in order to remove the oil pan

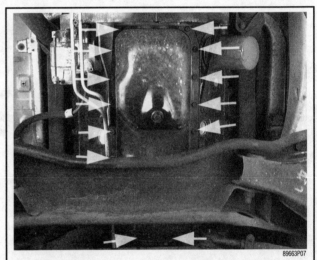
Fig. 104 Most of the oil pan bolts are visible in this photo; others are blocked by the front crossmember

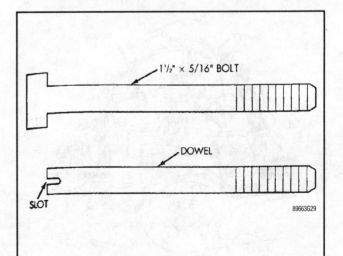
Fig. 105 Fabricate alignment dowels from the appropriate size bolts to appear as shown

8. Remove the engine to transmission support braces.
9. Remove the starter.
10. Remove the transmission inspection cover.
11. Support the right side of the engine.
12. Remove the nut on the passenger side motor mount. Loosen but do not remove the driver's side nut.
13. Remove the exhaust Y-pipe.
14. Support the transmission.
15. Remove the transmission support insulator bolts.
16. Remove the oil pan bolts.
17. Raise the engine and transmission enough to allow the oil pan to be removed.

➡The engine may have to be rotated for the pan to clear the number 1 and 2 journal counterweight on removal.

To install:
18. Thoroughly clean the gasket surfaces on the oil pan and the block.
19. Fabricate four dowels using 1½ x ⁵⁄₁₆ inch bolts. Cut the heads off the bolts and cut a slot into the top of each one. This will allow easier installation of the pan and gasket.
20. Install the four dowels in the four corners of the block-to-oil pan mating surface.

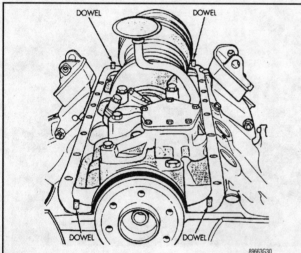

Fig. 106 Position the dowels at the 4 corners of the engine block as shown

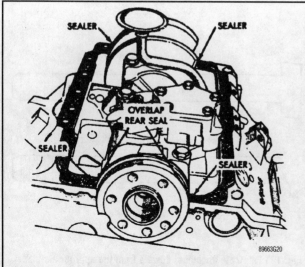

Fig. 107 Apply RTV sealer to the indicated locations

21. Apply a small amount of RTV sealant in the corner of the cap and the cylinder block.
22. Position the gasket over the dowels and onto the engine block. Position the oil pan over the dowels and onto the block. Hand start a couple of the oil pan bolts to hold it in place.
23. Tighten the oil pan bolts to 200 inch lbs. (23 Nm). Remove the dowels and install the remaining bolts.
24. Lower the engine and transmission into place. Tighten the engine mount nuts to 75 ft. lbs. (102 Nm). Tighten the transmission support bolts to 50 ft. lbs. (68 Nm). Remove the engine and transmission supports.
25. Install the exhaust Y-pipe.
26. Install the transmission inspection cover.
27. Install the starter, and tighten bolts to 50 ft. lbs. (68 Nm).
28. Install the engine to transmission support braces.
29. Place the transmission oil cooler line back into its clips on the oil pan.
30. Lower the vehicle.
31. Install the upper fan shroud.
32. Install the engine controller.
33. Install the engine oil dipstick.
34. Install the air cleaner intake tube.
35. Connect the negative battery cable.
36. Refill the engine with oil.

✳✳ WARNING

Operating the engine without the proper amount and type of engine oil will result in severe engine damage.

37. Start the engine and check for leaks. Turn the engine off and check the oil level.

Oil Pump

REMOVAL & INSTALLATION

1. Disconnect the negative battery cable.
2. Raise and support the vehicle.
3. Drain the engine oil.

✳✳ CAUTION

The EPA warns that prolonged contact with used engine oil may cause a number of skin disorders, including cancer! You should make every effort to minimize your exposure to used engine oil. Protective gloves should be worn when changing the oil. Wash your hands and any other exposed skin areas as soon as possible after exposure to used engine oil. Soap and water, or waterless hand cleaner should be used.

4. Remove the oil pan.
5. Remove the pick-up tube from the oil pump.
6. Remove the oil pump mounting bolts and remove the oil pump from the rear main bearing cap.
To install:
7. Install the oil pump onto the rear main bearing cap. Hold the pump base flush against the mating surface on the main bearing cap. finger tighten the pump attaching bolts. Tighten to 30 ft. lbs. (41 Nm).
8. Install the pick-up tube.
9. Install the oil pan.
10. Lower the vehicle.
11. Refill the engine with oil.

✳✳ WARNING

Operating the engine without the proper amount and type of engine oil will result in severe engine damage.

12. Connect the negative battery cable.

13. Start the engine and check the oil pressure.
14. Check for oil leaks.
15. Turn the engine off and check the engine oil level.

Crankshaft Damper

REMOVAL & INSTALLATION

▶ See Figures 108 thru 114

➡ Crankshaft Vibration Damper Puller/Installer Kit, Tool C-3688 and C-3732A, or equivalent is required.

1. Disconnect the negative battery cable.
2. Remove the fan shroud.
3. Remove the engine fan.
4. Remove the drive belt(s).
5. Raise and support the vehicle.
6. Remove the crankshaft pulley.
7. Remove the vibration damper bolt and washer from the crank-shaft.
8. Install the puller assembly on the vibration damper, and thread the forcing screw into the crankshaft. Install two bolts and washers through the

Fig. 110 Unfasten the damper retaining bolt and washer. To do so, it may be necessary to keep the crankshaft from turning

Fig. 108 The crankshaft pulley is attached to the damper by retaining bolts

Fig. 111 Withdraw the bolt and washer that retain the damper to the crankshaft

Fig. 109 After unfastening the retaining bolts, remove the crank-shaft pulley from the damper and set it aside

Fig. 112 Attach a puller to the damper, then tighten the center bolt to press off the damper

Fig. 113 When sufficiently loosened, remove the damper from the crankshaft

Fig. 114 Inspect the damper for wear on its front seal surface. If worn, be sure to replace it, or the engine may leak oil

puller and into the damper. Remove the vibration damper by turning the forcing screw.

9. When loosened, pull the damper off of the crankshaft

To install:

10. Using tool C-3688, or equivalent, press the damper onto the shaft. Remove the tool and install the damper bolt. Tighten the bolt to 135 ft. lbs. (183 Nm).

11. Install the crankshaft pulley.
12. Lower the vehicle.
13. Install the drive belt(s).
14. Install the engine fan.
15. Install the fan shroud.
16. Connect the negative battery cable.

Timing Chain Cover and Seal

REMOVAL & INSTALLATION

▶ See Figures 115 thru 120

1. Disconnect the negative battery cable.
2. Drain and recycle the engine coolant.

⁑ CAUTION

Never open, service or drain the radiator or cooling system when hot; serious burns can occur from the steam and hot coolant. Also, when draining engine coolant, keep in mind that cats and dogs are attracted to ethylene glycol antifreeze and could drink any that is left in an uncovered container or in puddles on the ground. This will prove fatal in sufficient quantities. Always drain coolant into a sealable container. Coolant should be reused unless it is contaminated or is several years old.

3. Remove the water pump.
4. Remove the power steering pump (if not removed during water pump removal).
5. Raise and support the vehicle.
6. Remove the crankshaft pulley.
7. Remove the vibration damper.
8. If replacing the seal only:
   a. Using a suitable tool, pry the seal from out of the timing cover. Use caution as to not damage the seal surface of the timing cover. Proceed to the installation steps.
9. Remove the bracket that retains the transmission cooler lines.

Fig. 115 You can use a seal puller, such as this one from Lisle®, to remove the front seal from the timing cover

Fig. 116 The bracket that retains the cooler lines must be removed to access the timing cover

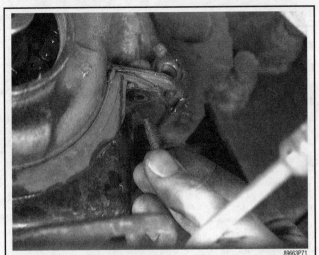

Fig. 117 The two front oil pan bolts pass through the bottom of the timing cover; remove them in order to detach the cover

Fig. 118 Remove the timing cover with care; avoid damage to the oil pan gasket, or the vehicle may leak oil

Fig. 119 Make sure the seal area of the cover is clean and smooth before installing a new seal

Fig. 120 A large socket can be used if the proper tool is unavailable; however, this is not the recommended method

10. Remove the two front oil pan bolts on each side of the crankshaft that retain the cover.

11. Remove the bolts that retain the timing cover to the engine block.

12. Remove the cover, using caution to avoid damaging the oil pan gasket.

13. Remove the seal from the timing cover using a suitable tool. Take care not to damage the seal surface of the timing cover.

To install:

14. Using a new timing cover gasket, place the timing cover on the engine block.

15. Install the timing cover bolts to the engine block. Tighten to 30 ft. lbs. (41 Nm).

16. Install the front two oil pan bolts, tighten to 215 inch lbs. (24 Nm).

17. Using tool C-4251or equivalent, install the threaded shaft into the crankshaft. Place seal in opening, with spring side down. Place the installing adapter C-4251-3 with the thrust bearing and nut over threaded shaft. Tighten nut until tool bottoms on timing cover.

18. Install the vibration damper.

19. Install the crankshaft pulley.

20. Lower the vehicle.

21. Install the power steering pump.

22. Install the water pump.

23. Refill the cooling system with the proper coolant mixture and bleed the system.

24. Connect the negative battery cable.

25. Start the vehicle and check for leaks.

Timing Chain and Sprockets

REMOVAL & INSTALLATION

▶ See Figures 121 and 122

1. Disconnect the negative battery cable.

2. Raise and support the vehicle.

3. Remove the timing chain cover.

4. Rotate the engine until No. 1 cylinder is at Top Dead Center (TDC) on its compression stroke.

5. Remove the camshaft sprocket attaching bolt and cup washer.

6. Remove the timing chain with both the camshaft and crankshaft sprockets.

1. Camshaft sprocket
2. Crankshaft sprocket
3. Timing chain

Fig. 121 View of the timing chain and sprockets, with the cover removed

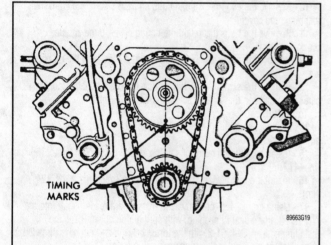

Fig. 122 Be sure to maintain proper alignment of the timing marks

To install:

7. Place the camshaft and crankshaft sprockets on a flat surface with the timing indicator marks on an imaginary centerline through both sprocket bosses.

8. Place the timing chain around both sprockets. Be sure that the timing marks are in alignment.

9. If necessary, turn the crankshaft and camshaft to align them with the keyway location in the crankshaft sprocket and the keyway or dowel hole in the camshaft sprocket.

10. Lift the sprockets and timing chain while keeping the sprockets tight against the chain in the correct position. Slide both sprockets evenly onto their respective shafts.

11. Use a straightedge to measure the alignment of the sprocket timing marks. They must be perfectly aligned.

12. Install the cup washer and camshaft sprocket bolt. Tighten to 35 ft. lbs. (47 Nm).

13. If camshaft end-play exceeds 0.010 in., install a new thrust plate. It should be 0.002–0.006 in. with the new plate.

14. Install the timing chain cover.

15. Lower the vehicle.

16. Connect the negative battery cable.

INSPECTION

Timing Chain Slack

▶ See Figure 123

1. Position a scale (ruler or straightedge) next to the timing chain to detect any movement in the chain.

2. Place a torque wrench and socket on the camshaft sprocket attaching bolt. Apply 30 ft. lbs. (41 Nm) of torque if the cylinder heads are installed on the engine, or 15 ft. lbs. (20 Nm) if the cylinder heads are removed, and rotate the bolt in the direction of crankshaft rotation in order to remove all slack from the chain.

3. While applying torque to the camshaft sprocket bolt, the crankshaft should not be allowed to rotate. It may be necessary to block the crankshaft to prevent rotation.

4. Position the scale over the edge of a timing chain link and apply an equal amount of torque in the opposite direction. If the movement of the chain exceeds 1/8 in. (3.175mm), replace the chain.

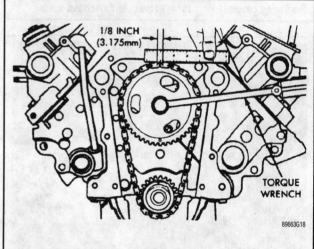

Fig. 123 Measuring timing chain slack with a torque wrench and ruler

Camshaft, Bearings and Lifters

REMOVAL & INSTALLATION

Camshaft and Lifters

▶ See Figures 124 thru 131

1. Disconnect the negative battery cable.
2. Remove the engine cover.
3. Remove the intake manifold.
4. Remove the valve covers.
5. Remove and label the rocker arm shafts (if equipped) or rocker arms and pivots.
6. Remove and label the pushrods.
7. Remove the lifters (tappets) as follows:

   a. Remove the yoke retainer and label the aligning yokes for each cylinder, keeping them in order to insure installation in their original locations.

   b. Slide a hydraulic valve tappet remover/installer into the bore and remove each lifter keeping them in order to insure the installation in their original locations.

   c. If the lifter or bore in the cylinder block is scored, ream the bore to the next oversize and replace with oversize lifters.

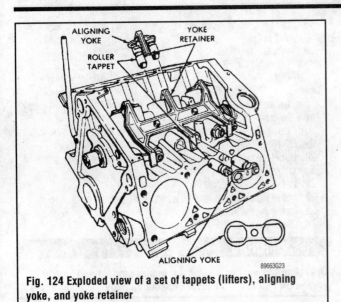

Fig. 124 Exploded view of a set of tappets (lifters), aligning yoke, and yoke retainer

Fig. 127 Remove the aligning yoke for each lifter you are servicing, noting its location

Fig. 125 Remove the bolts that hold the yoke retainer to the engine block

Fig. 128 Inspect the lifter for wear after removing; also inspect the bore for wear

Fig. 126 Lift the yoke retainer off of the engine block

Fig. 129 The camshaft, as seen through the top of the engine block

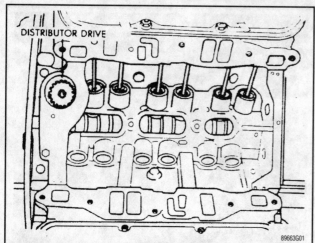

Fig. 130 The distributor drive gear is located in the distributor bore and is driven by the camshaft; the distributor must first be removed in order to access the drive gear

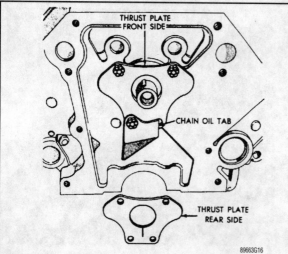

Fig. 131 The camshaft thrust plate is located on the front of the engine block, under the timing chain camshaft sprocket

8. Remove the timing gear cover, the camshaft and the crankshaft sprockets, and the timing chain.

9. Remove the distributor and lift out the oil pump and distributor driveshaft.

10. Remove the camshaft thrust plate (on 5.2L and 5.9L engines).

11. Install a long bolt into the front of the camshaft and remove the camshaft, being careful not to damage the cam bearings with the cam lobes.

12. See camshaft bearing section if replacing camshaft and bearings.

To install:

13. Prior to installation, lubricate the camshaft lobes and bearings journals. It is recommended that 1 pt. of Crankcase Conditioner be added to the initial crankcase oil fill.

14. Insert the camshaft into the engine block within 2 in. (51mm) of its final position in the block.

15. Have an assistant support the camshaft with a suitable tool to prevent the camshaft from contacting the plug in the rear of the engine block.

16. Position the suitable tool against the rear side of the cam gear and be careful not to damage the cam lobes.

17. Replace the camshaft thrust plate. If camshaft end-play exceeds 0.010 in. (0.254mm), install a new thrust plate. It should be 0.002–0.006 in. (0.051–0.152mm) with the new plate.

18. Install the timing chain and sprockets, timing gear cover, vibration damper, and pulley.

19. To install the lifters:
   a. Lubricate the lifters.
   b. Install the lifters in their original locations if installing the old ones.
   c. Insure that the oil feed hole in the side of the lifter faces up (away from the crankshaft).
   d. Install the yokes and yoke retainer. Tighten the bolts to 200 inch lbs. (23 Nm).

20. Install the pushrods, rocker arms and pivots or the rocker shafts (if equipped), and valve covers.

21. Install the intake manifold.

22. Install the distributor and oil pump driveshaft.

23. Install the distributor.

24. Check the engine oil level.

✴✴ WARNING

Operating the engine without the proper amount and type of engine oil will result in severe engine damage.

25. Connect the negative battery cable.

26. Start the engine and check for leaks.

27. Install the engine cover.

Camshaft Bearings

♦ See Figure 132

1. Remove the engine.

2. Remove the camshaft, flywheel and crankshaft.

3. Push the pistons to the top of the cylinder.

4. Remove the camshaft rear bearing bore plug.

5. Remove the camshaft bearings with a bearing removal tool. Select the proper size expanding collet and back-up nut and assemble on the mandrel. With the expanding collet collapsed, install the collet assembly in the camshaft bearing and tighten the back-up nut on the expanding mandrel until the collet fits the camshaft bearing.

Assemble the puller screw and extension (if necessary) and install on the expanding mandrel. Wrap a cloth around the threads of the puller screw to protect the front bearing or journal. Tighten the pulling nut against the thrust bearing and pulling plate to remove the camshaft bearing. Be sure to hold a wrench on the end of the puller screw to prevent it from turning.

6. To remove the front bearing, install the puller from the rear of the cylinder block.

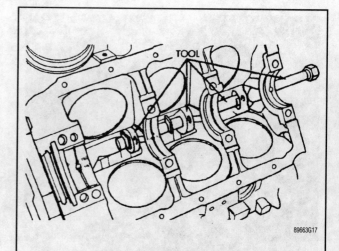

Fig. 132 Removal/installation of the camshaft bearings using a bearing installer/remover tool kit

To install:

7. Position the new bearings at the bearing bores, and press them in place. Be sure to center the pulling plate and puller screw to avoid damage to the bearing. Failure to use the correct expanding collet can cause severe bearing damage. Align the oil holes in the bearings with the oil holes in the cylinder block before pressing bearings into place.

8. Install the camshaft rear bearing bore plug.
9. Install the camshaft, crankshaft, flywheel and related parts.
10. Install the engine.

INSPECTION

Camshaft Lobe Lift

➡**Check the lift of each lobe in consecutive order and make a note of the reading.**

1. Disconnect the negative battery cable.
2. Remove the engine cover.
3. Remove the valve cover(s).
4. Remove the intake manifold.
5. Remove the rocker arm stud nut or fulcrum bolts, fulcrum seat and rocker arm.
6. Make sure the pushrod is in the valve tappet socket. Install a dial indicator so that the actuating point of the indicator is in the push rod socket (or the indicator ball socket adapter is on the end of the pushrod) and in the same plane as the pushrod movement.
7. Disconnect the I terminal and the S terminal at the starter relay. Install an auxiliary starter switch between the battery and S terminals of the start relay.
8. Crank the engine with the ignition switch off. Turn the crankshaft over until the tappet is on the base circle of the camshaft lobe. At this position, the push rod will be in its lowest position.
9. Zero the dial indicator. Continue to rotate the crankshaft slowly until the push rod is in the fully raised position.
10. Compare the total lift recorded on the dial indicator with the specification shown on the Camshaft Specification chart.
11. To check the accuracy of the original indicator reading, continue to rotate the crankshaft until the indicator reads zero. If the left on any lobe is below specified wear limits listed, the camshaft and the valve lifter operating on the worn lobe(s) must be replaced.
12. Remove the dial indicator and auxiliary starter switch.
13. Install the rocker arm, fulcrum seat and stud nut or fulcrum bolts. Check the valve clearance. Adjust if required.
14. Install the intake manifold.
15. Install the valve cover(s).
16. Install the engine cover.
17. Connect the negative battery cable.

Rear Main Seal

REMOVAL & INSTALLATION

▶ **See Figures 133, 134 and 135**

1. Disconnect the negative battery cable.
2. Raise and support the vehicle.
3. Drain the engine oil.

❉ CAUTION

The EPA warns that prolonged contact with used engine oil may cause a number of skin disorders, including cancer! You should make every effort to minimize your exposure to used engine oil. Protective gloves should be worn when changing the oil. Wash your hands and any other exposed skin areas as soon as possi-

ble after exposure to used engine oil. Soap and water, or waterless hand cleaner should be used.

4. Remove the oil pan.
5. Remove the oil pump.
6. Loosen all the main bearing cap bolts, thereby lowering the crankshaft slightly but not to exceed 1/32 in. (0.8mm).
7. Remove the rear main bearing cap, and remove the oil seal from the bearing cap and cylinder block. On the block half of the seal use a seal removal tool, or install a small metal screw in one end of the seal, and pull on the screw to remove the seal. Exercise caution to prevent scratching or damaging the crankshaft seal surfaces.
8. Remove the oil seal retaining pin from the bearing cap (if equipped). The pin is not used with the split-lip seal.

To install:

9. Thoroughly clean the seal groove in the cap and block.
10. Dip the split lip-type seal halves in clean engine oil.
11. Carefully install the upper seal (cylinder block) into its groove with undercut side of the seal (rubber type) toward the FRONT of the engine, by rotating it on the seal journal of the crankshaft until approximately 3/8 in.

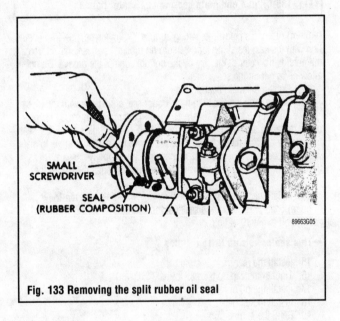

Fig. 133 Removing the split rubber oil seal

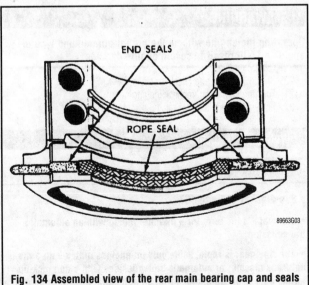

Fig. 134 Assembled view of the rear main bearing cap and seals

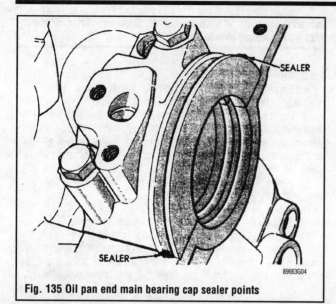

Fig. 135 Oil pan end main bearing cap sealer points

(9.5mm) protrudes below the parting surface. On rope type, pull into position with the seal installing tool. Be sure no rubber has been shaved from the outside diameter of the seal by the bottom edge of the groove. Do not allow oil to get on the sealer area.

12. Tighten the main bearing cap bolts.

13. On the rope type seal, trim the upper seal ends flush with the block surface. Install the lower seal (rubber type) in the rear main bearing cap under undercut side of seal toward the FRONT of the engine, allow the seal to protrude approximately ⅜ in. (9.5mm) above the parting surface to mate with the upper seal when the cap is installed. With rope type seals, press the seal full and firmly into the cap groove. Trim the ends flush with the cap.

14. Install the side seals into the bearing cap. Apply an even ¹⁄₁₆ in. (1.6mm) bead of RTV silicone sealer at the bearing cap to block joint to provide oil pan end sealing.

➡ **This sealer sets up in 15 minutes.**

15. Install the rear main bearing cap.
16. Tighten the cap bolts to 85 ft. lbs. (115 Nm).
17. Install the oil pump.
18. Install the oil pan.
19. Refill the engine oil.

※ WARNING

Operating the engine without the proper amount and type of engine oil will result in severe engine damage.

20. Start the engine and check for leaks.
21. Turn the engine off, recheck the engine oil.
22. Lower the vehicle.

Flywheel/Flexplate

REMOVAL & INSTALLATION

▶ **See Figures 136 and 137**

➡ **Flexplate is the term for a flywheel mated with an automatic transmission.**

➡ **The ring gear is replaceable only on engines mated with a manual transmission, or automatic transmissions with a non lock-up torque converter. On engines with an automatic transmission and lock-up torque converter, the ring gear is not replaceable, so you must replace the torque converter assembly.**

1. Disconnect the negative battery cable.
2. Raise and support the vehicle.
3. Remove the transmission.
4. If your vehicle has a manual transmission:
   a. Remove the clutch assembly.

➡ **The bolts should be loosened a little at a time in a crisscross pattern to avoid warping the pressure plate.**

   b. Remove the flywheel bolts.

➡ **The flywheel bolts should be loosened a little at a time in a crisscross pattern to avoid warping the flywheel.**

   c. Replace the pilot bearing in the end of the crankshaft after removing the flywheel.
   d. The flywheel should be checked for cracks and glazing. It can be resurfaced by a machine shop.
5. If the ring gear is to be replaced, drill a hole in the gear between two teeth, being careful not to contact the flywheel surface. Using a cold chisel at this point, crack the ring gear and remove it.

Polish the inner surface of the new ring gear and heat it in an oven to about 600°F (316°C). Quickly place the ring gear on the flywheel and tap it into place, making sure that it is fully seated.

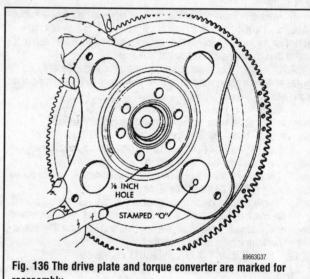

Fig. 136 The drive plate and torque converter are marked for reassembly

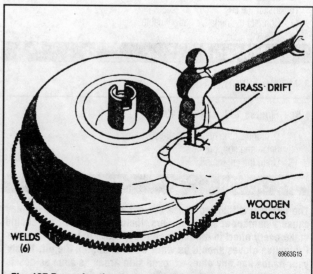

Fig. 137 Removing the starter ring gear with a cold chisel

6. If your vehicle has an automatic transmission:

a. Remove the torque converter from the transmission. This is done by removing the c-clamp from the edge of the bell-housing, and carefully sliding the torque converter off of the input shaft of the transmission.

b. The converter is mated to the engine by a drive plate. To unbolt it, remove the retaining bolts from the crankshaft.

To install:

7. If your vehicle has a manual transmission:

a. Position the flywheel on the end of the crankshaft. Tighten the bolts a little at a time, in a cross pattern, to 55 ft. lbs. (75 Nm).

b. Install the clutch assembly.

8. If your vehicle has a automatic transmission:

a. Install the torque converter on the input shaft..

b. Install the c-clamp that retains the converter to the bell housing.

9. Install the transmission.

10. Lower the vehicle.

11. Connect the negative battery cable.

12. Check the transmission fluid level.

EXHAUST SYSTEM

Inspection

▶ **See Figures 138 thru 145**

➡Safety glasses should be worn at all times when working on or near the exhaust system. Older exhaust systems will almost always be covered with loose rust particles which will shower you when disturbed. These particles are more than a nuisance and could injure your eye.

Your vehicle must be raised and supported safely to inspect the exhaust system properly. By placing 4 safety stands under the vehicle for support should provide enough room for you to slide under the vehicle and inspect

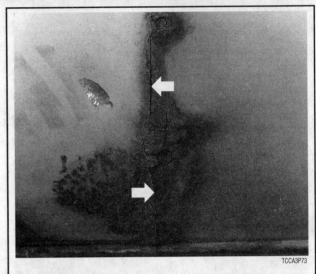

TCCA3P73

Fig. 139 Cracks in the muffler are a guaranteed leak

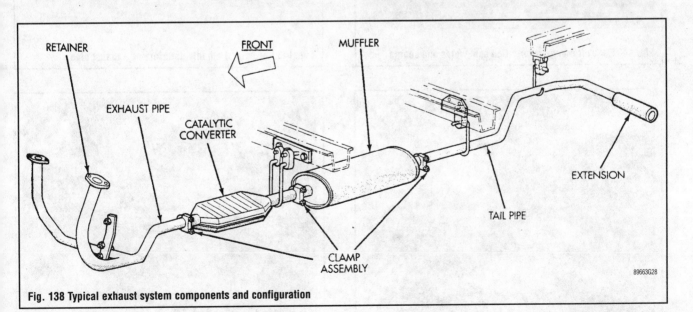

Fig. 138 Typical exhaust system components and configuration

89663G28

the system completely. Start the inspection at the exhaust manifold or turbocharger pipe where the header pipe is attached and work your way to the back of the vehicle. On dual exhaust systems, remember to inspect both sides of the vehicle. Check the complete exhaust system for open seams, holes loose connections, or other deterioration which could permit exhaust

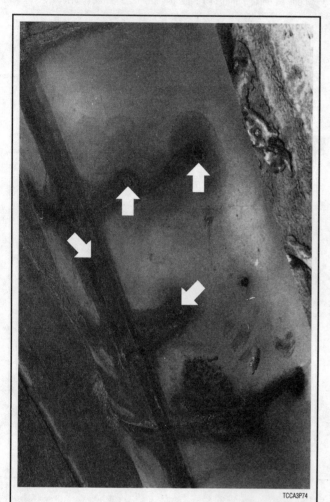

Fig. 140 Check the muffler for rotted spot welds and seams

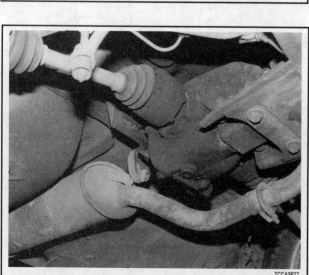

Fig. 141 Make sure the exhaust components are not contacting the body or suspension

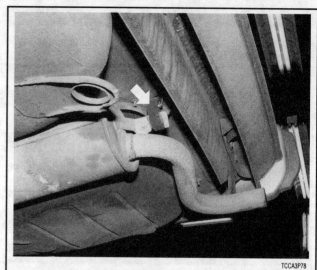

Fig. 142 Check for overstretched or torn exhaust hangers

Fig. 143 Example of a badly deteriorated exhaust pipe

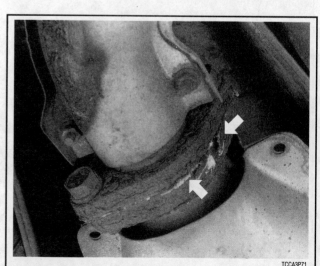

Fig. 144 Inspect flanges for gaskets that have deteriorated and need replacement

Fig. 145 Some systems, like this one, use large O-rings (donuts) in between the flanges

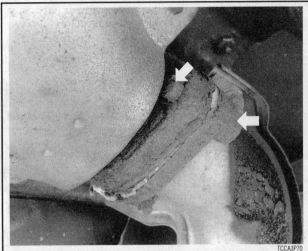

Fig. 146 Nuts and bolts will be extremely difficult to remove when deteriorated with rust

fumes to seep into the passenger compartment. Inspect all mounting brackets and hangers for deterioration, some models may have rubber O-rings that can be overstretched and non-supportive. These components will need to be replaced if found. It has always been a practice to use a pointed tool to poke up into the exhaust system where the deterioration spots are to see whether or not they crumble. Some models may have heat shield covering certain parts of the exhaust system , it will be necessary to remove these shields to have the exhaust visible for inspection also.

REPLACEMENT

▶ See Figure 146

There are basically two types of exhaust systems. One is the flange type where the component ends are attached with bolts and a gasket in-between. The other exhaust system is the slip joint type. These components slip into one another using clamps to retain them together.

✳✳ CAUTION

Allow the exhaust system to cool sufficiently before spraying a solvent exhaust fasteners. Some solvents are highly flammable and could ignite when sprayed on hot exhaust components.

Before removing any component of the exhaust system, ALWAYS squirt a liquid rust dissolving agent onto the fasteners for ease of removal. A lot of knuckle skin will be saved by following this rule. It may even be wise to spray the fasteners and allow them to sit overnight.

Flange Type

▶ See Figure 147

✳✳ CAUTION

Do NOT perform exhaust repairs or inspection with the engine or exhaust hot. Allow the system to cool completely before attempting any work. Exhaust systems are noted for sharp edges, flaking metal and rusted bolts. Gloves and eye protec-

Fig. 147 Example of a flange type exhaust system joint

tion are required. A healthy supply of penetrating oil and rags is highly recommended. Never spray liquid rust dissolving agent onto a hot exhaust component.

Before removing any component on a flange type system, ALWAYS squirt a liquid rust dissolving agent onto the fasteners for ease of removal. Start by unbolting the exhaust piece at both ends (if required). When unbolting the headpipe from the manifold, make sure that the bolts are free before trying to remove them. if you snap a stud in the exhaust manifold, the stud will have to be removed with a bolt extractor, which often means removal of the manifold itself. Next, disconnect the component from the mounting; slight twisting and turning may be required to remove the component completely from the vehicle. You may need to tap on the component with a rubber mallet to loosen the component. If all else fails, use a hacksaw to separate the parts. An oxy-acetylene cutting torch may be faster but the sparks are DANGEROUS near the fuel tank, and at the very least, accidents could happen, resulting in damage to the under-car parts, not to mention yourself.

Slip Joint Type

◆ **See Figure 148**

Before removing any component on the slip joint type exhaust system, ALWAYS squirt a liquid rust dissolving agent onto the fasteners for ease of removal. Start by unbolting the exhaust piece at both ends (if required). When unbolting the headpipe from the manifold, make sure that the bolts are free before trying to remove them. if you snap a stud in the exhaust manifold, the stud will have to be removed with a bolt extractor, which often means removal of the manifold itself. Next, remove the mounting U-bolts from around the exhaust pipe you are extracting from the vehicle. Don't be surprised if the U-bolts break while removing the nuts. Loosen the exhaust pipe from any mounting brackets retaining it to the floor pan and separate the components.

TCCA3P79

Fig. 148 Example of a common slip joint type system

ENGINE RECONDITIONING

Determining Engine Condition

Anything that generates heat and/or friction will eventually burn or wear out (i.e. a light bulb generates heat, therefore its life span is limited). With this in mind, a running engine generates tremendous amounts of both; friction is encountered by the moving and rotating parts inside the engine and heat is created by friction and combustion of the fuel. However, the engine has systems designed to help reduce the effects of heat and friction and provide added longevity. The oiling system reduces the amount of friction encountered by the moving parts inside the engine, while the cooling system reduces heat created by friction and combustion. If either system is not maintained, a break-down will be inevitable. Therefore, you can see how regular maintenance can affect the service life of your vehicle. If you do not drain, flush and refill your cooling system at the proper intervals, deposits will begin to accumulate in the radiator, thereby reducing the amount of heat it can extract from the coolant. The same applies to your oil and filter; if it is not changed often enough it becomes laden with contaminates and is unable to properly lubricate the engine. This increases friction and wear.

There are a number of methods for evaluating the condition of your engine. A compression test can reveal the condition of your pistons, piston rings, cylinder bores, head gasket(s), valves and valve seats. An oil pressure test can warn you of possible engine bearing, or oil pump failures. Excessive oil consumption, evidence of oil in the engine air intake area and/or bluish smoke from the tail pipe may indicate worn piston rings, worn valve guides and/or valve seals. As a general rule, an engine that uses no more than one quart of oil every 1000 miles is in good condition. Engines that use one quart of oil or more in less than 1000 miles should first be checked for oil leaks. If any oil leaks are present, have them fixed before determining how much oil is consumed by the engine, especially if blue smoke is not visible at the tail pipe.

COMPRESSION TEST

A noticeable lack of engine power, excessive oil consumption and/or poor fuel mileage measured over an extended period are all indicators of internal engine wear. Worn piston rings, scored or worn cylinder bores, blown head gaskets, sticking or burnt valves, and worn valve seats are all possible culprits. A check of each cylinder's compression will help locate the problem.

Gasoline Engines

◆ **See Figure 149**

➡A screw-in type compression gauge is more accurate than the type you simply hold against the spark plug hole. Although it takes slightly longer to use, it's worth the effort to obtain a more accurate reading.

1. Make sure that the proper amount and viscosity of engine oil is in the crankcase, then ensure the battery is fully charged.
2. Warm-up the engine to normal operating temperature, then shut the engine **OFF**.
3. Disable the ignition system.
4. Label and disconnect all of the spark plug wires from the plugs.
5. Thoroughly clean the cylinder head area around the spark plug ports, then remove the spark plugs.
6. Set the throttle plate to the fully open (wide-open throttle) position. You can block the accelerator linkage open for this, or you can have an assistant fully depress the accelerator pedal.
7. Install a screw-in type compression gauge into the No. 1 spark plug hole until the fitting is snug.

✳✳ WARNING

Be careful not to crossthread the spark plug hole.

8. According to the tool manufacturer's instructions, connect a remote starting switch to the starting circuit.
9. With the ignition switch in the **OFF** position, use the remote starting switch to crank the engine through at least five compression strokes (approximately 5 seconds of cranking) and record the highest reading on the gauge.
10. Repeat the test on each cylinder, cranking the engine approximately the same number of compression strokes and/or time as the first.
11. Compare the highest readings from each cylinder to that of the others. The indicated compression pressures are considered within specifications if the lowest reading cylinder is within 75 percent of the pressure recorded for the highest reading cylinder. For example, if your highest reading cylinder pressure was 150 psi (1034 kPa), then 75 percent of that would be 113 psi (779 kPa). So the lowest reading cylinder should be no less than 113 psi (779 kPa).

Fig. 149 A screw-in type compression gauge is more accurate and easier to use without an assistant

12. If a cylinder exhibits an unusually low compression reading, pour a tablespoon of clean engine oil into the cylinder through the spark plug hole and repeat the compression test. If the compression rises after adding oil, it means that the cylinder's piston rings and/or cylinder bore are damaged or worn. If the pressure remains low, the valves may not be seating properly (a valve job is needed), or the head gasket may be blown near that cylinder. If compression in any two adjacent cylinders is low, and if the addition of oil doesn't help raise compression, there is leakage past the head gasket. Oil and coolant in the combustion chamber, combined with blue or constant white smoke from the tail pipe, are symptoms of this problem. However, don't be alarmed by the normal white smoke emitted from the tail pipe during engine warm-up or from cold weather driving. There may be evidence of water droplets on the engine dipstick and/or oil droplets in the cooling system if a head gasket is blown.

OIL PRESSURE TEST

Check for proper oil pressure at the sending unit passage with an externally mounted mechanical oil pressure gauge (as opposed to relying on a factory installed dash-mounted gauge). A tachometer may also be needed, as some specifications may require running the engine at a specific rpm.

1. With the engine cold, locate and remove the oil pressure sending unit.
2. Following the manufacturer's instructions, connect a mechanical oil pressure gauge and, if necessary, a tachometer to the engine.
3. Start the engine and allow it to idle.
4. Check the oil pressure reading when cold and record the number. You may need to run the engine at a specified rpm, so check the specifications chart located earlier in this section.
5. Run the engine until normal operating temperature is reached (upper radiator hose will feel warm).
6. Check the oil pressure reading again with the engine hot and record the number. Turn the engine **OFF**.
7. Compare your hot oil pressure reading to that given in the chart. If the reading is low, check the cold pressure reading against the chart. If the cold pressure is well above the specification, and the hot reading was lower than the specification, you may have the wrong viscosity oil in the engine. Change the oil, making sure to use the proper grade and quantity, then repeat the test.

Low oil pressure readings could be attributed to internal component wear, pump related problems, a low oil level, or oil viscosity that is too low. High oil pressure readings could be caused by an overfilled crankcase, too high of an oil viscosity or a faulty pressure relief valve.

Buy or Rebuild?

Now that you have determined that your engine is worn out, you must make some decisions. The question of whether or not an engine is worth rebuilding is largely a subjective matter and one of personal worth. Is the engine a popular one, or is it an obsolete model? Are parts available? Will it get acceptable gas mileage once it is rebuilt? Is the car it's being put into worth keeping? Would it be less expensive to buy a new engine, have your engine rebuilt by a pro, rebuild it yourself or buy a used engine from a salvage yard? Or would it be simpler and less expensive to buy another car? If you have considered all these matters and more, and have still decided to rebuild the engine, then it is time to decide how you will rebuild it.

➤**The editors at Chilton feel that most engine machining should be performed by a professional machine shop. Don't think of it as wasting money, rather, as an assurance that the job has been done right the first time. There are many expensive and specialized tools required to perform such tasks as boring and honing an engine block or having a valve job done on a cylinder head. Even inspecting the parts requires expensive micrometers and gauges to properly measure wear and clearances. Also, a machine shop can deliver to you clean, and ready to assemble parts, saving you time and aggravation. Your maximum savings will come from performing the removal, disassembly, assembly and installation of the engine and purchasing or renting only the tools required to perform the above tasks. Depending on the particular circumstances, you may save 40 to 60 percent of the cost doing these yourself.**

A complete rebuild or overhaul of an engine involves replacing all of the moving parts (pistons, rods, crankshaft, camshaft, etc.) with new ones and machining the non-moving wearing surfaces of the block and heads. Unfortunately, this may not be cost effective. For instance, your crankshaft may have been damaged or worn, but it can be machined undersize for a minimal fee.

So, as you can see, you can replace everything inside the engine, but, it is wiser to replace only those parts which are really needed, and, if possible, repair the more expensive ones. Later in this section, we will break the engine down into its two main components: the cylinder head and the engine block. We will discuss each component, and the recommended parts to replace during a rebuild on each.

Engine Overhaul Tips

Most engine overhaul procedures are fairly standard. In addition to specific parts replacement procedures and specifications for your individual engine, this section is also a guide to acceptable rebuilding procedures. Examples of standard rebuilding practice are given and should be used along with specific details concerning your particular engine.

Competent and accurate machine shop services will ensure maximum performance, reliability and engine life. In most instances it is more profitable for the do-it-yourself mechanic to remove, clean and inspect the component, buy the necessary parts and deliver these to a shop for actual machine work.

Much of the assembly work (crankshaft, bearings, piston rods, and other components) is well within the scope of the do-it-yourself mechanic's tools and abilities. You will have to decide for yourself the depth of involvement you desire in an engine repair or rebuild.

TOOLS

The tools required for an engine overhaul or parts replacement will depend on the depth of your involvement. With a few exceptions, they will be the tools found in a mechanic's tool kit (see Section 1 of this manual). More in-depth work will require some or all of the following:

- A dial indicator (reading in thousandths) mounted on a universal base
- Micrometers and telescope gauges
- Jaw and screw-type pullers

- Scraper
- Valve spring compressor
- Ring groove cleaner
- Piston ring expander and compressor
- Ridge reamer
- Cylinder hone or glaze breaker
- Plastigage®
- Engine stand

The use of most of these tools is illustrated in this section. Many can be rented for a one-time use from a local parts jobber or tool supply house specializing in automotive work.

Occasionally, the use of special tools is called for. See the information on Special Tools and the Safety Notice in the front of this book before substituting another tool.

OVERHAUL TIPS

Aluminum has become extremely popular for use in engines, due to its low weight. Observe the following precautions when handling aluminum parts:
- Never hot tank aluminum parts (the caustic hot tank solution will eat the aluminum.
- Remove all aluminum parts (identification tag, etc.) from engine parts prior to the tanking.
- Always coat threads lightly with engine oil or anti-seize compounds before installation, to prevent seizure.
- Never overtighten bolts or spark plugs especially in aluminum threads.

When assembling the engine, any parts that will be exposed to frictional contact must be prelubed to provide lubrication at initial start-up. Any product specifically formulated for this purpose can be used, but engine oil is not recommended as a prelube in most cases.

When semi-permanent (locked, but removable) installation of bolts or nuts is desired, threads should be cleaned and coated with Loctite® or another similar, commercial non-hardening sealant.

CLEANING

▶ See Figures 150, 151, 152 and 153

Before the engine and its components are inspected, they must be thoroughly cleaned. You will need to remove any engine varnish, oil sludge and/or carbon deposits from all of the components to insure an accurate inspection. A crack in the engine block or cylinder head can easily become overlooked if hidden by a layer of sludge or carbon.

Most of the cleaning process can be carried out with common hand tools and readily available solvents or solutions. Carbon deposits can be chipped away using a hammer and a hard wooden chisel. Old gasket material and varnish or sludge can usually be removed using a scraper and/or cleaning solvent. Extremely stubborn deposits may require the use of a power drill with a wire brush. If using a wire brush, use extreme care around any critical machined surfaces (such as the gasket surfaces, bearing saddles, cylinder bores, etc.). USE OF A WIRE BRUSH IS NOT RECOMMENDED ON ANY ALUMINUM COMPONENTS. Always follow any safety recommendations given by the manufacturer of the tool and/or solvent. You should always wear eye protection during any cleaning process involving scraping, chipping or spraying of solvents.

An alternative to the mess and hassle of cleaning the parts yourself is to drop them off at a local garage or machine shop. They will, more than likely, have the necessary equipment to properly clean all of the parts for a nominal fee.

✳✳ CAUTION

Always wear eye protection during any cleaning process involving scraping, chipping or spraying of solvents.

Remove any oil galley plugs, freeze plugs and/or pressed-in bearings and carefully wash and degrease all of the engine components including the fasteners and bolts. Small parts such as the valves, springs, etc., should be placed in a metal basket and allowed to soak. Use pipe cleaner type brushes,

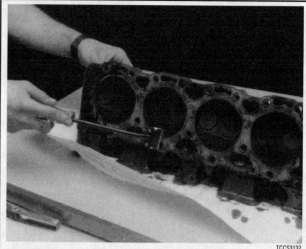
Fig. 150 Use a gasket scraper to remove the old gasket material from the mating surfaces

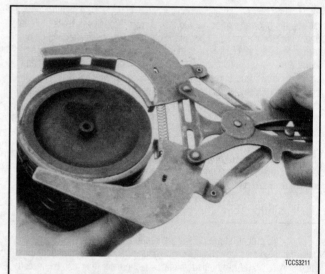
Fig. 151 Use a ring expander tool to remove the piston rings

Fig. 152 Clean the piston ring grooves using a ring groove cleaner tool, or . . .

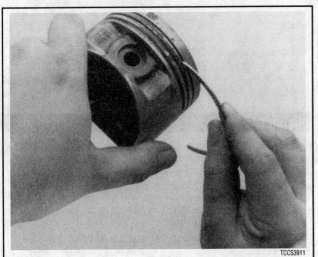

Fig. 153 . . . use a piece of an old ring to clean the grooves. Be careful, the ring can be quite sharp

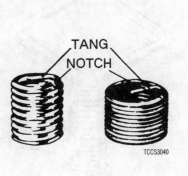

Fig. 155 Standard thread repair insert (left), and spark plug thread insert

and clean all passageways in the components. Use a ring expander and remove the rings from the pistons. Clean the piston ring grooves with a special tool or a piece of broken ring. Scrape the carbon off of the top of the piston. You should never use a wire brush on the pistons. After preparing all of the piston assemblies in this manner, wash and degrease them again.

❊❊ WARNING

Use extreme care when cleaning around the cylinder head valve seats. A mistake or slip may cost you a new seat.

When cleaning the cylinder head, remove carbon from the combustion chamber with the valves installed. This will avoid damaging the valve seats.

REPAIRING DAMAGED THREADS

▶ **See Figures 154, 155, 156, 157 and 158**

Several methods of repairing damaged threads are available. Heli-Coil® (shown here), Keenserts® and Microdot® are among the most widely used. All involve basically the same principle—drilling out stripped threads, tapping the hole and installing a prewound insert—making welding, plugging and oversize fasteners unnecessary.

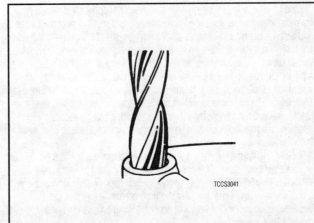

Fig. 156 Drill out the damaged threads with the specified size bit. Be sure to drill completely through the hole or to the bottom of a blind hole

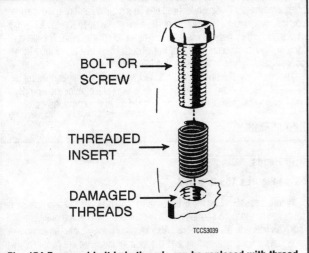

Fig. 154 Damaged bolt hole threads can be replaced with thread repair inserts

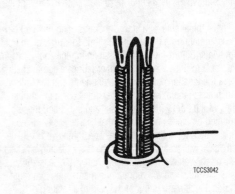

Fig. 157 Using the kit, tap the hole in order to receive the thread insert. Keep the tap well oiled and back it out frequently to avoid clogging the threads

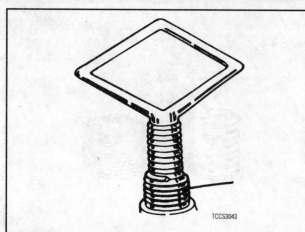

Fig. 158 Screw the insert onto the installer tool until the tang engages the slot. Thread the insert into the hole until it is ¼–½ turn below the top surface, then remove the tool and break off the tang using a punch

Two types of thread repair inserts are usually supplied: a standard type for most inch coarse, inch fine, metric course and metric fine thread sizes and a spark lug type to fit most spark plug port sizes. Consult the individual tool manufacturer's catalog to determine exact applications. Typical thread repair kits will contain a selection of prewound threaded inserts, a tap (corresponding to the outside diameter threads of the insert) and an installation tool. Spark plug inserts usually differ because they require a tap equipped with pilot threads and a combined reamer/tap section. Most manufacturers also supply blister-packed thread repair inserts separately in addition to a master kit containing a variety of taps and inserts plus installation tools.

Before attempting to repair a threaded hole, remove any snapped, broken or damaged bolts or studs. Penetrating oil can be used to free frozen threads. The offending item can usually be removed with locking pliers or using a screw/stud extractor. After the hole is clear, the thread can be repaired, as shown in the series of accompanying illustrations and in the kit manufacturer's instructions.

Engine Preparation

To properly rebuild an engine, you must first remove it from the vehicle, then disassemble and diagnose it. Ideally you should place your engine on an engine stand. This affords you the best access to the engine components. Follow the manufacturer's directions for using the stand with your particular engine. Remove the flywheel or flexplate before installing the engine to the stand.

Now that you have the engine on a stand, and assuming that you have drained the oil and coolant from the engine, it's time to strip it of all but the necessary components. Before you start disassembling the engine, you may want to take a moment to draw some pictures, or fabricate some labels or containers to mark the locations of various components and the bolts and/or studs which fasten them. Modern day engines use a lot of little brackets and clips which hold wiring harnesses and such, and these holders are often mounted on studs and/or bolts that can be easily mixed up. The manufacturer spent a lot of time and money designing your vehicle, and they wouldn't have wasted any of it by haphazardly placing brackets, clips or fasteners on the vehicle. If it's present when you disassemble it, put it back when you assemble, you will regret not remembering that little bracket which holds a wire harness out of the path of a rotating part.

You should begin by unbolting any accessories still attached to the engine, such as the water pump, power steering pump, alternator, etc. Then, unfasten any manifolds (intake or exhaust) which were not removed during the engine removal procedure. Finally, remove any covers remaining on the engine such as the rocker arm, front or timing cover and oil pan. Some front covers may require the vibration damper and/or crank pulley to be

removed beforehand. The idea is to reduce the engine to the bare necessities (cylinder head(s), valve train, engine block, crankshaft, pistons and connecting rods), plus any other `in block' components such as oil pumps, balance shafts and auxiliary shafts.

Finally, remove the cylinder head(s) from the engine block and carefully place on a bench. Disassembly instructions for each component follow later in this section.

Cylinder Head

There are two basic types of cylinder heads used on today's automobiles: the Overhead Valve (OHV) and the Overhead Camshaft (OHC). The latter can also be broken down into two subgroups: the Single Overhead Camshaft (SOHC) and the Dual Overhead Camshaft (DOHC). Generally, if there is only a single camshaft on a head, it is just referred to as an OHC head. Also, an engine with an OHV cylinder head is also known as a pushrod engine.

Most cylinder heads these days are made of an aluminum alloy due to its light weight, durability and heat transfer qualities. However, cast iron was the material of choice in the past, and is still used on many vehicles today. Whether made from aluminum or iron, all cylinder heads have valves and seats. Some use two valves per cylinder, while the more hi-tech engines will utilize a multi-valve configuration using 3, 4 and even 5 valves per cylinder. When the valve contacts the seat, it does so on precision machined surfaces, which seals the combustion chamber. All cylinder heads have a valve guide for each valve. The guide centers the valve to the seat and allows it to move up and down within it. The clearance between the valve and guide can be critical. Too much clearance and the engine may consume oil, lose vacuum and/or damage the seat. Too little, and the valve can stick in the guide causing the engine to run poorly if at all, and possibly causing severe damage. The last component all cylinder heads have are valve springs. The spring holds the valve against its seat. It also returns the valve to this position when the valve has been opened by the valve train or camshaft. The spring is fastened to the valve by a retainer and valve locks (sometimes called keepers). Aluminum heads will also have a valve spring shim to keep the spring from wearing away the aluminum.

An ideal method of rebuilding the cylinder head would involve replacing all of the valves, guides, seats, springs, etc. with new ones. However, depending on how the engine was maintained, often this is not necessary. A major cause of valve, guide and seat wear is an improperly tuned engine. An engine that is running too rich, will often wash the lubricating oil out of the guide with gasoline, causing it to wear rapidly. Conversely, an engine which is running too lean will place higher combustion temperatures on the valves and seats allowing them to wear or even burn. Springs fall victim to the driving habits of the individual. A driver who often runs the engine rpm to the redline will wear out or break the springs faster then one that stays well below it. Unfortunately, mileage takes it toll on all of the parts. Generally, the valves, guides, springs and seats in a cylinder head can be machined and re-used, saving you money. However, if a valve is burnt, it may be wise to replace all of the valves, since they were all operating in the same environment. The same goes for any other component on the cylinder head. Think of it as an insurance policy against future problems related to that component.

Unfortunately, the only way to find out which components need replacing, is to disassemble and carefully check each piece. After the cylinder head(s) are disassembled, thoroughly clean all of the components.

DISASSEMBLY

OHV Heads

▶ **See Figures 159 thru 164**

Before disassembling the cylinder head, you may want to fabricate some containers to hold the various parts, as some of them can be quite small (such as keepers) and easily lost. Also keeping yourself and the components organized will aid in assembly and reduce confusion. Where possible, try to maintain a components original location; this is especially important if there is not going to be any machine work performed on the components.

Fig. 159 When removing an OHV valve spring, use a compressor tool to relieve the tension from the retainer

1. If you haven't already removed the rocker arms and/or shafts, do so now.
2. Position the head so that the springs are easily accessed.
3. Use a valve spring compressor tool, and relieve spring tension from the retainer.

➡**Due to engine varnish, the retainer may stick to the valve locks. A gentle tap with a hammer may help to break it loose.**

4. Remove the valve locks from the valve tip and/or retainer. A small magnet may help in removing the locks.
5. Lift the valve spring, tool and all, off of the valve stem.
6. If equipped, remove the valve seal. If the seal is difficult to remove with the valve in place, try removing the valve first, then the seal. Follow the steps below for valve removal.
7. Position the head to allow access for withdrawing the valve.

➡**Cylinder heads that have seen a lot of miles and/or abuse may have mushroomed the valve lock grove and/or tip, causing difficulty in removal of the valve. If this has happened, use a metal file to carefully remove the high spots around the lock grooves and/or tip. Only file it enough to allow removal.**

Fig. 160 A small magnet will help in removal of the valve locks

Fig. 162 Remove the valve seal from the valve stem—O-ring type seal shown

Fig. 161 Be careful not to lose the small valve locks (keepers)

Fig. 163 Removing an umbrella/positive type seal

Fig. 164 Invert the cylinder head and withdraw the valve from the valve guide bore

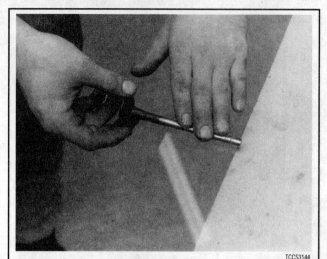

Fig. 165 Valve stems may be rolled on a flat surface to check for bends

8. Remove the valve from the cylinder head.

9. If equipped, remove the valve spring shim. A small magnetic tool or screwdriver will aid in removal.

10. Repeat Steps 3 though 9 until all of the valves have been removed.

INSPECTION

Now that all of the cylinder head components are clean, it's time to inspect them for wear and/or damage. To accurately inspect them, you will need some specialized tools:

- A 0–1 in. micrometer for the valves
- A dial indicator or inside diameter gauge for the valve guides
- A spring pressure test gauge

If you do not have access to the proper tools, you may want to bring the components to a shop that does.

Valves

▶ See Figures 165 and 166

The first thing to inspect are the valve heads. Look closely at the head, margin and face for any cracks, excessive wear or burning. The margin is the best place to look for burning. It should have a squared edge with an even width all around the diameter. When a valve burns, the margin will look melted and the edges rounded. Also inspect the valve head for any signs of tulipping. This will show as a lifting of the edges or dishing in the center of the head and will usually not occur to all of the valves. All of the heads should look the same, any that seem dished more than others are probably bad. Next, inspect the valve lock grooves and valve tips. Check for any burrs around the lock grooves, especially if you had to file them to remove the valve. Valve tips should appear flat, although slight rounding with high mileage engines is normal. Slightly worn valve tips will need to be machined flat. Last, measure the valve stem diameter with the micrometer. Measure the area that rides within the guide, especially towards the tip where most of the wear occurs. Take several measurements along its length and compare them to each other. Wear should be even along the length with little to no taper. If no minimum diameter is given in the specifications, then the stem should not read more than 0.001 in. (0.025mm) below the specification. Any valves that fail these inspections should be replaced.

Springs, Retainers and Valve Locks

▶ See Figures 167 and 168

The first thing to check is the most obvious, broken springs. Next check the free length and squareness of each spring. If applicable, insure to distinguish between intake and exhaust springs. Use a ruler and/or carpenters

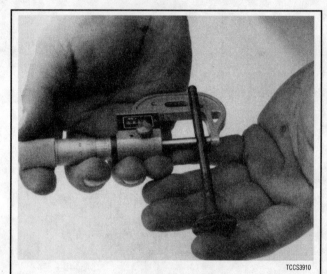

Fig. 166 Use a micrometer to check the valve stem diameter

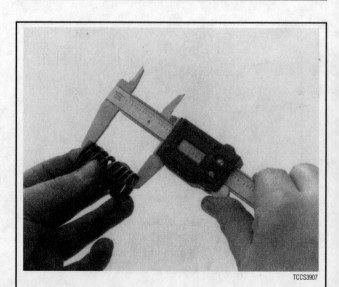

Fig. 167 Use a caliper to check the valve spring free-length

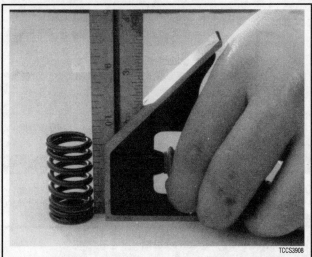

Fig. 168 Check the valve spring for squareness on a flat surface; a carpenter's square can be used

square to measure the length. A carpenters square should be used to check the springs for squareness. If a spring pressure test gauge is available, check each springs rating and compare to the specifications chart. Check the readings against the specifications given. Any springs that fail these inspections should be replaced.

The spring retainers rarely need replacing, however they should still be checked as a precaution. Inspect the spring mating surface and the valve lock retention area for any signs of excessive wear. Also check for any signs of cracking. Replace any retainers that are questionable.

Valve locks should be inspected for excessive wear on the outside contact area as well as on the inner notched surface. Any locks which appear worn or broken and its respective valve should be replaced.

Cylinder Head

There are several things to check on the cylinder head: valve guides, seats, cylinder head surface flatness, cracks and physical damage.

VALVE GUIDES

▶ See Figure 169

Now that you know the valves are good, you can use them to check the guides, although a new valve, if available, is preferred. Before you measure anything, look at the guides carefully and inspect them for any cracks, chips or breakage. Also if the guide is a removable style (as in most aluminum heads), check them for any looseness or evidence of movement. All of the guides should appear to be at the same height from the spring seat. If any seem lower (or higher) from another, the guide has moved. Mount a dial indicator onto the spring side of the cylinder head. Lightly oil the valve stem and insert it into the cylinder head. Position the dial indicator against the valve stem near the tip and zero the gauge. Grasp the valve stem and wiggle towards and away from the dial indicator and observe the readings. Mount the dial indicator 90 degrees from the initial point and zero the gauge and again take a reading. Compare the two readings for a out of round condition. Check the readings against the specifications given. An Inside Diameter (I.D.) gauge designed for valve guides will give you an accurate valve guide bore measurement. If the I.D. gauge is used, compare the readings with the specifications given. Any guides that fail these inspections should be replaced or machined.

VALVE SEATS

A visual inspection of the valve seats should show a slightly worn and pitted surface where the valve face contacts the seat. Inspect the seat carefully for severe pitting or cracks. Also, a seat that is badly worn will be recessed into the cylinder head. A severely worn or recessed seat may need to be replaced. All cracked seats must be replaced. A seat concentricity gauge, if available, should be used to check the seat run-out. If run-out exceeds specifications the seat must be machined (if no specification is given use 0.002 in. or 0.051mm).

CYLINDER HEAD SURFACE FLATNESS

▶ See Figures 170 and 171

After you have cleaned the gasket surface of the cylinder head of any old gasket material, check the head for flatness.

Place a straightedge across the gasket surface. Using feeler gauges, determine the clearance at the center of the straightedge and across the cylinder head at several points. Check along the centerline and diagonally on the head surface. If the warpage exceeds 0.003 in. (0.076mm) within a 6.0 in. (15.2cm) span, or 0.006 in. (0.152mm) over the total length of the head, the cylinder head must be resurfaced. After resurfacing the heads of a V-type engine, the intake manifold flange surface should be checked, and if necessary, milled proportionally to allow for the change in its mounting position.

CRACKS AND PHYSICAL DAMAGE

Generally, cracks are limited to the combustion chamber, however, it is not uncommon for the head to crack in a spark plug hole, port, outside of

Fig. 169 A dial gauge may be used to check valve stem-to-guide clearance; read the gauge while moving the valve stem

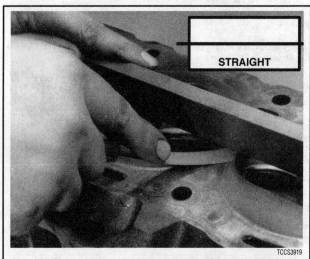

Fig. 170 Check the head for flatness across the center of the head surface using a straightedge and feeler gauge

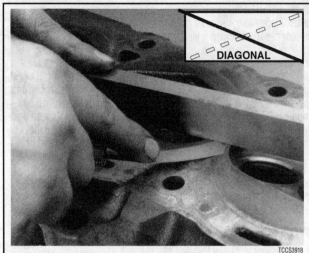

DIAGONAL

Fig. 171 Checks should also be made along both diagonals of the head surface

the head or in the valve spring/rocker arm area. The first area to inspect is always the hottest: the exhaust seat/port area.

A visual inspection should be performed, but just because you don't see a crack does not mean it is not there. Some more reliable methods for inspecting for cracks include Magnaflux®, a magnetic process or Zyglo®, a dye penetrant. Magnaflux® is used only on ferrous metal (cast iron) heads. Zyglo® uses a spray on fluorescent mixture along with a black light to reveal the cracks. It is strongly recommended to have your cylinder head checked professionally for cracks, especially if the engine was known to have overheated and/or leaked or consumed coolant. Contact a local shop for availability and pricing of these services.

Physical damage is usually very evident. For example, a broken mounting ear from dropping the head or a bent or broken stud and/or bolt. All of these defects should be fixed or, if unrepairable, the head should be replaced.

REFINISHING & REPAIRING

Many of the procedures given for refinishing and repairing the cylinder head components must be performed by a machine shop. Certain steps, if the inspected part is not worn, can be performed yourself inexpensively. However, you spent a lot of time and effort so far, why risk trying to save a couple bucks if you might have to do it all over again?

Valves

Any valves that were not replaced should be refaced and the tips ground flat. Unless you have access to a valve grinding machine, this should be done by a machine shop. If the valves are in extremely good condition, as well as the valve seats and guides, they may be lapped in without performing machine work.

It is a recommended practice to lap the valves even after machine work has been performed and/or new valves have been purchased. This insures a positive seal between the valve and seat.

LAPPING THE VALVES

➡Before lapping the valves to the seats, read the rest of the cylinder head section to insure that any related parts are in acceptable enough condition to continue.

➡Before any valve seat machining and/or lapping can be performed, the guides must be within factory recommended specifications.

1. Invert the cylinder head.
2. Lightly lubricate the valve stems and insert them into the cylinder head in their numbered order.

3. Raise the valve from the seat and apply a small amount of fine lapping compound to the seat.
4. Moisten the suction head of a hand-lapping tool and attach it to the head of the valve.
5. Rotate the tool between the palms of both hands, changing the position of the valve on the valve seat and lifting the tool often to prevent grooving.
6. Lap the valve until a smooth, polished circle is evident on the valve and seat.
7. Remove the tool and the valve. Wipe away all traces of the grinding compound and store the valve to maintain its lapped location.

✳✳ WARNING

Do not get the valves out of order after they have been lapped. They must be put back with the same valve seat with which they were lapped.

Springs, Retainers and Valve Locks

There is no repair or refinishing possible with the springs, retainers and valve locks. If they are found to be worn or defective, they must be replaced with new (or known good) parts.

Cylinder Head

Most refinishing procedures dealing with the cylinder head must be performed by a machine shop. Read the sections below and review your inspection data to determine whether or not machining is necessary.

VALVE GUIDES

➡If any machining or replacements are made to the valve guides, the seats must be machined.

Unless the valve guides need machining or replacing, the only service to perform is to thoroughly clean them of any dirt or oil residue.

There are only two types of valve guides used on automobile engines: the replaceable-type (all aluminum heads) and the cast-in integral-type (most cast iron heads). There are four recommended methods for repairing worn guides.
• Knurling
• Inserts
• Reaming oversize
• Replacing

Knurling is a process in which metal is displaced and raised, thereby reducing clearance, giving a true center, and providing oil control. It is the least expensive way of repairing the valve guides. However, it is not necessarily the best, and in some cases, a knurled valve guide will not stand up for more than a short time. It requires a special knurlizer and precision reaming tools to obtain proper clearances. It would not be cost effective to purchase these tools, unless you plan on rebuilding several of the same cylinder head.

Installing a guide insert involves machining the guide to accept a bronze insert. One style is the coil-type which is installed into a threaded guide. Another is the thin-walled insert where the guide is reamed oversize to accept a split-sleeve insert. After the insert is installed, a special tool is then run through the guide to expand the insert, locking it to the guide. The insert is then reamed to the standard size for proper valve clearance.

Reaming for oversize valves restores normal clearances and provides a true valve seat. Most cast-in type guides can be reamed to accept an valve with an oversize stem. The cost factor for this can become quite high as you will need to purchase the reamer and new, oversize stem valves for all guides which were reamed. Oversizes are generally 0.003 to 0.030 in. (0.076 to 0.762mm), with 0.015 in. (0.381mm) being the most common.

To replace cast-in type valve guides, they must be drilled out, then reamed to accept replacement guides. This must be done on a fixture which will allow centering and leveling off of the original valve seat or guide, otherwise a serious guide-to-seat misalignment may occur making it impossible to properly machine the seat.

Replaceable-type guides are pressed into the cylinder head. A hammer and a stepped drift or punch may be used to install and remove the guides. Before removing the guides, measure the protrusion on the spring side of the head and record it for installation. Use the stepped drift to hammer out the old guide from the combustion chamber side of the head. When installing, determine whether or not the guide also seals a water jacket in the head, and if it does, use the recommended sealing agent. If there is no water jacket, grease the valve guide and its bore. Use the stepped drift, and hammer the new guide into the cylinder head from the spring side of the cylinder head. A stack of washers the same thickness as the measured protrusion may help the installation process.

VALVE SEATS

➡**Before any valve seat machining can be performed, the guides must be within factory recommended specifications.**

➡**If any machining or replacements were made to the valve guides, the seats must be machined.**

If the seats are in good condition, the valves can be lapped to the seats, and the cylinder head assembled. See the valves section for instructions on lapping.

If the valve seats are worn, cracked or damaged, they must be serviced by a machine shop. The valve seat must be perfectly centered to the valve guide, which requires very accurate machining.

CYLINDER HEAD SURFACE

If the cylinder head is warped, it must be machined flat. If the warpage is extremely severe, the head may need to be replaced. In some instances, it may be possible to straighten a warped head enough to allow machining. In either case, contact a professional machine shop for service.

CRACKS AND PHYSICAL DAMAGE

Certain cracks can be repaired in both cast iron and aluminum heads. For cast iron, a tapered threaded insert is installed along the length of the crack. Aluminum can also use the tapered inserts, however welding is the preferred method. Some physical damage can be repaired through brazing or welding. Contact a machine shop to get expert advice for your particular dilemma.

ASSEMBLY

The first step for any assembly job is to have a clean area in which to work. Next, thoroughly clean all of the parts and components that are to be assembled. Finally, place all of the components onto a suitable work space and, if necessary, arrange the parts to their respective positions.

OHV Engines

1. Lightly lubricate the valve stems and insert all of the valves into the cylinder head. If possible, maintain their original locations.
2. If equipped, install any valve spring shims which were removed.
3. If equipped, install the new valve seals, keeping the following in mind:
   • If the valve seal presses over the guide, lightly lubricate the outer guide surfaces.
   • If the seal is an O-ring type, it is installed just after compressing the spring but before the valve locks.
4. Place the valve spring and retainer over the stem.
5. Position the spring compressor tool and compress the spring.
6. Assemble the valve locks to the stem.
7. Relieve the spring pressure slowly and insure that neither valve lock becomes dislodged by the retainer.
8. Remove the spring compressor tool.
9. Repeat Steps 2 through 8 until all of the springs have been installed.

Engine Block

GENERAL INFORMATION

A thorough overhaul or rebuild of an engine block would include replacing the pistons, rings, bearings, timing belt/chain assembly and oil pump. For OHV engines also include a new camshaft and lifters. The block would then have the cylinders bored and honed oversize (or if using removable cylinder sleeves, new sleeves installed) and the crankshaft would be cut undersize to provide new wearing surfaces and perfect clearances. However, your particular engine may not have everything worn out. What if only the piston rings have worn out and the clearances on everything else are still within factory specifications? Well, you could just replace the rings and put it back together, but this would be a very rare example. Chances are, if one component in your engine is worn, other components are sure to follow, and soon. At the very least, you should always replace the rings, bearings and oil pump. This is what is commonly called a "freshen up".

Cylinder Ridge Removal

Because the top piston ring does not travel to the very top of the cylinder, a ridge is built up between the end of the travel and the top of the cylinder bore.

Pushing the piston and connecting rod assembly past the ridge can be difficult, and damage to the piston ring lands could occur. If the ridge is not removed before installing a new piston or not removed at all, piston ring breakage and piston damage may occur.

➡**It is always recommended that you remove any cylinder ridges before removing the piston and connecting rod assemblies. If you know that new pistons are going to be installed and the engine block will be bored oversize, you may be able to forego this step. However, some ridges may actually prevent the assemblies from being removed, necessitating its removal.**

There are several different types of ridge reamers on the market, none of which are inexpensive. Unless a great deal of engine rebuilding is anticipated, borrow or rent a reamer.

1. Turn the crankshaft until the piston is at the bottom of its travel.
2. Cover the head of the piston with a rag.
3. Follow the tool manufacturers instructions and cut away the ridge, exercising extreme care to avoid cutting too deeply.
4. Remove the ridge reamer, the rag and as many of the cuttings as possible. Continue until all of the cylinder ridges have been removed.

DISASSEMBLY

◆ See Figures 172 and 173

The engine disassembly instructions following assume that you have the engine mounted on an engine stand. If not, it is easiest to disassemble the engine on a bench or the floor with it resting on the bell-housing or transmission mounting surface. You must be able to access the connecting rod fasteners and turn the crankshaft during disassembly. Also, all engine covers (timing, front, side, oil pan, whatever) should have already been removed. Engines which are seized or locked up may not be able to be completely disassembled, and a core (salvage yard) engine should be purchased.

Pushrod Engines

If not done during the cylinder head removal, remove the pushrods and lifters, keeping them in order for assembly. Remove the timing gears and/or timing chain assembly, then remove the oil pump drive assembly and withdraw the camshaft from the engine block. Remove the oil pick-up and pump assembly. If equipped, remove any balance or auxiliary shafts. If necessary, remove the cylinder ridge from the top of the bore. See the cylinder ridge removal procedure earlier in this section.

All Engines

Rotate the engine over so that the crankshaft is exposed. Use a number punch or scribe and mark each connecting rod with its respective cylinder number. The cylinder closest to the front of the engine is always number 1. However, depending on the engine placement, the front of the engine could either be the flywheel or damper/pulley end. Generally the front of the engine faces the front of the vehicle. Use a number punch or scribe and also mark the main bearing caps from front to rear with the front most cap being number 1 (if there are five caps, mark them 1 through 5, front to rear).

> ### ✳✳ WARNING
>
> **Take special care when pushing the connecting rod up from the crankshaft because the sharp threads of the rod bolts/studs will score the crankshaft journal. Insure that special plastic caps are installed over them, or cut two pieces of rubber hose to do the same.**

Again, rotate the engine, this time to position the number one cylinder bore (head surface) up. Turn the crankshaft until the number one piston is at the bottom of its travel, this should allow the maximum access to its connecting rod. Remove the number one connecting rods fasteners and cap and place two lengths of rubber hose over the rod bolts/studs to protect the crankshaft from damage. Using a sturdy wooden dowel and a hammer, push the connecting rod up about 1 in. (25mm) from the crankshaft and remove the upper bearing insert. Continue pushing or tapping the connecting rod up until the piston rings are out of the cylinder bore. Remove the piston and rod by hand, put the upper half of the bearing insert back into the rod, install the cap with its bearing insert installed, and hand-tighten the cap fasteners. If the parts are kept in order in this manner, they will not get lost and you will be able to tell which bearings came form what cylinder if any problems are discovered and diagnosis is necessary. Remove all the other piston assemblies in the same manner. On V-style engines, remove all of the pistons from one bank, then reposition the engine with the other cylinder bank head surface up, and remove that banks piston assemblies.

The only remaining component in the engine block should now be the crankshaft. Loosen the main bearing caps evenly until the fasteners can be turned by hand, then remove them and the caps. Remove the crankshaft from the engine block. Thoroughly clean all of the components.

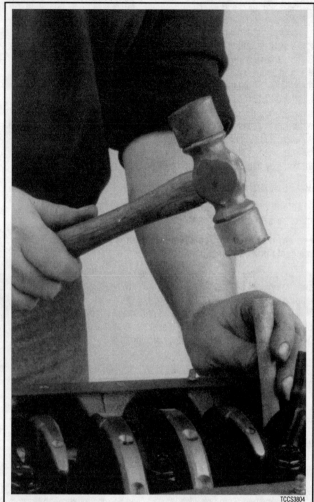

Fig. 173 Carefully tap the piston out of the bore using a wooden dowel

Fig. 172 Place rubber hose over the connecting rod studs to protect the crankshaft and cylinder bores from damage

INSPECTION

Now that the engine block and all of its components are clean, it's time to inspect them for wear and/or damage. To accurately inspect them, you will need some specialized tools:

• Two or three separate micrometers to measure the pistons and crankshaft journals
• A dial indicator
• Telescoping gauges for the cylinder bores
• A rod alignment fixture to check for bent connecting rods

If you do not have access to the proper tools, you may want to bring the components to a shop that does.

Generally, you shouldn't expect cracks in the engine block or its components unless it was known to leak, consume or mix engine fluids, it was severely overheated, or there was evidence of bad bearings and/or crankshaft damage. A visual inspection should be performed on all of the components, but just because you don't see a crack does not mean it is not there. Some more reliable methods for inspecting for cracks include Magnaflux®, a magnetic process or Zyglo®, a dye penetrant. Magnaflux® is used only on ferrous metal (cast iron). Zyglo® uses a spray on fluorescent mixture along with a black light to reveal the cracks. It is strongly recommended to have your engine block checked professionally for cracks, especially if the engine was known to have overheated and/or leaked or consumed coolant. Contact a local shop for availability and pricing of these services.

Engine Block

ENGINE BLOCK BEARING ALIGNMENT

Remove the main bearing caps and, if still installed, the main bearing inserts. Inspect all of the main bearing saddles and caps for damage, burrs or high spots. If damage is found, and it is caused from a spun main bearing, the block will need to be align-bored or, if severe enough, replacement. Any burrs or high spots should be carefully removed with a metal file.

Place a straightedge on the bearing saddles, in the engine block, along the centerline of the crankshaft. If any clearance exists between the straightedge and the saddles, the block must be align-bored.

Align-boring consists of machining the main bearing saddles and caps by means of a flycutter that runs through the bearing saddles.

DECK FLATNESS

The top of the engine block where the cylinder head mounts is called the deck. Insure that the deck surface is clean of dirt, carbon deposits and old gasket material. Place a straightedge across the surface of the deck along its centerline and, using feeler gauges, check the clearance along several points. Repeat the checking procedure with the straightedge placed along both diagonals of the deck surface. If the reading exceeds 0.003 in. (0.076mm) within a 6.0 in. (15.2cm) span, or 0.006 in. (0.152mm) over the total length of the deck, it must be machined.

CYLINDER BORES

▶ See Figure 174

The cylinder bores house the pistons and are slightly larger than the pistons themselves. A common piston-to-bore clearance is 0.0015–0.0025 in. (0.0381mm–0.0635mm). Inspect and measure the cylinder bores. The bore should be checked for out-of-roundness, taper and size. The results of this inspection will determine whether the cylinder can be used in its existing size and condition, or a rebore to the next oversize is required (or in the case of removable sleeves, have replacements installed).

The amount of cylinder wall wear is always greater at the top of the cylinder than at the bottom. This wear is known as taper. Any cylinder that has a taper of 0.0012 in. (0.305mm) or more, must be rebored. Measurements are taken at a number of positions in each cylinder: at the top, middle and bottom and at two points at each position; that is, at a point 90 degrees from the crankshaft centerline, as well as a point parallel to the

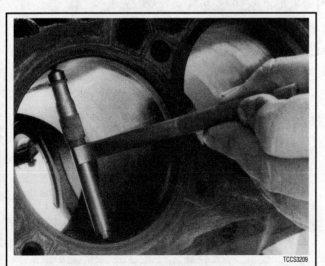

Fig. 174 Use a telescoping gauge to measure the cylinder bore diameter—take several readings within the same bore

crankshaft centerline. The measurements are made with either a special dial indicator or a telescopic gauge and micrometer. If the necessary precision tools to check the bore are not available, take the block to a machine shop and have them mike it. Also if you don't have the tools to check the cylinder bores, chances are you will not have the necessary devices to check the pistons, connecting rods and crankshaft. Take these components with you and save yourself an extra trip.

For our procedures, we will use a telescopic gauge and a micrometer. You will need one of each, with a measuring range which covers your cylinder bore size.

1. Position the telescopic gauge in the cylinder bore, loosen the gauges lock and allow it to expand.

➡ **Your first two readings will be at the top of the cylinder bore, then proceed to the middle and finally the bottom, making a total of six measurements.**

2. Hold the gauge square in the bore, 90 degrees from the crankshaft centerline, and gently tighten the lock. Tilt the gauge back to remove it from the bore.

3. Measure the gauge with the micrometer and record the reading.

4. Again, hold the gauge square in the bore, this time parallel to the crankshaft centerline, and gently tighten the lock. Again, you will tilt the gauge back to remove it from the bore.

5. Measure the gauge with the micrometer and record this reading. The difference between these two readings is the out-of-round measurement of the cylinder.

6. Repeat steps 1 through 5, each time going to the next lower position, until you reach the bottom of the cylinder. Then go to the next cylinder, and continue until all of the cylinders have been measured.

The difference between these measurements will tell you all about the wear in your cylinders. The measurements which were taken 90 degrees from the crankshaft centerline will always reflect the most wear. That is because at this position is where the engine power presses the piston against the cylinder bore the hardest. This is known as thrust wear. Take your top, 90 degree measurement and compare it to your bottom, 90 degree measurement. The difference between them is the taper. When you measure your pistons, you will compare these readings to your piston sizes and determine piston-to-wall clearance.

Crankshaft

Inspect the crankshaft for visible signs of wear or damage. All of the journals should be perfectly round and smooth. Slight scores are normal for a used crankshaft, but you should hardly feel them with your fingernail. When measuring the crankshaft with a micrometer, you will take readings at the front and rear of each journal, then turn the micrometer 90 degrees and take two more readings, front and rear. The difference between the front-to-rear readings is the journal taper and the first-to-90 degree reading is the out-of-round measurement. Generally, there should be no taper or out-of-roundness found, however, up to 0.0005 in. (0.0127mm) for either can be overlooked. Also, the readings should fall within the factory specifications for journal diameters.

If the crankshaft journals fall within specifications, it is recommended that it be polished before being returned to service. Polishing the crankshaft insures that any minor burrs or high spots are smoothed, thereby reducing the chance of scoring the new bearings.

Pistons and Connecting Rods

PISTONS

▶ See Figure 175

The piston should be visually inspected for any signs of cracking or burning (caused by hot spots or detonation), and scuffing or excessive wear on the skirts. The wristpin attaches the piston to the connecting rod. The piston should move freely on the wrist pin, both sliding and pivoting. Grasp the connecting rod securely, or mount it in a vise, and try to rock the piston back and forth along the centerline of the wristpin. There should not

Fig. 175 Measure the piston's outer diameter, perpendicular to the wrist pin, with a micrometer

be any excessive play evident between the piston and the pin. If there are C-clips retaining the pin in the piston then you have wrist pin bushings in the rods. There should not be any excessive play between the wrist pin and the rod bushing. Normal clearance for the wrist pin is approx. 0.001–0.002 in. (0.025mm–0.051mm).

Use a micrometer and measure the diameter of the piston, perpendicular to the wrist pin, on the skirt. Compare the reading to its original cylinder measurement obtained earlier. The difference between the two readings is the piston-to-wall clearance. If the clearance is within specifications, the piston may be used as is. If the piston is out of specification, but the bore is not, you will need a new piston. If both are out of specification, you will need the cylinder rebored and oversize pistons installed. Generally if two or more pistons/bores are out of specification, it is best to rebore the entire block and purchase a complete set of oversize pistons.

CONNECTING RODS

You should have the connecting rod checked for straightness at a machine shop. If the connecting rod is bent, it will unevenly wear the bearing and piston, as well as place greater stress on these components. Any bent or twisted connecting rods must be replaced. If the rods are straight and the wrist pin clearance is within specifications, then only the bearing end of the rod need be checked. Place the connecting rod into a vice, with the bearing inserts in place, install the cap to the rod and torque the fasteners to specifications. Use a telescoping gauge and carefully measure the inside diameter of the bearings. Compare this reading to the rods original crankshaft journal diameter measurement. The difference is the oil clearance. If the oil clearance is not within specifications, install new bearings in the rod and take another measurement. If the clearance is still out of specifications, and the crankshaft is not, the rod will need to be reconditioned by a machine shop.

➡You can also use Plastigage® to check the bearing clearances. The assembling section has complete instructions on its use.

Camshaft

Inspect the camshaft and lifters/followers as described earlier in this section.

Bearings

All of the engine bearings should be visually inspected for wear and/or damage. The bearing should look evenly worn all around with no deep scores or pits. If the bearing is severely worn, scored, pitted or heat blued, then the bearing, and the components that use it, should be brought to a machine shop for inspection. Full-circle bearings (used on most camshafts,

auxiliary shafts, balance shafts, etc.) require specialized tools for removal and installation, and should be brought to a machine shop for service.

Oil Pump

➡The oil pump is responsible for providing constant lubrication to the whole engine and so it is recommended that a new oil pump be installed when rebuilding the engine.

Completely disassemble the oil pump and thoroughly clean all of the components. Inspect the oil pump gears and housing for wear and/or damage. Insure that the pressure relief valve operates properly and there is no binding or sticking due to varnish or debris. If all of the parts are in proper working condition, lubricate the gears and relief valve, and assemble the pump.

REFINISHING

▶ See Figure 176

Almost all engine block refinishing must be performed by a machine shop. If the cylinders are not to be rebored, then the cylinder glaze can be removed with a ball hone. When removing cylinder glaze with a ball hone, use a light or penetrating type oil to lubricate the hone. Do not allow the hone to run dry as this may cause excessive scoring of the cylinder bores and wear on the hone. If new pistons are required, they will need to be installed to the connecting rods. This should be performed by a machine shop as the pistons must be installed in the correct relationship to the rod or engine damage can occur.

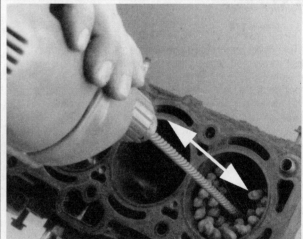

Fig. 176 Use a ball type cylinder hone to remove any glaze and provide a new surface for seating the piston rings

Pistons and Connecting Rods

▶ See Figure 177

Only pistons with the wrist pin retained by C-clips are serviceable by the home-mechanic. Press fit pistons require special presses and/or heaters to remove/install the connecting rod and should only be performed by a machine shop.

All pistons will have a mark indicating the direction to the front of the engine and the must be installed into the engine in that manner. Usually it is a notch or arrow on the top of the piston, or it may be the letter F cast or stamped into the piston.

C-CLIP TYPE PISTONS

1. Note the location of the forward mark on the piston and mark the connecting rod in relation.
2. Remove the C-clips from the piston and withdraw the wrist pin.

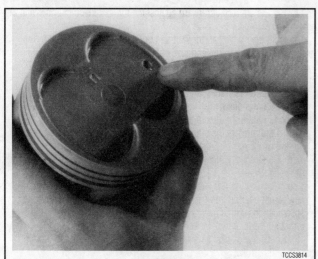

Fig. 177 Most pistons are marked to indicate positioning in the engine (usually a mark means the side facing the front)

➡Varnish build-up or C-clip groove burrs may increase the difficulty of removing the wrist pin. If necessary, use a punch or drift to carefully tap the wrist pin out.

3. Insure that the wrist pin bushing in the connecting rod is usable, and lubricate it with assembly lube.

4. Remove the wrist pin from the new piston and lubricate the pin bores on the piston.

5. Align the forward marks on the piston and the connecting rod and install the wrist pin.

6. The new C-clips will have a flat and a rounded side to them. Install both C-clips with the flat side facing out.

7. Repeat all of the steps for each piston being replaced.

ASSEMBLY

Before you begin assembling the engine, first give yourself a clean, dirt free work area. Next, clean every engine component again. The key to a good assembly is cleanliness.

Mount the engine block into the engine stand and wash it one last time using water and detergent (dishwashing detergent works well). While washing it, scrub the cylinder bores with a soft bristle brush and thoroughly clean all of the oil passages. Completely dry the engine and spray the entire assembly down with an anti-rust solution such as WD-40® or similar product. Take a clean lint-free rag and wipe up any excess anti-rust solution from the bores, bearing saddles, etc. Repeat the final cleaning process on the crankshaft. Replace any freeze or oil galley plugs which were removed during disassembly.

Crankshaft

▶ See Figures 178, 179, 180 and 181

1. Remove the main bearing inserts from the block and bearing caps.

2. If the crankshaft main bearing journals have been refinished to a definite undersize, install the correct undersize bearing. Be sure that the bearing inserts and bearing bores are clean. Foreign material under inserts will distort bearing and cause failure.

3. Place the upper main bearing inserts in bores with tang in slot.

➡The oil holes in the bearing inserts must be aligned with the oil holes in the cylinder block.

4. Install the lower main bearing inserts in bearing caps.

5. Clean the mating surfaces of block and rear main bearing cap.

6. Carefully lower the crankshaft into place. Be careful not to damage bearing surfaces.

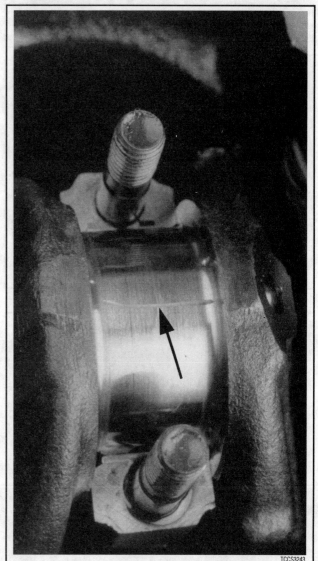

Fig. 178 Apply a strip of gauging material to the bearing journal, then install and torque the cap

Fig. 179 After the cap is removed again, use the scale supplied with the gauging material to check the clearance

Fig. 180 A dial gauge may be used to check crankshaft end-play

Fig. 181 Carefully pry the crankshaft back and forth while reading the dial gauge for end-play

7. Check the clearance of each main bearing by using the following procedure:

a. Place a piece of Plastigage® or its equivalent, on bearing surface across full width of bearing cap and about ¼ in. off center.

b. Install cap and tighten bolts to specifications. Do not turn crankshaft while Plastigage® is in place.

c. Remove the cap. Using the supplied Plastigage® scale, check width of Plastigage® at widest point to get maximum clearance. Difference between readings is taper of journal.

d. If clearance exceeds specified limits, try a 0.001 in. or 0.002 in. undersize bearing in combination with the standard bearing. Bearing clearance must be within specified limits. If standard and 0.002 in. undersize bearing does not bring clearance within desired limits, refinish crankshaft journal, then install undersize bearings.

8. Install the rear main seal.

9. After the bearings have been fitted, apply a light coat of engine oil to the journals and bearings. Install the rear main bearing cap. Install all bearing caps except the thrust bearing cap. Be sure that main bearing caps are installed in original locations. Tighten the bearing cap bolts to specifications.

10. Install the thrust bearing cap with bolts finger-tight.

11. Pry the crankshaft forward against the thrust surface of upper half of bearing.

12. Hold the crankshaft forward and pry the thrust bearing cap to the rear. This aligns the thrust surfaces of both halves of the bearing.

13. Retain the forward pressure on the crankshaft. Tighten the cap bolts to specifications.

14. Measure the crankshaft end-play as follows:

a. Mount a dial gauge to the engine block and position the tip of the gauge to read from the crankshaft end.

b. Carefully pry the crankshaft toward the rear of the engine and hold it there while you zero the gauge.

c. Carefully pry the crankshaft toward the front of the engine and read the gauge.

d. Confirm that the reading is within specifications. If not, install a new thrust bearing and repeat the procedure. If the reading is still out of specifications with a new bearing, have a machine shop inspect the thrust surfaces of the crankshaft, and if possible, repair it.

15. Rotate the crankshaft so as to position the first rod journal to the bottom of its stroke.

Pistons and Connecting Rods

▶ See Figures 182, 183, 184 and 185

1. Before installing the piston/connecting rod assembly, oil the pistons, piston rings and the cylinder walls with light engine oil. Install connecting rod bolt protectors or rubber hose onto the connecting rod bolts/studs. Also perform the following:

a. Select the proper ring set for the size cylinder bore.

b. Position the ring in the bore in which it is going to be used.

c. Push the ring down into the bore area where normal ring wear is not encountered.

d. Use the head of the piston to position the ring in the bore so that the ring is square with the cylinder wall. Use caution to avoid damage to the ring or cylinder bore.

Fig. 182 Checking the piston ring-to-ring groove side clearance using the ring and a feeler gauge

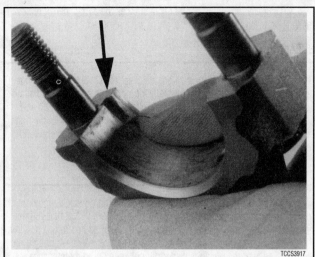

TCCS3917

Fig. 183 The notch on the side of the bearing cap matches the tang on the bearing insert

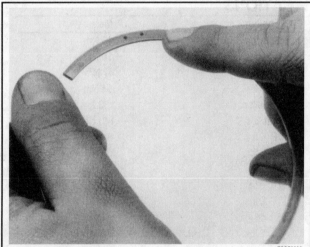

TCCS3222

Fig. 184 Most rings are marked to show which side of the ring should face up when installed to the piston

TCCS3914

Fig. 185 Install the piston and rod assembly into the block using a ring compressor and the handle of a hammer

e. Measure the gap between the ends of the ring with a feeler gauge. Ring gap in a worn cylinder is normally greater than specification. If the ring gap is greater than the specified limits, try an oversize ring set.

f. Check the ring side clearance of the compression rings with a feeler gauge inserted between the ring and its lower land according to specification. The gauge should slide freely around the entire ring circumference without binding. Any wear that occurs will form a step at the inner portion of the lower land. If the lower lands have high steps, the piston should be replaced.

2. Unless new pistons are installed, be sure to install the pistons in the cylinders from which they were removed. The numbers on the connecting rod and bearing cap must be on the same side when installed in the cylinder bore. If a connecting rod is ever transposed from one engine or cylinder to another, new bearings should be fitted and the connecting rod should be numbered to correspond with the new cylinder number. The notch on the piston head goes toward the front of the engine.

3. Install all of the rod bearing inserts into the rods and caps.

4. Install the rings to the pistons. Install the oil control ring first, then the second compression ring and finally the top compression ring. Use a piston ring expander tool to aid in installation and to help reduce the chance of breakage.

5. Make sure the ring gaps are properly spaced around the circumference of the piston. Fit a piston ring compressor around the piston and slide the piston and connecting rod assembly down into the cylinder bore, pushing it in with the wooden hammer handle. Push the piston down until it is only slightly below the top of the cylinder bore. Guide the connecting rod onto the crankshaft bearing journal carefully, to avoid damaging the crankshaft.

6. Check the bearing clearance of all the rod bearings, fitting them to the crankshaft bearing journals. Follow the procedure in the crankshaft installation above.

7. After the bearings have been fitted, apply a light coating of assembly oil to the journals and bearings.

8. Turn the crankshaft until the appropriate bearing journal is at the bottom of its stroke, then push the piston assembly all the way down until the connecting rod bearing seats on the crankshaft journal. Be careful not to allow the bearing cap screws to strike the crankshaft bearing journals and damage them.

9. After the piston and connecting rod assemblies have been installed, check the connecting rod side clearance on each crankshaft journal.

10. Prime and install the oil pump and the oil pump intake tube.

OHV Engines

CAMSHAFT, LIFTERS AND TIMING ASSEMBLY

1. Install the camshaft.
2. Install the lifters/followers into their bores.
3. Install the timing gears/chain assembly.

CYLINDER HEAD(S)

1. Install the cylinder head(s) using new gaskets.
2. Assemble the rest of the valve train (pushrods and rocker arms and/or shafts).

Engine Covers and Components

Install the timing cover(s) and oil pan. Refer to your notes and drawings made prior to disassembly and install all of the components that were removed. Install the engine into the vehicle.

Engine Start-up and Break-in

STARTING THE ENGINE

Now that the engine is installed and every wire and hose is properly connected, go back and double check that all coolant and vacuum hoses are connected. Check that you oil drain plug is installed and properly tightened. If not already done, install a new oil filter onto the engine. Fill the crankcase with the proper amount and grade of engine oil. Fill the cooling system with a 50/50 mixture of coolant/water.

1. Connect the vehicle battery.
2. Start the engine. Keep your eye on your oil pressure indicator; if it does not indicate oil pressure within 10 seconds of starting, turn the vehicle off.

✳✳ WARNING

Damage to the engine can result if it is allowed to run with no oil pressure. Check the engine oil level to make sure that it is full. Check for any leaks and if found, repair the leaks before continuing. If there is still no indication of oil pressure, you may need to prime the system.

3. Confirm that there are no fluid leaks (oil or other).
4. Allow the engine to reach normal operating temperature (the upper radiator hose will be hot to the touch).
5. If necessary, set the ignition timing.

6. Install any remaining components such as the air cleaner (if removed for ignition timing) or body panels which were removed.

BREAKING IT IN

Make the first miles on the new engine, easy ones. Vary the speed but do not accelerate hard. Most importantly, do not lug the engine, and avoid sustained high speeds until at least 100 miles. Check the engine oil and coolant levels frequently. Expect the engine to use a little oil until the rings seat. Change the oil and filter at 500 miles, 1500 miles, then every 3000 miles past that.

KEEP IT MAINTAINED

Now that you have just gone through all of that hard work, keep yourself from doing it all over again by thoroughly maintaining it. Not that you may not have maintained it before, heck you could have had one to two hundred thousand miles on it before doing this. However, you may have bought the vehicle used, and the previous owner did not keep up on maintenance. Which is why you just went through all of that hard work. See?

TORQUE SPECIFICATIONS

Components	English	Metric
3.9L Intake manifold bolts	12 ft. lbs.	16 Nm
5.2L/5.9L intake manifold bolts	12 ft. lbs.	16 Nm
Camshaft sprocket bolt	35 ft. lbs.	47 Nm
Converter Y-pipe-to-exhaust manifold	25 ft. lbs.	34 Nm
Crankshaft damper bolt	135 ft. lbs.	183 Nm
Cylinder head bolts	105 ft. lbs.**	143 Nm
Engine mount nuts	75 ft. lbs.	102 Nm
Exhaust manifold	25 ft. lbs.	34 Nm
Exhaust manifold-to-cylinder head	25 ft. lbs.	34 Nm
Exhaust pipe-to-manifold junction flange	19 ft. lbs.	26 Nm
Fan blade assembly-to-viscous fan clutch	17 ft. lbs.	23 Nm
Fan shroud mounting nuts	95 inch lbs.	11 Nm
Flywheel-to-driveplate	55 ft. lbs.	75 Nm
Heat shields	55 inch lbs.	6 Nm
Lifter yokes	200 inch lbs.	23 Nm
Main cap bolts	85 ft. lbs.	115 Nm
Oil pan bolts	200 inch lbs.	23 Nm
Oil pump bolts	30 ft. lbs.	41 Nm
Plenum pan bolts	84 inch lbs. **	9.5 Nm
Radiator mounting bolts	95 inch lbs.	2 Nm
Rocker arm retaining bolts	21 ft. lbs.	28 Nm
Rocker shaft bolts	200 inch lbs.	23 Nm
Starter bolts	50 ft. lbs.	68 Nm
Thermostat housing bolts	200 inch lbs.	23 Nm
Throttle body-to-intake manifold	200 inch lbs.	23 Nm
Timing cover bolts	30 ft. lbs.	41 Nm
Torque converter-to-drive plate	23 ft. lbs.	31 Nm
Transmission support bolts	50 ft. lbs.	68 Nm
Valve cover bolts	95 inch lbs.	11 Nm
Water pump bolts	30 ft. lbs.	40 Nm
Water pump pulley bolts	20 ft. lbs.	27 Nm
Yoke retainer	200 inch lbs.	23 Nm

** See Procedure

USING A VACUUM GAUGE

White needle = steady needle   *Dark needle = drifting needle*

The vacuum gauge is one of the most useful and easy-to-use diagnostic tools. It is inexpensive, easy to hook up, and provides valuable information about the condition of your engine.

Indication: Normal engine in good condition

Gauge reading: Steady, from 17–22 in./Hg.

Indication: Sticking valve or ignition miss

Gauge reading: Needle fluctuates from 15–20 in./Hg. at idle

Indication: Late ignition or valve timing, low compression, stuck throttle valve, leaking carburetor or manifold gasket.

Gauge reading: Low (15–20 in./Hg.) but steady

Indication: Improper carburetor adjustment, or minor intake leak at carburetor or manifold

NOTE: Bad fuel injector O-rings may also cause this reading.

Gauge reading: Drifting needle

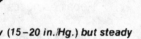
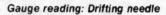

Indication: Weak valve springs, worn valve stem guides, or leaky cylinder head gasket (vibrating excessively at all speeds).

NOTE: A plugged catalytic converter may also cause this reading.

Gauge reading: Needle fluctuates as engine speed increases

Indication: Burnt valve or improper valve clearance. The needle will drop when the defective valve operates.

Gauge reading: Steady needle, but drops regularly

Indication: Choked muffler or obstruction in system. Speed up the engine. Choked muffler will exhibit a slow drop of vacuum to zero.

Gauge reading: Gradual drop in reading at idle

Indication: Worn valve guides

Gauge reading: Needle vibrates excessively at idle, but steadies as engine speed increases

TCCS3C01

Troubleshooting Engine Mechanical Problems

Problem	Cause	Solution
External oil leaks	• Cylinder head cover RTV sealant broken or improperly seated	• Replace sealant; inspect cylinder head cover sealant flange and cylinder head sealant surface for distortion and cracks
	• Oil filler cap leaking or missing	• Replace cap
	• Oil filter gasket broken or improperly seated	• Replace oil filter
	• Oil pan side gasket broken, improperly seated or opening in RTV sealant	• Replace gasket or repair opening in sealant; inspect oil pan gasket flange for distortion
	• Oil pan front oil seal broken or improperly seated	• Replace seal; inspect timing case cover and oil pan seal flange for distortion
	• Oil pan rear oil seal broken or improperly seated	• Replace seal; inspect oil pan rear oil seal flange; inspect rear main bearing cap for cracks, plugged oil return channels, or distortion in seal groove
	• Timing case cover oil seal broken or improperly seated	• Replace seal
	• Excess oil pressure because of restricted PCV valve	• Replace PCV valve
	• Oil pan drain plug loose or has stripped threads	• Repair as necessary and tighten
	• Rear oil gallery plug loose	• Use appropriate sealant on gallery plug and tighten
	• Rear camshaft plug loose or improperly seated	• Seat camshaft plug or replace and seal, as necessary
Excessive oil consumption	• Oil level too high	• Drain oil to specified level
	• Oil with wrong viscosity being used	• Replace with specified oil
	• PCV valve stuck closed	• Replace PCV valve
	• Valve stem oil deflectors (or seals) are damaged, missing, or incorrect type	• Replace valve stem oil deflectors
	• Valve stems or valve guides worn	• Measure stem-to-guide clearance and repair as necessary
	• Poorly fitted or missing valve cover baffles	• Replace valve cover
	• Piston rings broken or missing	• Replace broken or missing rings
	• Scuffed piston	• Replace piston
	• Incorrect piston ring gap	• Measure ring gap, repair as necessary
	• Piston rings sticking or excessively loose in grooves	• Measure ring side clearance, repair as necessary
	• Compression rings installed upside down	• Repair as necessary
	• Cylinder walls worn, scored, or glazed	• Repair as necessary

Troubleshooting Engine Mechanical Problems

Problem	Cause	Solution
Excessive oil consumption (cont.)	· Piston ring gaps not properly staggered · Excessive main or connecting rod bearing clearance	· Repair as necessary · Measure bearing clearance, repair as necessary
No oil pressure	· Low oil level · Oil pressure gauge, warning lamp or sending unit inaccurate · Oil pump malfunction · Oil pressure relief valve sticking · Oil passages on pressure side of pump obstructed · Oil pickup screen or tube obstructed · Loose oil inlet tube	· Add oil to correct level · Replace oil pressure gauge or warning lamp · Replace oil pump · Remove and inspect oil pressure relief valve assembly · Inspect oil passages for obstruction · Inspect oil pickup for obstruction · Tighten or seal inlet tube
Low oil pressure	· Low oil level · Inaccurate gauge, warning lamp or sending unit · Oil excessively thin because of dilution, poor quality, or improper grade · Excessive oil temperature · Oil pressure relief spring weak or sticking · Oil inlet tube and screen assembly has restriction or air leak · Excessive oil pump clearance · Excessive main, rod, or camshaft bearing clearance	· Add oil to correct level · Replace oil pressure gauge or warning lamp · Drain and refill crankcase with recommended oil · Correct cause of overheating engine · Remove and inspect oil pressure relief valve assembly · Remove and inspect oil inlet tube and screen assembly. (Fill inlet tube with lacquer thinner to locate leaks.) · Measure clearances · Measure bearing clearances, repair as necessary
High oil pressure	· Improper oil viscosity · Oil pressure gauge or sending unit inaccurate · Oil pressure relief valve sticking closed	· Drain and refill crankcase with correct viscosity oil · Replace oil pressure gauge · Remove and inspect oil pressure relief valve assembly
Main bearing noise	· Insufficient oil supply · Main bearing clearance excessive · Bearing insert missing · Crankshaft end-play excessive · Improperly tightened main bearing cap bolts · Loose flywheel or drive plate · Loose or damaged vibration damper	· Inspect for low oil level and low oil pressure · Measure main bearing clearance, repair as necessary · Replace missing insert · Measure end-play, repair as necessary · Tighten bolts with specified torque · Tighten flywheel or drive plate attaching bolts · Repair as necessary

TCCS3C03

Troubleshooting Engine Mechanical Problems

Problem	Cause	Solution
Connecting rod bearing noise	• Insufficient oil supply	• Inspect for low oil level and low oil pressure
	• Carbon build-up on piston	• Remove carbon from piston crown
	• Bearing clearance excessive or bearing missing	• Measure clearance, repair as necessary
	• Crankshaft connecting rod journal out-of-round	• Measure journal dimensions, repair or replace as necessary
	• Misaligned connecting rod or cap	• Repair as necessary
	• Connecting rod bolts tightened improperly	• Tighten bolts with specified torque
Piston noise	• Piston-to-cylinder wall clearance excessive (scuffed piston)	• Measure clearance and examine piston
	• Cylinder walls excessively tapered or out-of-round	• Measure cylinder wall dimensions, rebore cylinder
	• Piston ring broken	• Replace all rings on piston
	• Loose or seized piston pin	• Measure piston-to-pin clearance, repair as necessary
	• Connecting rods misaligned	• Measure rod alignment, straighten or replace
	• Piston ring side clearance excessively loose or tight	• Measure ring side clearance, repair as necessary
	• Carbon build-up on piston is excessive	• Remove carbon from piston
Valve actuating component noise	• Insufficient oil supply	• Check for: (a) Low oil level (b) Low oil pressure (c) Wrong hydraulic tappets (d) Restricted oil gallery (e) Excessive tappet to bore clearance
	• Rocker arms or pivots worn	• Replace worn rocker arms or pivots
	• Foreign objects or chips in hydraulic tappets	• Clean tappets
	• Excessive tappet leak-down	• Replace valve tappet
	• Tappet face worn	• Replace tappet; inspect corresponding cam lobe for wear
	• Broken or cocked valve springs	• Properly seat cocked springs; replace broken springs
	• Stem-to-guide clearance excessive	• Measure stem-to-guide clearance, repair as required
	• Valve bent	• Replace valve
	• Loose rocker arms	• Check and repair as necessary
	• Valve seat runout excessive	• Regrind valve seat/valves
	• Missing valve lock	• Install valve lock
	• Excessive engine oil	• Correct oil level

TCCS3C04

Troubleshooting Engine Performance

Problem	Cause	Solution
Hard starting (engine cranks normally)	• Faulty engine control system component	• Repair or replace as necessary
	• Faulty fuel pump	• Replace fuel pump
	• Faulty fuel system component	• Repair or replace as necessary
	• Faulty ignition coil	• Test and replace as necessary
	• Improper spark plug gap	• Adjust gap
	• Incorrect ignition timing	• Adjust timing
	• Incorrect valve timing	• Check valve timing; repair as necessary
Rough idle or stalling	• Incorrect curb or fast idle speed	• Adjust curb or fast idle speed (If possible)
	• Incorrect ignition timing	• Adjust timing to specification
	• Improper feedback system operation	• Refer to Chapter 4
	• Faulty EGR valve operation	• Test EGR system and replace as necessary
	• Faulty PCV valve air flow	• Test PCV valve and replace as necessary
	• Faulty TAC vacuum motor or valve	• Repair as necessary
	• Air leak into manifold vacuum	• Inspect manifold vacuum connections and repair as necessary
	• Faulty distributor rotor or cap	• Replace rotor or cap (Distributor systems only)
	• Improperly seated valves	• Test cylinder compression, repair as necessary
	• Incorrect ignition wiring	• Inspect wiring and correct as necessary
	• Faulty ignition coil	• Test coil and replace as necessary
	• Restricted air vent or idle passages	• Clean passages
	• Restricted air cleaner	• Clean or replace air cleaner filter element
Faulty low-speed operation	• Restricted idle air vents and passages	• Clean air vents and passages
	• Restricted air cleaner	• Clean or replace air cleaner filter element
	• Faulty spark plugs	• Clean or replace spark plugs
	• Dirty, corroded, or loose ignition secondary circuit wire connections	• Clean or tighten secondary circuit wire connections
	• Improper feedback system operation	• Refer to Chapter 4
	• Faulty ignition coil high voltage wire	• Replace ignition coil high voltage wire (Distributor systems only)
	• Faulty distributor cap	• Replace cap (Distributor systems only)
Faulty acceleration	• Incorrect ignition timing	• Adjust timing
	• Faulty fuel system component	• Repair or replace as necessary
	• Faulty spark plug(s)	• Clean or replace spark plug(s)
	• Improperly seated valves	• Test cylinder compression, repair as necessary
	• Faulty ignition coil	• Test coil and replace as necessary

TCCS3C05

Troubleshooting Engine Performance

Problem	Cause	Solution
Faulty acceleration (cont.)	• Improper feedback system operation	• Refer to Chapter 4
Faulty high speed operation	• Incorrect ignition timing • Faulty advance mechanism	• Adjust timing (if possible) • Check advance mechanism and repair as necessary (Distributor systems only)
	• Low fuel pump volume • Wrong spark plug air gap or wrong plug	• Replace fuel pump • Adjust air gap or install correct plug
	• Partially restricted exhaust manifold, exhaust pipe, catalytic converter, muffler, or tailpipe	• Eliminate restriction
	• Restricted vacuum passages • Restricted air cleaner	• Clean passages • Cleaner or replace filter element as necessary
	• Faulty distributor rotor or cap	• Replace rotor or cap (Distributor systems only)
	• Faulty ignition coil • Improperly seated valve(s)	• Test coil and replace as necessary • Test cylinder compression, repair as necessary
	• Faulty valve spring(s)	• Inspect and test valve spring tension, replace as necessary
	• Incorrect valve timing	• Check valve timing and repair as necessary
	• Intake manifold restricted	• Remove restriction or replace manifold
	• Worn distributor shaft	• Replace shaft (Distributor systems only)
	• Improper feedback system operation	• Refer to Chapter 4
Misfire at all speeds	• Faulty spark plug(s) • Faulty spark plug wire(s) • Faulty distributor cap or rotor	• Clean or relace spark plug(s) • Replace as necessary • Replace cap or rotor (Distributor systems only)
	• Faulty ignition coil • Primary ignition circuit shorted or open intermittently	• Test coil and replace as necessary • Troubleshoot primary circuit and repair as necessary
	• Improperly seated valve(s)	• Test cylinder compression, repair as necessary
	• Faulty hydraulic tappet(s) • Improper feedback system operation	• Clean or replace tappet(s) • Refer to Chapter 4
	• Faulty valve spring(s)	• Inspect and test valve spring tension, repair as necessary
	• Worn camshaft lobes • Air leak into manifold	• Replace camshaft • Check manifold vacuum and repair as necessary
	• Fuel pump volume or pressure low • Blown cylinder head gasket • Intake or exhaust manifold passage(s) restricted	• Replace fuel pump • Replace gasket • Pass chain through passage(s) and repair as necessary
Power not up to normal	• Incorrect ignition timing • Faulty distributor rotor	• Adjust timing • Replace rotor (Distributor systems only)

TCCS3C06

Troubleshooting Engine Performance

Problem	Cause	Solution
Power not up to normal (cont.)	• Incorrect spark plug gap • Faulty fuel pump • Faulty fuel pump • Incorrect valve timing • Faulty ignition coil • Faulty ignition wires • Improperly seated valves • Blown cylinder head gasket • Leaking piston rings • Improper feedback system operation	• Adjust gap • Replace fuel pump • Replace fuel pump • Check valve timing and repair as necessary • Test coil and replace as necessary • Test wires and replace as necessary • Test cylinder compression and repair as necessary • Replace gasket • Test compression and repair as necessary • Refer to Chapter 4
Intake backfire	• Improper ignition timing • Defective EGR component • Defective TAC vacuum motor or valve	• Adjust timing • Repair as necessary • Repair as necessary
Exhaust backfire	• Air leak into manifold vacuum • Faulty air injection diverter valve • Exhaust leak	• Check manifold vacuum and repair as necessary • Test diverter valve and replace as necessary • Locate and eliminate leak
Ping or spark knock	• Incorrect ignition timing • Distributor advance malfunction • Excessive combustion chamber deposits • Air leak into manifold vacuum • Excessively high compression • Fuel octane rating excessively low • Sharp edges in combustion chamber • EGR valve not functioning properly	• Adjust timing • Inspect advance mechanism and repair as necessary (Distributor systems only) • Remove with combustion chamber cleaner • Check manifold vacuum and repair as necessary • Test compression and repair as necessary • Try alternate fuel source • Grind smooth • Test EGR system and replace as necessary
Surging (at cruising to top speeds)	• Low fuel pump pressure or volume • Improper PCV valve air flow • Air leak into manifold vacuum • Incorrect spark advance • Restricted fuel filter • Restricted air cleaner • EGR valve not functioning properly • Improper feedback system operation	• Replace fuel pump • Test PCV valve and replace as necessary • Check manifold vacuum and repair as necessary • Test and replace as necessary • Replace fuel filter • Clean or replace air cleaner filter element • Test EGR system and replace as necessary • Refer to Chapter 4

Troubleshooting the Serpentine Drive Belt

Problem	Cause	Solution
Tension sheeting fabric failure (woven fabric on outside circumference of belt has cracked or separated from body of belt)	• Grooved or backside idler pulley diameters are less than minimum recommended • Tension sheeting contacting (rubbing) stationary object • Excessive heat causing woven fabric to age • Tension sheeting splice has fractured	• Replace pulley(s) not conforming to specification • Correct rubbing condition • Replace belt • Replace belt
Noise (objectional squeal, squeak, or rumble is heard or felt while drive belt is in operation)	• Belt slippage • Bearing noise • Belt misalignment • Belt-to-pulley mismatch • Driven component inducing vibration • System resonant frequency inducing vibration	• Adjust belt • Locate and repair • Align belt/pulley(s) • Install correct belt • Locate defective driven component and repair • Vary belt tension within specifications. Replace belt.
Rib chunking (one or more ribs has separated from belt body)	• Foreign objects imbedded in pulley grooves • Installation damage • Drive loads in excess of design specifications • Insufficient internal belt adhesion	• Remove foreign objects from pulley grooves • Replace belt • Adjust belt tension • Replace belt
Rib or belt wear (belt ribs contact bottom of pulley grooves)	• Pulley(s) misaligned • Mismatch of belt and pulley groove widths • Abrasive environment • Rusted pulley(s) • Sharp or jagged pulley groove tips • Rubber deteriorated	• Align pulley(s) • Replace belt • Replace belt • Clean rust from pulley(s) • Replace pulley • Replace belt
Longitudinal belt cracking (cracks between two ribs)	• Belt has mistracked from pulley groove • Pulley groove tip has worn away rubber-to-tensile member	• Replace belt • Replace belt
Belt slips	• Belt slipping because of insufficient tension • Belt or pulley subjected to substance (belt dressing, oil, ethylene glycol) that has reduced friction • Driven component bearing failure • Belt glazed and hardened from heat and excessive slippage	• Adjust tension • Replace belt and clean pulleys • Replace faulty component bearing • Replace belt
"Groove jumping" (belt does not maintain correct position on pulley, or turns over and/or runs off pulleys)	• Insufficient belt tension • Pulley(s) not within design tolerance • Foreign object(s) in grooves	• Adjust belt tension • Replace pulley(s) • Remove foreign objects from grooves

TCCS3C09

Troubleshooting the Serpentine Drive Belt

Problem	Cause	Solution
"Groove jumping" (belt does not maintain correct position on pulley, or turns over and/or runs off pulleys)	• Excessive belt speed • Pulley misalignment • Belt-to-pulley profile mismatched • Belt cordline is distorted	• Avoid excessive engine acceleration • Align pulley(s) • Install correct belt • Replace belt
Belt broken (Note: identify and correct problem before replacement belt is installed)	• Excessive tension • Tensile members damaged during belt installation • Belt turnover • Severe pulley misalignment • Bracket, pulley, or bearing failure	• Replace belt and adjust tension to specification • Replace belt • Replace belt • Align pulley(s) • Replace defective component and belt
Cord edge failure (tensile member exposed at edges of belt or separated from belt body)	• Excessive tension • Drive pulley misalignment • Belt contacting stationary object • Pulley irregularities • Improper pulley construction • Insufficient adhesion between tensile member and rubber matrix	• Adjust belt tension • Align pulley • Correct as necessary • Replace pulley • Replace pulley • Replace belt and adjust tension to specifications
Sporadic rib cracking (multiple cracks in belt ribs at random intervals)	• Ribbed pulley(s) diameter less than minimum specification • Backside bend flat pulley(s) diameter less than minimum • Excessive heat condition causing rubber to harden • Excessive belt thickness • Belt overcured • Excessive tension	• Replace pulley(s) • Replace pulley(s) • Correct heat condition as necessary • Replace belt • Replace belt • Adjust belt tension

TCCS3C10

Troubleshooting the Cooling System

Problem	Cause	Solution
High temperature gauge indication—overheating	• Coolant level low • Improper fan operation • Radiator hose(s) collapsed • Radiator airflow blocked • Faulty pressure cap • Ignition timing incorrect • Air trapped in cooling system • Heavy traffic driving • Incorrect cooling system component(s) installed • Faulty thermostat • Water pump shaft broken or impeller loose • Radiator tubes clogged • Cooling system clogged • Casting flash in cooling passages • Brakes dragging • Excessive engine friction • Antifreeze concentration over 68% • Missing air seals • Faulty gauge or sending unit • Loss of coolant flow caused by leakage or foaming • Viscous fan drive failed	• Replenish coolant • Repair or replace as necessary • Replace hose(s) • Remove restriction (bug screen, fog lamps, etc.) • Replace pressure cap • Adjust ignition timing • Purge air • Operate at fast idle in neutral intermittently to cool engine • Install proper component(s) • Replace thermostat • Replace water pump • Flush radiator • Flush system • Repair or replace as necessary. Flash may be visible by removing cooling system components or removing core plugs. • Repair brakes • Repair engine • Lower antifreeze concentration percentage • Replace air seals • Repair or replace faulty component • Repair or replace leaking component, replace coolant • Replace unit
Low temperature indication—undercooling	• Thermostat stuck open • Faulty gauge or sending unit	• Replace thermostat • Repair or replace faulty component
Coolant loss—boilover	• Overfilled cooling system • Quick shutdown after hard (hot) run • Air in system resulting in occasional "burping" of coolant • Insufficient antifreeze allowing coolant boiling point to be too low • Antifreeze deteriorated because of age or contamination • Leaks due to loose hose clamps, loose nuts, bolts, drain plugs, faulty hoses, or defective radiator	• Reduce coolant level to proper specification • Allow engine to run at fast idle prior to shutdown • Purge system • Add antifreeze to raise boiling point • Replace coolant • Pressure test system to locate source of leak(s) then repair as necessary

TCCS3C11

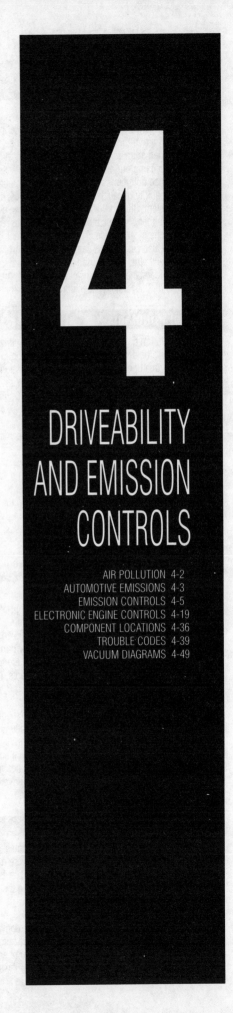

4

DRIVEABILITY
AND EMISSION
CONTROLS

AIR POLLUTION

The earth's atmosphere, at or near sea level, consists approximately of 78 percent nitrogen, 21 percent oxygen and 1 percent other gases. If it were possible to remain in this state, 100 percent clean air would result. However, many varied sources allow other gases and particulates to mix with the clean air, causing our atmosphere to become unclean or polluted.

Some of these pollutants are visible while others are invisible, with each having the capability of causing distress to the eyes, ears, throat, skin and respiratory system. Should these pollutants become concentrated in a specific area and under certain conditions, death could result due to the displacement or chemical change of the oxygen content in the air. These pollutants can also cause great damage to the environment and to the many man made objects that are exposed to the elements.

To better understand the causes of air pollution, the pollutants can be categorized into 3 separate types, natural, industrial and automotive.

Natural Pollutants

Natural pollution has been present on earth since before man appeared and continues to be a factor when discussing air pollution, although it causes only a small percentage of the overall pollution problem. It is the direct result of decaying organic matter, wind born smoke and particulates from such natural events as plain and forest fires (ignited by heat or lightning), volcanic ash, sand and dust which can spread over a large area of the countryside.

Such a phenomenon of natural pollution has been seen in the form of volcanic eruptions, with the resulting plume of smoke, steam and volcanic ash blotting out the sun's rays as it spreads and rises higher into the atmosphere. As it travels into the atmosphere the upper air currents catch and carry the smoke and ash, while condensing the steam back into water vapor. As the water vapor, smoke and ash travel on their journey, the smoke dissipates into the atmosphere while the ash and moisture settle back to earth in a trail hundreds of miles long. In some cases, lives are lost and millions of dollars of property damage result.

Industrial Pollutants

Industrial pollution is caused primarily by industrial processes, the burning of coal, oil and natural gas, which in turn produce smoke and fumes. Because the burning fuels contain large amounts of sulfur, the principal ingredients of smoke and fumes are sulfur dioxide and particulate matter. This type of pollutant occurs most severely during still, damp and cool weather, such as at night. Even in its less severe form, this pollutant is not confined to just cities. Because of air movements, the pollutants move for miles over the surrounding countryside, leaving in its path a barren and unhealthy environment for all living things.

Working with federal, state and local mandated regulations and by carefully monitoring emissions, big business has greatly reduced the amount of pollutant introduced from its industrial sources, striving to obtain an acceptable level. Because of the mandated industrial emission clean up, many land areas and streams in and around the cities that were formerly barren of vegetation and life, have now begun to move back in the direction of nature's intended balance.

Automotive Pollutants

The third major source of air pollution is automotive emissions. The emissions from the internal combustion engines were not an appreciable problem years ago because of the small number of registered vehicles and the nation's small highway system. However, during the early 1950's, the trend of the American people was to move from the cities to the surrounding suburbs. This caused an immediate problem in transportation because the majority of suburbs were not afforded mass transit conveniences. This lack of transportation created an attractive market for the automobile manufacturers, which resulted in a dramatic increase in the number of vehicles produced and sold, along with a marked increase in highway construction

between cities and the suburbs. Multi-vehicle families emerged with a growing emphasis placed on an individual vehicle per family member. As the increase in vehicle ownership and usage occurred, so did pollutant levels in and around the cities, as suburbanites drove daily to their businesses and employment, returning at the end of the day to their homes in the suburbs.

It was noted that a smoke and fog type haze was being formed and at times, remained in suspension over the cities, taking time to dissipate. At first this "smog," derived from the words "smoke" and "fog," was thought to result from industrial pollution but it was determined that automobile emissions shared the blame. It was discovered that when normal automobile emissions were exposed to sunlight for a period of time, complex chemical reactions would take place.

It is now known that smog is a photo chemical layer which develops when certain oxides of nitrogen (NOx) and unburned hydrocarbons (HC) from automobile emissions are exposed to sunlight. Pollution was more severe when smog would become stagnant over an area in which a warm layer of air settled over the top of the cooler air mass, trapping and holding the cooler mass at ground level. The trapped cooler air would keep the emissions from being dispersed and diluted through normal air flows. This type of air stagnation was given the name "Temperature Inversion."

TEMPERATURE INVERSION

In normal weather situations, surface air is warmed by heat radiating from the earth's surface and the sun's rays. This causes it to rise upward, into the atmosphere. Upon rising it will cool through a convection type heat exchange with the cooler upper air. As warm air rises, the surface pollutants are carried upward and dissipated into the atmosphere.

When a temperature inversion occurs, we find the higher air is no longer cooler, but is warmer than the surface air, causing the cooler surface air to become trapped. This warm air blanket can extend from above ground level to a few hundred or even a few thousand feet into the air. As the surface air is trapped, so are the pollutants, causing a severe smog condition. Should this stagnant air mass extend to a few thousand feet high, enough air movement with the inversion takes place to allow the smog layer to rise above ground level but the pollutants still cannot dissipate. This inversion can remain for days over an area, with the smog level only rising or lowering from ground level to a few hundred feet high. Meanwhile, the pollutant levels increase, causing eye irritation, respiratory problems, reduced visibility, plant damage and in some cases, even disease.

This inversion phenomenon was first noted in the Los Angeles, California area. The city lies in terrain resembling a basin and with certain weather conditions, a cold air mass is held in the basin while a warmer air mass covers it like a lid.

Because this type of condition was first documented as prevalent in the Los Angeles area, this type of trapped pollution was named Los Angeles Smog, although it occurs in other areas where a large concentration of automobiles are used and the air remains stagnant for any length of time.

HEAT TRANSFER

Consider the internal combustion engine as a machine in which raw materials must be placed so a finished product comes out. As in any machine operation, a certain amount of wasted material is formed. When we relate this to the internal combustion engine, we find that through the input of air and fuel, we obtain power during the combustion process to drive the vehicle. The by-product or waste of this power is, in part, heat and exhaust gases with which we must dispose.

The heat from the combustion process can rise to over 4000°F (2204°C). The dissipation of this heat is controlled by a ram air effect, the use of cooling fans to cause air flow and a liquid coolant solution surrounding the combustion area to transfer the heat of combustion through the cylinder walls and into the coolant. The coolant is then directed to a thin-finned, multi-tubed radiator, from which the excess heat is transferred to the atmosphere by 1 of the 3 heat transfer methods, conduction, convection or radiation.

The cooling of the combustion area is an important part in the control of exhaust emissions. To understand the behavior of the combustion and transfer of its heat, consider the air/fuel charge. It is ignited and the flame front burns progressively across the combustion chamber until the burning charge reaches the cylinder walls. Some of the fuel in contact with the walls is not hot enough to burn, thereby snuffing out or quenching the combustion process. This leaves unburned fuel in the combustion chamber. This unburned fuel is then forced out of the cylinder and into the exhaust system, along with the exhaust gases.

Many attempts have been made to minimize the amount of unburned fuel in the combustion chambers due to quenching, by increasing the coolant temperature and lessening the contact area of the coolant around the combustion area. However, design limitations within the combustion chambers prevent the complete burning of the air/fuel charge, so a certain amount of the unburned fuel is still expelled into the exhaust system, regardless of modifications to the engine.

AUTOMOTIVE EMISSIONS

Before emission controls were mandated on internal combustion engines, other sources of engine pollutants were discovered along with the exhaust emissions. It was determined that engine combustion exhaust produced approximately 60 percent of the total emission pollutants, fuel evaporation from the fuel tank and carburetor vents produced 20 percent, with the final 20 percent being produced through the crankcase as a by-product of the combustion process.

Exhaust Gases

The exhaust gases emitted into the atmosphere are a combination of burned and unburned fuel. To understand the exhaust emission and its composition, we must review some basic chemistry.

When the air/fuel mixture is introduced into the engine, we are mixing air, composed of nitrogen (78 percent), oxygen (21 percent) and other gases (1 percent) with the fuel, which is 100 percent hydrocarbons (HC), in a semi-controlled ratio. As the combustion process is accomplished, power is produced to move the vehicle while the heat of combustion is transferred to the cooling system. The exhaust gases are then composed of nitrogen, a diatomic gas (N_2), the same as was introduced in the engine, carbon dioxide (CO_2), the same gas that is used in beverage carbonation, and water vapor (H_2O). The nitrogen (N_2), for the most part, passes through the engine unchanged, while the oxygen (O_2) reacts (burns) with the hydrocarbons (HC) and produces the carbon dioxide (CO_2) and the water vapors (H_2O). If this chemical process would be the only process to take place, the exhaust emissions would be harmless. However, during the combustion process, other compounds are formed which are considered dangerous. These pollutants are hydrocarbons (HC), carbon monoxide (CO), oxides of nitrogen (NOx) oxides of sulfur (SOx) and engine particulates.

HYDROCARBONS

Hydrocarbons (HC) are essentially fuel which was not burned during the combustion process or which has escaped into the atmosphere through fuel evaporation. The main sources of incomplete combustion are rich air/fuel mixtures, low engine temperatures and improper spark timing. The main sources of hydrocarbon emission through fuel evaporation on most vehicles used to be the vehicle's fuel tank and carburetor float bowl.

To reduce combustion hydrocarbon emission, engine modifications were made to minimize dead space and surface area in the combustion chamber. In addition, the air/fuel mixture was made more lean through the improved control which feedback carburetion and fuel injection offers and by the addition of external controls to aid in further combustion of the hydrocarbons outside the engine. Two such methods were the addition of air injection systems, to inject fresh air into the exhaust manifolds and the installation of catalytic converters, units that are able to burn traces of hydrocarbons without affecting the internal combustion process or fuel economy.

To control hydrocarbon emissions through fuel evaporation, modifications were made to the fuel tank to allow storage of the fuel vapors during periods of engine shut-down. Modifications were also made to the air intake system so that at specific times during engine operation, these vapors may be purged and burned by blending them with the air/fuel mixture.

CARBON MONOXIDE

Carbon monoxide is formed when not enough oxygen is present during the combustion process to convert carbon (C) to carbon dioxide (CO_2). An increase in the carbon monoxide (CO) emission is normally accompanied by an increase in the hydrocarbon (HC) emission because of the lack of oxygen to completely burn all of the fuel mixture.

Carbon monoxide (CO) also increases the rate at which the photo chemical smog is formed by speeding up the conversion of nitric oxide (NO) to nitrogen dioxide (NO_2). To accomplish this, carbon monoxide (CO) combines with oxygen (O_2) and nitric oxide (NO) to produce carbon dioxide (CO_2) and nitrogen dioxide (NO_2). ($CO + O_2 + NO = CO_2 + NO_2$).

The dangers of carbon monoxide, which is an odorless and colorless toxic gas are many. When carbon monoxide is inhaled into the lungs and passed into the blood stream, oxygen is replaced by the carbon monoxide in the red blood cells, causing a reduction in the amount of oxygen supplied to the many parts of the body. This lack of oxygen causes headaches, lack of coordination, reduced mental alertness and, should the carbon monoxide concentration be high enough, death could result.

NITROGEN

Normally, nitrogen is an inert gas. When heated to approximately 2500°F (1371°C) through the combustion process, this gas becomes active and causes an increase in the nitric oxide (NO) emission.

Oxides of nitrogen (NOx) are composed of approximately 97–98 percent nitric oxide (NO). Nitric oxide is a colorless gas but when it is passed into the atmosphere, it combines with oxygen and forms nitrogen dioxide (NO_2). The nitrogen dioxide then combines with chemically active hydrocarbons (HC) and when in the presence of sunlight, causes the formation of photo-chemical smog.

Ozone

To further complicate matters, some of the nitrogen dioxide (NO_2) is broken apart by the sunlight to form nitric oxide and oxygen. (NO_2 + sunlight = NO + O). This single atom of oxygen then combines with diatomic (meaning 2 atoms) oxygen (O_2) to form ozone (O_3). Ozone is one of the smells associated with smog. It has a pungent and offensive odor, irritates the eyes and lung tissues, affects the growth of plant life and causes rapid deterioration of rubber products. Ozone can be formed by sunlight as well as electrical discharge into the air.

The most common discharge area on the automobile engine is the secondary ignition electrical system, especially when inferior quality spark plug cables are used. As the surge of high voltage is routed through the secondary cable, the circuit builds up an electrical field around the wire, which acts upon the oxygen in the surrounding air to form the ozone. The faint glow along the cable with the engine running that may be visible on a dark night, is called the "corona discharge." It is the result of the electrical field passing from a high along the cable, to a low in the surrounding air, which forms the ozone gas. The combination of corona and ozone has been a major cause of cable deterioration. Recently, different and better quality insulating materials have lengthened the life of the electrical cables.

Although ozone at ground level can be harmful, ozone is beneficial to the earth's inhabitants. By having a concentrated ozone layer called the "ozonosphere," between 10 and 20 miles (16–32 km) up in the atmosphere, much of the ultra violet radiation from the sun's rays are absorbed and screened. If this ozone layer were not present, much of the earth's surface would be burned, dried and unfit for human life.

OXIDES OF SULFUR

Oxides of sulfur (SOx) were initially ignored in the exhaust system emissions, since the sulfur content of gasoline as a fuel is less than $\frac{1}{10}$ of 1 percent. Because of this small amount, it was felt that it contributed very little to the overall pollution problem. However, because of the difficulty in solving the sulfur emissions in industrial pollution and the introduction of catalytic converter to the automobile exhaust systems, a change was mandated. The automobile exhaust system, when equipped with a catalytic converter, changes the sulfur dioxide (SO_2) into sulfur trioxide (SO_3).

When this combines with water vapors (H_2O), a sulfuric acid mist (H_2SO_4) is formed and is a very difficult pollutant to handle since it is extremely corrosive. This sulfuric acid mist that is formed, is the same mist that rises from the vents of an automobile battery when an active chemical reaction takes place within the battery cells.

When a large concentration of vehicles equipped with catalytic converters are operating in an area, this acid mist may rise and be distributed over a large ground area causing land, plant, crop, paint and building damage.

PARTICULATE MATTER

A certain amount of particulate matter is present in the burning of any fuel, with carbon constituting the largest percentage of the particulates. In gasoline, the remaining particulates are the burned remains of the various other compounds used in its manufacture. When a gasoline engine is in good internal condition, the particulate emissions are low but as the engine wears internally, the particulate emissions increase. By visually inspecting the tail pipe emissions, a determination can be made as to where an engine defect may exist. An engine with light gray or blue smoke emitting from the tail pipe normally indicates an increase in the oil consumption through burning due to internal engine wear. Black smoke would indicate a defective fuel delivery system, causing the engine to operate in a rich mode. Regardless of the color of the smoke, the internal part of the engine or the fuel delivery system should be repaired to prevent excess particulate emissions.

Diesel and turbine engines emit a darkened plume of smoke from the exhaust system because of the type of fuel used. Emission control regulations are mandated for this type of emission and more stringent measures are being used to prevent excess emission of the particulate matter. Electronic components are being introduced to control the injection of the fuel at precisely the proper time of piston travel, to achieve the optimum in fuel ignition and fuel usage. Other particulate after-burning components are being tested to achieve a cleaner emission.

Good grades of engine lubricating oils should be used, which meet the manufacturers specification. Cut-rate oils can contribute to the particulate emission problem because of their low flash or ignition temperature point. Such oils burn prematurely during the combustion process causing emission of particulate matter.

The cooling system is an important factor in the reduction of particulate matter. The optimum combustion will occur, with the cooling system operating at a temperature specified by the manufacturer. The cooling system must be maintained in the same manner as the engine oiling system, as each system is required to perform properly in order for the engine to operate efficiently for a long time.

Crankcase Emissions

Crankcase emissions are made up of water, acids, unburned fuel, oil fumes and particulates. These emissions are classified as hydrocarbons (HC) and are formed by the small amount of unburned, compressed air/fuel mixture entering the crankcase from the combustion area (between the cylinder walls and piston rings) during the compression and power strokes. The head of the compression and combustion help to form the remaining crankcase emissions.

Since the first engines, crankcase emissions were allowed into the atmosphere through a road draft tube, mounted on the lower side of the engine block. Fresh air came in through an open oil filler cap or breather. The air passed through the crankcase mixing with blow-by gases. The motion of the vehicle and the air blowing past the open end of the road draft tube caused a low pressure area (vacuum) at the end of the tube. Crankcase emissions were simply drawn out of the road draft tube into the air.

To control the crankcase emission, the road draft tube was deleted. A hose and/or tubing was routed from the crankcase to the intake manifold so the blow-by emission could be burned with the air/fuel mixture. However, it was found that intake manifold vacuum, used to draw the crankcase emissions into the manifold, would vary in strength at the wrong time and not allow the proper emission flow. A regulating valve was needed to control the flow of air through the crankcase.

Testing, showed the removal of the blow-by gases from the crankcase as quickly as possible, was most important to the longevity of the engine. Should large accumulations of blow-by gases remain and condense, dilution of the engine oil would occur to form water, soots, resins, acids and lead salts, resulting in the formation of sludge and varnishes. This condensation of the blow-by gases occurs more frequently on vehicles used in numerous starting and stopping conditions, excessive idling and when the engine is not allowed to attain normal operating temperature through short runs.

Evaporative Emissions

Gasoline fuel is a major source of pollution, before and after it is burned in the automobile engine. From the time the fuel is refined, stored, pumped and transported, again stored until it is pumped into the fuel tank of the vehicle, the gasoline gives off unburned hydrocarbons (HC) into the atmosphere. Through the redesign of storage areas and venting systems, the pollution factor was diminished, but not eliminated, from the refinery standpoint. However, the automobile still remained the primary source of vaporized, unburned hydrocarbon (HC) emissions.

Fuel pumped from an underground storage tank is cool but when exposed to a warmer ambient temperature, will expand. Before controls were mandated, an owner might fill the fuel tank with fuel from an underground storage tank and park the vehicle for some time in warm area, such as a parking lot. As the fuel would warm, it would expand and should no provisions or area be provided for the expansion, the fuel would spill out of the filler neck and onto the ground, causing hydrocarbon (HC) pollution and creating a severe fire hazard. To correct this condition, the vehicle manufacturers added overflow plumbing and/or gasoline tanks with built in expansion areas or domes.

However, this did not control the fuel vapor emission from the fuel tank. It was determined that most of the fuel evaporation occurred when the vehicle was stationary and the engine not operating. Most vehicles carry 5–25 gallons (19–95 liters) of gasoline. Should a large concentration of vehicles be parked in one area, such as a large parking lot, excessive fuel vapor emissions would take place, increasing as the temperature increases.

To prevent the vapor emission from escaping into the atmosphere, the fuel systems were designed to trap the vapors while the vehicle is stationary, by sealing the system from the atmosphere. A storage system is used to collect and hold the fuel vapors from the carburetor (if equipped) and the fuel tank when the engine is not operating. When the engine is started, the storage system is then purged of the fuel vapors, which are drawn into the engine and burned with the air/fuel mixture.

EMISSION CONTROLS

Crankcase Ventilation System

OPERATION

▶ **See Figures 1, 2, 3 and 4**

When the engine is running, a small portion of the gases which are formed in the combustion chamber leak by the piston rings and enter the crankcase. Since these gases are under pressure they tend to escape from the crankcase and enter into the atmosphere. If these gases are allowed to remain in the crankcase for any length of time, they would contaminate the engine oil and cause sludge to build up. If the gases are allowed to escape into the atmosphere, they would pollute the air, as they contain unburned hydrocarbons. The crankcase emission control equipment recycles these gases back into the engine combustion chamber, where they are burned.

Crankcase gases are recycled in the following manner. While the engine is running, clean filtered air is drawn into the crankcase through the intake

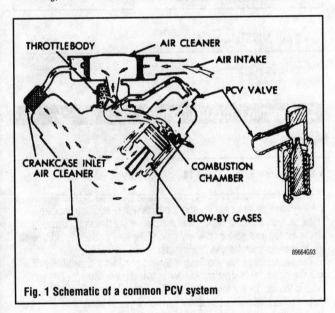

Fig. 1 Schematic of a common PCV system

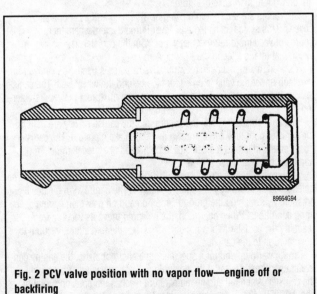

Fig. 2 PCV valve position with no vapor flow—engine off or backfiring

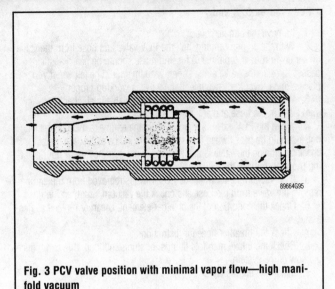

Fig. 3 PCV valve position with minimal vapor flow—high manifold vacuum

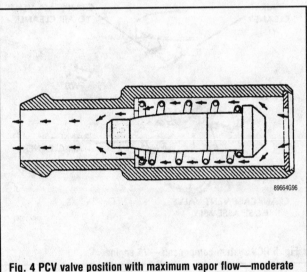

Fig. 4 PCV valve position with maximum vapor flow—moderate intake manifold vacuum

air filter and then through a hose leading to the oil filler cap or the valve cover. As the air passes through the crankcase it picks up the combustion gases and carries them out of the crankcase, up through the PCV valve and into the intake manifold. After they enter the intake manifold they are drawn into the combustion chamber and are burned.

The most critical component of the system is the PCV valve. This vacuum-controlled valve regulates the amount of gases which are recycled into the combustion chamber. At low engine speeds the valve is partially closed, limiting the flow of gases into the intake manifold. As engine speed increases, the valve opens to admit greater quantities of the gases into the intake manifold. If the valve should become blocked or plugged, the gases will be prevented from escaping the crankcase by the normal route. Since these gases are under pressure, they will find their own way out of the crankcase. This alternate route is usually a weak oil seal or gasket in the engine. As the gas escapes by the gasket, it also creates an oil leak. Besides causing oil leaks, a clogged PCV valve also allows these gases to remain in the crankcase for an extended period of time, promoting the formation of sludge in the engine.

COMPONENT TESTING

▶ See Figures 5, 6 and 7

1. Remove the engine cover.
2. With the engine running, pull the PCV valve and hose from the valve rocker cover rubber grommet. A hissing noise should be heard as air passes through the valve and a strong vacuum should be felt when you place a finger over the valve inlet if the valve is working properly.
3. While you have your finger over the PCV valve inlet, check for vacuum leaks in the hose and at the connections.
4. When the PCV valve is removed from the engine, a metallic clicking noise should be heard when it is shaken. This indicates that the metal check ball inside the valve is still free and is not gummed up. If not operating properly, replace the valve.
5. If no vacuum is felt when the PCV valve is removed from the engine, remove the valve from the hose and check the vacuum supply in the hose.
6. Check the condition of the breather element. Clean or replace as necessary.
7. Check the breather hose for restrictions.
8. Check the intake manifold fittings for sludge buildup, this can reduce the flow of the system.
9. Install the engine cover.

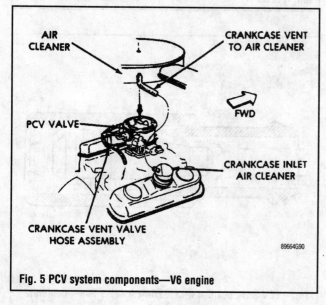

Fig. 5 PCV system components—V6 engine

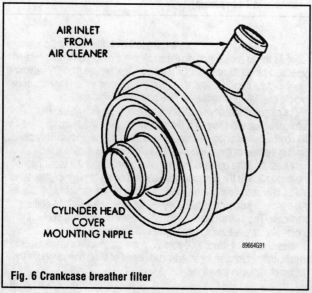

Fig. 6 Crankcase breather filter

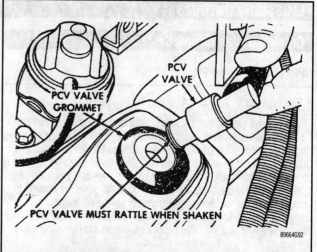

Fig. 7 The PCV valve fits into a grommet on the valve cover; replace the grommet if it leaks

REMOVAL & INSTALLATION

Refer to Section 1 for removal and installation of the PCV valve and breather element.

Evaporative Emission Controls

OPERATION

▶ See Figures 8, 9, 10 and 11

Changes in atmospheric temperature cause fuel tanks to breathe, that is, the air within the tank expands and contracts with outside temperature changes. If an unsealed system was used, when the temperature rises, air would escape through the tank vent tube or the vent in the tank cap. The air which escapes contains gasoline vapors.

The Evaporative Emission Control System provides a sealed fuel system with the capability to store and condense fuel vapors. When the fuel evaporates in the fuel tank, the vapor passes through vent hoses or tubes to a carbon filled evaporative canister. When the engine is operating the vapors are drawn into the intake manifold.

The vapors are drawn into the engine at idle as well as at operating speeds. This system is called a Bi-level Purge System where there is a dual source of vacuum to remove fuel vapor from the canister. The source of vacuum at idle is a tee in the PCV system.

A sealed, maintenance free evaporative canister is used. The canister is mounted under the vehicle on either side behind the wheel well. The canister is filled with granules of an activated carbon mixture. Fuel vapors entering the canister are absorbed by the charcoal granules.

Fuel tank pressure vents fuel vapors into the canister. They are held in the canister until they can be drawn into the intake manifold. The canister purge solenoid allows the canister to be purged at a predetermined time and engine operating conditions.

Vacuum for the canister is controlled by the canister purge solenoid. The solenoid is operated by the engine controller. The controller regulates the solenoid by switching the ground circuit on and off based on engine operating conditions. When energized, the solenoid prevents vacuum from reaching the canister. When not energized the solenoid allows vacuum to flow through to the canister.

During warm up and for a specified time after hot starts, the engine controller energizes (grounds) the solenoid preventing vacuum from reaching the canister. When the engine temperature reaches the operating level of about 120°F (49°C), the engine controller removes the ground from the solenoid allowing vacuum to flow through the canister and purges vapors through the throttle body. During certain idle conditions, the purge solenoid may be grounded to control fuel mix calibrations.

The fuel tank is sealed with a pressure-vacuum relief filler cap. The relief valves in the cap are a safety feature, preventing excessive pressure or vacuum in the fuel tank. If the cap is malfunctioning, and needs to be replaced, ensure that the replacement is the identical cap to ensure correct system operation.

During warm up and for a specified time after hot starts, the engine controller energizes (grounds) the solenoid preventing vacuum from reaching the canister. When the engine temperature reaches the operating level of about 120°F (49°C), the engine controller removes the ground from the solenoid allowing vacuum to flow through the canister and purges vapors through the throttle body. During certain idle conditions, the purge solenoid may be grounded to control fuel mix calibrations.

1996–98 vehicles have added system components due to the EVAP system monitor incorporated in the OBD-II engine control system used on these years. Two, instead of one, EVAP canisters are used and they are mounted on the drivers side of the vehicle instead of the passenger side. The canister purge solenoid is located on the bracket with the canisters. A Leak Detection Pump (LDP) is used to actually monitor the EVAP system for leaks. It is located on the driver's side inner fender wheelhouse. A test port for pressurizing the EVAP system is included and located below the

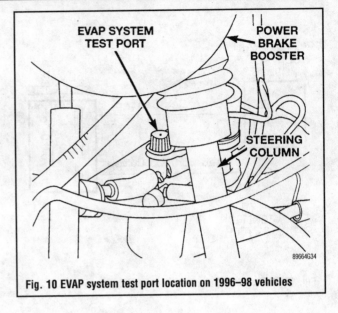

Fig. 10 EVAP system test port location on 1996–98 vehicles

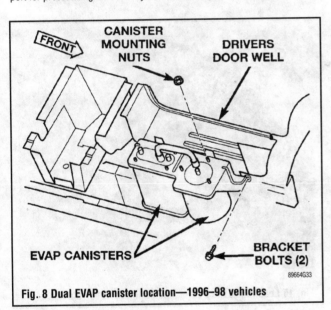

Fig. 8 Dual EVAP canister location—1996–98 vehicles

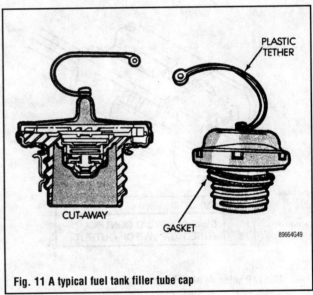

Fig. 11 A typical fuel tank filler tube cap

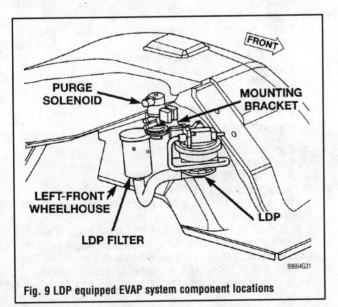

Fig. 9 LDP equipped EVAP system component locations

brake booster on a tube that comes off the LDP. The test port is used to pressurize the system with a special gas and serious precautions must be taken to avoid damage to the EVAP system and the fuel tank. This is a procedure best suited to a professional shop, due to the precautions and the equipment needed to test this system. The ECM can store trouble codes for EVAP system performance, a list of the codes is provided later in this section. Normal testing procedure can be used for any component listed in EVAP testing in this book.

COMPONENT TESTING

➡To relieve fuel tank pressure, the filler cap must be removed before disconnecting any fuel system component.

Canister Purge Solenoid

◗ See Figures 12 and 13

1. Remove the engine cover.
2. With the ignition off, unplug the connector on the EVAP solenoid.
3. Turn ignition on, measure the voltage at the ignition switch output line, voltage should be 10.0v or more. If voltage is not 10.0v or more, repair circuit from ignition switch to EVAP solenoid.

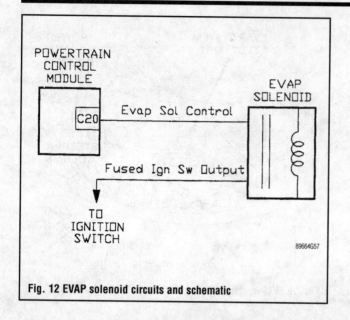

Fig. 12 EVAP solenoid circuits and schematic

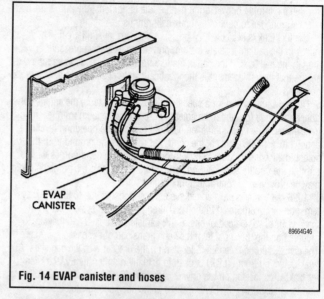

Fig. 14 EVAP canister and hoses

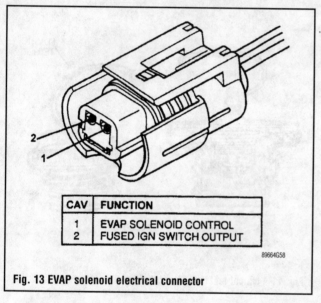

CAV	FUNCTION
1	EVAP SOLENOID CONTROL
2	FUSED IGN SWITCH OUTPUT

Fig. 13 EVAP solenoid electrical connector

Fig. 15 Location of the EVAP canister on pre-1996 vehicles

4. Disconnect the negative battery cable.
5. Disconnect the ECM harness from the ECM.
6. Check the resistance of the EVAP solenoid control circuit between the ECM harness connector and the EVAP solenoid connector. Resistance should be less than 5.0 ohms; if not, repair the opening in the circuit.
7. Install the engine cover.
8. Connect the negative battery cable.

REMOVAL & INSTALLATION

➡To relieve fuel tank pressure, the filler cap must be removed before disconnecting any fuel system component.

Evaporative (Carbon) Canister

▶ See Figures 14 thru 19

1. Disconnect the negative battery cable.
2. Raise and support the vehicle.
3. Label and disconnect the hoses on the top of the canister.
4. Remove the bolt on the canister retaining strap.
5. Remove the two-piece strap and canister together.

To install:
6. Install the two-piece strap and canister in the mounting bracket.
7. Install and tighten the retaining strap bolt to 95 inch lbs. (10 Nm).
8. Install the hoses in their proper locations.
9. Lower the vehicle.
10. Connect the negative battery cable.

Canister Purge Solenoid

▶ See Figures 20 and 21

1. Disconnect the negative battery cable.
2. Remove the engine cover.
3. Disconnect the solenoid wiring harness.
4. Disconnect the vacuum harness.
5. The rest of the procedure is different for some model years. The differences are as follows:

a. On 1989–92 TBI vehicles, remove the solenoid mounting pack as an assembly. Depress the tab on top of the purge solenoid and slide the solenoid downward to release it from the bracket.

b. On 1993–95 MFI vehicles, remove the solenoid and support bracket as an assembly.

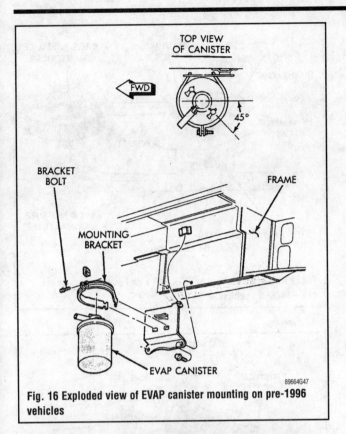

Fig. 16 Exploded view of EVAP canister mounting on pre-1996 vehicles

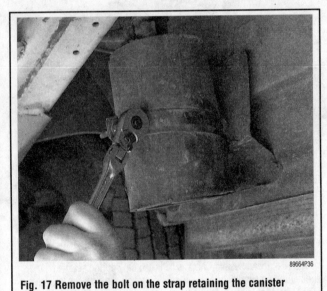

Fig. 17 Remove the bolt on the strap retaining the canister

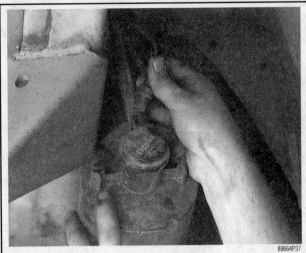

Fig. 18 Mark the lines connected to the EVAP canister before removal to ease installation

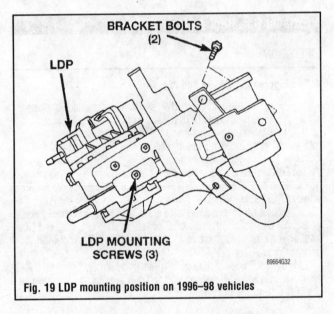

Fig. 19 LDP mounting position on 1996–98 vehicles

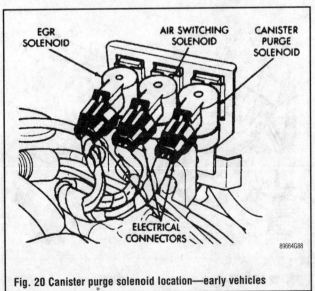

Fig. 20 Canister purge solenoid location—early vehicles

    c. On 1996–98 vehicles, remove the solenoid from the support bracket.

To install:

6. The procedures for the different model years are as follows:

    a. On 1989–92 TBI vehicles, install a new solenoid onto the solenoid pack bracket, and snap the retaining tab into place. Mount the solenoid pack onto the vehicle and tighten the retaining bolts.

    b. On 1993–95 MFI vehicles, install the bracket and solenoid assembly onto the vehicle and tighten the retaining bolts.

    c. On 1996–98 vehicles, install the solenoid onto the support bracket.

7. Connect the vacuum harness.

8. Connect the wiring harness.

9. Install the engine cover.

10. Connect the negative battery cable.

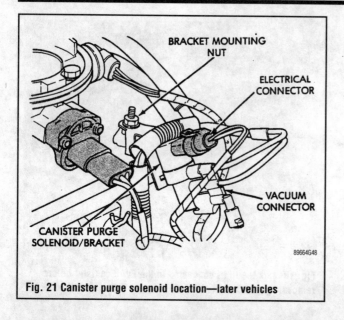

Fig. 21 Canister purge solenoid location—later vehicles

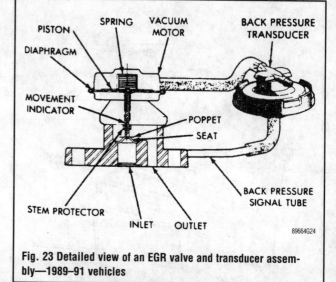

Fig. 23 Detailed view of an EGR valve and transducer assembly—1989–91 vehicles

Exhaust Gas Recirculation System

OPERATION

▶ See Figures 22, 23, 24 and 25

The Exhaust Gas Recirculation (EGR) system reduces oxides of nitrogen (NOx) in engine exhaust and helps prevent spark knock. This is accomplished by allowing a predetermined amount of hot exhaust gas to recirculate and dilute the incoming fuel/air mixture. This dilution reduces peak flame temperature during combustion.

The EGR system is a backpressure type. A backpressure transducer measures the amount of exhaust backpressure on the exhaust side of the EGR valve and varies the strength of the vacuum signal applied to the EGR valve. The transducer uses this backpressure signal to provide the correct amount of Exhaust Gas Recirculation under all conditions. The 3.9L, 5.2L and 5.9L engines use manifold vacuum controlled by a electronically controlled vacuum solenoid.

EGR System On-Board Diagnostics (California Vehicles Only): All California vehicles with EGR systems have an On-Board Diagnostic System for the EGR system. The Diagnostic System uses a solenoid in the vacuum sig-

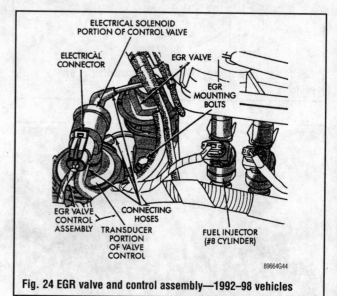

Fig. 24 EGR valve and control assembly—1992–98 vehicles

nal line to the EGR valve. The system is monitored by the ECM during certain driving conditions, and if a fault is detected, turns on the Check Engine Light and stores a DTC. If a EGR fault is retrieved from the ECM, use the testing procedures provided later to diagnose the system.

The Diagnostic System Check is activated only during selected engine/driving conditions to avoid mis-diagnosis, and checks the entire EGR system for failures. The engine controller monitors EGR system performance and registers a fault code if the system has failed or degraded, and the dash-mounted check engine light is turned on indicating immediate service is required.

If a malfunction is indicated by a check engine light and a fault code for EGR system, proper operation of the EGR system should be checked. If the EGR system is found to be functioning correctly, the on-board diagnostics system should then be checked.

COMPONENT TESTING

EGR Control System Test

1. Remove the engine cover.
2. Start and warm up the engine.

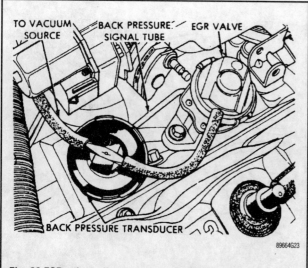

Fig. 22 EGR valve and transducer—1989–91 vehicles

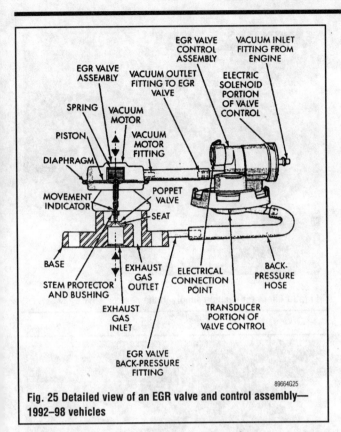

Fig. 25 Detailed view of an EGR valve and control assembly—1992–98 vehicles

Fig. 27 Using a hand held vacuum pump to verify EGR diaphragm operation

3. Allow it to idle with the parking brake firmly set.

4. Allow the engine to idle in Neutral with the throttle closed, then quickly accelerate the engine speed to approximately 2000 rpm.

5. Watch the EGR movement indicator (groove) on the valve stem. If the valve stem moves, the EGR system is operating correctly.

6. If no movement is noted, continue diagnosis with other EGR tests.

EGR Gas Flow Test

▶ See Figures 26 and 27

1. Remove the engine cover.
2. Connect a tachometer to the engine.
3. Remove the vacuum hose or rubber elbow from the EGR valve and connect a hand vacuum pump to the EGR valve vacuum nipple.

Fig. 26 Disconnect the EGR vacuum line

4. Start the engine and slowly apply vacuum to the EGR valve diaphragm.

5. The engine speed should drop as vacuum reaches 3–5 in. Hg and continue to drop as more vacuum is applied. The engine may even stall. This means EGR gas is flowing through the system.

6. If the engine speed doesn't drop, check for a failed EGR valve or plugged EGR passage. Remove the EGR valve and inspect/repair as necessary.

EGR Valve Leakage Test

1. Disconnect the negative battery cable.
2. Remove the engine cover.
3. Disconnect the hose from the fitting from the top of the EGR valve.
4. Connect a hand-held vacuum pump to the fitting and apply 15 inches of vacuum to the valve. Observe the gauge reading on the pump; if vacuum falls off, the diaphragm in the EGR valve has ruptured, and the EGR valve must be replaced. If vacuum remains, proceed to next step.
5. Remove the hose from the bottom of the EGR valve. Using compressed air (if available) and an air nozzle with rubber tip, apply 50 psi of regulated air pressure to the fitting.
6. Using your hand, open the throttle all the way, and listen inside the throttle body, if air is escaping, the poppet valve in the base of the EGR valve is leaking. Replace the EGR valve.

EGR Vacuum Transducer Valve Control

▶ See Figures 28, 29, 30 and 31

1. Remove the engine cover.
2. Remove the hose on the bottom of the EGR valve control.
3. Connect a hand-held vacuum pump to the fitting and apply 10 inches of vacuum. If the vacuum falls off, the valve control diaphragm is leaking. Replace the EGR valve control and retest. If OK, connect hose proceed to next step.
4. Remove the hose at the EGR valve control inlet.
5. Connect a vacuum gauge to this hose.
6. Start the engine and bring it to operating temperature.
7. Hold the engine speed at approximately 1500 RPM. Check for steady manifold vacuum at this hose.

➡ To figure out what the vacuum should be, remove a vacuum hose directly from the intake manifold and measure the vacuum at 1500 RPM.

8. If manifold vacuum is not present, check for vacuum leaks on line or lack of manifold vacuum. Repair as necessary and retest. If manifold vacuum was OK, shut off engine, connect hose, and proceed to next step.

9. Disconnect the hose at the vacuum valve control outlet fitting.

10. Connect a vacuum gauge to this fitting.

11. Disconnect the electrical connector on the valve control. This will simulate an open circuit at the valve control.

12. Start the engine and bring it to operating temperature.

13. Hold the engine speed at approximately 2000 RPM while checking for vacuum flow through the valve control.

14. The gauge reading will be low, at idle speed the gauge reading should be erratic. This is normal.

15. To allow full manifold vacuum to flow through the valve control, exhaust backpressure must be present. It must be high enough to hold the bleed valve in the transducer portion of the valve control closed. Have a helper momentarily (a few seconds) block the exhaust with a rag or other suitable device.

✳✳ CAUTION

Make sure to have the helper wear heavy gloves to reduce the risk of burns from the exhaust gas or exhaust pipes.

16. As temporary backpressure is built, full manifold vacuum should be observed.

Fig. 30 Check for vacuum supply to the control valve

Fig. 28 Disconnect the EGR backpressure hose

Fig. 31 Detach the electrical connector from the EGR control valve

17. If full vacuum was present at the inlet fitting, but is not present at the outlet fitting, replace the valve control.

18. Install the engine cover.

REMOVAL & INSTALLATION

EGR Valve

▶ See Figures 32, 33, 34, 35 and 36

1. Disconnect the negative battery cable.

2. Remove the engine cover.

3. Disconnect the vacuum line to the EGR valve. Inspect for damage.

4. Remove the two EGR valve mounting bolts from the intake manifold.

5. Remove the EGR valve from the intake manifold.

6. Clean the gasket surface and discard the old gasket. Check for any signs of leakage or cracked surfaces.

To install:

7. Assemble the EGR valve with a new gasket onto the intake manifold.

8. Install the EGR valve mounting bolts and tighten them to 200 inch lbs. (22 Nm).

Fig. 29 Remove the vacuum feed line to the EGR control valve

Fig. 32 Unfasten the EGR valve retaining bolts

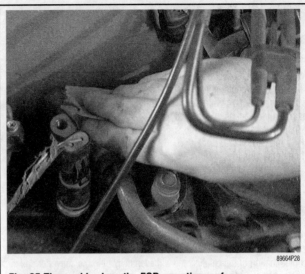

Fig. 35 Thoroughly clean the EGR mounting surface

Fig. 33 Remove the EGR valve

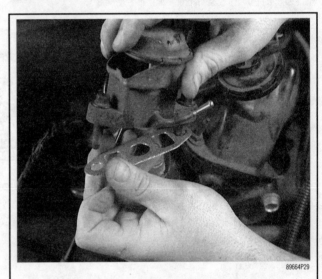

Fig. 36 Be sure to install a new gasket with the EGR valve

Fig. 34 Look inside the EGR passages of the intake manifold for blockage

9. Reconnect the vacuum line.
10. Connect the negative battery cable.
11. Start the engine and check for exhaust leaks.
12. Install the engine cover.

EGR Solenoid

1. Disconnect the negative battery cable.
2. Remove the engine cover.
3. Label and remove the vacuum hoses and electrical connectors from the solenoid(s).
4. Remove the fasteners and remove the solenoid pack.
5. Depress the tab on top of the solenoid to be replaced and slide the solenoid down out of the mounting bracket.
   To install:
6. Place the new solenoid it position and slide in up into the bracket until the mounting tab is secure.
7. Mount the solenoid in position and secure it with the mounting fasteners.
8. Attach the vacuum lines and wiring connectors to the solenoid(s).
9. Connect the negative battery cable.

Catalytic Converter

OPERATION

The catalytic converter, mounted in the exhaust system, is a muffler-shaped device containing a ceramic honeycomb shaped material coated with alumina and impregnated with catalytically active precious metals such as platinum, palladium and rhodium.

The catalyst's job is to reduce air pollutants by oxidizing hydrocarbons (HC) and carbon monoxide (CO). Catalysts containing palladium and rhodium also oxidize nitrous oxides (NOx).

On some trucks, the catalyst is also fed by the secondary air system, via a small supply tube in the side of the catalyst.

No maintenance is possible on the converter, other than keeping the heat shield clear of flammable debris, such as leaves and twigs.

Other than external damage, the only significant damage possible to a converter is through the use of leaded gasoline, or by way of a too rich fuel/air mixture. Both of these problems will ruin the converter through contamination of the catalyst and will eventually plug the converter causing loss of power and engine performance.

When this occurs, the catalyst must be replaced. For catalyst replacement, see the Exhaust System procedures in Section 3.

Air Injection System

OPERATION

▶ **See Figures 37 and 38**

The air injection system is used to inject fresh air into the exhaust manifolds or catalytic converters via an air control valve. The air is created by an air pump that is driven by the engine, it is located in the front of the engine and is propelled by a belt. Under some operating conditions, the air can be dumped back into the atmosphere via an air bypass valve. On some applications the two valves are combined into one unit. The air bypass valve can be either the normally closed type, when the valves are separate, or the normally open type, when the valves are combined.

The system uses a diverter valve which is used to prevent backfire in the exhaust system during sudden deceleration. When the throttle is suddenly closed, a too-rich air/fuel mixture may be created which could not normally be burned. This mixture becomes burnable when it reaches the exhaust area and combines with the injected air. The diverter valve senses the sudden increase in the intake manifold vacuum causing the valve to open, allowing air from the air pump to pass through the valve and silencer into the atmosphere.

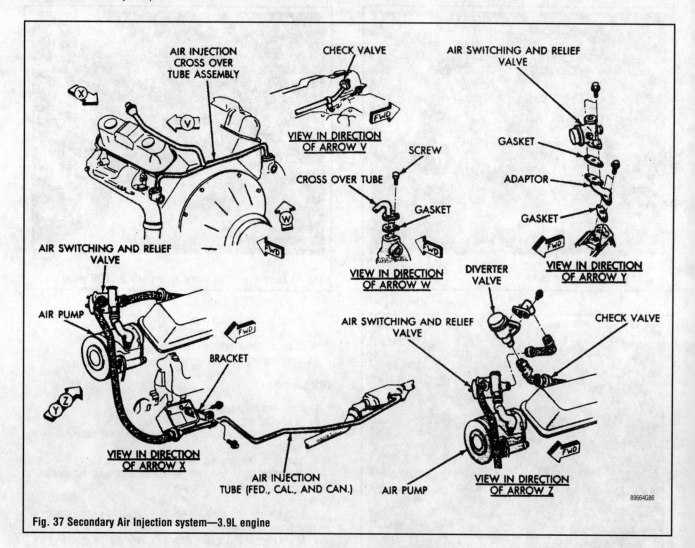

Fig. 37 Secondary Air Injection system—3.9L engine

89664G86

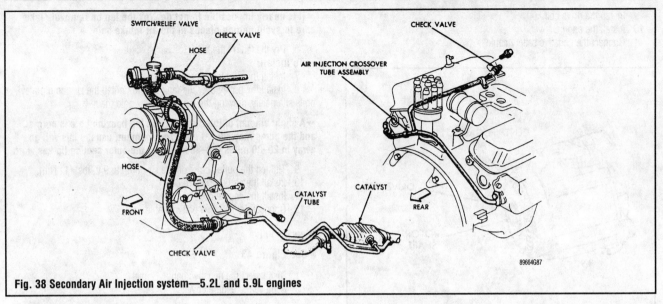

Fig. 38 Secondary Air Injection system—5.2L and 5.9L engines

COMPONENT TESTING

➡ **Do not attempt to correct pump noise by lubricating the air pump. Never lubricate the air pump. Do not assume a pump is bad just because it's noisy.**

Normally Closed Air Bypass Valve Functional Test

1. Remove the engine cover.
2. Disconnect the air supply hose at the valve.
3. Run the engine to normal operating temperature.
4. Disconnect the vacuum line and make sure vacuum is present. If no vacuum is present, remove or bypass any restrictors or delay valves in the vacuum line.
5. Run the engine at 1,500 rpm with the vacuum line connected. Air pump supply air should be heard and felt at the valve outlet.
6. With the engine still at 1,500 rpm, disconnect the vacuum line. Air at the outlet should shut off or dramatically decrease. Air pump supply air should now be felt or heard at the silencer ports.
7. If the valve doesn't pass each of these tests, replace it.
8. Install the engine cover.

Normally Open Air Bypass Valve Functional Test

1. Remove the engine cover.
2. Disconnect the air supply hose at the valve.
3. Run the engine to normal operating temperature.
4. Disconnect the vacuum lines from the valve.
5. Run the engine at 1,500 rpm with the vacuum lines disconnected. Air pump supply air should be heard and felt at the valve outlet.
6. Shut off the engine. Using a spare length of vacuum hose, connect the vacuum nipple of the valve to direct manifold vacuum.
7. Run the engine at 1,500 rpm. Air at the outlet should shut off or dramatically decrease. Air pump supply air should now be felt or heard at the silencer ports.
8. With the engine still in this mode, cap the vacuum vent. Accelerate the engine to 2,000 rpm and suddenly release the throttle. A momentary interruption of air pump supply air should be felt at the valve outlet.
9. If the valve doesn't pass each of these tests, replace it. Reconnect all lines.
10. Install the engine cover.

Air Control Valve Functional Test

1. Remove the engine cover.
2. Run the engine to normal operating temperature, then increase the speed to 1,500 rpm.

3. Disconnect the air supply hose at the valve inlet and verify that there is airflow present.
4. Reconnect the air supply hose.
5. Disconnect both air supply hoses.
6. Disconnect the vacuum hose from the valve.
7. With the engine running at 1,500 rpm, airflow should be felt and heard at the outlet on the side of the valve, with no airflow heard or felt at the outlet opposite the vacuum nipple.
8. Shut off the engine.
9. Using a spare piece of vacuum hose, connect direct manifold vacuum to the valve's vacuum fitting. Airflow should be heard and felt at the outlet opposite the vacuum nipple, and no airflow should be present at the other outlet.
10. If the valve is not functioning properly, replace it.
11. Install the engine cover.

Air Supply Pump Functional Check

1. Check and, if necessary, adjust the belt tension. Press at the midpoint of the belt's longest straight run. You should be able to depress the belt about ½ in. (13mm) at most.
2. Remove the engine cover.
3. Run the engine to normal operating temperature and let it idle.
4. Disconnect the air supply hose from the bypass control valve. If the pump is operating properly, airflow should be felt at the pump outlet. The flow should increase as you increase the engine speed. The pump is not serviceable and should be replaced if it is not functioning properly.
5. Install the engine cover.

REMOVAL & INSTALLATION

Air Injection Pump

▶ See Figures 39 and 40

1. Disconnect the negative battery cable.
2. Remove the engine cover.
3. Remove the drive belt.
4. Remove the air hose from the air pump control valve (the elbow protruding from the pump).
5. Remove the pivot and adjusting bolts from the pump and bracket.
6. Remove the pump from the vehicle.

To install:

7. Install the pump on the mounting bracket and tighten the bolts to 30 ft. lbs. (41 Nm).
8. Install the air hose onto the pump control valve.

9. Install the drive belt.
10. Install the engine cover.
11. Connect the negative battery cable.

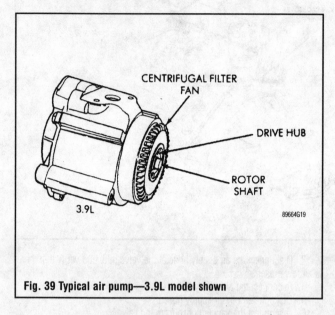

Fig. 39 Typical air pump—3.9L model shown

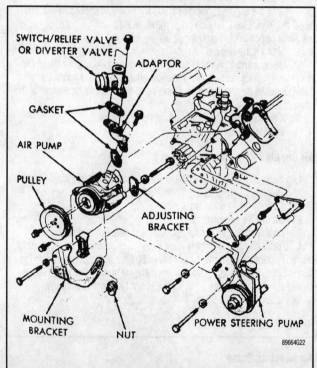

Fig. 40 Exploded view of an air pump mounting at the front of an engine

Centrifugal Filter Fan

▶ See Figures 41 and 42

1. Disconnect the negative battery cable.
2. Remove the engine cover.
3. Remove the air pump drive belt.
4. Remove the air pump pulley.
5. Insert a pair of needlenose pliers between the plastic filter fins and break the fan from the hub.

➡It is nearly impossible to not destroy the fan on removal. Take care to avoid getting pieces in the air intake hole.

6. Pry the fan off the hub.

To install:

7. Install the new fan over the hub.
8. Install the pulley over the fan. Start to tighten the air pump pulley bolts alternately, drawing the fan all the way onto the hub.

➡A slight amount of interference with the housing bore is normal, and the pump may squeal upon replacement, usually this will go away in 20–30 miles (32–48 km) after the outer sealing lip has worn.

9. Tighten the pulley bolts on the air pump to 9 ft. lbs. (11 Nm).
10. Install the air pump drive belt.
11. Install the engine cover.
12. Connect the negative battery cable.

Diverter Valve

▶ See Figure 43

1. Disconnect the negative battery cable.
2. Remove the engine cover.

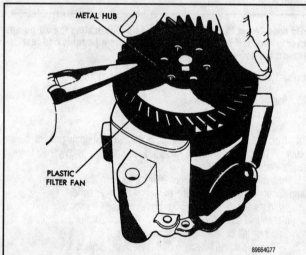

Fig. 41 Use needlenose pliers to break away a damaged fan from the hub

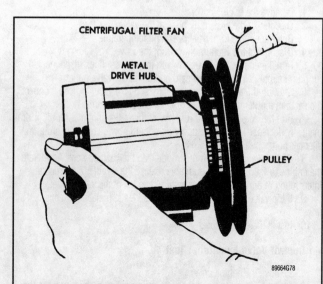

Fig. 42 Tighten down the air pump pulley to seat the fan

3. Remove the air and vacuum hoses from the diverter valve.
4. Remove the valve mounting bolts.
5. Remove the valve from the mounting flange.

To install:

6. Thoroughly clean gasket material off the mounting flange.
7. Position new gasket on the mounting flange.
8. Position diverter valve on mounting flange and tighten bolts to 95 inch lbs. (11 Nm).
9. Install the air and vacuum hoses.
10. Install the engine cover.
11. Connect the negative battery cable.

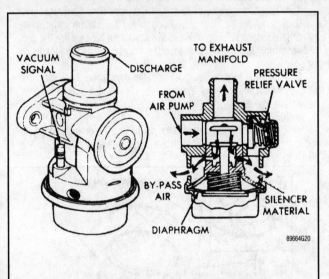

Fig. 43 Internal and external details of the diverter valve

Switch/Relief Valve

▶ See Figure 44

1. Disconnect the negative battery cable.
2. Remove the engine cover.
3. Remove the air and vacuum hoses from pump.
4. Remove the valve mounting bolts.
5. Remove the valve.

To install:

6. Thoroughly clean the valve mounting flange of gasket material.

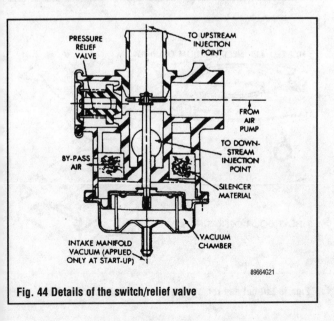

Fig. 44 Details of the switch/relief valve

7. Position new gasket on mounting flange.
8. Position new relief valve on flange and tighten to 95 inch lbs. (11 Nm).
9. Install air and vacuum hoses to valve.
10. Install the engine cover.
11. Connect the negative battery cable.

Check Valve

NON-THREADED TYPE

1. Disconnect the negative battery cable.
2. Remove the engine cover.
3. Release the clamp, and remove the hose from check valve inlet.
4. Remove the bolts or tube nut securing injection tube to the exhaust manifolds or exhaust pipe.
5. Remove the infection tube assembly from the vehicle.

To install:

6. Thoroughly clean the gasket surface on the exhaust manifold and injection tube flanges.
7. Install new gaskets on exhaust manifold flanges and install injection tube assembly.
8. Tighten the tube bracket and flange mounting bolts to 200 inch lbs. (23 Nm). Tighten the tube nut joint assembly to 24–35 ft. lbs. (34–37 Nm).
9. Install the inlet hose and tighten clamp.
10. Install the engine cover.
11. Connect the negative battery cable.

THREADED TYPE

1. Disconnect the negative battery cable.
2. Remove the engine cover.
3. Release clamp and remove hose from valve inlet.
4. Unscrew the check valve from the injection tube.

To install:

5. Install check valve onto injection tube assembly and tighten to 25 ft. lbs. (34 Nm).
6. Install the air hose onto the valve inlet and tighten the clamp.
7. Install the engine cover.
8. Connect the negative battery cable.

Heated Air Intake System

OPERATION

▶ See Figure 45

The heated air intake system is part of the air cleaner assembly. It controls the intake air temperature so the air/fuel mixture can be calibrated leaner when ambient temperatures are low. The system improves engine warm-up characteristics and minimizes icing problems in the cold.

When ambient air temperature is 15°F (8°C) or more above the control temperature, air flow is deflected through the outside air inlet. When the ambient temperature is below these values, warm intake air flow is taken from the heat stove on the exhaust manifold. The colder the temperature, the greater the amount of air taken through the stove. Air flow is controlled by a vacuum-operated door in the snorkel.

Modulation of induction air temperature is controlled by intake manifold vacuum, a temperature sensor and vacuum diaphragm. Temperature modulation only occurs at road load throttle positions or when the intake manifold vacuum is above the operating vacuum of the diaphragm.

Improper operation of the heated air intake system will cause driveability problems and high emissions. Make sure all vacuum hoses and the stove to the air cleaner flexible connector are properly attached and in good condition. With a cold engine and ambient temperature below 110°F (44°C), the heat control door in the snorkel should be in the UP position. With the engine warmed up and running, or when the intake air temperature goes above 130°F (54°C), the control door should be in the DOWN position.

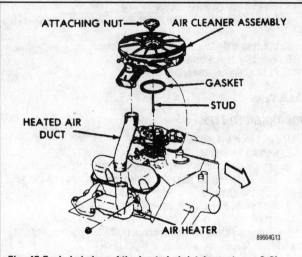

Fig. 45 Exploded view of the heated air intake system—3.9L engine

TESTING

System Test

▶ See Figure 46

1. Disconnect the negative battery cable.
2. Remove the engine cover.
3. Use a hand held vacuum pump to apply 25 in. Hg to the diaphragm.
4. The diaphragm should not bleed down more than 10 in. Hg in 5 minutes.
5. The door should not lift off the bottom of the snorkel with less than 2 in. Hg of vacuum applied.
6. The door should be in the full UP position with 4 in. Hg applied.
7. If the vacuum diaphragm does not perform as described, replace it. If it operates normally, proceed to the next step.
8. Remove the air cleaner from the engine. If the temperature of the air cleaner is not 112°F (45°C) or less, allow it to cool.
9. Apply 20 inches of vacuum to the temperature sensor, if the air door is not in the closed position, the diaphragm is suspect. If the vacuum diaphragm performs correctly, but the proper temperature is not maintained, replace the temperature sensor.

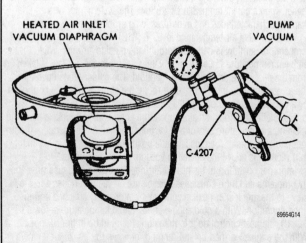

Fig. 46 Use a hand held vacuum pump to test the air cleaner vacuum diaphragm

10. Install the engine cover.
11. Connect the negative battery cable.

REMOVAL & INSTALLATION

Vacuum Diaphragm

▶ See Figures 47 and 48

1. Disconnect the negative battery cable.
2. Remove the engine cover.
3. Remove the air cleaner from the vehicle.
4. Disconnect the vacuum hose from the blend door diaphragm.
5. Drill out the diaphragm mounting rivet. Tip the diaphragm slightly forward to disengage the lock. When the diaphragm is free, slide the complete assembly to one side to disengage the operating rod from the blend air door.
6. With the diaphragm removed from the air cleaner, check the blend air door for freedom of travel. When the door is raised, it should fall freely. Adjust as necessary.

To install:

7. Place the diaphragm in position on the air cleaner and engage the rod to the blend air door. Mount the diaphragm with a rivet.

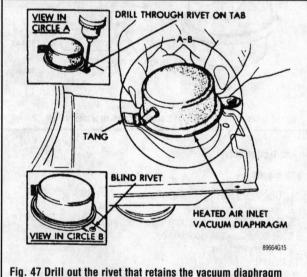

Fig. 47 Drill out the rivet that retains the vacuum diaphragm

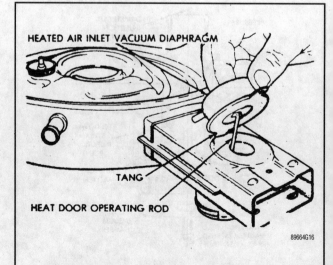

Fig. 48 Lift out and remove the vacuum diaphragm assembly

8. Apply 4 inches of vacuum to the diaphragm. The control door should operate freely.

9. Install the air cleaner, start the engine and check the blend air door operation.

10. Install the engine cover.

11. Disconnect the negative battery cable.

Heated Air Temperature Sensor

▶ See Figure 49

1. Disconnect the negative battery cable.
2. Remove the engine cover.
3. Remove the air cleaner assembly from the vehicle.
4. Remove and discard the sensor mounting clip. Remove the sensor.
5. Position the mounting gasket on the sensor. Install the sensor in position on the air cleaner.
6. Support the sensor and slide the new retainer into position. Make sure the sensor is secure and in the proper position with the mounting gasket to ensure a tight air seal.
7. Install the air cleaner assembly.
8. Install the engine cover.
9. Connect the negative battery cable.

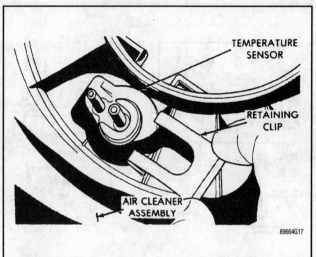

Fig. 49 Slide off the retaining clip to remove the air temperature sensor

Maintenance Reminder Light

The Service Reminder Light (SRL), also known as an Emission Maintenance Reminder (EMR) lamp, comes on at certain mileage intervals when illuminated by the ECM. The ECM monitors the mileage and, when such mileage is reached, illuminates the SRL to alert the driver that maintenance is recommended at that mileage. For more information on the required service, and how to turn off the SRL, refer to Section 1.

ELECTRONIC ENGINE CONTROLS

Engine Control Module

OPERATION

▶ See Figures 50, 51 and 52

The Engine Control Module (ECM) performs many functions on your vehicle. The module accepts information from various engine sensors and computes the required fuel flow rate necessary to maintain the correct amount of air/fuel ratio throughout the entire engine operational range.

Based on the information that is received and programmed into the ECM's memory, the ECM generates output signals to control relays, actuators and solenoids. The ECM also sends out a command to the fuel injectors that meters the appropriate quantity of fuel. The module automatically senses and compensates for any changes in altitude when driving your vehicle.

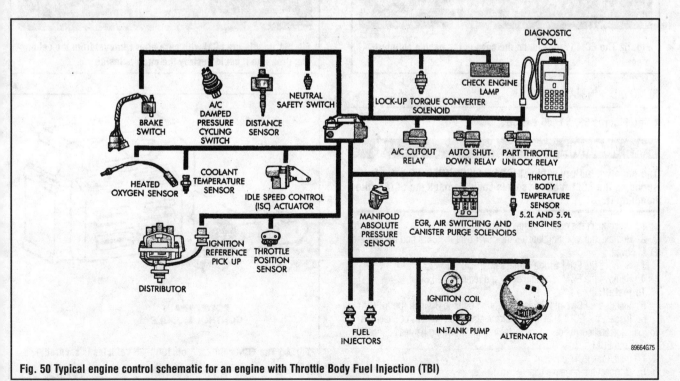

Fig. 50 Typical engine control schematic for an engine with Throttle Body Fuel Injection (TBI)

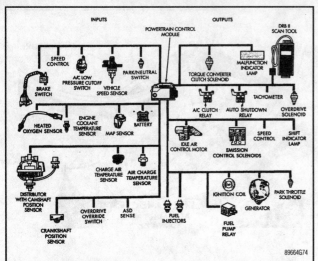

Fig. 51 Typical engine control schematic for an engine with Multi-port Fuel Injection (MFI)

Fig. 53 The ECM with its connector and cover removed

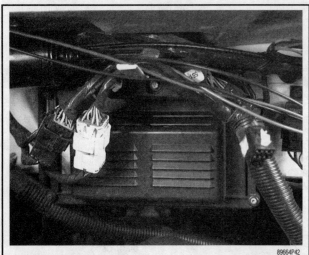

Fig. 52 The ECM is located on the cowl in the engine compartment

Fig. 54 Handle the ECM with care after removal from the vehicle; dropping it could destroy the circuits inside

REMOVAL & INSTALLATION

▶ See Figures 53, 54, 55 and 56

⁘ WARNING

The negative battery cable MUST BE DISCONNECTED prior to servicing the ECM. Voltage spikes could damage the ECM while handling it.

1. Disconnect the negative battery cable.
2. Remove the retaining tabs on the cover over the ECM and remove the ECM cover.
3. Remove the ECM wiring harness connector(s).
4. Remove the ECM retaining bolts and remove the ECM.

To install:

5. Install the ECM and tighten mounting bolts to 35 inch lbs. (4 Nm).
6. Inspect the ECM pins and the terminals on the harness connector(s) for damage and corrosion before installing. Install wiring harness connector(s) onto ECM.
7. Install the ECM cover.
8. Connect the negative battery cable.

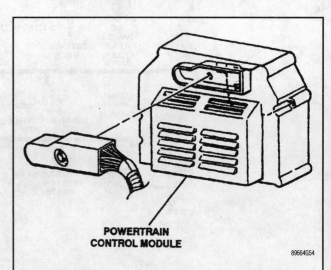

POWERTRAIN CONTROL MODULE

Fig. 55 The ECM connector on 1989–95 vehicles is secured by a bolt

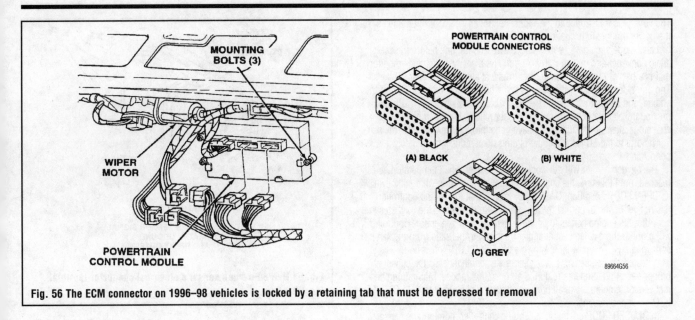

Fig. 56 The ECM connector on 1996–98 vehicles is locked by a retaining tab that must be depressed for removal

→ If replacing the ECM on 1996–98 vehicles, the DRB-II scan tool or equivalent must be used to program the new processor with the vehicle's VIN number and original mileage. If this step is not done, a DTC can be set.

Oxygen Sensor

OPERATION

▶ See Figures 57, 58 and 59

The oxygen sensor (O2) is a device which produces an electrical voltage when exposed to the oxygen present in the exhaust gases. The sensor is mounted in the exhaust manifold. Some oxygen sensors are electrically heated internally for faster switching when the engine is running. The oxygen sensor produces a voltage within 0 and 1 volt. When there is a large amount of oxygen present (lean mixture), the sensor produces a low voltage (less than 0.4v). When there is a lesser amount present (rich mixture) it produces a higher voltage (0.6–1.0v). The stoichiometric or correct fuel to air ratio will read between 0.4 and 0.6v. By monitoring the oxygen content and converting it to electrical voltage, the sensor acts as a rich-lean switch.

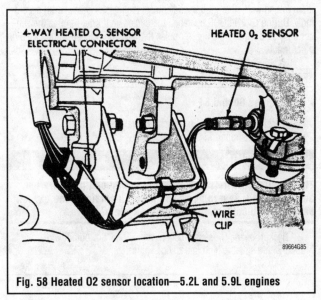

Fig. 58 Heated O2 sensor location—5.2L and 5.9L engines

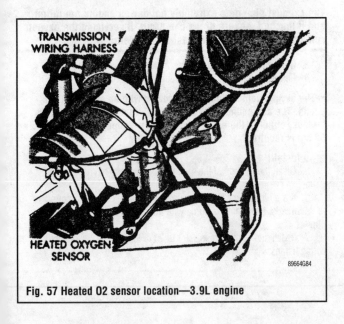

Fig. 57 Heated O2 sensor location—3.9L engine

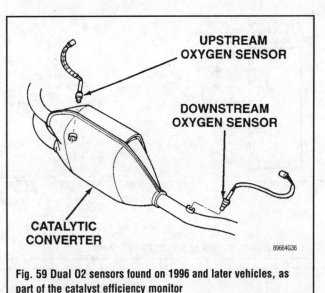

Fig. 59 Dual O2 sensors found on 1996 and later vehicles, as part of the catalyst efficiency monitor

The voltage is transmitted to the engine controller. The controller signals the power module to trigger the fuel injector.

Later models, namely 1996–98 have two sensors, one before the catalytic converter and one after. This is done for a catalyst efficiency monitor that is a part of the OBD-II engine controls that are on these year vehicles. The one before the catalyst measures the exhaust emissions right out of the engine, and sends the signal to the ECM about the state of the mixture as previously talked about. The second sensor reports the difference in the emissions after the exhaust gases have gone through the catalyst. This sensor reports to the ECM the amount of emissions reduction the catalyst is performing.

The oxygen sensor will not work until a predetermined temperature is reached, until this time the engine controller is running in what as known as OPEN LOOP operation. OPEN LOOP means that the engine controller has not yet begun to correct the air-to-fuel ratio by reading the oxygen sensor. After the engine comes to operating temperature, the engine controller will monitor the oxygen sensor and correct the air/fuel ratio from the sensor's readings. This is what is known as CLOSED LOOP operation.

A heated oxygen sensor has a heating element that keeps the sensor at proper operating temperature during all operating modes. Maintaining correct sensor temperature at all times allows the system to enter into CLOSED LOOP operation sooner.

In CLOSED LOOP operation the engine controller monitors the sensor input (along with other inputs) and adjusts the injector pulse width accordingly. During OPEN LOOP operation the engine controller ignores the sensor input and adjusts the injector pulse to a preprogrammed value based on other inputs.

TESTING

♦ **See Figures 60 and 61**

1. Start the engine and bring it up to operating temperature.
2. Raise and support the vehicle.

❊❊ CAUTION

The exhaust pipe gets extremely hot during engine operation, and if touched, severe burns can occur. If servicing the oxygen sensor, avoid contacting the exhaust system.

3. Backprobe the O2 sensor between the O2 sensor output wire and ground with a suitable high impedance voltmeter.

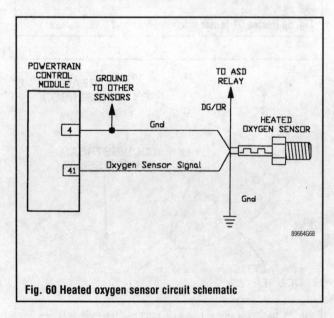

Fig. 60 Heated oxygen sensor circuit schematic

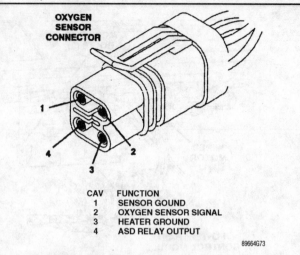

CAV	FUNCTION
1	SENSOR GOUND
2	OXYGEN SENSOR SIGNAL
3	HEATER GROUND
4	ASD RELAY OUTPUT

Fig. 61 Heated oxygen sensor's electrical connector terminal identification

4. The O2 sensor should be rapidly switching between 0 and 1v. If working properly, it should be switching from a lean mixture (less than 0.4v) to a rich mixture (0.6–1.0v), and back. The average voltage should fall between 0.4–0.6v.
5. If the sensor switches slowly, or is stuck in the middle of the range, the O2 may be faulty.
6. If the sensor is stuck rich or lean, it most likely indicates a problem with the engine; for example, a vacuum leak would cause the O2 to read a lean mixture, and a malfunctioning fuel pressure regulator would cause a rich mixture.
7. If the O2 sensor is above or below the specified range (0–1v), a wiring or computer problem is most likely the cause.
8. Lower the vehicle.
9. Turn the engine off.

REMOVAL & INSTALLATION

♦ **See Figures 62, 63, 64 and 65**

1. Disconnect the negative battery cable.
2. Raise and support the vehicle.

❊❊ CAUTION

The exhaust pipe gets extremely hot during engine operation, and if touched, severe burns can occur. If servicing the oxygen sensor, avoid contacting the exhaust system.

3. Disconnect the wiring harness from the oxygen sensor.
4. Remove the sensor using the appropriate tool.

➡**The oxygen sensor threads are coated with an anti-seize compound. The compound must be removed from the mounting boss threads, either in the exhaust manifold or Y-pipe. An 18mm x 1.5 x 6E tap is required.**

To install:
5. Clean the threads of the mount to remove any old anti-seize compound.
6. If the old sensor is to be reused, apply anti-seize compound to its threads. New sensors come with the compound already applied.
7. Install and tighten the sensor to 20 ft. lbs. (27 Nm). Connect the wiring harness.

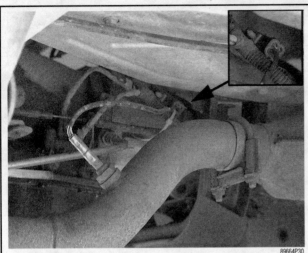

Fig. 62 The O2 sensor is located in front of the catalytic converter. The sensor's electrical connector is shown in the inset

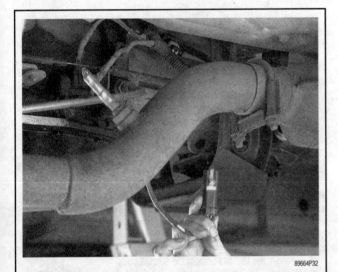

Fig. 63 Detach the O2 sensor's electrical connector

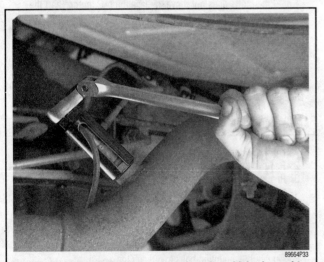

Fig. 64 A special socket, like the one here from Lisle, is used to remove the O2 sensor

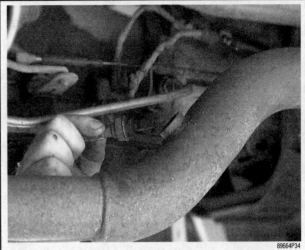

Fig. 65 When fully loosened, remove the O2 sensor from the exhaust pipe

8. If vehicle has two O2 sensors, repeat procedure for second sensor.

9. Lower the vehicle.

10. Connect the negative battery cable.

Idle Air Control Motor

OPERATION

The Idle Air Control (IAC) motor is mounted to the throttle body and is operated by the engine controller. The throttle body has an air control passage that provides air for the engine at idle(when the throttle plate is closed). The IAC motor pintle protrudes into the air control passage and regulates air flow through it. Based on various sensor inputs, the engine controller adjusts engine speed by moving the pintle in and out of the air control passage. The IAC motor is positioned when the ignition is turned to the **ON** position.

➡The IAC motor is used on 1992 MFI, as well as all 1993 and later vehicles. For 1989–92 TBI vehicles, refer to the Idle Speed Control (ISC) Actuator procedure, later in this section.

TESTING

♦ See Figures 66, 67, 68 and 69

To perform a complete test of the IAC motor, you will need the DRB-II scan tool, or equivalent. This test is a test of the IAC motor only. You will need access to the special factory IAC motor exerciser tool No. 7558 or equivalent.

Take the following precautions before beginning:

• Set the parking brake and block the drive wheels.

• Route all tester cables away from the cooling fan, drive belt(s), pulleys and exhaust system.

• Do not operate the engine indoors, but provide proper ventilation.

• Always return the engine idle speed to normal before disconnecting the exerciser tool.

1. Remove the engine cover.

2. With the engine **OFF**, unplug the IAC motor wire connector.

3. Plug the exerciser tool No. 7558 harness connector onto the IAC motor.

4. Connect the red clip of the exerciser tool to the positive battery terminal, and the black to the negative battery terminal. The red lamp will illuminate when the tool is properly connected.

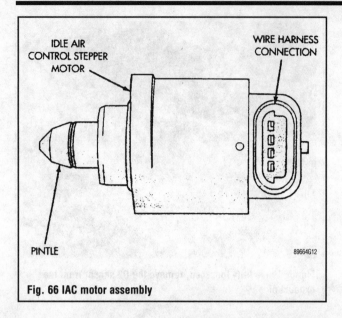

Fig. 66 IAC motor assembly

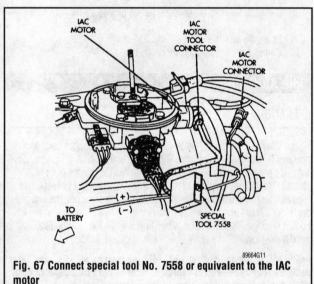

Fig. 67 Connect special tool No. 7558 or equivalent to the IAC motor

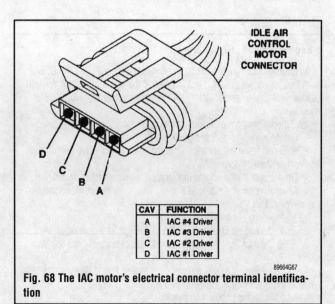

Fig. 68 The IAC motor's electrical connector terminal identification

CAV	FUNCTION
A	IAC #4 Driver
B	IAC #3 Driver
C	IAC #2 Driver
D	IAC #1 Driver

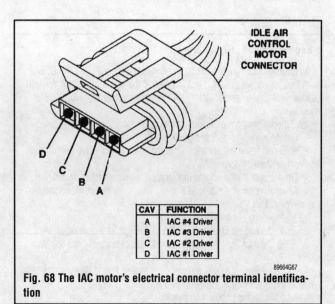

Fig. 69 The IAC motor and driver circuits

5. Start the engine. When the switch is in the high or low position, the lamp on the exerciser tool will flash. This indicates that the voltage pulses are being sent to the IAC stepper motor.

6. Move the switch to the HIGH position. The engine speed should increase. Move the switch to the LOW position. The engine speed should decrease.

a. If the engine speed changed predictably while using the exerciser tool, the IAC motor is working correctly. Disconnect the exerciser tool and install the IAC motor wiring connector on IAC motor.

b. If the engine speed does not change, turn the ignition **OFF** and proceed to Step 6.

✳✳ WARNING

When the IAC motor is removed from the throttle body, do not extend the pintle more than 0.250 inch (6.35mm). If the pintle is extended more than this amount, it may separate from the IAC motor and the motor will have to be replaced.

7. Remove the IAC motor from the throttle body.

8. With the ignition **OFF**, cycle the exerciser tool switch between the HIGH and LOW positions. Keep your attention on the pintle. It should move in-and-out of the motor.

a. If the pintle does not move, replace the IAC motor. Start the engine and test the replacement motor operation as described in Step 5.

b. If the pintle operates properly, check the IAC motor bore in the throttle body for blockage and clean as needed. Install the IAC motor and retest. If blockage is not found, more complete testing will be required using the DRB-II scan tool or equivalent, and the appropriate Powertrain Diagnostics Procedures service manual.

REMOVAL & INSTALLATION

1. Disconnect the negative battery cable.
2. Remove the engine cover.
3. Remove the air cleaner assembly.
4. Unplug the IAC motor connector.
5. Remove the mounting bolts.
6. Remove the IAC motor from the throttle body.

To install:

7. Install the IAC motor in the throttle body.
8. Tighten the mounting bolts to 60 inch lbs. (7 Nm).
9. Plug the IAC electrical connector in.
10. Install the air cleaner assembly.

11. Install the engine cover.
12. Connect the negative battery cable.

Idle Speed Control Actuator

OPERATION

▶ **See Figure 70**

The Idle Speed Control (ISC) actuator is mounted to the throttle body and is controlled by the ECM. The ISC contains the idle contact switch and provides an input signal to the ECM. Various other sensors on the car give input to the ECM which help to control the ISC. The ECM supplies current and a ground path to the ISC actuator. This enables the ECM to increase or decrease the throttle stop angle by extending or retracting the ISC actuator. The throttle lever rests against an adjustment screw at the end of the actuator. The actuator extends or retracts to control engine speed and to set throttle stop angle during deceleration.

➡ **The ISC actuator is used on 1989–92 TBI vehicles. For 1992 MFI, as well as all 1993 and later vehicles, refer to the Idle Air Control (IAC) Motor procedure, earlier in this section.**

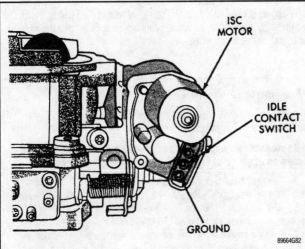

Fig. 70 ISC actuator with its electrical connector removed—note the Idle Contact Switch circuit

TESTING

▶ **See Figures 71 and 72**

1. Remove the engine cover.
2. Remove the air cleaner assembly.
3. While watching the ISC actuator, have an assistant start the engine, shut it off and turn the ignition **OFF**. The ISC actuator should move outward to preset a fast idle after the next start, after the ignition is turned **OFF**. If it does not move outward, continue diagnostics. If the actuator moves outward, start engine and let idle to verify proper idle speed, if idle speed is out of specifications, set the idle speed using the procedure on reinstallation of the ISC later in this section.
4. Check the ISC actuator to see if it is frozen or sticking, if it is, replace it and retest. If it is OK, continue diagnostics.
5. Start the engine and backprobe the ISC connector to voltage is getting to ISC actuator. Voltage should be fluctuating between 2.0 and 6.0 volts. If voltage is OK, continue diagnostics. If voltage is not OK, repair circuit and retest.
6. Shut the engine off.

7. Disconnect the negative battery cable.
8. Disconnect the ECM wiring harness.

※※ WARNING

Testing the wiring harness with the ECM still connected can cause serious damage to the processor. ALWAYS disconnect the ECM before testing the wiring harness., unless instructed otherwise.

9. Using an ohmmeter, measure the resistance on the ground circuit, using the supplied wiring diagrams, between the ISC connector and ECM harness connector. Resistance should be less than 5.0 ohms, if not repair ground circuit and retest. If resistance is OK, replace ISC motor.

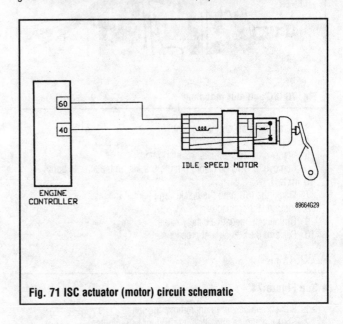

Fig. 71 ISC actuator (motor) circuit schematic

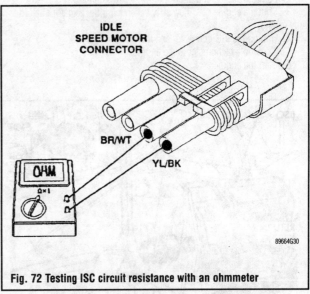

Fig. 72 Testing ISC circuit resistance with an ohmmeter

REMOVAL & INSTALLATION

▶ **See Figure 73**

1. Disconnect the negative battery cable.
2. Remove the engine cover.

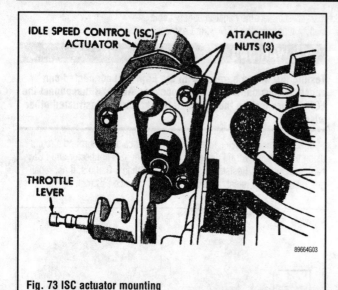

Fig. 73 ISC actuator mounting

3. Remove the air cleaner assembly.
4. Unplug the ISC connector.
5. Remove the ISC actuator retaining nuts.
6. Remove the ISC actuator from the bracket on the throttle body.
To install:
7. Install the ISC onto the bracket and tighten the retaining nuts.
8. Plug in ISC connector.
9. Connect the negative battery cable.
10. Perform the adjustment procedure.

ADJUSTMENT

▶ **See Figure 74**

1. If the engine cover is on, remove the engine cover.
2. Start the engine and allow it to run for two minutes.
3. Shut the engine off. Allow sixty seconds for the actuator shaft to fully extend.
4. Unplug the ISC connector and the ECT connector.
5. Hook up a tachometer to the engine.
6. Start the engine.

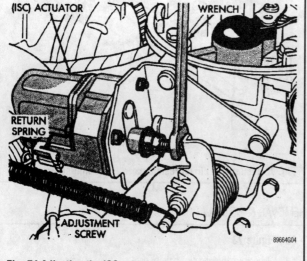

Fig. 74 Adjusting the ISC actuator

7. Adjust the extension screw on the ISC actuator shaft until the RPM is within the specifications.
8. On the 3.9L engine:
   a. If the vehicle has less than 1000 miles, set to 2400–2500 RPM.
   b. If the vehicle has more than 1000 miles, set to 2500–2600 RPM
9. On 5.2L and 5.9L engines:
   a. If the vehicle has less than 1000 miles, set to 2650–2750 rpm.
   b. If the vehicle has more than 1000 miles, set to 2750–2850 rpm.
10. Shut off the engine.
11. Remove the tachometer from the engine.
12. Plug in the ECT and ISC connectors.
13. Install the air cleaner assembly.
14. Start engine and ensure that the idle is at specification.
15. Install the engine cover.

Engine Coolant Temperature Sensor

OPERATION

The Engine Coolant Temperature (ECT) sensor resistance changes in response to engine coolant temperature. The sensor resistance decreases as the coolant temperature increases, and increases as the coolant temperature decreases. This provides a reference signal to the ECM, which indicates engine coolant temperature. The signal sent to the ECM by the ECT sensor helps the ECM to determine spark advance, EGR flow rate, air/fuel ratio, and engine temperature.

TESTING

▶ **See Figures 75, 76 and 77**

1. Disconnect the negative battery cable.
2. Remove the engine cover.

➡**Be sure you are unplugging and checking the ECT, and not the temperature gauge sending unit; they are two different parts.**

3. Unplug the connector on the sensor.
4. Test the resistance of the sensor across the two terminals of the sensor.
5. With the engine cold, and ambient temperature below 90°F (32°C), the resistance should be between 500–1100 ohms.
6. With the engine at normal operating temperature, the resistance should be greater than 1300 ohms.
7. If the sensor is not within specifications, replace it.

Fig. 75 The coolant temperature sensor can be tested using the Auto Xray or equivalent tool's data display feature

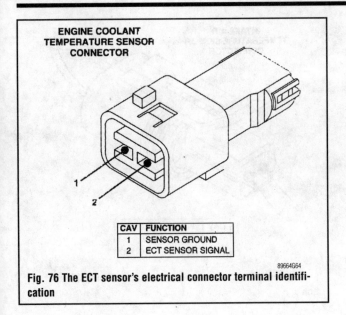

Fig. 76 The ECT sensor's electrical connector terminal identification

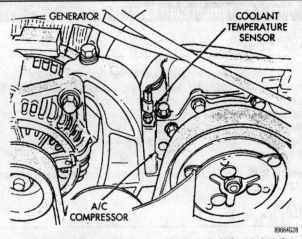

Fig. 78 The engine coolant temperature sensor is located at the base of the intake manifold, between the A/C compressor and alternator (generator)

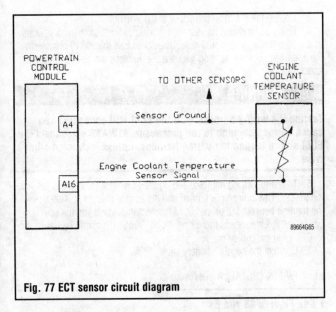

Fig. 77 ECT sensor circuit diagram

Fig. 79 Location of the ECT sensor with neighboring components removed

REMOVAL & INSTALLATION

▶ See Figures 78 and 79

1. Disconnect the negative battery cable.
2. Remove the engine cover.

❄ CAUTION

Never open, service or drain the radiator or cooling system when hot; serious burns can occur from the steam and hot coolant. Also, when draining engine coolant, keep in mind that cats and dogs are attracted to ethylene glycol antifreeze and could drink any that is left in an uncovered container or in puddles on the ground. This will prove fatal in sufficient quantities. Always drain coolant into a sealable container. Coolant should be reused unless it is contaminated or is several years old.

3. Drain and recycle the engine coolant.
4. Remove the air cleaner assembly.
5. On vehicles with air conditioning:
   a. Remove the A/C compressor to intake manifold bracket.
   b. Fabricate a 8 inch long hook tool from a coat hanger to remove the wiring harness connector.
6. Remove the connector from the sensor.
7. Remove the sensor from the intake manifold.

To install:

8. Install the sensor in the manifold and tighten to 8 ft. lbs. (11 Nm).
9. Install the connector on the sensor.
10. On vehicles with air conditioning:
    a. Install the A/C bracket.
11. Replace the air cleaner assembly.
12. Refill and bleed the engine cooling system.
13. Connect the negative battery cable.
14. Inspect for leaks.
15. Install the engine cover.

Intake Air Temperature Sensor

OPERATION

The Intake Air Temperature (IAT) sensor determines the air temperature inside the intake manifold. Resistance changes in response to the ambient air temperature. The sensor resistance decreases as the air temperature increases. This provides a signal to the ECM indicating the temperature of the incoming air charge. This sensor helps the ECM to determine spark timing and air/fuel ratio. The IAT is threaded and screws into the intake manifold.

➡ Only Multi-port Fuel Injected (MFI) vehicles are equipped with an IAT sensor.

TESTING

▶ See Figures 80, 81 and 82

1. Disconnect the negative battery cable.
2. Remove the engine cover.

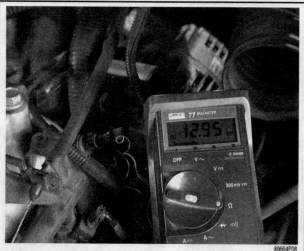

Fig. 80 Using an ohmmeter, test the intake air temperature sensor for resistance across its two terminals

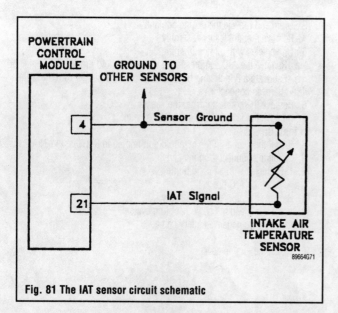

Fig. 81 The IAT sensor circuit schematic

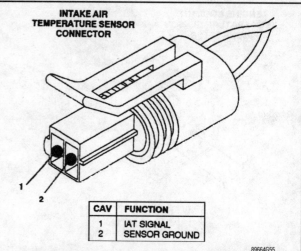

CAV	FUNCTION
1	IAT SIGNAL
2	SENSOR GROUND

Fig. 82 The IAT sensor's electrical connector terminal identification

3. Unplug the electrical connector at the sensor.
4. Using a ohmmeter, measure the resistance across the two terminals of the sensor. The sensor resistance should be less than 1340 ohms with the engine at normal operating temperature. Replace the sensor if not within specifications.

✳✳ WARNING

Testing the wiring harness with the ECM still connected can cause serious damage to the processor. ALWAYS disconnect the ECM before testing the wiring harness, unless instructed otherwise.

5. To test the wiring harness, unplug the ECM, test the harness between the proper ECM connector terminal and the sensor connector. Also check the harness between the proper ECM connector terminal and the sensor connector. If resistance is more than 1 ohm, repair the wiring harness.
6. Install the engine cover.
7. Connect the negative battery cable.

REMOVAL & INSTALLATION

▶ See Figures 83 and 84

1. Disconnect the negative battery cable.
2. Remove the engine cover.
3. Unplug the electrical connector from the sensor.
4. Unscrew the sensor out of the intake manifold.

To install:

5. Install the sensor into the intake manifold and tighten it to 20 ft. lbs. (28 Nm).
6. Plug the connector into the sensor.
7. Install the engine cover.
8. Connect the negative battery cable.

Throttle Body Temperature Sensor

OPERATION

Throttle Body Injected (TBI) vehicles equipped with a 5.2L or 5.9L engine have a Throttle Body Temperature (TBT) sensor. The sensor monitors throttle body temperature, which is the same as fuel temperature. It is mounted on the throttle body. This sensor provides the ECM with information on fuel temperature, which allows the ECM to richen the air/fuel mixture for a hot restart condition.

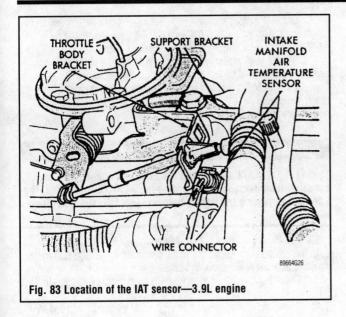

Fig. 83 Location of the IAT sensor—3.9L engine

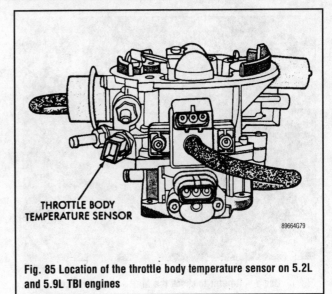

Fig. 85 Location of the throttle body temperature sensor on 5.2L and 5.9L TBI engines

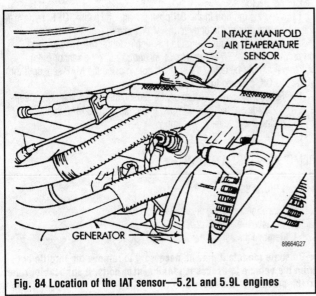

Fig. 84 Location of the IAT sensor—5.2L and 5.9L engines

TESTING

▶ See Figure 85

1. Disconnect the negative battery cable.
2. Remove the engine cover.
3. Unplug the electrical connector at the sensor.
4. Using a ohmmeter, measure the resistance across the two terminals of the sensor. The sensor resistance should be less than 1340 ohms with the engine at normal operating temperature. Replace the sensor if not within specifications.

✳✳ WARNING

Testing the wiring harness with the ECM still connected can cause serious damage to the processor. ALWAYS disconnect the ECM before testing the wiring harness, unless instructed otherwise.

5. To test the wiring harness, unplug the ECM, test the harness between the proper ECM connector terminal and the sensor connector. If resistance is more than 1 ohm, repair the wiring harness.

6. Install the engine cover.
7. Connect the negative battery cable.

REMOVAL & INSTALLATION

▶ See Figure 85

1. Disconnect the negative battery cable.
2. Remove the engine cover.
3. Remove the air cleaner assembly.
4. Unplug the TBT sensor connector.
5. Remove the TBT from the throttle body by unscrewing it from its bore.

To install:

6. Thread the TBT sensor into its bore on the throttle body and tighten to 110 inch lbs. (12 Nm).
7. Plug in the TBT connector.
8. Install the air cleaner assembly.
9. Install the engine cover.
10. Connect the negative battery cable.

Manifold Absolute Pressure Sensor

OPERATION

The Manifold Absolute Pressure (MAP) sensor measures the pressure inside the intake manifold, by measuring the vacuum level. It sends a voltage signal to the ECM in relation to the pressure inside the manifold, which varies according to engine load and altitude. The ECM uses this signal to adjust the air/fuel ratio.

TESTING

▶ See Figures 86, 87 and 88

1. Remove the engine cover.
2. Remove the air cleaner assembly.
3. Inspect the L shaped tube from the throttle body to the MAP for cracks, blockage, and damage. Repair as necessary.
4. Unplug the MAP sensor connector.
5. Test the MAP sensor output voltage at the MAP sensor connector between terminals A and B. With ignition **ON** and the engine **OFF**, the voltage should be between 4–5 volts. If no voltage is present, proceed to Step 8.

Fig. 86 Use a voltmeter to check the MAP sensor for signal

6. Test MAP sensor supply voltage at sensor connector between terminals A and C with the ignition **ON** and engine off, voltage should be 4.5–5.0 volts. If no voltage is present, proceed to Step 8.

7. Test the MAP sensor ground circuit at terminal A of the MAP connector, voltage should be less than 0.2 volts. If not inspect for open harness from pin 4 of ECM harness and terminal A. If no voltage is present, proceed to the next step.

8. Turn the ignition **OFF**.

9. Disconnect the ECM harness from the ECM.

✳✳ WARNING

Testing the wiring harness with the ECM still connected can cause serious damage to the processor. ALWAYS disconnect the ECM before testing the wiring harness, unless instructed otherwise.

10. Test the MAP sensor output voltage at the ECM connector. At the ECM harness connector test pin 1 of the connector, the voltage should be the same as at the MAP sensor in Step 5.

11. Check ECM harness connector pin 6 for the same voltage as in Step 6.

12. If all of the above tests pass, plug in ECM wiring harness and MAP sensor connector.

13. With the ignition in the **ON** position, and the engine **OFF**, remove the tube from the throttle body to the MAP sensor.

14. Connect a vacuum pump to the nipple on the MAP sensor, and pump the sensor to 20–27 in. Hg. of vacuum. Check the sensor output voltage, it should be below 1.8 volts. If not , replace the MAP sensor. If the voltage is OK, proceed to next step.

15. Relieve vacuum pressure on the sensor, then check the output voltage. The voltage should be 4–5 volts; if not, replace the MAP sensor.

16. Install the air cleaner assembly.

17. Install the engine cover.

REMOVAL & INSTALLATION

▶ **See Figure 89**

1. Disconnect the negative battery cable.
2. Remove the engine cover.
3. Remove the air cleaner assembly.

➡On some models it may be necessary to remove the throttle body from the vehicle to access the MAP sensor bolts. If applicable, refer to the procedure in Section 5.

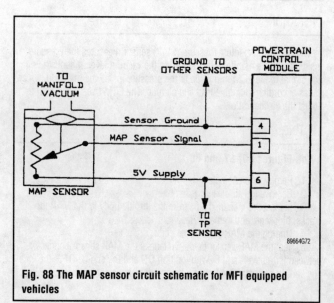

Fig. 87 The MAP sensor's electrical connector terminal identification—MFI vehicles

CAV	FUNCTION
1	SENSOR GROUND
2	MAP SENSOR SIGNAL
3	5-VOLT SUPPLY

Fig. 88 The MAP sensor circuit schematic for MFI equipped vehicles

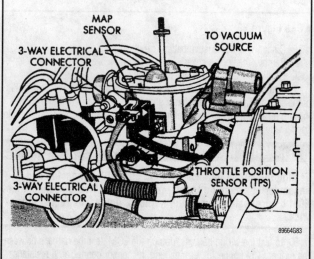

Fig. 89 The MAP sensor location for TBI equipped vehicles

4. Remove the two MAP sensor retaining bolts.
5. Slide the L-shaped tube to the MAP sensor from the throttle body off while removing the MAP sensor from the throttle body.

To install:
6. Install the L-shaped tube onto the MAP sensor.
7. Install the MAP sensor onto the throttle body assembly. Tighten the retaining bolts to 25 inch lbs. (3 Nm). If applicable, install the throttle body.
8. Install the air cleaner assembly.
9. Install the engine cover.
10. Connect the negative battery cable.

Throttle Position Sensor

OPERATION

The Throttle Position (TP) sensor is a potentiometer that provides a signal to the ECM that is directly proportional to the throttle plate position. The TP sensor is mounted on the side of the throttle body and is connected to the throttle plate shaft. The TP sensor monitors throttle plate movement and position, and transmits an appropriate electrical signal to the ECM. These signals are used by the ECM to adjust the air/fuel mixture, spark timing and EGR operation according to engine load at idle, part throttle, or full throttle. The TP sensor is not adjustable.

TESTING

▶ **See Figures 90, 91, 92, 93 and 94**

1. Remove the engine cover.
2. Remove the air cleaner assembly.
3. With the engine **OFF** and the ignition **ON**, check the voltage at the center terminal of the TP sensor by carefully backprobing the connector.
4. Voltage should be between 0.2 and 1.4 volts at idle, and less than 4.8v at Wide Open Throttle (WOT). If the TP sensor does not meet these specifications, replace it.
5. If no voltage is present, check the wiring harness for supply voltage (5.0v) and ground (0.3v or less), by referring to your corresponding wiring guide. If supply voltage and ground are present, but no output voltage from TP, replace the TP sensor. If supply voltage and ground do not meet specifications, make necessary repairs to the harness or ECM.
6. Replace the air cleaner assembly.
7. Replace the engine cover.

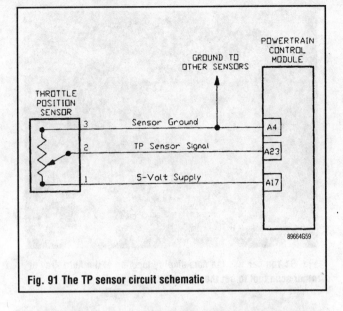

Fig. 91 The TP sensor circuit schematic

Fig. 92 Using a voltmeter to check the TP sensor for signal voltage

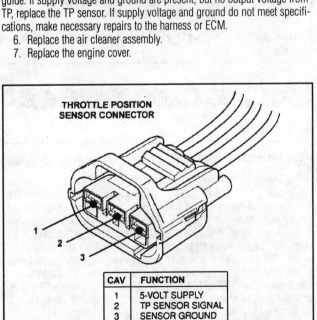

Fig. 90 The TP sensor's electrical connector terminal identification—MFI engines

CAV	FUNCTION
1	5-VOLT SUPPLY
2	TP SENSOR SIGNAL
3	SENSOR GROUND

Fig. 93 Using a voltmeter to check the TP sensor for reference (supply) voltage

Fig. 94 You can use the data display function of the Auto Xray or other scan tool to get the TP sensor readings

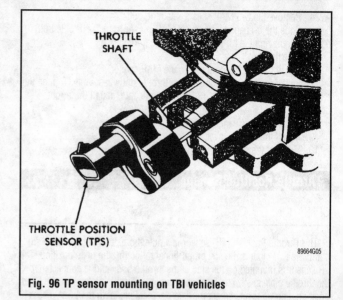

Fig. 96 TP sensor mounting on TBI vehicles

REMOVAL & INSTALLATION

▶ See Figures 95, 96 and 97

1. Disconnect the negative battery cable.
2. Remove the engine cover.
3. Remove the air cleaner assembly.
4. Unplug the TP sensor connector.
5. Remove the two retaining bolts.
6. Remove the TP sensor from the throttle body.

To install:

7. Install the TP sensor on the throttle body.
8. Tighten the TP sensor bolts to 60 inch lbs. (7 Nm) on 1993 and later vehicles, and 27 inch lbs. (3 Nm) on 1989–92 vehicles.
9. Open the throttle to WOT and back again several times to check for binding.
10. Plug in the connector for the TP sensor.
11. Install the air cleaner assembly.
12. Install the engine cover.
13. Connect the negative battery cable.

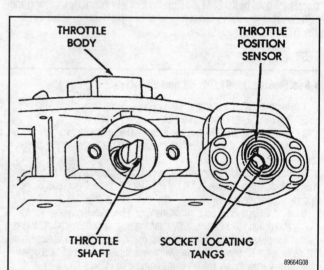

Fig. 97 Align the locating tangs on the TP sensor with the throttle shaft

Camshaft Position Sensor

OPERATION

▶ See Figure 98

The Camshaft Position (CMP) sensor provides camshaft position information which is used by the ECM for fuel and ignition system synchronization. The sensor is a Hall effect digital sensor. It has a metal pulse ring and a pickup assembly located inside the distributor. The CMP signal is a digital on/off type signal. When the pulse ring travels through the pickup, a permanent magnet inside the pickup creates magnetism, which induces voltage. The pulse ring has slots, or one large slot; as the slot(s) pass, the pickup loses its magnetism and voltage is lost, thereby generating the on/off signal. The CMP and Crankshaft Position (CKP) sensor let the ECM know the position of the camshaft and crankshaft, so the engine can be properly timed.

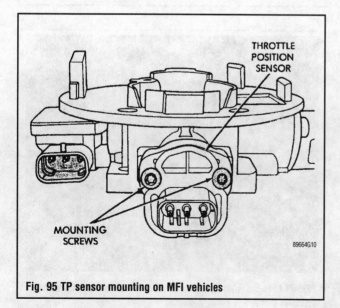

Fig. 95 TP sensor mounting on MFI vehicles

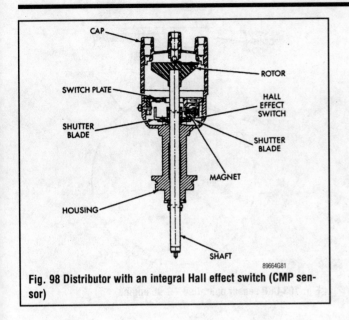

Fig. 98 Distributor with an integral Hall effect switch (CMP sensor)

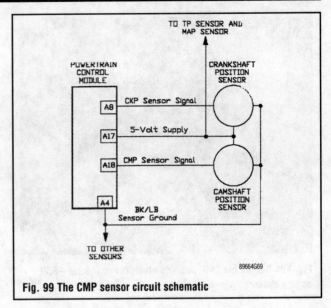

Fig. 99 The CMP sensor circuit schematic

TESTING

♦ **See Figures 99 and 100**

1. Remove the engine cover.
2. With the DRB-II scan tool or equivalent, plug in to diagnostic connector.
3. Using the DRB-II, erase all DTC's and turn the ignition off and on again.
4. Crank the engine and observe CAM SYNC; if NO CAM SYNC is shown, proceed to the next step. If CAM SYNC was present, the CMP sensor is operational.
5. Inspect the wiring and connectors, repair as necessary and retest or if OK, proceed to next step.
6. Unplug the CMP sensor connector.
7. Turn the ignition **ON** and, using a voltmeter, probe the CMP connector to verify the supply voltage using supplied wiring schematic.
   a. On 1995 and earlier vehicles, if voltage is 7.0v or above, proceed to the next step; if no voltage or insufficient voltage is detected, repair the circuit and retest.
   b. On 1996–98 vehicles, the voltage should be 4.5v or above. If voltage does not met specifications, repair circuit and retest, if OK, proceed to next step.
8. Connect a jumper between the CMP signal circuit and CMP ground circuit (use supplied schematic). Without turning key off, attempt to start vehicle while making and breaking connection. If vehicle starts, replace CMP sensor. If vehicle does not start proceed to next step.
9. Remove the distributor cap and ensure that distributor turns while cranking engine. If distributor turns, proceed to next step, if it does not turn, repair as necessary and retest.
10. Disconnect the negative battery cable.
11. Using an ohmmeter, probe the ground circuit between the CMP sensor connector and a engine ground. If resistance is less than 5.0 ohms, proceed to next step, if not, repair circuit and retest.
12. Disconnect the ECM wiring harness.

✳✳ WARNING

Testing the wiring harness with the ECM still connected can cause serious damage to the processor. ALWAYS disconnect the ECM before testing the wiring harness., unless instructed otherwise.

13. Using an ohmmeter, test the CMP signal circuit for resistance between the CMP sensor connector and the ECM harness connector. If

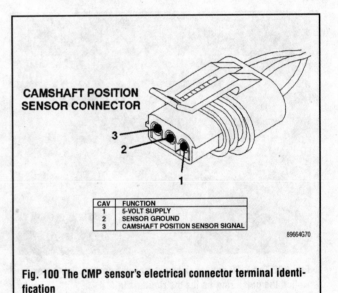

Fig. 100 The CMP sensor's electrical connector terminal identification

resistance is less than 5.0 ohms, proceed to next step, if not, repair circuit and retest.

14. Using an ohmmeter measure the CMP signal circuit resistance between CMP connector and ground, if resistance is less than 5.0 ohms, repair the CMP signal circuit for a short ground. If the resistance is more than 5.0 ohms, replace the ECM.
15. Install the engine cover.
16. Connect the negative battery cable.

REMOVAL & INSTALLATION

♦ **See Figures 101 and 102**

1. Disconnect the negative battery cable.
2. Remove the engine cover.
3. Remove the distributor cap from the distributor.
4. Remove the distributor rotor from the distributor shaft.
5. Unplug the CMP sensor's electrical connector.
6. Lift the CMP sensor out of the distributor assembly.

To install:

7. Install the CMP sensor into distributor, aligning sensor with notch in distributor.

Fig. 101 Detach the CMP sensor's electrical connector—5.2L engine shown

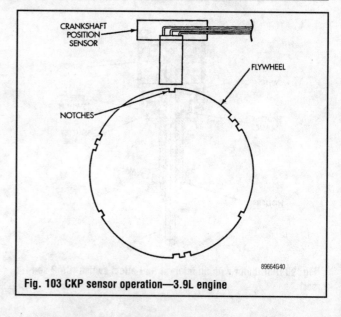

Fig. 103 CKP sensor operation—3.9L engine

Fig. 102 The CMP sensor pickup removed from the distributor. Notice the pulse ring on the distributor shaft

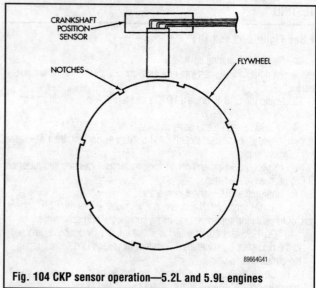

Fig. 104 CKP sensor operation—5.2L and 5.9L engines

8. Plug connector in.
9. Install rotor.
10. Install distributor cap and tighten screws.
11. Install engine cover.
12. Connect the negative battery cable.

Crankshaft Position Sensor

OPERATION

▶ **See Figures 103 and 104**

The CKP sensor, located on the back of the engine, runs off the flywheel/driveplate and provides the ECM with crankshaft position and engine speed. The sensor is a Hall effect type which senses the passing of teeth on a flywheel/driveplate, because the teeth disrupt the magnetic field of the sensor. This disruption creates a pulse generation, which is monitored by the ECM. On the 3.9L engine, the flywheel/driveplate has three sets of double notches and three sets of single notches. On the 5.2L and the 5.9L, the flywheel/driveplate has 8 single notches spaced every 45 degrees. The ECM uses these pulses to properly set the ignition timing. With out these signals, the vehicles will crank but not start.

TESTING

▶ **See Figures 105 and 106**

1. Remove the engine cover.
2. Using the DRB-II scan tool or equivalent, plug into diagnostic connector and erase DTC's.
3. Turn ignition **OFF** and then **ON** again.
4. Crank engine until starts or for 10 seconds, whichever first. Monitor Crank Signal on scan tool. If Crank Signal is detected, CKP sensor is OK, if No Crank Signal is detected, proceed with diagnostics.
5. Inspect wiring and connectors and repair as necessary and retest, if wiring and connectors are OK, proceed to next step.
6. With the ignition **OFF**, unplug the CKP sensor signal. Using a voltmeter, check the supply voltage using supplied schematics.
   a. On 1995 and earlier vehicles, it should be 7.0v or more; if not, repair circuit and retest. If voltage is OK, proceed to next step.
   b. On 1996–98 vehicles, it should be 4.5v or more; if not, repair circuit and retest. If voltage is OK, proceed to the next step.
7. Using the scan tool, erase DTC's in the ECM, then turn the ignition **OFF** and install a jumper wire on the CKP signal circuit. Turn the ignition **ON**.

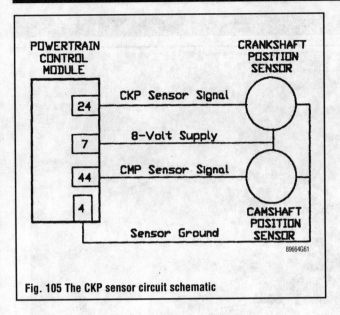

Fig. 105 The CKP sensor circuit schematic

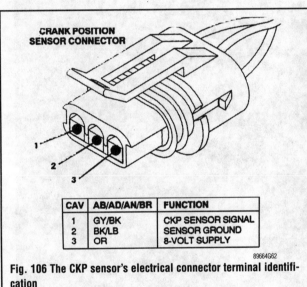

CAV	AB/AD/AN/BR	FUNCTION
1	GY/BK	CKP SENSOR SIGNAL
2	BK/LB	SENSOR GROUND
3	OR	8-VOLT SUPPLY

Fig. 106 The CKP sensor's electrical connector terminal identification

8. While observing the display on scan tool, tap the other end of the jumper wire to the sensor ground. If the scan tool shows No Cam Sync, replace the CKP sensor. If the scan tool shows a Cam Sync, proceed to next step.

9. With the ignition **OFF**, using an ohmmeter probe the ground signal on the CKP sensor connector, measure the resistance between the connector and ground. If it is less than 5.0 ohms, proceed to the next step; if it is more than 5.0v, repair the circuit and retest.

10. Disconnect the negative battery cable.

11. Disconnect the ECM wiring harness. Inspect for any damaged pins or connector terminals and repair and retest if necessary.

Testing the wiring harness with the ECM still connected can cause serious damage to the processor. ALWAYS disconnect the ECM before testing the wiring harness., unless instructed otherwise.

12. Using an ohmmeter, test the CKP signal circuit between CKPconnector and ECM connector for resistance. If it is less than 5.0 ohms, proceed to next step, if it is more than 5.0 ohms, repair the circuit and retest.

13. Plug in the CKP sensor connector.

14. Using an ohmmeter, measure the resistance between the CKP signal circuit and CKP ground at the ECM connector. If resistance is less than 5ohms, repair the short in the CKP signal wire. If the resistance is more than 5 ohms, replace the CKP sensor.

REMOVAL & INSTALLATION

▶ See Figure 107

1. Disconnect the negative battery cable.
2. Remove the engine cover.
3. Unplug the CKP sensor connector.
4. Remove the two sensor retaining bolts.
5. Remove the sensor from the engine block.

To install:

6. Install the sensor on the engine block and tighten retaining bolts to 70 inch lbs. (8 Nm).
7. Plug the CKP sensor connector in.
8. Install the engine cover.
9. Connect the negative battery cable.

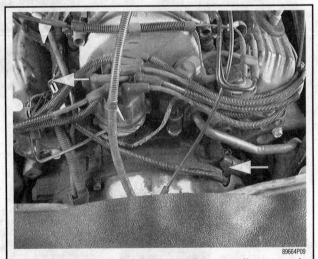

Fig. 107 Location of the crankshaft position sensor (lower arrow) and electrical connector (upper arrow)—5.2L engine shown

COMPONENT LOCATIONS

EMISSION CONTROL COMPONENT LOCATIONS

1. Breather element assembly
2. PCV valve and hose
3. EVAP purge solenoid
4. EGR valve

ELECTRONIC ENGINE CONTROL AND EGR SYSTEM COMPONENT LOCATIONS

1. Intake Air Temperature (IAT) sensor
2. Crankshaft Position (CKP) sensor
3. EGR valve transducer
4. Camshaft Position (CMP) sensor (inside distributor)

ELECTRONIC ENGINE CONTROL COMPONENT LOCATIONS

1. Manifold Absolute Pressure (MAP) sensor
2. Throttle Position (TP) sensor
3. Idle Air Control (IAC) motor
4. Engine Coolant Temperature (ECT) sensor
   (in front of intake manifold)

TROUBLE CODES

General Information

The Engine Control Module (ECM) is given responsibility for the operation of the emission control devices, cooling fans, ignition and advance and in some cases, automatic transmission functions. Because the ECM oversees both the ignition timing and the fuel injector operation, a precise air/fuel ratio will be maintained under all operating conditions. The ECM is a microprocessor or small computer which receives electrical inputs from several sensors, switches and relays on and around the engine.

Based on combinations of these inputs, the ECM controls outputs to various devices concerned with engine operation and emissions. The ECM relies on the signals to form a correct picture of current vehicle operation. If any of the input signals is incorrect, the ECM reacts to what ever picture is painted for it. For example, if the coolant temperature sensor is inaccurate and reads too low, the ECM may see a picture of the engine never warming up. Consequently, the engine settings will be maintained as if the engine were cold. Because so many inputs can affect one output, correct diagnostic procedures are essential on these systems.

One part of the ECM is devoted to monitoring both input and output functions within the system. This ability forms the core of the self-diagnostic system. If a problem is detected within a circuit, the control module will recognize the fault, assign it an Diagnostic Trouble Code (DTC), and store the code in memory. The stored code(s) may be retrieved during diagnosis.

While the ECM is capable of recognizing many internal faults, certain faults will not be recognized. Because the ECM sees only electrical signals, it cannot sense or react to mechanical or vacuum faults affecting engine operation. Some of these faults may affect another component which will set a code. For example, the ECM monitors the output signal to the fuel injectors, but cannot detect a partially clogged injector. As long as the output driver responds correctly, the computer will read the system as functioning correctly. However, the improper flow of fuel may result in a lean mixture. This would, in turn, be detected by the oxygen sensor and noticed as a constantly lean signal by the ECM. Once the signal falls outside the pre-programmed limits, the ECM would notice the fault and set an trouble code.

Additionally, the ECM employs adaptive fuel logic. This process is used to compensate for normal wear and variability within the fuel system. Once the engine enters steady-state operation, the ECM watches the oxygen sensor signal for a bias or tendency to run slightly rich or lean. If such a bias is detected, the adaptive logic corrects the fuel delivery to bring the air/fuel mixture towards a centered or 14.7:1 ratio. This compensating shift is stored in a non-volatile memory which is retained by battery power even with the ignition switched **OFF**. The correction factor is then available the next time the vehicle is operated.

➡️**If the battery cable(s) is disconnected for longer than 5 minutes, the adaptive fuel factor will be lost. After repair it will be necessary to drive the truck at least 10 miles to allow the processor to relearn the correct factors. The driving period should include steady-throttle open road driving if possible. During the drive, the vehicle may exhibit driveability symptoms not noticed before. These symptoms should clear as the control module computes the correction factor.**

There are two electronic engine control systems used. The first is used on 1989–95 vehicles and is referred to as OBD-I. The second is used on 1996–98 vehicles, and is called OBD-II. OBD-I is slightly more basic than OBD-II, the main difference is the monitors that are incorporated into the engine controls on OBD-II. OBD-II vehicles are able to monitor certain systems of the vehicle through various new input sensors and output hardware. These monitors include the Catalyst Efficiency, Engine Misfire Detection, Comprehensive Component, EGR System Flow, EVAP System Integrity, Secondary Air (if equipped), Fuel System, and Heated O2 Sensor Monitors.

Some of the new hardware included with these monitors are another O2 sensor behind the catalyst, an LDP on the EVAP system, and a High Data Rate CKP sensor to help monitor engine misfires. All monitors in the OBD-II system have separate trouble codes and are diagnosed by standard diagnostic methods.

MALFUNCTION INDICATOR LAMP (MIL)

▶ See Figure 108

The Malfunction Indicator Lamp (MIL) is located on the instrument panel. The lamp is connected to the control unit and will alert the driver to certain malfunctions detected by the ECM. When the lamp is illuminated, the ECM has detected a fault and stored an DTC in memory.

The light will stay illuminated as long as the fault is present. Should the fault self-correct, the MIL will extinguish but the stored code will remain in memory.

Under normal operating conditions, the MIL should illuminate briefly when the ignition key is turned **ON**. This is commonly known as a bulb check. As soon as the ECM receives a signal that the engine is cranking, the lamp should extinguish. The lamp should remain extinguished during the normal operating cycle.

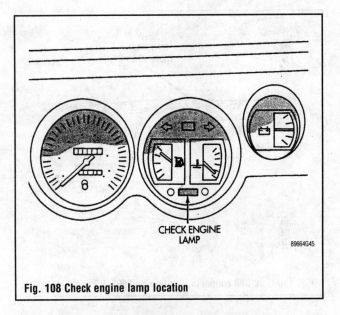

CHECK ENGINE
LAMP

89664G45

Fig. 108 Check engine lamp location

Diagnostic Connector

▶ See Figures 109, 110 and 111

The diagnostic connector is located in the engine compartment on the firewall, near the ECM on 1989–95 vehicles. On 1996–98 vehicles, it is located under the dashboard, on the driver's side, next to the steering column.

Reading Codes

▶ See Figures 112 and 113

There are two kinds of codes stored in the ECM: hard faults and continuous faults. A hard fault is a fault detected that is malfunctioning at the time of testing. A continuos fault is a fault that was detected by the ECM, but is not malfunctioning at the moment. The ECM will erase this code if the fault does not recur within a set amount of time; different year models take differ-

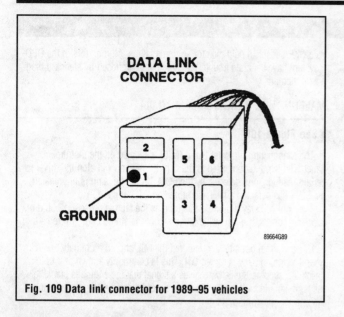

Fig. 109 Data link connector for 1989–95 vehicles

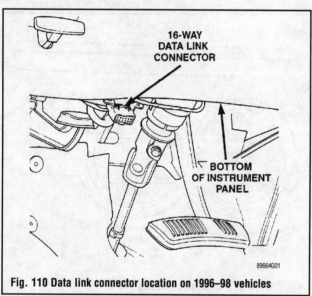

Fig. 110 Data link connector location on 1996–98 vehicles

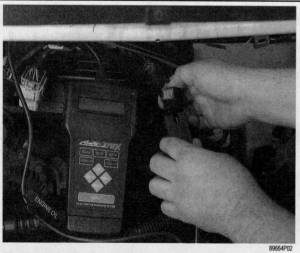

Fig. 111 Plug the scan tool right into the connector to retrieve DTC's or to perform other tests

Fig. 112 Although sometimes no DTC's are found, that does not rule out a potential problem

Fig. 113 When you find a DTC, proceed to diagnostics

ent amounts of time to clear these code, however it usually is around 50 starts.

When the MIL lamp (Check Engine light) illuminates while the engine is running, it indicates a detected fault by the ECM. To retrieve this information from the ECM you can use two methods. The first is to use the DRB-II scan tool, or equivalent, and retrieve the codes. The second way to retrieve the codes is to cycle the ignition switch as follows:**ON-OFF-ON-OFF-ON** within five seconds. The MIL lamp will then flash the DTC(s). Each code, if there is more than one, will be preceded by a four-second pause to distinguish it from the previous code. An example of a DTC flashed by the MIL would be:

1. Lamp on for two seconds, then turns off.
2. Lamp flashes two times, then pauses, then flashes seven times.
3. Lamp pauses for four seconds.
4. Lamp flashes three times, then pauses, then flashes one time.
5. Lamp pauses for four seconds.
6. Lamp flashes five times, then pauses, then flashes five times.

In this ECM, the DTC's stored were 27, and 31. The ECM will then flash code 55 after it has reached the last code stored in its memory.

➡**The second method of DTC retrieval will not work on 1996–98 OBD-II vehicles. OBD-II DTC's must be retrieved using the DRB-II scan tool or equivalent.**

1989–92 FAULT CODE DESCRIPTION

Fault Code	DRBII Display	Description of Fault Condition
11	Ign Reference Signal	No distributor reference signal detected during engine cranking.
12	N/A (See Key-On Info)	Direct battery input to controller disconnected within the last 50 ignition key on cycles.
13	MAP Pneumatic Signal or MAP Voltage Too Low	No variation in MAP sensor signal is detected. No difference is recognized between the engine MAP reading and the stored barometric pressure reading.
14	MAP Voltage Too Low or MAP Voltage Too High	MAP sensor input below minimum acceptable voltage. MAP sensor input above maximum acceptable voltage.
15	Vehicle Speed Signal	No distance sensor signal detected during road load conditions.
17	Low Engine Temp	Engine coolant temperature remains below normal operating temperatures during vehicle travel (thermostat).
21	Oxygen Sensor Signal or O₂ Sensor Shorted High	Neither rich or lean condition is detected from the oxygen sensor input. Oxygen sensor input voltage maintained above normal operating range.
22	Coolant Voltage Low or Coolant Voltage High	Coolant temperature sensor input below the minimum acceptable voltage. Coolant temperature sensor input above the maximum acceptable voltage.
23	T/B Temp Voltage Low or T/B Temp Voltage High	Throttle body temperature sensor input below the minimum acceptable voltage (5.2L and 5.9L engines). Throttle body temperature sensor input above the maximum acceptable voltage (5.2L and 5.9L Engines).

89664C01

1989–92 FAULT CODE DESCRIPTION

FAULT CODE	DRBII DISPLAY	DESCRIPTION OF FAULT CONDITION
24	TPS Voltage Low or TPS Voltage High	Throttle position sensor input below the minimum acceptable voltage. Throttle position sensor input above the maximum acceptable voltage.
25	AIS Motor Circuits	A shorted condition detected in one or more of the AIS control circuits.
27	INJ 1 Control Ckt	Injector output driver #1 or #2 does not respond properly to the control signal.
31	Purge Solenoid Ckt	An open or shorted condition detected in the purge solenoid circuit.
32	EGR Solenoid Circuit or EGR System Failure	An open or shorted condition detected in the EGR solenoid circuit. Required change in air-fuel ratio not detected during diagnostic test (California emission packages only).
33	A/C Clutch Relay Ckt	An open or shorted condition detected in the A/C clutch relay circuit.
34	S/C Servo Solenoids	An open or shorted condition detected in the speed control vacuum or vent solenoid circuits.
35	Idle Switch Shorted or Idle Switch Opened	Idle contact switch input circuit shorted to ground. Idle contact switch input circuit opened.
36	Air Switch Solenoid	An open or shorted condition detected in the air switching solenoid circuit.
37	PTU Solenoid Circuit	An open or shorted condition detected in the torque convertor part throttle unlock circuit (Engine packages with A-999 or A-500 automatic transmissions only).

89664C02

1989–92 FAULT CODE DESCRIPTION

FAULT CODE	DRBII DISPLAY	DESCRIPTION OF FAULT CONDITION
41	Alternator Field Ckt	An open or shorted condition detected in the alternator control circuit.
42	ASD Relay Circuit or Z1 Voltage Sense	An open or shorted condition detected in the auto shutdown relay circuit. No Z1 voltage sensed when the auto shutdown relay circuit.
45	Overdrive Solenoid	An open or shorted condition detected in the overdrive solenoid circuit (engine packages with A-500 or A-518 automatic transmissions only).
46	Battery Voltage High	Battery voltage sensor input above target charging voltage during engine operation.
47	Charging Output Low	Battery voltage sense input below target charging voltage during engine operation and no significant change in voltage detected during active test of alternator output.
51	Lean F/A Condition	Oxygen sensor signal input indicates lean fuel/air ratio condition during engine operation.
52	Rich F/A Condition or Excessive Leaning	Oxygen sensor signal input indicates rich fuel/air ratio condition during engine operation. Adaptive fuel valve leaned excessively due to a sustained rich condition.
53	Internal Self Test	Internal engine controller fault condition detected.
62	EMR Miles Not Stored	Unsuccessful attempt to update EMR mileage in the controller EEPROM.
63	EEPROM Write Denied	Unsuccessful attempt to write to an EEPROM location by the controller.
55	N/A	Completion of fault code display on the CHECK ENGINE lamp.

89664C03

1993–95 *DIAGNOSTIC TROUBLE CODE (DTC) DESCRIPTION*

Diagnostic Trouble Code	DRB II Display	Description of Trouble Code Condition
11	No Crank Reference Signal at PCM	No distributor reference signal detected during engine cranking.
13+••	No Change in MAP From Start to Run	No variation in MAP sensor signal is detected. No difference is recognized between the engine MAP reading and the barometric pressure reading at start up.
14+••	MAP Voltage Too Low or MAP Voltage Too High	MAP sensor input below minimum acceptable voltage. MAP sensor input above maximum acceptable voltage.
15••	No Vehicle Speed Sensor Signal	No speed sensor signal detected during road load conditions.
17	Engine is Cold Too Long	Engine coolant temperature remains below normal operating temperatures during vehicle travel (thermostat).
21••	O$_2$ Signal Stays at Center or O$_2$ Signal Shorted to Voltage	Neither rich or lean condition is detected from the oxygen sensor input. Oxygen sensor input voltage maintained above normal operating range.
22+••	ECT Sensor Voltage Too Low or ECT Sensor Voltage Too High	Coolant temperature sensor input below the minimum acceptable voltage. Coolant temperature sensor input above the maximum acceptable voltage.
23	Charge Air Temperature Sensor Voltage High or Charge Air Temperature Sensor Voltage Low	Charge Air Temperature Sensor input above/below acceptable minimum.
24+••	Throttle Position Sensor Voltage High or Throttle Position Sensor Voltage Low	Throttle position sensor (TPS) input above the maximum acceptable voltage. Throttle position sensor (TPS) input below the minimum acceptable voltage.
25••	Idle Air Control Motor Circuits (ISC Actuator)	A shorted condition detected in one or more of the idle air control actuator circuits.
27+••	Control Circuit	Injector output driver does not respond properly to the control signal.
31••	EVAP Purge Solenoid Circuit	An open or shorted condition detected in the purge solenoid circuit.
32••	EGR System Failure	An open or shorted condition detected in the EGR solenoid circuit. Required change in air-fuel ratio not detected during diagnostic test (California emissions packages only).

89664C04

1993–95 *DIAGNOSTIC TROUBLE CODE (DTC) DESCRIPTION—CONTINUED*

Diagnostic Trouble Code	DRB II Display	Description of Trouble Code Condition
33	A/C Clutch Relay Circuit	An open or shorted condition detected in the A/C clutch relay circuit.
34	Speed Control Solenoid Circuits	An open or shorted condition detected in the speed control vacuum or vent solenoid circuits.
37	Torque Converter Clutch Solenoid Circuit (CKT)	An open or shorted condition detected in the torque converter clutch solenoid circuit (vehicles with automatic transmissions only).
41+**	Generator Field Not Switching Properly	Generator field not switching properly.
42	Auto Shutdown Relay Control Circuit or No ASD Relay Voltage Sense at Controller	An open or short condition detected in the auto shutdown relay circuit. No ASD voltage sensed at PCM.
44	Battery Temperature Voltage	Battery temperature sensor volts out of limit.
45	Overdrive Solenoid	An open or shorted condition detected in overdrive solenoid circuit.
46+**	Charging System Voltage Too High	Charging system voltage too high.
47+**	Charging System Voltage Too Low	Charging system voltage too low.
51**	O_2 Signal Stays Below Center (Lean) or Additive Adaptive Memory at Rich Limit	O_2 sensor signal stays lean. Additive adaptive memory at rich limit.
52**	O_2 Signal Stays Above Center (Rich) or Additive Adaptive Memory at Lean Limit	O_2 sensor signal stays rich. Additive adaptive memory at lean limit.
53	Internal PCM Failure	Internal failure in the PCM (Powertrain Control Module)
54	Sync Pick-up Signal	No fuel sync signal detected during crankshaft rotation.
55	NA	Completion of trouble code display on the Malfunction Indicator (MIL) lamp.
62	PCM Failure SRI Miles Not Stored	PCM (Powertrain Control Module) failure – SRI miles not stored.
63	PCM Failure EEprom Write Denied	PCM (Powertrain Control Module) failure – EEprom write denied.

** Check Engine Lamp ON (California only)
+ Check Engine Lamp ON

89664C05

1996–98 *DIAGNOSTIC TROUBLE CODE DESCRIPTIONS*

Generic Scan Tool Code	DRB Scan Tool Display	Description of Diagnostic Trouble Code
		DTC Error
P0340	No Cam Signal at PCM	No camshaft signal detected during engine cranking.
P0601	Internal Controller Failure	PCM Internal fault condition detected.
P0162	Charging System Voltage Too Low	Battery voltage sense input below target charging during engine operation. Also, no significant change detected in battery voltage during active test of generator output circuit.
P1594	Charging System Voltage Too High	Battery voltage sense input above target charging voltage during engine operation.
P1388	Auto Shutdown Relay Control Circuit	An open or shorted condition detected in the auto shutdown relay circuit.
P0622	Generator Field Not Switching Properly	An open or shorted condition detected in the generator field control circuit.
P0743	Torque Converter Clutch Soleniod/Trans Relay Circuits	An open or shorted condition detected in the torque converter part throttle unlock solenoid control circuit (3 speed auto RH trans. only).
P1595	Speed Control Solenoid Circuits	An open or shorted condition detected in the Speed Control vacuum or vent solenoid circuits.
P0645	A/C Clutch Relay Circuit	An open or shorted condition detected in the A/C clutch relay circuit.
P0443	EVAP Purge Solenoid Circuit	An open or shorted condition detected in the duty cycle purge solenoid circuit.
P0203 or	Injector #3 Control Circuit	Injector #3 output driver does not respond properly to the control signal.
P0202 or	Injector #2 Control Circuit	Injector #2 output driver does not respond properly to the control signal.
P0201	Injector #1 Control Circuit	Injector #1 output driver does not respond properly to the control signal.
P0505	Idle Air Control Motor Circuits	A shorted or open condition detected in one or more of the idle air control motor circuits.
P0122 or	Throttle Position Sensor Voltage Low	Throttle position sensor input below the minimum acceptable voltage.
P0123	Throttle Position Sensor Voltage High	Throttle position sensor input above the maximum acceptable voltage.
P0117 or	ECT Sensor Voltage Too Low	Engine coolant temperature sensor input below minimum acceptable voltage.
P0118	ECT Sensor Voltage Too High	Engine coolant temperature sensor input above maximum acceptable voltage.

89664C07

1996–98 DIAGNOSTIC TROUBLE CODES

Generic Scan Tool Code	DRB Scan Tool Display	Description of Diagnostic Trouble Code
1281	Engine Is Cold Too Long	Engine did not reach operating temperature within acceptable limits.
P0107 or	MAP Sensor Voltage Too Low	MAP sensor input below minimum acceptable voltage.
P0108	MAP Sensor Voltage Too High	MAP sensor input above maximum acceptable voltage.
P1297	No Change in MAP From Start to Run	No difference recognized between the engine MAP reading and the barometric (atmospheric) pressure reading from start-up.
P0320	No Crank Reference Signal at PCM	No crank reference signal detected during engine cranking.
P0351	Ignition Coil #1 Primary Circuit	Peak primary circuit current not achieved with maximum dwell time.
P1389	No ASD Relay Output Voltage at PCM	An Open condition Detected In The ASD Relay Output Circuit.
P1696	PCM Failure EEPROM Write Denied	Unsuccessful attempt to write to an EEPROM location by the PCM.
P0753	Trans 3-4 Shift Sol/Trans Relay Circuits	Current state of output port for the solenoid is different from expected state.
P0112 or	Intake Air Temp Sensor Voltage Low	Intake air temperature sensor input below the maximum acceptable voltage.
P0113	Intake Air Temp Sensor Voltage High	Intake air temperature sensor input above the minimum acceptable voltage.
P0204	Injector #4 Control Circuit	Injector #4 output driver does not respond properly to the control signal.
P0132	Left Upstream O2S Shorted to Voltage	Oxygen sensor input voltage maintained above the normal operating range.
P0154	O2 2/1 Signal Inactive	No signal at O2 2/1 sensor
P0152	O2 2/1 Shorted High	Oxygen sensor input voltage sustained above the normal operating range.
PO600	PCM Failure SPI Communications	PCM internal fault condition detected.
P0205 or	Injector #5 Control Circuit	Injector #5 output driver does not respond properly to the control signal.
P0206	Injector #6 Control Circuit	Injector #6 output driver does not respond properly to the control signal.
P0712 or	Trans Temp Sensor Voltage Too Low	Voltage less than 1.55 volts.
P0713	Trans Temp Sensor Voltage Too High	Voltage greater than 3.76 volts.
P0207	Injector #7 Control Circuit	Injector #7 output driver does not respond properly to the control signal.

89664C08

1996–98 DIAGNOSTIC TROUBLE CODES

Generic Scan Tool Code	DRB Scan Tool Display	Description of Diagnostic Trouble Code
or P0208	Injector #8 Control Circuit	Injector #8 output driver does not respond properly to the control signal.
P1683	SPD CTRL PWR RLY; or S/C 12V Driver CKT	Malfuntion detected with power feed to speed control servo solenoids.
P1596	MUX S/C Switch High	Speed control switch input above the maximum acceptable voltage.
or P1597	MUX S/C Switch Low	Speed control switch input below the minimum acceptable voltage.
P1282	Fuel Pump Relay Control Circuit	An open or shorted condition detected in the fuel pump relay control circuit.
P0133 or P0152	O2 1/1 Slow Response	Oxygen sensor response slower than minimum required switching frequency.
or P0135	O2 1/1 Heater Circuit	Upstream oxygen sensor heating element circuit malfunction.
P0139	O2 1/1 Slow Response	Oxygen sensor response slower than minimum required switching frequency.
P0141	O2 1/2 Heater Circuit	Oxygen sensor heating element circuit malfunction.
P0300 or	Multiple Cylinder Mis-fire	Misfire detected in multiple cylinders.
P0301 or	Cylinder #1 Mis-fire	Misfire detected in cylinder #1.
P0302 or	Cylinder #2 Mis-fire	Misfire detected in cylinder #2.
P0303 or	Cylinder #3 Mis-fire	Misfire detected in cylinder #3.
P0304	Cylinder #4 Mis-fire	Misfire detected in cylinder #4.
P0420	Catalyst 1/1 Effic	Catalyst efficiency below required level.
P0441	Incorrect Purge Flow	Insufficient or excessive vapor flow detected during evaporative emission system operation.
P1899	P/N Switch Stuck in Park or in Gear	Incorrect input state detected for the Park/Neutral switch, auto. trans. only.
P0172	Left Bank or Fuel System Rich	A rich air/fuel mixture has been indicated by an abnormally lean correction factor.
P0171	Right Rear (or just) Fuel System Lean	A lean air/fuel mixture has been indicated by an abnormally rich correction factor.
P0175	Fuel System 2/1 Rich	A rich air/fuel mixture has been indicated by an abnormally lean correction factor.
P0174	Fuel System 2/1 Lean	A lean air/fuel mixture has been indicated by an abnormally lean correction factor.

89664C09

Clearing Codes

CONTINUOUS MEMORY CODES

These codes are retained in memory for usually around 50 warm-up cycles. To clear the codes for the purposes of testing or confirming repair, perform the code reading procedure. Use the DRB-II scan tool or equivalent to erase the memory. Disconnecting the negative battery cable will not erase the code completely from the memory, it will remain as a continuous fault. The MIL lamp will remain out if you disconnect the battery, and the malfunction that lit the MIL lamp is repaired. After 50 warm-up cycles or so are reached, the code will be erased from the ECM's memory.

KEEP ALIVE MEMORY

The Keep Alive Memory (KAM) contains the adaptive factors used by the processor to compensate for component tolerances and wear. It should not be routinely cleared during diagnosis. If an emissions related part is replaced during repair, the KAM must be cleared. Failure to clear the KAM may cause severe driveability problems since the correction factor for the old component will be applied to the new component.

To clear the Keep Alive Memory, disconnect the negative battery cable for at least 5 minutes. After the memory is cleared and the battery reconnected, the vehicle must be driven at least 10 miles so that the processor may relearn the needed correction factors. The distance to be driven depends on the engine and vehicle, but all drives should include steady-throttle cruise on open roads. Certain driveability problems may be noted during the drive because the adaptive factors are not yet functioning.

VACUUM DIAGRAMS

▶ **See Figures 114 thru 120**

Following are vacuum diagrams for most of the engine and emissions package combinations covered by this manual. Because vacuum circuits will vary based on various engine and vehicle options, always refer first to the vehicle emission control information label, if present. Should the label

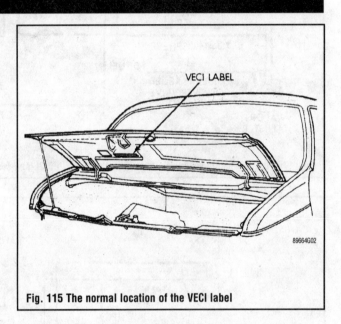

Fig. 115 The normal location of the VECI label

be missing, or should the vehicle be equipped with a different engine from the vehicle's original equipment, refer to the diagrams below for the same or similar configuration.

If you wish to obtain a replacement emissions label, most manufacturers make the labels available for purchase.

The labels can usually be ordered from a local dealer.

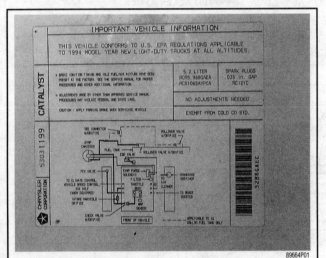

Fig. 114 The Vehicle Emission Control Information (VECI) label contains information critical to its performance

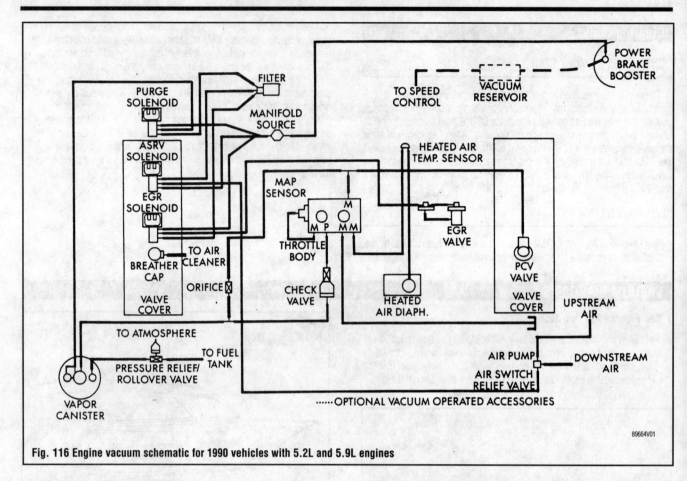

Fig. 116 Engine vacuum schematic for 1990 vehicles with 5.2L and 5.9L engines

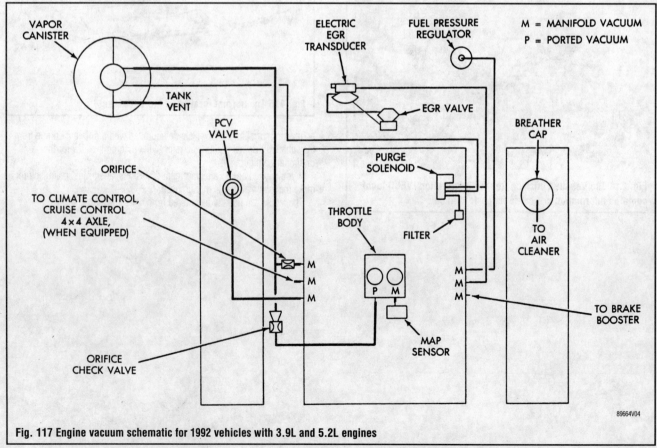

Fig. 117 Engine vacuum schematic for 1992 vehicles with 3.9L and 5.2L engines

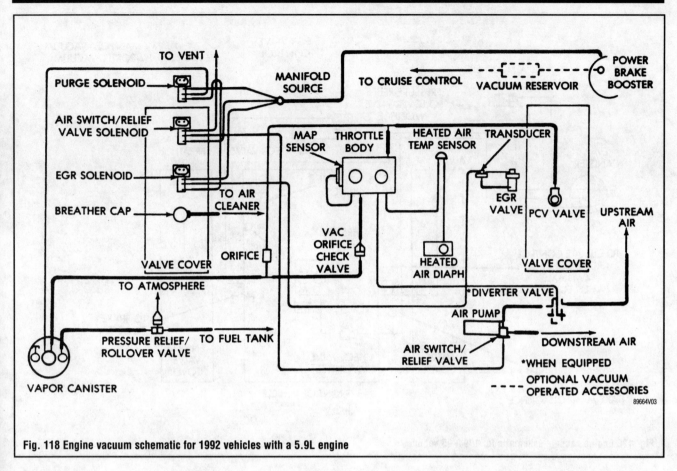

Fig. 118 Engine vacuum schematic for 1992 vehicles with a 5.9L engine

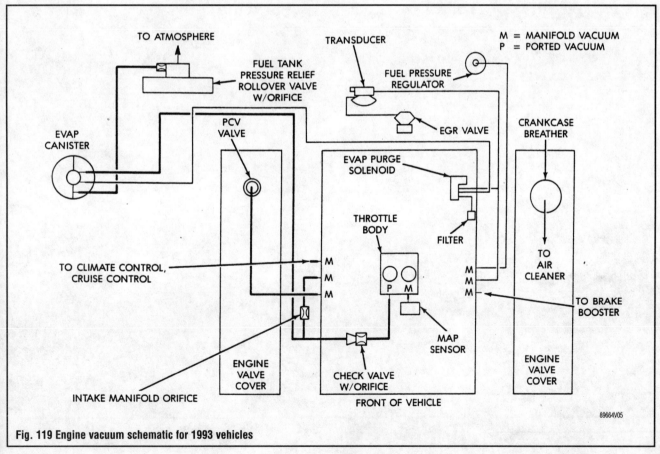

Fig. 119 Engine vacuum schematic for 1993 vehicles

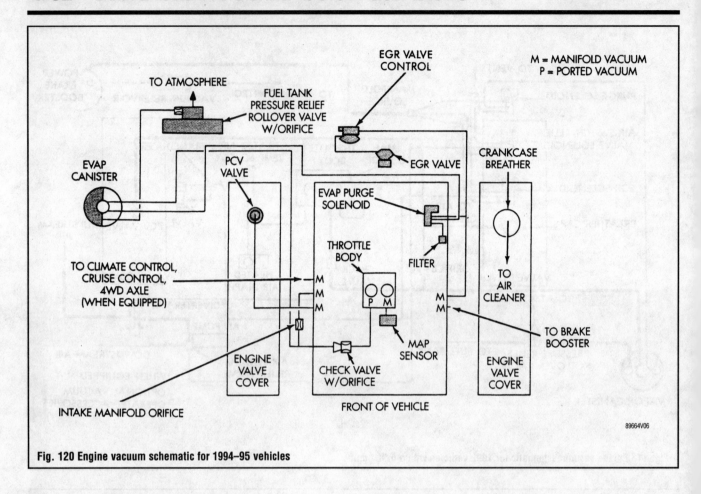

Fig. 120 Engine vacuum schematic for 1994–95 vehicles

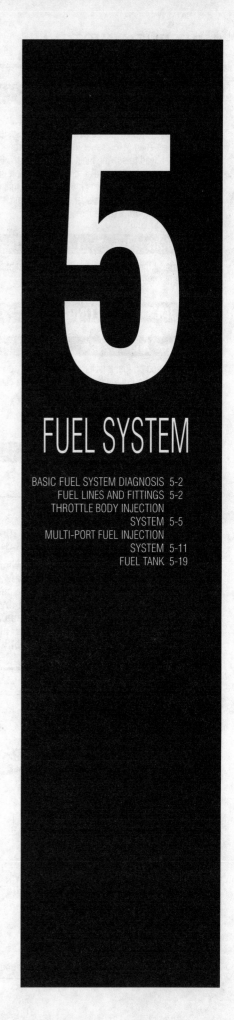

5

FUEL SYSTEM

BASIC FUEL SYSTEM DIAGNOSIS

When there is a problem starting or driving a vehicle, two of the most important checks involve the ignition and the fuel systems. The questions most mechanics attempt to answer first, "is there spark?" and "is there fuel?" will often lead to solving most basic problems. For ignition system diagnosis and testing, please refer to the information on engine electrical components and ignition systems found earlier in this manual. If the ignition system checks out (there is spark), then you must determine if the fuel system is operating properly (is there fuel?).

Precautions

• Disconnect the negative battery terminal, except for testing when battery voltage is required.

FUEL LINES AND FITTINGS

Fuel Lines and Hoses

The hoses used on fuel injected vehicles are of special construction to prevent contamination of the fuel system. The hose clamps used are of a special construction. The clamps have a rolled edge design to prevent the edges from cutting the hose when tightened down. Only these type of clamps may be used on the fuel system hoses.

Conventional Type Fuel Fitting

REMOVAL & INSTALLATION

▶ See Figure 1

※ CAUTION

Observe all applicable safety precautions when working around fuel. Whenever servicing the fuel system, always work in a well ventilated area. Do not allow fuel spray or vapors to come in contact with a spark or open flame. Keep a dry chemical fire extinguisher near the work area. Always keep fuel in a container specifically designed for fuel storage; also, always properly seal fuel containers to avoid the possibility of fire or explosion.

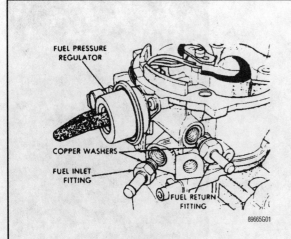

Fig. 1 The fuel line fittings on a TBI throttle body assembly

• Whenever possible, use a flashlight instead of a drop light to inspect fuel system components or connections.
• Keep all open flames and smoking material out of the area and make sure there is adequate ventilation to remove fuel vapors.
• Use a clean shop cloth to catch fuel when opening a fuel system. Dispose of gasoline-soaked rags properly.
• Relieve the fuel system pressure before any service procedures are attempted that require disconnecting a fuel line.
• Use eye protection.
• Always keep a dry chemical (class B) fire extinguisher near the area.

1. Remove the engine cover.
2. Remove the air cleaner assembly.
3. Perform the fuel system pressure release.
4. Disconnect the negative battery cable.
5. Loosen the fuel intake and return hose clamps. Wrap a shop towel around each hose, twist and pull off each hose.
6. Remove each fitting and note the inlet diameter. Remove the copper washers.
   To install:
7. Replace the copper washers with new washers.
8. Install the fuel fittings in the proper ports and tighten to 175 inch lbs. (20 Nm).
9. Using new original equipment type hose clamps, install the fuel return and supply hoses.
10. Reconnect the negative battery cable.
11. Start the engine and check for leaks.
12. Install the air cleaner assembly.
13. Install the engine cover.

Quick-Connect Fuel Fittings

REMOVAL & INSTALLATION

Single-Tab Type

▶ See Figure 2

※ CAUTION

Observe all applicable safety precautions when working around fuel. Whenever servicing the fuel system, always work in a well ventilated area. Do not allow fuel spray or vapors to come in contact with a spark or open flame. Keep a dry chemical fire extinguisher near the work area. Always keep fuel in a container specifically designed for fuel storage; also, always properly seal fuel containers to avoid the possibility of fire or explosion.

1. Remove the engine cover.
2. Remove the air cleaner assembly.
3. Properly relieve the fuel system pressure.
4. Disconnect the negative battery cable.
5. Clean the fitting of any foreign material before disassembly.
6. Press the release tab on the side of the fitting to release the pull tab.

※ WARNING

The release tab must be pressed prior to releasing the pull tab or the tab will be damaged.

7. While pressing the release tab on the side of the fitting, use a small prytool to pry up the pull tab.

8. Raise the pull tab until it separates from the quick-disconnect fitting. Discard the old pull tab.

9. Disconnect the quick-connect fitting.

10. Inspect the fitting body and the fuel system component for damage. Replace as necessary.

To install:

11. Insert the quick-connect fitting into the fuel tube or component until the built-on stop on the fuel tube or component rests against the back of the fitting.

12. Obtain a new pull tab. Push the new tab down until it locks into place in the quick-connect fitting.

13. Pull firmly on the fitting to verify the fitting is secure.

14. Connect the negative battery cable.

15. Start the engine and check for leaks.

16. Install the air cleaner assembly.

17. Install the engine cover.

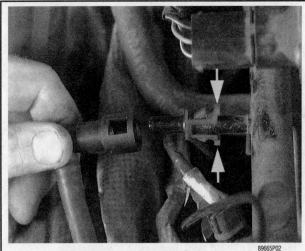

Fig. 3 Remove the fuel line connection by pressing down on its tabs (arrows) and pulling the line outward

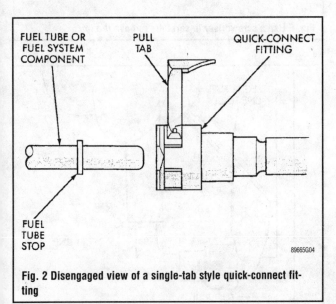

Fig. 2 Disengaged view of a single-tab style quick-connect fitting

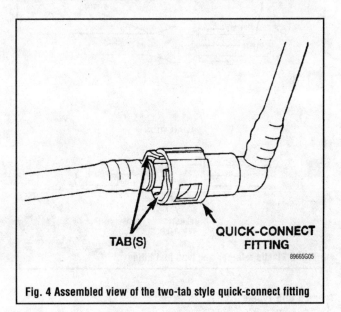

Fig. 4 Assembled view of the two-tab style quick-connect fitting

Two-Tab Type

⬩ See Figures 3 and 4

❋❋ CAUTION

Observe all applicable safety precautions when working around fuel. Whenever servicing the fuel system, always work in a well ventilated area. Do not allow fuel spray or vapors to come in contact with a spark or open flame. Keep a dry chemical fire extinguisher near the work area. Always keep fuel in a container specifically designed for fuel storage; also, always properly seal fuel containers to avoid the possibility of fire or explosion.

1. Remove the engine cover.
2. Remove the air cleaner assembly.
3. Properly relieve the fuel system pressure.
4. Disconnect the negative battery cable.
5. Clean the fitting of any foreign material before disassembly.
6. Squeeze the plastic retaining tabs against the sides of the fitting with your fingers.
7. Pull the fitting from the component or tube being disconnected. The plastic retainer will stay on the component or tube. The O-rings and spacer will remain in the fitting connector body.
8. Inspect the fitting body and the fuel system component for damage. Replace as necessary.

To install:

9. Insert the quick-connect fitting to the component or fuel tube and into the plastic retainer. When a connection is made, a click will be heard.

10. Pull firmly on the fitting to verify the fitting is secure.

11. Connect the negative battery cable.

12. Start the engine and check for leaks.

13. Install the air cleaner assembly.

14. Install the engine cover.

Plastic Retainer Ring Type

⬩ See Figure 5

❋❋ CAUTION

Observe all applicable safety precautions when working around fuel. Whenever servicing the fuel system, always work in a well ventilated area. Do not allow fuel spray or vapors to come in contact with a spark or open flame. Keep a dry chemical fire extinguisher near the work area. Always keep fuel in a container specifically designed for fuel storage; also, always properly seal fuel containers to avoid the possibility of fire or explosion.

1. Remove the engine cover.
2. Remove the air cleaner assembly.
3. Properly relieve the fuel system pressure.
4. Disconnect the negative battery cable.
5. Clean the fitting of any foreign material before disassembly.
6. To release the fitting, firmly push the fitting towards the component it's attached to while firmly pushing the plastic retainer ring into the fitting.
7. Pull the fitting from the component or tube being disconnected. The plastic retainer will stay on the component or tube.
8. Inspect the fitting body and the fuel system component for damage. Replace as necessary.

To install:

9. Insert the quick-connect fitting to the component or fuel tube and into the plastic retainer. When a connection is made, a click will be heard.
10. Pull firmly on the fitting to verify the fitting is secure.
11. Connect the negative battery cable.
12. Start the engine and check for leaks.
13. Install the air cleaner assembly.
14. Install the engine cover.

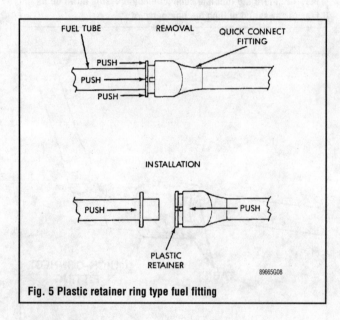

Fig. 5 Plastic retainer ring type fuel fitting

Latch Clip Type

▶ See Figures 6 and 7

※※ CAUTION

Observe all applicable safety precautions when working around fuel. Whenever servicing the fuel system, always work in a well ventilated area. Do not allow fuel spray or vapors to come in contact with a spark or open flame. Keep a dry chemical fire extinguisher near the work area. Always keep fuel in a container specifically designed for fuel storage; also, always properly seal fuel containers to avoid the possibility of fire or explosion.

1. Remove the engine cover.
2. Remove the air cleaner assembly.
3. Properly relieve the fuel system pressure.
4. Disconnect the negative battery cable.
5. Clean the fitting of any foreign material before disassembly.

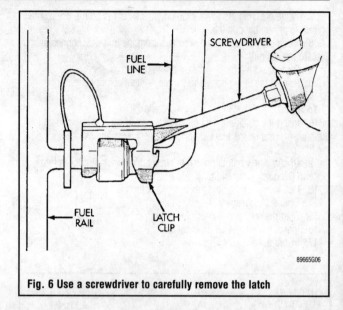

Fig. 6 Use a screwdriver to carefully remove the latch

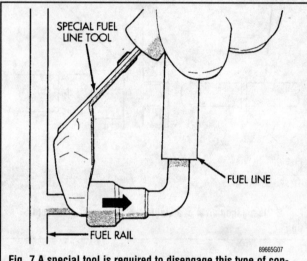

Fig. 7 A special tool is required to disengage this type of connection

6. Pry up on the latch clip with a screwdriver and remove the clip from the quick-connect fitting.
7. Insert a proper fuel line removal tool, available from such companies as Lisle, into the fuel line.
8. With the tool inserted inside the line releasing the locking fingers, pull the line releasing the connection.
9. Inspect the fitting, locking fingers and fuel line for damage, repair as necessary.

To install:

10. Insert the fitting end onto the line or component until a click is heard.
11. Pull firmly on the fitting to verify the fitting is secure.
12. Install the latch clip onto the fitting.
13. Connect the negative battery cable.
14. Start the engine and check for leaks.
15. Install the air cleaner assembly.
16. Install the engine cover.

THROTTLE BODY INJECTION SYSTEM

General Information

※※ CAUTION

The fuel injection system is under a constant pressure of approximately 14.5 psi. Before servicing any part of the fuel injection system, the system pressure must be released. Use a clean shop towel to catch any fuel spray and take precautions to avoid the risk of fire.

A Throttle Body Injection (TBI) system is used on all 1989–91, as well as some 1992 model engines. The TBI system is controlled by a pre-programmed digital computer known as the Engine Control Module (ECM). The ECM controls ignition timing, air/fuel ratio, emission control devices, charging system and idle speed. The ECM constantly varies timing, fuel delivery and idle speed to meet changing engine operating conditions.

Various sensors provide the input necessary for the ECM to correctly regulate the fuel flow at the fuel injector. These include the manifold absolute pressure, throttle position, oxygen sensor, coolant temperature, charge temperature, vehicle speed (distance) sensors and throttle body temperature. In addition to the sensors, various switches also provide important information. These include the neutral safety, heated backlite, air conditioning, air conditioning clutch switches, and an electronic idle switch.

All inputs to the ECM are converted into signals which are used to calculate and adjust the fuel flow at the injector or ignition timing or both. The ECM accomplishes this by sending signals to the power module.

The ECM tests many of its own input and output circuits. If a fault is found in a major system this information is stored in the ECM as a Diagnostic Trouble Code (DTC). Information on this fault can be displayed to a technician by means of the grounding a terminal and reading the check engine lamp flashes or by connecting a scan tool and reading the DTCs (see Section 4 for a more complete procedure).

Relieving Fuel System Pressure

※※ CAUTION

Observe all applicable safety precautions when working around fuel. Whenever servicing the fuel system, always work in a well ventilated area. Do not allow fuel spray or vapors to come in contact with a spark or open flame. Keep a dry chemical fire extinguisher near the work area. Always keep fuel in a container specifically designed for fuel storage; also, always properly seal fuel containers to avoid the possibility of fire or explosion.

1. Loosen the fuel filler cap to release tank pressure.
2. Remove the engine cover.
3. Remove the air cleaner assembly.
4. Remove the wiring harness connector from the injector.
5. Ground one terminal of the injector.
6. Connect a jumper wire to the second terminal and touch the battery positive post for no longer than ten seconds. This releases system pressure.
7. Remove the jumper wire and continue fuel system service.

Testing Fuel System Pressure

※※ CAUTION

Observe all applicable safety precautions when working around fuel. Whenever servicing the fuel system, always work in a well ventilated area. Do not allow fuel spray or vapors to come in contact with a spark or open flame. Keep a dry chemical fire

extinguisher near the work area. Always keep fuel in a container specifically designed for fuel storage; also, always properly seal fuel containers to avoid the possibility of fire or explosion.

1. Remove the engine cover.
2. Properly relieve the fuel system pressure.
3. Remove the fuel intake hose from the throttle body and connect fuel system pressure testers C-3292, and C-4749, C-4799B or equivalent, between the fuel filter hose and the throttle body.
4. Start the engine and read the gauge; the pressure should be 14.5 psi.
5. If the fuel pressure is below specifications:
   a. Install the tester on the fuel filter inlet hose between the fuel filter and the fuel pump.
   b. Start the engine. If the pressure is now correct, replace the fuel filter. If no change is observed, gently squeeze the return hose. If the pressure increases, replace the pressure regulator. If no change is observed, the problem is either a plugged pump filter sock or a defective fuel pump.
6. If the pressure is above specifications:
   a. Remove the fuel return hose from the throttle body. Connect a substitute hose and place the other end of the hose in a clean container.
   b. Start the engine. If the pressure is now correct, check for a restricted fuel return line. If no change is observed, replace the fuel regulator.

Fuel Pump

♦ See Figure 8

The fuel pump used in this system is a positive displacement, roller vane immersible pump with a permanent magnet electric motor. The fuel is drawn in through a filter sock and pushed through the electric motor to the outlet. The pump contains two check valves. One valve is used to relieve internal fuel pump pressure and regulate maximum pump output. The other check valve, located near the pump outlet, restricts fuel movement in either direction when the pump is not operational. Voltage to operate the pump is supplied through the Auto Shut Down (ASD) relay.

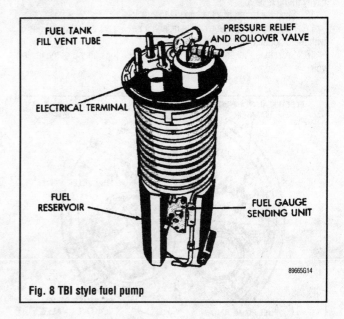

FUEL TANK FILL VENT TUBE — PRESSURE RELIEF AND ROLLOVER VALVE — ELECTRICAL TERMINAL — FUEL RESERVOIR — FUEL GAUGE SENDING UNIT

89665G14

Fig. 8 TBI style fuel pump

TESTING

Refer to the preceding Fuel System Pressure testing procedure.

REMOVAL & INSTALLATION

♦ See Figures 9 thru 15

✷✷ CAUTION

Observe all applicable safety precautions when working around fuel. Whenever servicing the fuel system, always work in a well ventilated area. Do not allow fuel spray or vapors to come in contact with a spark or open flame. Keep a dry chemical fire extinguisher near the work area. Always keep fuel in a container specifically designed for fuel storage; also, always properly seal fuel containers to avoid the possibility of fire or explosion.

1. Properly relieve the fuel system pressure.
2. Disconnect the negative battery cable.
3. Raise and support vehicle.
4. Remove the fuel tank from the vehicle.
5. Remove the holding clamp and lift out the fuel pump module.
6. Remove the sending unit attaching screws from the mounting bracket located on the drain tube.
7. Disconnect the wires from the sending unit and remove the sending unit.
8. Remove the drain tube from the mounting lug at the bottom of the reservoir.
9. Remove the lowermost coil of the drain tube from the mounting lugs on top of the reservoir. Be careful to avoid unsnapping the return line check valve cover from the bottom of the reservoir.
10. Release the pump mounting bracket from the reservoir. Press the bracket with both thumbs toward the center of the reservoir.
11. Remove the pump mounting bracket and rubber collar from the hose. Cut the hose clamp on the supply line and discard the clamp. Remove the pump/filter assembly. Pry the filter from the pump.
   To install:
12. Press a new filter onto the pump.
13. Using a new clamp, attach the supply hose.
14. Position the pump mounting bracket and rubber collar on the supply hose between the bulge in the hose and the pump.
15. Position the pump in the reservoir so that the filter aligns with the cavity in the reservoir.
16. Snap the pump bracket into the reservoir.
17. Position the coil tube on the reservoir so that the drain tube aligns with the mounting lugs on the reservoir.
18. Snap the lower-most coil into the mounting lugs on top of the reservoir.

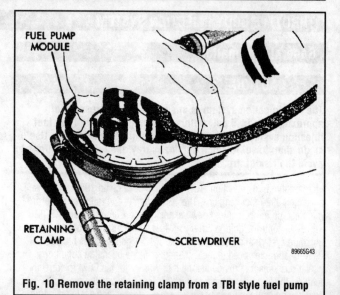

Fig. 10 Remove the retaining clamp from a TBI style fuel pump

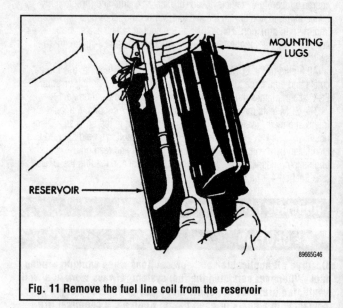

Fig. 11 Remove the fuel line coil from the reservoir

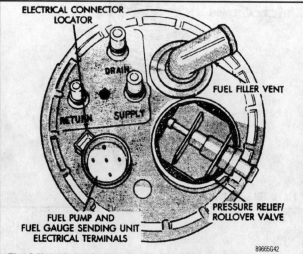

Fig. 9 Note the various components on top of a TBI style fuel pump assembly

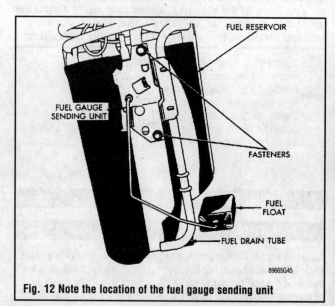

Fig. 12 Note the location of the fuel gauge sending unit

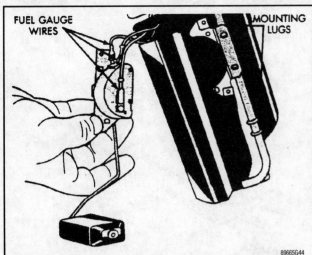

Fig. 13 Mark them for identification, then detach the wires from the terminals on the sending unit

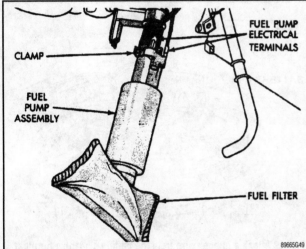

Fig. 14 View of an exposed fuel pump assembly (with the surrounding components removed)

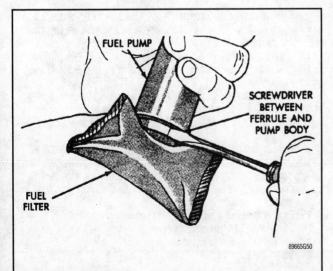

Fig. 15 Removing the fuel pump filter, also known as the "sock"

19. Snap the drain tube into the lugs on the bottom of the reservoir.
20. Connect the wires to the new sending unit.
21. Align the index tab on the level unit with the index hole in the mounting bracket.
22. Install the level unit screws.
23. Install the assembly in the tank.
24. Lower the vehicle.
25. Connect the negative battery cable.

Throttle Body

REMOVAL & INSTALLATION

✻✻ CAUTION

Observe all applicable safety precautions when working around fuel. Whenever servicing the fuel system, always work in a well ventilated area. Do not allow fuel spray or vapors to come in contact with a spark or open flame. Keep a dry chemical fire extinguisher near the work area. Always keep fuel in a container specifically designed for fuel storage; also, always properly seal fuel containers to avoid the possibility of fire or explosion.

1. Remove the engine cover.
2. Remove the air cleaner assembly.
3. Properly relieve the fuel system pressure.
4. Disconnect the negative battery cable.
5. Disconnect and label the vacuum hoses and electrical connectors.
6. Remove the throttle cable and, if so equipped, speed control and kickdown cables.
7. Remove the return spring.
8. Remove the fuel intake and return hoses.
9. Remove the throttle body mounting screws and lift the throttle body from the engine.
To install:
10. When installing the throttle body, use a new gasket. Install the throttle body and tighten the mounting screws to 175 inch lbs. (20.5 Nm).
11. Install the fuel intake and return hoses using new original equipment type clamps.
12. Install the return spring.
13. Install the throttle cable and, if so equipped, install the kickdown and speed control cables.
14. Install the wiring connectors and vacuum hoses.
15. Install the air cleaner assembly.
16. Reconnect the negative battery cable.
17. Start the engine and check for leaks.
18. Install the engine cover.

Fuel Injector(s)

TESTING

▶ See Figures 16, 17, 18 and 19

✻✻ CAUTION

Observe all applicable safety precautions when working around fuel. Whenever servicing the fuel system, always work in a well ventilated area. Do not allow fuel spray or vapors to come in contact with a spark or open flame. Keep a dry chemical fire extinguisher near the work area. Always keep fuel in a container specifically designed for fuel storage; also, always properly seal fuel containers to avoid the possibility of fire or explosion.

1. Remove the engine cover.
2. Remove the air cleaner assembly.
3. Disconnect the injector harness connector. Inspect the connector; if damaged, repair or replace it as necessary.
4. Probe the injector connector, using the schematics supplied in this manual, into the circuits from the ASD relay. Turn the ignition to **RUN**, and the fuel pump will run for a few seconds until the ECM ungrounds it. (Voltage will only be present for a few seconds.) If voltage is above 10.0v, proceed to the next test; if voltage is not 10.0v or above, repair the circuit and retest.

➡**There are two ASD relay circuits in the injector harness connector, and both have to be checked for voltage. Use the schematics supplied in this manual to find them.**

5. Turn the ignition **OFF**.
6. Disconnect the negative battery cable.
7. Unfasten the ECM harness connector.
8. Using the schematics supplied in this manual, probe the ECM connector and injector connector driver circuits and check for resistance. If resistance is more than 10.0 ohms, repair circuit(s) and retest. If resistance is less than 10.0 ohms, proceed to the next test.

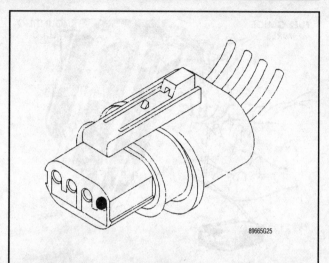

Fig. 18 Terminal view of the TBI system's fuel injector electrical connector

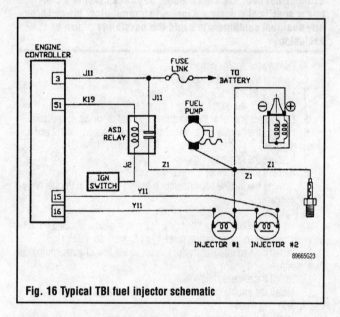

Fig. 16 Typical TBI fuel injector schematic

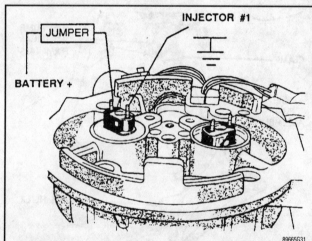

Fig. 19 Attach a jumper wire from the battery's positive terminal and momentarily ground the injector's other terminal to test injector operation

9. Remove the injector caps and inspect the injector terminals. If the terminals are damaged, repair as necessary. If the terminals are OK, proceed to the next test.
10. Connect the negative battery cable.
11. Connect a jumper wire between either terminal of injector #1 and the positive battery terminal.
12. Watch the injector for fuel spray while grounding the other terminal of the injector for no more than three seconds. If there is fuel spray, proceed to the next test; if no spray was detected, replace the injector and retest.
13. Connect the positive battery lead to either terminal on injector #2. Ground the other terminal for no more than three seconds, while watching for fuel spray. If no spray was detected, replace the injector and retest; if spray occurred, replace the ECM and retest.
14. Install the caps on the injectors.
15. Plug in the injector wiring harness connector.
16. Fasten the ECM harness connector.
17. Install the air cleaner assembly.
18. Install the engine cover.

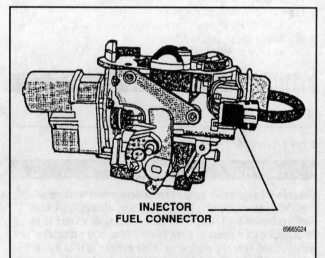

Fig. 17 Location of the fuel injector electrical connector on a TBI system

REMOVAL & INSTALLATION

♦ **See Figures 20, 21 and 22**

✳✳ CAUTION

Observe all applicable safety precautions when working around fuel. Whenever servicing the fuel system, always work in a well ventilated area. Do not allow fuel spray or vapors to come in contact with a spark or open flame. Keep a dry chemical fire extinguisher near the work area. Always keep fuel in a container specifically designed for fuel storage; also, always properly seal fuel containers to avoid the possibility of fire or explosion.

1. Remove the engine cover.
2. Properly relieve the fuel system pressure.
3. Disconnect the negative battery cable.
4. Remove the air cleaner assembly.
5. Remove the fuel pressure regulator.
6. Remove the retaining clamp on the injector caps.
7. With two small screwdrivers, lift the cap off the injector using the slots provided.

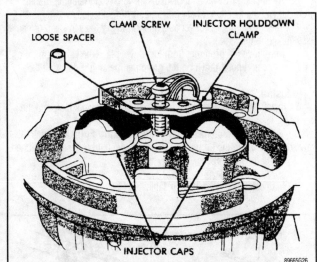

Fig. 20 The TBI injectors are covered by caps, and the caps are retained by a hold-down clamp

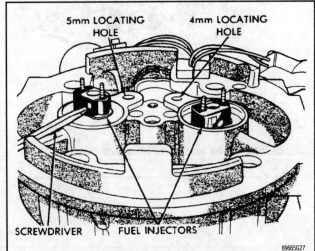

Fig. 21 After the caps are removed, the injectors can be removed by gently prying them out of the throttle body

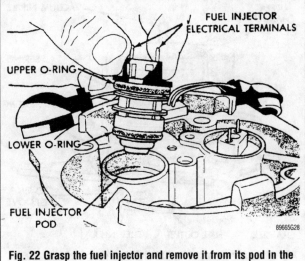

Fig. 22 Grasp the fuel injector and remove it from its pod in the throttle body

8. Using a small screwdriver placed in the hole in the front of the electrical connector, gently pry the injector from pod.
9. Make sure the injector lower O-ring has been removed from the pod.

To install:

10. Place a new lower O-ring on the injector and a new O-ring on the injector cap. The injector will have the upper O-ring already installed.
11. Put the injector cap on the injector. (The injector and cap are keyed). The cap should sit on the injector without interference. Apply a light coating of castor oil or petroleum jelly on the O-rings. Place the assembly in the pod.
12. Rotate the cap and injector to line up the attachment hole.
13. Push down on the cap until it contacts the injector pod.
14. Install the retaining screws and tighten them to 35–45 inch lbs. (4–5 Nm).
15. Install the fuel pressure regulator.
16. Connect the negative battery cable.
17. Start the engine and check for leaks.
18. Reinstall the air cleaner assembly.
19. Install the engine cover.

Fuel Pressure Regulator

REMOVAL & INSTALLATION

♦ **See Figures 23 and 24**

✳✳ CAUTION

Observe all applicable safety precautions when working around fuel. Whenever servicing the fuel system, always work in a well ventilated area. Do not allow fuel spray or vapors to come in contact with a spark or open flame. Keep a dry chemical fire extinguisher near the work area. Always keep fuel in a container specifically designed for fuel storage; also, always properly seal fuel containers to avoid the possibility of fire or explosion.

1. Remove the engine cover.
2. Properly relieve the fuel system pressure.
3. Disconnect the negative battery cable.
4. Remove the air cleaner assembly.
5. Remove the three screws attaching the pressure regulator to the throttle body. Place a shop towel around the inlet chamber to contain any fuel remaining in the system.

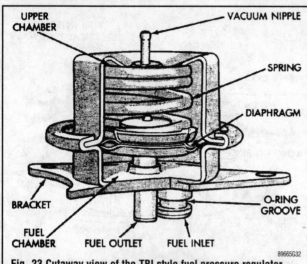

Fig. 23 Cutaway view of the TBI style fuel pressure regulator, which mounts on the throttle body

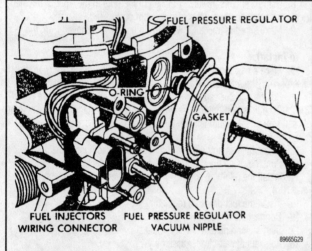

Fig. 24 Removing the fuel pressure regulator on a TBI equipped vehicle

6. Pull the pressure regulator from the throttle body.

7. Carefully remove the O-ring from the pressure regulator and remove the gasket.

To install:

8. Thoroughly clean the gasket surfaces.

9. Place a new gasket on the pressure regulator and carefully install a new O-ring.

10. Position the pressure regulator on the throttle body press it into place.

11. Install the three screws and tighten them to 40 inch lbs. (4.5 Nm).

12. Connect the negative battery cable.

13. Start the vehicle and check for leaks.

14. Install the air cleaner assembly.

15. Install the engine cover.

Pressure Relief Valve

REMOVAL & INSTALLATION

▶ See Figure 25

> ❉❉ **CAUTION**
>
> Observe all applicable safety precautions when working around fuel. Whenever servicing the fuel system, always work in a well ventilated area. Do not allow fuel spray or vapors to come in contact with a spark or open flame. Keep a dry chemical fire extinguisher near the work area. Always keep fuel in a container specifically designed for fuel storage; also, always properly seal fuel containers to avoid the possibility of fire or explosion.

1. Properly relieve the fuel system pressure.
2. Disconnect the negative battery cable.
3. Raise and support the vehicle.
4. Remove the fuel tank.
5. Wedge the blade of a flat bladed screwdriver between the rubber grommet and the fuel tank where the support rib is located.
6. Use a second screwdriver as a support to pry the valve and grommet assembly from the tank.
7. To remove the grommet from the valve, place the valve upright on a flat surface and push down on the grommet, peeling it down off the valve.

To install:

8. Install the rubber grommet in the fuel tank and work it around the curled lip.
9. Lubricate the grommet with **Power Steering Fluid** and push the valve downward into the grommet. Twist the valve until properly positioned.
10. Install the fuel tank.
11. Lower the vehicle.
12. Connect the negative battery cable.

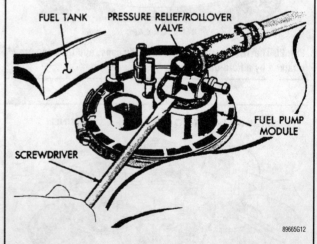

Fig. 25 Removing the pressure relief/rollover valve on a TBI style fuel pump

MULTI-PORT FUEL INJECTION SYSTEM

General Information

A Multi-port Fuel Injection (MFI) system is used on some 1992 and all 1993–98 model engines. The MFI system is controlled by a pre-programmed digital computer known as the Engine Control Module (ECM). The ECM controls ignition timing, air/fuel ratio, emission control devices, charging system and idle speed. The ECM constantly varies timing, fuel delivery and idle speed to meet changing engine operating conditions.

Various sensors provide the input necessary for the ECM to correctly regulate the fuel flow at the fuel injectors. These include the manifold absolute pressure, throttle position, oxygen sensor, coolant temperature, intake air temperature, and camshaft and crankshaft position sensors. In addition to the sensors, various switches also provide important information. These include the neutral safety, air conditioning, air conditioning clutch, and brake light switches.

All inputs to the ECM are converted into signals which are used to calculate and adjust the fuel flow at the injectors or ignition timing or both. The ECM accomplishes this by varying the pulse width of the injectors to adjust the fuel/air ratio, or advancing or retarding timing. The ECM tests many of its own input and output circuits. If a fault is found in a major system, this information is stored in the ECM as a Diagnostic Trouble Code (DTC). Information on this fault can be displayed to a technician by means of the grounding a terminal and reading the check engine lamp flashes or by connecting a scan tool and reading the DTCs (see Section 4 for a more complete procedure).

Relieving Fuel System Pressure

✳✳ CAUTION

Observe all applicable safety precautions when working around fuel. Whenever servicing the fuel system, always work in a well ventilated area. Do not allow fuel spray or vapors to come in contact with a spark or open flame. Keep a dry chemical fire extinguisher near the work area. Always keep fuel in a container specifically designed for fuel storage; also, always properly seal fuel containers to avoid the possibility of fire or explosion.

1. Disconnect the negative battery cable.
2. Remove the fuel filler cap.
3. Remove the engine cover.
4. Remove the air cleaner assembly.
5. Remove the protective cap from the fuel pressure test port on the fuel rail.
6. Install fuel pressure gauge with relief hose attached onto the test port. Place the vent hose into a suitable container and relieve the fuel pressure by venting the pressure out the hose.
7. Remove the gauge set.
8. Install protective cap on fuel pressure test port.
9. Install removed components after servicing the fuel system.

Testing Fuel System Pressure

▶ See Figures 26, 27, 28 and 29

✳✳ CAUTION

Observe all applicable safety precautions when working around fuel. Whenever servicing the fuel system, always work in a well ventilated area. Do not allow fuel spray or vapors to come in contact with a spark or open flame. Keep a dry chemical fire extinguisher near the work area. Always keep fuel in a container specifically designed for fuel storage; also, always properly seal fuel containers to avoid the possibility of fire or explosion.

1. Remove the engine cover.
2. Remove the air cleaner assembly.
3. Remove the protective cap from the fuel pressure test port on the fuel rail.
4. Install fuel pressure gauge C-5069 or equivalent to the test port fitting.
5. Start the engine and check fuel pressure; at idle, the pressure should be 35–45 psi.
6. If pressure fails to meet specifications, perform normal diagnostics.
7. Install all removed components after servicing the fuel system.

Fuel Pump

TESTING

Refer to the preceding Fuel System Pressure testing procedure.

Fig. 26 On 5.2L and 5.9L engines, the fuel pressure test port is located on the driver's side fuel rail. Remove the cap to test fuel pressure

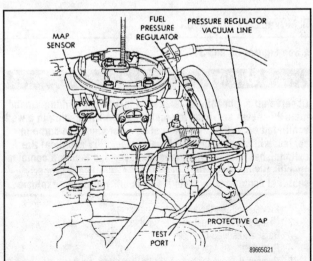

Fig. 27 Location of the fuel pressure test port on a 3.9L MFI engine

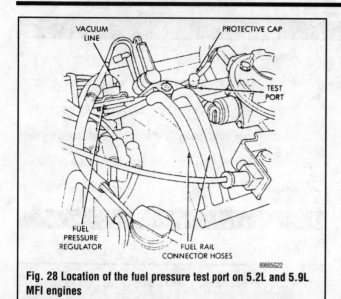

Fig. 28 Location of the fuel pressure test port on 5.2L and 5.9L MFI engines

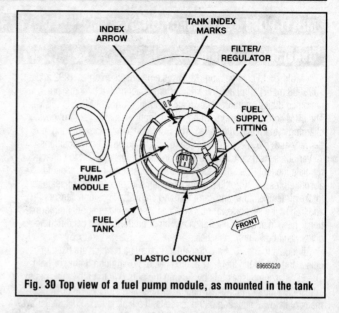

Fig. 30 Top view of a fuel pump module, as mounted in the tank

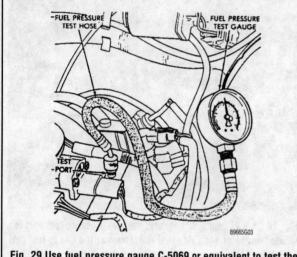

Fig. 29 Use fuel pressure gauge C-5069 or equivalent to test the fuel pressure on an MFI equipped vehicle

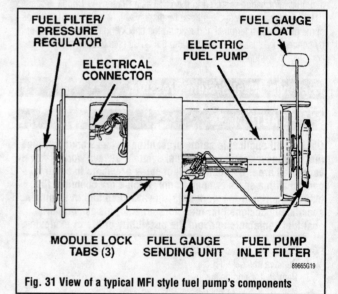

Fig. 31 View of a typical MFI style fuel pump's components

REMOVAL & INSTALLATION

▶ See Figures 30 and 31

✳✳ CAUTION

Observe all applicable safety precautions when working around fuel. Whenever servicing the fuel system, always work in a well ventilated area. Do not allow fuel spray or vapors to come in contact with a spark or open flame. Keep a dry chemical fire extinguisher near the work area. Always keep fuel in a container specifically designed for fuel storage; also, always properly seal fuel containers to avoid the possibility of fire or explosion.

1. Properly relieve the fuel system pressure.
2. Disconnect the negative battery cable.
3. Raise and support vehicle.
4. Remove the fuel tank.
5. Remove the locknut and lift out the fuel pump module.

6. Perform the following if you need to remove the sending unit:
   a. Remove the sending unit attaching screws from the mounting bracket located on the drain tube.
   b. Label disconnect the wires from the sending unit and remove the sending unit.
   of the reservoir.
7. If you need to remove the in-tank filter (sock) perform the following:
   a. Pry the mounting tabs back and remove the in-tank fuel filter (sock).

To install:

8. If removed, press a new filter (sock) onto the pump.
9. If removed connect the wires to the new sending unit, and install the sending unit onto the pump.
10. Using a new gasket, position the fuel pump module into the tank.
11. Position the locknut over the fuel pump module, and tighten the locknut.
12. Install the fuel tank.
13. Lower the vehicle.
14. Connect the negative battery cable.

Throttle Body

REMOVAL & INSTALLATION

▶ **See Figures 32 thru 44**

1. Disconnect the negative battery cable.
2. Remove the engine cover.
3. Remove the air cleaner assembly.
4. Disconnect and label the vacuum hoses and electrical connectors.
5. Remove the throttle and kickdown cables and if so equipped, the speed control cable.
6. Remove the throttle body mounting screws and lift the throttle body from the engine.

To install:

7. Thoroughly clean the intake manifold and the throttle body gasket surfaces.
8. When installing the throttle body, use a new gasket. Install the throttle body and tighten the mounting screws to 200 inch lbs. (23 Nm).
9. Install the throttle and kickdown cables and, if so equipped, the speed control cable.

Fig. 34 Unfasten the electrical connector from the TP sensor

Fig. 32 Remove the vacuum line to the throttle body

Fig. 35 Detach the electrical connector from the MAP sensor

Fig. 33 Separate the electrical connector from the IAC valve

Fig. 36 Squeeze the tabs on the transmission kickdown cable and pull it through the bracket

Fig. 37 Remove the throttle cable from the bracket

Fig. 40 Remove the bolts retaining the throttle body to the intake manifold

Fig. 38 Disconnect the transmission kickdown cable by pushing it forward to release from the eyelet

Fig. 41 Remove the throttle body from the intake manifold

Fig. 39 Disconnect the throttle cable barrel end from the throttle body

Fig. 42 Placing a rag in the port for the throttle body will reduce the chance of something falling into the intake manifold

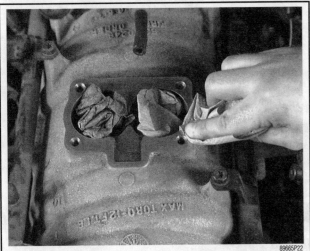

Fig. 43 Thoroughly clean the gasket surface before reinstalling the throttle body

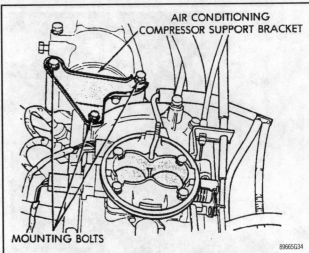

Fig. 45 The A/C compressor support bracket must be removed to access the fuel rail on MFI vehicles equipped with A/C

Fig. 44 Install a new gasket on the intake manifold, and remove the rag blocking the port, before reinstalling the throttle body

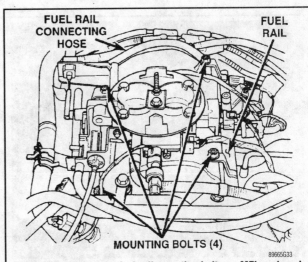

Fig. 46 Location of the fuel rail mounting bolts on MFI equipped vehicles

10. Install the wiring connectors and vacuum hoses.
11. Install the air cleaner assembly.
12. Reconnect the negative battery cable.
13. Start the engine and check for leaks.
14. Install the engine cover.

Fuel Rail Assembly

REMOVAL & INSTALLATION

▶ See Figures 45, 46, 47, 48 and 49

✳✳ CAUTION

Observe all applicable safety precautions when working around fuel. Whenever servicing the fuel system, always work in a well ventilated area. Do not allow fuel spray or vapors to come in contact with a spark or open flame. Keep a dry chemical fire extinguisher near the work area. Always keep fuel in a container specifically designed for fuel storage; also, always properly seal fuel containers to avoid the possibility of fire or explosion.

Fig. 47 Remove the fuel rail's retaining bolts

Fig. 48 Unplug the fuel injector connectors

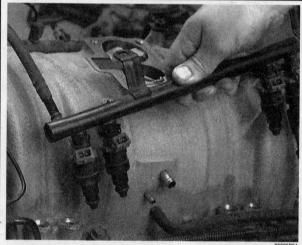

Fig. 49 Pull straight up on the injector rail to unseat it from the intake manifold

1. Disconnect the negative battery cable.
2. Remove the engine cover.
3. Remove the air cleaner assembly.
4. Properly relieve the fuel system pressure.
5. Remove the throttle body assembly.
6. If equipped with A/C, remove the A-shaped A/C compressor-to-intake manifold bracket.
7. On the 3.9L engine only, remove the IAT sensor wiring connector.
8. Remove the EVAP canister purge solenoid/bracket assembly from the intake manifold.
9. Disconnect the fuel line at the fuel rail.
10. Disconnect and label all the injector wiring harness connectors.
11. Remove the fuel rail attaching bolts.
12. Gently rock and pull the driver's side fuel rail until the injectors unseat themselves from the intake manifold. Repeat this procedure for the passenger's side and then remove the fuel rail from the engine with the injectors attached.

To install:

13. Apply a small amount of engine oil to each injector O-ring.
14. Install the fuel rail onto intake aligning injectors into the openings. Guide the injectors into intake, taking care not to tear O-rings.

15. Push down passenger's side of fuel rail until the injectors have bottomed on injector shoulder. Repeat for the driver's side.
16. Install the fuel rail mounting bolts.
17. Plug in all the injector wiring harness connectors.
18. Connect the fuel line onto fuel rail.
19. Install the EVAP canister purge solenoid and bracket onto intake manifold.
20. On the 3.9L engine, plug in the IAT sensor connector.
21. On vehicles with A/C, install the A/C compressor support bracket.
22. Install the throttle body assembly.
23. Install the air cleaner assembly.
24. Connect the negative battery cable.
25. Start the engine and check for leaks.
26. Install the engine cover.

Fuel Injector(s)

TESTING

▶ **See Figure 50**

Refer to the following Injector Diagnosis Chart.

REMOVAL & INSTALLATION

▶ **See Figures 51, 52, 53 and 54**

❊❊ CAUTION

Observe all applicable safety precautions when working around fuel. Whenever servicing the fuel system, always work in a well ventilated area. Do not allow fuel spray or vapors to come in contact with a spark or open flame. Keep a dry chemical fire extinguisher near the work area. Always keep fuel in a container specifically designed for fuel storage; also, always properly seal fuel containers to avoid the possibility of fire or explosion.

1. Disconnect the negative battery cable.
2. Remove the engine cover.
3. Remove the air cleaner assembly.
4. Remove the fuel rail assembly.
5. Remove the clip(s) retaining the injector(s).
6. Remove the injector(s) from the fuel rail.

To install:

7. Apply a small amount of engine oil to each injector O-ring.
8. Install the injector(s) onto the fuel rail and install the clip(s).
9. Install the fuel rail assembly.
10. Install the air cleaner assembly.
11. Connect the negative battery cable.
12. Start the engine and check for leaks.
13. Install the engine cover.

Fuel Pressure Regulator/Filter Assembly

REMOVAL & INSTALLATION

▶ **See Figure 55**

❊❊ CAUTION

Observe all applicable safety precautions when working around fuel. Whenever servicing the fuel system, always work in a well ventilated area. Do not allow fuel spray or vapors to come in contact with a spark or open flame. Keep a dry chemical fire extinguisher near the work area. Always keep fuel in a container specifically designed for fuel storage; also, always properly seal fuel containers to avoid the possibility of fire or explosion.

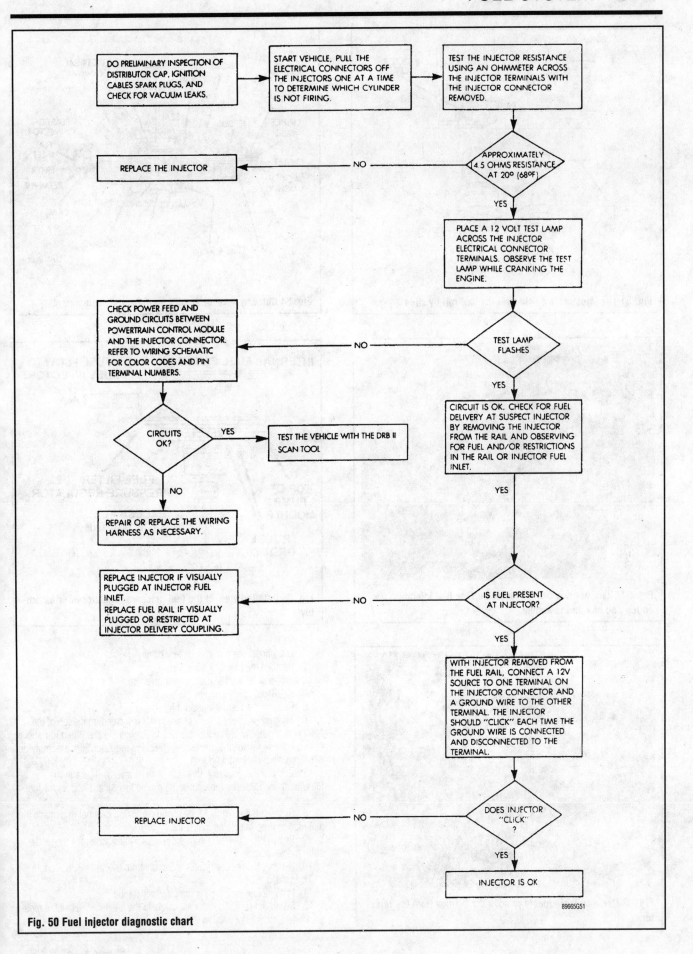

Fig. 50 Fuel injector diagnostic chart

89665G51

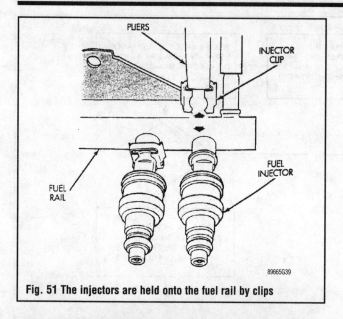

Fig. 51 The injectors are held onto the fuel rail by clips

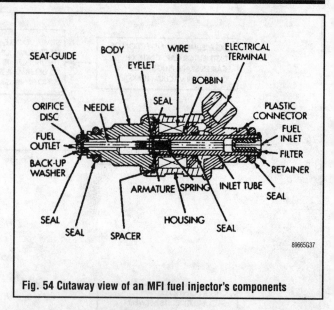

Fig. 54 Cutaway view of an MFI fuel injector's components

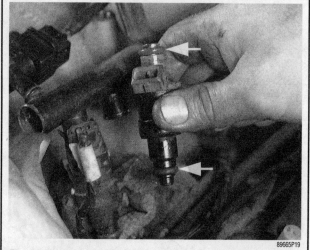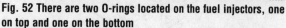

Fig. 52 There are two O-rings located on the fuel injectors, one on top and one on the bottom

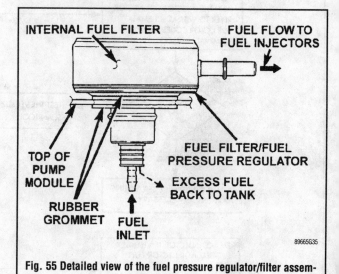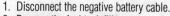

Fig. 55 Detailed view of the fuel pressure regulator/filter assembly

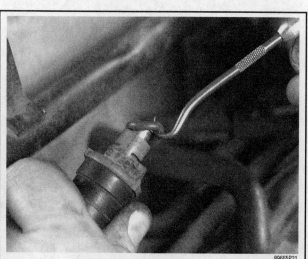

Fig. 53 Use a suitable tool to remove the O-rings from the injector

1. Disconnect the negative battery cable.
2. Remove the fuel tank filler cap.
3. Properly relieve the fuel system pressure.
4. Raise and safely support the vehicle.
5. Remove the fuel tank assembly.
6. The fuel pressure regulator assembly is located on the top of the fuel pump assembly. It is not necessary to remove the fuel pump to remove the pressure regulator/filter assembly. Twist the regulator/filter assembly out of it's grommet on the fuel pump.
7. Remove the snap ring that retains the convoluted tube to the filter/regulator. Slide the tube down the plastic fuel tube to access the fuel tube clamp.
8. Gently cut the old fuel tube clamp off, taking care not to damage the fuel tube or drop the clamp inside the tank.
9. Remove the fuel tube from the regulator/filter assembly by gently pulling downward.
10. Remove the regulator/filter assembly from the fuel pump module.
To install:
11. Install a new clamp over the plastic fuel tube.
12. Install the regulator/filter assembly to the fuel tube. Rotate the regulator/filter until it is pointed in the 10 o'clock position.

13. Tighten the clamp to fuel line using Hose Clamp Pliers C-4124 or equivalent.

14. Slide the convoluted plastic tube up to the bottom of the regulator/filter and install the snap ring.

15. Press the regulator/filter assembly into the rubber grommet making sure it is pointed in the 10 o'clock position.

16. Install the fuel tank.

17. Lower the vehicle.

18. Connect the negative battery cable.

19. Install the fuel filler cap.

Pressure Relief Valve

REMOVAL & INSTALLATION

♦ See Figure 56

✳ CAUTION

Observe all applicable safety precautions when working around fuel. Whenever servicing the fuel system, always work in a well ventilated area. Do not allow fuel spray or vapors to come in contact with a spark or open flame. Keep a dry chemical fire extinguisher near the work area. Always keep fuel in a container specifically designed for fuel storage; also, always properly seal fuel containers to avoid the possibility of fire or explosion.

1. Disconnect the negative battery cable.
2. Remove the engine cover.
3. Remove the air cleaner assembly.
4. Properly relieve the fuel system pressure.
5. Raise and support the vehicle.
6. Remove the fuel tank.
7. Wedge the blade of a flatblade screwdriver between the rubber grommet and the fuel tank where the support rib is located.

FUEL TANK

Tank Assembly

REMOVAL & INSTALLATION

♦ See Figures 57 thru 62

✳ CAUTION

Observe all applicable safety precautions when working around fuel. Whenever servicing the fuel system, always work in a well ventilated area. Do not allow fuel spray or vapors to come in contact with a spark or open flame. Keep a dry chemical fire extinguisher near the work area. Always keep fuel in a container specifically designed for fuel storage; also, always properly seal fuel containers to avoid the possibility of fire or explosion.

1. Properly relieve the fuel system pressure.
2. Disconnect the negative battery cable.
3. Remove the fuel tank filler cap.
4. Pump all fuel from the tank into an approved holding tank.
5. Raise and safely support the vehicle.
6. Disconnect the fuel line and wire lead to the gauge unit. Remove the ground strap.

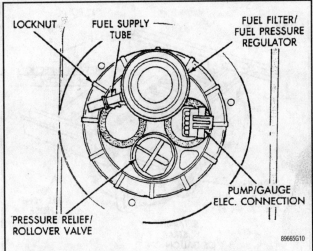

Fig. 56 Top view of the fuel pump module, including the pressure relief/rollover valve

8. Use a second screwdriver as a support to pry the valve and grommet assembly from the tank.

9. To remove the grommet from the valve, place the valve upright on a flat surface and push down on the grommet peeling it down off the valve.

To install:

10. Install the rubber grommet in the fuel tank and work it around the curled lip.

11. Lubricate the grommet with **Power Steering Fluid** and push the valve downward into the grommet. Twist valve until properly positioned.

12. Install the fuel tank.
13. Lower the vehicle.
14. Install the air cleaner and engine cover.
15. Connect the negative battery cable.

7. Remove the vent hose shield and the hose clamps from the hoses running to the vapor vent tube.

8. Remove the filler tube hose clamps and disconnect the hose from the tank.

9. Place a transmission jack or other proper support device under the center of the tank and apply sufficient pressure to support the tank.

10. Disconnect the two J-bolts and remove the retaining straps at the rear of the tank. Lower the tank from the vehicle. Feed the two vent tube hoses and filler tube vent hose through the grommets in the frame as the tank is being lowered. Remove the tank gauge unit.

To install:

11. Inspect the fuel pump filter (sock), and if it is clogged or damaged, replace it.

12. Install fuel pump assembly.

13. Position the tank on a transmission jack and hoist it into place, feeding the vent hoses through the grommets on the way up.

14. Connect the J-bolts and retaining straps, and tighten to 40 inch lbs. Remove the jack.

15. Connect the filler tube and all vent hoses.

16. Connect the fuel supply line, ground strap, and gauge unit wire lead.

17. Refill the tank and inspect it for leaks. Connect the battery ground cable.

18. Reconnect the battery cable ground cable.

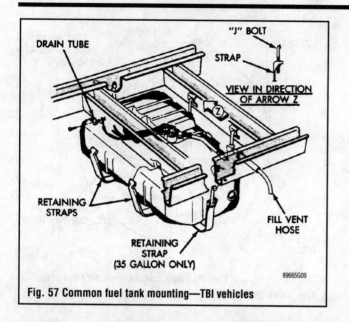

Fig. 57 Common fuel tank mounting—TBI vehicles

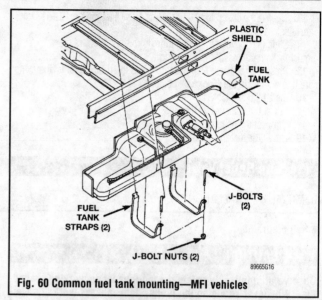

Fig. 60 Common fuel tank mounting—MFI vehicles

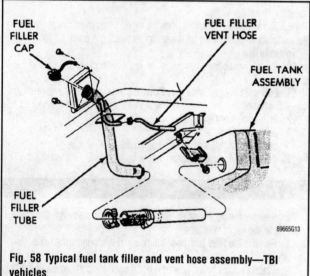

Fig. 58 Typical fuel tank filler and vent hose assembly—TBI vehicles

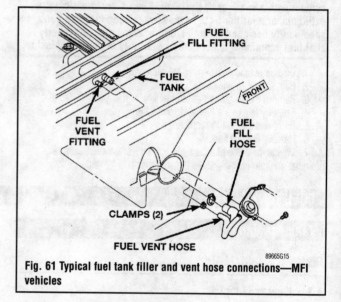

Fig. 61 Typical fuel tank filler and vent hose connections—MFI vehicles

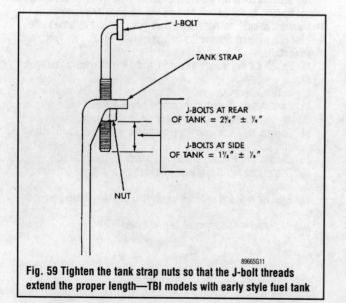

Fig. 59 Tighten the tank strap nuts so that the J-bolt threads extend the proper length—TBI models with early style fuel tank

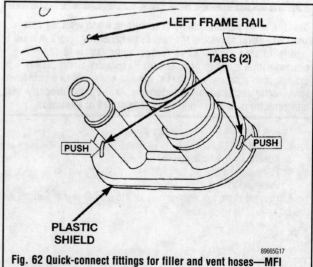

Fig. 62 Quick-connect fittings for filler and vent hoses—MFI vehicles

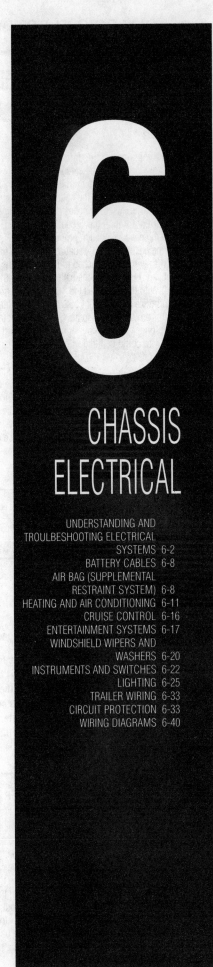

6

CHASSIS ELECTRICAL

UNDERSTANDING AND TROUBLESHOOTING ELECTRICAL SYSTEMS

Basic Electrical Theory

▶ **See Figure 1**

For any 12 volt, negative ground, electrical system to operate, the electricity must travel in a complete circuit. This simply means that current (power) from the positive (+) terminal of the battery must eventually return to the negative (-) terminal of the battery. Along the way, this current will travel through wires, fuses, switches and components. If, for any reason, the flow of current through the circuit is interrupted, the component fed by that circuit will cease to function properly.

Perhaps the easiest way to visualize a circuit is to think of connecting a light bulb (with two wires attached to it) to the battery—one wire attached to the negative (-) terminal of the battery and the other wire to the positive (+) terminal. With the two wires touching the battery terminals, the circuit would be complete and the light bulb would illuminate. Electricity would follow a path from the battery to the bulb and back to the battery. It's easy to see that with longer wires on our light bulb, it could be mounted anywhere. Further, one wire could be fitted with a switch so that the light could be turned on and off.

The normal automotive circuit differs from this simple example in two ways. First, instead of having a return wire from the bulb to the battery, the current travels through the frame of the vehicle. Since the negative (-) battery cable is attached to the frame (made of electrically conductive metal), the frame of the vehicle can serve as a ground wire to complete the circuit. Secondly, most automotive circuits contain multiple components which receive power from a single circuit. This lessens the amount of wire needed to power components on the vehicle.

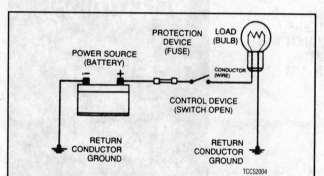

Fig. 1 This example illustrates a simple circuit. When the switch is closed, power from the positive (+) battery terminal flows through the fuse and the switch, and then to the light bulb. The light illuminates and the circuit is completed through the ground wire back to the negative (-) battery terminal. In reality, the two ground points shown in the illustration are attached to the metal frame of the vehicle, which completes the circuit back to the battery

HOW DOES ELECTRICITY WORK: THE WATER ANALOGY

Electricity is the flow of electrons—the subatomic particles that constitute the outer shell of an atom. Electrons spin in an orbit around the center core of an atom. The center core is comprised of protons (positive charge) and neutrons (neutral charge). Electrons have a negative charge and balance out the positive charge of the protons. When an outside force causes the number of electrons to unbalance the charge of the protons, the electrons will split off the atom and look for another atom to balance out. If this imbalance is kept up, electrons will continue to move and an electrical flow will exist.

Many people have been taught electrical theory using an analogy with water. In a comparison with water flowing through a pipe, the electrons would be the water and the wire is the pipe.

The flow of electricity can be measured much like the flow of water through a pipe. The unit of measurement used is amperes, frequently abbreviated as amps (a). You can compare amperage to the volume of water flowing through a pipe. When connected to a circuit, an ammeter will measure the actual amount of current flowing through the circuit. When relatively few electrons flow through a circuit, the amperage is low. When many electrons flow, the amperage is high.

Water pressure is measured in units such as pounds per square inch (psi); The electrical pressure is measured in units called volts (v). When a voltmeter is connected to a circuit, it is measuring the electrical pressure.

The actual flow of electricity depends not only on voltage and amperage, but also on the resistance of the circuit. The higher the resistance, the higher the force necessary to push the current through the circuit. The standard unit for measuring resistance is an ohm (omega). Resistance in a circuit varies depending on the amount and type of components used in the circuit. The main factors which determine resistance are:

• Material—some materials have more resistance than others. Those with high resistance are said to be insulators. Rubber materials (or rubber-like plastics) are some of the most common insulators used in vehicles as they have a very high resistance to electricity. Very low resistance materials are said to be conductors. Copper wire is among the best conductors. Silver is actually a superior conductor to copper and is used in some relay contacts, but its high cost prohibits its use as common wiring. Most automotive wiring is made of copper.

• Size—the larger the wire size being used, the less resistance the wire will have. This is why components which use large amounts of electricity usually have large wires supplying current to them.

• Length—for a given thickness of wire, the longer the wire, the greater the resistance. The shorter the wire, the less the resistance. When determining the proper wire for a circuit, both size and length must be considered to design a circuit that can handle the current needs of the component.

• Temperature—with many materials, the higher the temperature, the greater the resistance (positive temperature coefficient). Some materials exhibit the opposite trait of lower resistance with higher temperatures (negative temperature coefficient). These principles are used in many of the sensors on the engine.

OHM'S LAW

There is a direct relationship between current, voltage and resistance. The relationship between current, voltage and resistance can be summed up by a statement known as Ohm's law.

Voltage (E) is equal to amperage (I) times resistance (R): $E = I \times R$
Other forms of the formula are $R = E/I$ and $I = E/R$

In each of these formulas, E is the voltage in volts, I is the current in amps and R is the resistance in ohms. The basic point to remember is that as the resistance of a circuit goes up, the amount of current that flows in the circuit will go down, if voltage remains the same.

The amount of work that the electricity can perform is expressed as power. The unit of power is the watt (w). The relationship between power, voltage and current is expressed as:

Power (W) is equal to amperage (I) times voltage (E): $W = I \times E$

This is only true for direct current (DC) circuits; the alternating current formula is a tad different, but since the electrical circuits in most vehicles are DC type, we need not get into AC circuit theory.

Electrical Components

POWER SOURCE

Power is supplied to the vehicle by two devices: The battery and the alternator. The battery supplies electrical power during starting or during periods when the current demand of the vehicle's electrical system exceeds the output capacity of the alternator. The alternator supplies electrical current when the engine is running. Just not does the alternator supply the current needs of the vehicle, but it recharges the battery.

The Battery

In most modern vehicles, the battery is a lead/acid electrochemical device consisting of six 2 volt subsections (cells) connected in series, so that the unit is capable of producing approximately 12 volts of electrical pressure. Each subsection consists of a series of positive and negative plates held a short distance apart in a solution of sulfuric acid and water.

The two types of plates are of dissimilar metals. This sets up a chemical reaction, and it is this reaction which produces current flow from the battery when its positive and negative terminals are connected to an electrical load. The power removed from the battery is replaced by the alternator, restoring the battery to its original chemical state.

The Alternator

On some vehicles there isn't an alternator, but a generator. The difference is that an alternator supplies alternating current which is then changed to direct current for use on the vehicle, while a generator produces direct current. Alternators tend to be more efficient and that is why they are used.

Alternators and generators are devices that consist of coils of wires wound together making big electromagnets. One group of coils spins within another set and the interaction of the magnetic fields causes a current to flow. This current is then drawn off the coils and fed into the vehicles electrical system.

GROUND

Two types of grounds are used in automotive electric circuits. Direct ground components are grounded to the frame through their mounting points. All other components use some sort of ground wire which is attached to the frame or chassis of the vehicle. The electrical current runs through the chassis of the vehicle and returns to the battery through the ground (-) cable; if you look, you'll see that the battery ground cable connects between the battery and the frame or chassis of the vehicle.

➡️**It should be noted that a good percentage of electrical problems can be traced to bad grounds.**

PROTECTIVE DEVICES

▶ See Figure 2

It is possible for large surges of current to pass through the electrical system of your vehicle. If this surge of current were to reach the load in the circuit, the surge could burn it out or severely damage it. It can also overload the wiring, causing the harness to get hot and melt the insulation. To prevent this, fuses, circuit breakers and/or fusible links are connected into the supply wires of the electrical system. These items are nothing more than a built-in weak spot in the system. When an abnormal amount of current flows through the system, these protective devices work as follows to protect the circuit:
- Fuse—when an excessive electrical current passes through a fuse, the fuse "blows" (the conductor melts) and opens the circuit, preventing the passage of current.
- Circuit Breaker—a circuit breaker is basically a self-repairing fuse. It will open the circuit in the same fashion as a fuse, but when the surge subsides, the circuit breaker can be reset and does not need replacement.
- Fusible Link—a fusible link (fuse link or main link) is a short length of special, high temperature insulated wire that acts as a fuse. When an excessive electrical current passes through a fusible link, the thin gauge wire inside the link melts, creating an intentional open to protect the circuit. To repair the circuit, the link must be replaced. Some newer type fusible links are housed in plug-in modules, which are simply replaced like a fuse, while older type fusible links must be cut and spliced if they melt. Since this link is very early in the electrical path, it's the first place to look if nothing on the vehicle works, yet the battery seems to be charged and is properly connected.

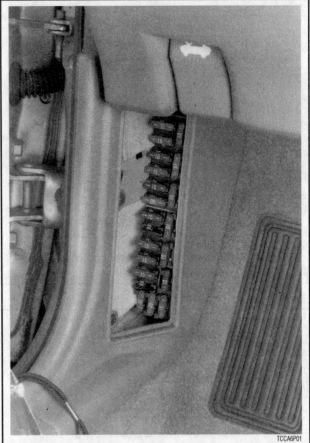

TCCA6P01

Fig. 2 Most vehicles use one or more fuse panels. This one is located on the driver's side kick panel

SWITCHES & RELAYS

▶ See Figures 3 and 4

Switches are used in electrical circuits to control the passage of current. The most common use is to open and close circuits between the battery and the various electric devices in the system. Switches are rated according to the amount of amperage they can handle. If a sufficient amperage rated switch is not used in a circuit, the switch could overload and cause damage.

Some electrical components which require a large amount of current to operate use a special switch called a relay. Since these circuits carry a large amount of current, the thickness of the wire in the circuit is also greater. If this large wire were connected from the load to the control switch, the switch would have to carry the high amperage load and the fairing or dash would be twice as large to accommodate the increased size of the wiring harness. To prevent these problems, a relay is used.

Relays are composed of a coil and a set of contacts. When the coil has a current passed though it, a magnetic field is formed and this field causes the contacts to move together, completing the circuit. Most relays are normally open, preventing current from passing through the circuit, but they can take any electrical form depending on the job they are intended to do. Relays can be considered "remote control switches." They allow a smaller current to operate devices that require higher amperages. When a small

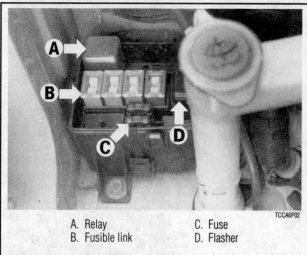

A. Relay   C. Fuse
B. Fusible link   D. Flasher

TCCA6P02

Fig. 3 The underhood fuse and relay panel usually contains fuses, relays, flashers and fusible links

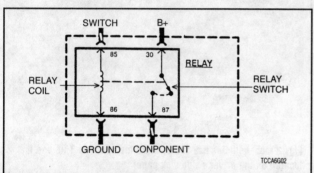

TCCA6G02

Fig. 4 Relays are composed of a coil and a switch. These two components are linked together so that when one operates, the other operates at the same time. The large wires in the circuit are connected from the battery to one side of the relay switch (B+) and from the opposite side of the relay switch to the load (component). Smaller wires are connected from the relay coil to the control switch for the circuit and from the opposite side of the relay coil to ground

current operates the coil, a larger current is allowed to pass by the contacts. Some common circuits which may use relays are the horn, headlights, starter, electric fuel pump and other high draw circuits.

LOAD

Every electrical circuit must include a "load" (something to use the electricity coming from the source). Without this load, the battery would attempt to deliver its entire power supply from one pole to another. This is called a "short circuit." All this electricity would take a short cut to ground and cause a great amount of damage to other components in the circuit by developing a tremendous amount of heat. This condition could develop sufficient heat to melt the insulation on all the surrounding wires and reduce a multiple wire cable to a lump of plastic and copper.

WIRING & HARNESSES

The average vehicle contains meters and meters of wiring, with hundreds of individual connections. To protect the many wires from damage and to keep them from becoming a confusing tangle, they are organized into bundles, enclosed in plastic or taped together and called wiring harnesses. Dif-

ferent harnesses serve different parts of the vehicle. Individual wires are color coded to help trace them through a harness where sections are hidden from view.

Automotive wiring or circuit conductors can be either single strand wire, multi-strand wire or printed circuitry. Single strand wire has a solid metal core and is usually used inside such components as alternators, motors, relays and other devices. Multi-strand wire has a core made of many small strands of wire twisted together into a single conductor. Most of the wiring in an automotive electrical system is made up of multi-strand wire, either as a single conductor or grouped together in a harness. All wiring is color coded on the insulator, either as a solid color or as a colored wire with an identification stripe. A printed circuit is a thin film of copper or other conductor that is printed on an insulator backing. Occasionally, a printed circuit is sandwiched between two sheets of plastic for more protection and flexibility. A complete printed circuit, consisting of conductors, insulating material and connectors for lamps or other components is called a printed circuit board. Printed circuitry is used in place of individual wires or harnesses in places where space is limited, such as behind instrument panels.

Since automotive electrical systems are very sensitive to changes in resistance, the selection of properly sized wires is critical when systems are repaired. A loose or corroded connection or a replacement wire that is too small for the circuit will add extra resistance and an additional voltage drop to the circuit.

The wire gauge number is an expression of the cross-section area of the conductor. Vehicles from countries that use the metric system will typically describe the wire size as its cross-sectional area in square millimeters. In this method, the larger the wire, the greater the number. Another common system for expressing wire size is the American Wire Gauge (AWG) system. As gauge number increases, area decreases and the wire becomes smaller. An 18 gauge wire is smaller than a 4 gauge wire. A wire with a higher gauge number will carry less current than a wire with a lower gauge number. Gauge wire size refers to the size of the strands of the conductor, not the size of the complete wire with insulator. It is possible, therefore, to have two wires of the same gauge with different diameters because one may have thicker insulation than the other.

It is essential to understand how a circuit works before trying to figure out why it doesn't. An electrical schematic shows the electrical current paths when a circuit is operating properly. Schematics break the entire electrical system down into individual circuits. In a schematic, usually no attempt is made to represent wiring and components as they physically appear on the vehicle; switches and other components are shown as simply as possible. Face views of harness connectors show the cavity or terminal locations in all multi-pin connectors to help locate test points.

CONNECTORS

◆ See Figures 5 and 6

Three types of connectors are commonly used in automotive applications—weatherproof, molded and hard shell.

• Weatherproof—these connectors are most commonly used where the connector is exposed to the elements. Terminals are protected against moisture and dirt by sealing rings which provide a weathertight seal. All repairs require the use of a special terminal and the tool required to service it. Unlike standard blade type terminals, these weatherproof terminals cannot be straightened once they are bent. Make certain that the connectors are properly seated and all of the sealing rings are in place when connecting leads.

• Molded—these connectors require complete replacement of the connector if found to be defective. This means splicing a new connector assembly into the harness. All splices should be soldered to insure proper contact. Use care when probing the connections or replacing terminals in them, as it is possible to create a short circuit between opposite terminals. If this happens to the wrong terminal pair, it is possible to damage certain components. Always use jumper wires between connectors for circuit checking and NEVER probe through weatherproof seals.

• Hard Shell—unlike molded connectors, the terminal contacts in hard-shell connectors can be replaced. Replacement usually involves the use of

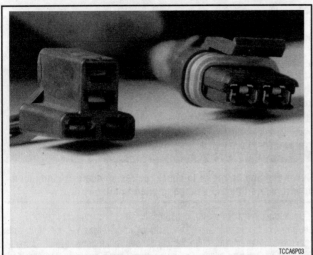

Fig. 5 Hard shell (left) and weatherproof (right) connectors have replaceable terminals

Fig. 6 Weatherproof connectors are most commonly used in the engine compartment or where the connector is exposed to the elements

a special terminal removal tool that depresses the locking tangs (barbs) on the connector terminal and allows the connector to be removed from the rear of the shell. The connector shell should be replaced if it shows any evidence of burning, melting, cracks, or breaks. Replace individual terminals that are burnt, corroded, distorted or loose.

Test Equipment

Pinpointing the exact cause of trouble in an electrical circuit is most times accomplished by the use of special test equipment. The following describes different types of commonly used test equipment and briefly explains how to use them in diagnosis. In addition to the information covered below, the tool manufacturer's instructions booklet (provided with the tester) should be read and clearly understood before attempting any test procedures.

JUMPER WIRES

✳✳ CAUTION

Never use jumper wires made from a thinner gauge wire than the circuit being tested. If the jumper wire is of too small a

gauge, it may overheat and possibly melt. Never use jumpers to bypass high resistance loads in a circuit. Bypassing resistance, in effect, creates a short circuit. This may, in turn, cause damage and fire. Jumper wires should only be used to bypass lengths of wire or to simulate switches.

Jumper wires are simple, yet extremely valuable, pieces of test equipment. They are basically test wires which are used to bypass sections of a circuit. Although jumper wires can be purchased, they are usually fabricated from lengths of standard automotive wire and whatever type of connector (alligator clip, spade connector or pin connector) that is required for the particular application being tested. In cramped, hard-to-reach areas, it is advisable to have insulated boots over the jumper wire terminals in order to prevent accidental grounding. It is also advisable to include a standard automotive fuse in any jumper wire. This is commonly referred to as a "fused jumper". By inserting an in-line fuse holder between a set of test leads, a fused jumper wire can be used for bypassing open circuits. Use a 5 amp fuse to provide protection against voltage spikes.

Jumper wires are used primarily to locate open electrical circuits, on either the ground (-) side of the circuit or on the power (+) side. If an electrical component fails to operate, connect the jumper wire between the component and a good ground. If the component operates only with the jumper installed, the ground circuit is open. If the ground circuit is good, but the component does not operate, the circuit between the power feed and component may be open. By moving the jumper wire successively back from the component toward the power source, you can isolate the area of the circuit where the open is located. When the component stops functioning, or the power is cut off, the open is in the segment of wire between the jumper and the point previously tested.

You can sometimes connect the jumper wire directly from the battery to the "hot" terminal of the component, but first make sure the component uses 12 volts in operation. Some electrical components, such as fuel injectors or sensors, are designed to operate on about 4 to 5 volts, and running 12 volts directly to these components will cause damage.

TEST LIGHTS

▶ See Figure 7

The test light is used to check circuits and components while electrical current is flowing through them. It is used for voltage and ground tests. To use a 12 volt test light, connect the ground clip to a good ground and probe wherever necessary with the pick. The test light will illuminate when voltage is detected. This does not necessarily mean that 12 volts (or any particular amount of voltage) is present; it only means that some voltage is

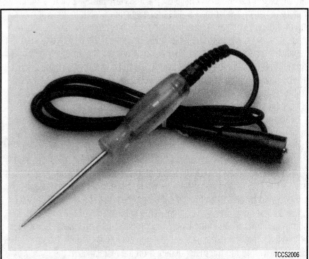

Fig. 7 A 12 volt test light is used to detect the presence of voltage in a circuit

present. It is advisable before using the test light to touch its ground clip and probe across the battery posts or terminals to make sure the light is operating properly.

❄❄ WARNING

Do not use a test light to probe electronic ignition, spark plug or coil wires. Never use a pick-type test light to probe wiring on computer controlled systems unless specifically instructed to do so. Any wire insulation that is pierced by the test light probe should be taped and sealed with silicone after testing.

Like the jumper wire, the 12 volt test light is used to isolate opens in circuits. But, whereas the jumper wire is used to bypass the open to operate the load, the 12 volt test light is used to locate the presence of voltage in a circuit. If the test light illuminates, there is power up to that point in the circuit; if the test light does not illuminate, there is an open circuit (no power). Move the test light in successive steps back toward the power source until the light in the handle illuminates. The open is between the probe and a point which was previously probed.

The self-powered test light is similar in design to the 12 volt test light, but contains a 1.5 volt penlight battery in the handle. It is most often used in place of a multimeter to check for open or short circuits when power is isolated from the circuit (continuity test).

The battery in a self-powered test light does not provide much current. A weak battery may not provide enough power to illuminate the test light even when a complete circuit is made (especially if there is high resistance in the circuit). Always make sure that the test battery is strong. To check the battery, briefly touch the ground clip to the probe; if the light glows brightly, the battery is strong enough for testing.

➡**A self-powered test light should not be used on any computer controlled system or component. The small amount of electricity transmitted by the test light is enough to damage many electronic automotive components.**

MULTIMETERS

Multimeters are an extremely useful tool for troubleshooting electrical problems. They can be purchased in either analog or digital form and have a price range to suit any budget. A multimeter is a voltmeter, ammeter and ohmmeter (along with other features) combined into one instrument. It is often used when testing solid state circuits because of its high input impedance (usually 10 megaohms or more). A brief description of the multimeter main test functions follows:

• Voltmeter—the voltmeter is used to measure voltage at any point in a circuit, or to measure the voltage drop across any part of a circuit. Voltmeters usually have various scales and a selector switch to allow the reading of different voltage ranges. The voltmeter has a positive and a negative lead. To avoid damage to the meter, always connect the negative lead to the negative (-) side of the circuit (to ground or nearest the ground side of the circuit) and connect the positive lead to the positive (+) side of the circuit (to the power source or the nearest power source). Note that the negative voltmeter lead will always be black and that the positive voltmeter will always be some color other than black (usually red).

• Ohmmeter—the ohmmeter is designed to read resistance (measured in ohms) in a circuit or component. Most ohmmeters will have a selector switch which permits the measurement of different ranges of resistance (usually the selector switch allows the multiplication of the meter reading by 10, 100, 1,000 and 10,000). Some ohmmeters are "auto-ranging" which means the meter itself will determine which scale to use. Since the meters are powered by an internal battery, the ohmmeter can be used like a self-powered test light. When the ohmmeter is connected, current from the ohmmeter flows through the circuit or component being tested. Since the ohmmeter's internal resistance and voltage are known values, the amount of current flow through the meter depends on the resistance of the circuit or

component being tested. The ohmmeter can also be used to perform a continuity test for suspected open circuits. In using the meter for making continuity checks, do not be concerned with the actual resistance readings. Zero resistance, or any ohm reading, indicates continuity in the circuit. Infinite resistance indicates an opening in the circuit. A high resistance reading where there should be none indicates a problem in the circuit. Checks for short circuits are made in the same manner as checks for open circuits, except that the circuit must be isolated from both power and normal ground. Infinite resistance indicates no continuity, while zero resistance indicates a dead short.

❄❄ WARNING

Never use an ohmmeter to check the resistance of a component or wire while there is voltage applied to the circuit.

• Ammeter—an ammeter measures the amount of current flowing through a circuit in units called amperes or amps. At normal operating voltage, most circuits have a characteristic amount of amperes, called "current draw" which can be measured using an ammeter. By referring to a specified current draw rating, then measuring the amperes and comparing the two values, one can determine what is happening within the circuit to aid in diagnosis. An open circuit, for example, will not allow any current to flow, so the ammeter reading will be zero. A damaged component or circuit will have an increased current draw, so the reading will be high. The ammeter is always connected in series with the circuit being tested. All of the current that normally flows through the circuit must also flow through the ammeter; if there is any other path for the current to follow, the ammeter reading will not be accurate. The ammeter itself has very little resistance to current flow and, therefore, will not affect the circuit, but it will measure current draw only when the circuit is closed and electricity is flowing. Excessive current draw can blow fuses and drain the battery, while a reduced current draw can cause motors to run slowly, lights to dim and other components to not operate properly.

Troubleshooting Electrical Systems

When diagnosing a specific problem, organized troubleshooting is a must. The complexity of a modern automotive vehicle demands that you approach any problem in a logical, organized manner. There are certain troubleshooting techniques, however, which are standard:

• Establish when the problem occurs. Does the problem appear only under certain conditions? Were there any noises, odors or other unusual symptoms? Isolate the problem area. To do this, make some simple tests and observations, then eliminate the systems that are working properly. Check for obvious problems, such as broken wires and loose or dirty connections. Always check the obvious before assuming something complicated is the cause.

• Test for problems systematically to determine the cause once the problem area is isolated. Are all the components functioning properly? Is there power going to electrical switches and motors. Performing careful, systematic checks will often turn up most causes on the first inspection, without wasting time checking components that have little or no relationship to the problem.

• Test all repairs after the work is done to make sure that the problem is fixed. Some causes can be traced to more than one component, so a careful verification of repair work is important in order to pick up additional malfunctions that may cause a problem to reappear or a different problem to arise. A blown fuse, for example, is a simple problem that may require more than another fuse to repair. If you don't look for a problem that caused a fuse to blow, a shorted wire (for example) may go undetected.

Experience has shown that most problems tend to be the result of a fairly simple and obvious cause, such as loose or corroded connectors, bad grounds or damaged wire insulation which causes a short. This makes careful visual inspection of components during testing essential to quick and accurate troubleshooting.

Testing

OPEN CIRCUITS

♦ See Figure 8

This test already assumes the existence of an open in the circuit and it is used to help locate the open portion.

1. Isolate the circuit from power and ground.
2. Connect the self-powered test light or ohmmeter ground clip to the ground side of the circuit and probe sections of the circuit sequentially.
3. If the light is out or there is infinite resistance, the open is between the probe and the circuit ground.
4. If the light is on or the meter shows continuity, the open is between the probe and the end of the circuit toward the power source.

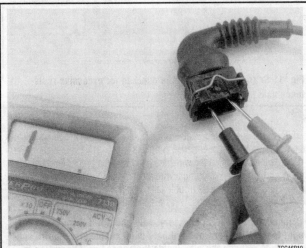

Fig. 8 The infinite reading on this multimeter (1 .) indicates that the circuit is open

SHORT CIRCUITS

➡Never use a self-powered test light to perform checks for opens or shorts when power is applied to the circuit under test. The test light can be damaged by outside power.

1. Isolate the circuit from power and ground.
2. Connect the self-powered test light or ohmmeter ground clip to a good ground and probe any easy-to-reach point in the circuit.
3. If the light comes on or there is continuity, there is a short somewhere in the circuit.
4. To isolate the short, probe a test point at either end of the isolated circuit (the light should be on or the meter should indicate continuity).
5. Leave the test light probe engaged and sequentially open connectors or switches, remove parts, etc. until the light goes out or continuity is broken.
6. When the light goes out, the short is between the last two circuit components which were opened.

VOLTAGE

This test determines voltage available from the battery and should be the first step in any electrical troubleshooting procedure after visual inspection. Many electrical problems, especially on computer controlled systems, can be caused by a low state of charge in the battery. Excessive corrosion at the battery cable terminals can cause poor contact that will prevent proper charging and full battery current flow.

1. Set the voltmeter selector switch to the 20V position.
2. Connect the multimeter negative lead to the battery's negative (-) post or terminal and the positive lead to the battery's positive (+) post or terminal.
3. Turn the ignition switch **ON** to provide a load.
4. A well charged battery should register over 12 volts. If the meter reads below 11.5 volts, the battery power may be insufficient to operate the electrical system properly.

VOLTAGE DROP

♦ See Figure 9

When current flows through a load, the voltage beyond the load drops. This voltage drop is due to the resistance created by the load and also by small resistances created by corrosion at the connectors and damaged insulation on the wires. The maximum allowable voltage drop under load is critical, especially if there is more than one load in the circuit, since all voltage drops are cumulative.

1. Set the voltmeter selector switch to the 20 volt position.
2. Connect the multimeter negative lead to a good ground.
3. Operate the circuit and check the voltage prior to the first component (load).
4. There should be little or no voltage drop in the circuit prior to the first component. If a voltage drop exists, the wire or connectors in the circuit are suspect.
5. While operating the first component in the circuit, probe the ground side of the component with the positive meter lead and observe the voltage readings. A small voltage drop should be noticed. This voltage drop is caused by the resistance of the component.
6. Repeat the test for each component (load) down the circuit.
7. If a large voltage drop is noticed, the preceding component, wire or connector is suspect.

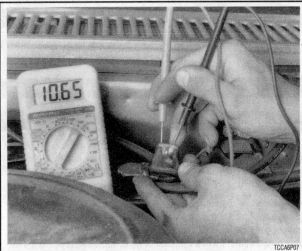

Fig. 9 This voltage drop test revealed high resistance (low voltage) in the circuit

RESISTANCE

♦ See Figures 10 and 11

✳✳ WARNING

Never use an ohmmeter with power applied to the circuit. The ohmmeter is designed to operate on its own power supply. The normal 12 volt electrical system voltage could damage the meter!

Fig. 10 Checking the resistance of a coolant temperature sensor with an ohmmeter. Reading is 1.04 kilohms

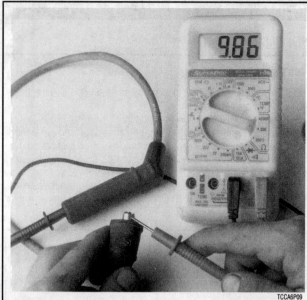

Fig. 11 Spark plug wires can be checked for excessive resistance using an ohmmeter

1. Isolate the circuit from the vehicle's power source.
2. Ensure that the ignition key is **OFF** when disconnecting any components or the battery.
3. Where necessary, also isolate at least one side of the circuit to be checked, in order to avoid reading parallel resistance. Parallel circuit resistance will always give a lower reading than the actual resistance of either of the branches.
4. Connect the meter leads to both sides of the circuit (wire or component) and read the actual measured ohms on the meter scale. Make sure the selector switch is set to the proper ohm scale for the circuit being tested, to avoid misreading the ohmmeter test value.

Wire and Connector Repair

Almost anyone can replace damaged wires, as long as the proper tools and parts are available. Wire and terminals are available to fit almost any

need. Even the specialized weatherproof, molded and hard shell connectors are now available from aftermarket suppliers.

Be sure the ends of all the wires are fitted with the proper terminal hardware and connectors. Wrapping a wire around a stud is never a permanent solution and will only cause trouble later. Replace wires one at a time to avoid confusion. Always route wires exactly the same as the factory.

➡**If connector repair is necessary, only attempt it if you have the proper tools. Weatherproof and hard shell connectors require special tools to release the pins inside the connector. Attempting to repair these connectors with conventional hand tools will damage them.**

BATTERY CABLES

Disconnecting the Cables

When working on any electrical component on the vehicle, it is always a good idea to disconnect the negative (-) battery cable. This will prevent potential damage to many sensitive electrical components such as the Engine Control Module (ECM), radio, alternator, etc.

➡**Any time you disengage the battery cables, it is recommended that you disconnect the negative (-) battery cable first. This will prevent your accidentally grounding the positive (+) terminal to the body of the vehicle when disconnecting it, thereby preventing damage to the above mentioned components.**

Before you disconnect the cable(s), first turn the ignition to the **OFF** position. This will prevent a draw on the battery which could cause arcing

(electricity trying to ground itself to the body of a vehicle, just like a spark plug jumping the gap) and, of course, damaging some components such as the alternator diodes.

When the battery cable(s) are reconnected (negative cable last), be sure to check that your lights, windshield wipers and other electrically operated safety components are all working correctly. If your vehicle contains an Electronically Tuned Radio (ETR), don't forget to also reset your radio stations. Ditto for the clock.

Anytime the battery cables have been disconnected and then reconnected, some abnormal drive symptoms could occur. The is due to the ECM losing the memory voltage and its learned adaptive strategy. The vehicle will need to be driven for 10 miles (16 km) or more until the ECM relearns its adaptive strategy, and acclimates the engine and transmission functions to your driving style.

AIR BAG (SUPPLEMENTAL RESTRAINT SYSTEM)

General Information

✳✳ CAUTION

This system is a sensitive, complex electro-mechanical unit. Before attempting to diagnose or service, you must first disconnect the negative battery cable and wait 2 minutes for the sys-

tem capacitor to discharge. Failure to do so could result in accidental deployment which could cause personal injury.

SYSTEM OPERATION

The air bag or Supplemental Restraint System (SRS) is a safety device designed to be used in conjunction with the seat belt. Its purpose is to help protect the driver in a frontal impact exceeding a certain set limit. The system consists of the air bag module, three impact sensors, a clockspring and a dedicated air bag control module.

The air bag is a fabric bag or balloon with an explosive inflator unit attached. The system employs impact sensors and a safing sensor, as well as an inflator circuit and control module.

When the control unit receives the sensor signals, power is supplied to the inflator circuit, either from the battery or backup system. A small heater causes a chemical reaction in the igniter; the non-toxic gas from the chemical mixture expands very rapidly (in milliseconds), filling the bag and forcing it through the cover pad. Since all this is happening very rapidly, the expanding bag should reach the occupant before he/she reaches the steering wheel/dashboard during a frontal collision. The chemical reaction is complete by the time the air bag is fully inflated; as the occupant hits the bag, the gas is allowed to escape slowly through vents in the back of the bag.

SYSTEM COMPONENTS

Air Bag Module

The air bag module is mounted directly to the steering wheel beneath a protective cover. Under the air bag module protective cover, the air bag cushion and its supporting components are contained. The air bag module contains a housing to which the cushion and inflator are attached and sealed. The air bag module is non-repairable. If it is dropped or damaged, it must be replaced.

The inflator assembly is mounted to the back of the module. The inflator seals the hole in the air bag cushion so it can discharge the gas it produces directly into the cushion when supplied with the proper electrical signal. Upon deployment, the protective cover will split horizontally.

Impact Sensors

The three impact sensors used in the SRS system verify the direction and severity of an impact. One of the sensors is called the safing sensor. It is located in the Air Bag Control Module (ACM), which is mounted to a bracket under the instrument panel, on top of the floor pan transmission tunnel. The other two are impact sensors and are mounted on the left and right inner fender extension panels behind the grille. The sensors are calibrated for the particular vehicle that they serve.

The impact sensors are threshold-sensitive switches that complete an electrical circuit when an impact provides a sufficient deceleration force to close the switch. The safing sensor is an accelerometer that senses the rate of deceleration. The microprocessor in the ACM monitors the sensor signals. A pre-programmed decision algorithm in the microprocessor determines when the deceleration rate indicates an impact that is severe enough to require air bag system protection.

The two impact sensors are available for service replacement. The safing sensor is only serviced as part of the ACM.

Clockspring
♦ See Figure 12

The clockspring is mounted on the steering column behind the steering wheel. Its purpose is to maintain a continuous electrical circuit between the wiring harness and the driver's side air bag module. This assembly consists of a flat, ribbon-like electrically conductive tape that winds and unwinds with the steering wheel rotation.

Air Bag Control Module (ACM)
♦ See Figure 13

The ACM contains the safing sensor, and a microprocessor that monitors the air bag system to determine readiness. It also monitors the impact sensors to determine when the proper conditions exist to provide the electrical signal that deploys the air bag. The ACM contains On-Board Diagnostics (OBD), and will light the air bag warning lamp on the instrument

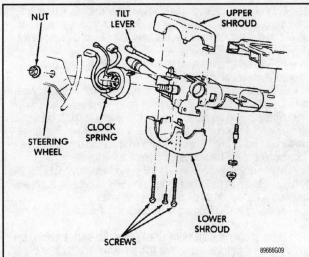

Fig. 12 The clockspring assembly is mounted to the end of the column, behind the steering wheel

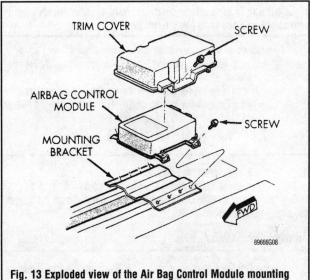

Fig. 13 Exploded view of the Air Bag Control Module mounting

panel if a (monitored) air bag system fault occurs. If the light does not come on, does not go out or comes on when driving, the system must be diagnosed and repaired by a Dodge dealer or reputable shop. The system is NOT repairable at home.

The ACM also contains an energy-storage capacitor. The capacitor stores enough electrical energy to deploy the air bag for up to two minutes following a battery disconnect or failure. The purpose of the capacitor is to provide air bag system protection in a severe secondary impact if the initial impact somehow damaged or disconnected the battery, but did not deploy the air bag.

SERVICE PRECAUTIONS

➡**This manual does not cover SRS repairs or replacement as such work should be left to a trained professional. The following precautions then, are only to inform the do-it-yourselfer and give him a greater appreciation for the system when required to work in proximity to SRS components.**

• Replace air bag system components only with parts specified in the Chrysler Mopar parts catalog. Substitute parts may appear interchangeable, but internal differences may result in inferior occupant protection.

- The fasteners, screws and bolts have special coatings and are specially designed for use in the air bag system. Never replace them with substitutes. Always use the correct replacement fasteners as supplied by the Chrysler Mopar parts catalog.
- No SRS component should be used if it shows any sign of being dropped, dented or otherwise damaged.
- SRS components formerly installed in another vehicle should never be used. Only new components should be installed.
- Whenever working on SRS components (except for electrical inspections), always disconnect the negative battery cable and then wait at least two minutes before beginning (and taking other precautions as necessary). Once the air bag has been deployed, replace the SRS unit.
- Whenever the ignition switch is **ON** or has been turned **OFF** for less than two minutes, be careful not to bump the SRS unit; the air bag could accidentally deploy and do damage or cause injuries.
- Do not try to take apart the air bag assembly. Once deployed, it cannot be re-used or repaired.
- For temporary storage of the air bag assembly while servicing the vehicle, place it with the pad surface **UP**. Store the air bag assembly on a secure, clean, flat surface away from heat, oil, grease, water or detergent.

❄❄ CAUTION

If the air bag is stored face down, it could spontaneously deploy and cause serious injury and damage.

- Take extra care when doing paint or body work near the air bag assembly and keep heat guns, welding and spray equipment away from the air bag assembly.
- Make sure SRS wiring harnesses are not pinched, and that all ground contacts are clean. Poor grounding can cause intermittent problems that are difficult to diagnose.

DISARMING THE SYSTEM

1. First read the system precautions.
2. Disconnect and isolate the negative battery cable.
3. If the air bag module is undeployed, wait two minutes for the system capacitor to discharge.

ARMING THE SYSTEM

Assuming that the system components (air bag control module, sensors, air bag, etc.) are installed correctly and are in good working order, the system is armed whenever the battery's positive and negative battery cables are connected.

❄❄ WARNING

If you have disarmed the air bag system for any reason, and are re-arming the system, make sure no one is in the vehicle (as an added safety measure), then connect the negative battery cable.

HANDLING A LIVE MODULE

At no time should any source of electricity be permitted near the inflator on the back of the module. When carrying a live module (such as when removing the steering wheel), the trim cover should be pointed away from the body to minimize injury in the event of accidental deployment. In addition, if the module is placed on a bench or other surface, the plastic trim cover should be face up to minimize movement in case of accidental deployment.

When handling a steering column with an air bag module attached, never place the column on the floor or other surface with the steering wheel or module face down.

DEPLOYED MODULE

The vehicle interior may contain a very small amount of sodium hydroxide powder, a by-product of air bag deployment. Since this powder can irritate the skin, eyes, nose or throat, be sure to wear safety glasses, rubber gloves and long sleeves during cleanup.

If you find that the cleanup is irritating your skin, run cool water over the affected area. Also, if you experience nasal or throat irritation, exit the vehicle for fresh air until the irritation ceases. If irritation continues, see a physician.

Clean-Up Procedure

▶ See Figure 14

Begin the clean-up by putting tape over the two air bag exhaust vents so that no additional powder will find its way into the vehicle interior. Then, remove the air bag and air bag module from the vehicle.

Use a vacuum cleaner to remove any residual powder from the vehicle interior. Work from the outside in so that you avoid kneeling or sitting in a unclean area.

Be sure to vacuum the heater and A/C outlets as well; in fact, it's a good idea to run the blower on LOW and to vacuum up any powder expelled from the plenum. You may need to vacuum the interior of the vehicle a second time to recover all of the powder.

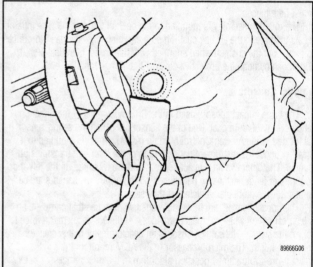

Fig. 14 Applying tape to the vent holes in a deployed module

Servicing a Deployed Air Bag

After an air bag has been deployed, the air bag module and clockspring must be replaced because they cannot be reused. Other air bag system components must also be replaced if damaged.

AIR BAG SYSTEM CHECK

❄❄ WARNING

Disconnect and isolate the battery negative cable before beginning any air bag system component removal or installation procedure. This will disable the air bag system. Failure to disconnect the battery could result in accidental air bag deployment and possible personal injury. Allow the system capacitor to discharge for 2 minutes before removing any air bag components.

1. Disconnect and isolate the negative battery cable.
2. Remove the cover as necessary.

3. Connect a DRB-II or equivalent scan tool to the ACM data link 6-way connector, located at the right of the steering column.

4. Turn the ignition key to the **ON** position.

5. Exit the vehicle with the DRB-II or equivalent tool.

6. After checking that no one is inside the vehicle, connect the battery negative cable.

7. Using the DRB-II or equivalent, read and record the active diagnostic data.

8. Read and record any stored diagnostic codes.

9. Correct any problems found in Steps 6 and 7.

10. Erase stored diagnostic codes if there are no active diagnostic codes. If problems remain, the diagnostic codes will not erase.

11. Turn the ignition key to **OFF** then **ON** and observe the message center air bag lamp. It should go on for six to eight seconds, then go out, indicating that the system is functioning normally.

12. If the air bag warning lamp either fails to light, blinks on and off, or goes on and stays on, there is a system malfunction.

HEATING AND AIR CONDITIONING

Blower Motor

REMOVAL & INSTALLATION

▶ **See Figure 15**

1. Disconnect the negative battery cable.
2. Remove the top half of the radiator fan shroud.

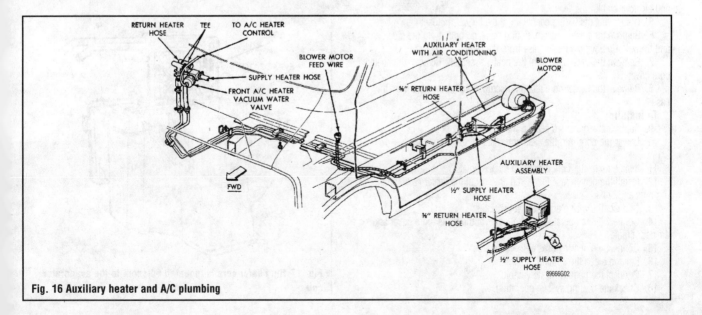

Fig. 15 The location of the front blower motor on a vehicle with A/C

3. Move the top half of the shroud out of the way. Remove the blower motor cooler tube from the blower.

4. Disconnect the blower motor wiring connector.

5. Remove the blower motor cooling tube from the nipple on the blower housing cover.

6. Remove the blower motor mounting plate screws or nuts and washers.

7. While holding the suction and discharge lines inboard and upward (if equipped with A/C), remove the blower motor from the housing.

8. Inspect and replace any damaged sealing material.

9. Remove the retaining clip that retains the blower motor fan wheel to the blower motor shaft.

To install:

10. Install the blower motor fan wheel over the blower motor shaft and install the retaining clip.

11. Place a bead of RTV sealant around the blower motor side of the rubber seal.

12. Position the rubber seal on the blower motor mounting plate.

13. Place the blower motor in position and secure it with the mounting screws or nuts and washers. Tighten the nuts to 20 inch lbs. (2.2 Nm).

14. Install the blower motor vent cooling tube and connect the wiring harness.

15. Install the top shroud.

16. Connect the negative battery cable.

Auxiliary Heater/Air Conditioner Blower Motor

▶ **See Figure 16**

1. Disconnect the negative battery cable.
2. Raise and support the vehicle.
3. Remove the cover from the auxiliary heater-A/C unit.
4. Remove the vertical duct from the auxiliary heater-A/C unit.

Fig. 16 Auxiliary heater and A/C plumbing

5. Remove the horizontal duct from the auxiliary heater-A/C unit.
6. Remove the upper housing from the auxiliary heater-A/C unit.
7. Disconnect the blower motor wiring connector.
8. Remove the blower motor cooling tube from the nipple on the blower housing cover.
9. Remove the blower motor mounting plate screws or nuts and washers.
10. Inspect and replace any damaged sealing material.
11. Remove the retaining clip that retains the blower motor fan wheel to the blower motor shaft.
To install:
12. Install the blower motor fan wheel over the blower motor shaft and install the retaining clip.
13. Place a bead of RTV sealant around the blower motor side of the rubber seal.
14. Position the rubber seal on the blower motor mounting plate.
15. Place the blower motor in position and secure it with the mounting screws or nuts and washers. Tighten the nuts to 20 inch lbs. (2.2 Nm).
16. Install the upper housing on the auxiliary heater-A/C unit.
17. Install the horizontal duct on the auxiliary heater-A/C unit.
18. Install the vertical duct on the auxiliary heater-A/C unit.
19. Install the cover on the auxiliary heater-A/C unit.
20. Lower the vehicle.
21. Connect the negative battery cable.

Heater Core

REMOVAL & INSTALLATION

Front Heater Core—Without Air Conditioning

1. Disconnect the negative battery ground cable.
2. Drain the cooling system.

✳ CAUTION

When draining the coolant, keep in mind that cats and dogs are attracted by the ethylene glycol antifreeze, and are quite likely to drink any that is left in an uncovered container or in puddles on the ground. This will prove fatal in sufficient quantity. Always drain the coolant into a sealable container. Coolant should be reused unless it is contaminated or several years old.

3. Disconnect the heater hoses at the core tubes.
4. Disconnect the temperature control cable at the heater core cover and air door crank.
5. Disconnect the wiring connector at the blower motor.
6. Remove the heater case mounting nuts and bolts from the side cowl and firewall. Remove the heater case from the vehicle.
7. Remove the back plate from the heater assembly. Remove the heater core cover
8. Remove the heater core retaining screws and lift the core from the case.
To install:
9. Replace any damaged sealing material.
10. Lower the core into the case and install the core retaining screws.
11. Install the heater core cover and backing plate.
12. Install the heater case in the van and install the heater case mounting nuts and bolts.
13. Connect the wiring at the blower resistor.
14. Connect the temperature control cable at the heater core cover and air door crank.
15. Connect the heater hoses at the core tubes.
16. Fill and bleed the cooling system.
17. Connect the negative battery cable.
18. Check the heating system operation.

Front Heater Core—With Air Conditioning

♦ See Figure 17

1. Have the vehicle's air conditioning system discharged by a certified MVAC technician.
2. Disconnect the negative battery ground cable.
3. Drain the cooling system. Disconnect the freeze control connector from the wiring harness at the H-expansion valve (years equipped).

✳ CAUTION

Never open, service or drain the radiator or cooling system when hot; serious burns can occur from the steam and hot coolant. Also, when draining engine coolant, keep in mind that cats and dogs are attracted to ethylene glycol antifreeze and could drink any that is left in an uncovered container or in puddles on the ground. This will prove fatal in sufficient quantities. Always drain coolant into a sealable container. Coolant should be reused unless it is contaminated or is several years old.

4. Cover the alternator with a plastic bag.
5. Disconnect the heater hoses at the core tubes.
6. Using a back-up wrench on the fittings, disconnect the refrigerant lines at the H-valve. Cap all openings at once!
7. Remove the mounting screws from the filter-drier bracket and swing the piping out of the way, towards the center of the van. Cap all openings at once!
8. Remove the temperature control cable from the case cover.
9. Remove the glove box.
10. Remove the spot cooler bezel and appearance shield.
11. Working through the glove box, remove the evaporator housing-to-dash panel attaching screws and nuts.
12. Remove the mounting screws from the flange connection at the blower housing. Separate the evaporator housing from the blower motor housing and carefully remove it from the van.
13. Remove the cover from the housing.
14. Remove the screw from the strap on the heater core tubes and pull the core from the housing.
To install:
15. Put the core in the housing. Install the screw in the strap on the heater core tubes.
16. Install the cover on the housing. Place the housing into position in the van.
17. Join the evaporator housing to the blower motor housing. Install the mounting screws in the flange connection at the blower housing.

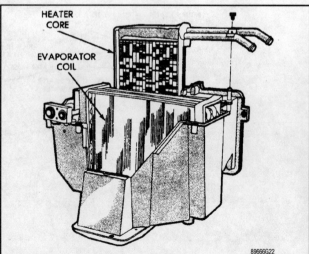

Fig. 17 The heater core is mounted adjacent to the evaporator coil

18. Working through the glove box, install the evaporator housing-to-dash panel attaching screws and nuts.

19. Install the spot cooler bezel and appearance shield.

20. Install the glove box.

21. Install the temperature control cable on the case cover.

22. Install the mounting screws from the filter-drier bracket.

23. Connect the refrigerant lines at the H-valve.

24. Connect the heater hoses at the core tubes.

25. Uncover the alternator.

26. Fill and bleed the cooling system.

27. Connect the freeze control wiring harness.

28. Connect the negative battery cable.

29. Have a certified MVAC service technician evacuate, charge and leak test the A/C system.

Auxiliary Heater Core

▶ See Figures 18, 19 and 20

➡The rear heater core and evaporator core are one unit and are serviced as a single unit, called a combination coil.

1. Have the system discharged by a certified MVAC technician.

2. Disconnect the negative battery ground cable.

3. Drain and recycle the engine coolant.

4. Raise and support the vehicle.

5. Remove the expansion valve from the combination coil.

6. Disconnect the rear heater hoses and the A/C lines from the combination coil and plug or cover the combination coil tubes.

7. Remove the cover from the auxiliary heater-A/C unit.

8. Remove the vertical duct from the auxiliary heater-A/C unit.

9. Remove the horizontal duct from the auxiliary heater-A/C unit.

10. Remove the upper housing from the auxiliary heater-A/C unit.

11. Remove the combination coil from the auxiliary heater-A/C unit lower housing.

To install:

12. Install the combination coil into the auxiliary heater-A/C unit lower housing.

13. Install the upper housing on the auxiliary heater-A/C unit.

14. Install the horizontal duct on the auxiliary heater-A/C unit.

15. Install the vertical duct on the auxiliary heater-A/C unit.

16. Install the cover on the auxiliary heater-A/C unit.

Fig. 19 Unfasten the retainers and remove the unit's cover

Fig. 20 The auxiliary heater water control valve

17. Remove the plugs and connect the heater hoses and A/C lines to the combination coil.

18. Install the expansion valve on the combination coil.

19. Lower the vehicle.

20. Fill and bleed the cooling system.

21. Connect the negative battery cable.

22. Have a certified MVAC service technician evacuate, charge and leak test the system.

Heater Water Control Valve

REMOVAL & INSTALLATION

▶ See Figure 21

1. Disconnect the negative battery cable.

2. Drain the cooling system so that the level (of the system) is below the control valve.

Fig. 18 View of the auxiliary heater-A/C unit with its cover installed

Fig. 21 The heater water control valve; note the vacuum line and the two heater hose connections

✳✳ CAUTION

Never open, service or drain the radiator or cooling system when hot; serious burns can occur from the steam and hot coolant. Also, when draining engine coolant, keep in mind that cats and dogs are attracted to ethylene glycol antifreeze and could drink any that is left in an uncovered container or in puddles on the ground. This will prove fatal in sufficient quantities. Always drain coolant into a sealable container. Coolant should be reused unless it is contaminated or is several years old.

3. Loosen the heater hose clamps and remove the hoses.
4. Disconnect the vacuum line to the valve vacuum control.
5. Remove the mounting screws and remove the valve.
6. On models with an auxiliary heater, the water control valve is "teed" from the main control valve. The removal and installation procedure is the same except for more hose clamps to loosen and an extra vacuum line to remove and connect.
7. Place the control in position and secure it. Connect the heater hoses (replace any hoses that show wear) and secure the hose clamps. Connect the vacuum line(s).
8. Fill the cooling system and check the control valve operation.

Air Conditioning Components

REMOVAL & INSTALLATION

Repair or service of air conditioning components is not covered by this manual, because of the risk of personal injury or death, and because of the legal ramifications of servicing these components without the proper EPA certification and experience. Cost, personal injury or death, environmental damage, and legal considerations (such as the fact that it is a federal crime to vent refrigerant into the atmosphere) dictate that the A/C components on your vehicle should be serviced only by a Motor Vehicle Air Conditioning (MVAC) trained, and EPA certified automotive technician.

➡️**If your vehicle's A/C system uses R-12 refrigerant and is in need of recharging, the A/C system can be converted over to R-134a refrigerant (less environmentally harmful and expensive). Refer to Section 1 for additional information on R-12 to R-134a conversions, and for additional considerations dealing with your vehicle's A/C system.**

Control Cables

REMOVAL & INSTALLATION

▶ **See Figures 22 and 23**

➡️**Later vehicles have vacuum controlled motors and do not have a control cable. Look on the evaporator/heater core case of your vehicle to see if there is a cable attached or vacuum motors are used.**

1. Disconnect the negative battery cable.
2. Remove the engine cover.
3. Depress tab on the self-adjusting clip and remove cable from the blend door.
4. Remove heater control panel.
5. Depress tab and remove the cable from the heater control panel.
6. To remove the self-adjusting clip, hold core wire firmly at both ends of clip and place a ¼ inch I.D. tube over the clip and pry the clip off the wire.

To install:
7. Position self-adjusting clip on core wire 2 inches from the loop at blend door. With a ¼ inch I.D. tube, pry the clip into the locked position.
8. Properly route the cable, as illustrated.
9. Slide the cable core wire loop on control panel lever and snap into place.
10. Install the heater control panel.
11. Place the control lever on the control panel to the **OFF** position.
12. Insert the self-adjusting clip onto the blend door and snap into place.
13. Adjust the cable by moving the control lever all the way to the right.
14. Install the engine cover.
15. Connect the negative battery cable.

Control Panel

REMOVAL & INSTALLATION

▶ **See Figures 24, 25 and 26**

1. Disconnect the negative battery cable.
2. Remove the engine cover.
3. If your vehicle has a control cable:
   a. Depress tab on the self-adjusting clip and remove cable from the blend door.
4. If your vehicle has vacuum motors:

Fig. 22 A distribution door vacuum motor indicates that this system is vacuum rather than cable controlled

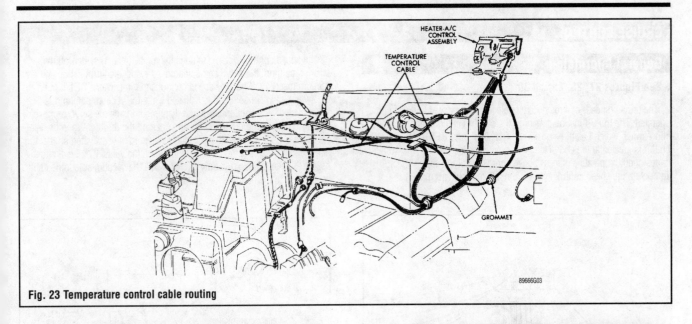

Fig. 23 Temperature control cable routing

Fig. 24 The A/C and heater control panel, as mounted in the dashboard

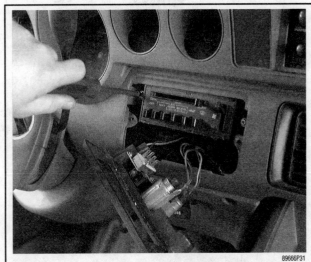

Fig. 26 Remove the retaining screws from the control panel

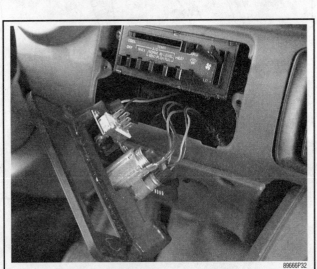

Fig. 25 Unfasten the screws and move the control panel trim out of the way to access the control panel

    a. Reach between the upper dash panel engine housing extension and the bottom of the dash panel to access and unplug the vacuum harness connector, which is located near the driver's side defroster outlet of the distribution duct.

5. Remove the control panel trim from the dash panel.
6. Remove the retaining screws from the control panel.
7. Pull the control panel out of the dash panel far enough to access the connections on the back of the control.
8. Label and disconnect all the connections on the back of the control panel and remove the panel from the dash completely.

To install:

9. Install the connections onto the control panel.
10. Place control panel into opening in dash panel.
11. Tighten the retaining screws to 20 inch lbs. (2.2 Nm).
12. Install the control panel trim onto the dash panel.
13. If your vehicle has vacuum motors, plug-in the vacuum harness connector.
14. If your vehicle has a control cable plug the control cable in at the blend door.
15. Install the engine cover.
16. Connect the negative battery cable.

CRUISE CONTROL

General Information

▶ See Figures 27, 28, 29 and 30

The cruise (speed) control system is electrically actuated and vacuum operated. The multi-function switch on the steering column incorporates a slide-switch which has three positions: **ON**, **OFF**, and **RESUME**. The **SET** button is located at the end of the three position slide switch. This system is designed to operate at speeds above approximately 35 mph (58 km/h). To operate the speed control system, consult your owner's manual.

The speed control system includes the multi-function switch on the steering column, the servo and solenoids, the speed control cable, and a vacuum reservoir. When the speed control servo receives a **SET** input from the switch, the vent solenoid is actuated while the vacuum solenoid is "duty-cycled". This action cause the diaphragm inside the servo to move, pulling on the speed control cable and opening the throttle. When the vehicle reaches its target speed, the vacuum solenoid is deactivated so that the diaphragm holds, and the cable is held. When the vehicle is above target speed, the vent solenoid is duty-cycled, while the vacuum solenoid is still deactivated to maintain the target speed.

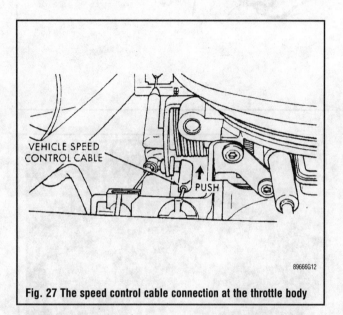

Fig. 27 The speed control cable connection at the throttle body

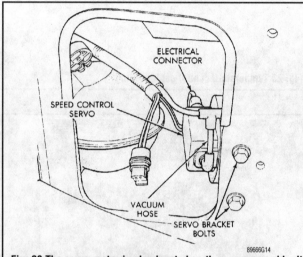

Fig. 29 The servo motor is also located on the passenger side; it is held by a fender extension

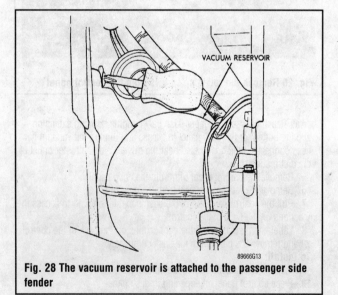

Fig. 28 The vacuum reservoir is attached to the passenger side fender

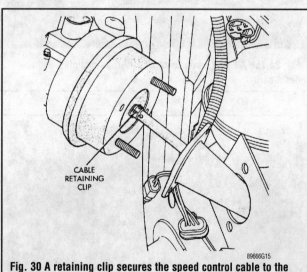

Fig. 30 A retaining clip secures the speed control cable to the servo

CRUISE CONTROL TROUBLESHOOTING

Problem	Possible Cause
Will not hold proper speed	Incorrect cable adjustment Binding throttle linkage Leaking vacuum servo diaphragm Leaking vacuum tank Faulty vacuum or vent valve Faulty stepper motor Faulty transducer Faulty speed sensor Faulty cruise control module
Cruise intermittently cuts out	Clutch or brake switch adjustment too tight Short or open in the cruise control circuit Faulty transducer Faulty cruise control module
Vehicle surges	Kinked speedometer cable or casing Binding throttle linkage Faulty speed sensor Faulty cruise control module
Cruise control inoperative	Blown fuse Short or open in the cruise control circuit Faulty brake or clutch switch Leaking vacuum circuit Faulty cruise control switch Faulty stepper motor Faulty transducer Faulty speed sensor Faulty cruise control module

Note: Use this chart as a guide. Not all systems will use the components listed.

TCCA6C01

ENTERTAINMENT SYSTEMS

Radio Receiver/Tape Player/CD Player

REMOVAL & INSTALLATION

▶ **See Figures 31 and 32**

1. Disconnect the negative battery cable.
2. Remove the cluster bezel from the dash panel.
3. Remove the retaining screws from the radio.
4. Pull the radio far enough away from the dashboard to reach the connections.
5. Label and unplug all connections on the back of the radio.
6. Remove the radio from the dash panel.
To install:
7. Plug all connections into the back of the radio.
8. Place the radio in dash opening.
9. Tighten the radio mounting screws to 30 inch lbs. (3.3 Nm).
10. Install the cluster bezel.
11. Connect the negative battery cable.

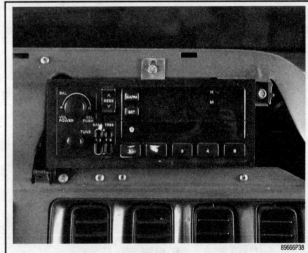
89666P38

Fig. 31 The radio as mounted in the dashboard (with the cluster bezel removed)

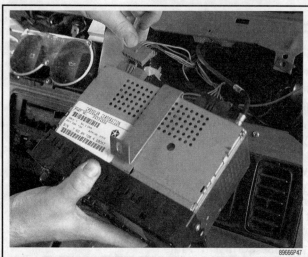

Fig. 32 Label the connectors at the back of the radio before removal for proper installation

Speakers

REMOVAL & INSTALLATION

Dash Panel Speakers

▶ See Figure 33

1. Disconnect the negative battery cable.
2. Remove the top cover from the dash panel.
3. Remove the speaker retaining screws.
4. Pull the speaker out of the opening in the dash panel.
5. Unplug the connector from the back of the speaker.
6. Remove the speaker from the dash panel.

To install:

7. Plug in the connector to the back of the speaker.
8. Install the speaker into the dash opening.

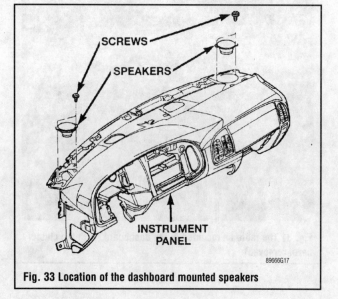

Fig. 33 Location of the dashboard mounted speakers

9. Tighten the retaining screws to 17 inch lbs. (2 Nm).
10. Install the dash panel top cover.
11. Connect the negative battery cable.

Door Speakers

▶ See Figures 34, 35 and 36

1. Disconnect the negative battery cable.
2. Remove the door panel.
3. Remove the speaker retaining screws.
4. Pull the speaker from the door opening.
5. Unplug the connector on the back of the speaker.

To install:

6. Plug in the connector on the back of the speaker.
7. Install the speaker in the door opening.
8. Tighten the speaker retaining screws to 35 inch lbs. (4 Nm).
9. Install the door panel.
10. Connect the negative battery cable.

Fig. 34 The speaker rests in a cutout in the door frame. Remove the speaker's retaining screws . . .

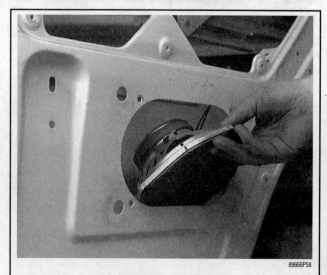

Fig. 35 . . . and pull the speaker out of the door

Fig. 36 Unplug the speaker's electrical connector

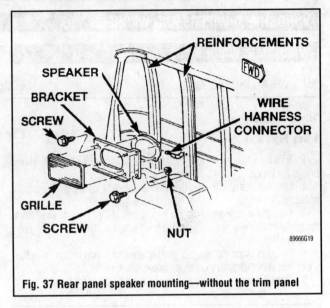

Fig. 37 Rear panel speaker mounting—without the trim panel

Rear Panel Speakers

WITHOUT REAR COMPARTMENT TRIM

▶ See Figure 37

1. Disconnect the negative battery cable.
2. Remove the speaker mounting bracket retaining screws.
3. Pull the speaker mounting bracket out far enough to access and unplug the connector on the back of the speaker.
4. Remove the nuts that retain the speaker grille from the back.
5. Remove the grille from the speaker mounting bracket.
6. Remove the screws that secure the speaker from the front of the mounting bracket.
7. Remove the speaker from the mounting bracket.

To install:

8. Install the speaker onto the mounting bracket and tighten the screws to 20 inch lbs. (2.2 Nm).
9. Install the grille onto the speaker mounting bracket and tighten the nuts to 20 inch lbs. (2.2 Nm).
10. Plug the connector into the back of the speaker.
11. Install the speaker mounting bracket onto the vehicle and tighten the retaining screws to 20 inch lbs. (2.2 Nm).
12. Connect the negative battery cable.

WITH REAR COMPARTMENT TRIM

▶ See Figure 38

1. Disconnect the negative battery cable.
2. Remove the inside trim panel from the rear panel.
3. Unplug the connector on the back of the speaker.
4. Remove the nuts that retain the speaker grille from the back of the trim panel.
5. Remove the grille from the front of the trim panel.

6. Remove the screws that secure the speaker from the front of the trim panel.
7. Remove the speaker from the trim panel.

To install:

8. Install the speaker onto the trim panel and tighten the screws to 20 inch lbs. (2.2 Nm).
9. Install the grille onto the trim panel and tighten the nuts to 20 inch lbs. (2.2 Nm).
10. Plug the connector into the back of the speaker.
11. Install the trim panel onto the rear panel.
12. Connect the negative battery cable

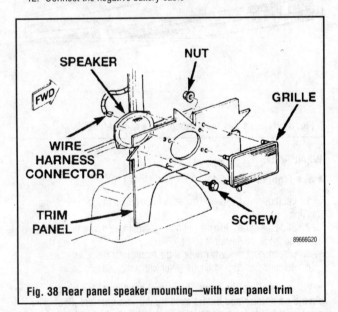

Fig. 38 Rear panel speaker mounting—with rear panel trim

WINDSHIELD WIPERS AND WASHERS

Windshield Wiper Blade and Arm

REMOVAL & INSTALLATION

Wiper Blades

▶ See Figure 39

1. Turn the wiper switch **ON**, then turn the ignition **ON** and **OFF**. This brings the wipers to a more convenient working position.
2. Lift the wiper arm to raise the wiper blade and element off of the windshield.
3. Push the release tab under the arm tip and slide the blade away from the tip (towards the pivot), and remove the blade from the arm.
   To install:
4. Slide the blade retainer into the U-shaped formation on the tip of the wiper arm until the release tab snaps into position.
5. Place the arm and blade assembly back onto the windshield.

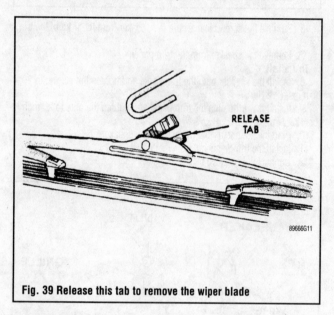

Fig. 39 Release this tab to remove the wiper blade

Wiper Arms

▶ See Figures 40 and 41

1. Lift the arm(s) to permit the latch to be pulled out to the holding position.
2. Slide the spring-like washer hose guard, located near the wiper pivot, up the hose toward the wiper blade.
3. Disconnect the washer hose at the nipple near the wiper pivot.
4. Remove the arm(s) from the pivot with a rocking motion.

➡When installing the arms, the at-rest position of the blades should be determined before pushing the arm onto the pivot. The driver's side blade should be 1.84 in. (47mm) above the windshield weatherstripping at the heel of the blade; the passenger's side blade should be 2.24 in. (57mm) above the weatherstripping.

To install:
5. Mount the arm(s) on the pivot shafts.
6. Lift the wiper arm(s) away from the windshield slightly to relieve the spring tension on the latch.
7. Push the latch into the locked position and slowly release the arm until the wiper blade rests on the windshield.
8. Install the washer hoses to the nipples near the wiper pivots and slide the hose guards back into position.

Fig. 40 Use a screwdriver to release the latch on the wiper arm

1. Wiper pivot　　　2. Wiper arm splines

Fig. 41 The wiper pivot splines engage those on the wiper arm

9. Operate the wipers and put them in **PARK**. Check for proper wiper arm positioning and adjust if necessary.

Windshield Wiper Motor

REMOVAL & INSTALLATION

▶ See Figures 42, 43, 44 and 45

1. Raise the hood.
2. Disconnect the negative battery ground cable.
3. Unplug the wiring at the motor.
4. Remove the wiper motor mounting bolts.
5. Lower the motor to gain access to the crank arm-to-drive link bushing.
6. Disconnect the crank arm from the drive link by prying the bushing off.
7. Remove the motor.

Fig. 42 Disengage the electrical connector from the wiper motor

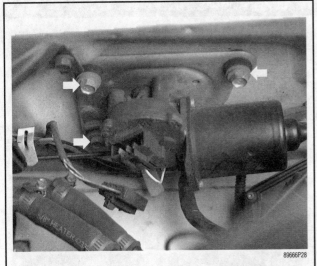

Fig. 43 The wiper motor is usually retained by three bolts

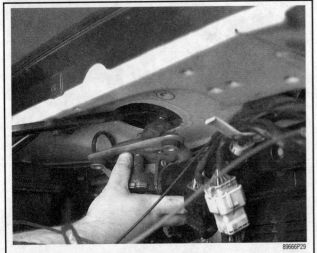

Fig. 44 Use a suitable tool to release the linkage from the motor crank arm

Fig. 45 Remove the nut that retains the crank arm if you are replacing the motor; usually, the new motor doesn't come with one

8. Remove the nut securing the crank arm to the motor.
9. Remove the crank arm.

To install:

10. Install the crank arm. Tighten the retaining nut to 95 inch lbs. (11 Nm).
11. Connect the drive link to the crank arm.
12. Position the wiper motor and install and secure the mounting bolts.
13. Tighten the mounting bolts to 65 inch lbs. (7 Nm).
14. Connect the wiring harness to the wiper motor.
15. Connect the battery cable.
16. Close the hood.

Windshield Washer Motor

REMOVAL & INSTALLATION

▶ See Figures 46 and 47

1. Disconnect the negative battery cable.
2. Remove the bolts mounting the washer reservoir to the mounting bracket.

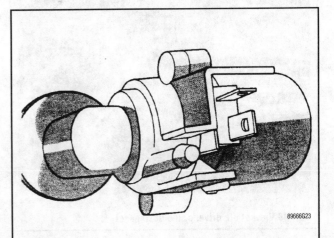

Fig. 46 The washer pump, shown removed from the washer bottle

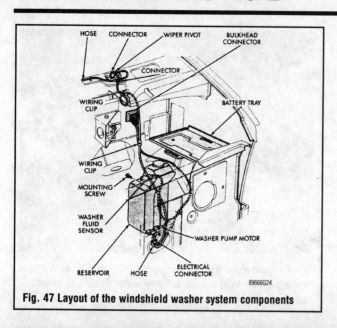

Fig. 47 Layout of the windshield washer system components

3. Hold the reservoir and disconnect the wiring leads to the washer pump.

4. Empty the washer solvent out of the washer reservoir.

5. Remove the pump from the reservoir by gently prying it to release it from the rubber grommet.

6. Remove the pump from the bottom of the washer reservoir.

7. Discard the rubber grommet.

To install:

8. Install a new mounting grommet.

9. Install the washer pump and secure it with the washer and nut.

10. Connect the wiring leads and secure the reservoir to its mounting bracket.

11. Fill the reservoir.

12. Check for leaks and pump operation.

13. Connect the negative battery cable.

INSTRUMENTS AND SWITCHES

Instrument Cluster

REMOVAL & INSTALLATION

▶ **See Figures 48 thru 55**

1. Disconnect the negative battery ground cable.

2. Remove the screws securing the dash panel cluster bezel.

3. Pull the bezel off of the upper retaining clips.

4. On model equipped, disconnect the message center electrical connector.

5. Disconnect the gear shift pointer cable from the steering column (if automatic transmission equipped).

6. Remove the cluster mounting screws.

7. Pull the cluster out just far enough to disconnect the speedometer cable (if equipped).

8. Unplug the wiring connectors at the back of the cluster.

9. Remove the cluster.

To install:

10. Position the cluster at the panel opening.

11. Connect the wiring harness connectors and speedometer(if equipped).

12. Place the cluster into position.

13. Tighten the mounting screws to 20 inch lbs. (2.2 Nm).

14. Connect the gearshift pointer cable to arm on the steering column.

15. Connect the message center wiring harness.

16. Install the dash panel cluster bezel.

17. Connect the negative battery cable.

Fig. 48 View of the driver's side dash panel

Fig. 49 Removing the instrument cluster bezel

Fig. 50 Disengage the connector from the message center (if so equipped)

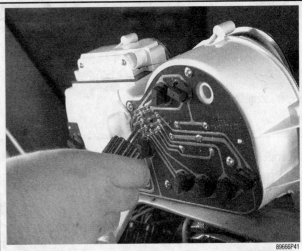

Fig. 53 On most clusters, there are two electrical connectors—one behind the speedometer . . .

Fig. 51 View of the instrument cluster, installed in the dash panel

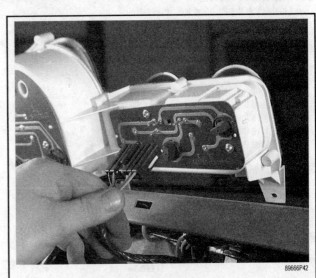

Fig. 54 . . . and one behind the voltmeter

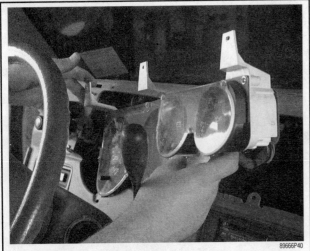

Fig. 52 Pull the cluster out enough to detach the electrical connectors on the back

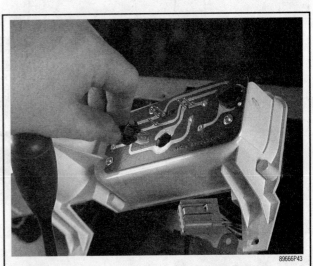

Fig. 55 The cluster is illuminated by small bulbs that are replaceable from the back

Gauges

On some models, the gauges are serviced separately. Other models require complete instrument cluster replacement. The way to tell if your gauges are separately replaceable is if the cluster bezel has circular holes around each gauge; if it does, you can replace each gauge separately. If your entire cluster is visible behind one lens, you must replace the entire cluster assembly.

REMOVAL & INSTALLATION

Separately Replaceable Gauges

▶ See Figure 56

1. Disconnect the negative battery cable.
2. Remove the instrument cluster.
3. Remove the gauge mounting screws or nuts and remove the gauge(s).

To install:

4. Install and secure the gauge(s) in its mounted position.
5. Install the gauge mask, small lens and shroud assembly (install the cluster assembly if removed).
6. Install the cluster hood and bezel.
7. Connect the negative battery cable.

Cluster Replacement

▶ See Figure 57

1. Disconnect the negative battery cable.
2. Remove the cluster assembly from the dash panel.
3. Remove the cluster lens assembly.
4. Remove the cluster housing rear cover.
5. Remove the cluster from the cluster housing.

To install:

6. Install the cluster into the cluster housing.
7. Install the cluster rear housing cover.
8. Install the cluster lens assembly.
9. Install the cluster assembly into the dash panel.
10. Connect the negative battery cable.

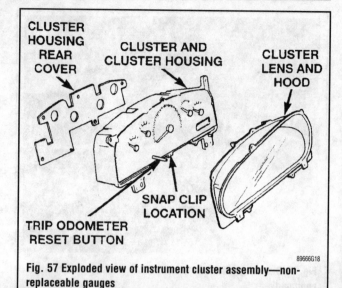

Fig. 57 Exploded view of instrument cluster assembly—non-replaceable gauges

Windshield Wiper Switch

REMOVAL & INSTALLATION

The windshield wiper switch is part of a multi-function switch on the steering column. Please refer to Section 8.

Headlight Switch

REMOVAL & INSTALLATION

▶ See Figure 58

1. Disconnect the negative battery cable.
2. Remove the knee bolster panel (not necessary on 1998 models).

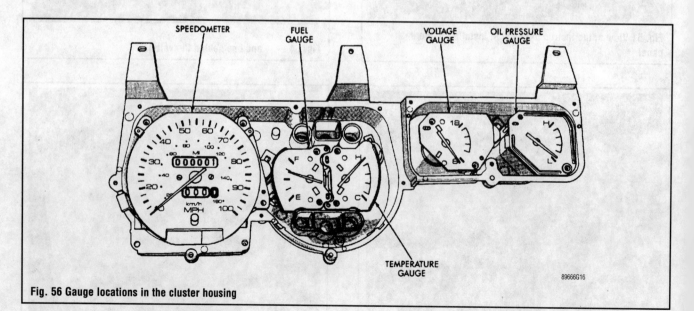

Fig. 56 Gauge locations in the cluster housing

Fig. 58 The headlamp switch is located at the upper left side of the instrument panel (cluster trim bezel removed)

3. Working under the instrument panel, depress the locking button on the switch and pull the knob and stem from the switch (not necessary on 1998 models).
4. Remove the instrument cluster bezel.
5. Remove the switch bezel mounting screws.
6. Remove the switch mounting nut, remove the switch and disconnect the wiring.

To install:
7. Place the light switch into position after connect the wiring harness.
8. Secure the switch with the mounting nut.
9. Install the switch bezel and secure it with the mounting screws.
10. Install the instrument cluster bezel.
11. Push the headlamp switch knob and stem into the switch until it is locked into position.
12. Install the knee bolster panel (if necessary).
13. Connect the negative battery cable.

LIGHTING

Headlights

REMOVAL & INSTALLATION

1989–93 Models (Sealed Beams)

▶ See Figure 59

1. Open and secure the hood.
2. Remove the headlamp trim bezel retaining screws and remove the bezel.

➡ The parking lamp assembly is attached to the bezel.

3. Remove the parking lamp and turn signal bulb sockets from the bezel.
4. Set the bezel down in a safe place.
5. Remove the screws from the retaining ring around the headlamp.
6. Pull the headlamp out of the front of the vehicle.
7. Unplug the headlamp electrical connector.

To install:
8. Plug the headlamp connector into the headlamp assembly.
9. Install the headlamp into the front of the vehicle.
10. Install the retaining ring and tighten the screws.
11. Pick up the bezel and install the sockets into the parking lamp on the bezel.
12. Install the bezel and lamp assembly into the front of the vehicle.
13. Tighten the retaining screws on the bezel assembly.
14. Lower the hood.

1994–98 Models (Halogen Bulbs)

▶ See Figures 60, 61, 62, 63 and 64

1. Open and secure the hood.
2. Press in and pull up on the headlamp release levers to remove the headlamp assembly.
3. Unplug the electrical connector from the bulb/socket assembly.
4. Unfasten the locking ring which secures the bulb assembly, then withdraw the assembly rearward.

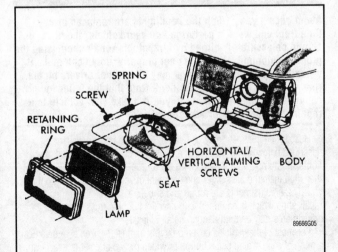

Fig. 59 Sealed beam style headlamp mounting

Fig. 60 Pull straight up to loosen the headlight retaining tabs

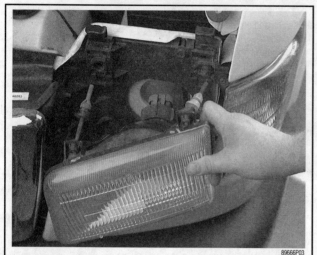

Fig. 61 Pull the headlight straight out after its retaining tabs are loosened

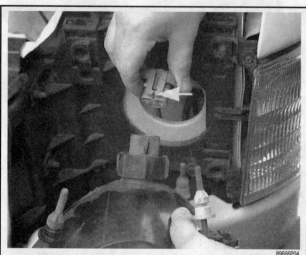

Fig. 62 Lift the tab on the headlight connector while pulling to disengage it

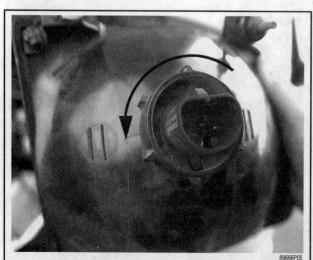

Fig. 63 Turn the headlamp locking ring to remove the bulb assembly

Fig. 64 Pull straight out to release the bulb assembly from the headlamp

To install:

✳✳ WARNING

Do not touch the glass bulb with your fingers. Oil from your fingers can severely shorten the life of the bulb. If necessary, wipe off any dirt or oil from the bulb with rubbing alcohol before completing installation.

5. Position the replacement halogen headlamp bulb and secure it with the locking ring.
6. Plug the electrical connector into the headlamp.
7. Place the headlamp assembly into place and secure the levers.
8. Close the vehicle's hood.

AIMING THE HEADLIGHTS

▶ See Figures 65, 66, 67, 68 and 69

The headlights must be properly aimed to provide the best, safest road illumination. The lights should be checked for proper aim and adjusted as necessary. Certain state and local authorities have requirements for headlight aiming; these should be checked before adjustment is made.

✳✳ CAUTION

About once a year, when the headlights are replaced or any time front end work is performed on your vehicle, the headlight should be accurately aimed by a reputable repair shop using the proper equipment. Headlights not properly aimed can make it virtually impossible to see and may blind other drivers on the road, possibly causing an accident. Note that the following procedure is a temporary fix, until you can take your vehicle to a repair shop for a proper adjustment.

Headlight adjustment may be temporarily made using a wall, as described below, or on the rear of another vehicle. When adjusted, the lights should not glare in oncoming car or truck windshields, nor should they illuminate the passenger compartment of vehicles driving in front of you. These adjustments are rough and should always be fine-tuned by a repair shop which is equipped with headlight aiming tools. Improper adjustments may be both dangerous and illegal.

For most of the vehicles covered by this manual, horizontal and vertical aiming of each sealed beam unit is provided by two adjusting screws which move the retaining ring and adjusting plate against the tension of a coil spring. There is no adjustment for focus; this is done during headlight manufacturing.

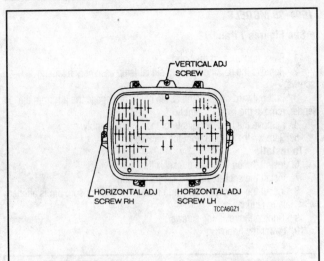

Fig. 65 Location of the aiming screws on most vehicles with sealed beam headlights

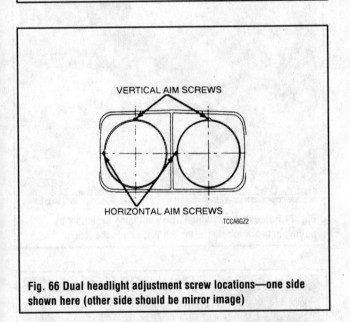

Fig. 66 Dual headlight adjustment screw locations—one side shown here (other side should be mirror image)

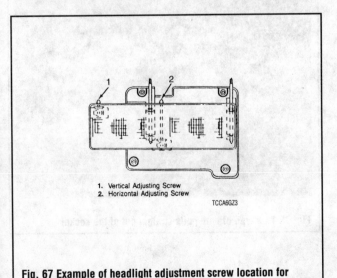

1. Vertical Adjusting Screw
2. Horizontal Adjusting Screw

Fig. 67 Example of headlight adjustment screw location for composite headlamps

➡ **Because the composite headlight assembly is bolted into position, no adjustment should be necessary or possible. Some applications, however, may be bolted to an adjuster plate or may be retained by adjusting screws. If so, follow this procedure when adjusting the lights, BUT always have the adjustment checked by a reputable shop.**

Before removing the headlight bulb or disturbing the headlamp in any way, note the current settings in order to ease headlight adjustment upon reassembly. If the high or low beam setting of the old lamp still works, this can be done using the wall of a garage or a building:

1. Park the vehicle on a level surface, with the fuel tank about ½ full and with the vehicle empty of all extra cargo (unless normally carried). The vehicle should be facing a wall which is no less than 6 feet (1.8m) high and 12 feet (3.7m) wide. The front of the vehicle should be about 25 feet (7.7m) from the wall.

2. If aiming is to be performed outdoors, it is advisable to wait until dusk in order to properly see the headlight beams on the wall. If done in a garage, darken the area around the wall as much as possible by closing shades or hanging cloth over the windows.

3. Turn the headlights **ON** and mark the wall at the center of each light's low beam, then switch on the bright lights and mark the center of each

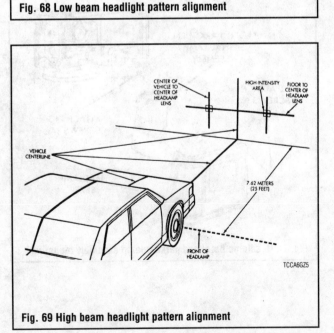

Fig. 68 Low beam headlight pattern alignment

Fig. 69 High beam headlight pattern alignment

light's high beam. A short length of masking tape which is visible from the front of the vehicle may be used. Although marking all four positions is advisable, marking one position from each light should be sufficient.

4. If neither beam on one side is working, and if another like-sized vehicle is available, park the second one in the exact spot where the vehicle was and mark the beams using the same-side light. Then switch the vehicles so the one to be aimed is back in the original spot. It must be parked no closer to or farther away from the wall than the second vehicle.

5. Perform any necessary repairs, but make sure the vehicle is not moved, or is returned to the exact spot from which the lights were marked. Turn the headlights **ON** and adjust the beams to match the marks on the wall.

6. Have the headlight adjustment checked as soon as possible by a reputable repair shop.

Signal and Parking Lights

REMOVAL & INSTALLATION

Front Turn Signal and Parking Lights

1989–93 MODELS

▶ **See Figure 70**

1. Raise and support the hood.
2. Remove the headlamp trim bezel retaining screws and remove the bezel.

➡ **The parking lamp assembly is attached to the bezel.**

3. Remove the parking lamp and turn signal bulb sockets from the bezel.
4. Set the bezel down in a safe place.
5. Remove the bulb(s) from the socket(s).

To install:

6. Install the bulb(s) into the socket(s).
7. Pick up the bezel and install the sockets into the bezel.
8. Install the bezel and lamp assembly into the front of the vehicle.
9. Tighten the retaining screws on the bezel assembly.
10. Lower the hood.

1994–98 MODELS

▶ **See Figures 71 and 72**

1. Raise and support the hood.
2. Remove the parking and turn signal lamp assembly retaining screws.
3. Pull outward on the lamp assembly to disengage the pin from the fender, remove the lamp assembly.
4. Remove the bulb sockets from the lamp assembly.
5. Remove the bulb(s) from the socket(s).

To install:

6. Install the bulb(s) into the socket(s).
7. Install the sockets into the lamp assembly.
8. Install the lamp assembly into the fender, making sure pin is aligned with hole in fender.
9. Tighten the retaining screws.
10. Lower the hood.

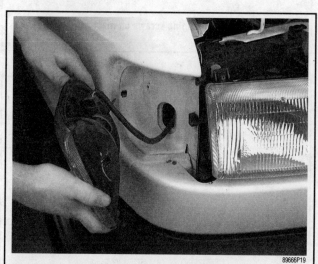

Fig. 71 Remove the parking/turn signal lamp assembly by pulling outward to release the pin that enters the fender

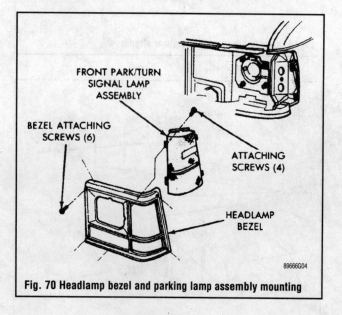

Fig. 70 Headlamp bezel and parking lamp assembly mounting

Fig. 72 This type of bulb pulls straight out of the socket

Rear Turn Signal, Brake, Side Marker and Parking Lights

▶ **See Figures 73, 74, 75, 76 and 77**

1. Remove the tail lamp assembly retaining screws.
2. Remove the tail lamp assembly from the vehicle.
3. Remove the bulb sockets from the tail lamp assembly.
4. Remove the bulb(s) from their socket(s).

To install:

5. Install the bulb(s) into the sockets.
6. Install the bulb sockets into the tail lamp assembly.
7. Install the tail lamp onto vehicle.
8. Tighten the tail lamp retaining screws.

High-Mount Brake Light

▶ **See Figures 78 and 79**

1. Remove the retaining screws on the high-mount brake lamp lens.
2. Remove the bulb socket from the lens assembly by twisting out.
3. Grasp the bulb and remove it from the socket.

To install:

4. Install a new bulb into the socket, and install the socket into the lens.

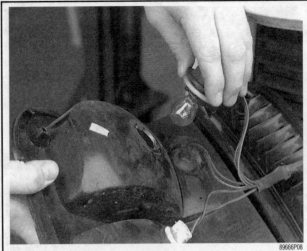

Fig. 75 Twist the sockets on the back of the tail lamp assembly a quarter turn counterclockwise to remove them

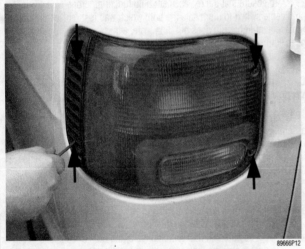

Fig. 73 Unfasten the retaining screws to remove the tail lamp assembly

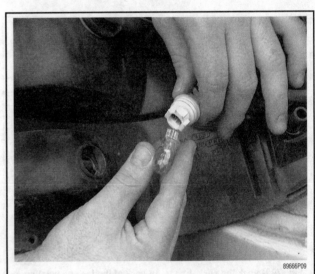

Fig. 76 These small light bulbs pull straight out of their sockets

Fig. 74 Be careful removing the tail lamp; after the screws are removed, the lamp is not supported

Fig. 77 Here is an example of a burned out bulb—note the dark, silvery color

Fig. 78 Remove the retaining screws to remove the lens and access the bulb

Fig. 80 Disengage the spring clip which retains one tapered end of this dome light bulb, then withdraw the bulb

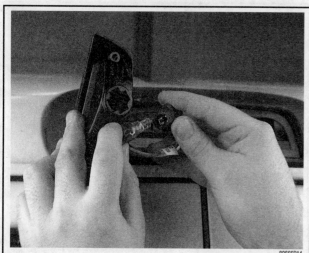

Fig. 79 Unlock the socket from the back of the lens by twisting a quarter turn counterclockwise, then pull out the bulb

5. Install the lens into the lamp assembly.
6. Tighten the retaining screws.

Dome Light

▶ See Figure 80

1. Using a small prytool, carefully remove the cover lens from the lamp assembly.
2. Remove the bulb from its retaining clip contacts. If the bulb has tapered ends, gently depress the spring clip/metal contact and disengage the light bulb, then pull it free of the two metal contacts.
To install:
3. Before installing the light bulb into the metal contacts, ensure that all electrical conducting surfaces are free of corrosion or dirt.
4. Position the bulb between the two metal contacts. If the contacts have small holes, be sure that the tapered ends of the bulb are situated in them.

5. To ensure that the replacement bulb functions properly, activate the applicable switch to illuminate the bulb which was just replaced. If the replacement light bulb does not illuminate, either it is faulty or there is a problem in the bulb circuit or switch. Correct as necessary.
6. Install the cover lens until its retaining tabs are properly engaged.

Cargo or Passenger Area Lamps (Rear of Cargo and Club Wagons)

1. Using a small prytool, carefully remove the cover lens from the lamp assembly.
2. Remove the bulb from its retaining clip contacts. If the bulb has tapered ends, gently depress the spring clip/metal contact and disengage the light bulb, then pull it free of the two metal contacts.
To install:
3. Before installing the light bulb into the metal contacts, ensure that all electrical conducting surfaces are free of corrosion or dirt.
4. Position the bulb between the two metal contacts. If the contacts have small holes, be sure that the tapered ends of the bulb are situated in them.
5. To ensure that the replacement bulb functions properly, activate the applicable switch to illuminate the bulb which was just replaced. If the replacement light bulb does not illuminate, either it is faulty or there is a problem in the bulb circuit or switch. Correct as necessary.
6. Install the cover lens until its retaining tabs are properly engaged.

License Plate Lights

BASE AND STANDARD BUMPER

▶ See Figures 81, 82, 83 and 84

1. Remove the license plate.
2. Remove the bolts attaching the lamp assembly to the bumper.
3. Bring the lamp assembly down to access the lens cover retaining screws.
4. Remove the lens retaining screws.
5. Remove the lens from the lamp.
6. Remove the bulb from the socket.
To install:
7. Install the bulb into the socket.
8. Install the lens over the lamp and tighten the retaining screws.

Fig. 81 The license plate lamp is located above the license plate, and behind the bumper

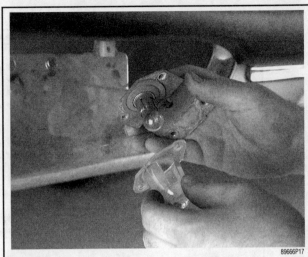

Fig. 83 Be sure to place the lens out of harm's way until you are ready to reinstall it

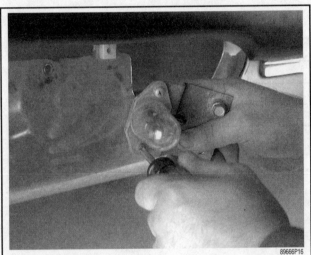

Fig. 82 Unfasten the screws to remove the lens, so you can access the bulb

Fig. 84 Turn the bulb until the tang on it aligns with the slot in the socket, then withdraw the bulb

9. Install the lamp assembly onto the bumper.
10. Tighten the bolts attaching the lamp assembly to the bumper.
11. Install the license plate.

STEP BUMPER

1. Remove the lamp retaining screws.
2. Remove the lamp(s) assembly from the bumper.

3. Remove the bulb(s) from the socket.
To install:
4. Install the bulb into the socket.
5. Install the lamp on the bumper and tighten the retaining screws.

1989–93 Light Bulb Application Chart

INTERIOR LAMP BULBS			
Headlight Switch Rheostat Dimming		**Non-Dimming**	
Air Conditioning Control Illumination	#161	Brake Indicator Lamp	#194
Ashtray Lamp	#161	Dome Lamp	#211-2
Auxiliary Heater Control Illumination	#161	Door Lamp	#211-2
Cigar Lighter Illumination	#161	Maintenance Required	#161
Clock Electronic (Note A)		Fasten Seat Belt Indicator Lamp	#161
Gear Shift Selector (Note B)	#194	Glove Compartment Lamp	#1891
Headlamp Switch Illumination	#161	Rear Window Defogger Indicator	#161
Rear Window Defogger Control Illumination	#161	High Beam Indicator Lamp	#194
Heater Control Illumination	#161	Ignition Switch Lamp	#53
Instrument Cluster Illumination	#194	Low Washer Fluid Lamp	#161
Radio All (ETSR) (Note) Illumination	#74	Oil Pressure Indicator Lamp	#194
Radio Ultimate Sound System (Note C)		Dome/Reading Lamp	1, #211-2 and 2, #906
Speedometer Illumination	#194	Rear Cargo Lamp	#211-2
Windshield Wiper Switch Illumination	#161	Turn Signal Indicator Lamp	#194
		Visor Vanity Lamp	#74
		Stepwell Courtesy Lamp	#212-2

NOTE: (A) Included in Radio.
(B) Included in instrument cluster lighting.
(C) Warranty service by authorized service dealer only.

EXTERIOR LIGHT BULBS	
Back-Up Lamps	#1156
Front Park Turn Signal Lamps	#2057
Front Side Marker Is Also Park Lamp	
License Plate Lamp Standard Bumper	#1155
License Plate Lamp Step Bumper	#168
Headlamps Rectangular	#H6054
Side Marker Lamps (Rear)	#194
Tail, Stop and Turn Signal Lamps	#1157
Underhood Lamp	#105

CIRCUIT BREAKER	
Circuit	Headlamps
Amp	20
Location	Integral with Switch

89666C01

1994–98 Light Bulb Application Chart

EXTERIOR LAMPS

Back-up	921
Center High Mounted Stoplamp	922
Front Side Marker	3157NA
Headlamp	9004
License Plate-Step Bumper	168
License Plate-Std. Bumper	1155
Park/Turn Signal	3157NA
Rear Side Marker	168
Tail/Stop/Turn Signal	3157

INTERIOR LAMPS

DIMMER CONTROLLED LAMPS

Ash Receiver	161
Aux. Heater	161
Cigar Lighter	161
Instrument Cluster	PC194
Radio	ASC
Underpanel Courtesy	211-2
Ignition Key	53

INDICATOR LAMPS

A/C Control	158
Airbag	PC194
Anti-lock Brake	PC194
Brake Warning	PC194
Check Engine	PC194
Engine Oil Pressure	PC194
Fasten Seat Belts	PC194
Heater Control	161
High Beam	PC194
Illumination	PC194
Low Fuel	PC194
Low Washer Fluid	PC194
Turn Signal	PC194

NON-DIMMING LAMPS

Dome	211-2
Door Lamp	211-2
Glove Compartment	194
Map/reading	212-2 & 906
Stepwell	212-2
Under Hood	105
Visor Vanity	74

89666C02

TRAILER WIRING

Wiring the vehicle for towing is fairly easy. There are a number of good wiring kits available and these should be used, rather than trying to design your own.

All trailers will need brake lights and turn signals as well as tail lights and side marker lights. Most areas require extra marker lights for overwide trailers. Also, most areas have recently required back-up lights for trailers, and most trailer manufacturers have been building trailers with back-up lights for several years.

Additionally, some Class I, most Class II and just about all Class III and IV trailers will have electric brakes. Add to this number an accessories wire, to operate trailer internal equipment or to charge the trailer's battery, and you can have as many as seven wires in the harness.

Determine the equipment on your trailer and buy the wiring kit necessary. The kit will contain all the wires needed, plus a plug adapter set which includes the female plug, mounted on the bumper or hitch, and the male plug, wired into, or plugged into the trailer harness.

When installing the kit, follow the manufacturer's instructions. The color coding of the wires is usually standard throughout the industry. One point to note: some domestic vehicles, and most imported vehicles, have separate turn signals. On most domestic vehicles, the brake lights and rear turn signals operate with the same bulb. For those vehicles without separate turn signals, you can purchase an isolation unit so that the brake lights won't blink whenever the turn signals are operated.

One, final point, the best kits are those with a spring loaded cover on the vehicle mounted socket. This cover prevents dirt and moisture from corroding the terminals. Never let the vehicle socket hang loosely; always mount it securely to the bumper or hitch.

CIRCUIT PROTECTION

Fuses

⏵ **See Figures 85, 86 and 87**

The fuse block is located under the glove box door. Most models use blade-type fuses, but some earlier models may use glass tubular type fuses. Be sure to always try to determine the cause of a blown fuse before replacing, and visually check the protected circuit before replacing the fuse. If no problem was found during the visual inspection, replace the fuse. If it blows again, a short exists in the system; repair the short before replacing the fuse.

Some models have a power distribution box located in the engine compartment. The box is located adjacent to the battery and contains additional fuses for circuits such as the Anti-lock Braking System (ABS), trailer towing, alternator, A/C compressor, and other circuits.

REPLACEMENT

Interior Fuse Block

1. Open the glove box door.
2. Lift the fuse block cover.

Fig. 85 The interior fuse block is located alongside the glove box on most models

Fig. 86 The fuse block is located beneath the black cover, which is behind the glove box door

3. Remove the appropriate fuse from the fuse block, noting its location for installation.

To install:

4. Install the proper type and rated fuse into location.
5. Close the fuse block cover.
6. Close the glove box door.

Power Distribution Box

1. Open the hood.
2. Remove the power distribution box cover.
3. Remove the appropriate fuse from the power distribution box, noting its location for installation.

To install:

4. Install the proper type and rated fuse into location.
5. Install the cover on the power distribution box.
6. Close the hood.

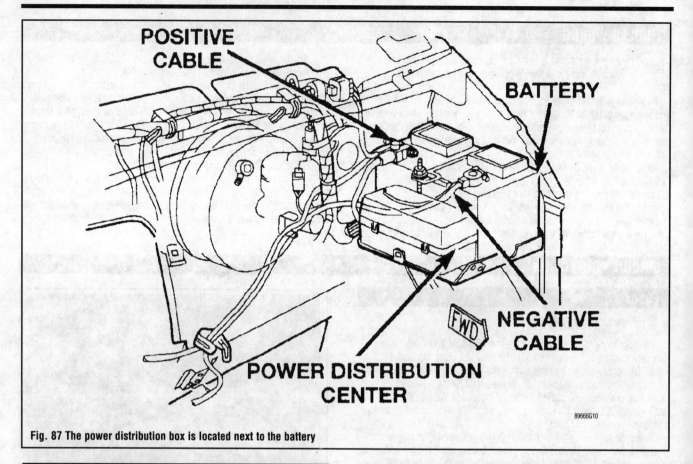

POSITIVE CABLE

BATTERY

NEGATIVE CABLE

FWD

POWER DISTRIBUTION CENTER

89666G10

Fig. 87 The power distribution box is located next to the battery

Fusible Links

❊❊ WARNING

DO NOT replace blown fusible links with standard wire. Use only fusible type wire with hypalon insulation or damage to the electrical system could occur. Make sure the correct gauge of wiring is used.

When a fusible link blows it is very important to find out the cause. Do not just replace the link to correct the problem. The fusible links are placed in the system for protection against dead shorts to ground.

In some instances the link may be blown and it will not show through the insulation. Check the entire length of the fusible wire when the link is suspect of failure.

REPLACEMENT

To repair any blown fuse link use the following procedure:
1. Determine which circuit is damaged, its location and the cause of the open fuse link. If the damaged fuse link is one of three fed by a common No. 10 or 12 gauge feed wire, determine the specific affected circuit.
2. Disconnect the negative battery cable.
3. Cut the damaged fuse link from the wiring harness and discard it. If the fuse link is one of three circuits fed by a single feed wire, cut it out of the harness at each splice end and discard it.
4. Identify and procure the proper fuse link and butt connectors for attaching the fuse link to the harness.
5. To repair any fuse link in a 3-link group with one feed: After cutting the open link out of the harness, cut each of the remaining undamaged fuse links close to the feed wire weld.
6. Strip approximately ½ in. (13mm) of insulation from the detached ends of the two good fuse links. Then insert two wire ends into one end of a butt

connector and carefully push one stripped end of the replacement fuse link into the same end of the butt connector and crimp all three firmly together.

➡**Care must be taken when fitting the three fuse links into the butt connector as the internal diameter is a snug it for three wires. Make sure to use a proper crimping tool. Pliers, side cutters, etc. will not apply the proper crimp to retain the wires and withstand a pull test.**

7. After crimping the butt connector to the three fuse links, cut the weld portion from the feed wire and strip approximately ½ in. (13mm) of insulation from the cut end. Insert the stripped end into the open end of the butt connector and crimp very firmly.
8. To attach the remaining end of the replacement fuse link, strip approximately ½ in. (13mm) of insulation from the wire end of the circuit from which the blown fuse link was removed, and firmly crimp a butt connector or equivalent to the stripped wire. Then, insert the end of the replacement link into the other end of the butt connector and crimp firmly.
9. Using rosin core solder with a consistency of 60 percent tin and 40 percent lead, solder the connectors and the wires at the repairs and insulate with electrical tape.
10. To replace any fuse link on a single circuit in a harness, cut out the damaged portion, strip approximately ½ in. (13mm) of insulation from the two wire ends and attach the appropriate replacement fuse link to the stripped wire ends with two proper size butt connectors. Solder the connectors and wires and insulate the tape.
11. To repair any fuse link which has an eyelet terminal on one end such as the charging circuit, cut off the open fuse link behind the weld, strip approximately ½ in. (13mm) of insulation from the cut end and attach the appropriate new eyelet fuse link to the cut stripped wire with an appropriate size butt connector. Solder the connectors and wires at the repair and insulate with tape.
12. Connect the negative battery cable to the battery and test the system for proper operation.

→ Do not mistake a resistor wire for a fuse link. The resistor wire is generally longer and has print stating, "Resistor: don't cut or splice." DO NOT replace blown fusible links with standard wire. Use only fusible type wire with hypalon insulation or damage to the electrical system could occur. Make sure the correct gauge of wiring is used.

Circuit Breakers

RESETTING AND/OR REPLACEMENT

The circuit breakers are located inside the fuse box, under the glove box door, or next to the fuse box on 1998 models. The circuit breakers are automatically reset when the failure corrects itself, however, that does not mean that the problem is repaired. If a circuit such as the power windows, has a window motor that is going bad, the resistance will be high and eventually the circuit breaker trips and power is shut off to the circuit. When the circuit cools down, and the circuit breaker works again, so will the windows, however the breaker will trip again when the resistance builds. Circuits that might be needed in case of an emergency or to operate the vehicle like the power door locks and power windows have circuit breakers instead of fuses. A circuit breaker is replaced exactly like a fuse.

Flashers

REPLACEMENT

▶ See Figures 88, 89 and 90

The flashers are located at the back of the dash panel on 1989–97 models, and at the driver's side of the dash panel on 1998 models.
To replace the flasher(s):
1. On 1989–97 models:
   a. Open the glove box door.
   b. Remove the glove box assembly.

c. Reach through the opening, the flashers are located in the passenger side corner.
2. On 1998 models:
   a. Remove the end cap from the dash panel.
3. Remove the flasher(s) from the vehicle.
To install:
4. Push new flasher into socket.
5. Verify operation of the flasher(s).
6. On 1989–97 models:
   a. Install the glove box assembly.
   b. Close the glove box door.
7. On 1998 models:
   a. Install the dash panel end cap.

Fig. 89 The flasher is located at the far passenger side of the dash panel in most models

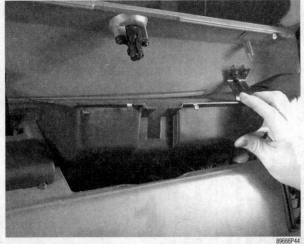

Fig. 88 Removing the glove box to access the flasher(s) is necessary on some models

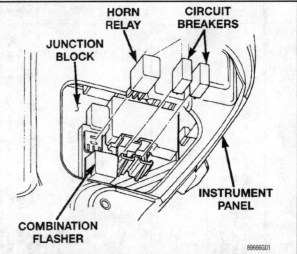

Fig. 90 The flasher is located at the driver's side of the dashboard on 1998 models

89666C03

AMPS	FUSE	COLOR CODE
3	VT	VIOLET
4	PK	PINK
5	TN	TAN
10	RD	RED
20	YL	YELLOW
25	NAT	NATURAL
30	LG	LIGHT GREEN

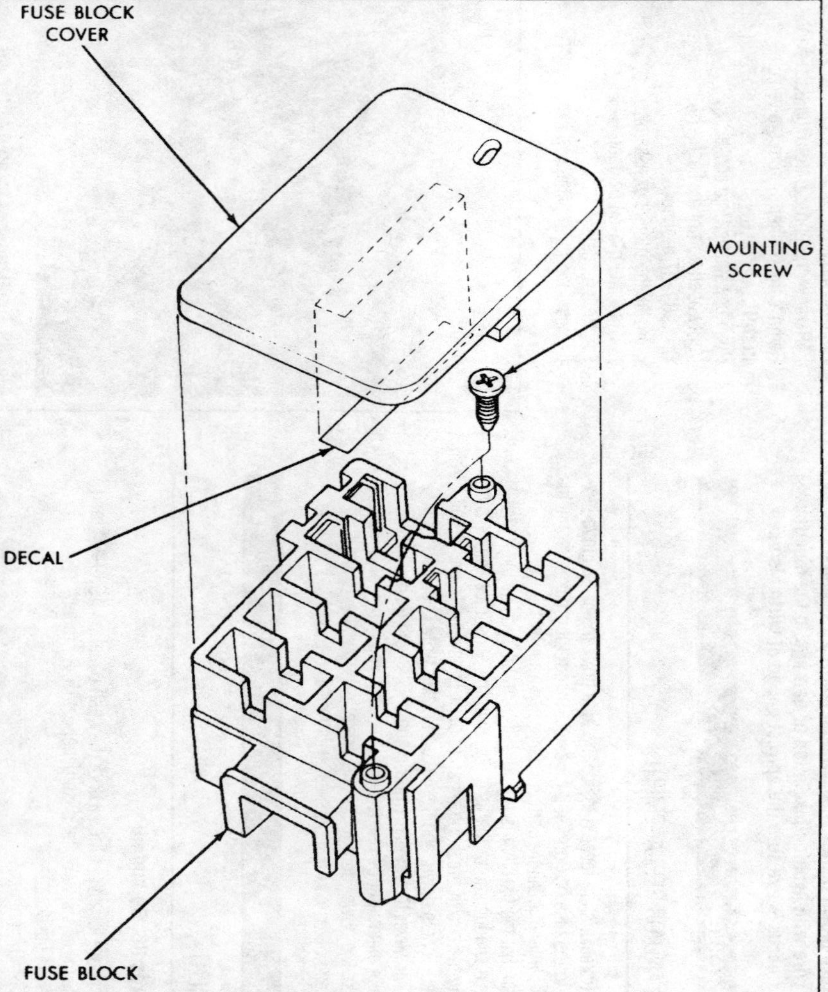

CAUTION: WHEN REPLACING A BLOWN FUSE, IT IS IMPORTANT TO REPLACE IT WITH A FUSE HAVING THE CORRECT AMPERAGE RATING. THE USE OF A FUSE WITH A RATING OTHER THAN INDICATED MAY RESULT IN A DANGEROUS ELECTRICAL OVERLOAD. IF A PROPERLY RATED FUSE CONTINUES TO BLOW, IT INDICATES A PROBLEM THAT SHOULD BE CORRECTED.

MOUNTING SCREW

FUSE BLOCK COVER

DECAL

FUSE BLOCK

1989–90 Fuse Block Circuits

CAVITY	FUSE/COLOR	ITEMS FUSED	MODE
1	3 AMP	ILLUMINATION LAMPS, RADIO, A/C & HEATER, CIGAR LIGHTER, AUXILIARY A/C HEATER, REAR DEFOGGER & CLOCK DISPLAY DIMMING	
2	10 AMP	RADIO AND CLOCK	IGNITION ACC & RUN
3	20 AMP	WINDSHIELD WIPER SWITCH	
4	20 AMP	BACK-UP LAMPS, TURN SIGNALS, & A/C CLUTCH	
5	5 AMP	GAUGES (AMPS, FUEL, TEMPERATURE & OIL) OIL LAMP, EMR LAMP, BRAKE WARNING LAMP, REAR DEFOGGER SWITCH & RELAY, WINDOW LIFT RELAY, SEAT BELT WARNING LAMP & BUZZER, SPEED CONTROL, EMR FEED & OVERDRIVE MODULE	IGNITION RUN AND START
6	20 AMP	ILLUMINATION LAMPS, FUSE #1, PARK, TAIL, SIDE MARKER & LICENSE LAMP, CLOCK DISPLAY INTENSITY HORNS	
7	25 AMP	CIGAR LIGHTER, AUXILIARY A/C & HEATER, KEY-IN & HEADLAMP ON BUZZER, STOP LAMPS	BATTERY FEED
8	20 AMP	RADIO & CLOCK MEMORY, DOME LAMP, COURTESY READING LAMP, GLOVE BOX LAMP, IGNITION TIME DELAY RELAY AND LAMPS	
9	30 AMP	AIR CONDITIONING BLOWER MOTOR AND HEATER BLOWER MOTOR	IGNITION ACC & RUN
10	20 AMP	HAZARD FLASHERS	

89666C04

CAVITY	FUSE/COLOR	ITEMS FUSED
1		NOT USED
2	20 AMP YELLOW	RADIO ELECTRONICS, GLOVE BOX; TIME DELAY; DOOR COURTESY; DOME; READING; AND UNDER-HOOD LAMPS, POWER MIRRORS
3	20 AMP YELLOW	HAZARD FLASHER
4		OPEN
5		OPEN
6	10 AMP RED	BACK-UP LAMPS, HEATED REAR WINDOW SWITCH
7	30 AMP LT. GREEN	A/C & HEATER BLOWER MOTOR, AUXILIARY A/C HEATER RELAY
8	30 AMP C/BRKR	POWER WINDOWS
9	15 AMP LT. BLUE	CIGAR LIGHTER
10	20 AMP YELLOW	WINDSHIELD WIPERS
11	10 AMP RED	RADIO AND CLOCK
12	20 AMP YELLOW	TURN SIGNAL FLASHER, VAN CONVERSION RELAY, REAR WHEEL ANTI-LOCK MODULE
13	20 AMP YELLOW	HORNS
14	20 AMP YELLOW	EXTERIOR LAMPS
15	20 AMP YELLOW	STOP LAMPS, KEY-IN & HEADLAMP ON BUZZER, REAR WHEEL ANTI-LOCK, AUXILIARY AC & HEATER
16	30 AMP C/BRKR	POWER DOOR LOCKS, DOOR LOCK RELAY
17	5 AMP TAN	GAUGES, BRAKE LAMP, SEAT BELT BUZZER AND LAMP, SRI LAMP, LOW WASHER FLUID LAMP, LOW OIL LAMP, MIL LAMP, ANTI-LOCK LAMP TRANSMISSION OVERDRIVE MODULE
18	2 AMP GRAY	VEHICLE SPEED CONTROL
19		OPEN
20	3 AMP VIOLET	CLUSTER LAMPS, RADIO LAMPS, A/C HEATER CONTROL LAMP, CIGAR LIGHTER LAMP, HEATED REAR WINDOW SWITCH LAMP, REAR A/C HEATER SWITCH LAMP

AMPS	FUSE	COLOR CODE
2	GY	GREY
3	VT	VIOLET
5	TN	TAN
10	RD	RED
15	LB	LIGHT BLUE
20	YL	YELLOW
30	LG	LIGHT GREEN

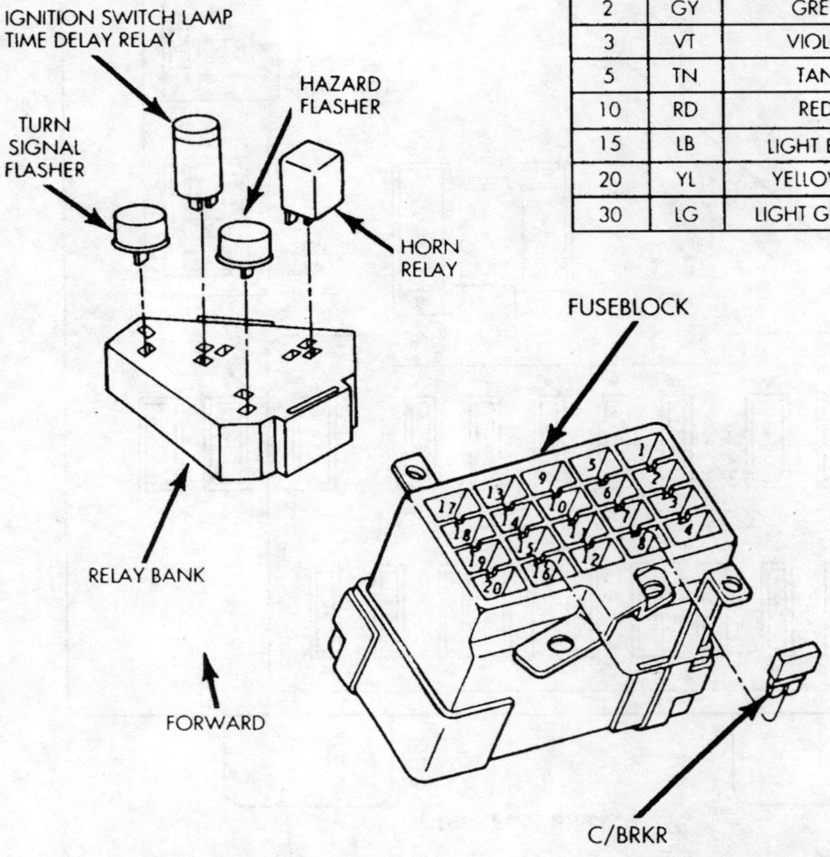

FUSEBLOCK

C/BRKR

HORN RELAY

HAZARD FLASHER

IGNITION SWITCH LAMP TIME DELAY RELAY

TURN SIGNAL FLASHER

RELAY BANK

FORWARD

1991–94 Fuse Block Circuits

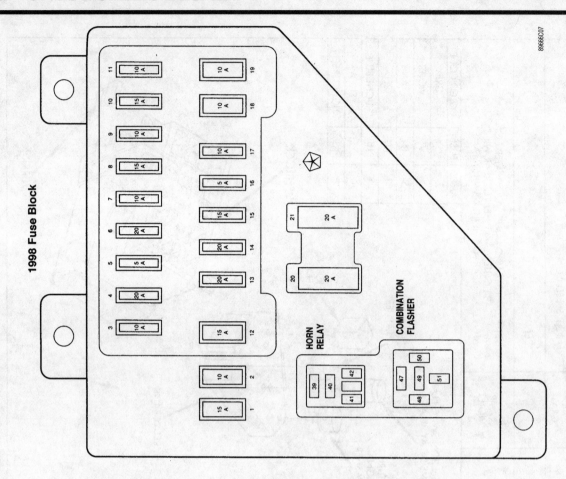

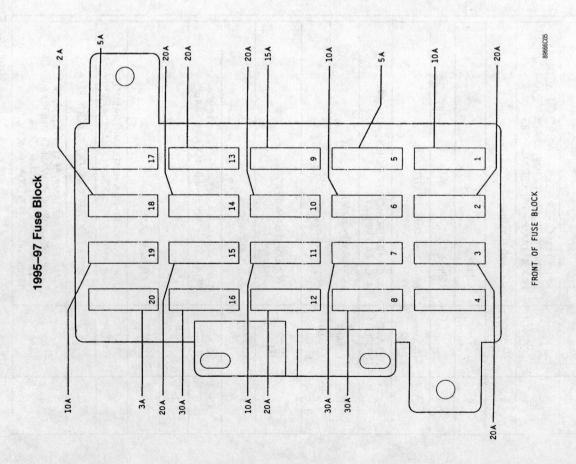

Power Distribution Center Component Location Chart

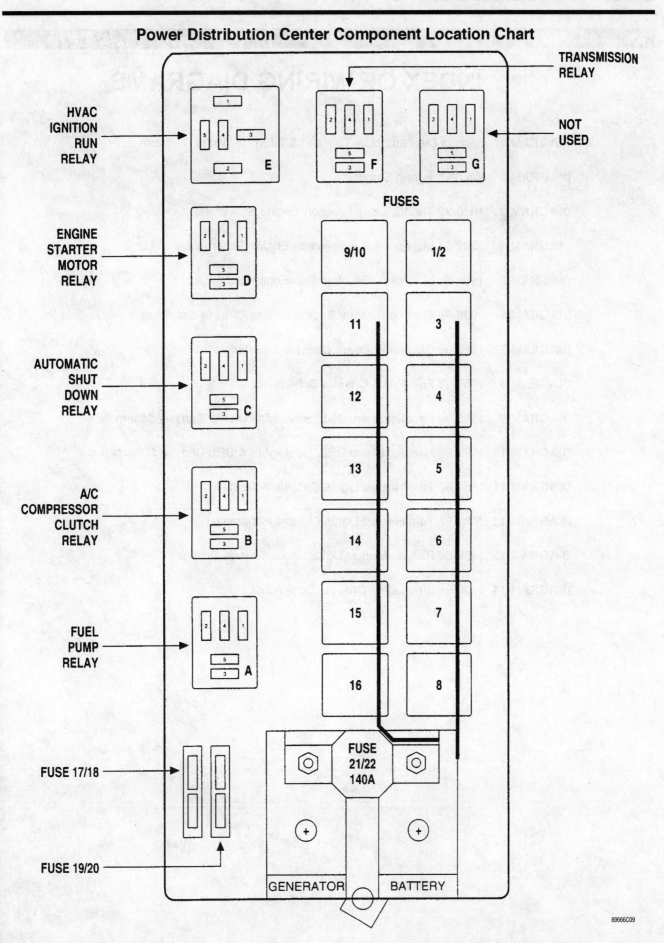

TRANSMISSION RELAY

NOT USED

HVAC IGNITION RUN RELAY

ENGINE STARTER MOTOR RELAY

AUTOMATIC SHUT DOWN RELAY

A/C COMPRESSOR CLUTCH RELAY

FUEL PUMP RELAY

FUSE 17/18

FUSE 19/20

FUSES

9/10   1/2

11   3

12   4

13   5

14   6

15   7

16   8

FUSE 21/22 140A

GENERATOR   BATTERY

89666C09

INDEX OF WIRING DIAGRAMS

89666W01

SAMPLE DIAGRAM: HOW TO READ & INTERPRET WIRING DIAGRAMS

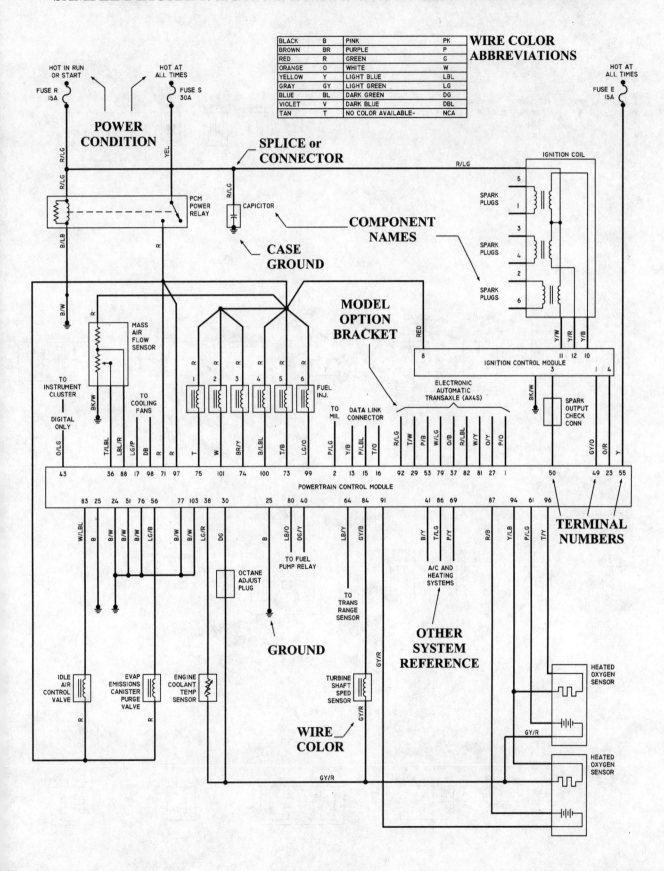

DIAGRAM 1

TCCA6W01

WIRING DIAGRAM SYMBOLS

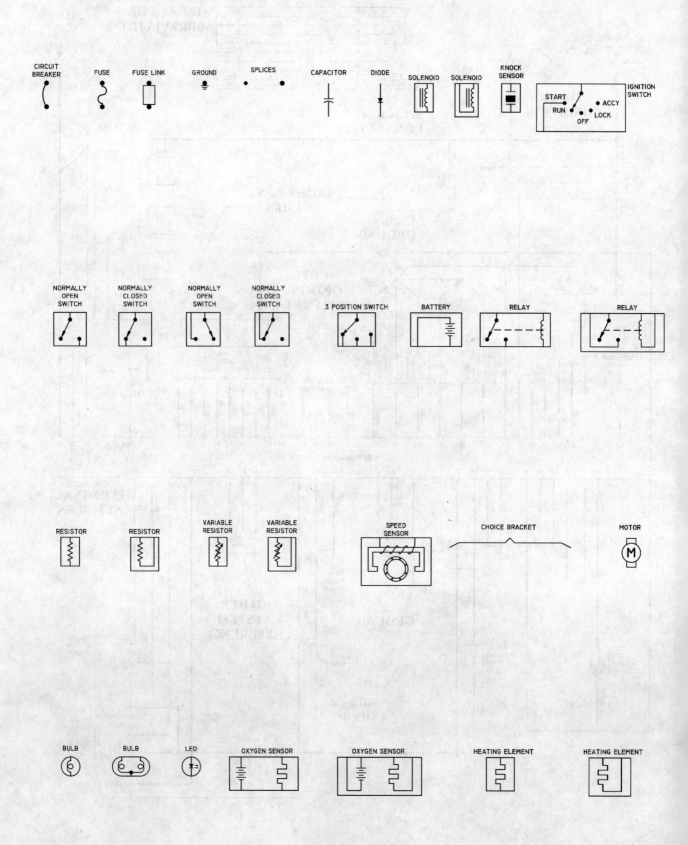

DIAGRAM 2

TCCA6W02

1989-92 Throttle Body Injection Engine Schematics

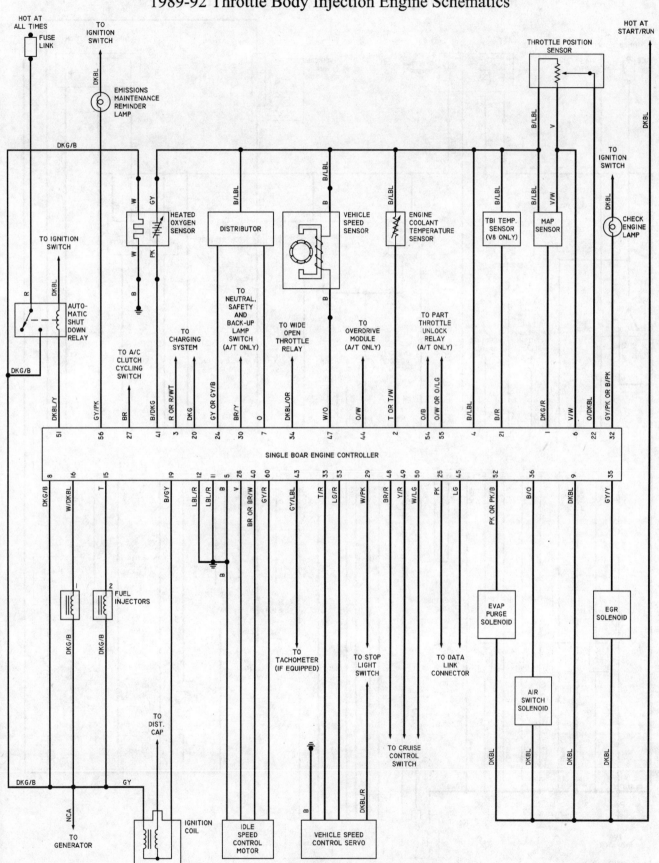

DIAGRAM 3

89666E01

1992-95 Multi-point Fuel Injection Engine Schematics

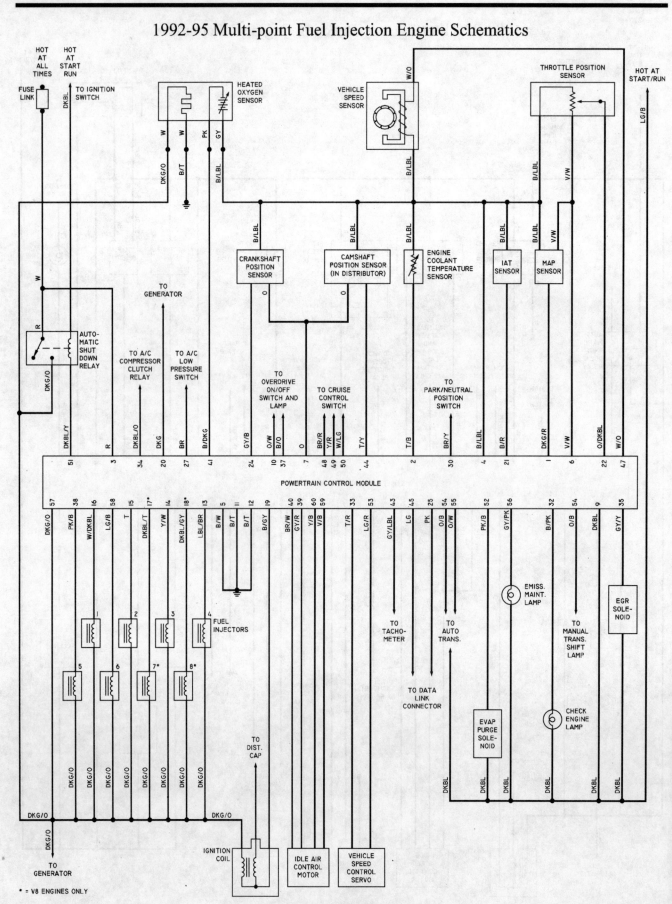

DIAGRAM 4

89666E02

1996-98 Multi-point Fuel Injection Engine Schematics

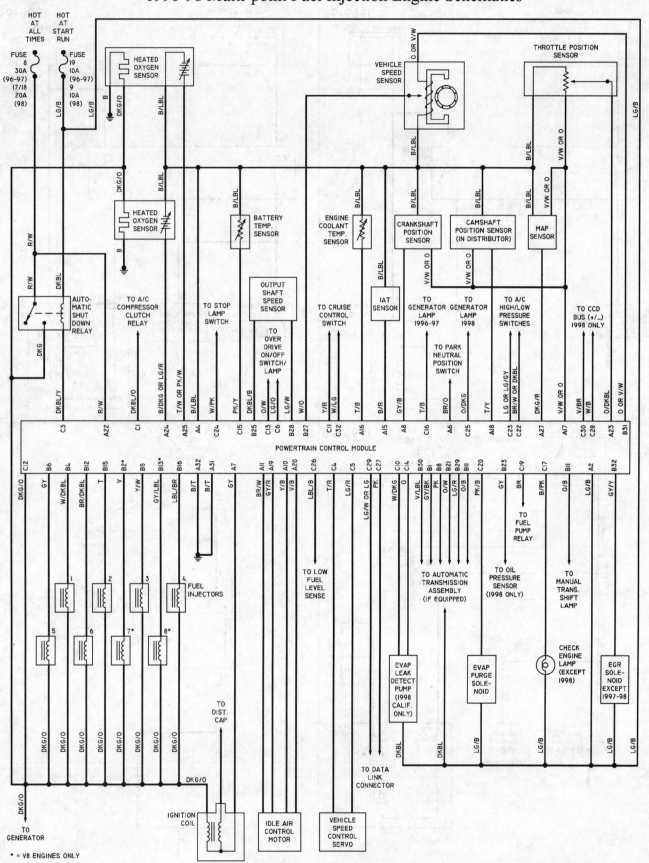

DIAGRAM 5

89666E03

1989-98 Chrysler Full Size Vans

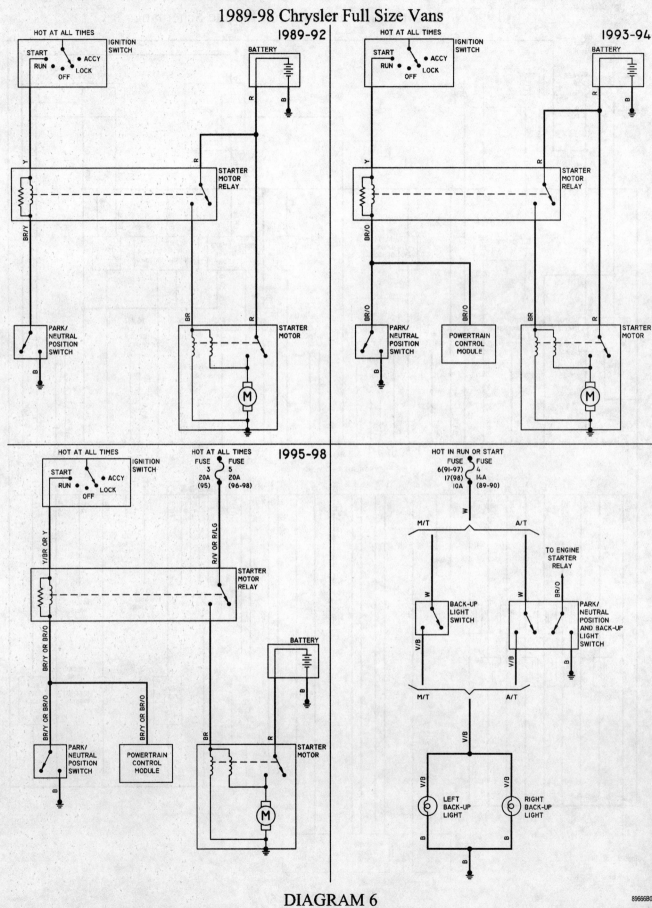

DIAGRAM 6

89666B01

1989-98 Chrysler Full Size Vans

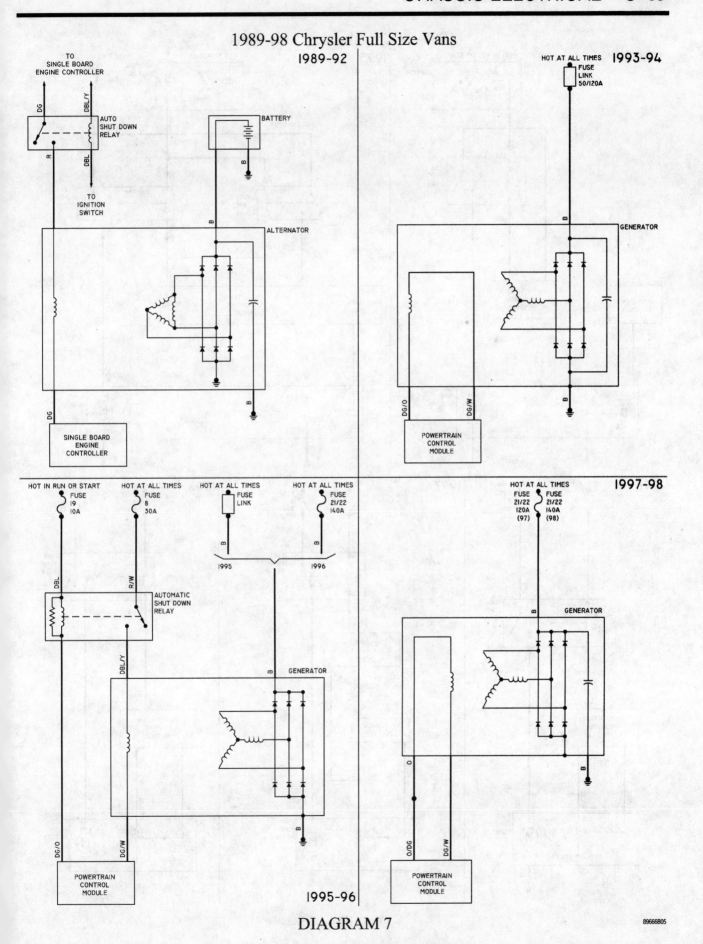

DIAGRAM 7

89666805

1989-98 Chrysler Full Size Vans

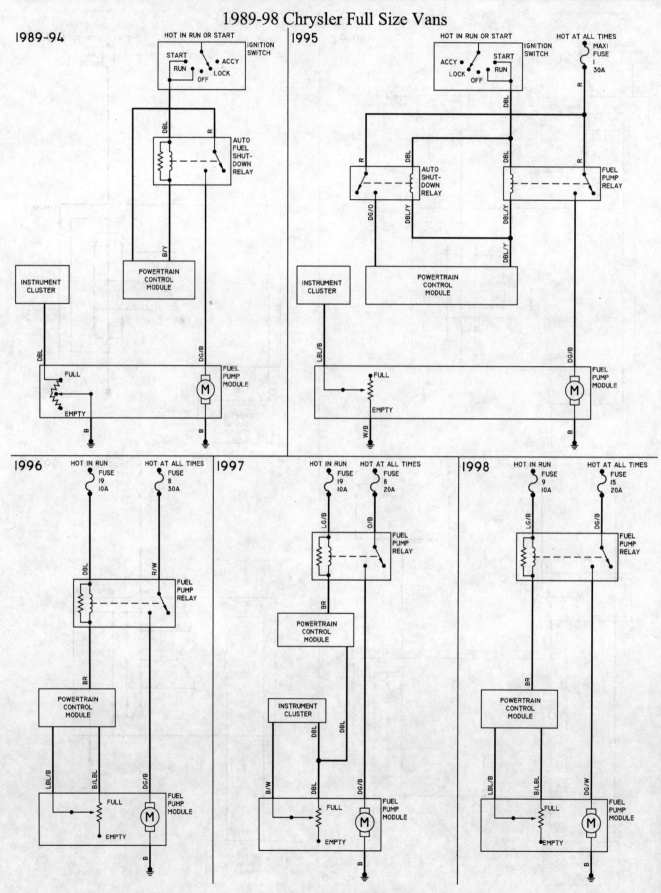

DIAGRAM 8

89666B06

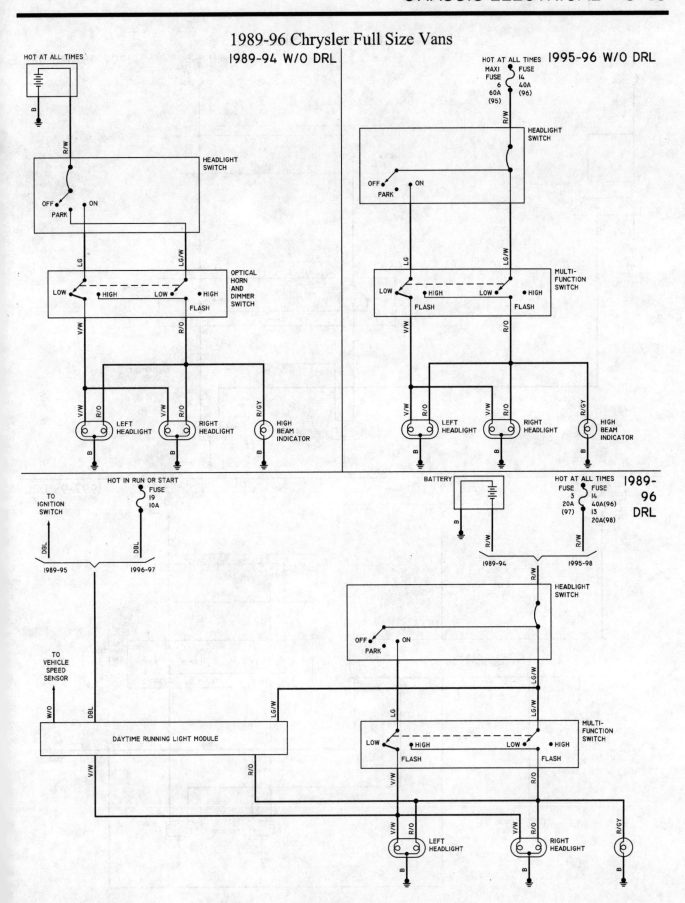

DIAGRAM 9

89666B07

1997-98 Chrysler Full Size Vans

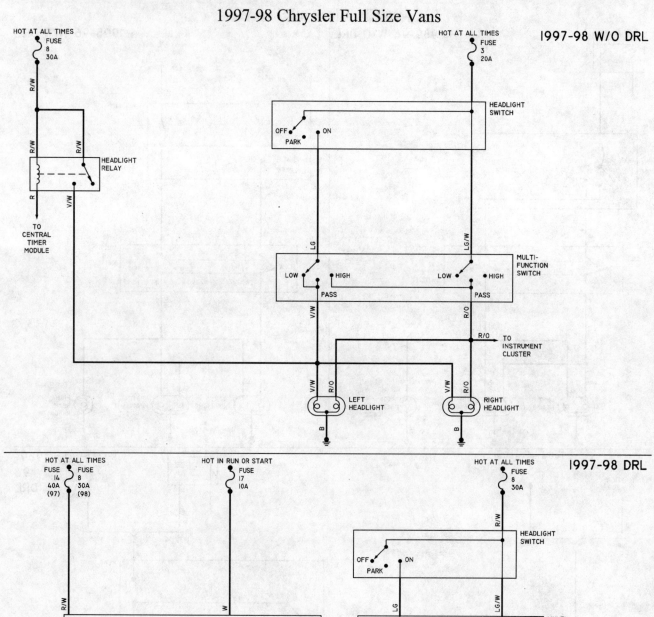

DIAGRAM 10

89666B02

1989-90 Chrysler Full Size Vans

1989-90

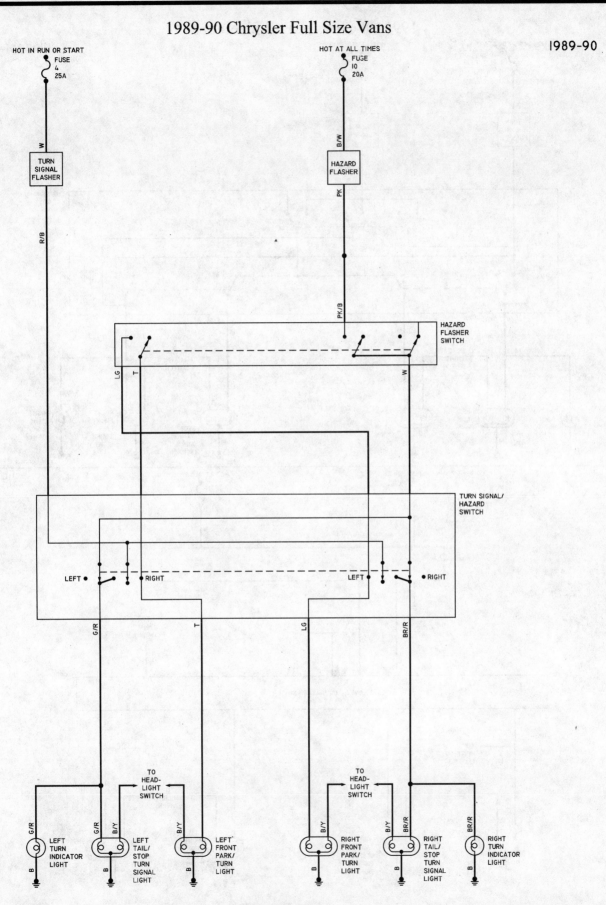

DIAGRAM 11

89666B08

1991-98 Chrysler Full Size Vans

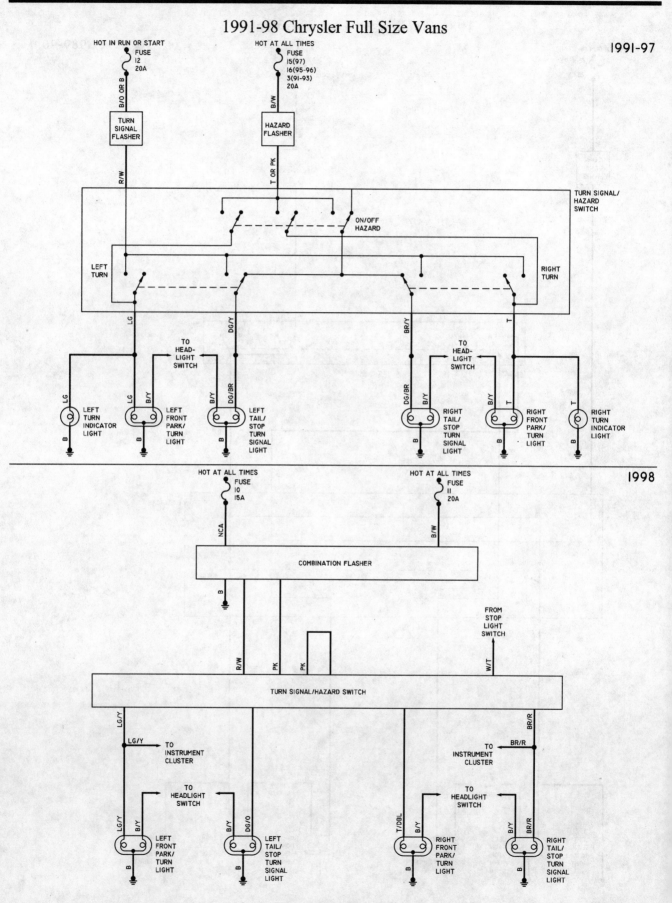

DIAGRAM 12

89666B04

1989-98 Chrysler Full Size Vans

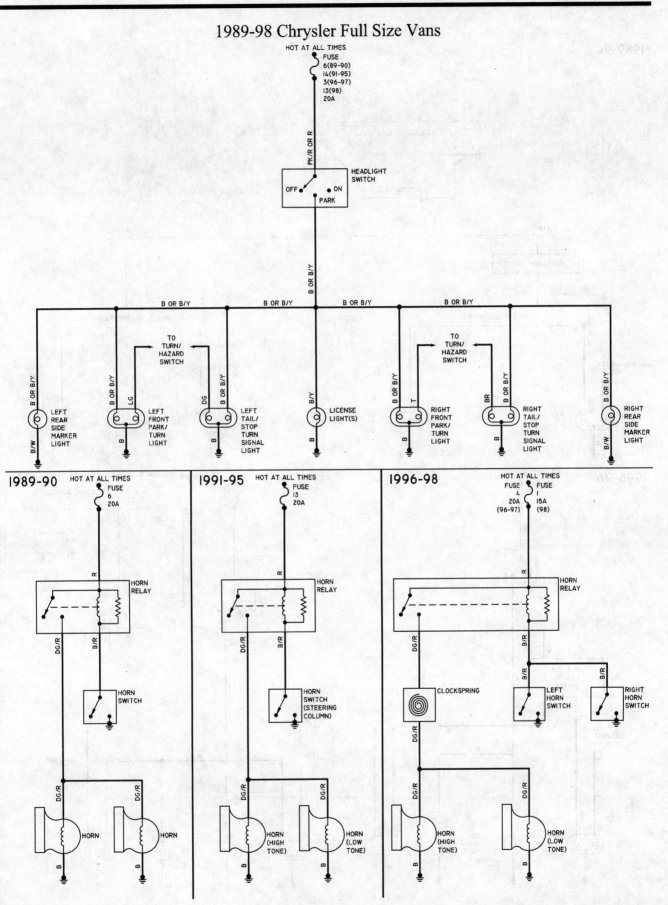

DIAGRAM 13

89666B09

1989-98 Chrysler Full Size Vans

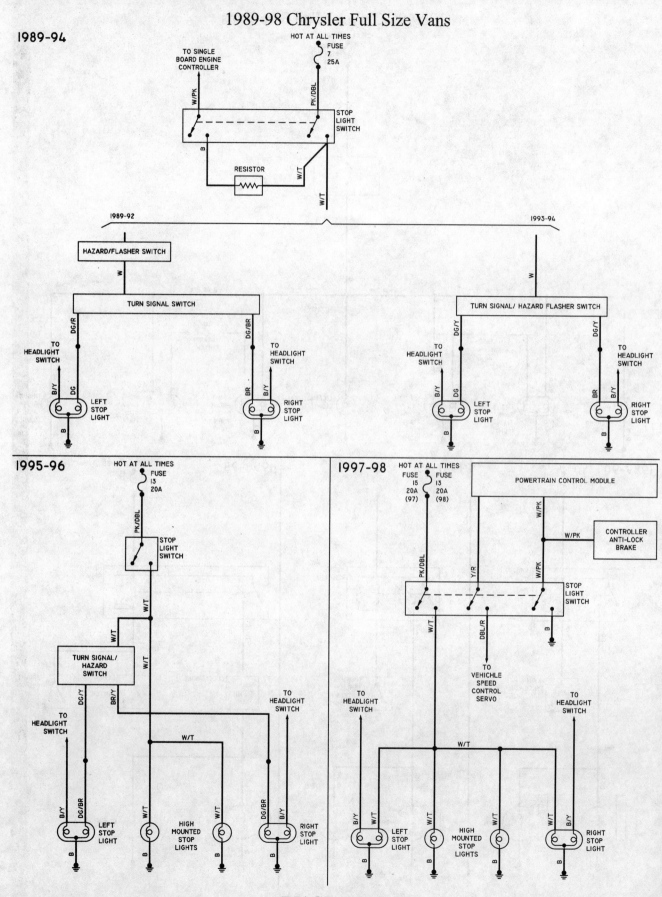

DIAGRAM 14

89666B03

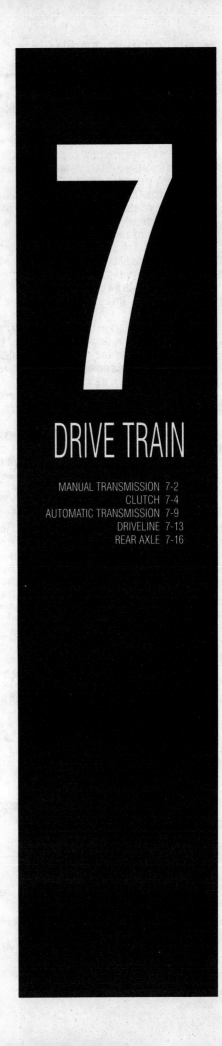

7

DRIVE TRAIN

MANUAL TRANSMISSION

Understanding the Manual Transmission

Because of the way an internal combustion engine breathes, it can produce torque (or twisting force) only within a narrow speed range. Most overhead valve pushrod engines must turn at about 2500 rpm to produce their peak torque. Often by 4500 rpm, they are producing so little torque that continued increases in engine speed produce no power increases.

The torque peak on overhead camshaft engines is, generally, much higher, but much narrower.

The manual transmission and clutch are employed to vary the relationship between engine RPM and the speed of the wheels so that adequate power can be produced under all circumstances. The clutch allows engine torque to be applied to the transmission input shaft gradually, due to mechanical slippage. The vehicle can, consequently, be started smoothly from a full stop.

The transmission changes the ratio between the rotating speeds of the engine and the wheels by the use of gears. 4-speed or 5-speed transmissions are most common. The lower gears allow full engine power to be applied to the rear wheels during acceleration at low speeds.

The clutch driveplate is a thin disc, the center of which is splined to the transmission input shaft. Both sides of the disc are covered with a layer of material which is similar to brake lining and which is capable of allowing slippage without roughness or excessive noise.

The clutch cover is bolted to the engine flywheel and incorporates a diaphragm spring which provides the pressure to engage the clutch. The cover also houses the pressure plate. When the clutch pedal is released, the driven disc is sandwiched between the pressure plate and the smooth surface of the flywheel, thus forcing the disc to turn at the same speed as the engine crankshaft.

The transmission contains a mainshaft which passes all the way through the transmission, from the clutch to the driveshaft. This shaft is separated at one point, so that front and rear portions can turn at different speeds.

Power is transmitted by a countershaft in the lower gears and reverse. The gears of the countershaft mesh with gears on the mainshaft, allowing power to be carried from one to the other. Countershaft gears are often integral with that shaft, while several of the mainshaft gears can either rotate independently of the shaft or be locked to it. Shifting from one gear to the next causes one of the gears to be freed from rotating with the shaft and locks another to it. Gears are locked and unlocked by internal dog clutches which slide between the center of the gear and the shaft. The forward gears usually employ synchronizers; friction members which smoothly bring gear and shaft to the same speed before the toothed dog clutches are engaged.

Two types of 5-speed manual transmissions are used in these vehicles. The NP-2500 is used from 1989–91 and the AX-15 is used from 1992–98.

Adjustments

Both the NP-2500 and AX-15 transmission shift mechanisms consist of a single unit, top mounted shift lever and internal mounted shift rails. Since the shift mechanism is internally mounted, no linkage adjustments are necessary.

Shift Lever

REMOVAL & INSTALLATION

NP-2500

♦ See Figure 1

The gearshift lever is a two-piece design. The upper part of the lever is threaded to the transmission stub lever. The upper lever can be removed for service without having to remove the entire shift lever assembly or the transmission.

1. Remove the boot mounting screws, the support and trim bezel for access to the lower end of the shifter.

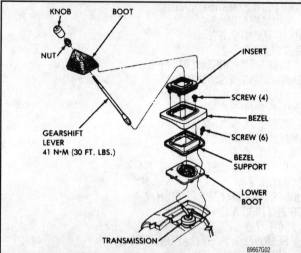

Fig. 1 The two-piece NP-2500 shifter can be serviced from the passenger compartment

2. Unthread and remove the upper end of the shift lever.
To install:
3. Service the lever as required.
4. Thread the upper lever to the stud end and secure the shift boot and components.

AX-15

♦ See Figure 2

The gearshift lever is a one-piece design which must be disconnected from under the vehicle.
1. Lower the transmission slightly.
2. Reach up and around the transmission case and press the shift lever retainer downward with your fingers.
3. Turn the retainer counterclockwise to release it.
4. Lift the lever and retainer out of the shift tower.

➡If is not necessary to remove the shift lever from the floorpan boot. Simply leave the lever in place for later installation.

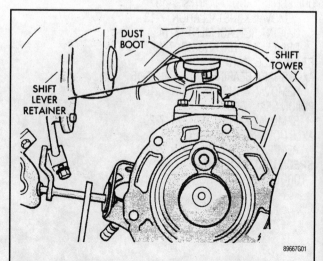

Fig. 2 The AX-15 shifter must be disconnected from under the vehicle

To install:
5. Position the transmission in the vehicle.
6. Reach up and around the transmission.
7. Position the lever and retainer in the shift tower.
8. Turn the retainer clockwise to install it.

Back-up Light Switch

REMOVAL & INSTALLATION

▶ **See Figures 3 and 4**

On all manual transmissions, the switch is located on the driver's side of the transmission, just below and behind the shifter.
1. Raise and safely support the vehicle securely on jackstands.
2. Locate the switch on the transmission.
3. Disconnect the switch electrical harness.

➡**Place a drain pan under the transmission to catch any fluid that may leak out.**

4. Using a properly sized wrench, loosen and remove the switch.

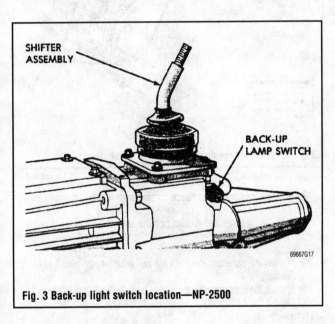

Fig. 3 Back-up light switch location—NP-2500

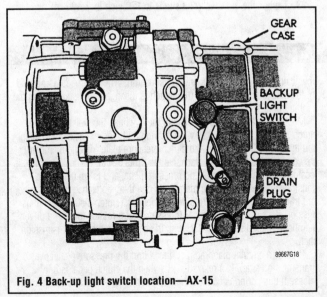

Fig. 4 Back-up light switch location—AX-15

To install:
5. Coat the switch threads with Teflon® tape and install the switch.
6. Carefully tighten the switch.
7. Connect the switch electrical harness.
8. Lower the vehicle.

Extension Housing Seal

REMOVAL & INSTALLATION

▶ **See Figures 5 and 6**

➡**A special seal removal/installation tool is required.**

1. Raise and safely support the vehicle securely on jackstands.
2. Place a drain pan under the end of the extension housing.
3. Mark the position of the driveshaft for installation reference.
4. Disconnect the driveshaft at the rear universal joint and carefully slide the shaft out of the transmission extension housing.
5. Remove the extension housing seal with the special tool.
6. Clean the end and inside of the extension housing.

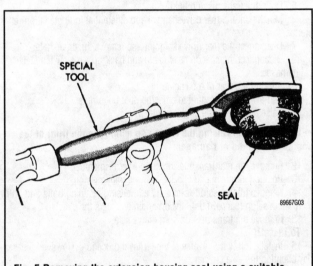

Fig. 5 Removing the extension housing seal using a suitable seal removal fork

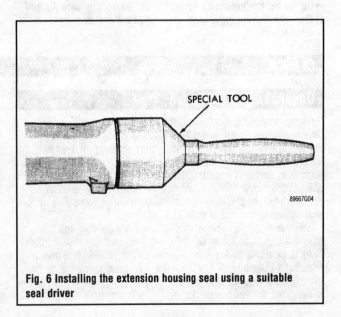

Fig. 6 Installing the extension housing seal using a suitable seal driver

7. Start the new seal into position and, with the installing tool, tap the seal into place.

8. Check the condition of the driveshaft slip yoke. Repair or replace as necessary.

9. Lubricate the lips of the seal and the slip yoke.

10. Align and install the driveshaft, taking care when guiding the slip yoke into the extension housing.

11. Remove the drain pan.

12. Check and correct the transmission fluid level.

13. Lower the vehicle.

Manual Transmission Assembly

REMOVAL & INSTALLATION

▶ **See Figure 7**

1. Disconnect the negative battery cable.
2. Remove the engine cover.
3. Disconnect the gear shift lever. On AX-15 transmissions, this step should be performed after the vehicle has been raised.
4. Raise and safely support the vehicle securely on jackstands.
5. Drain the transmission fluid.
6. Matchmark the rear driveshaft yoke to differential for installation reference.
7. Disconnect the rear universal joint and remove the driveshaft.
8. Disconnect the speedometer cable and back-up lamp switch electrical harnesses.
9. Support the rear of the engine.
10. Remove the rear mount to crossmember bolts/nuts.
11. Raise the rear of the engine slightly.

➡ **Take care when raising the engine so nothing in the front of the engine is strained or damaged.**

12. Remove the rear transmission support crossmember.
13. Position a transmission jack under the transmission.
14. Remove transmission-to-clutch bell housing retaining bolts and pull the transmission rearward until the drive pinion clears the clutch.
15. Remove the transmission from the vehicle.

To install:

16. Installation is the reverse of the removal procedure. However, please pay attention to these special steps.

17. Place a small amount of multi-purpose grease into the clutch pilot bushing and on the clutch release bearing sleeve.

➡ **Do not get any grease on flywheel face. Do not lubricate the end of the transmission input shaft, clutch disc splines, or clutch release levers.**

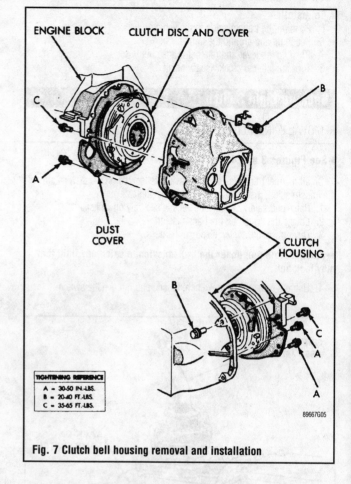

Fig. 7 Clutch bell housing removal and installation

18. Align the clutch disc and backing plate with a spare drive pinion shaft or clutch aligning tool.

19. With the transmission in gear, turn the splines until they are aligned, then push the transmission input shaft into the clutch until it mates to the bell housing.

20. Tighten the transmission-to-clutch bell housing retaining bolts to 50 ft. lbs. (68 Nm).

21. Tighten the crossmember mounting bolts to 30 ft. lbs. (40 Nm).

22. Tighten the transmission mount-to-crossmember bolts to 50 ft. lbs. (68 Nm).

23. Tigthen the universal joint straps to 170 inch lbs. (19 Nm).

CLUTCH

Understanding the Clutch

The purpose of the clutch is to disconnect and connect engine power at the transmission. A vehicle at rest requires a lot of engine torque to get all that weight moving. An internal combustion engine does not develop a high starting torque (unlike steam engines) so it must be allowed to operate without any load until it builds up enough torque to move the vehicle. To a point, torque increases with engine rpm. The clutch allows the engine to build up torque by physically disconnecting the engine from the transmission, relieving the engine of any load or resistance.

The transfer of engine power to the transmission (the load) must be smooth and gradual; if it weren't, driveline components would wear out or break quickly. This gradual power transfer is made possible by gradually releasing the clutch pedal. The clutch disc and pressure plate are the connecting link between the engine and transmission. When the clutch pedal is released, the disc and plate contact each other (the clutch is engaged)

physically joining the engine and transmission. When the pedal is pushed in, the disc and plate separate (the clutch is disengaged) disconnecting the engine from the transmission.

Most clutch assemblies consists of the flywheel, the clutch disc, the clutch pressure plate, the throw out bearing and fork, the actuating linkage and the pedal. The flywheel and clutch pressure plate (driving members) are connected to the engine crankshaft and rotate with it. The clutch disc is located between the flywheel and pressure plate, and is splined to the transmission shaft. A driving member is one that is attached to the engine and transfers engine power to a driven member (clutch disc) on the transmission shaft. A driving member (pressure plate) rotates (drives) a driven member (clutch disc) on contact and, in so doing, turns the transmission shaft.

There is a circular diaphragm spring within the pressure plate cover (transmission side). In a relaxed state (when the clutch pedal is fully released) this spring is convex; that is, it is dished outward toward the transmission. Pushing in the clutch pedal actuates the attached linkage. Connected to the other end of this is the throw out fork, which hold the throw out bearing. When the clutch pedal is depressed, the clutch linkage pushes the fork and bearing forward to contact the diaphragm spring of the pressure plate. The outer edges of the spring are secured to the pressure plate and are pivoted on rings so that when the center of the spring is compressed by the throwout bearing, the outer edges bow outward and, by so doing, pull the pressure plate in the same direction—away from the clutch disc. This action separates the disc from the plate, disengaging the clutch and allowing the transmission to be shifted into another gear. A coil type clutch return spring attached to the clutch pedal arm permits full release of the pedal. Releasing the pedal pulls the throw out bearing away from the diaphragm spring resulting in a reversal of spring position. As bearing pressure is gradually released from the spring center, the outer edges of the spring bow outward, pushing the pressure plate into closer contact with the clutch disc. As the disc and plate move closer together, friction between the two increases and slippage is reduced until, when full spring pressure is applied (by fully releasing the pedal) the speed of the disc and plate are the same. This stops all slipping, creating a direct connection between the plate and disc which results in the transfer of power from the engine to the transmission. The clutch disc is now rotating with the pressure plate at engine speed and, because it is splined to the transmission shaft, the shaft now turns at the same engine speed.

The clutch is operating properly if:

1. It will stall the engine when released with the vehicle held stationary.
2. The shift lever can be moved freely between 1st and reverse gears when the vehicle is stationary and the clutch disengaged.

❊❊ CAUTION

The clutch driven disc may contain asbestos, which has been determined to be a cancer causing agent. Never clean clutch surfaces with compressed air! Avoid inhaling any dust from any clutch surface! When cleaning clutch surfaces, use a commercially available brake cleaning fluid.

Driven Disc and Pressure Plate

REMOVAL & INSTALLATION

▶ See Figures 8 thru 23

1. Remove the transmission.
2. Remove the clutch housing.
3. Remove the clutch fork and release bearing assembly.

Fig. 9 Loosen and remove the clutch and pressure plate bolts evenly, a little at a time . . .

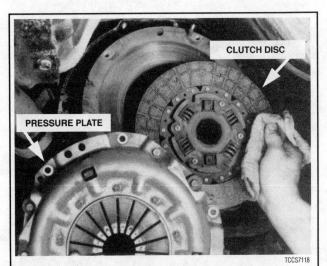

Fig. 10 . . . then carefully remove the clutch and pressure plate assembly from the flywheel

Fig. 8 Typical clutch alignment tool; note how the splines match the transmission's input shaft

Fig. 11 Check across the flywheel surface; it should be flat

Fig. 12 If necessary, lock the flywheel in place and remove the retaining bolts . . .

Fig. 15 Check the pressure plate for excessive wear

Fig. 13 . . . then remove the flywheel from the crankshaft in order to replace it or have it machined

Fig. 16 Be sure that the flywheel surface is clean, before installing the clutch

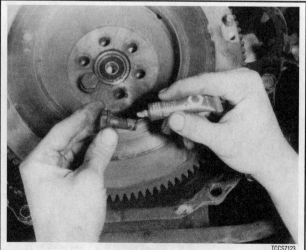

Fig. 14 Upon installation, it is usually a good idea to apply a threadlocking compound to the flywheel bolts

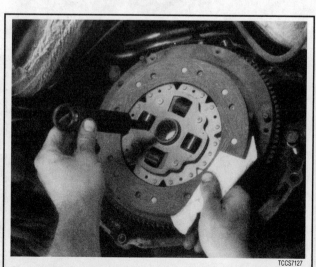

Fig. 17 Install a clutch alignment arbor, to align the clutch assembly during installation

Fig. 18 Clutch plate installed with the arbor in place

Fig. 21 You may want to use a threadlocking compound on the clutch assembly bolts

Fig. 19 Clutch plate and pressure plate installed with the alignment arbor in place

Fig. 22 Install the clutch assembly bolts and tighten in steps, using an X pattern

Fig. 20 The pressure plate-to-flywheel bolt holes should align

Fig. 23 Be sure to use a torque wrench to accurately tighten all bolts

4. Matchmark the clutch cover and flywheel for installation reference.

5. Remove the pressure plate retaining bolts, loosening them evenly so the clutch cover will not be distorted.

6. Pull the pressure plate assembly clear of the flywheel and, while supporting the pressure plate, slide the clutch disc from between the flywheel and pressure plate.

To install:

7. Thoroughly clean all working surfaces of the flywheel and pressure plate.

8. Grease radius at back of bushing.

9. Rotate clutch cover and pressure plate assembly for maximum clearance between flywheel and frame crossmember if crossmember was not removed during clutch removal.

10. Tilt top edge of clutch cover and pressure plate assembly back and move it up into the clutch housing. Support the clutch cover and pressure plate assembly and slide clutch disc into position.

11. Position clutch disc and plate against flywheel and insert clutch alignment tool through clutch disc hub and into main drive pilot bearing.

12. Rotate clutch cover until the punch marks on cover and flywheel line up.

13. Bolt the pressure plate loosely to flywheel. Tighten the bolts a few turns at a time, in progression, until tight. Then tighten the 5/16 in. bolts to 20 ft. lbs. (27 Nm) and the 3/8 in. bolts to 30 ft. lbs. (41 Nm).

14. Install the transmission.

ADJUSTMENTS

All vehicles are equipped with a hydraulic operating linkage system. No adjustment is required. The hydraulic linkage system is serviced as an assembly only. The individual components that form the system cannot be overhauled or serviced separately.

Master and Slave Cylinders

REMOVAL & INSTALLATION

▶ **See Figure 24**

1. Raise and safely support the vehicle securely on jackstands.
2. Remove the nuts attaching the slave cylinder to the bell housing.
3. Remove the slave cylinder and clip from the housing.
4. Lower the vehicle.
5. Remove the locating clip from the clutch master cylinder mounting bracket.
6. Remove the retaining ring, flat washer, and wave washer that attach the clutch master cylinder pushrod to the clutch pedal. Slide the pushrod off the pedal pin.
7. Inspect the bushing on the pedal pin and replace if it is excessively worn.

➡ **Verify that the cap on the clutch master cylinder reservoir is tight so that fluid will not spill during removal.**

8. Remove the screws attaching the reservoir and bracket to the dash panel and remove the reservoir.
9. Pull the clutch master cylinder rubber seal from the dash panel.
10. Rotate the clutch master cylinder, remote reservoir, slave cylinder and connecting lines from the vehicle.

To install:

11. Verify that the cap on the fluid reservoir is tight so that fluid will not spill during installation.
12. Insert the master cylinder in the dash. Rotate it 45° to lock it in place.
13. Lubricate the rubber seal to ease installation.

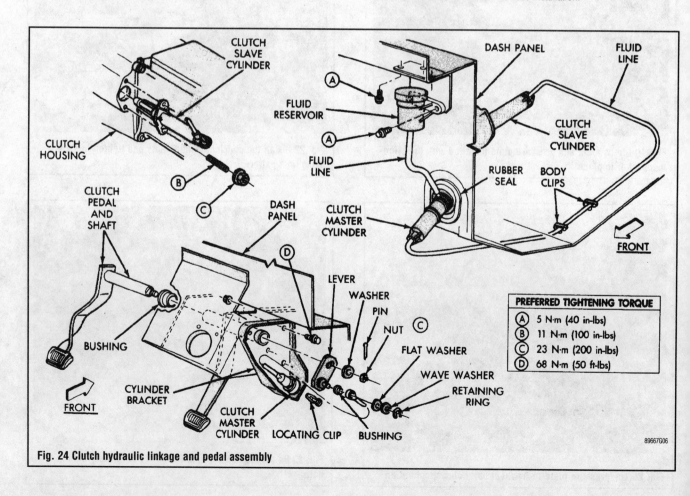

Fig. 24 Clutch hydraulic linkage and pedal assembly

PREFERRED TIGHTENING TORQUE	
Ⓐ	5 N·m (40 in-lbs)
Ⓑ	11 N·m (100 in-lbs)
Ⓒ	23 N·m (200 in-lbs)
Ⓓ	68 N·m (50 ft-lbs)

89667G06

14. Seat the seal around the cylinder in the dash.
15. Install the fluid reservoir and bracket, if equipped, to the dash panel. Tighten screws to 40 inch lbs. (5 Nm).
16. Install the master cylinder pushrod to the clutch pedal pin. Secure the rod with the wave washer, flat washer and retaining ring. Install the locating clip.

➡ **Do not remove the plastic shipping stop from the pushrod until the slave cylinder has been installed.**

17. Raise and safely support the vehicle securely on jackstands.
18. Insert the slave cylinder pushrod through the opening and make sure the cap on the end of the pushrod is securely engaged in the release lever before tightening the attaching nuts. Tighten the nuts to 17 ft. lbs. (23 Nm).

19. Lower the vehicle.
20. Remove the plastic shipping stop from the master cylinder pushrod.
21. Bleed the hydraulic system.
22. Operate the clutch pedal a few times to verify proper operation of the system.

HYDRAULIC SYSTEM BLEEDING

The hydraulic linkage system is serviced as an assembly only. The individual components that form the system cannot be overhauled or serviced separately. The cylinders and connecting lines are sealed units.

AUTOMATIC TRANSMISSION

Understanding the Automatic Transmission

The automatic transmission allows engine torque and power to be transmitted to the rear wheels within a narrow range of engine operating speeds. It will allow the engine to turn fast enough to produce plenty of power and torque at very low speeds, while keeping it at a sensible rpm at high vehicle speeds (and it does this job without driver assistance). The transmission uses a light fluid as the medium for the transmission of power. This fluid also works in the operation of various hydraulic control circuits and as a lubricant. Because the transmission fluid performs all of these functions, trouble within the unit can easily travel from one part to another. For this reason, and because of the complexity and unusual operating principles of the transmission, a very sound understanding of the basic principles of operation will simplify troubleshooting.

TORQUE CONVERTER

▶ **See Figure 25**

The torque converter replaces the conventional clutch. It has three functions:
1. It allows the engine to idle with the vehicle at a standstill, even with the transmission in gear.
2. It allows the transmission to shift from range-to-range smoothly, without requiring that the driver close the throttle during the shift.
3. It multiplies engine torque to an increasing extent as vehicle speed drops and throttle opening is increased. This has the effect of making the transmission more responsive and reduces the amount of shifting required.

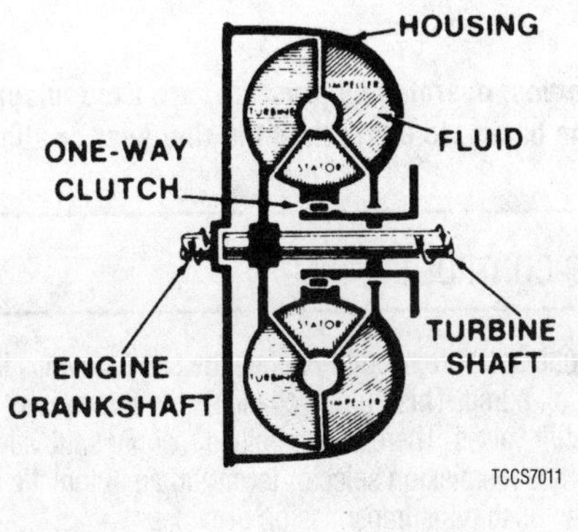

Fig. 25 The torque converter housing is rotated by the engine's crankshaft, and turns the impeller—the impeller then spins the turbine, which gives motion to the turbine shaft, driving the gears

The torque converter is a metal case which is shaped like a sphere that has been flattened on opposite sides. It is bolted to the rear end of the engine's crankshaft. Generally, the entire metal case rotates at engine speed and serves as the engine's flywheel.

The case contains three sets of blades. One set is attached directly to the case. This set forms the torus or pump. Another set is directly connected to the output shaft, and forms the turbine. The third set is mounted on a hub which, in turn, is mounted on a stationary shaft through a one-way clutch. This third set is known as the stator.

A pump, which is driven by the converter hub at engine speed, keeps the torque converter full of transmission fluid at all times. Fluid flows continuously through the unit to provide cooling.

Under low speed acceleration, the torque converter functions as follows:
The torus is turning faster than the turbine. It picks up fluid at the center of the converter and, through centrifugal force, slings it outward. Since the outer edge of the converter moves faster than the portions at the center, the fluid picks up speed.

The fluid then enters the outer edge of the turbine blades. It then travels back toward the center of the converter case along the turbine blades. In impinging upon the turbine blades, the fluid loses the energy picked up in the torus.

If the fluid was now returned directly into the torus, both halves of the converter would have to turn at approximately the same speed at all times, and torque input and output would both be the same.

In flowing through the torus and turbine, the fluid picks up two types of flow, or flow in two separate directions. It flows through the turbine blades, and it spins with the engine. The stator, whose blades are stationary when the vehicle is being accelerated at low speeds, converts one type of flow into another. Instead of allowing the fluid to flow straight back into the torus, the stator's curved blades turn the fluid almost 90° toward the direction of rotation of the engine. Thus the fluid does not flow as fast toward the torus, but is already spinning when the torus picks it up. This has the effect of allowing the torus to turn much faster than the turbine. This difference in speed may be compared to the difference in speed between the smaller and larger gears in any gear train. The result is that engine power output is higher, and engine torque is multiplied.

As the speed of the turbine increases, the fluid spins faster and faster in the direction of engine rotation. As a result, the ability of the stator to redirect the fluid flow is reduced. Under cruising conditions, the stator is eventually forced to rotate on its one-way clutch in the direction of engine rotation. Under these conditions, the torque converter begins to behave almost like a solid shaft, with the torus and turbine speeds being almost equal.

PLANETARY GEARBOX

▶ **See Figures 26, 27 and 28**

The ability of the torque converter to multiply engine torque is limited. Also, the unit tends to be more efficient when the turbine is rotating at relatively high speeds. Therefore, a planetary gearbox is used to carry the power output of the turbine to the driveshaft.

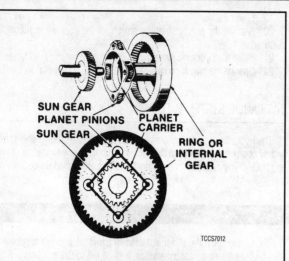

Fig. 26 Planetary gears work in a similar fashion to manual transmission gears, but are composed of three parts

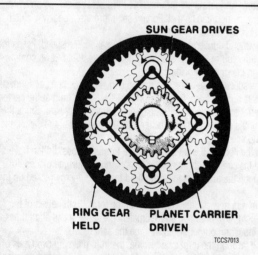

Fig. 27 Planetary gears in the maximum reduction (low) range. The ring gear is held and a lower gear ratio is obtained

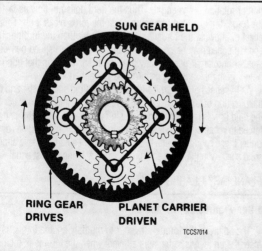

Fig. 28 Planetary gears in the minimum reduction (drive) range. The ring gear is allowed to revolve, providing a higher gear ratio

Planetary gears function very similarly to conventional transmission gears. However, their construction is different in that three elements make up one gear system, and, in that all three elements are different from one another. The three elements are: an outer gear that is shaped like a hoop, with teeth cut into the inner surface; a sun gear, mounted on a shaft and located at the very center of the outer gear; and a set of three planet gears, held by pins in a ring-like planet carrier, meshing with both the sun gear and the outer gear. Either the outer gear or the sun gear may be held stationary, providing more than one possible torque multiplication factor for each set of gears. Also, if all three gears are forced to rotate at the same speed, the gearset forms, in effect, a solid shaft.

Most automatics use the planetary gears to provide various reductions ratios. Bands and clutches are used to hold various portions of the gearsets to the transmission case or to the shaft on which they are mounted. Shifting is accomplished, then, by changing the portion of each planetary gearset which is held to the transmission case or to the shaft.

SERVOS & ACCUMULATORS

▶ **See Figure 29**

The servos are hydraulic pistons and cylinders. They resemble the hydraulic actuators used on many other machines, such as bulldozers. Hydraulic fluid enters the cylinder, under pressure, and forces the piston to move to engage the band or clutches.

The accumulators are used to cushion the engagement of the servos. The transmission fluid must pass through the accumulator on the way to the servo. The accumulator housing contains a thin piston which is sprung away from the discharge passage of the accumulator. When fluid passes through the accumulator on the way to the servo, it must move the piston against spring pressure, and this action smooths out the action of the servo.

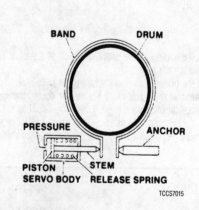

Fig. 29 Servos, operated by pressure, are used to apply or release the bands, to either hold the ring gear or allow it to rotate

HYDRAULIC CONTROL SYSTEM

The hydraulic pressure used to operate the servos comes from the main transmission oil pump. This fluid is channeled to the various servos through the shift valves. There is generally a manual shift valve which is operated by the transmission selector lever and an automatic shift valve for each automatic upshift the transmission provides.

➡**Many new transmissions are electronically controlled. On these models, electrical solenoids are used to better control the hydraulic fluid. Usually, the solenoids are regulated by an electronic control module.**

There are two pressures which affect the operation of these valves. One is the governor pressure which is effected by vehicle speed. The other is the modulator pressure which is effected by intake manifold vacuum or throttle position. Governor pressure rises with an increase in vehicle speed, and modulator pressure rises as the throttle is opened wider. By responding to these two pressures, the shift valves cause the upshift points to be delayed with increased throttle opening to make the best use of the engine's power output.

Most transmissions also make use of an auxiliary circuit for downshifting. This circuit may be actuated by the throttle linkage the vacuum line which actuates the modulator, by a cable or by a solenoid. It applies pressure to a special downshift surface on the shift valve or valves.

The transmission modulator also governs the line pressure, used to actuate the servos. In this way, the clutches and bands will be actuated with a force matching the torque output of the engine.

Neutral Safety Switch

The neutral safety switch, otherwise known as the park/neutral position switch, prevents the vehicle from being started in any position other than PARK and NEUTRAL. It also functions as the back-up lamp switch.

REMOVAL & INSTALLATION

▶ See Figures 30, 31 and 32

1. Raise and safely support the vehicle securely on jackstands.
2. Place a drain pan under the switch.
3. Label and disconnect the electrical harness.
4. Using the proper size wrench, unscrew the switch

To install:

5. Move the selector lever to the PARK and NEUTRAL positions. Verify that the switch operating lever fingers are centered in the switch opening in the transmission.
6. Using a new seal, install the new switch and tighten it to 25 ft. lbs. (34 Nm).
7. Test continuity of the switch using a multimeter or 12 volt test lamp.
8. Connect the electrical harness.
9. Lower the vehicle.

ADJUSTMENT

The park/neutral switch is not adjustable.

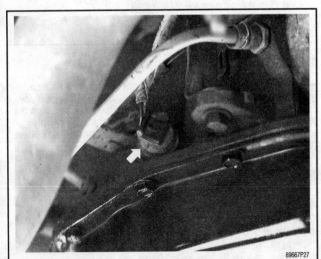

Fig. 30 The park/neutral switch is usually located on the driver's side of the transmission

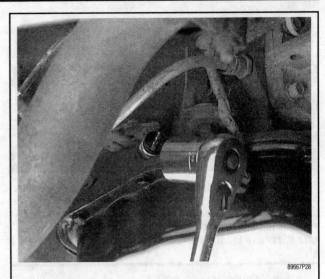

Fig. 31 Remove the switch using an appropriately sized socket

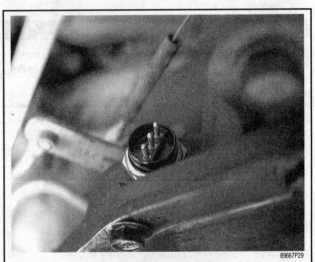

Fig. 32 The park/neutral position switch contains three terminals, and controls both the park/neutral function and the back-up lamps

Extension Housing Seal

REMOVAL & INSTALLATION

➡A special seal removal/installation tool is required.

1. Raise and safely support the vehicle securely on jackstands.
2. Place a drain pan under the end of the extension housing.
3. Mark the position of the driveshaft for installation reference.
4. Disconnect the driveshaft at the rear universal joint and carefully slide the shaft out of the transmission extension housing.
5. Remove the extension housing seal with the special tool.
6. Clean the end and inside of the extension housing.
7. Start the new seal into position and with the installing tool, tap the seal into place.
8. Check the condition of the driveshaft slip yoke. Repair or replace as necessary.
9. Lubricate the lips of the seal and the slip yoke.
10. Align and install the driveshaft taking care when guiding the slip yoke into the extension housing.

11. Remove the drain pan.
12. Check and correct the transmission fluid level.
13. Lower the vehicle.

Automatic Transmission Assembly

REMOVAL & INSTALLATION

▶ See Figure 33

✳✳ WARNING

The transmission and torque converter must be removed as an assembly to avoid component damage. The converter drive plate, pump bushing, or oil seal can be damaged if the converter is left attached to the driveplate during removal. Be sure to remove the transmission and converter as an assembly.

1. Disconnect the negative battery cable.
2. Raise and safely support the vehicle securely on jackstands.
3. Remove engine-to-transmission struts.
4. Remove starter motor and cooler line bracket.

✳✳ WARNING

The crankshaft position sensor can be damaged if the transmission is removed (or installed) with the sensor still bolted to the engine block. To avoid damage, remove the sensor before removing the transmission.

5. Disconnect and remove the crankshaft position sensor. Retain the sensor attaching bolts.
6. Remove the torque converter access cover.
7. Remove the transmission oil pan and drain the fluid. Temporarily install the pan after the fluid has drained.
8. Remove transmission fluid fill tube. Discard fill tube O-ring it should not be reused.
9. Mark the torque converter and drive plate for assembly alignment. Use a scriber or paint for this purpose.
10. Rotate the crankshaft in a clockwise direction until the converter bolts are accessible. Then, remove the bolts one at a time. Rotate the crankshaft with a socket wrench on the damper bolt.
11. Matchmark propeller shaft and axle yokes for assembly alignment. Then, disconnect and remove the propeller shaft.

Fig. 33 The speedometer's electrical harness is connected to the driver's side of the transmission

12. Disconnect wires from the park/neutral position switch, transmission solenoid, and vehicle speed sensor.
13. Disconnect gearshift cable from transmission shift lever.
14. Disconnect throttle valve cable from transmission throttle lever.
15. Disconnect overdrive connector wires from the plug on the driver's side of the transmission.
16. Remove transmission wire harnesses from clips on transmission. Also, disconnect the oxygen sensor wire if necessary.
17. Support the rear of the engine using jackstands.
18. Raise transmission slightly with floor jack to relieve load on supports.
19. Remove bolts securing transmission mount to crossmember and crossmember to frame and crossmember.
20. Remove engine oil filter.
21. Remove all converter housing bolts.
22. Disconnect fluid cooler lines at transmission.

✳✳ CAUTION

Do not dip the front of transmission downward during removal process, since the torque converter can fall out, causing damage or injury.

23. Carefully work the transmission and torque converter assembly rearward off the engine block dowels and disengage the torque converter hub from the end of the crankshaft. If necessary, attach a small C-clamp to edge of bell housing to hold torque converter in place during transmission removal.
24. Lower transmission and remove assembly from under the vehicle.

To install:

25. Installation is the reverse of the removal procedure. However, please keep in mind these important steps.

➡**It is important that the correct length bolts be used to attach the converter to the driveplate. Bolts that are too long will damage the lockup surface within the converter. If new bolts are required, use the bolt specified by the manufacturer .**

26. Tighten the transmission bell housing-to-engine bolts as illustrated.
27. Verify the torque converter bolts length as follows:
- 9.5 in. 3 lug converter—0.46 in. (11.7mm)
- 9.5 in. 4 lug converter—0.52 in. (13.2mm)
- 10.0 in. 4 lug converter—0.52 in. (13.2mm)
- 10.75 in. 4 lug converter—0.44 in. (11.2mm)
28. Tighten the torque converter bolts to the following specification:
- 9.5 in. 3 lug converter—40 ft. lbs. (54 Nm)
- 9.5 in. 4 lug converter—55 ft. lbs. (74 Nm)
- 10.0 in. 4 lug converter—55 ft. lbs. (74 Nm)
- 10.75 in. 4 lug converter—23 ft. lbs. (31 Nm)

ADJUSTMENTS

Throttle Linkage

➡**To insure proper adjustment, it is suggested that new linkage grommets be installed. Do not attempt to adjust the linkage if any of the parts are excessively worn. If any rods are removed from the plastic grommets, new grommets should be installed. Pry only where the grommet and rod attach, not on the rod itself. Use pliers to snap the rod into the new grommet.**

1. Shift the transmission into PARK.
2. Raise and safely support the vehicle securely on jackstands.
3. Loosen the shift rod adjusting swivel lock screw. Make sure the swivel turns freely on the rod.
4. Make sure the valve body is in the PARK position by moving it all the way rearward.
5. Adjust the swivel position on the shift rod to obtain a free pin fit in the torque shaft lever. Tighten the lock screw.
6. If the vehicle starts in any gear other than PARK or NEUTRAL, or does not start in both **P** and **N**, either the adjustment is wrong or another problem exists.

DRIVELINE

Driveshaft and U-Joints

REMOVAL & INSTALLATION

▶ See Figures 34, 35, 36, 37 and 38

➡Do not allow the propeller shaft to drop or hang from any U-joint during removal. Attach the propeller shaft to the vehicle underside with wire to prevent damage to the joints.

1. Raise and safely support the vehicle securely on jackstands.
2. Matchmark the driveshaft and the rear axle drive yoke.
3. Remove the rear U-joint attaching bolts and both strap clamps from the rear axle drive yoke.
4. Use a suitable prybar to gently pry the U-joint out of the yoke.
5. Wrap the U-joint caps with tape to prevent them from falling off the U-joint.
6. Fluid may run from the rear of the extension housing when the shaft

is removed, so position a suitable drain pan under the area.

➡It is very important to protect the external machined surface of the Slip yoke from damage during and after propeller shaft removal. If the yoke is damaged, the transmission extension seal may be damaged and therefore cause a leak.

7. Remove the driveshaft from the transmission or transfer case.

➡Extension housing plugs are available to prevent a constant stream of fluid from escaping the transmission.

To install:
8. Lubricate the front yoke of the driveshaft with transmission fluid and insert it into the transmission.
9. Align the U-joint with the rear axle drive yoke and position the U-joint in the yoke.
10. Install the yoke strap clamps and tighten the ¼ inch bolts to 14 ft. lbs. (19 Nm) and the 5⁄16 inch bolts to 25 ft. lbs. (34 Nm).
11. Lower the vehicle.

Fig. 34 Driveshafts are balanced and must be matchmarked with the differential yoke for installation reference

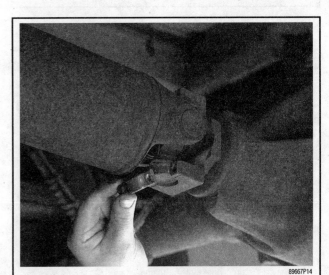
Fig. 36 . . . and remove the straps from the yoke

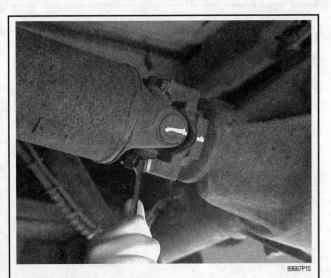
Fig. 35 Loosen the U-joint strap bolts . . .

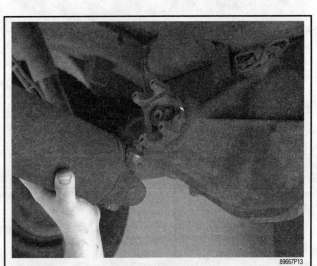
Fig. 37 Remove the U-joint from the rear yoke. It may be necessary to use a prybar to free the U-joint

Fig. 38 Carefully remove the front yoke from the transmission

U-JOINT REPLACEMENT

▶ **See Figures 39, 40, 41 and 42**

1. Remove the driveshaft from the vehicle.

➡**Do not clamp the driveshaft tube in a vise. Clamp only the forged portion of the yoke in a vise. Do not overtighten the vise jaws.**

2. Clamp the yoke in a vise and remove the bearing cap retainers.

3. Place a socket which has an inside diameter larger than the outside diameter of the bearing cap, against the yoke around the perimeter of the first cap to be removed. Place a socket which is slightly smaller than the cap, on the cap, opposite the cap to be removed. Then position the yoke in a vise.

4. Compress the jaws until the smaller socket has driven the other cap into the larger socket.

5. Release the jaws and remove the cap that is partially out of the yoke.

6. Repeat the procedure for the remaining cap(s).

To install:

7. Clean and remove and rust from the yoke bores and lubricate lightly with suitable lithium based grease.

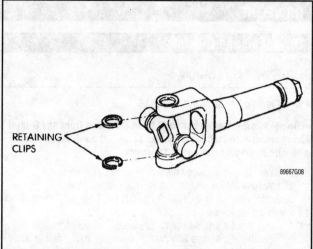

Fig. 40 Some U-joints use circlips to prevent the caps from moving in the yoke

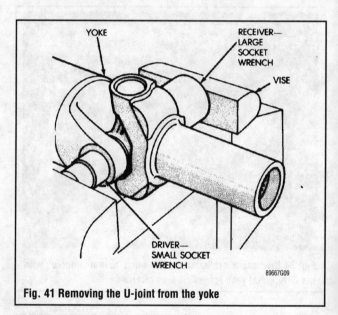

Fig. 41 Removing the U-joint from the yoke

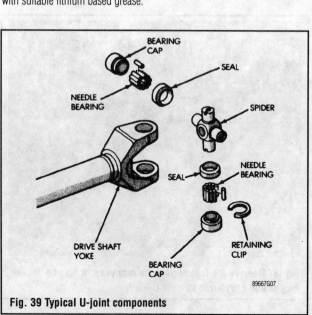

Fig. 39 Typical U-joint components

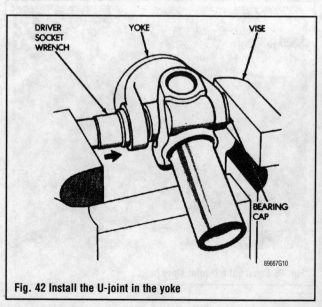

Fig. 42 Install the U-joint in the yoke

8. Position the spider cylinders in the yoke bores. Insert the seals into the yoke bore and against the spider cylinders. Tap the bearing caps into the yoke bores far enough to keep the spider in place.

9. Place the socket that is slightly smaller than the cap against the first cap and position the assembly in a vise.

10. Compress the jaws to force the bearing caps into the yoke bores far enough so the retainer grooves are visible.

11. Repeat the procedure for the remaining caps if necessary.

12. Install the retaining clips.

13. Install the driveshaft assembly to the vehicle.

DRIVESHAFT BALANCING

▶ See Figures 43, 44 and 45

Unbalance

Propeller shaft vibration increases as the vehicle speed is increased. A vibration that occurs within a specific speed range is not usually caused by a propeller shaft being unbalanced. Defective universal joints, or an incorrect propeller shaft angle, are usually the cause of such a vibration.

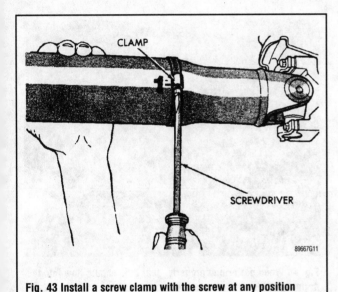

Fig. 43 Install a screw clamp with the screw at any position

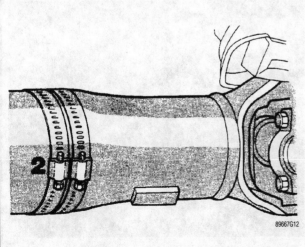

Fig. 44 If the vibration decreases, install a second clamp

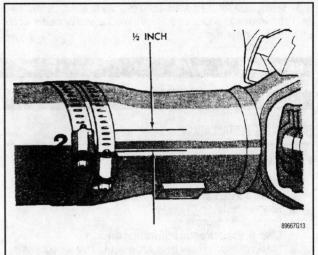

Fig. 45 If the second clamp causes additional vibration, rotate the clamps in opposite directions

If propeller shaft is suspected of being unbalanced, it can be verified with the following procedure.

➡Removing and re-indexing the propeller shaft 180° relative to the yoke may eliminate some vibrations.

1. Raise and safely support the vehicle securely on jackstands.

2. Clean all the foreign material from the propeller shaft and the universal joints.

3. Inspect the propeller shaft for missing balance weights, broken welds, and bent areas. If the propeller shaft is dented or bent, it must be replaced.

4. Inspect the universal joints to ensure that they are not worn, are properly installed, and are correctly aligned with the shaft.

5. Check the universal joint clamp bolt torque.

6. Remove the wheels and tires. Install the wheel lug nuts to retain the brake drums or rotors.

7. Mark and number the shaft six inches (15.24cm) from the yoke end at four positions 90° apart.

8. Run and accelerate the vehicle until vibration occurs. Note the intensity and speed the vibration occurred. Stop the engine.

9. Install a screw clamp at any position.

10. Start the engine and re-check for vibration. If there is little or no change in vibration, move the clamp to one of the other three positions. Repeat the vibration test.

11. If there is no difference in vibration at the other positions, the source of the vibration may not be propeller shaft.

12. If the vibration decreased, install a second clamp and repeat the test.

13. If the additional clamp causes additional vibration, rotate the clamps (¼ inch above and below the mark). Repeat the vibration test.

14. Increase distance between the clamp screws and repeat the test until the amount of vibration is at the lowest level. Bend the slack end of the clamps so the screws will not loosen.

15. If the vibration remains unacceptable, apply the same steps to the front end of the propeller shaft.

16. Install the wheel and tires.

17. Lower the vehicle.

Run-out

1. Remove dirt, rust, paint, and undercoating from the propeller shaft surface where the dial indicator will contact the shaft.

2. The dial indicator must be installed perpendicular to the shaft surface.

➡Measure front/rear run-out approximately 3 inches (76mm) from the weld seem at each end of the shaft tube for tube lengths over 30 inches (76.2cm). Under 30 inches, the maximum run-out is 0.20 inch (5.08mm) for the full length of the tube.

3. Measure run-out at the center and ends of the shaft sufficiently far away from weld areas to ensure that the effects of the weld process will not enter into the measurements.

4. Replace the propeller shaft if the run-out exceeds 0.010 in. (0.25mm) at the front of shaft, 0.015 in. (0.38mm) at the center of the shaft or 0.010 in. (0.25mm) at the rear of the shaft.

REAR AXLE

Axle Shaft, Bearing and Seal

REMOVAL & INSTALLATION

▶ **See Figures 46 thru 67**

1. Raise and safely support the vehicle securely on jackstands.
2. Ensure that the transmission is in Neutral.
3. Remove wheels.
4. Remove brake drums.
5. Clean all foreign material from housing cover area.
6. Loosen all housing cover bolts, and remove all but two bolts on the top and two on the bottom.
7. Use a prybar to pry the cover loose from the axle.
8. Allow the gear oil to drain from the housing and axle shaft tubes.

9. Remove the axle housing cover.
10. Rotate the differential case so that the pinion mate gear shaft lock screw is accessible. Remove the lock screw and pinion mate gear shaft from the differential case.
11. Remove the axle shaft.
12. Remove the axle shaft seal from the end of the axle tube with a small prybar.

➡**The seal and bearing can be removed at the same time with the bearing removal tool.**

13. Remove the axle shaft bearing from the axle tube using an appropriate puller.

To install:

➡**Always install a new axle bearing seal.**

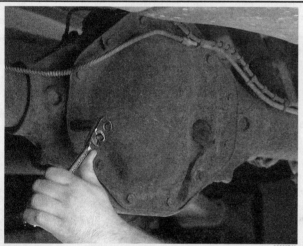

Fig. 46 Loosen the cover bolts and remove all of them, except two at the top and two at the bottom

Fig. 48 When performed properly, gear fluid should flow into the drain pan without causing a mess

Fig. 47 Use a prybar to carefully pry the cover from the axle housing

Fig. 49 Once the gear oil drains, remove the remaining bolts, then remove the axle housing cover

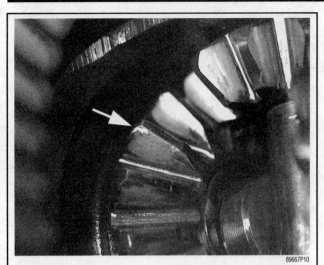

Fig. 50 Any time the differential cover is removed, inspect the gears for damage (arrow) and replace as necessary

Fig. 53 . . . push the pinion gear shaft up from the bottom . . .

Fig. 51 Rotate the differential case so that the pinion gear shaft lock screw is accessible

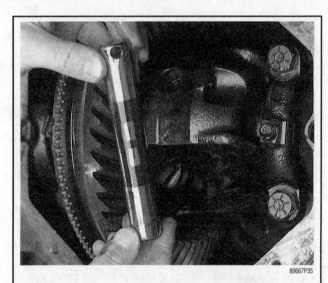

Fig. 54 . . . and remove it from the differential case

Fig. 52 Remove the lock screw . . .

Fig. 55 Once the shaft is removed, the C-clip is visible. Push the axle in slightly to remove the C-clip . . .

Fig. 56 . . . and the axle can then be removed from the housing

Fig. 59 Use a scraper to remove gasket material from the axle housing . . .

Fig. 57 Take care not to damage the seal or bearing during axle removal

Fig. 60 . . . and the axle housing cover

Fig. 58 When installing the axle shaft lock screw, always use a threadlocking compound to hold the screw in place

Fig. 61 Wipe the cover clean, as sealer will not adhere to an oily surface

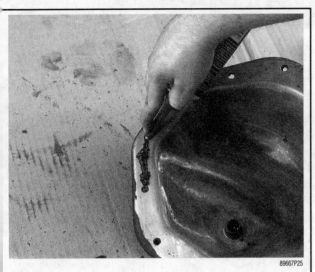

Fig. 62 Apply sealer in a continuous bead around the cover

Fig. 65 Fill the axle housing through the filler hole with the proper type and amount of gear oil

Fig. 63 When installing the axle cover, always replace the metal identification tag. This tag provides the only means of externally identifying the axle ratio

Fig. 66 When checking the gear oil level, stick your finger inside the filler/inspection hole

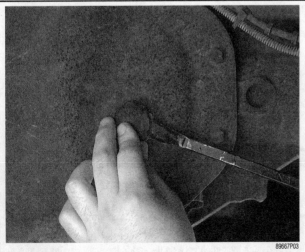

Fig. 64 The rear axle fluid can be checked after removing a plug in the rear cover

Fig. 67 The gear oil level should be ⅜ in. (10mm) below the bottom of the filler hole

14. Wipe the axle tube bore clean. Remove any old sealer or burrs from the tube.

15. Install the axle shaft bearing. Ensure that the bearing part number is facing outward. Verify that the bearing is installed straight and flush with the axle tube when fully seated.

16. Inspect axle shaft seal for leakage or damage

17. Inspect roller bearing contact surface on axle shaft for signs of brinelling, galling and pitting. If any of these conditions exist, the axle shaft and/or bearing and seal must be replaced.

18. Lubricate bearing bore and seal lip with gear lubricant. Insert axle shaft through seal, bearing, and engage it into side gear splines.

➡ **Use care to prevent shaft splines from damaging axle shaft seal lip.**

19. Insert C-clip lock in end of axle shaft.
20. Push axle shaft outward to seat C-clip lock in side gear.
21. Insert pinion mate shaft into the differential case and through the thrust washers and pinion gears.
22. Align the hole in the shaft with the hole in the differential case, and install the lock screw with Loctite® on the threads. Tighten the lock screw to 8 ft. lbs. (11 Nm).
23. Install cover and fill the differential with gear oil.
24. Install the brake drum.
25. Install the wheel and tire.
26. Lower the vehicle.

Pinion Seal

REMOVAL & INSTALLATION

♦ **See Figures 68, 69 and 70**

1. Raise and safely support the vehicle securely on jackstands.
2. Scribe a mark on the universal joint, pinion yoke, and pinion shaft for installation reference.
3. Disconnect the propeller shaft from the pinion yoke.
4. Secure the propeller shaft in an upright position to prevent damage to the rear universal joint.
5. Remove the wheel and tire assemblies.
6. Remove the brake drums to prevent any drag. The drag may cause a false bearing rotating torque measurement.
7. Rotate the pinion yoke three or four times.
8. Measure the amount of torque necessary to rotate the pinion gear with a inch pound dial-type torque wrench. Record the torque reading for installation reference.

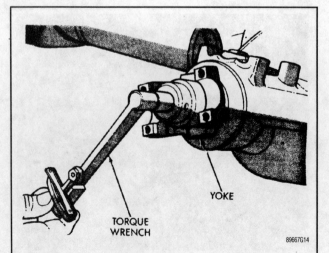

Fig. 68 Always measure bearing preload prior to loosening the pinion nut

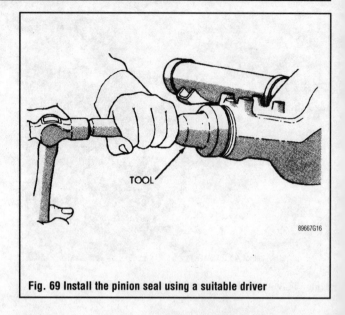

Fig. 69 Install the pinion seal using a suitable driver

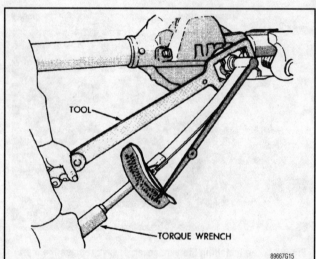

Fig. 70 Hold the pinion yoke with a suitable tool and tighten the shaft nut, then recheck the pinion preload

9. Hold the yoke in position with a pipe wrench or other suitable tool. Remove the pinion shaft nut and washer.
10. Remove the yoke.
11. Remove the pinion shaft seal with suitable prytool or slide-hammer mounted screw.
To install:
12. Clean the seal contact surface in the housing bore.
13. Examine the splines on the pinion shaft for burrs or wear. Remove any burrs and clean the shaft.
14. Inspect pinion yoke for cracks, worn splines and worn seal contact surface. Replace yoke if necessary.

➡ **The outer perimeter of the seal is pre-coated with a special sealant. An additional application of sealant is not required.**

15. Apply a light coating of gear lubricant on the lip of pinion seal.
16. Install the new pinion shaft seal.

➡ **The seal is correctly installed when the seal flange contacts the face of the differential housing flange.**

17. Position the pinion yoke on the end of the shaft with the reference marks aligned.
18. Seat the yoke on the pinion shaft.

19. Remove the tools and install the pinion yoke washer. The convex side of the washer must face outward.

※※ WARNING

Do not exceed the minimum tightening torque when installing the pinion yoke retaining nut at this point. Damage to the collapsible spacer or bearings may result.

20. Hold the pinion yoke with pipe wrench or other suitable tool and tighten shaft nut to 210 ft. lbs. (285 Nm).
21. Rotate the pinion shaft several revolutions to ensure the bearing rollers are seated.
22. Rotate the pinion shaft using an inch pounds beam type torque wrench. Rotating torque should be equal to the reading recorded during removal, plus an additional 5 inch lbs. (0.56 Nm).

※※ WARNING

Never loosen the pinion gear nut to decrease pinion gear bearing rotating torque, and never exceed the specified preload torque. If preload torque is exceeded, a new collapsible spacer must be installed.

23. Install the brake drums.
24. Install the wheel and tire assemblies.
25. Align the propeller shaft with the pinion yoke and install.
26. Lower the vehicle.

Axle Housing Assembly

REMOVAL & INSTALLATION

1. Raise and safely support the vehicle securely on jackstands.
2. Position a floor jack under the axle and secure axle to jack.

3. Remove the wheels and tires.
4. Secure brake drums to the axle shaft using the lug nuts.
5. Remove the Rear Wheel Anti-lock Lock (RWAL) sensor from the differential housing, if necessary.
6. Disconnect the brake hose at the axle junction block. Do not disconnect the brake hydraulic lines at the wheel cylinders.
7. Disconnect the parking brake cables and cable brackets.
8. Disconnect the vent hose from the axle shaft tube.
9. Mark the propeller shaft and yoke for installation alignment reference.
10. Remove propeller shaft.
11. Disconnect the shock absorbers from the axle.
12. Remove the spring clamps and spring brackets.
13. Separate the axle from the vehicle.
To install:
14. Raise the axle with lifting device and align to the leaf spring centering bolts.
15. Install the spring clamps and spring brackets.
16. Install the shock absorbers and tighten the mounting nuts to 60 ft. lbs. (82 Nm).
17. Install the RWAL sensor to the differential housing, if necessary.
18. Install the brake drums.
19. Connect the brake hose to the axle junction block.
20. Install the axle vent hose.
21. Align propeller shaft and pinion with reference marks.
22. Install universal joint straps and bolts. Tighten to 14 ft. lbs. (19 Nm).
23. Install the wheels and tires.
24. Add gear lubricant, if necessary.
25. Remove the jack and lower the vehicle.

TORQUE SPECIFICATIONS

Components	English	Metric
Manual Transmission		
Back-up light switch		
NP-2500	15 ft. lbs.	20 Nm
AX-15	27 ft. lbs.	37 Nm
Transmission Assembly		
Transmission-to-clutch bell housing	50 ft. lbs.	68 Nm
Crossmember	30 ft. lbs.	40 Nm
Transmission mount-to-crossmember	50 ft. lbs.	68 Nm
Universal joint straps	170 inch lbs.	19 Nm
Clutch		
Pressure Plate		
5/16 inch bolts	20 ft. lbs.	27 Nm
3/8 inch bolts	30 ft. lbs.	41 Nm
Master Cylinder		
Fluid reservoir	40 inch lbs.	5 Nm
Slave cylinder	17 ft. lbs.	23 Nm
Automatic Transmission		
Park/Neutral switch	25 ft. lbs.	34 Nm
Torque Converter		
9.5 inch 3 lug converter	40 ft. lbs.	54 Nm
9.5 inch. 4 lug converter	55 ft. lbs.	74 Nm
10.0 inch 4 lug converter	55 ft. lbs.	74 Nm
10.75 inch 4 lug converter	23 ft. lbs.	31 Nm
Driveline		
1/4 inch bolts	14 ft. lbs.	19 Nm
5/16 inch bolts	25 ft. lbs.	34 Nm

89667C01

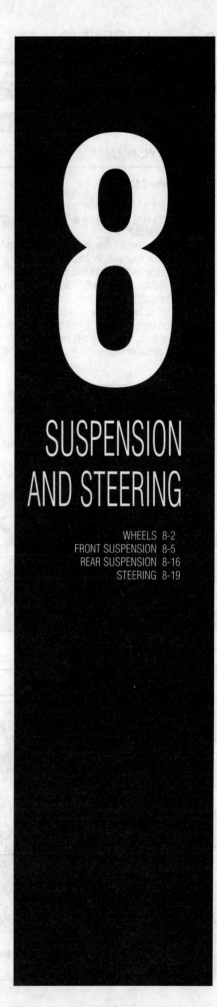

8

SUSPENSION
AND STEERING

WHEELS

Wheels

REMOVAL & INSTALLATION

♦ **See Figures 1 thru 7**

1. Park the vehicle on a level surface.
2. Remove the jack, tire iron and, if necessary, the spare tire from their storage compartments.
3. Check the owner's manual or refer to Section 1 of this manual for the jacking points on your vehicle. Then, place the jack in the proper position.
4. If equipped with lug nut trim caps, remove them by either unscrewing or pulling them off the lug nuts, as appropriate. Consult the owner's manual, if necessary.
5. If equipped with a wheel cover or hub cap, insert the tapered end of the tire iron in the groove and pry off the cover.
6. Apply the parking brake and block the diagonally opposite wheel with a wheel chock or two.

➡Wheel chocks may be purchased at your local auto parts store, or a block of wood cut into wedges may be used. If possible, keep one or two of the chocks in your tire storage compartment, in case any of the tires has to be removed on the side of the road.

7. If equipped with an automatic transmission, place the selector lever in **P** or Park; with a manual transmission, place the shifter in Reverse.
8. With the tires still on the ground, use the tire iron/wrench to break the lug nuts loose.

➡If a nut is stuck, never use heat to loosen it, or damage to the wheel and bearings may occur. If the nuts are seized, one or two heavy hammer blows directly on the end of the bolt usually loosens the rust. Be careful, as continued pounding will likely damage the brake drum or rotor.

9. Using the jack, raise the vehicle until the tire is clear of the ground. Support the vehicle safely using jackstands.
10. Remove the lug nuts, then remove the tire and wheel assembly.

TCCA8P00

Fig. 1 Place the jack at the proper lifting point on your vehicle

TCCA8P02

Fig. 3 With the vehicle still on the ground, break the lug nuts loose using the wrench end of the tire iron

TCCA8P01

Fig. 2 Before jacking the vehicle, block the diagonally opposite wheel with one or, preferably, two chocks

TCCA8P03

Fig. 4 After the lug nuts have been loosened, raise the vehicle using the jack until the tire is clear of the ground

Fig. 5 Remove the lug nuts from the studs

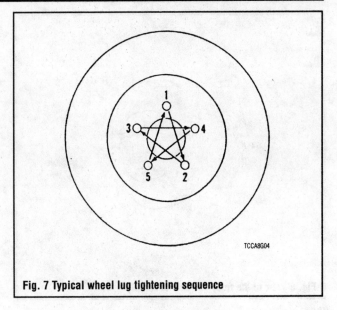

Fig. 7 Typical wheel lug tightening sequence

Fig. 6 Remove the wheel and tire assembly from the vehicle

16. If so equipped, install the wheel cover or hub cap. Make sure the valve stem protrudes through the proper opening before tapping the wheel cover into position.

17. If equipped, install the lug nut trim caps by pushing them or screwing them on, as applicable.

18. Remove the jack from under the vehicle, and place the jack and tire iron/wrench in their storage compartments. Remove the wheel chock(s).

19. If you have removed a flat or damaged tire, place it in the storage compartment of the vehicle and take it to your local repair station to have it fixed or replaced as soon as possible.

INSPECTION

Inspect the tires for lacerations, puncture marks, nails and other sharp objects. Repair or replace as necessary. Also check the tires for treadwear and air pressure as outlined in Section 1 of this manual.

Check the wheel assemblies for dents, cracks, rust and metal fatigue. Repair or replace as necessary.

Wheel Lug Studs

REMOVAL & INSTALLATION

With Disc Brakes

▶ See Figures 8, 9 and 10

1. Raise and support the appropriate end of the vehicle safely using jackstands, then remove the wheel.

2. Remove the brake pads and caliper. Support the caliper aside using wire or a coat hanger. For details, please refer to Section 9 of this manual.

3. Remove the outer wheel bearing and lift off the rotor. For details on wheel bearing removal, installation and adjustment, please refer to Section 1 of this manual.

4. Properly support the rotor using press bars, then drive the stud out using an arbor press.

➡If a press is not available, CAREFULLY drive the old stud out using a blunt drift. MAKE SURE the rotor is properly and evenly supported or it may be damaged.

To install:

5. Clean the stud hole with a wire brush and start the new stud with a hammer and drift pin. Do not use any lubricant or thread sealer.

6. Finish installing the stud with the press.

To install:

11. Make sure the wheel and hub mating surfaces, as well as the wheel lug studs, are clean and free of all foreign material. Always remove rust from the wheel mounting surface and the brake rotor or drum. Failure to do so may cause the lug nuts to loosen in service.

12. Install the tire and wheel assembly and hand-tighten the lug nuts.

13. Using the tire wrench, tighten all the lug nuts, in a crisscross pattern, until they are snug.

14. Raise the vehicle and withdraw the jackstand, then lower the vehicle.

15. Using a torque wrench, tighten the lug nuts in a crisscross pattern to the following specifications:
- 15 inch wheels—80–110 ft. lbs. (109–150 Nm)
- 16 inch wheels with ½ inch studs—85–115 ft. lbs. (115–155 Nm)
- 16 inch wheels with ⅝ inch studs—175–225 ft. lbs. (240–305 Nm)

➡Check your owner's manual or refer to Section 1 of this manual for the proper tightening sequence.

✳ WARNING

Do not overtighten the lug nuts, as this may cause the wheel studs to stretch or the brake disc (rotor) to warp.

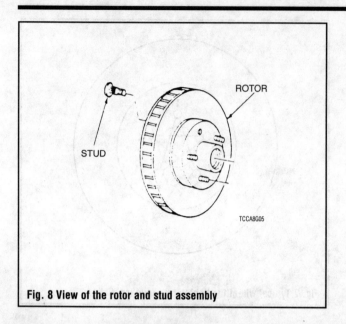

Fig. 8 View of the rotor and stud assembly

→If a press is not available, start the lug stud through the bore in the hub, then position about 4 flat washers over the stud and thread the lug nut. Hold the hub/rotor while tightening the lug nut, and the stud should be drawn into position. **MAKE SURE THE STUD IS FULLY SEATED, then remove the lug nut and washers.**

7. Install the rotor and adjust the wheel bearings.
8. Install the brake caliper and pads.
9. Install the wheel, then remove the jackstands and carefully lower the vehicle.
10. Tighten the lug nuts to the proper torque.

With Drum Brakes

▸ **See Figures 11, 12 and 13**

1. Raise the vehicle and safely support it with jackstands, then remove the wheel.
2. Remove the brake drum.
3. If necessary to provide clearance, remove the brake shoes, as outlined in Section 9 of this manual.
4. Using a large C-clamp and socket, press the stud from the axle flange.

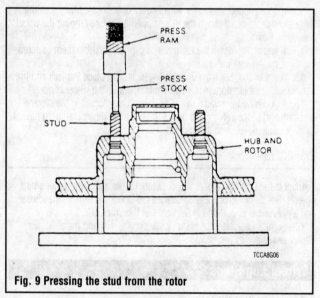

Fig. 9 Pressing the stud from the rotor

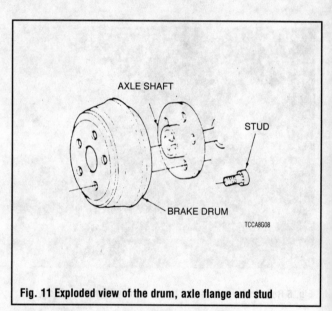

Fig. 11 Exploded view of the drum, axle flange and stud

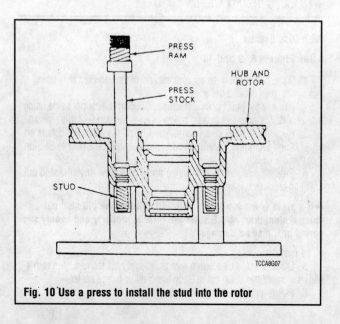

Fig. 10 Use a press to install the stud into the rotor

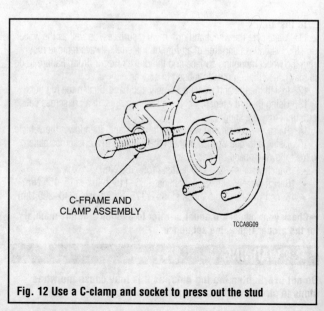

Fig. 12 Use a C-clamp and socket to press out the stud

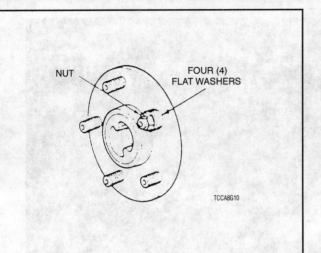

Fig. 13 Force the stud onto the axle flange using washers and a lug nut

5. Coat the serrated part of the stud with liquid soap and place it into the hole.

To install:

6. Position about 4 flat washers over the stud and thread the lug nut. Hold the flange while tightening the lug nut, and the stud should be drawn into position. MAKE SURE THE STUD IS FULLY SEATED, then remove the lug nut and washers.

7. If applicable, install the brake shoes.

8. Install the brake drum.

9. Install the wheel, then remove the jackstands and carefully lower the vehicle.

10. Tighten the lug nuts to the proper torque.

FRONT SUSPENSION

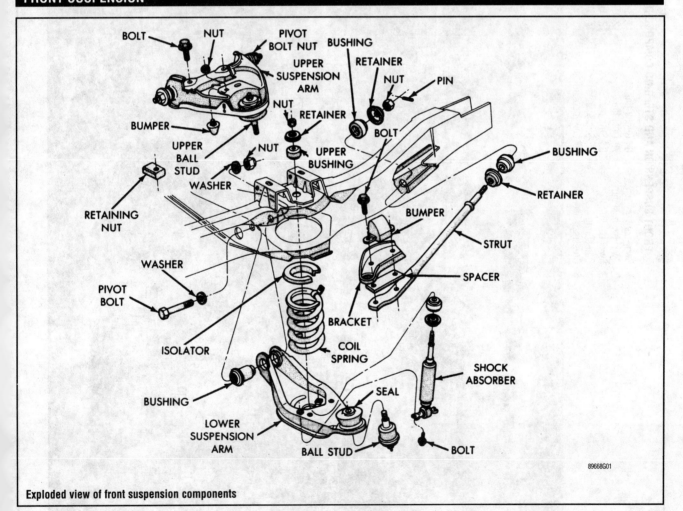

Exploded view of front suspension components

FRONT SUSPENSION AND STEERING COMPONENTS

1. Sway bar
2. Sway bar bushing
3. Sway bar link
4. Coil spring
5. Crossmember
6. Center link
7. Drag link
8. Strut bar
9. Shock absorber
10. Lower control arm
11. Lower ball joint
12. Tie rod end (outer)
13. Upper ball joint
14. Upper control arm
15. Idler arm

Coil Springs

REMOVAL & INSTALLATION

▶ **See Figure 14**

1. Raise and safely support the vehicle securely on jackstands.
2. Remove the wheels.
3. Remove the brake calipers and suspend them out of the way.

➡ **Do not disconnect the brake lines.**

4. Remove the shock absorbers.
5. Disconnect the sway bar, if so equipped.
6. Remove the lower control arm strut bar.
7. Install an appropriate spring compressor following the manufacturer's instructions.

➡ **This will retain the spring in place until the lower control arm is disconnected and lowered for spring removal.**

8. Remove the ball joint nuts.
9. Using ball joint separator, separate the ball joint from the steering knuckle.
10. Slowly loosen the spring compressor until all tension is relieved from the coil.
11. Remove the compressor and spring.

To install:

12. Position the spring on the control arm and install the compressor.
13. Compress the spring until the ball joint is properly positioned.
14. Install the ball joint nuts and tighten them to 135 ft. lbs. (183 Nm) for $^{11}\!/_{16}$ nuts, or 175 ft. lbs. (237 Nm) for $^{3}\!/_{4}$ nuts. Install new cotter pins.
15. Install the lower control arm strut bar.
16. Connect the sway bar.
17. Remove the spring compressor.
18. Install the shock absorber.
19. Install the brake caliper.
20. Install the wheels
21. Lower the vehicle.

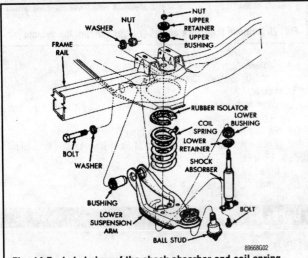

Fig. 14 Exploded view of the shock absorber and coil spring assembly

Shock Absorbers

TESTING

▶ **See Figure 15**

The purpose of the shock absorber is simply to limit the motion of the spring during compression and rebound cycles. If the vehicle is not equipped with these motion dampers, the up and down motion would multiply until the vehicle was alternately trying to leap off the ground and to pound itself into the pavement.

Contrary to popular rumor, the shocks do not affect the ride height of the vehicle. This is controlled by other suspension components such as springs and tires. Worn shock absorbers can affect handling; if the front of the vehicle is rising or falling excessively, the "footprint" of the tires changes on the pavement and steering is affected.

The simplest test of the shock absorber is simply push down on one corner of the unladen vehicle and release it. Observe the motion of the body as it is released. In most cases, it will come up beyond it original rest position, dip back below it and settle quickly to rest. This shows that the damper is controlling the spring action. Any tendency to excessive pitch (up-and-down) motion or failure to return to rest within 2–3 cycles is a sign of poor function within the shock absorber. Oil-filled shocks may have a light film of oil around the seal, resulting from normal breathing and air exchange. This should NOT be taken as a sign of failure, but any sign of thick or running oil definitely indicates failure. Gas filled shocks may also show some film at the shaft; if the gas has leaked out, the shock will have almost no resistance to motion.

While each shock absorber can be replaced individually, it is recommended that they be changed as a pair (both front or both rear) to maintain equal response on both sides of the vehicle. Chances are quite good that if one has failed, its mate is weak also.

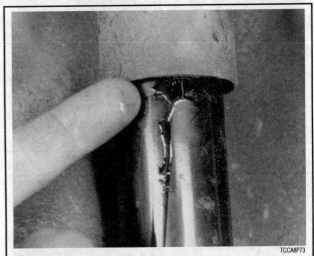

Fig. 15 When fluid is seeping out of the shock absorber, it's time to replace it

REMOVAL & INSTALLATION

▶ **See Figures 16, 17, 18, 19 and 20**

1. Raise and safely support the vehicle securely on jackstands.
2. Remove the wheels.
3. Remove the upper nut and retainer.

89668P24

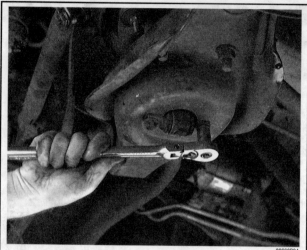

Fig. 16 Front shock absorbers are attached to the lower control arm with two bolts

89668P25

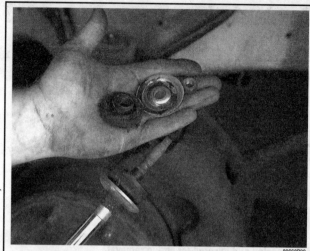

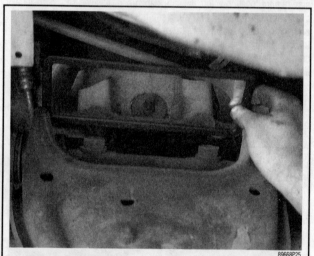

Fig. 17 After positioning a mirror, the upper shock absorber nut and retainer can be seen

89668P26

Fig. 18 The use of a special shock rod holding tool may be necessary to retain the rod while removing the upper nut

89668P29

Fig. 19 The upper end of the shock absorber is secured by a bushing, retainer and nut

89668P28

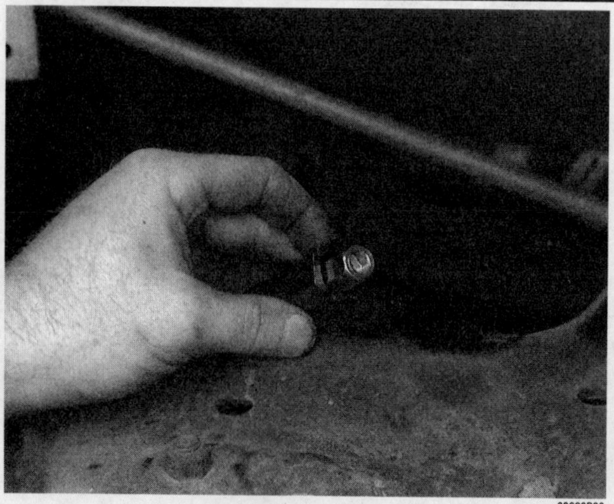

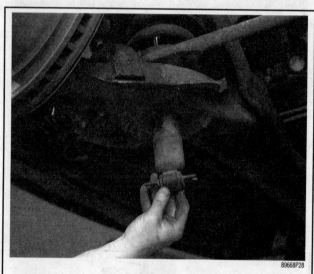

Fig. 20 Remove the shock absorber from beneath the vehicle

4. Remove the two lower mounting bolts.
5. Remove the shock absorber.

To install:

6. When installing the shock absorber, make sure the upper bushings are in the correct position.
7. Replace any worn or cracked bushing.
8. Tighten the top nut to 25 ft. lbs. (34 Nm). Then, tighten the lower bolts to 17 ft. lbs. (23 Nm).
9. Install the wheels.
10. Lower the vehicle.

Upper Ball Joint

INSPECTION

Front end noise, front wheel shimmy and difficult steering could be caused by a worn upper ball joint. Jack up the vehicle beneath the lower control arm. Position a suitable prybar under the tire and pry upward. Observe any free travel and determine what piece of the suspension has excessive play. Lateral movement in the ball joint should be less than 0.030 in. (0.8mm) or less.

REMOVAL & INSTALLATION

▶ See Figure 21

➡The upper ball joint is screwed into the upper control arm. A special ball joint socket (C-3561), or equivalent, is necessary to unscrew the ball joint.

1. Raise and safely support the vehicle securely on jackstands.
2. Remove the wheel.
3. Remove the ball joint-to-knuckle cotter pin and nut.
4. Using a ball joint separator, loosen the upper ball joint.
5. Unscrew the ball joint from the control arm.

To install:

6. Screw a new ball joint into the control arm and tighten to 125 ft. lbs. (170 Nm).
7. Install the new ball joint seal, using a 2 in. (51mm) socket. Be sure that the seal is seated on the ball joint housing.
8. Insert the ball joint into the steering knuckle and install the ball joint nut. Tighten the 11/16 in. nut to 135 ft. lbs. (183 Nm), or the 3/4 in. nut to 175 ft. lbs. (237 Nm).
9. Insert a new cotter pin.
10. Install the wheel and lower the van.

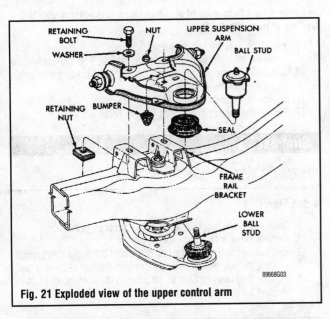

Fig. 21 Exploded view of the upper control arm

Lower Ball Joint

INSPECTION

Front end noise, front wheel shimmy and difficult steering could be caused by a worn lower ball joint. Jack the vehicle up under the lower control arm. Position a suitable prybar under the tire and pry upward. Observe any free travel and determine what piece of the suspension has excessive play. Lateral movement in the ball joint should be no more than 0.020 in. (0.5mm).

REMOVAL & INSTALLATION

▶ See Figure 22

1. Remove the lower control arm.
2. Remove the ball joint seal.
3. Using an arbor press and an appropriately sized driver, press the ball joint from the control arm.

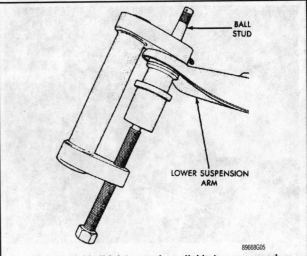

Fig. 22 A special ball joint press is available to remove and install the ball joint on the vehicle

To install:

4. Press the new ball joint into the lower control arm.
5. Ensure the ball joint is fully seated.
6. Install a new ball joint seal.
7. Install the lower control arm.

Sway Bar

REMOVAL & INSTALLATION

▶ See Figures 23, 24, 25, 26 and 27

1. Raise and safely support the vehicle securely on jackstands.
2. Remove the nut and washer from the link bolt at the lower control arm.
3. Remove the link bolt, retainers, insulators and spacer from each control arm.
4. Remove the bolts from the sway bar retainers.
5. Remove the sway bar from the vehicle.

To install:

6. Carefully inspect the retainer and link bushings. Replace as necessary.
7. Position the sway bar on the vehicle.

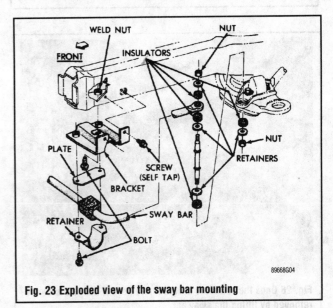

Fig. 23 Exploded view of the sway bar mounting

Fig. 24 Disconnect the sway bar link by removing the upper and lower nuts (wrench shown on lower one)

Fig. 25 The link is retained to the lower control arm by a nut and washer

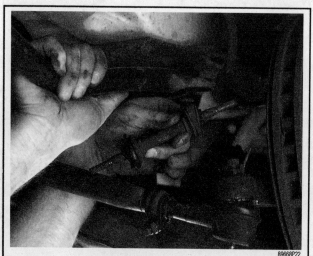

Fig. 26 Once the retainers have been removed, the link is easily removed by lifting the sway bar

Fig. 27 The sway bar is attached to the chassis by a bracket

➡Perform final tightening of all suspension components with the vehicle at ride height.

    8. Install the sway bar retainers bolts.
    9. Install the link bolt, retainers, insulators and spacer on each control arm.
    10. Install the nut and washer on the link bolt at the lower control arm.
    11. Lower the vehicle.
    12. Tighten the retainer bolts to 16 ft. lbs. (23 Nm).
    13. Tighten the link nut to 100 inch lbs. (11 Nm).

Strut Bar

REMOVAL & INSTALLATION

◆ See Figure 28

    1. Raise and safely support the vehicle securely on jackstands.
    2. Remove the wheels.
    3. Remove the roll pin from the rear of the strut bar with a small punch.
    4. Remove the nut, retainer and bushing from the rear of the strut bar.
    5. Remove the bolts attaching the strut bar to the lower control arm.
    6. Remove the strut bar from the vehicle.

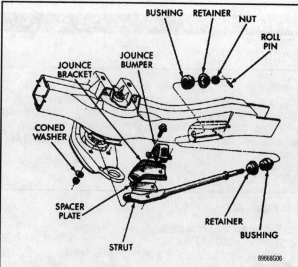

Fig. 28 Exploded view of the strut bar and lower control arm

To install:

7. Position the strut bar in the vehicle.

8. Install the bolts attaching the strut bar to the lower control arm and tighten to 100 ft. lbs. (136 Nm).

9. Install the nut, retainer and bushing from the rear of the strut bar. Tighten the nut to 52 ft. lbs. (71 Nm).

10. Install the roll pin from the rear of the strut bar with a small punch.

11. Install the wheels.

12. Lower the vehicle.

Upper Control Arm

REMOVAL & INSTALLATION

➡**Any time the control arm is removed, it is necessary to perform a front end alignment.**

1. Raise and safely support the vehicle securely on jackstands.

2. Remove the wheel.

3. Remove the brake caliper and rotor.

4. Remove the shock absorber.

5. Install an appropriate spring compressor, following the manufacturer's instructions.

➡**This will retain the spring in place until the upper control arm is disconnected and removed.**

6. Remove the ball joint-to-knuckle cotter pin and nut.

7. Using a ball joint separator, loosen the upper ball joint.

8. Separate the ball joint from the steering knuckle.

9. Remove the eccentric pivot bolts, after marking their relative positions in the control arm.

10. Remove the upper control arm.

To install:

11. Install the upper control arm.

12. Install the pivot bolts and finger-tighten them for now.

➡**Tightening the pivot bolts to the specified torque at this point may damage the bushings once the vehicle returns to normal ride height. Only tighten pivot bolts to specification with the vehicle at normal ride height.**

13. Position the spring on the control arm and install the spring compressor.

14. Compress the spring until the ball joint is properly positioned.

15. Install the ball joint nut and tighten to 135 ft. lbs. (183 Nm) for $^{11}\!/_{16}$ nuts, or 175 ft. lbs. (237 Nm) for $^3\!/_4$ nuts. Install new cotter pins.

16. Remove the spring compressor.

17. Install the shock absorber.

18. Install the brake caliper and rotor.

19. Install the wheels.

20. Lower the vehicle.

21. Tighten the pivot upper control arm bolts to 220 ft. lbs. (298 Nm).

22. Perform a front end alignment.

Lower Control Arm

REMOVAL & INSTALLATION

1. Raise and safely support the vehicle securely on jackstands.

2. Remove the wheels.

3. Remove the brake calipers and suspend them out of the way.

➡**Do not disconnect the brake lines.**

4. Remove the shock absorbers.

5. Disconnect the sway bar, if equipped.

6. Remove the lower control arm strut bar.

7. Install an appropriate spring compressor following the manufacturer's instructions.

➡**This will retain the spring in place until the lower control arm is disconnected and lowered for spring removal.**

8. Remove the ball joint nuts.

9. Using ball joint separator, separate the ball joint from the steering knuckle.

10. Slowly loosen the spring compressor until all tension is relieved from the coil.

11. Remove the compressor and spring.

12. Remove the lower control arm pivot bolts.

13. Remove the lower control arm from the vehicle.

To install:

14. Loosely attach the lower control arm to the crossmember. Hand-tighten the pivot bolts.

➡**Tightening the pivot bolts to the specified torque at this point may damage the bushings once the vehicle returns to normal ride height. Only tighten pivot bolts to specification with the vehicle at normal ride height.**

15. Position the spring on the control arm and install the compressor.

16. Compress the spring until the ball joint is properly positioned.

17. Install the ball joint nuts and tighten them to 135 ft. lbs. (183 Nm) for $^{11}\!/_{16}$ nuts, or 175 ft. lbs. (237 Nm) for $^3\!/_4$ nuts. Install new cotter pins.

18. Install the lower control arm strut bar.

19. Connect the sway bar.

20. Remove the spring compressor.

21. Install the shock absorber.

22. Install the brake caliper.

23. Install the wheels

24. Lower the vehicle.

25. Tighten the lower control arm pivot bolts to 175 ft. lbs. (237 Nm) once the vehicle is at ride height.

CONTROL ARM BUSHING REPLACEMENT

1. Remove the lower control arm, as previously detailed.

2. Use an arbor press and an appropriate size sleeve (driver) to force out the old bushing.

3. Use an arbor press and an appropriate size sleeve (driver) to install the new bushing. Make sure that the bushing is completely seated.

4. Install the lower control arm, as previously detailed.

Knuckle and Spindle

REMOVAL & INSTALLATION

▶ **See Figure 29**

1. Raise and safely support the vehicle securely on jackstands.

2. Remove the wheels.

3. Remove the brake calipers and suspend them out of the way.

➡**Do not disconnect the brake lines.**

4. Remove the brake rotor.

5. Remove the brake splash shield.

6. Support the lower control arm with a floor jack.

7. Disconnect the tie rod from the knuckle.

8. Disconnect the ball joints from the knuckle.

9. Remove the knuckle.

10. Unbolt the brake adapter from the knuckle.

To install:

11. Install the adapter on the knuckle and tighten bolts to 100 ft. lbs. (136 Nm).

12. Align the steering arm and the knuckle, then tighten $^5\!/_8$ inch nuts to 217 ft. lbs. (294 Nm) and $^3\!/_4$ inch nuts to 225 ft. lbs. (330 Nm).

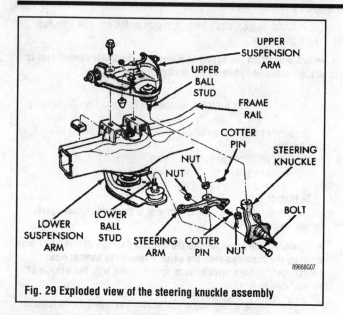

Fig. 29 Exploded view of the steering knuckle assembly

13. Install the knuckle assembly on the control arms and connect the ball joints.

14. Connect the tie rod ends.

15. Install the splash shield and new dust seal. Tighten the bolts to 18 ft. lbs. (24 Nm).

16. Install the brake rotor.

17. Install the brake calipers.

18. Install the wheels.

19. Lower the vehicle.

Front Wheel Bearings

REMOVAL & INSTALLATION

▶ **See Figures 30 thru 41**

1. Raise and safely support the vehicle securely on jackstands.

2. Remove the wheels.

3. Remove the caliper assembly and support it using a piece of mechanic's wire attached to the frame.

➡ **Do not disconnect the brake fluid hose or allow the caliper to hang by the hose.**

Fig. 30 Remove the dust cap to access the rotor retaining hardware

Fig. 31 Remove the cotter pin

Fig. 32 Remove the locknut

Fig. 33 Use a suitable tool to loosen the retaining nut

Fig. 34 After the nut is removed, place it and the washer in a safe place

Fig. 37 The wheel bearing grease seal, as installed on the rotor

Fig. 35 Remove the outer wheel bearing and set it aside for later inspection

Fig. 38 Use a suitable tool, such as this seal remover from Lisle®, to remove the grease seal from the rotor

Fig. 36 Remove the rotor from the spindle with care; be ready for the sudden weight when the rotor is no longer supported

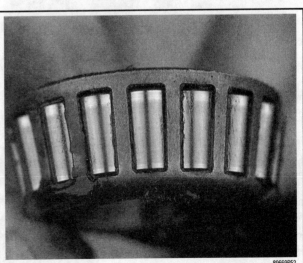

Fig. 39 Inspect the bearing rollers for wear

Fig. 40 This bearing is an example of one that wasn't properly maintained; notice the sludge build-up from the old grease

Fig. 41 Always spin the rotor while tightening the retaining nut to ensure proper wheel bearing adjustment

4. Remove the grease cap from the hub.

5. Remove the cotter pin, nut lock, adjusting nut and flat washer from the spindle.

6. Tilt the rotor slightly to remove the outer bearing assembly from the hub.

7. Pull the rotor assembly off the wheel spindle.

8. Remove and discard the old grease seal at the rear of the rotor.

9. Remove the inner bearing cone and roller assembly from the hub.

To install:

10. Clean all grease from the inner and outer bearing cups with solvent. Inspect the bearing races for pits, scratches, or excessive wear. If the races are damaged, remove them with a drift.

11. Clean the inner and outer cone and roller assemblies with solvent and dry them. If the cone and roller assemblies show excessive wear or damage, replace them as an assembly with new bearing races.

➡**Do not dry the bearings with compressed air. Spinning the bearing without lubrication may cause damage.**

12. Clean the spindle and the inside of the hub with solvent to thoroughly remove all old grease.

13. If the inner and/or outer bearing cups were removed, install the replacement cups on the hub. Be sure that the cups seat properly in the hub.

14. It is imperative that all old grease be removed from the bearings and surrounding surfaces before repacking. The new EP High Temperature Grease is not compatible with the sodium base grease used in the past.

15. Use a bearing packer, if available, to pack the new bearings with grease. If not, work the grease in between the rollers and the outer and inner races of the bearing, using the palm of your hand. Work from the larger diameter of the bearing. Make sure the grease goes through the width of the bearing to the small diameter. Pack and install the inner bearing first.

16. Install the inner bearing grease seal with an appropriate driver.

17. Install the hub and disc on the wheel spindle. To prevent damage to the grease retainer and spindle threads, keep the hub centered on the spindle.

18. Install the outer bearing cone and roller assembly and the flat washer on the spindle. Install the adjusting nut.

19. Adjust the wheel bearings. Rotate the wheel, hub and rotor assembly while tightening the adjusting nut to 240–300 inch lbs. (27–34 Nm) in order to seat the bearings. Back off the adjusting nut ¼ turn (90°), then finger-tighten the adjusting nut.

20. Locate the nut lock on the adjusting nut so that the castellations on the lock are lined up with the cotter pin hole in the spindle. Install the new cotter pin, bending the ends of the cotter pin around the castellated flange of the nut lock.

➡**Bend the ends of the cotter pin around the castellations of the locknut to prevent interference.**

21. Check the wheel for proper rotation, then install the grease cap.
22. Install the wheels.

➡**Failure to tighten the lug nuts to the proper torque in a star pattern may result in damage to the brake rotor.**

23. Lower the vehicle

Wheel Alignment

If the tires are worn unevenly, if the vehicle is not stable on the highway or if the handling seems uneven in spirited driving, the wheel alignment should be checked. If an alignment problem is suspected, first check for improper tire inflation and other possible causes. These can be worn suspension or steering components, accident damage or even unmatched tires. If any worn or damaged components are found, they must be replaced before the wheels can be properly aligned. Wheel alignment requires very expensive equipment and involves minute adjustments which must be accurate; it should only be performed by a trained technician. Take your vehicle to a properly equipped shop.

Following is a description of the alignment angles which are adjustable on most vehicles and how they affect vehicle handling. Although these angles can apply to both the front and rear wheels, usually only the front suspension is adjustable.

CASTER

◆ **See Figure 42**

Looking at a vehicle from the side, caster angle describes the steering axis rather than a wheel angle. The steering knuckle is attached to a control arm or strut at the top and a control arm at the bottom. The wheel pivots around the line between these points to steer the vehicle. When the upper point is tilted back, this is described as positive caster. Having a positive caster tends to make the wheels self-centering, increasing directional stability. Excessive positive caster makes the wheels hard to steer, while an uneven caster will cause a pull to one side. Overloading the vehicle or sagging rear springs will affect caster, as will raising the rear of the vehicle. If the rear of the vehicle is lower than normal, the caster becomes more positive.

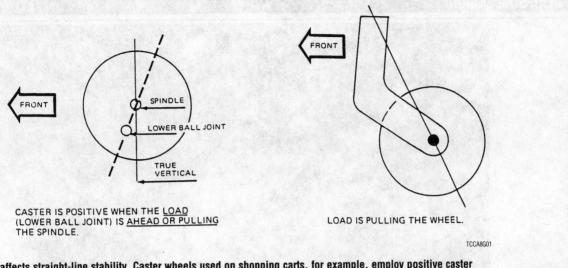

CASTER IS POSITIVE WHEN THE <u>LOAD</u>
(LOWER BALL JOINT) IS <u>AHEAD OR PULLING</u>
THE SPINDLE.

LOAD IS PULLING THE WHEEL.

TCCA8G01

Fig. 42 Caster affects straight-line stability. Caster wheels used on shopping carts, for example, employ positive caster

CAMBER

▶ **See Figure 43**

Looking from the front of the vehicle, camber is the inward or outward tilt of the top of wheels. When the tops of the wheels are tilted in, this is negative camber; if they are tilted out, it is positive. In a turn, a slight amount of negative camber helps maximize contact of the tire with the road. However, too much negative camber compromises straight-line stability, increases bump steer and torque steer.

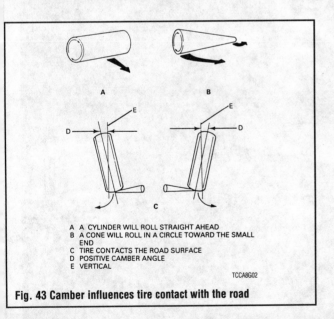

A A CYLINDER WILL ROLL STRAIGHT AHEAD
B A CONE WILL ROLL IN A CIRCLE TOWARD THE SMALL
   END
C TIRE CONTACTS THE ROAD SURFACE
D POSITIVE CAMBER ANGLE
E VERTICAL

TCCA8G02

Fig. 43 Camber influences tire contact with the road

TOE

▶ **See Figures 44 and 45**

Looking down at the wheels from above the vehicle, toe angle is the distance between the front of the wheels, relative to the distance between the back of the wheels. If the wheels are closer at the front, they are said to be toed-in or to have negative toe. A small amount of negative toe enhances directional stability and provides a smoother ride on the highway.

89668P10

Fig. 44 Toe is adjusted by turning the link between the inner and outer tie rod ends

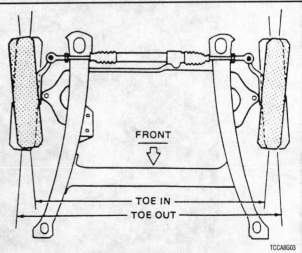

FRONT

TOE IN
TOE OUT

TCCA8G03

Fig. 45 With toe-in, the distance between the wheels is closer at the front than at the rear

REAR SUSPENSION

REAR SUSPENSION AND DRIVE TRAIN COMPONENTS

1. Leaf spring shackle
2. Shock absorber
3. Differential housing
4. Rear axle tube
5. U-bolt plate
6. U-bolt
7. Leaf spring

Leaf Springs

REMOVAL & INSTALLATION

▶ **See Figures 46, 47, 48 and 49**

1. Raise the van and support the rear with jackstands under the frame.

➡**Ensure the front wheels are chocked and that the parking brake is set.**

2. The rear wheels should now be touching the floor, with all the weight off of the springs.
3. Remove the nuts, lockwashers and U-bolts that hold the axle to the springs.
4. Remove the front pivot bolts.
5. Remove the rear shackle bolt nuts and the rear shackle plate.
6. Remove the front shackle bolt nuts and the rear shackle plate.
7. Remove the spring.

To install:

8. Position the spring in place and install the eye bolt and nut. Ensure that the rear spring eye is located above the shackle bracket pivot bolt.

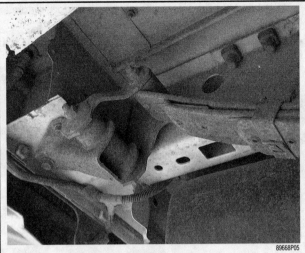

Fig. 47 . . . and a shackle at the rear. Note that the spring is attached above the shackle

Fig. 46 The leaf spring is mounted in a chassis bracket at the front . . .

Fig. 48 The leaf spring attaches to the axle with two U-bolts. Be sure that the spring is properly centered before tightening the bolts

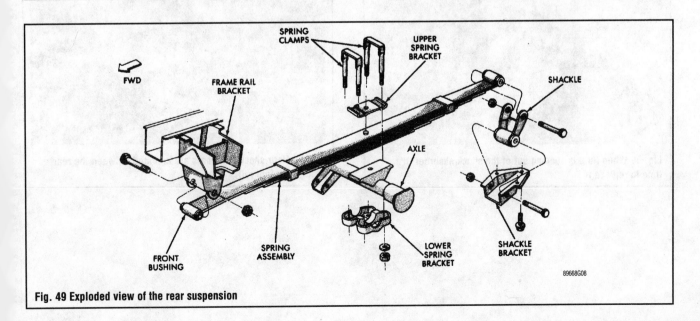

Fig. 49 Exploded view of the rear suspension

9. Install the shackles and bolts. Tighten them just enough to make them snug.

➡**Do not final-tighten any of the shackle bolts until the vehicle is at ride height.**

10. Make sure that the spring center bolt enters the locating hole in the axle pad. On headless-type spring bolts, install the bolts with the lock groove lined up with the lock bolt hole in the bracket. Install the lock bolt and tighten the lock bolt nut. Install the lubrication fittings.

11. Install the U-bolts, lockwashers and nuts. Make them just snug for now. Align the auxiliary spring parallel with the main spring.

12. Lower the vehicle to its normal position with the weight back on the springs. Now tighten all bolts and nuts as follows:
- U-bolt nuts, except on the 350 model—45 ft. lbs. (61 Nm)
- U-bolt nuts on the 350 model—110 ft. lbs. (149 Nm)
- Shackle nuts (two-piece shackle)—35 ft. lbs. (47 Nm)
- Shackle nuts (one-piece shackle)—155 ft. lbs. (210 Nm)
- Fixed end—100 ft. lbs. (135 Nm)

Shock Absorbers

TESTING

▶ **See Figure 50**

The purpose of the shock absorber is simply to limit the motion of the spring during compression and rebound cycles. If the vehicle is not equipped with these motion dampers, the up and down motion would multiply until the vehicle was alternately trying to leap off the ground and to pound itself into the pavement.

Contrary to popular belief, the shocks do not affect the ride height of the vehicle. This is controlled by other suspension components such as springs and tires. Worn shock absorbers can affect handling; if the front of the vehicle is rising or falling excessively, the "footprint" of the tires changes on the pavement and steering is affected.

The simplest test of the shock absorber is simply push down on one corner of the unladen vehicle and release it. Observe the motion of the body as it is released. In most cases, it will come up beyond its original rest position, dip back below it and settle quickly to rest. This shows that the damper is controlling the spring action. Any tendency to excessive pitch (up-and-down) motion or failure to return to rest within 2–3 cycles is a sign of poor function within the shock absorber. Oil-filled shocks may have a light film of oil around the seal, resulting from normal breathing and air exchange. This should NOT be taken as a sign of failure, but any sign of thick or running oil definitely indicates failure. Gas filled shocks may also show some film at the shaft; if the gas has leaked out, the shock will have almost no resistance to motion.

While each shock absorber can be replaced individually, it is recommended that they be changed as a pair (both front or both rear) to maintain equal response on both sides of the vehicle. Chances are quite good that if one has failed, its mate is weak also.

REMOVAL & INSTALLATION

▶ **See Figure 51**

1. Raise and safely support the vehicle securely on jackstands.
2. Remove the wheels.
3. Remove the upper nut and retainer.
4. Remove the lower mounting bolt.
5. Remove the shock absorber.

To install:

6. When installing the shock absorber, make sure the upper bushings are in the correct position.
7. Replace any worn or cracked bushings.
8. Hand-tighten the shock absorber fasteners.
9. Install the wheels.
10. Lower the vehicle.
11. Once the vehicle is at normal ride height, final-tighten the shock absorber fasteners to 60 ft. lbs. (82 Nm).

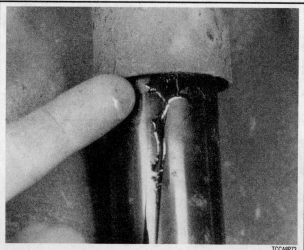

TCCA8P73

Fig. 50 When fluid is seeping out of the shock absorber, it's time to replace it

89668P03

Fig. 51 Rear shock absorbers are mounted between the rear axle and frame rail

STEERING

✳✳✳ CAUTION

Some models covered by this manual are equipped with a Supplemental Restraint System (SRS), which uses an air bag. Whenever working near any of the SRS components, such as the impact sensors, air bag module, steering column and instrument panel, disable the SRS, as described in Section 6.

Steering Wheel

REMOVAL & INSTALLATION

▶ See Figures 52 and 53

Without Air Bag

1. Ensure the steering wheel and the vehicle's front wheels are in the straight ahead position.
2. Disconnect the negative battery cable.
3. Working through the access holes in the back of the wheel, remove the attaching screws and push the horn pad off the wheel.

➡Do not attempt to pry the pad off the steering wheel front the front side.

4. Disconnect the horn wire.
5. Matchmark the steering wheel and shaft.
6. Remove the steering wheel retaining nut.
7. Using a steering wheel puller, remove the steering wheel from the shaft.

To install:

8. Align and install the steering wheel on the column shaft.
9. Install a new retaining nut and tighten the nut to 45 ft. lbs. (61 Nm).
10. Connect the horn wire.
11. Install the horn pad on the steering wheel and tighten the attaching screws securely.
12. Connect the negative battery cable.

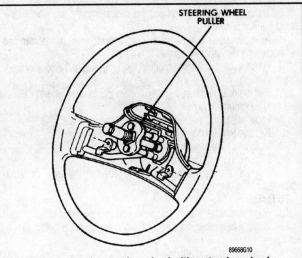

Fig. 53 Removing the steering wheel with a steering wheel puller

With Air Bag

✳✳✳ CAUTION

Some models covered by this manual may be equipped with a Supplemental Restraint System (SRS), which uses an air bag. Whenever working near any of the SRS components, such as the impact sensors, the air bag module, steering column and instrument panel, disable the SRS, as described in Section 6.

➡Do not move the front wheels or steering shaft once the steering wheel is removed. Moving the front wheels or steering shaft will disturb the relationship between the clock spring and the shaft. If the relationship has been disturbed, the clock spring must be centered prior to reinstalling the steering wheel.

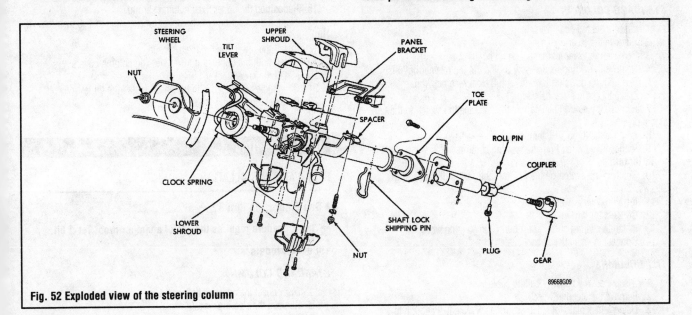

Fig. 52 Exploded view of the steering column

1. Disconnect the negative battery cable.
2. Wait two minutes. This time is required to discharge the capacitor and prevent unintended air bag deployment. The system is now disarmed.
3. Ensure the steering wheel and the vehicle's front wheels are in the straight ahead position.
4. As required, remove the speed control switches from the horn pad by unscrewing the attaching screws.
5. Remove the four air bag module retaining nuts at the back of the steering wheel.
6. Pull the module far enough away from the steering wheel to disconnect the clockspring wire harness.
7. Label and disconnect the clockspring wire harness.
8. Remove the air bag module from the steering wheel.
9. Matchmark the steering wheel and shaft.
10. Remove the steering wheel retaining nut.
11. Using a steering wheel puller, remove the steering wheel from the shaft.

To install:
12. Align and install the steering wheel on the column shaft.
13. Install a new retaining nut and tighten the nut to 45 ft. lbs. (61 Nm).
14. Connect the clockspring wire harness.
15. Install the four air bag module retaining nuts and tighten to 80–100 inch lbs. (9–11 Nm).
16. As required, install the speed control switches on the horn pad.
17. Connect the negative battery cable.
18. Check the air bag system for proper function prior to driving the vehicle.

Combination Switch

REMOVAL & INSTALLATION

The multi-function (combination) switch contains electrical circuitry for turn signal, hazard warning, headlamp beam selection, windshield wiper and windshield washer switching.

➡This procedure requires the use of a tamper proof Torx® bit.

1989–90 Models

STANDARD COLUMNS

1. Disconnect the negative battery cable.
2. Remove the steering wheel.
3. Remove the lower instrument panel bezel.
4. Remove the wiring retainers by prying out the retainer buttons.
5. Position the gearshift lever to its full clockwise position.
6. Disconnect the electrical wiring harness.
7. Remove the screw that attaches the combination switch to the turn signal pivot.
8. Remove the three switch mounting screws.
9. Remove the switch from the steering column.

To install:
10. Position the switch on the column and install the attaching screws.
11. Install the wiper-washer switch.
12. Connect the wiring.
13. Install the wiring cover, lower bezel and steering wheel.
14. Connect the negative battery cable.

TILT COLUMNS

1. Disconnect the negative battery cable.
2. Remove the steering wheel.
3. Using a lock plate tool, depress the lock plate just enough to remove the retaining ring, and pry the retaining ring out of the grove.
4. Remove the lock plate and upper bearing spring.
5. Place the turn signal switch in the right turn position.

6. Remove the screw which attaches the link between the turn signal switch and wiper/washer switch pivot.
7. Remove the screw which attaches the hazard switch knob.
8. Remove the 3 screws securing the turn signal switch.
9. Gently pull the switch and wiring from the column.

To install:
10. Position the switch and wiring in the column.
11. Install the 3 screws securing the turn signal switch.
12. Install the screw which attaches the hazard switch knob.
13. Install the screw which attaches the link between the turn signal switch and wiper/washer switch pivot.
14. Place the turn signal switch in the normal position.
15. Install the lock plate and upper bearing spring.
16. Using a lock plate tool, depress the lock plate just enough to install the retaining ring.
17. Install the steering wheel.
18. Connect the negative battery cable.
19. Check switch operation.

1991–98 Models

1. Disconnect the negative battery cable.
2. On vehicles equipped with tilt wheel, remove the tilt lever.
3. Remove the knee blocker.
4. Remove both the upper and lower steering column covers.
5. Remove the lower column fixed shroud.
6. Loosen, but do not remove the steering column upper bracket nuts.
7. Move the upper fixed column shroud to gain access to the rear of the combination switch.
8. Remove the multi-function switch tamper proof Torx® screws.
9. Pull the switch away from the column carefully.
10. Loosen the connector screw (the screw will remain in the connector).
11. Remove the wiring connector from the multi-function switch.
12. Remove the switch from the steering column.

To install:
13. Position the switch on the steering column.
14. Install the wiring connector on the multi-function switch and tighten the connector screw to 17 inch lbs. (2 Nm).
15. Install the multi-function switch tamper proof Torx® screws and tighten to 17 inch lbs. (2 Nm).
16. Reposition the upper fixed column shroud.
17. Tighten the steering column upper bracket nuts to 110 inch lbs. (12 Nm).
18. Install the lower column fixed shroud.
19. Install both the upper and lower steering column covers.
20. Install the knee blocker.
21. On vehicles equipped with tilt wheel, install the tilt lever.
22. Connect the negative battery cable.
23. Check switch operation.

Ignition Switch

REMOVAL & INSTALLATION

▶ **See Figures 54 thru 59**

➡This procedure requires the use of a tamper proof Torx® bit.

1989–90 Models

STANDARD COLUMN

1. Disconnect the negative battery cable.
2. Remove the steering wheel.
3. Remove the turn signal switch.
4. Remove the retaining screw and lift the ignition lock cylinder lamp out of the way.

5. Remove the bearing housing.

6. Remove the coil spring.

7. Remove the lock plate from the shaft.

8. Remove the 2 retaining screws and lift the lock lever guide plate to expose the lock cylinder release hole.

9. Insert the key and place the lock cylinder in the **LOCK** position. Remove the key.

10. Insert a thin punch into the lock cylinder release hole and push inward to release the spring-loaded lock retainer. At the same time, pull the lock cylinder out of the column.

11. Remove the 3 retaining screws and lift out the ignition switch.

To install:

12. Position the ignition switch in the center detent position (**OFF**).

13. Place the shift lever in **PARK**.

14. Feed the wires down through the space between the housing and jacket. Position the switch in the housing and install the 3 retaining screws.

15. Place the lock cylinder in the **LOCK** position and press it into place in the column. It will snap into position.

16. The remainder of assembly is the reverse of disassembly.

TILT COLUMN

1. Disconnect the negative battery cable.

2. Remove the steering wheel.

3. Remove the tilt lever and turn signal lever.

4. If equipped, remove the turn signal lever.

5. Remove the turn signal switch.

6. Using the key, place the lock cylinder in the **LOCK** position. Remove the key.

7. Insert a thin punch in the slot next to the switch mounting screw boss and depress the spring latch at the bottom of the slot. Hold the spring latch depressed and pull the lock cylinder out of the column.

8. Place the ignition switch in the **ACCESSORY** position and remove the mounting screws. Lift off the switch. The **ACCESSORY** position is the one opposite the spring-loaded end position.

To install:

9. Install the lock cylinder. Place the cylinder in the **LOCK** position and push it into the housing. It will snap into place.

10. Rotate the lock cylinder to the **ACCESSORY** position.

11. Fit the actuator rod in the slider hole and position the switch on the column. Insert the mounting screws, but don't tighten them yet.

12. Push the switch gently down the column to remove all lash from the actuator rod. Tighten the mounting screws. Make sure that you didn't take the switch out of the **ACCESSORY** detent!

13. Complete the remainder of installation in reverse order.

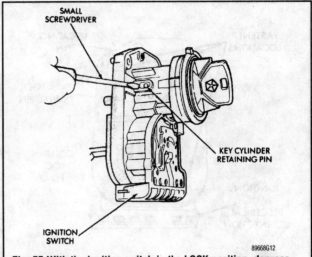

Fig. 55 With the ignition switch in the LOCK position, depress the key cylinder retaining pin

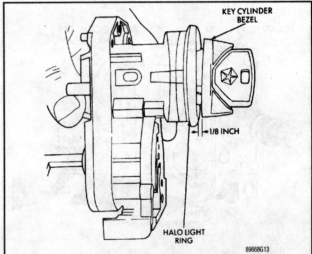

Fig. 56 With the ignition switch in the OFF position, unseat the cylinder about ⅛ inch above the ignition switch halo light ring . . .

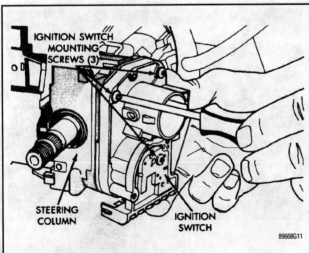

Fig. 54 Remove the ignition switch screws using a Torx® bit screwdriver

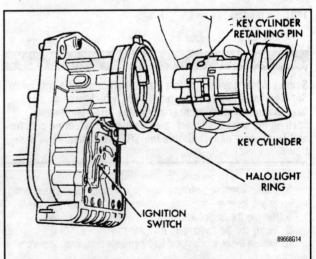

Fig. 57 . . . then return the switch to the LOCK position, and remove the key cylinder—1991–98 models

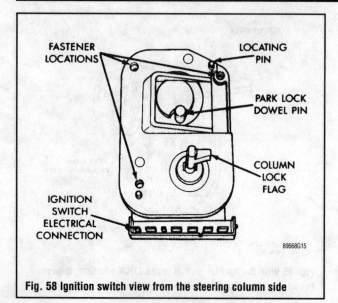

Fig. 58 Ignition switch view from the steering column side

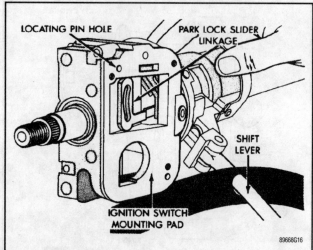

Fig. 59 On column shift models, be sure to properly engage the park lock slider linkage

1991–98 Models

1. Disconnect the negative battery cable.

✷✷ CAUTION

Some models covered by this manual are equipped with a Supplemental Restraint System (SRS), which uses an air bag. Whenever working near any of the SRS components, such as the impact sensors, air bag module, steering column and instrument panel, disable the SRS, as described in Section 6.

2. Remove the tilt column lever, as required.
3. Carefully remove both the tamper proof column cover screws and lift the upper and lower steering column covers off the column.
4. Remove the tamper proof ignition switch mounting screws.
5. Gently pull the switch away from the column.
6. Release the connector locks and then unplug the connector from the switch.
7. Release the connector lock on the key in switch and halo light connector, then remove the connector from the ignition switch.

8. With the key inserted and the ignition switch in the **LOCK** position, use a small screwdriver to depress the key cylinder retaining pin flush with the key cylinder surface.
9. Rotate the key clockwise to the **OFF** position. The key cylinder should now be unseated from the ignition switch assembly. Do not attempt to remove the key cylinder yet.

➡The unseated position is with the key cylinder bezel about ⅛ inch (3mm) above the ignition switch halo light ring.

10. With the key cylinder in the unseated position, rotate the key counterclockwise to the **LOCK** position and remove the key.
11. Remove the key cylinder.

To install:
12. Install the electrical connectors to the switch. Make sure that the switch locking tabs are fully seated in the wiring connectors.
13. Mount the ignition switch to the column. On column shift columns, the shifter must be in the **PARK** position, and the park lock dowel pin on the ignition switch assembly must engage with the column park lock slider linkage.
14. Verify that the ignition switch is in the **LOCK** position. The flag should be parallel with the ignition switch terminals.
15. Apply a dab of grease to the flag and pin.
16. Position the park lock link and slider to mid-travel.
17. Position the ignition switch against the lock housing face, making sure the pin is inserted into the park lock link contour slot.
18. Tighten the tamper proof retaining screws to 12–22 inch lbs. (1.3–2.5 Nm).
19. Assemble the column covers and tighten the tamper proof screws to 17 inch lbs. (2 Nm).
20. Install the tilt column lever, as required.
21. Connect the negative battery cable.
22. With the key cylinder and the ignition in the **LOCK** position, gently insert the key cylinder into the ignition switch assembly until it bottoms.
23. Insert the key, and while gently pushing inward on the key cylinder toward the ignition switch, rotate the key clockwise to the end of its travel.
24. Check for proper operation.

Steering Linkage

REMOVAL & INSTALLATION

▶ **See Figures 60 and 61**

1. Raise and safely support the vehicle securely on jackstands.
2. Remove the front wheels.

1. Drag link 3. Tie rod
2. Center link 4. Pitman arm

Fig. 60 Steering linkage components

Fig. 61 The center link is attached to an idler arm at each side of the vehicle

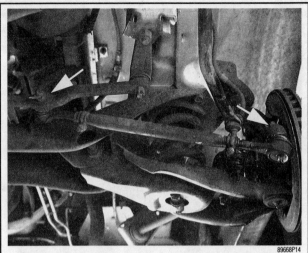

Fig. 62 The tie rod connects the center link (left arrow) to the steering knuckle (right arrow)

3. Remove the cotter pins and retaining nuts from the tie rod end, idler arm and Pitman arm pivot ball studs.

➡Use care to avoid damaging seals while removing steering components.

4. Remove the outer tie rod ends from the steering knuckles, using a tie rod end separator.

5. Remove the inner tie rod ball studs from the center link. Once again using a tie rod end separator.

6. Remove the idler arm ball studs from the center link.

7. Remove the idler arm retaining nuts from the frame bracket bolts.

8. Remove the drag link ball studs from the Pitman arm and the center link bore.

9. Remove the retaining nut and the Pitman arm from the steering gear, using a Pitman arm puller.

10. Examine all the steering linkage components. Replace as necessary.

To install:

11. Examine all the steering linkage components. Replace as necessary.

12. Position the idler arms at the frame brackets and install the retaining nuts. Tighten them to 70 ft. lbs. (95 Nm).

13. Place the center link on the idler arm ball studs. Install and tighten the retaining nuts to 47 ft. lbs. (64 Nm). Install new cotter pins.

14. Connect the tie rod end ball studs to the steering knuckles and to the center link. Tighten the ⁹⁄₁₆ nuts to 18–55 ft. lbs. (75 Nm) and the ⅝ inch nuts to 18–75 ft. lbs. (102 Nm). Install new cotter pins.

15. Install the Pitman arm on the steering gear and tighten the nut to 175 ft. lbs. (237 Nm).

16. Connect the drag link ball studs to the Pitman arm and to the center link. Tighten the nuts to 55 ft. lbs. (75 Nm), then install new cotter pins.

17. Install the front wheels and lower the vehicle.

18. Have the front end alignment checked.

Tie Rod Ends

▶ See Figures 62 thru 68

➡Only the tie rod end (outer tie rod) can be removed from heavy duty tie rods.

1. Raise and safely support the vehicle securely on jackstands.

2. Loosen the tie rod adjusting nut.

3. Remove the cotter pin and nut from the tie rod end.

4. Using a separator, free the tie rod end from the knuckle arm or center link.

5. Count the exact number of threads visible between the tie rod end and the sleeve. Loosen the clamp bolts and unscrew the tie rod end.

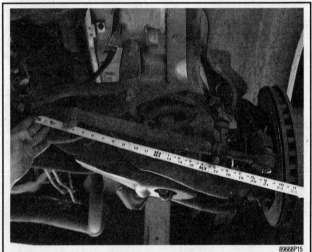

Fig. 63 Prior to removing the tie rod, measure the tie rod length. Record this figure for installation reference

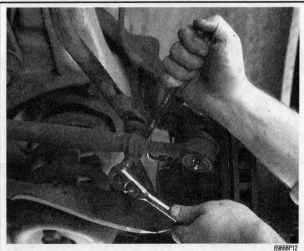

Fig. 64 Loosen the tie rod adjusting nut prior to disconnecting the tie rod end from the steering knuckle

Fig. 65 Using a pair of needlenose pliers, remove the cotter pin from the tie rod end's castle nut

Fig. 66 Unscrew the castle nut to the end of the stud. The nut will prevent the tie rod tool from damaging the end of the stud

Fig. 67 Install the tie rod tool and tighten to press the tie rod end from the steering knuckle

Fig. 68 Remove the castle nut and separate the tie rod end from the steering knuckle

To install:

6. Screw the end into the sleeve until the exact number of threads originally noted is showing.

7. Tighten the clamp nuts to 200 inch lbs. (22 Nm) on all vehicles except HD, or to 26 ft. lbs. (35 Nm) on HD models.

8. Tighten the 9/16 nuts to 18 –55 ft. lbs. (75 Nm) and the 5/8 inch nuts to 18– 75 ft. lbs. (102 Nm). Install new cotter pins.

Power Steering Gear

REMOVAL & INSTALLATION

▶ **See Figures 69 and 70**

1. Position the front wheel in the straight ahead position.
2. Place a drain pan under the gear.
3. Disconnect and cap the fluid hoses from the steering gear.
4. Matchmark the coupler for installation reference.
5. Remove the coupler retaining bolts and disconnect the coupler from the steering gear.
6. Matchmark the Pitman shaft and Pitman arm for installation reference.

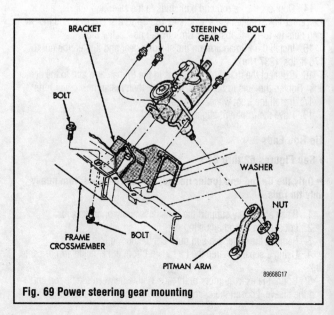

Fig. 69 Power steering gear mounting

Fig. 70 The steering gear is connected to the drag link by a Pitman arm

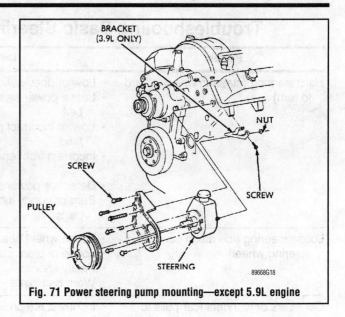

Fig. 71 Power steering pump mounting—except 5.9L engine

7. Remove the Pitman arm from the shaft, using a Pitman arm puller.
8. Remove the gear-to-frame mounting bolts and remove the gear.

To install:

9. Position the gear and tighten the gear-to-frame mounting bolts to 100 ft. lbs. (136 Nm).
10. Align the coupler and install new retaining bolts. Tighten the retaining bolts to 36 ft. lbs. (49 Nm).
11. Align and install the Pitman arm on the shaft. Tighten the retaining nut to 185 ft. lbs. (251 Nm).
12. Connect the fluid hoses to the steering gear.
13. Fill the steering gear with fresh power steering fluid.

Power Steering Pump

REMOVAL & INSTALLATION

▶ See Figures 71, 72 and 73

1. If the pump is to be replaced or disassembled, remove the pulley nut before removing the belt.
2. Remove the accessory drive belt.
3. Place a drain pan under the pump.
4. Disconnect and cap both hoses at the pump.
5. Remove the mounting and adjusting bolts.
6. Lift the pump from the engine compartment.

To install:

7. Position the pump in the engine compartment and tighten the bolts to 40 ft. lbs. (54 Nm) on 3.9L and 5.2L engines or 21 ft. lbs. (28 Nm) on the 5.9L engine.
8. Connect the fluid lines.
9. Ensure hoses are routed at least 1 in. (25mm) from all surfaces and at least 2 in. (51mm) from the exhaust manifold.
10. Install the accessory drive belt and tension properly.
11. Start the engine and bleed the power steering system.
12. Adjust fluid level, as necessary, using fresh power steering fluid.

BLEEDING

After filling the power steering reservoir to the correct level, start the engine and turn the steering wheel slowly from lock to lock several times. Do not force the steering wheel against the stops. Stop the engine and check the fluid level. Add fluid if necessary. Continue until bubbles in the fluid disappear.

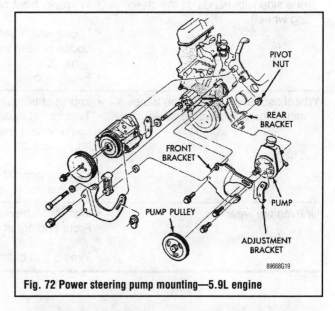

Fig. 72 Power steering pump mounting—5.9L engine

Fig. 73 Some power steering pumps use a separate cooler to control fluid temperature and increase pump life

Troubleshooting Basic Steering and Suspension Problems

Problem	Cause	Solution
Hard steering (steering wheel is hard to turn)	• Low or uneven tire pressure • Loose power steering pump drive belt • Low or incorrect power steering fluid • Incorrect front end alignment • Defective power steering pump • Bent or poorly lubricated front end parts	• Inflate tires to correct pressure • Adjust belt • Add fluid as necessary • Have front end alignment checked/adjusted • Check pump • Lubricate and/or replace defective parts
Loose steering (too much play in the steering wheel)	• Loose wheel bearings • Loose or worn steering linkage • Faulty shocks • Worn ball joints	• Adjust wheel bearings • Replace worn parts • Replace shocks • Replace ball joints
Car veers or wanders (car pulls to one side with hands off the steering wheel)	• Incorrect tire pressure • Improper front end alignment • Loose wheel bearings • Loose or bent front end components • Faulty shocks	• Inflate tires to correct pressure • Have front end alignment checked/adjusted • Adjust wheel bearings • Replace worn components • Replace shocks
Wheel oscillation or vibration transmitted through steering wheel	• Improper tire pressures • Tires out of balance • Loose wheel bearings • Improper front end alignment • Worn or bent front end components	• Inflate tires to correct pressure • Have tires balanced • Adjust wheel bearings • Have front end alignment checked/adjusted • Replace worn parts
Uneven tire wear	• Incorrect tire pressure • Front end out of alignment • Tires out of balance	• Inflate tires to correct pressure • Have front end alignment checked/adjusted • Have tires balanced

TCCA8C01

Torque Specifications

Components	English	Metric
Wheels		
15 inch wheels	80–110 ft. lbs.	109–150 Nm
16 inch wheels with 1/2 inch studs	85–115 ft. lbs.	115–155 Nm
16 inch wheels with 5/8 inch studs	175–225 ft. lbs.	240–305 Nm
Front Suspension		
Ball Joints		
11/16 inch nuts	135 ft. lbs.	183 Nm
3/4 inch nuts	175 ft. lbs.	237 Nm
Screw in upper ball joint	125 ft. lbs.	170 Nm
Shock Absorber		
Upper	25 ft. lbs.	34 Nm
Lower	17 ft. lbs.	23 Nm
Sway Bar		
Retainer	16 ft. lbs.	23 Nm
Link	100 inch lbs.	11 Nm
Strut Bar		
Strut bar-to-lower control arm	100 ft. lbs.	136 Nm
Strut bar-to-frame bracket	52 ft. lbs.	71 Nm
Control Arm		
Upper pivot bolts	220 ft. lbs.	298 Nm
Lower pivot bolts	175 ft. lbs.	237 Nm
Knuckle		
Adapter	100 ft. lbs.	136 Nm
Splash shield	18 ft. lbs.	24 Nm
Wheel Bearings		
Step 1:	240-300 inch lbs.	27-34 Nm
Step 2:	Back off 1/4 turn (90 degrees)	
Step 3:	finger-tighten	
Rear Suspension		
Leaf Springs		
U-bolt nuts (exc. 350 models)	45 ft. lbs.	61 Nm
U-bolt nuts (350 models)	110 ft. lbs.	149 Nm
Shackle nuts (two-piece shackle)	35 ft. lbs.	47 Nm
Shackle nuts (one-piece shackle)	155 ft. lbs.	210 Nm
Fixed end	100 ft. lbs.	135 Nm
Shock Absorbers	60 ft. lbs.	82 Nm

89668C01

Torque Specifications

Components	English	Metric
Steering		
Steering wheel	45 ft. lbs.	61 Nm
Air bag module	80–100 inch lbs.	9–11 Nm
Combination Switch	17 inch lbs.	2 Nm
Ignition Switch	12–22 inch lbs.	1.3–2.5 Nm
Steering Linkage		
Idler arms	70 ft. lbs.	95 Nm
Center link	47 ft. lbs.	64 Nm
Pitman arm	175 ft. lbs.	237 Nm
Drag Link	55 ft. lbs.	75 Nm
Tie Rod End		
Clamp nuts (Except HD Suspension)	200 inch lbs.	22 Nm
Clamp nuts (HD Suspension)	26 ft. lbs.	35 Nm
Castle Nuts-9/16 inch nuts	55 ft. lbs.	75 Nm
Castle Nuts-5/8 inch nuts	75 ft. lbs.	102 Nm
Power Steering Gear		
Gear-to-frame bolts	100 ft. lbs.	136 Nm
Coupler bolts	36 ft. lbs.	49 Nm
Power Steering Pump		
3.9L and 5.2L engines	40 ft. lbs.	54 Nm
5.9L engine	21 ft. lbs.	28 Nm

89668C02

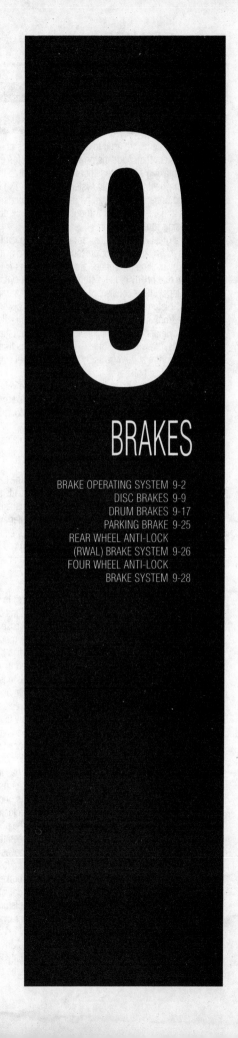

9

BRAKES

BRAKE OPERATING SYSTEM

Basic Operating Principles

Hydraulic systems are used to actuate the brakes of all modern automobiles. The system transports the power required to force the frictional surfaces of the braking system together from the pedal to the individual brake units at each wheel. A hydraulic system is used for two reasons.

First, fluid under pressure can be carried to all parts of an automobile by small pipes and flexible hoses without taking up a significant amount of room or posing routing problems.

Second, a great mechanical advantage can be given to the brake pedal end of the system, and the foot pressure required to actuate the brakes can be reduced by making the surface area of the master cylinder pistons smaller than that of any of the pistons in the wheel cylinders or calipers.

The master cylinder consists of a fluid reservoir along with a double cylinder and piston assembly. Double type master cylinders are designed to separate the front and rear braking systems hydraulically in case of a leak. The master cylinder coverts mechanical motion from the pedal into hydraulic pressure within the lines. This pressure is translated back into mechanical motion at the wheels by either the wheel cylinder (drum brakes) or the caliper (disc brakes).

Steel lines carry the brake fluid to a point on the vehicle's frame near each of the vehicle's wheels. The fluid is then carried to the calipers and wheel cylinders by flexible tubes in order to allow for suspension and steering movements.

In drum brake systems, each wheel cylinder contains two pistons, one at either end, which push outward in opposite directions and force the brake shoe into contact with the drum.

In disc brake systems, the cylinders are part of the calipers. At least one cylinder in each caliper is used to force the brake pads against the disc.

All pistons employ some type of seal, usually made of rubber, to minimize fluid leakage. A rubber dust boot seals the outer end of the cylinder against dust and dirt. The boot fits around the outer end of the piston on disc brake calipers, and around the brake actuating rod on wheel cylinders.

The hydraulic system operates as follows: When at rest, the entire system, from the piston(s) in the master cylinder to those in the wheel cylinders or calipers, is full of brake fluid. Upon application of the brake pedal, fluid trapped in front of the master cylinder piston(s) is forced through the lines to the wheel cylinders. Here, it forces the pistons outward, in the case of drum brakes, and inward toward the disc, in the case of disc brakes. The motion of the pistons is opposed by return springs mounted outside the cylinders in drum brakes, and by spring seals, in disc brakes.

Upon release of the brake pedal, a spring located inside the master cylinder immediately returns the master cylinder pistons to the normal position. The pistons contain check valves and the master cylinder has compensating ports drilled in it. These are uncovered as the pistons reach their normal position. The piston check valves allow fluid to flow toward the wheel cylinders or calipers as the pistons withdraw. Then, as the return springs force the brake pads or shoes into the released position, the excess fluid reservoir through the compensating ports. It is during the time the pedal is in the released position that any fluid that has leaked out of the system will be replaced through the compensating ports.

Dual circuit master cylinders employ two pistons, located one behind the other, in the same cylinder. The primary piston is actuated directly by mechanical linkage from the brake pedal through the power booster. The secondary piston is actuated by fluid trapped between the two pistons. If a leak develops in front of the secondary piston, it moves forward until it bottoms against the front of the master cylinder, and the fluid trapped between the pistons will operate the rear brakes. If the rear brakes develop a leak, the primary piston will move forward until direct contact with the secondary piston takes place, and it will force the secondary piston to actuate the front brakes. In either case, the brake pedal moves farther when the brakes are applied, and less braking power is available.

All dual circuit systems use a switch to warn the driver when only half of the brake system is operational. This switch is usually located in a valve body which is mounted on the firewall or the frame below the master cylinder. A hydraulic piston receives pressure from both circuits, each circuit's pressure being applied to one end of the piston. When the pressures are in balance, the piston remains stationary. When one circuit has a leak, however, the greater pressure in that circuit during application of the brakes will push the piston to one side, closing the switch and activating the brake warning light.

In disc brake systems, this valve body also contains a metering valve and, in some cases, a proportioning valve. The metering valve keeps pressure from traveling to the disc brakes on the front wheels until the brake pads on the rear wheels have contacted the drums, ensuring that the front brakes will never be used alone. The proportioning valve controls the pressure to the rear brakes to lessen the chance of rear wheel lock-up during very hard braking.

Warning lights may be tested by depressing the brake pedal and holding it while opening one of the wheel cylinder bleeder screws. If this does not cause the light to go on, substitute a new lamp, make continuity checks, and, finally, replace the switch as necessary.

The hydraulic system may be checked for leaks by applying pressure to the pedal gradually and steadily. If the pedal sinks very slowly to the floor, the system has a leak. This is not to be confused with a springy or spongy feel due to the compression of air within the lines. If the system leaks, there will be a gradual change in the position of the pedal with a constant pressure.

Check for leaks along all lines and at wheel cylinders. If no external leaks are apparent, the problem is inside the master cylinder.

DISC BRAKES

Instead of the traditional expanding brakes that press outward against a circular drum, disc brake systems utilize a disc (rotor) with brake pads positioned on either side of it. An easily-seen analogy is the hand brake arrangement on a bicycle. The pads squeeze onto the rim of the bike wheel, slowing its motion. Automobile disc brakes use the identical principle but apply the braking effort to a separate disc instead of the wheel.

The disc (rotor) is a casting, usually equipped with cooling fins between the two braking surfaces. This enables air to circulate between the braking surfaces making them less sensitive to heat buildup and more resistant to fade. Dirt and water do not drastically affect braking action since contaminants are thrown off by the centrifugal action of the rotor or scraped off the by the pads. Also, the equal clamping action of the two brake pads tends to ensure uniform, straight line stops. Disc brakes are inherently self-adjusting. There are three general types of disc brake:

1. A fixed caliper.
2. A floating caliper.
3. A sliding caliper.

The fixed caliper design uses two pistons mounted on either side of the rotor (in each side of the caliper). The caliper is mounted rigidly and does not move.

The sliding and floating designs are quite similar. In fact, these two types are often lumped together. In both designs, the pad on the inside of the rotor is moved into contact with the rotor by hydraulic force. The caliper, which is not held in a fixed position, moves slightly, bringing the outside pad into contact with the rotor. There are various methods of attaching floating calipers. Some pivot at the bottom or top, and some slide on mounting bolts. In any event, the end result is the same.

DRUM BRAKES

Drum brakes employ two brake shoes mounted on a stationary support plate. These shoes are positioned inside a circular drum which rotates with the wheel assembly. The shoes are held in place by springs. This allows them to slide toward the drums (when they are applied) while keeping the linings and drums in alignment. The shoes are actuated by a wheel cylinder which is mounted at the top of the support plate. When the brakes are applied, hydraulic pressure forces the wheel cylinder's actuating links outward. Since these links bear directly against the top of the brake shoes, the tops of the shoes are then forced against the inner side of the drum. This action forces the bottoms of the two shoes to contact the brake drum by rotating the entire assembly slightly (known as servo action). When pressure within the wheel cylinder is relaxed, return springs pull the shoes back away from the drum.

Most modern drum brakes are designed to self-adjust themselves during application when the vehicle is moving in reverse. This motion causes both shoes to rotate very slightly with the drum, rocking an adjusting lever, thereby causing rotation of the adjusting screw. Some drum brake systems are designed to self-adjust during application whenever the brakes are applied. This on-board adjustment system reduces the need for maintenance adjustments and keeps both the brake function and pedal feel satisfactory.

POWER BOOSTERS

Virtually all modern vehicles use a vacuum assisted power brake system to multiply the braking force and reduce pedal effort. Since vacuum is always available when the engine is operating, the system is simple and efficient. A vacuum diaphragm is located on the front of the master cylinder and assists the driver in applying the brakes, reducing both the effort and travel he must put into moving the brake pedal.

The vacuum diaphragm housing is normally connected to the intake manifold by a vacuum hose. A check valve is placed at the point where the hose enters the diaphragm housing, so that during periods of low manifold vacuum brakes assist will not be lost.

Depressing the brake pedal closes off the vacuum source and allows atmospheric pressure to enter on one side of the diaphragm. This causes the master cylinder pistons to move and apply the brakes. When the brake pedal is released, vacuum is applied to both sides of the diaphragm and springs return the diaphragm and master cylinder pistons to the released position.

If the vacuum supply fails, the brake pedal rod will contact the end of the master cylinder actuator rod and the system will apply the brakes without any power assistance. The driver will notice that much higher pedal effort is needed to stop the car and that the pedal feels harder than usual.

Power brake systems may be tested for hydraulic leaks just as ordinary systems are tested.

Vacuum Leak Test

1. Operate the engine at idle without touching the brake pedal for at least one minute.
2. Turn off the engine and wait one minute.
3. Test for the presence of assist vacuum by depressing the brake pedal and releasing it several times. If vacuum is present in the system, light application will produce less and less pedal travel. If there is no vacuum, air is leaking into the system.

System Operation Test

1. With the engine **OFF**, pump the brake pedal until the supply vacuum is entirely gone.
2. Put light, steady pressure on the brake pedal.
3. Start the engine and let it idle. If the system is operating correctly, the brake pedal should fall toward the floor if the constant pressure is maintained.

✳ WARNING

Clean, high quality brake fluid is essential to the safe and proper operation of the brake system. You should always buy the highest quality brake fluid that is available. If the brake fluid becomes contaminated, drain and flush the system, then refill the master cylinder with new fluid. Never reuse any brake fluid. Any brake fluid that is removed from the system should be discarded. Also, do not allow any brake fluid to come in contact with a painted surface; it will damage the paint.

Brake Light Switch

REMOVAL & INSTALLATION

The brake light switch is located on the brake pedal bracket, under the driver's side of the dashboard.

1. Remove the steering column trim cover for access to the brake pedal.
2. Press and hold the brake pedal in the applied position.
3. Rotate the switch counterclockwise to unlock. Then, pull the switch straight out of its mounting bracket and release the brake pedal.
4. Once the switch is removed, disconnect the electrical harness.

To install:

5. Connect the electrical harness to the switch.
6. Press and hold the brake pedal in the applied position.
7. Position the switch and rotate it clockwise to lock.
8. Install the steering column trim cover.

ADJUSTMENT

With Locknut

▶ **See Figure 1**

1. Loosen the switch-to-pedal bracket screw and slide the switch away from the pedal arm.
2. Push the pedal down by hand and allow it to return on its own to the free-hanging position. Do not pull it back!
3. Slide the switch towards the pedal until there is a gap of 0.140 in. (3.5mm) between the plunger and pedal arm.

➡ **The pedal must not move when measuring the gap.**

4. Tighten the switch screw to 82 inch lbs. (9 Nm). Recheck the gap.

Without Locknut

1. Push the switch through the clip in the mounting bracket until it is seated against the bracket. The pedal will move forward slightly.

➡ **Do not use more than 10 lbs. (44 N) of force when pulling the brake pedal rearward. Excessive force may damage components.**

2. Gently pull back on the pedal as far as it will go. The switch will ratchet backwards to the correct position.

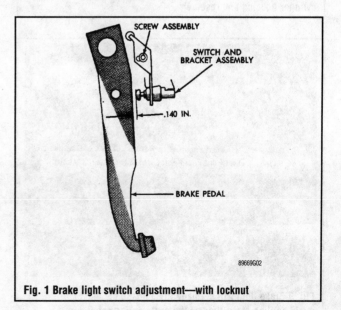

89669G02

Fig. 1 Brake light switch adjustment—with locknut

Master Cylinder

REMOVAL & INSTALLATION

♦ **See Figures 2 thru 7**

The body of the master cylinder is made of aluminum and the reservoir is made of nylon. The body of the master cylinder is not serviceable, and should be replaced as a unit if defective.

1. Using a flare nut wrench, loosen the brake line fittings on the master cylinder.
2. Disconnect and cap the brake lines to prevent dirt from entering the system.
3. On some vehicles, it will be necessary to remove the anti-lock brake valve or combination valve from the master cylinder.
4. Remove the master cylinder mounting nuts.
5. Slide the master cylinder off of the power brake booster.

To install:

6. If a new master cylinder is being installed, perform the master cylinder bleeding procedure, prior to installation.
7. Place the master cylinder in position on the brake booster and tighten the mounting nuts to 14–16 ft. lbs. (19–23 Nm).

Fig. 4 Make sure you label the lines to the master cylinder upon removal to ease installation

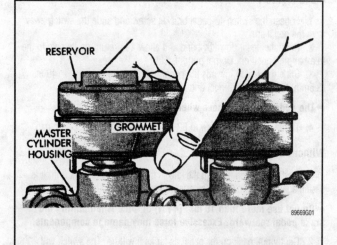

Fig. 2 Rubber grommets seal the junction between the master cylinder housing and reservoir

Fig. 5 The master cylinder is bolted to the booster, and is secured by two retaining bolts

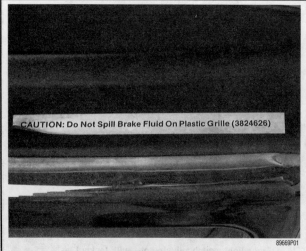

Fig. 3 Brake fluid will permanently damage the plastic grille, so avoid spilling brake fluid on the grille during servicing

Fig. 6 If so equipped, detach the anti-lock brake valve before removing the master cylinder

Fig. 7 Pull the master cylinder off the pushrod and power booster assembly

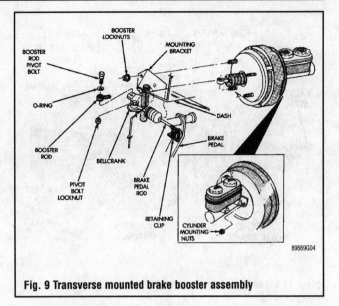

Fig. 9 Transverse mounted brake booster assembly

8. Install the anti-lock brake valve or combination valve, if removed. Tighten the mounting nut to 65–95 inch lbs. (7–11 Nm).

9. Connect the brake lines and tighten fittings with a flare nut wrench to 12–16 ft. lbs. (16–23 Nm).

10. Refill the brake master cylinder reservoir with clean, fresh brake fluid, meeting DOT 3 or DOT 4 specifications. Properly bleed the brake system.

Power Brake Booster

REMOVAL & INSTALLATION

▶ **See Figures 8 and 9**

1. Remove the rear anti-lock valve, combination valve and master cylinder.

2. Disconnect the vacuum hose from the power booster.

3. On transverse mounted boosters, remove the pivot bolt, O-ring and nut that attach the booster rod to the bell crank.

4. On inline mounted boosters, remove the steering column knee bolster for access to the brake pedal. Remove the clip that attaches the pushrod and disconnect the pushrod from the brake pedal.

5. Remove the power booster attaching nuts and remove the booster.

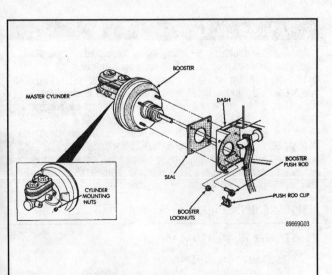

Fig. 8 In-line mounted brake booster assembly

To install:

6. Install the power booster and tighten to 18 ft. lbs. (23 Nm).

7. On inline mounted boosters, connect the pushrod to the brake pedal and install the clip. From inside the vehicle, install the steering column knee bolster.

8. On transverse mounted boosters, install the pivot bolt, O-ring and nut that attach the booster rod to the bell crank. Coat the eyelet with Lubriplate® or equivalent prior to assembly. Tighten the pivot bolt to 30 ft. lbs. (40 Nm).

9. Connect the vacuum hose to the power booster.

10. Install the master cylinder, combination valve and rear anti-lock valve.

11. Refill the brake master cylinder reservoir with clean, fresh brake fluid, meeting DOT 3 or DOT 4 specifications. Properly bleed the brake system.

Combination Valve

REMOVAL & INSTALLATION

▶ **See Figures 10, 11, 12, 13 and 14**

➡ **All models incorporate the brake safety switch into either the metering valve or combination metering/proportioning valve.**

1. Raise and safely support the vehicle securely on jackstands.

2. On transverse mount master cylinders, remove the windshield washer reservoir for access to the valve.

3. Remove the splash shield, as required.

4. Disconnect the wiring at the warning light switch.

5. On anti-lock brake equipped vehicles, remove the rear anti-lock valve.

6. Disconnect and plug the brake lines at the combination valve.

7. Unbolt and remove the valve from the frame.

To install:

8. Install the anti-lock brake valve or combination valve and tighten the mounting nut to 65–95 inch lbs. (7–11 Nm).

9. Connect the brake lines and tighten fittings with a flare nut wrench to 12–16 ft. lbs. (16–23 Nm).

10. Refill the brake master cylinder reservoir with clean, fresh brake fluid, meeting DOT 3 or DOT 4 specifications. Properly bleed the brake system.

11. Install the splash shield, as required.

12. On transverse mount master cylinders, install the windshield washer reservoir for access to the valve.

13. Lower the vehicle.

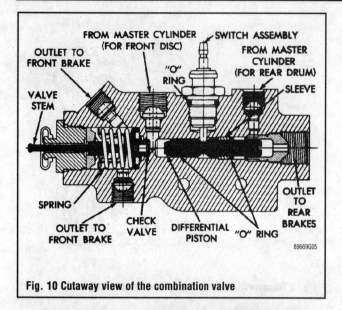

Fig. 10 Cutaway view of the combination valve

Fig. 13 Use a second wrench to hold the combination valve in place when loosening brake line fittings

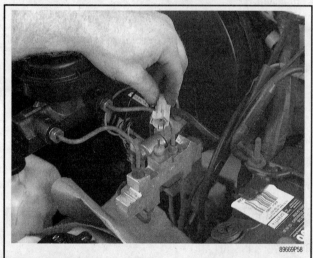

Fig. 11 The brake safety switch connector is located at the top of the combination valve

Fig. 14 Always use a line wrench when loosening brake line fittings

Fig. 12 The RWAL connector is located at the side of the combination valve

Brake Hoses and Lines

Metal lines and rubber brake hoses should be checked frequently for leaks and external damage. Metal lines are particularly prone to crushing and kinking under the vehicle. Any such deformation can restrict the proper flow of fluid and therefore impair braking at the wheels. Rubber hoses should be checked for cracking or scraping; such damage can create a weak spot in the hose and it could fail under pressure.

Any time the lines are removed or disconnected, extreme cleanliness must be observed. Clean all joints and connections before disassembly (use a stiff bristle brush and clean brake fluid); be sure to plug the lines and ports as soon as they are opened. New lines and hoses should be flushed clean with brake fluid before installation to remove any contamination.

REMOVAL & INSTALLATION

▶ See Figures 15, 16, 17 and 18

1. Disconnect the negative battery cable.
2. Raise and safely support the vehicle on jackstands.
3. Remove any wheel and tire assemblies necessary for access to the particular line you are removing.

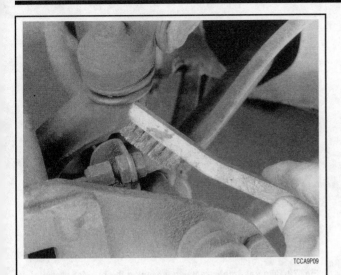

Fig. 15 Use a brush to clean the fittings of any debris

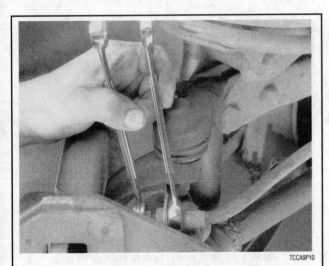

Fig. 16 Use two wrenches to loosen the fitting. If available, use flare nut type wrenches

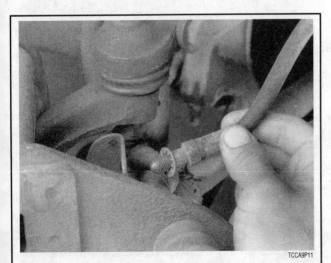

Fig. 17 Any gaskets/crush washers should be replaced with new ones during installation

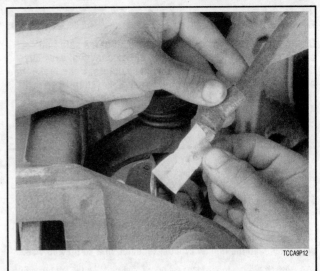

Fig. 18 Tape or plug the line to prevent contamination

4. Thoroughly clean the surrounding area at the joints to be disconnected.
5. Place a suitable catch pan under the joint to be disconnected.
6. Using two wrenches (one to hold the joint and one to turn the fitting), disconnect the hose or line to be replaced.
7. Disconnect the other end of the line or hose, moving the drain pan if necessary. Always use a back-up wrench to avoid damaging the fitting.
8. Disconnect any retaining clips or brackets holding the line and remove the line from the vehicle.

➡If the brake system is to remain open for more time than it takes to swap lines, tape or plug each remaining clip and port to keep contaminants out and fluid in.

To install:
9. Install the new line or hose, starting with the end farthest from the master cylinder. Connect the other end, then confirm that both fittings are correctly threaded and turn smoothly using finger pressure. Make sure the new line will not rub against any other part. Brake lines must be at least ½ in. (13mm) from the steering column and other moving parts. Any protective shielding or insulators must be reinstalled in the original location.

✳✳ WARNING

Make sure the hose is NOT kinked or touching any part of the frame or suspension after installation. These conditions may cause the hose to fail prematurely.

10. Using two wrenches as before, tighten each fitting.
11. Install any retaining clips or brackets on the lines.
12. If removed, install the wheel and tire assemblies, then carefully lower the vehicle to the ground.
13. Refill the brake master cylinder reservoir with clean, fresh brake fluid, meeting DOT 3 or DOT 4 specifications. Properly bleed the brake system.
14. Connect the negative battery cable.

Bleeding the Brake System

✳✳ CAUTION

Brake fluid contains polyglycol ethers and polyglycols. Avoid contact with the eyes and wash your hands thoroughly after handling brake fluid. If you do get brake fluid in your eyes, flush your eyes with clean, running water for 15 minutes. If eye irritation persists, or if you have taken brake fluid internally, IMMEDIATELY seek medical assistance.

Clean, high quality brake fluid is essential to the safe and proper operation of the brake system. You should always buy the highest quality brake fluid that is available. If the brake fluid becomes contaminated, drain and flush the system, then refill the master cylinder with new fluid. Never reuse any brake fluid. Any brake fluid that is removed from the system should be discarded. Also, do not allow any brake fluid to come in contact with a painted surface; it will damage the paint.

MASTER CYLINDER BLEEDING

▶ See Figure 19

➡This procedure can be performed with the master cylinder mounted in position on the vehicle. However, it is most commonly performed with the master cylinder mounted in a soft jawed vise.

1. Attach bleeder tubes to the cylinder outlet ports and insert tubes into the reservoir compartments. The bleeder tubes may be made up from brake line equipped with the correct master cylinder end fitting.

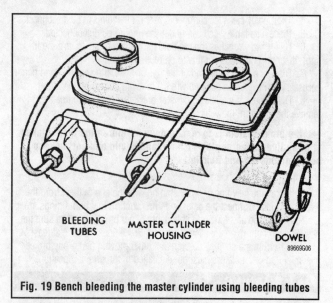

Fig. 19 Bench bleeding the master cylinder using bleeding tubes

2. Fill the brake master cylinder reservoir with clean, fresh brake fluid, meeting DOT 3 or DOT 4 specifications.
3. If performing this procedure off the vehicle, insert a wooden dowel into the piston end of the cylinder. Otherwise, use the brake pedal to operate the master cylinder piston.
4. Push the piston inward and release it. Continue this "pumping operation" until no air bubbles are visible in the brake fluid.
5. Correct the fluid level in the master cylinder as necessary.
6. Remove the bleeder lines, install the reservoir caps and install the master cylinder.

BRAKE SYSTEM BLEEDING

▶ See Figures 20, 21 and 22

When any part of the hydraulic system has been disconnected for repair or replacement, air may get into the lines and cause spongy pedal action (because air can be compressed and brake fluid cannot). To correct this condition, it is necessary to bleed the hydraulic system to be sure all air is purged.

When bleeding the brake system, bleed one brake component at a time, beginning at the wheel cylinder or caliper with the longest hydraulic line

Fig. 20 Take extreme care when loosening the bleeder screw, if rusted, to avoid rounding it off

Fig. 21 Attach a length of rubber hose to the bleeder screw and place the other end of the hose in a jar, submerged in brake fluid

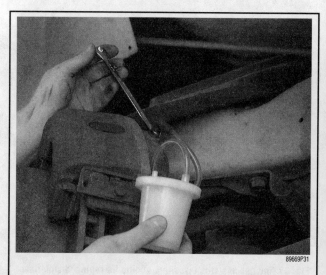

Fig. 22 Use a line wrench to open and close the bleeder screw

(farthest from the master cylinder). ALWAYS Keep the master cylinder reservoir filled with brake fluid during the bleeding operation. Never use brake fluid that has been drained from the hydraulic system, no matter how clean it is.

The primary and secondary hydraulic brake systems are separate and are bled independently. During the bleeding operation, do not allow the reservoir to run dry. Keep the master cylinder reservoir filled with brake fluid.

1. Clean all dirt from around the master cylinder fill cap
2. Fill the brake master cylinder reservoir with clean, fresh brake fluid, meeting DOT 3 or DOT 4 specifications, until the level is within ¼ in. (6mm) of the top edge of the reservoir.
3. Clean the bleeder screws at all 4 wheels, in addition to any bleeder screws located at the master cylinder or combination valve. The bleeder screws are located on the back of the brake support plate (drum brakes) and on the top of the brake calipers (disc brakes).
4. Attach a length of rubber hose over the bleeder screw and place the other end of the hose in a glass jar, submerged in brake fluid.

5. Open the bleeder screw ½–¾ turn. Have an assistant slowly depress the brake pedal.
6. Close the bleeder screw and tell your assistant to allow the brake pedal to return slowly. Continue this process to purge all air from the system.

➡ Do not pump the brake pedal during the bleeding procedure.

7. When bubbles cease to appear at the end of the bleeder hose, close the bleeder screw and remove the hose. Tighten the bleeder screw to 61–87 inch lbs. (7–9 Nm).
8. Check the master cylinder fluid level and add fluid accordingly. Do this after bleeding each wheel.
9. Repeat the bleeding operation at the remaining 3 wheels, ending with the one closet to the master cylinder.
10. Refill the brake master cylinder reservoir with clean, fresh brake fluid, meeting DOT 3 or DOT 4 specifications.

DISC BRAKES

✻✻ CAUTION

Older brake pads or shoes may contain asbestos, which has been determined to be cancer causing agent. Never clean the brake surfaces with compressed air! Avoid inhaling any dust from any brake surface! When cleaning brake surfaces, use a commercially available brake cleaning fluid.

Brake Pads

REMOVAL & INSTALLATION

▸ **See Figures 23, 24 and 25**

1. Drain some of the fluid from the master cylinder.
2. Raise and safely support the vehicle securely on jackstands.
3. Remove the wheels.
4. Remove the caliper from the adapter.
5. Suspend the caliper with wire to avoid damage to the flexible brake hose.

6. Remove the outboard pad from the caliper by prying between the pad and the caliper fingers.
7. Remove the inboard pad from the caliper support by the same method.

➡ Do not depress the brake pedal with the pads removed.

8. Push the caliper piston to the bottom of its bore. This may be done with a large C-clamp or a pair of large pliers by placing a flat metal bar against the piston and depressing the piston with a steady force. This operation will displace some of the fluid in the master cylinder.
9. Slide the new pads into the caliper and caliper support. The ears of the pad should rest on the bridges of the caliper.
10. Install the caliper on the adapter and tighten retaining bolts to 20 ft. lbs. (27 Nm).
11. Pump the brake pedal until it is firm.
12. Refill the brake master cylinder reservoir with clean, fresh brake fluid, meeting DOT 3 or DOT 4 specifications. As necessary, properly bleed the brake system.

➡ Failure to tighten the lug nuts to the proper torque in a star pattern may result in damage to the brake rotor.

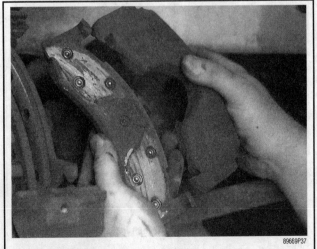

Fig. 23 Usually the outer pad will remain in the caliper when it is removed, while . . .

Fig. 24 . . . the inner pad will remain in the mounting bracket

Fig. 25 A suitable tool, like the one here from Lisle®, must be used to compress the piston into the caliper

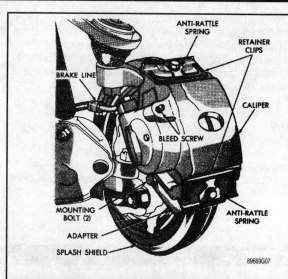

Fig. 26 Disc brake caliper mounting components

13. Install the wheels and lower the vehicle.
14. Check the brake pedal for a firm feel. Road test the vehicle.

INSPECTION

Inspect the brake pads for wear using a ruler or Vernier caliper. Compare measurements to the brake specifications chart. If the lining is thinner than specification on any part of the pad, or there is evidence of the lining being contaminated by brake fluid or oil, replace both brake pad assemblies (a complete axle set).

Brake Caliper

REMOVAL & INSTALLATION

▶ See Figures 26 thru 36

1. Raise and safely support the vehicle securely on jackstands.
2. Remove the wheels.
3. Disconnect the rubber brake hose from the tubing at the frame mount. Check the rubber hose for cracks or chafed spots.

➡If the piston is to be removed from the caliper, leave the brake hose connected to the caliper.

4. Plug the brake line to prevent loss of fluid.
5. Remove the retaining screw, clip and anti-rattle spring that attach the caliper to the adapter.
6. Carefully slide the caliper out and away from the disc. A small pry-bar may be necessary to free the caliper from the adapter.
7. If the old brake pads are being used, matchmark them for installation reference.
To install:
8. Position the outboard shoe in the caliper. The shoe should not rattle in the caliper. If it does, or if any movement is obvious, bend the shoe tabs over the caliper to tighten the fit.
9. Install the inboard shoe.
10. Lubricate the slide surfaces of the caliper with high temperature grease.
11. Slide the caliper into position on the adapter and over the rotor.

✳✳ WARNING

Take great care to avoid dislodging the piston dust boot!

12. Install the anti-rattle springs and retaining clips and tighten the retainer bolts to 20 ft. lbs. (27 Nm).
13. Connect the rubber brake hose to the tubing at the frame mount and tighten to 35 ft. lbs. (47 Nm).
14. Refill the brake master cylinder reservoir with clean, fresh brake fluid, meeting DOT 3 or DOT 4 specifications.
15. Properly bleed the brake system.
16. Install the wheels.

➡Failure to tighten the lug nuts to the proper torque in a star pattern may result in damage to the brake rotor.

17. Lower the vehicle.

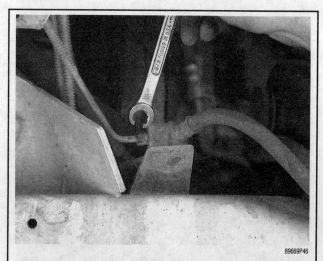

Fig. 27 Always use a line wrench when loosening brake line fittings

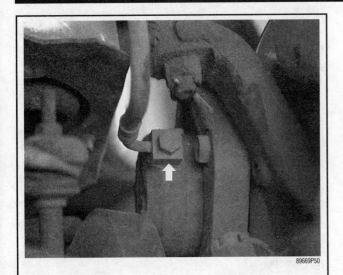

Fig. 28 The front brake caliper hose-to-caliper junction

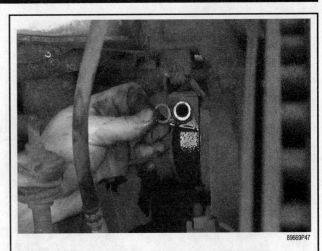

Fig. 31 There is a washer on the brake hose fitting at the caliper. Be sure not to lose this, since the hose will leak if it is not installed

Fig. 29 The front brake hose is attached to the caliper by a through-bolt

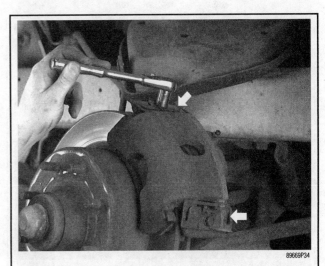

Fig. 32 On some models, the calipers are secured by retaining clips

Fig. 30 Disconnect the brake hose from the caliper

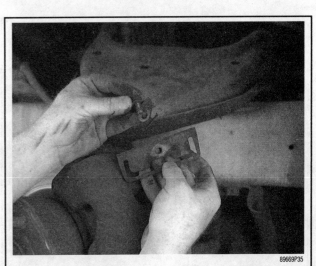

Fig. 33 View of the caliper retaining clip, along with the anti-rattle spring and bolt

Fig. 34 Slide the caliper off of the rotor

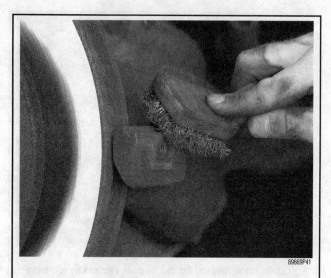

Fig. 35 Thoroughly clean the caliper slides before assembly

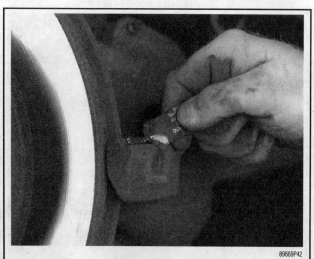

Fig. 36 Lubricate the caliper slides with the appropriate type of grease before installing the caliper

OVERHAUL

▶ See Figures 37 thru 44

➡ Some vehicles may be equipped dual piston calipers. The procedure to overhaul the caliper is essentially the same with the exception of multiple pistons, O-rings and dust boots.

1. Remove the caliper from the vehicle and place on a clean workbench.

✳✳ CAUTION

NEVER place your fingers in front of the pistons in an attempt to catch or protect the pistons when applying compressed air. This could result in personal injury!

➡ Depending upon the vehicle, there are two different ways to remove the piston from the caliper. Refer to the brake pad replacement procedure to make sure you have the correct procedure for your vehicle.

2. The first method is as follows:
   a. Stuff a shop towel or a block of wood into the caliper to catch the piston.

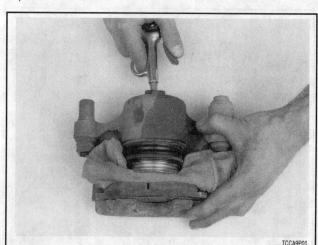

Fig. 37 For some types of calipers, use compressed air to drive the piston out of the caliper, but be sure to keep your fingers clear

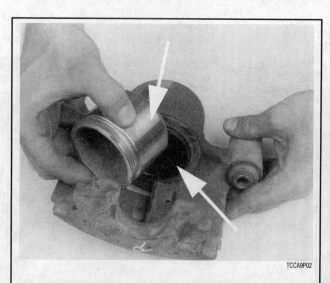

Fig. 38 Withdraw the piston from the caliper bore

b. Remove the caliper piston using compressed air applied into the caliper inlet hole. Inspect the piston for scoring, nicks, corrosion and/or worn or damaged chrome plating. The piston must be replaced if any of these conditions are found.

3. For the second method, you must rotate the piston to retract it from the caliper.

4. If equipped, remove the anti-rattle clip.

5. Use a prybar to remove the caliper boot, being careful not to scratch the housing bore.

6. Remove the piston seals from the groove in the caliper bore.

7. Carefully loosen the brake bleeder valve cap and valve from the caliper housing.

8. Inspect the caliper bores, pistons and mounting threads for scoring or excessive wear.

9. Use crocus cloth to polish out light corrosion from the piston and bore.

10. Clean all parts with denatured alcohol and dry with compressed air.

To assemble:

11. Lubricate and install the bleeder valve and cap.

12. Install the new seals into the caliper bore grooves, making sure they are not twisted.

13. Lubricate the piston bore.

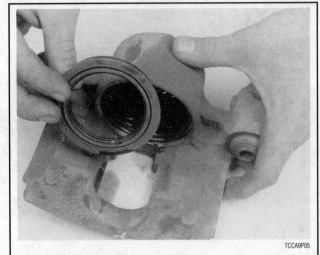

Fig. 41 . . . then remove the boot from the caliper housing, taking care not to score or damage the bore

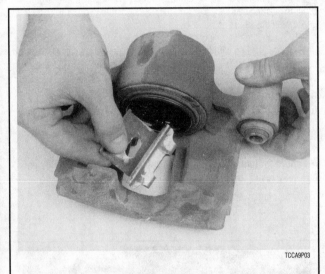

Fig. 39 On some vehicles, you must remove the anti-rattle clip

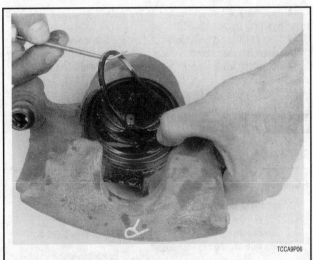

Fig. 42 Use extreme caution when removing the piston seal; DO NOT scratch the caliper bore

Fig. 40 Use a prybar to carefully pry around the edge of the boot . . .

Fig. 43 Use the proper size driving tool and a mallet to properly seal the boots in the caliper housing

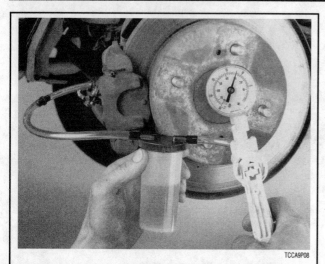

Fig. 44 There are tools, such as this Mighty-Vac, available to assist in proper brake system bleeding

14. Install the pistons and boots into the bores of the calipers and push to the bottom of the bores.

15. Use a suitable driving tool to seat the boots in the housing.

16. Install the caliper in the vehicle.

17. Install the wheel and tire assembly, then carefully lower the vehicle.

18. Properly bleed the brake system.

Brake Disc (Rotor)

REMOVAL & INSTALLATION

▶ **See Figures 45 thru 56**

1. Raise and safely support the vehicle securely on jackstands.
2. Remove the wheels.
3. Remove the caliper assembly and support it using a piece of mechanic's wire attached to the frame.

➡ **Do not disconnect the brake fluid hose or allow the caliper to hang by the hose.**

4. Remove the grease cap from the hub.
5. Remove the cotter pin, nut lock, adjusting nut and flat washer from the spindle.
6. Tilt the rotor slightly to remove the outer bearing assembly from the hub.
7. Pull the hub and disc assembly off the wheel spindle.
8. Remove and discard the old grease seal at the rear of the rotor.
9. Remove the inner bearing cone and roller assembly from the hub.

To install:

10. Clean all grease from the inner and outer bearing cups with solvent. Inspect the bearing races for pits, scratches, or excessive wear. If the races are damaged, remove them with a drift.

11. Clean the inner and outer cone and roller assemblies with solvent and dry them. If the cone and roller assemblies show excessive wear or damage, replace them as an assembly with new bearing races.

➡ **Do not dry the bearings with compressed air. Spinning the bearing without lubrication may cause damage.**

12. Clean the spindle and the inside of the hub with solvent to thoroughly remove all old grease.

13. If the inner and/or outer bearing cups were removed, install the replacement cups on the hub. Be sure that the cups seat properly in the hub.

➡ **It is imperative that all old grease be removed from the bearings and surrounding surfaces before repacking. The newer EP High Temperature Grease is not compatible with the sodium base grease used in the past.**

14. Use a bearing packer, if available, to pack the new bearings with grease. If not, work the grease in between the rollers and the outer and inner races of the bearing, using the palm of your hand. Work from the larger diameter of the bearing. Make sure the grease goes through the width of the bearing to the small diameter. Pack and install the inner bearing first.

15. Install the inner bearing grease seal with an appropriate driver.

16. Install the hub and disc on the wheel spindle. To prevent damage to the grease retainer and spindle threads, keep the hub centered on the spindle.

17. Install the outer bearing cone and roller assembly and the flat washer on the spindle. Install the adjusting nut.

18. Adjust the wheel bearings. Rotate the wheel, hub and rotor assembly while tightening the adjusting nut to 240–300 inch lbs. (27–34 Nm) in order to seat the bearings. Back off the adjusting nut ¼ turn (90°), then finger-tighten the adjusting nut.

19. Locate the nut lock on the adjusting nut so that the castellations on the lock are lined up with the cotter pin hole in the spindle. Install the new cotter pin, bending the ends of the cotter pin around the castellated flange of the nut lock.

➡ **Bend the ends of the cotter pin around the castellations of the locknut to prevent interference.**

20. Check the wheel for proper rotation, then install the grease cap.
21. Install the wheels.

➡ **Failure to tighten the lug nuts to the proper torque in a star pattern may result in damage to the brake rotor.**

22. Lower the vehicle.

Fig. 45 Pry off the dust cap to access the rotor retaining hardware

Fig. 46 Use needlenose pliers to remove the cotter pin

Fig. 47 Remove the nut lock

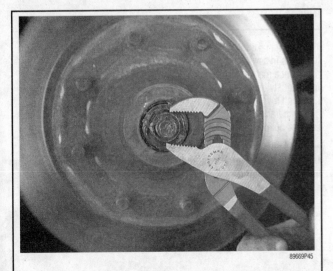

Fig. 48 Use a suitable tool to loosen the retaining nut

Fig. 49 After the nut is removed, place it and the washer in a safe place

Fig. 50 Remove the outer bearing and set it aside for a later inspection

Fig. 51 Remove the rotor from the spindle with care; be ready for the sudden weight when the rotor is no longer supported

Fig. 52 The wheel bearing grease seal, as installed on the rotor

Fig. 55 This bearing is an example of one that wasn't properly maintained; notice the sludge build-up from the old grease

Fig. 53 Use a suitable tool, such as this seal remover from Lisle®, to remove the grease seal from the rotor

Fig. 56 Always tighten the retaining nut to specifications after installing the rotor, to ensure proper wheel bearing adjustment

INSPECTION

Using a brake rotor micrometer or Vernier caliper measure the rotor thickness in several places around the rotor.

Mount a magnetic base dial indicator to the strut member and zero the indicator stylus on the face of the rotor. Rotate the rotor 360 degrees by hand and record the run-out.

Compare measurements to the brake specifications chart. If the thickness and run-out do not meet specifications, replace the rotor.

➡Rotor minimum thickness is cast or stamped into each rotor. If the value on the rotor disagrees with the values stated here, use the value on the rotor.

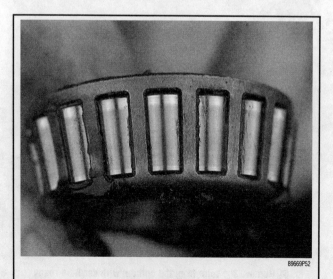

Fig. 54 Inspect the bearing rollers for wear

DRUM BRAKES

DRUM BRAKE COMPONENTS

1. Anchor bolt and spring
2. Parking brake lever
3. Primary brake shoe
4. Secondary brake shoe
5. Return spring (upper)
6. Hold-down spring
7. Hold-down pin
8. Wheel cylinder
9. Return spring (lower)
10. Automatic adjuster cable
11. Automatic adjuster
12. Automatic adjuster lever
13. Adjuster lever return spring

89669P69

✳✳ CAUTION

Older brake pads or shoes may contain asbestos, which has been determined to be cancer causing agent. Never clean the brake surfaces with compressed air! Avoid inhaling any dust from any brake surface! When cleaning brake surfaces, use a commercially available brake cleaning fluid.

Brake Drums

REMOVAL & INSTALLATION

▶ **See Figures 57, 58 and 59**

11 Inch Brakes

These brakes are used with a conventional axle assembly in 150 and 250 series vans.

1. Raise and safely support the vehicle securely on jackstands.
2. Remove the plug from the brake adjustment access hole.
3. Insert a thin bladed tool or a piece of stiff wire through the adjusting hole and hold the adjusting lever away from the star wheel.
4. Release the brake shoes by prying down against the star wheel with a brake adjusting tool.
5. Remove the rear wheel and clips from the wheel studs.

➡The brake drum may be filled with brake dust. Take all appropriate cautions to avoid inhaling the dust.

6. Remove the brake drum.

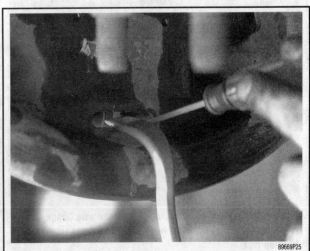

Fig. 57 Insert a screwdriver and adjusting tool through the access hole in the brake backing plate

89669P25

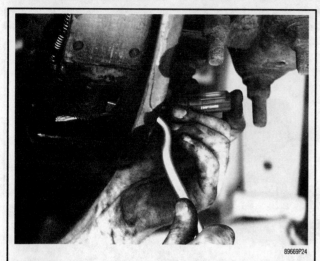

Fig. 58 Disengage the lever to relieve pressure from the star wheel

To install:

7. Position the brake drum on the hub.
8. Install the retaining clips on the studs.
9. Install the rear wheels.
10. Adjust the brake shoes prying up against the star wheel with a brake adjusting tool. The brakes should be adjusted so there is a slight drag on the wheel when rotated.
11. Lower the vehicle.

12 Inch Brakes

These brakes are used with a full floating axle assembly in 350 series vans.

1. Raise and safely support the vehicle securely on jackstands.
2. Remove the plug from the brake adjustment access hole.
3. Insert a thin bladed tool or a piece of stiff wire through the adjusting hole and hold the adjusting lever away from the star wheel.

4. Release the brake shoes by prying down against the star wheel with a brake adjusting tool.
5. Remove the axle shaft nuts, washers and cones. If the cones do not readily release, tap the axle shaft sharply in the center with a brass hammer.
6. Remove the axle shaft.
7. Remove the outer hub nut.
8. Straighten the lockwasher tab and remove it, along with the inner nut and bearing.

➡ The brake drum may be filled with brake dust. Take all appropriate precautions to avoid inhaling the dust.

9. Carefully remove the drum.
To install:
10. Position the drum on the axle housing.
11. Install the bearing and inner nut. While rotating the wheel and tire, tighten the adjusting nut until a slight drag is felt.
12. Back off the adjusting nut Z\n turn so that the wheel rotates freely without excessive end-play.
13. Install the lockrings and nut. Place a new gasket on the hub and install the axle shaft, cones, lockwashers and nuts.
14. Install the rear wheels.
15. Adjust the brake shoes prying up against the star wheel with a brake adjusting tool. The brakes should be adjusted so that there is a slight drag on the wheel when rotated.
16. Lower the vehicle.

INSPECTION

▶ **See Figure 60**

Check that there are no cracks or chips in the braking surface. Excessive bluing indicates overheating and a replacement drum is needed. The drum can be machined to remove minor damage and to establish a perfectly round braking surface on a warped drum. Never exceed the maximum oversize of the drum when machining the braking surface. The maximum inside diameter is stamped on the rim of the drum.

Fig. 59 Remove the drum by pulling it off the axle flange. It might be necessary to lightly tap with a hammer to remove built-up rust

Fig. 60 The maximum diameter stamping on the drum usually looks like this; you may have to clean it to read it clearly

Brake Shoes

INSPECTION

Inspect the brake pads for wear using a ruler or Vernier caliper. Compare measurements to the brake specifications chart. If the lining is thinner than specification on any part of the pad or there is evidence of the lining being contaminated by brake fluid or oil, replace both brake pad assemblies (a complete axle set).

REMOVAL & INSTALLATION

▶ **See Figures 61 thru 73**

1. Raise and safely support the vehicle securely on jackstands.
2. Remove the wheels.
3. Remove the brake drum. If the brake drum is difficult to remove, back off the brake pad self-adjuster.

➡**Never use compressed air to blow dust from brake components.**

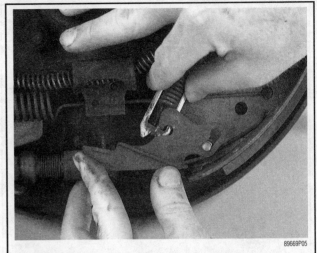

Fig. 63 Disconnect the automatic adjuster cable from the adjuster lever

Fig. 61 Brake shoe return springs are best removed by using brake spring pliers

Fig. 64 The adjuster cable is secured at the top of the support plate, near the wheel cylinder

Fig. 62 When removing the brake shoe return spring, note the direction it faces for installation reference

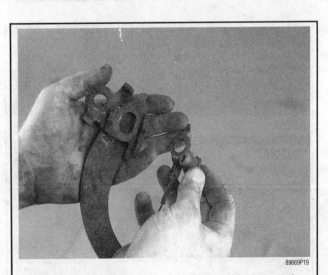

Fig. 65 Note the arrangement of the adjuster cable, lever and other components

Fig. 66 The adjuster lever is secured to the support plate with a pin

Fig. 69 The brake shoe retaining springs are composed of a hold-down spring and a pin

Fig. 67 Slide the adjuster lever down so the pin fits through the large end of the keyhole slot

Fig. 70 The parking brake cable fits into a slot on the parking brake lever

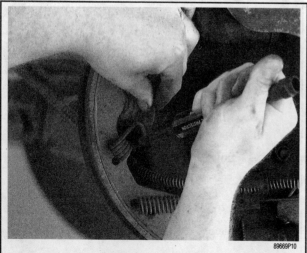

Fig. 68 Remove the brake shoe retaining springs using a suitable tool

Fig. 71 It is possible to remove both brake shoes simultaneously if the bottom brake spring and adjuster are left in place

Fig. 72 Always clean the brake shoe-to-support plate contact points . . .

Fig. 73 . . . and lubricate them with grease to prevent binding

4. Vacuum brake components to remove brake lining dust. If a vacuum is not available, use water dampened cloths or an appropriate brake cleaning fluid.

➡️**It is a good idea to only disassemble and assemble one side at a time, leaving the other side intact as a reference.**

5. Remove the brake shoe return springs, using suitable brake spring pliers.

6. Disconnect the automatic adjuster cable from the anchor and unhook it from the lever.

7. Remove the cable guide from the secondary shoe and anchor plate from the anchor pin.

8. Remove the adjuster lever. Disconnect the lever from the spring by sliding the lever down to clear the pivot and work the lever out from under the spring.

9. Disconnect and remove the brake shoe springs from the brake shoes.

10. Disconnect and remove the adjuster screw assembly from the brake shoes.

11. Remove the brake shoe retainers and springs.

12. Remove the secondary brake shoe from the support plate.

13. Remove the strut and spring.

14. Remove the parking brake lever from the secondary shoe.

15. Remove the primary shoe from the support plate

16. Disconnect the parking brake lever from the parking brake cable.

To install:

17. Thoroughly clean the support plate with brake cleaning solvent and dry completely.

18. Use silicone grease to lubricate the brake support plate-to-brake shoe contact areas.

19. Apply a light coating of grease to the threaded areas of the adjuster. Turn the adjuster in and out to spread the lubricant. Turn the adjuster all the way down on the screw and loosen one-half turn.

20. Connect the parking brake lever to the parking brake cable. Then connect the lever to the secondary shoe.

21. Install the primary shoe on the support plate

22. Install the spring on the parking brake strut and engage the strut on the primary shoe.

23. Install the secondary brake shoe on the support plate.

24. Insert strut into secondary shoe and guide shoe into anchor pin.

25. Install the anchor plate and adjuster cable eyelet on support plate anchor pin.

26. Install cable guide in secondary shoe and position cable in guide.

27. Assemble adjuster screw, then install between brake shoes.

➡️**Ensure the adjuster screws are installed on the correct side of the vehicle. The adjuster screws are marked "L" for left and "R" for right.**

28. Install the adjuster lever and spring and connect the adjuster cable to the lever.

29. Install the shoe retainers and springs.

30. Install the shoe return spring. Connect the spring to the secondary shoe first, and then to the primary shoe.

31. Verify adjuster operation. Pull adjuster cable upward, cable should lift lever and rotate star wheel.

➡️**Ensure that the adjuster lever properly engages the star wheel teeth.**

32. Install the brake drum and adjust the brake shoes.

33. Install the wheels.

34. Lower the vehicle.

ADJUSTMENTS

The drum brakes are self-adjusting and require a manual adjustment only after the brake shoes have been replaced, or when the length of the adjusting screw has been changed while performing some other service operation.

Drum Installed

▸ See Figures 57, 58 and 74

1. Raise and support the vehicle safely.

2. Remove the rubber plug from the adjusting slot on the support plate.

3. Insert a brake adjusting tool into the slot and engage the lowest possible tooth on the star wheel. Move the end of the brake spoon downward to move the star wheel upward and expand the adjusting screw. Repeat this operation until the brakes lock the wheels.

4. Insert a small screwdriver or piece of firm wire (coat hanger wire) into the adjusting slot and push the automatic adjusting lever out and free of the star wheel on the adjusting screw and hold it there.

5. Engage the topmost tooth possible on the star wheel with the brake adjusting spoon. Move the end of the adjusting spoon upward to move the adjusting screw star wheel downward and contract the adjusting screw. Back off the adjusting screw star wheel until the wheel spins freely with a minimum of drag. Keep track of the number of turns that the star wheel is backed off, or the number of strokes taken with the brake adjusting spoon.

6. Repeat this operation for the other side. When backing off the brakes on the other side, the star wheel adjuster must be backed off the same number of turns to prevent side-to-side brake pull.

7. When the brakes are adjusted, make several stops while backing the vehicle to equalize the brakes on both of the wheels.

8. Lower the vehicle.

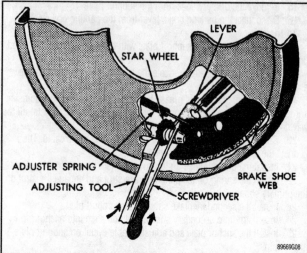

Fig. 74 Adjusting the service brakes—disengage the lever to relieve pressure from the star wheel

Drum Removed

1. Remove the brake drum.
2. Make sure that the shoe-to-contact pad areas are clean and properly lubricated.
3. Using a Brake Adjustment Gauge or equivalent, check the inside diameter of the drum.
4. Measure across the diameter of the assembled brake shoes, at their widest point.
5. Turn the adjusting screw so that the diameter of the shoes is 0.030 in. (0.76mm) less than the brake drum inner diameter.
6. Install the drum.

Wheel Cylinders

REMOVAL & INSTALLATION

◆ **See Figures 75, 76, 77 and 78**

1. Raise and safely support the vehicle securely on jackstands.
2. Remove the wheels.
3. Remove the brake drums and shoes.

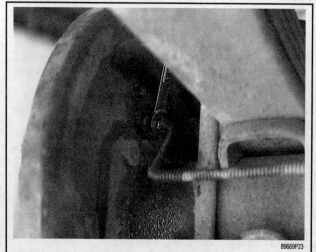

Fig. 75 The tool of choice for loosening brake line fittings is a line wrench

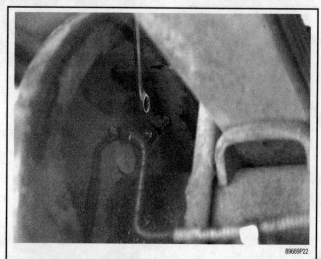

Fig. 76 Wheel cylinder mounting bolts are accessible from the rear of the support plate

Fig. 77 The hole in the support plate situates the wheel cylinder properly

Fig. 78 Take extreme care when loosening the bleeder screw, if rusted, as it can easily be rounded off

4. Loosen the brake fitting with a flare nut wrench. Disconnect and cap the brake hose.

5. Loosen the wheel cylinder attaching bolts and remove the wheel cylinder from the support plate.

To install:

6. Install the wheel cylinder and tighten the attaching bolts securely.

7. Uncap and connect and the brake hose. Tighten fitting securely with a flare nut wrench.

8. Install the brake drums and shoes.

9. Refill and bleed the brake system.

10. Install the wheels.

11. Lower the vehicle.

OVERHAUL

♦ **See Figures 79 thru 88**

Wheel cylinder overhaul kits may be available, but often at little or no savings over a reconditioned wheel cylinder. It often makes sense with

these components to substitute a new or reconditioned part instead of attempting an overhaul.

If no replacement is available, or you would prefer to overhaul your wheel cylinders, the following procedure may be used. When rebuilding and installing wheel cylinders, avoid getting any contaminants into the system. Always use clean, new, high quality brake fluid. If dirty or improper fluid has been used, it will be necessary to drain the entire system, flush the system with proper brake fluid, replace all rubber components, then refill and bleed the system.

1. Remove the wheel cylinder from the vehicle and place on a clean workbench.

2. First remove and discard the old rubber boots, then withdraw the pistons. Piston cylinders are equipped with seals and a spring assembly, all located behind the pistons in the cylinder bore.

3. Remove the remaining inner components, seals and spring assembly. Compressed air may be useful in removing these components. If no compressed air is available, be VERY careful not to score the wheel cylinder bore when removing parts from it. Discard all components for which replacements were supplied in the rebuild kit.

Fig. 79 Remove the outer boots from the wheel cylinder

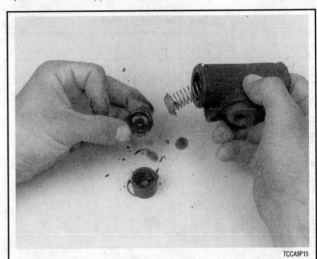

Fig. 81 Remove the pistons, cup seals and spring from the cylinder

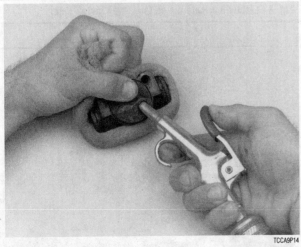

Fig. 80 Compressed air can be used to remove the pistons and seals

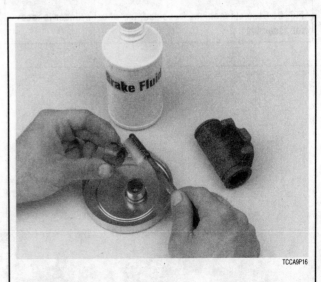

Fig. 82 Use brake fluid and a soft brush to clean the pistons . . .

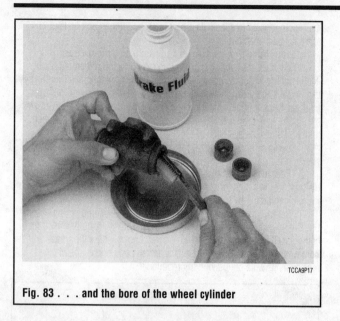

Fig. 83 . . . and the bore of the wheel cylinder

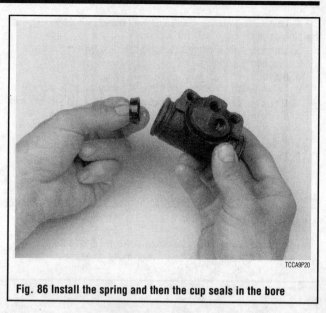

Fig. 86 Install the spring and then the cup seals in the bore

Fig. 84 Once cleaned and inspected, the wheel cylinder is ready for assembly

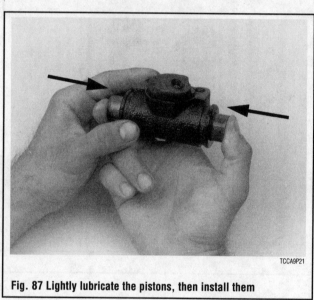

Fig. 87 Lightly lubricate the pistons, then install them

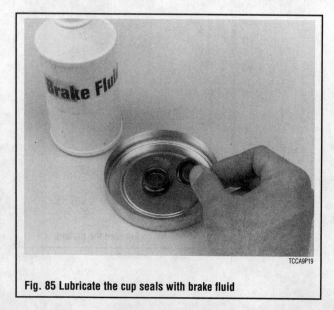

Fig. 85 Lubricate the cup seals with brake fluid

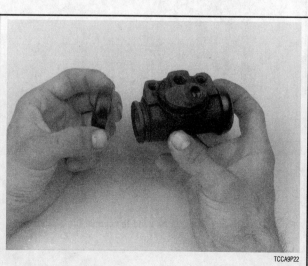

Fig. 88 The boots can now be installed over the wheel cylinder ends

4. Wash the cylinder and metal parts in denatured alcohol or clean brake fluid.

✳✳ WARNING

Never use a mineral-based solvent such as gasoline, kerosene or paint thinner for cleaning purposes. These solvents will swell rubber components and quickly deteriorate them.

PARKING BRAKE

Cables

REMOVAL & INSTALLATION

Front Cable

1. Raise and safely support the vehicle securely on jackstands.
2. Disconnect the cable spring.
3. Loosen the adjusting nut at the equalizer to create slack in the cable.
4. Remove the clips retaining the cable to the under side of the vehicle.
5. Lower the vehicle.
6. Remove the cable grommet on the floorboard inside the driver's compartment.
7. Compress and remove the cable retainer from the pedal bracket.
8. Loosen the cable retaining clamp screw and push the ball end of the cable out of the pedal assembly and slide the cable out.
9. Remove the front cable assembly from the vehicle through the engine compartment.
   To install:
10. Route the cable through the engine compartment and place the cable in position.
11. Insert the cable retainer into the hole in the pedal assembly and seat securely.
12. Engage the cable ball end in the cleaves on the pedal assembly.
13. Install the cable grommet.
14. Raise and safely support the vehicle securely on jackstands.
15. Route the cable under the vehicle, installing the retaining clips.
16. Connect the cable to the equalizer and tighten nut to take up slack in the cable.
17. Connect the cable spring.

Rear Cable

▶ See Figures 89 and 90

1. Release the parking brake.
2. Raise and safely support the vehicle securely on jackstands.
3. Loosen the rear cable adjuster nut and disconnect the rear cable from the equalizer.
4. Remove the clips that secure the rear cable to the under side of the vehicle.
5. Remove the rear wheel and brake drum and brake shoes.
6. Using a small (mini) hose clamp, compress the fingers on the cable retainer.
7. Pull the cable through the support plate just enough to clear the retaining fingers.
8. Remove the hose clamp and pull the cable through the support plate.
   To install:
9. Install the cable in the support plate and snap the attaching fingers into place.
10. Connect the cable to the parking brake lever.

11. Install the brake shoes and brake drum.
12. Connect the cable to the equalizer.
13. Mount the cable in the retaining clips under the vehicle.
14. Adjust the parking brake.
15. Lower the vehicle.

5. Allow the parts to air dry or use compressed air. Do not use rags for cleaning, since lint will remain in the cylinder bore.
6. Inspect the piston and replace it if it shows scratches.
7. Lubricate the cylinder bore and seals using clean brake fluid.
8. Position the spring assembly.
9. Install the inner seals, then the pistons.
10. Insert the new boots into the counterbores by hand. Do not lubricate the boots.
11. Install the wheel cylinder.

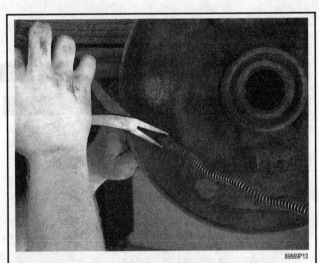

Fig. 89 A pair of pliers (shown) or a small hose clamp can be used to release the cable from the support plate

Fig. 90 The rear cable is shrouded in metal to prevent abrasion

ADJUSTMENT

◆ **See Figure 91**

➡Ensure that the service brakes are properly adjusted prior to adjusting the parking brakes.

1. Raise and safely support the vehicle securely on jackstands.
2. Release the parking brake lever and loosen the cable adjusting nut to be sure that the cable is slack.
3. Tighten the cable adjusting nut until a slight drag is felt while rotating the wheels.
4. Loosen the cable adjusting nut until the wheels can be rotated freely, then back off the cable adjusting nut two turns.
5. Apply the parking brake several times, then release it and check to be sure that the rear wheels rotate freely.

Fig. 91 Adjust the brake cable tension at the cable adjusting nut as illustrated

REAR WHEEL ANTI-LOCK (RWAL) BRAKE SYSTEM

General Information

The RWAL brake system uses a standard master cylinder and booster arrangement with a split hydraulic circuit. An electronic control module, rear wheel speed sensor and a hydraulic pressure valve are the major components of the system.

There are some minor changes in brake lines, hoses and electrical circuits to accommodate RWAL on models so equipped. No hydraulic pumps are used; brake pressure comes directly from the pedal application. The system provides stability by allowing at least one rear wheel to remain unlocked. It's still possible to lock the front wheels, since this system works on the rear wheels only.

An amber Anti-Lock warning light is installed on the instrument panel along with the standard red brake warning lights. Looking for this amber warning light is the quickest way of determining whether or not the vehicle is equipped with RWAL.

A speed sensor is mounted to the top of the rear differential housing. A toothed exciter ring is press fit onto the differential case next to the differential ring gear and provides the signal for the sensor.

The electronic control module is located on the lower right side cowl panel. The control module monitors the rear wheel speed and controls the dual solenoid valve. The module also performs a system self-check every time the ignition switch is turned from the **OFF** to the **ON** position.

The hydraulic pressure valve allows brake fluid to flow freely between the master cylinder and the rear brakes under normal operating conditions. Once anti-lock braking begins, the control module triggers the valve to either isolate or reduce pressure to the rear wheels.

Fault Codes

If a system fault is detected during the self-test, or at any other time, the control module will illuminate the Anti-Lock indicator lamp and store the fault code in the microprocessor memory. If a fault code is generated, the module will remember the code after the ignition is switched **OFF**. The microprocessor memory will store and display only one fault code at a time. The stored code can be displayed by grounding the RWAL diagnostic connector and counting the number of flashes on the indicator lamp. To clear the fault code, disconnect the control module connector or disconnect the battery for at least 5 seconds. During system retest, wait 30 seconds to make sure the fault code does not reappear.

FAULT CODE NUMBER	TYPICAL FAILURE DETECTED
1	Not used.
2	Open isolation valve wiring or bad control module.
3	Open dump valve wiring or bad control module.
4	Closed RWAL valve switch.
5	Over 16 dump pulses generated in 2WD vehicles (disabled for 4WD).
6	Erratic speed sensor reading while rolling.
7	Electronic control module fuse pellet open, isolation output missing, or valve wiring shorted to ground.
8	Dump output missing or valve wiring shorted to ground.
9	Speed sensor wiring/resistance (usually high reading).
10	Sensor wiring/resistance (usually low reading).
11	Brake switch always on. RWAL light comes on when speed exceeds 40 mph.
12	Not used.
13	Electronic control module phase lock loop failure.
14	Electronic control module program check failure.
15	Electronic control module RAM failure.

89669G09

Speed Sensor

TESTING

Resistance

1. Raise and safely support the vehicle securely on jackstands.
2. Ensure the ignition key is in the **OFF** position.
3. Disconnect the speed sensor electrical harness.
4. Measure resistance between the terminals on the speed sensor
5. Resistance should be 1000–2500 ohms.
6. If resistance is not within specification, check the harness for continuity.
7. If continuity exists, the sensor is faulty.

Air Gap

▶ **See Figures 92 and 93**

1. Raise and safely support the vehicle securely on jackstands.
2. Remove the sensor from the differential.
3. Measure and record the distance from the underside of the sensor flange to the end of the sensor pole piece. This distance represents dimen-

sion "B". This dimension should be 1.07–1.08 in. (27.18–27.43mm). If dimension is not within specification, replace the speed sensor.
4. Measure and record the distance between the sensor mounting surface of the differential case and the teeth at the top of the exciter ring. This distance represents dimension "A". This dimension should be 1.085–1.120 in. (27.56–28.45mm). If dimension is not within specification, replace the exciter ring.
5. Subtract dimension "B" from dimension "A" to determine sensor air gap. The gap should be 0.005–0.050 in. (0.127–1.27mm).

REMOVAL & INSTALLATION

▶ **See Figures 94, 95 and 96**

1. Raise the vehicle and support it safely.
2. Remove the sensor hold-down bolt.
3. Remove the sensor shield and sensor from the differential by pulling the sensor straight out.
4. Disconnect the wiring and remove the sensor.
To install:
5. Connect the wiring to the sensor. Make sure the seal is in place between the sensor and wiring connector.

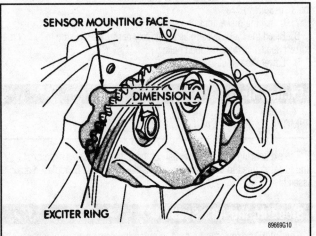

Fig. 92 Measure and record the distance between the sensor mounting surface of the differential case and the teeth at the top of the exciter ring

Fig. 94 The rear wheel speed sensor connector is located at the top of the rear axle's differential housing

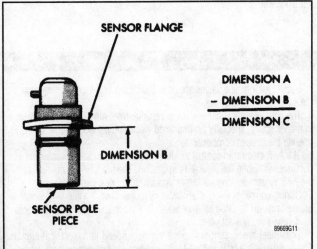

Fig. 93 Measure and record the distance from the underside of the sensor flange to the end of the sensor pole piece

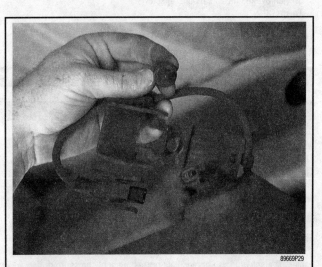

Fig. 95 The sensor wire harness is attached to the rear axle with a single bolt

89669P30

Fig. 96 The magnetic speed sensor fits inside a hole in the rear axle, and reads off a tone ring on the ring gear

6. Install the sensor into the differential housing, making sure the new O-ring is in place.
7. Install the sensor shield.
8. Install the sensor hold-down bolt and tighten it to 170–230 inch lbs. (19–29 Nm).
9. Lower the vehicle.

Control Module

TESTING

To properly diagnose the control module, a scan tool capable of reading ABS codes (DRB, DRB-II, DRB-III or equivalent) is necessary. Because of the complexity of the ABS system and the importance of correct system functioning, it is recommended to have a qualified automotive technician test the system if any problems have been detected.

REMOVAL & INSTALLATION

1. Disconnect the negative battery cable.
2. Label and disconnect the module electrical harness.
3. Remove the module mounting screws.
To install:
4. Position the module in the vehicle and tighten mounting screws to 21 inch lbs. (2 Nm).

FOUR WHEEL ANTI-LOCK BRAKE SYSTEM

General Information

The Four Wheel Anti-lock Brake System (ABS) is designed to prevent wheel lock-up during braking under virtually any road surface conditions. This allows the driver to retain greater control of the vehicle during braking. The Four Wheel ABS has a three-channel design. The front brake anti-lock valve provides two channel pressure control of the front brakes. Each front wheel brake unit is controlled separately. Two solenoid valves are used in each control channel.

The rear brake anti-lock valve controls the rear wheel brakes in tandem. The rear brake valve contains two solenoid valves.

The front and rear anti-lock valves contain electrically operated solenoid valves. The solenoid valves modulate brake fluid apply pressure during

5. Connect the electrical harness.
6. Connect the negative battery cable.

Hydraulic Valve

TESTING

To properly diagnose the hydraulic valve, a scan tool capable of reading ABS codes (DRB, DRB-II, DRB-III or equivalent) is necessary. Because of the complexity of the ABS system and the importance of correct system functioning, it is recommended to have a qualified automotive technician test the system if any problems have been detected.

REMOVAL & INSTALLATION

1. Raise the vehicle and support it safely.
2. Remove the brake lines from the hydraulic valve.
3. Remove the nuts attaching the valve to the frame rail.
4. Remove the valve from the frame and disconnect the wiring.
To install:
5. Connect the wiring to the control valve.
6. Install the valve on the frame. Tighten the mounting bolts to 16–25 ft. lbs. (21–34 Nm).
7. Install the brake lines.
8. Bleed the brake system as previously described. Be sure to follow the correct sequence, as described below.
9. Lower the vehicle.

Exciter Ring

REMOVAL & INSTALLATION

The exciter ring is an integral part of the differential case. If the exciter ring is determined to be faulty, the differential case must be replaced as an assembly.

Bleeding the ABS System

The RWAL system can be bled in much the same way as a conventional brake system. Bleeding can be performed manually or with vacuum/pressure equipment, as long as the recommended bleeding sequence is followed. Bleed only one brake component at a time. The recommended bleeding sequence is: master cylinder, combination valve, rear anti-lock valve, left rear wheel, right rear wheel, right front wheel, left front wheel.

anti-lock braking. The valves are operated by the anti-lock electronic module.

The anti-lock electrical system is separate from other electrical circuits in the vehicle. A specially programmed electronic control module is used to operate the system components.

The ABS electronic control module monitors wheel speed sensor inputs continuously while the vehicle is in motion. The module will not activate the ABS system as long as sensor inputs indicate normal braking.

During normal braking, the master cylinder, power booster and wheel brakes units all function as they would in a vehicle without ABS. The solenoid valves are not activated.

The wheel speed sensors converts wheel speed into electrical signals. These signals are transmitted to the module for processing and determine wheel lock-up and deceleration rate. When a wheel speed sensor signal indicate the onset of wheel lock-up the ABS braking is activated.

The anti-lock system retards the lockup conditions by modulating fluid apply pressure to the wheel brake units. The pressure is modulated according to wheel speed, degree of lock-up and rate of deceleration. The solenoid valves are cycled continuously to modulate pressure. Solenoid cycle time in anti-lock mode can be measured in milliseconds.

Fault Codes

If a system fault is detected during the self-test, or at any other time, the control module will illuminate the Anti-Lock indicator lamp and store the fault code in the microprocessor memory. If a fault code is generated, the module will remember the code after the ignition is switched **OFF**. The stored code can be only be displayed by using a scan tool.

FOUR WHEEL ANTI-LOCK BRAKE DIAGNOSTIC CODES

The anti-lock brake system module may report any of the following diagnostic trouble codes:

(21) Right Front Sensor Open
(22) No Signal From Right Front Sensor
(23) Intermittent Signal From Right Front Sensor

(25) Left Front Sensor Open
(26) No Signal From Left Front Sensor
(27) Intermittent Signal From Left Front Sensor

(35) Rear Sensor Open
(36) No Signal From Rear Sensor
(37) Intermittent Signal From Rear Sensor

(38) Wheel Speed Mismatch

(41) Right Front Isolation Solenoid Open
(42) Right Front Dump Solenoid Open
(43) Right Front Isolation Solenoid Shorted
(44) Right Front Dump Solenoid Shorted

(45) Left Front Isolation Solenoid Open
(46) Left Front Dump Solenoid Open
(47) Left Front Isolation Solenoid Shorted
(48) Left Front Dump Solenoid Shorted

(51) Rear Isolation Solenoid Open
(52) Rear Dump Solenoid Open
(53) Rear Isolation Solenoid Open
(54) Rear Dump Solenoid Shorted

(61) Right Front Reset Switch Closed
(62) Left Front Reset Switch Closed
(63) Rear Reset Switch Closed

(65) Main Relay Open
(66) Main Relay Shorted

(67) Pump Motor Circuit Open
(68) Pump Motor Stalled

(70) Controller/Vehicle Mismatch
(71) RAM Read/Write
(72) ROM Checksum
(73) Watchdog
(78) Foundation Brake

(81) Brake Switch Circuit
(88) Brake Warning Lamp (Red) Circuit
(89) ABS Warning Lamp Circuit

89669C02

Speed Sensors

TESTING

1. Raise and safely support the vehicle securely on jackstands.
2. Ensure the ignition key is in the **OFF** position.
3. Disconnect the speed sensor electrical harness.
4. Measure resistance between the terminals on the speed sensor
5. Resistance should be 1000–2500 ohms.
6. If resistance is not within specification, check harness for continuity.
7. If continuity exists, sensor is faulty.

REMOVAL & INSTALLATION

Front

▶ **See Figure 97**

1. Raise and safely support the vehicle securely on jackstands.
2. Remove the wheels.
3. Remove the disc brake caliper and rotor.
4. Remove the sensor mounting bolts.

➡ **The sensor uses special mounting bolts. These bolts have a unique shoulder, thread length and surface treatment. Use only factory replacement bolts; do NOT use substitute bolts.**

5. Label and disconnect the speed sensor harness.
6. Remove the sensor.
7. If sensor harness is to be replaced, remove the clips securing the sensor wire to the control arm and inner fender panel.

To install:

8. If the sensor harness was replaced, attach the sensor wire using clips.
9. Connect the speed sensor harness.
10. Install the sensor and tighten mounting bolts to 190 inch lbs. (21 Nm).
11. Install the disc brake caliper and rotor.
12. Install the wheels.
13. Lower the vehicle.

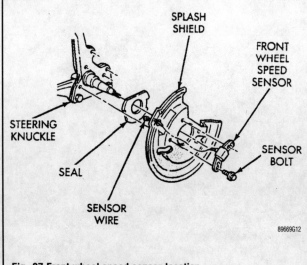

Fig. 97 Front wheel speed sensor location

Rear

▶ **See Figure 98**

1. Raise the vehicle and support it safely.
2. Remove the sensor hold-down bolt.
3. Remove the sensor shield and sensor from the differential by pulling the sensor straight out.
4. Disconnect the wiring and remove the sensor.

To install:

5. Connect the wiring to the sensor. Make sure the seal is in place between the sensor and wiring connector.
6. Install the sensor into the differential housing, making sure the new O-ring is in place.
7. Install the sensor shield.
8. Install the sensor hold-down bolt and tighten it to 170–230 inch lbs. (19–29 Nm).
9. Lower the vehicle.

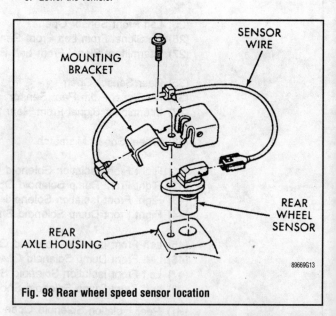

Fig. 98 Rear wheel speed sensor location

Control Module

TESTING

To properly diagnose the control module, a scan tool capable of reading ABS codes (DRB, DRB II, DRB III or equivalent) is necessary. Because of the complexity of the ABS system and the importance of correct system functioning, it is recommended to have a qualified automotive technician test the system if any problems have been detected.

REMOVAL & INSTALLATION

1. Disconnect the negative battery cable.
2. Remove the windshield washer and engine coolant recovery reservoirs, as necessary, to gain access to the module.
3. Label and disconnect the module electrical harness.
4. Remove the module mounting screws.

To install:

5. Position the module in the vehicle and tighten mounting screws to 21 inch lbs. (2 Nm).
6. Connect the electrical harness.

7. Install the windshield washer and engine coolant recovery reservoirs, if removed.

8. Connect the negative battery cable.

Hydraulic Valve

TESTING

To properly diagnose the hydraulic valve, a scan tool capable of reading ABS codes (DRB, DRB-II, DRB-III or equivalent) is necessary. Because of the complexity of the ABS system and the importance of correct system functioning, it is recommended to have a qualified automotive technician test the system if any problems have been detected.

REMOVAL & INSTALLATION

1. Raise the vehicle and support it safely.
2. Remove the brake lines from the hydraulic valve.
3. Remove the nuts attaching the valve to the frame rail.
4. Remove the valve from the frame and disconnect the wiring.

To install:

5. Connect the wiring to the control valve.
6. Install the valve on the frame. Tighten the mounting bolts to 16–25 ft. lbs. (21–34 Nm).
7. Install the brake lines.
8. Bleed the brake system as described below.
9. Lower the vehicle.

Exciter Ring

REMOVAL & INSTALLATION

The exciter ring is an integral part of the differential case. If the exciter ring is determined to be faulty, the differential case must be replaced as an assembly.

Bleeding the ABS System

♦ **See Figures 99 and 100**

The 4-Wheel Anti-Lock system can be bled in much the same way as a conventional brake system. Bleeding manually or with vacuum/pressure equipment can be performed as long as the recommended bleeding sequence is followed. Bleed only one brake component at a time. The recommended bleeding sequence is: master cylinder, combination valve, rear anti-lock valve, front anti-lock valve, left rear wheel, right rear wheel, right front wheel, left front wheel.

If a new front anti-lock valve assembly is installed, bleed the new valve as follows:

1. Loosen the bleed plug on the new front valve about ¼ to one full turn. The plug must be open to fully bleed the upper and lower sections of the front hydraulic valve.
2. Remove the cap from the bleed valve stem.
3. Install a valve depressor tool, or equivalent. A helper can also be used to hold the valve in the proper position. Insert the tool on the valve stem by sliding the notched side of tool onto the boss that surrounds the bleed valve stem.
4. Tighten the thumbscrew on the tool just enough to push the valve stem inward about 0.020–0.030 in. (0.51–0.76mm). The stem must be held

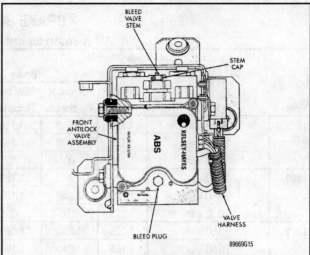

Fig. 99 Note the bleeding component locations of the front anti-lock valve assembly

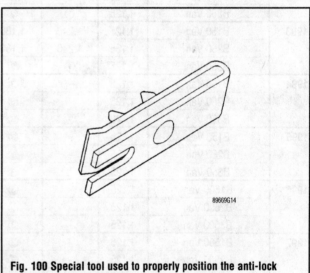

Fig. 100 Special tool used to properly position the anti-lock valve when bleeding the brakes

inward in an open position to fully bleed the upper section of the new valve assembly.

5. Apply the brake pedal. The pedal will fall off significantly when the bleed plug is properly open and the bleed valve stem is correctly unseated (pressed inward).
6. Rapidly depress the brake pedal 5–10 times. This action will fill the upper and lower sections of the valve rapidly.
7. Bleed the new valve assembly at each brake line. Only bleed one fitting at a time. Remember to close the valve bleeding plug before each brake pedal stroke. Continue bleeding until fluid flowing from the fittings is clear and free of bubbles.
8. Remove the depressor tool from the valve stem and install the cap on the stem. Then, tighten the bleed plug to 60–84 inch lbs. (7–9 Nm).

➡**If the original front anti-lock assembly is being used, the bleed plug and bleed valve do not have to be open during bleeding operations.**

BRAKE SPECIFICATIONS
All measurements in inches unless noted

Year	Model	Master Cylinder Bore	Brake Disc			Brake Drum Diameter			Minimum Lining Thickness	
			Original Thickness	Minimum Thickness	Maximum Run-out	Original Inside Diameter	Max. Wear Limit	Maximum Machine Diameter	Front	Rear
1989	B150 Van	1.125	1.240	1.180	0.004	11.00	11.09	11.06	0.062	0.062
	B250 Van	1.125	1.240	1.180	0.004	11.00	11.09	11.06	0.062	0.062
	B350 Van	1.125	①	②	0.004	12.00	12.09	12.06	0.062	0.062
1990	B150 Van	1.125	1.240	1.180	0.004	11.00	11.09	11.06	0.062	0.062
	B250 Van	1.125	1.240	1.180	0.004	11.00	11.09	11.06	0.062	0.062
	B350 Van	1.125	①	②	0.004	12.00	12.09	12.06	0.062	0.062
1991	B150 Van	1.125	1.240	1.180	0.004	11.00	11.09	11.06	0.062	0.062
	B250 Van	1.125	1.240	1.180	0.004	11.00	11.09	11.06	0.062	0.062
	B350 Van	1.125	①	②	0.004	12.00	12.09	12.06	0.062	0.062
1992	B150 Van	1.125	1.240	1.180	0.004	11.00	11.09	11.06	0.062	0.062
	B250 Van	1.125	1.240	1.180	0.004	11.00	11.09	11.06	0.062	0.062
	B350 Van	1.125	①	②	0.004	12.00	12.09	12.06	0.062	0.062
1993	B150 Van	1.125	1.240	1.180	0.004	11.00	11.09	11.06	0.062	0.062
	B250 Van	1.125	1.240	1.180	0.004	11.00	11.09	11.06	0.062	0.062
	B350 Van	1.125	①	②	0.004	12.00	12.09	12.06	0.062	0.062
1994	B150 Van	1.125	-	③	0.004	11.00	11.09	11.06	0.125	0.062 ④
	B250 Van	1.125	-	③	0.004	11.00	11.09	11.06	0.125	0.062 ④
	B350 Van	1.125	-	③	0.004	12.00	12.09	12.06	0.125	0.062 ④
1995	B150 Van	1.125	-	③	0.004	11.00	11.09	11.06	0.125	0.062 ④
	B250 Van	1.125	-	③	0.004	11.00	11.09	11.06	0.125	0.062 ④
	B350 Van	1.125	-	③	0.004	12.00	12.09	12.06	0.125	0.062 ④
1996	B1500 Van	1.125	-	③	0.004	11.00	11.09	11.06	0.125	0.062 ④
	B2500 Van	1.125	-	③	0.004	11.00	11.09	11.06	0.125	0.062 ④
	B3500 Van	1.125	-	③	0.004	12.00	12.09	12.06	0.125	0.062 ④
1997	B1500 Van	1.125	-	③	0.004	11.00	11.09	11.06	0.125	0.062 ④
	B2500 Van	1.125	-	③	0.004	11.00	11.09	11.06	0.125	0.062 ④
	B3500 Van	1.125	-	③	0.004	12.00	12.09	12.06	0.125	0.062 ④
1998	B1500 Van	1.125	-	③	0.004	11.00	11.09	11.06	0.125	0.062 ④
	B2500 Van	1.125	-	③	0.004	11.00	11.09	11.06	0.125	0.062 ④
	B3500 Van	1.125	-	③	0.004	12.00	12.09	12.06	0.125	0.062 ④

① Except 4000 lb. rear axle: 1.240 in.
With 4000 lb. rear axle: 1.180 in.
② With 3300 lb. or 3600 lb. rear axle: 1.180 in.
With 4000 lb. rear axle: 1.125 in.
③ Minimum thickness indicated on rotor hub
④ For riveted brake shoes: 0.031

89669C01

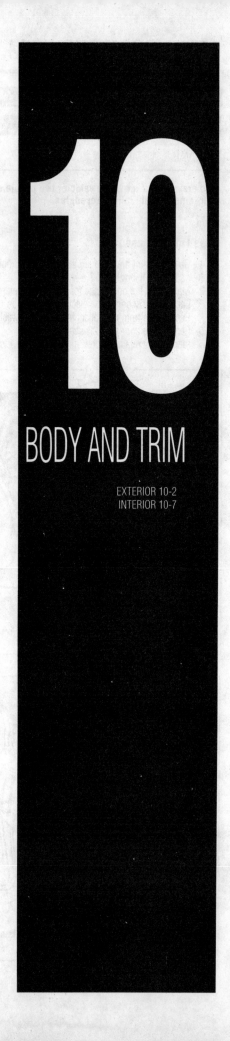

10

BODY AND TRIM

EXTERIOR

Doors

REMOVAL & INSTALLATION

➡ **To prevent damage to the vehicle, two people should perform the door removal/installation procedures.**

Front

▶ **See Figures 1 and 2**

1. Open the front door and support it using a floor jack. This is where a helper comes in handy.
2. Matchmark the door hinge for installation reference.
3. Label and disconnect the electrical harnesses.
4. Remove the front door attaching bolts and washers.
5. Remove the door from the vehicle.
6. Identify and retain the door hinge shims for installation.

To install:

7. Lubricate the door hinges with engine oil.
8. Position the door on the vehicle using the proper amount of shims and hand-tighten the attaching bolts.
9. Align the matchmarks and tighten the door attaching bolts to 26 ft. lbs. (35 Nm).
10. Carefully close the door to check for proper alignment.
11. Readjust door alignment as necessary.

Sliding Side

▶ **See Figures 3 thru 8**

1. Remove the lower rear screw from the roller track cover, body sheet metal side.
2. Remove the 2 bolts securing the upper hinge assembly mounting plate and remove the plate.
3. Remove the 2 screws securing the lower roller bracket to the door lower roller bracket support assembly.

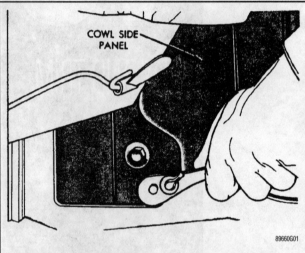

Fig. 1 The front door's lower attaching bolt is accessible after removing the cowl side panel

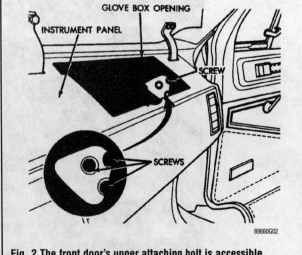

Fig. 2 The front door's upper attaching bolt is accessible through the glove box

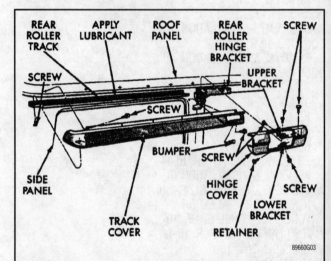

Fig. 3 Exploded view of the sliding door hinge and track components

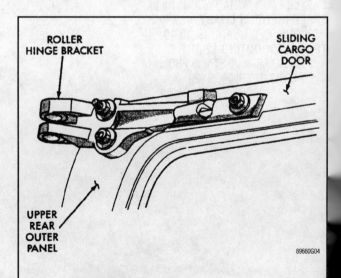

Fig. 4 View of the sliding door's rear, upper roller hinge bracket

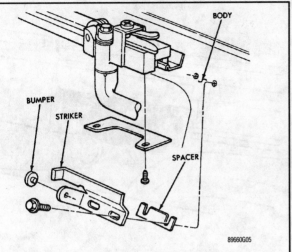

Fig. 5 Exploded view of the sliding door's closed position catch striker

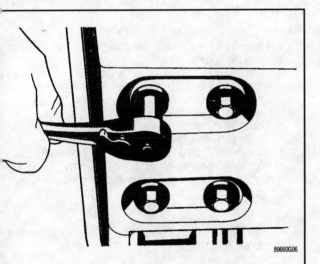

Fig. 6 Loosen the sliding door's lower attaching bolts

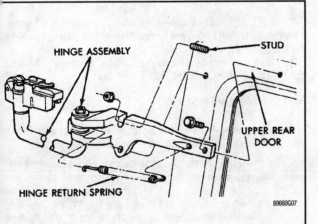

Fig. 7 Exploded view of the sliding door hinge support bracket assembly

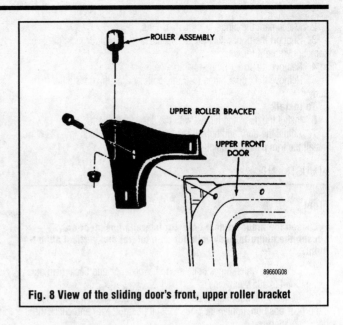

Fig. 8 View of the sliding door's front, upper roller bracket

4. Slide the door rearward, guiding the upper front and rear rollers out of the rails.

To install:

5. Lubricate both roller tracks with multi-purpose lubricant.

6. Insert the front and rear rollers into the tracks, slide the door forward to the front of each track.

7. Position the rear, upper roller hinge plate at the hinge and align the screw holes.

8. Install the retaining screws and tighten them to 200 inch lbs. (23 Nm).

9. Install the upper hinge cover.

10. Position the roller bracket under the support bracket with the screw holes aligned.

11. Install the retaining screws in the support bracket finger-tight.

12. Adjust the door as required.

13. Tighten the roller bracket screws to 30 ft. lbs. (41 Nm).

Side and Rear Cargo/Single Doors

▶ **See Figure 9**

1. Remove the interior trim panel (models equipped) to gain access to the door pillar to hinge screws.

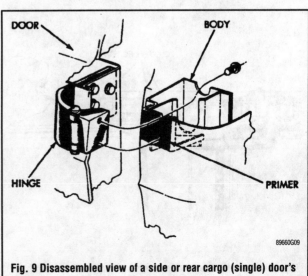

Fig. 9 Disassembled view of a side or rear cargo (single) door's hinge

2. Matchmark the hinge-to-body locations.
3. Support the door either on jackstands, a padded floor jack, or have somebody hold it for you.
4. Remove the lower hinge-to-frame bolts.
5. Remove the upper hinge-to-frame bolts and lift the door off of the body.

To install:

6. Install the door and hinges with the bolts finger tight.
7. Adjust the door and tighten the hinge bolts to 200 inch lbs. (23 Nm). Install the trim panel, if equipped.

ADJUSTMENT

Front

→Loosen the hinge-to-door bolts for lateral adjustment only. Loosen the hinge-to-body bolts for both lateral and vertical adjustment.

1. Determine which hinge bolts are to be loosened and back them out just enough to allow movement.
2. To move the door safely, use a padded pry bar. When the door is in the proper position, tighten the bolts to 24 ft. lbs. (32 Nm) and check the door operation.

→There should be no binding or interference when the door is closed and opened.

3. Door closing adjustment can also be affected by the position of the lock striker plate. Loosen the striker plate bolts and move the striker plate just enough to permit proper closing and locking of the door.

Sliding Side

FORE AND AFT

▶ **See Figures 10 and 11**

1. Remove the outer covers.
2. Loosen the hinge-roller screws and move the assembly to the desired position.
3. Tighten the screws and check the fit.
4. If necessary, shim the front striker to make sure that the pin enters the striker by 4.78 in. (121.5mm).
5. If it was necessary to shim the striker, loosen the striker screws so they are just snug, close the door and open it carefully so as not to move the striker. Tighten the screws.

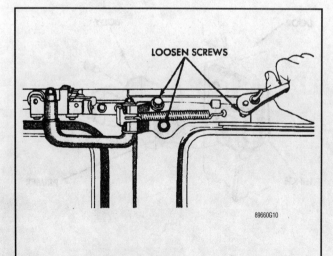

Fig. 10 Loosen the hinge-roller screws and move the assembly to the desired position

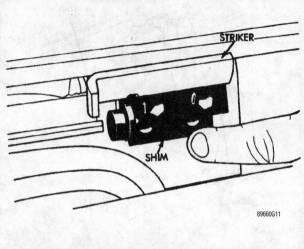

Fig. 11 Shim the front striker to make sure that the pin enters the striker correctly

VERTICAL

1. To adjust the front edge fit:
   a. Loosen the 3 upper roller bracket screws.
   b. Loosen the 4 lower attaching screws.
   c. Move the door to the correct position and tighten the lower bolts.
   d. Make sure that there is 0.059 in. (1.5mm) clearance between the top roller and the top of the track.
2. To adjust the rear edge fit:
   a. Loosen the rear center striker and move it up or down the amount the door is to be raised or lowered, and tighten the screws.
   b. Close the door so that the rear latch is caught, but not fully closed.
   c. Loosen the 3 hinge screws and fully close the door.
   d. Push the front edge of the hinge up as far as it will go and snug down the front screw.
   e. Pull down firmly on the swing arm and fully tighten all 3 screws.
   f. Make sure that there is 0.031 in. (0.8mm) clearance between the latch pawl and striker bar.

IN AND OUT

1. Front upper corner adjustments are made by loosening the roller stud nut and moving the door to the correct position. Maintain a 0.059 in. (1.5mm) clearance between the rollers and the top of the track. Tighten the screws.
2. Front lower corner adjustments are made by loosening the 2 lower roller support bracket screws and moving the door to the desired position. Tighten the screws.
3. Rear adjustments are made by loosening the rear center striker and moving it to the desired position. Tighten the screws.

Rear Doors/Single Cargo Door

→Loosen the hinge-to-door bolts for lateral adjustment only. Loosen the hinge-to-body bolts for both lateral and vertical adjustment.

1. Determine which hinge bolts are to be loosened and back them out just enough to allow movement.
2. To move the door safely, use a padded prybar. When the door is in the proper position, tighten the bolts to 24 ft. lbs. (32 Nm) and check the door operation. There should be no binding or interference when the door is closed and opened.
3. Door closing adjustment can also be affected by the position of the lock striker plate. Loosen the striker plate bolts and move the striker plate just enough to permit proper closing and locking of the door.

Hood

REMOVAL & INSTALLATION

▶ **See Figures 12 and 13**

➡ **To prevent damage to the vehicle, two people should perform this procedure.**

1. Open and prop up the hood. Disconnect the underhood light, if equipped. Remove the harness from the fasteners.
2. Scribe the hood hinge outline on the hood for installation reference. Place a protective cover over the cowl. Have an assistant support the hood. Remove the bolts from each hinge and lift off the hood.
3. Place the hood in position and line up the hinge retaining bolt holes. Insert the bolts and tighten them enough to support the hood, but allow enough "slack" for hood alignment. Align the hood and tighten the mounting bolts to 200 inch lbs. (23 Nm). Install the underhood harness and connect the lamp.

ALIGNMENT

The hood can be adjusted fore-aft and up-and-down to obtain a proper fit.

1. Loosen the hood-to-hinge bolts until they are finger-tight.
2. Reposition the hood as required.
3. Tighten the bolts.

Grille

REMOVAL & INSTALLATION

▶ **See Figures 14 thru 20**

1. Remove the headlamp trim and parking lamps, as necessary.
2. Remove the grille mounting screws and the grille.
To install:
3. Position the grille in place and install the mounting screws.

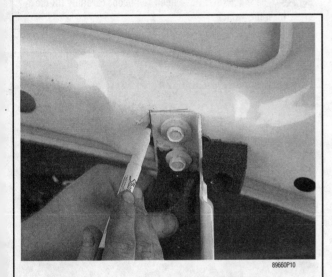

Fig. 12 Always matchmark the hood and hinges prior to removal

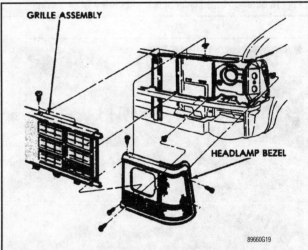

Fig. 14 On early model vehicles, the headlamp bezel must be removed prior to removing the grille

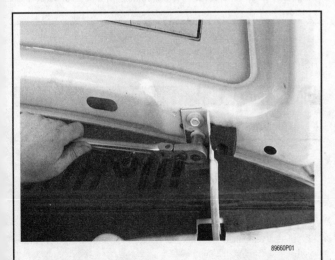

Fig. 13 Using one hand to steady the hood, remove the hinge retaining bolts

Fig. 15 A long screwdriver must be used to reach the grille retaining screws, especially toward the center of the grille

89660P12

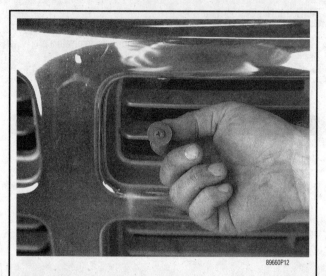

Fig. 16 Screws at the center of the grille use a large washer

89660P13

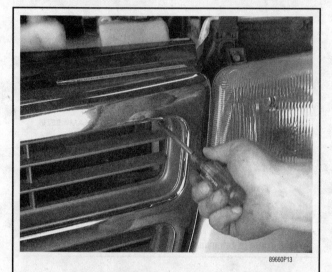

Fig. 17 Screws at the end of the grille are easily accessible . . .

89660P14

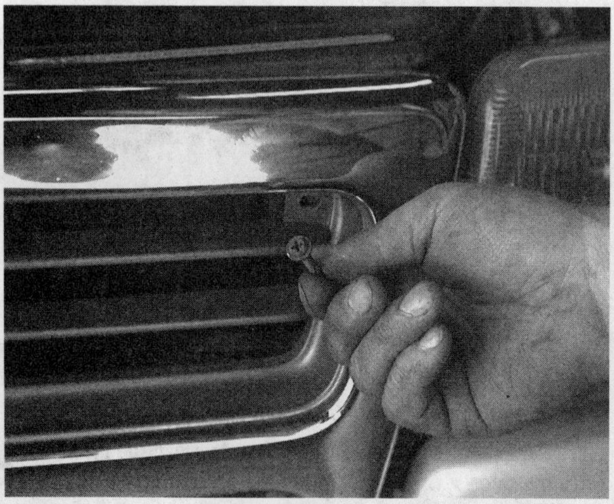

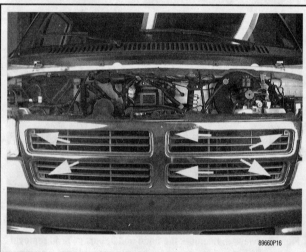

Fig. 18 . . . and do not use a washer

89660P15

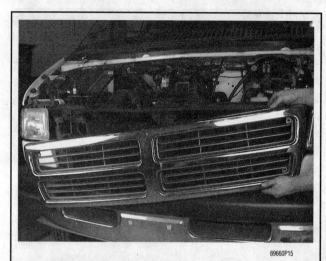

Fig. 19 Once the screws have been removed, carefully lift the grille from the vehicle

89660P16

Fig. 20 The grille is secured to the vehicle with several screws (arrows)

4. Tighten the mounting screws to 17 inch lbs. (2 Nm).
5. Install the headlamp trim and parking lamps, as necessary.

Outside Mirrors

REMOVAL & INSTALLATION

1. All mirrors are removed by unfastening the mounting screws and lifting off the mirror and gasket.
2. On 6–9 in. (152–229mm) wide "swing away" mirrors, remove the mounting cover from the base.
3. Remove the mirror base mounting screws, the mirror and reinforcement base.
4. Place the mounting bracket (if separate) and mirror in position, then install and tighten the mounting screws.
5. Install the base cover, if equipped.

Antenna

REPLACEMENT

♦ See Figure 21

1. Disconnect the negative battery cable.
2. Remove the windshield wiper arms and disconnect the windshield washer hoses.
3. Remove the cowl grille. Snap out the glove box.
4. On vehicles equipped with air conditioning, remove the right air duct.
5. Reaching through the glove box opening, unplug the antenna cable from the radio.

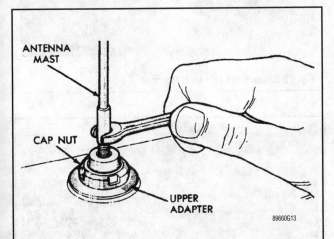

Fig. 21 Use a wrench to remove the antenna mast, if it cannot be unscrewed by hand

6. Working through the cowl opening, remove the antenna cable and mounting grommet.
7. Unscrew the antenna mast from the mounting adapter.
8. Reach through the cowl opening and hold the antenna body.
9. Remove the adapter cap nut and pull the antenna from the sheet metal.

To install:

10. Place the antenna in the sheet metal and install the adapter cap nut. Tighten the capnut to 100–150 inch lbs. (11–17 Nm).
11. Install the mast in the adapter.
12. Install the cable and grommet through the cowl.
13. Plug the antenna cable into the radio.
14. On vehicles equipped with air conditioning, install the right air duct.
15. Install the glove box.
16. Connect the washer hoses at the nozzles.
17. Install the cowl grille.
18. Install the windshield wiper arms.
19. Connect the battery ground cable.

Fenders

REMOVAL & INSTALLATION

1. Remove the headlight assembly, as required.
2. Remove the grille, as required.
3. Label and disconnect any electrical harnesses attached to the fender.
4. Remove the fender attaching screws.
5. Remove the fender.

To install:

6. Place the fender in position and install all the retainers finger-tight.
7. Adjust the fender until proper fit and appearance have been achieved, then tighten the retainers.
8. Install the grille, as required.
9. Install the headlight assembly, as required.

INTERIOR

Engine Cover

REMOVAL & INSTALLATION

♦ See Figures 22 thru 27

The inside engine cover is attached to the floor with retaining clips and with screws at the rear; it also latches to the firewall.

1. Remove the rear retaining screws.
2. Unfasten the latches at the front.
3. Remove the cover.

To install:

4. Place the cover in position.
5. Install the rear screws finger-tight.
6. Fasten the front latches, then tighten the mounting screws to 24 inch lbs. (3 Nm).

Fig. 22 The engine cover is fastened at several locations (arrows)

Fig. 23 To remove the engine cover, first unfasten the over-center clips at the firewall

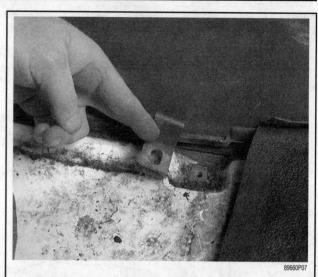

Fig. 26 Remove the clip from the cover . . .

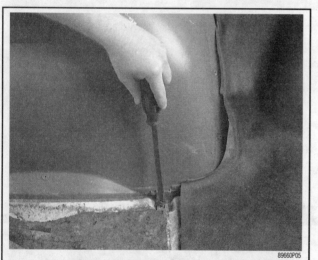

Fig. 24 Next, pull back the rug and remove the clips attaching the cover to the floor with either a screwdriver . . .

Fig. 27 . . . and lift the cover from the passenger compartment

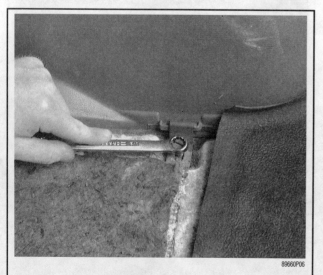

Fig. 25 . . . or a wrench

Instrument Panel

REMOVAL & INSTALLATION

▶ **See Figures 28, 29 and 30**

1. Disconnect the negative battery ground cable.
2. Remove the instrument panel hood and bezel. The bezel is retained by spring clips.
3. Remove the knee blocker from the underside of the dashboard.
4. Pull the instrument cluster out just far enough to disconnect the speedometer cable.
5. Unplug the wiring connectors at the back of the cluster.
6. Remove the instrument cluster.
7. Lower the steering column.
8. Remove the screws attaching the instrument panel to the body.
9. Remove the instrument panel.
10. Installation is the reverse of removal.

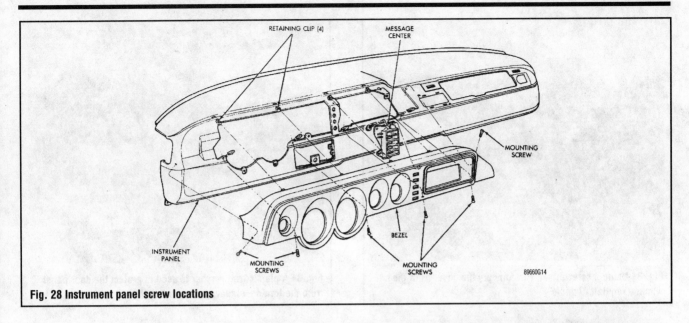

Fig. 28 Instrument panel screw locations

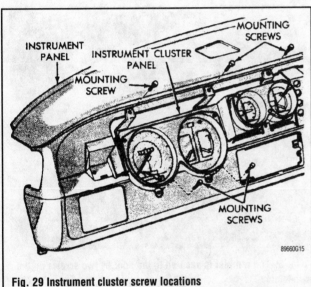

Fig. 29 Instrument cluster screw locations

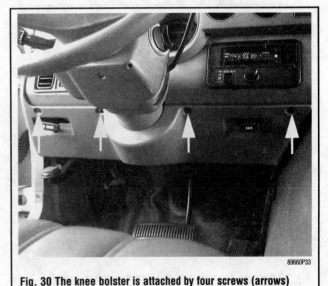

Fig. 30 The knee bolster is attached by four screws (arrows)

Console

REMOVAL & INSTALLATION

The console is attached to the engine cover with screws that are accessible through the ashtray housing. Open the ashtray and remove the console mounting screws and the console. To install, place the console in position on the engine cover and secure the mounting screws.

Door Panels

REMOVAL & INSTALLATION

▶ See Figures 31 thru 40

1. Remove the power window switch housing bezel or the window regulator handle.

2. Remove the armrest and inside latch handle and bezel.
3. Use a trim removal tool to pry the trim panel away from the door inner panel. Remove the trim or access panel from the door.
4. Carefully separate the water shield from the door inner panel. Remove the water shield from the door.
5. If necessary, remove the door pull handle and upper trim panel.

To install:
6. Apply adhesive to the water shield edges, prior to installation.
7. Install the water shield on the door inner panel.
8. Position the trim panel on the door inner panel and press inward around the edge of the panel to attach the retainers to the inner panel.
9. Install the inside latch release handle.
10. Install the door armrest and inside latch release handle bezel. Tighten the armrest retaining screws to 30 inch lbs. (3 Nm).
11. Install the window regulator handle or the power switch housing.
12. If removed, install the door upper trim panel and the pull handle. Tighten the retaining screws to 30 inch lbs. (3 Nm).

Fig. 31 Using a screwdriver, carefully pry the cover from the window regulator handle

89660P17

Fig. 34 A plastic trim washer is used to protect the door panel from the turning window regulator handle

89660P20

Fig. 32 With the cap removed, the retaining bolt is visible

89660P18

Fig. 35 The armrest is secured to the door by two screws on the underside . . .

89660P21

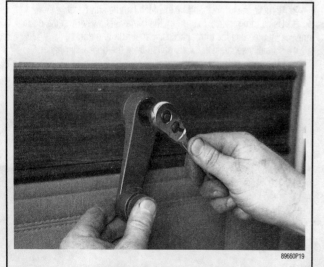

Fig. 33 Remove the bolt while holding the handle steady

89660P19

Fig. 36 . . . and one screw at the inside door handle

89660P22

Fig. 37 With the screw and handle removed, the inside door handle's pivot point is visible

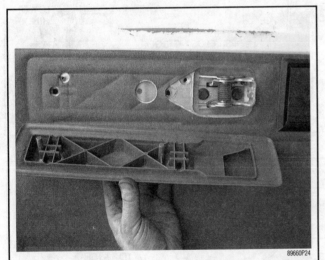

Fig. 38 After removing all the fasteners, the armrest is easily removed

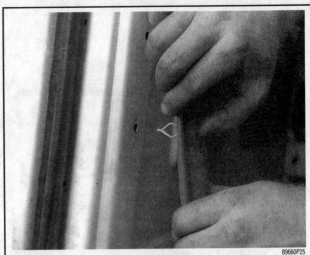

Fig. 39 Carefully pry the door panel away from the door, being careful not to damage the panel or its retaining clips

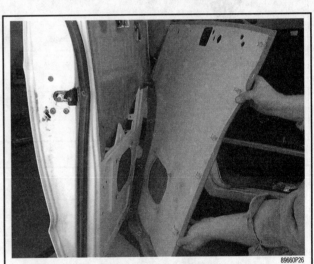

Fig. 40 Once all the door panel clips are unfastened, the door panel can be removed

Door Locks

REMOVAL & INSTALLATION

▶ **See Figures 41, 42 and 43**

Manual Lock Cylinder

1. Raise the window all the way.
2. Remove the door trim panel.
3. Disconnect the lock actuating rod from the lock control clip.
4. Remove the lock cylinder retaining clip and pull the lock cylinder from the door. On the side doors, it will be necessary to loosen the inside lock control knob setscrew and remove the knob.

5. Place the cylinder in position and install the retainer clip. Install the rods, controls and panel.

Power Lock Solenoid

1. Raise the glass to the full UP position.
2. Remove the door trim panel.
3. Unplug the wiring from the solenoid.
4. Disconnect the linkage from the solenoid.
5. Remove the mounting screws and lift out the solenoid.
6. Secure the solenoid with the mounting screws. Connect the linkage and wiring, then install the door panel.

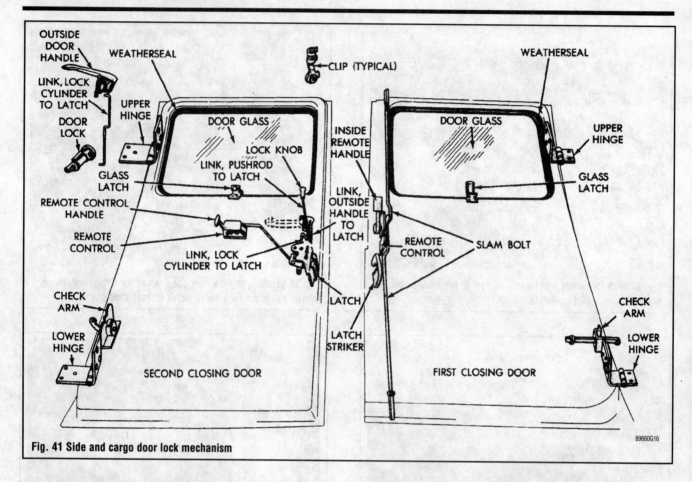

Fig. 41 Side and cargo door lock mechanism

89660G16

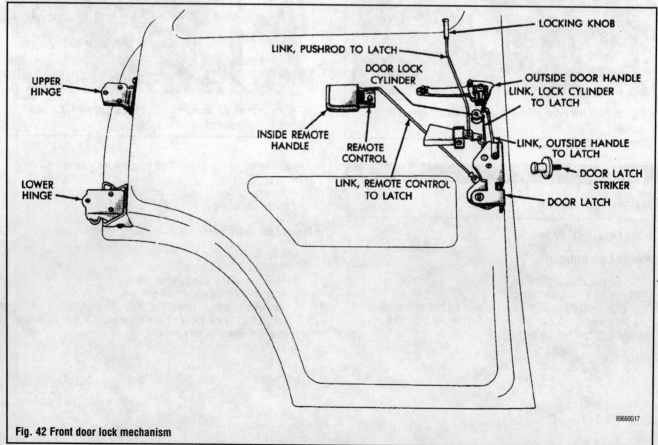

Fig. 42 Front door lock mechanism

89660G17

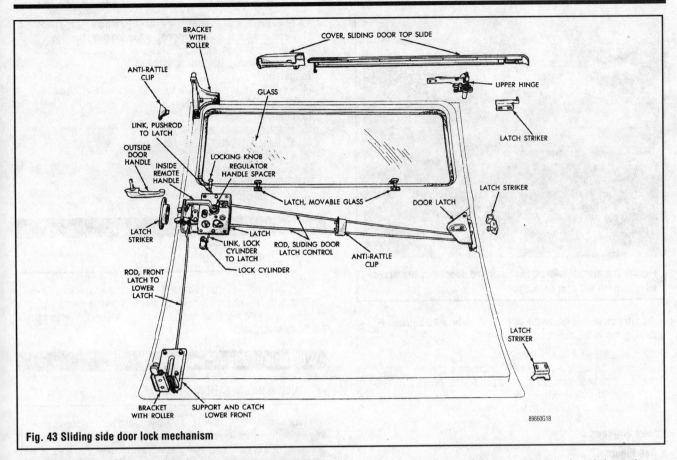

Fig. 43 Sliding side door lock mechanism

Door Glass and Regulator

REMOVAL & INSTALLATION

Manual Windows
▶ **See Figures 44, 45 and 46**

1. Remove the access or trim panel and the water shield.
2. Lower the glass all the way.
3. Remove the lower vent window support bolt.

4. Locate the vent window retaining clip screw through the weatherstripping and remove the screw.
5. Lower the door glass and tilt the vent window assembly rearward.
6. Remove the vent window.
7. Slide the door glass forward to disengage it from the regulator.
8. Remove the inside weatherstripping from the glass opening.
9. Lift the glass from the door.
10. Unbolt and remove the regulator. Later models have the regulator secured with rivets; if so equipped, drill them out.
To install:
11. Install the regulator.

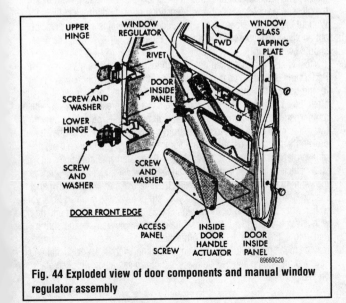

Fig. 44 Exploded view of door components and manual window regulator assembly

Fig. 45 To access the window regulator and door glass, first remove the water shield from the door

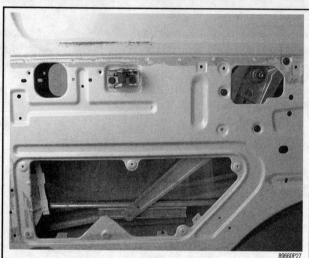

Fig. 46 The manual window regulator and door glass are accessible through the door openings

➡️**On later models, replace the rivets with ¼ in. x 20 bolts and nuts. Tighten to 90 inch lbs. (10 Nm).**

12. Lower the glass into the door.
13. Install the inside weatherstripping in the glass opening.
14. Slide the door glass rearward to attach it to the regulator.
15. Install the vent window.
16. Install the access panel and water shield.

Power Windows

▶ **See Figure 47**

1. Raise the glass to the full UP position.
2. Remove the trim panel and water shield.
3. Remove the down-stop bumper bracket.
4. Lower the glass all the way.
5. Remove the lower vent window support bolt.
6. Locate the vent window retaining clip screw through the weatherstripping and remove the screw.
7. Lower the door glass and tilt the vent window assembly rearward.
8. Remove the vent window.
9. Disconnect the regulator wiring from the harness.

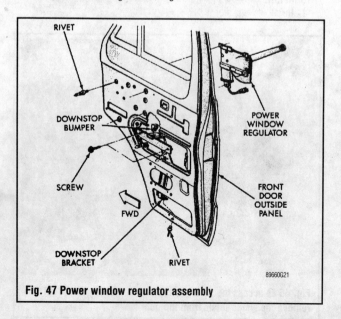

Fig. 47 Power window regulator assembly

10. Slide the door glass forward to disconnect it from the regulator.
11. Remove the inside weatherstripping from the glass opening.
12. Lift the glass from the door.
13. Drill out the regulator mounting rivets.
To install:
14. Install the regulator. Replace the rivets with ¼ in. x 20 bolts and nuts. Tighten to 90 inch lbs. (10 Nm).
15. Lower the glass into the door.
16. Install the inside weatherstripping in the glass opening.
17. Slide the door glass rearward to attach it to the regulator.
18. Connect the wiring.
19. Install the vent window.
20. Install the down-stop bumper.
21. Install the access panel and water shield.

Electric Window Motor

REMOVAL & INSTALLATION

The electric window motor is secured to the window regulator by three attaching bolts. To remove the motor, follow the preceding window regulator procedure. Once the regulator is removed, simply remove the motor from the regulator assembly.

Windshield and Fixed Glass

REMOVAL & INSTALLATION

If your windshield, or other fixed window, is cracked or chipped, you may decide to replace it with a new one yourself. However, there are two main reasons why replacement windshields and other window glass should be installed only by a professional automotive glass technician: safety and cost.

The most important reason a professional should install automotive glass is for safety. The glass in the vehicle, especially the windshield, is designed with safety in mind in case of a collision. The windshield is specially manufactured from two panes of specially-tempered glass with a thin layer of transparent plastic between them. This construction allows the glass to "give" in the event that a part of your body hits the windshield during the collision, and prevents the glass from shattering, which could cause lacerations, blinding and other harm to passengers of the vehicle. The other fixed windows are designed to be tempered so that if they break during a collision, they shatter in such a way that there are no large pointed glass pieces. The professional automotive glass technician knows how to install the glass in a vehicle so that it will function optimally during a collision. Without the proper experience, knowledge and tools, installing a piece of automotive glass yourself could lead to additional harm if an accident should ever occur.

Cost is also a factor when deciding to install automotive glass yourself. Performing this could cost you much more than a professional may charge for the same job. Since the windshield is designed to break under stress, an often life saving characteristic, windshields tend to break VERY easily when an inexperienced person attempts to install one. Do-it-yourselfers buying two, three or even four windshields from a salvage yard because they have broken them during installation are common stories. Also, since the automotive glass is designed to prevent the outside elements from entering your vehicle, improper installation can lead to water and air leaks. Annoying whining noises at highway speeds from air leaks or inside body panel rusting from water leaks can add to your stress level and subtract from your wallet. After buying two or three windshields, installing them and ending up with a leak that produces a noise while driving and water damage during rainstorms, the cost of having a professional do it correctly the first time may be much more alluring. We here at Chilton, therefore, advise that you have a professional automotive glass technician service any broken glass on your vehicle.

WINDSHIELD CHIP REPAIR

▶ See Figures 48 thru 62

➡Check with your state and local authorities on the laws for state safety inspection. Some states or municipalities may not allow chip repair as a viable option for correcting stone damage to your windshield.

Although severely cracked or damaged windshields must be replaced, there is something that you can do to prolong or even prevent the need for replacement of a chipped windshield. There are many companies which offer windshield chip repair products, such as Loctite's® Bullseye™ windshield repair kit. These kits usually consist of a syringe, pedestal and a sealing adhesive. The syringe is mounted on the pedestal and is used to create a vacuum which pulls the plastic layer against the glass. This helps make the chip transparent. The adhesive is then injected which seals the chip and helps to prevent further stress cracks from developing. Refer to the sequence of photos to get a general idea of what windshield chip repair involves.

➡Always follow the specific manufacturer's instructions.

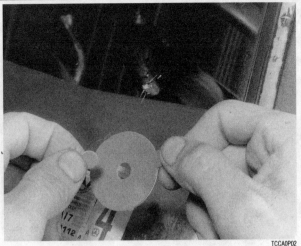

Fig. 50 Remove the center from the adhesive disc and peel off the backing from one side of the disc . . .

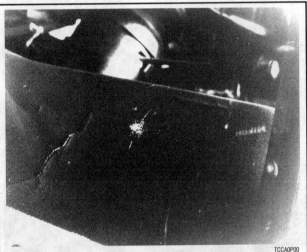

Fig. 48 Small chips on your windshield can be fixed with an aftermarket repair kit, such as the one from Loctite®

Fig. 51 . . . then press it on the windshield so that the chip is centered in the hole

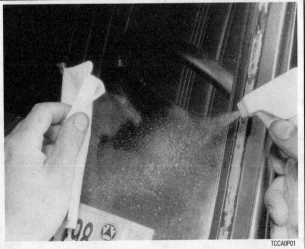

Fig. 49 To repair a chip, clean the windshield with glass cleaner and dry it completely

Fig. 52 Be sure that the tab points upward on the windshield

Fig. 53 Peel the backing off the exposed side of the adhesive disc . . .

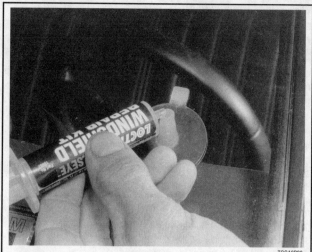

Fig. 56 . . . then install the applicator syringe nipple in the pedestal's hole

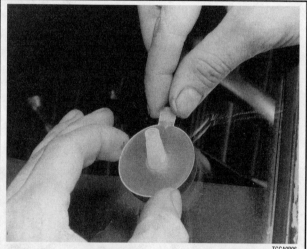

Fig. 54 . . . then position the plastic pedestal on the adhesive disc, ensuring that the tabs are aligned

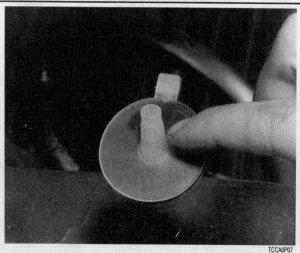

Fig. 55 Press the pedestal firmly on the adhesive disc to create an adequate seal . . .

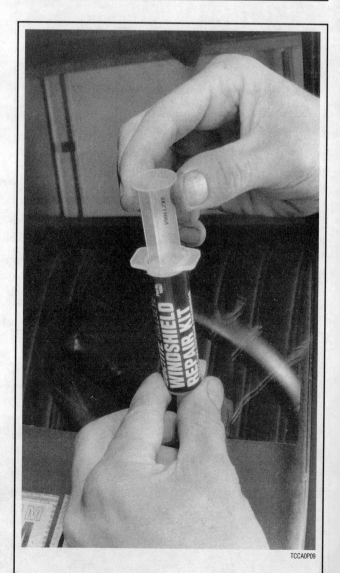

Fig. 57 Hold the syringe with one hand while pulling the plunger back with the other hand

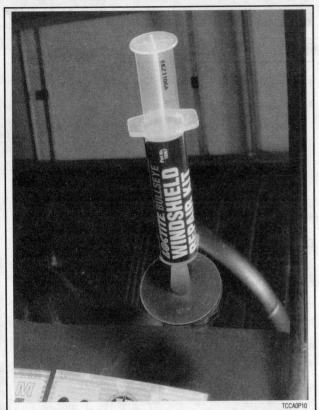

Fig. 58 After applying the solution, allow the entire assembly to sit until it has set completely

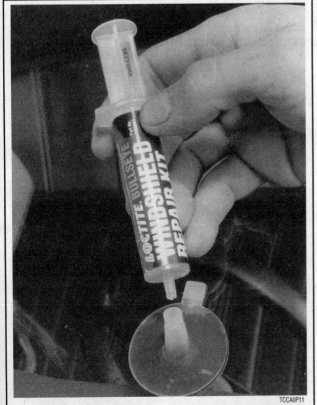

Fig. 59 After the solution has set, remove the syringe from the pedestal . . .

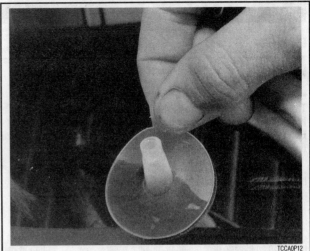

Fig. 60 . . . then peel the pedestal off of the adhesive disc . . .

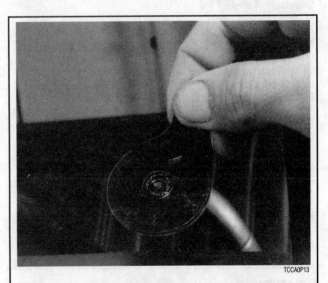

Fig. 61 . . . and peel the adhesive disc off of the windshield

Fig. 62 The chip will still be slightly visible, but it should be filled with the hardened solution

Inside Rear View Mirror

REPLACEMENT

▸ **See Figure 63**

➡ **Breakaway mounts are used with the inside rear view mirrors. The breakaway mounts are designed to detach from the mirror bracket in the event of an air bag deployment during a collision. Excessive force, up-and-down, or side-to-side movement can cause the mirror to detach from the windshield glass.**

1. Mark the mirror mounting bracket location on the outside surface of the windshield with a wax pencil.
2. Loosen the mirror assembly setscrew.
3. Remove the mirror assembly by sliding it upward and away from the mounting bracket.
4. If the bracket mounting pad remains on the windshield, apply low heat from an electric heat gun until the glue softens. Peel the mounting pad off the windshield and discard.

To install:

5. Make sure the glass, bracket and adhesive kit are at least at a room temperature of 65–75°F (18–24°C).
6. Thoroughly clean the bonding surfaces of the glass and bracket to remove the old adhesive. Use a mild abrasive cleaner on the glass and fine sandpaper on the bracket to lightly roughen the surface. Wipe it clean with the alcohol-moistened cloth.
7. Crush the accelerator vial of the rear view mirror repair kit, and apply the accelerator to the bonding surface of the bracket and windshield. Follow directions on drying time.
8. Apply two drops of adhesive to the mounting surface of the bracket. Quickly spread the adhesive evenly over the mounting surface of the bracket using the applicator.
9. Quickly position the mounting bracket on the windshield. The ⅜ in. (10mm) circular depression in the bracket must be facing you. Press the bracket firmly against the windshield and hold for the appropriate dry time stated in the directions.
10. Allow the bond to set. Remove any excess bonding material from the windshield with an alcohol dampened cloth.
11. Attach the mirror to the mounting bracket and tighten the setscrew to 10–20 inch lbs. (1–2 Nm).

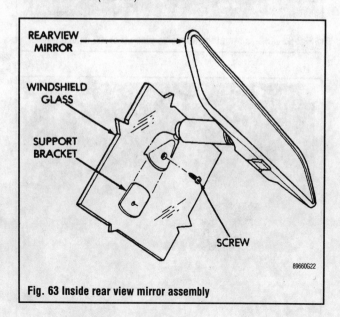

Fig. 63 Inside rear view mirror assembly

Seats

REMOVAL & INSTALLATION

Front Bucket Seat

▸ **See Figure 64**

1. Remove the anchor bolts and shoulder belt from the seat platform.
2. Remove the seat track-to-floor nuts and lift out the seat.
3. Separate the seat from the platform if necessary.

To install:

4. Install the seat to the platform.
5. Place the seat in position inside the vehicle and tighten the mounting bolts to 55 ft. lbs. (75 Nm).
6. Install the shoulder belt and anchors.

Center and Rear Seats

The 3-passenger seat is attached to the floor with hooks and anchors at the rear, and with latches and anchors at the front. The 4-passenger seat is attached to the floor with brackets, nuts and studs.

1. On 3-passenger seats: Lift up the release lever and push up on the seat.
2. While holding up the front of the seat, push rearward to unlatch the rear anchors.
3. Lift the seat up and out of the vehicle.
4. On 4-passenger seats: Remove the hold-down bolts and remove the seat.
5. Place the seat in position and mount it as required.

Travel Seat

A travel seat option is offered on some models. The package can be converted from a 6-passenger, forward facing seating arrangement to:
- a lounge/full size sleeper
- a 6-place dinette with table

The seat/cushions, and table are arranged by various lowering and platform placement. Removal is accomplished by simultaneously inserting small prybars in the opening at each side of the seat platform and raising the travel latch pin to disengage the latches from their stops.

Fig. 64 The front bucket seat frame is attached to the floor with four nuts

Power Seat Motor

REMOVAL & INSTALLATION

➡ **If the seat is in the raised position, it is possible to access and remove the seat and/or power seat adjuster and motors without removing the seat riser.**

1. Disconnect the negative battery cable.
2. Remove the rearward facing fasteners that secure the rear shield to the seat riser.
3. Label and disconnect the power seat feed and seat belt switch electrical harnesses.
4. Remove the nuts that secure the seat riser to the studs on the floor panel.

➡ **The rear nuts are accessed by lifting up the seat riser rear shield.**

5. Remove the seat, the power seat adjuster and motors and the seat riser as a unit.

6. Remove the screws that secure the power seat adjuster and motors to the seat cushion frame.
7. Label and disconnect the power seat switch electrical harness.
8. Remove the power seat adjuster and motors from the seat riser.

To install:

9. Install the power seat adjuster and motors on the seat riser. Tighten the screws to 200 inch lbs. (23 Nm).
10. Connect the power seat switch electrical harness.
11. Install the screws that secure the power seat adjuster and motors to the seat cushion frame. Tighten the screws to 200 inch lbs. (23 Nm).
12. Install the seat and tighten the nuts to 55 ft. lbs. (75 Nm).
13. Connect the power seat feed and seat belt switch electrical harnesses.
14. Install the rearward facing fasteners that secure the rear shield to the seat riser.
15. Connect the negative battery cable.

TORQUE SPECIFICATIONS

Components	English	Metric
Doors		
Front	26 ft. lbs.	35 Nm
Side	30 ft. lbs.	41 Nm
Rear	200 inch lbs.	23 Nm
Hood	200 inch lbs.	23 Nm
Engine Cover	24 inch lbs.	3 Nm
Door Panel	30 inch lbs.	3 Nm
Window Regulator	90 inch lbs.	10 Nm

89660C01

How to Remove Stains from Fabric Interior

For rest results, spots and stains should be removed as soon as possible. Never use gasoline, lacquer thinner, acetone, nail polish remover or bleach. Use a 3' x 3" piece of cheesecloth. Squeeze most of the liquid from the fabric and wipe the stained fabric from the outside of the stain toward the center with a lifting motion. Turn the cheesecloth as soon as one side becomes soiled. When using water to remove a stain, be sure to wash the entire section after the spot has been removed to avoid water stains. Encrusted spots can be broken up with a dull knife and vacuumed before removing the stain.

Type of Stain	How to Remove It
Surface spots	Brush the spots out with a small hand brush or use a commercial preparation such as K2R to lift the stain.
Mildew	Clean around the mildew with warm suds. Rinse in cold water and soak the mildew area in a solution of 1 part table salt and 2 parts water. Wash with upholstery cleaner.
Water stains	Water stains in fabric materials can be removed with a solution made from 1 cup of table salt dissolved in 1 quart of water. Vigorously scrub the solution into the stain and rinse with clear water. Water stains in nylon or other synthetic fabrics should be removed with a commercial type spot remover.
Chewing gum, tar, crayons, shoe polish (greasy stains)	Do not use a cleaner that will soften gum or tar. Harden the deposit with an ice cube and scrape away as much as possible with a dull knife. Moisten the remainder with cleaning fluid and scrub clean.
Ice cream, candy	Most candy has a sugar base and can be removed with a cloth wrung out in warm water. Oily candy, after cleaning with warm water, should be cleaned with upholstery cleaner. Rinse with warm water and clean the remainder with cleaning fluid.
Wine, alcohol, egg, milk, soft drink (non-greasy stains)	Do not use soap. Scrub the stain with a cloth wrung out in warm water. Remove the remainder with cleaning fluid.
Grease, oil, lipstick, butter and related stains	Use a spot remover to avoid leaving a ring. Work from the outisde of the stain to the center and dry with a clean cloth when the spot is gone.
Headliners (cloth)	Mix a solution of warm water and foam upholstery cleaner to give thick suds. Use only foam—liquid may streak or spot. Clean the entire headliner in one operation using a circular motion with a natural sponge.
Headliner (vinyl)	Use a vinyl cleaner with a sponge and wipe clean with a dry cloth.
Seats and door panels	Mix 1 pint upholstery cleaner in 1 gallon of water. Do not soak the fabric around the buttons.
Leather or vinyl fabric	Use a multi-purpose cleaner full strength and a stiff brush. Let stand 2 minutes and scrub thoroughly. Wipe with a clean, soft rag.
Nylon or synthetic fabrics	For normal stains, use the same procedures you would for washing cloth upholstery. If the fabric is extremely dirty, use a multi-purpose cleaner full strength with a stiff scrub brush. Scrub thoroughly in all directions and wipe with a cotton towel or soft rag.

TCCA0C01

GLOSSARY

AIR/FUEL RATIO: The ratio of air-to-gasoline by weight in the fuel mixture drawn into the engine.

AIR INJECTION: One method of reducing harmful exhaust emissions by injecting air into each of the exhaust ports of an engine. The fresh air entering the hot exhaust manifold causes any remaining fuel to be burned before it can exit the tailpipe.

ALTERNATOR: A device used for converting mechanical energy into electrical energy.

AMMETER: An instrument, calibrated in amperes, used to measure the flow of an electrical current in a circuit. Ammeters are always connected in series with the circuit being tested.

AMPERE: The rate of flow of electrical current present when one volt of electrical pressure is applied against one ohm of electrical resistance.

ANALOG COMPUTER: Any microprocessor that uses similar (analogous) electrical signals to make its calculations.

ARMATURE: A laminated, soft iron core wrapped by a wire that converts electrical energy to mechanical energy as in a motor or relay. When rotated in a magnetic field, it changes mechanical energy into electrical energy as in a generator.

ATMOSPHERIC PRESSURE: The pressure on the Earth's surface caused by the weight of the air in the atmosphere. At sea level, this pressure is 14.7 psi at 32°F (101 kPa at 0°C).

ATOMIZATION: The breaking down of a liquid into a fine mist that can be suspended in air.

AXIAL PLAY: Movement parallel to a shaft or bearing bore.

BACKFIRE: The sudden combustion of gases in the intake or exhaust system that results in a loud explosion.

BACKLASH: The clearance or play between two parts, such as meshed gears.

BACKPRESSURE: Restrictions in the exhaust system that slow the exit of exhaust gases from the combustion chamber.

BAKELITE: A heat resistant, plastic insulator material commonly used in printed circuit boards and transistorized components.

BALL BEARING: A bearing made up of hardened inner and outer races between which hardened steel balls roll.

BALLAST RESISTOR: A resistor in the primary ignition circuit that lowers voltage after the engine is started to reduce wear on ignition components.

BEARING: A friction reducing, supportive device usually located between a stationary part and a moving part.

BIMETAL TEMPERATURE SENSOR: Any sensor or switch made of two dissimilar types of metal that bend when heated or cooled due to the different expansion rates of the alloys. These types of sensors usually function as an on/off switch.

BLOWBY: Combustion gases, composed of water vapor and unburned fuel, that leak past the piston rings into the crankcase during normal engine operation. These gases are removed by the PCV system to prevent the buildup of harmful acids in the crankcase.

BRAKE PAD: A brake shoe and lining assembly used with disc brakes.

BRAKE SHOE: The backing for the brake lining. The term is, however, usually applied to the assembly of the brake backing and lining.

BUSHING: A liner, usually removable, for a bearing; an anti-friction liner used in place of a bearing.

CALIPER: A hydraulically activated device in a disc brake system, which is mounted straddling the brake rotor (disc). The caliper contains at least one piston and two brake pads. Hydraulic pressure on the piston(s) forces the pads against the rotor.

CAMSHAFT: A shaft in the engine on which are the lobes (cams) which operate the valves. The camshaft is driven by the crankshaft, via a belt, chain or gears, at one half the crankshaft speed.

CAPACITOR: A device which stores an electrical charge.

CARBON MONOXIDE (CO): A colorless, odorless gas given off as a normal byproduct of combustion. It is poisonous and extremely dangerous in confined areas, building up slowly to toxic levels without warning if adequate ventilation is not available.

CARBURETOR: A device, usually mounted on the intake manifold of an engine, which mixes the air and fuel in the proper proportion to allow even combustion.

CATALYTIC CONVERTER: A device installed in the exhaust system, like a muffler, that converts harmful byproducts of combustion into carbon dioxide and water vapor by means of a heat-producing chemical reaction.

CENTRIFUGAL ADVANCE: A mechanical method of advancing the spark timing by using flyweights in the distributor that react to centrifugal force generated by the distributor shaft rotation.

CHECK VALVE: Any one-way valve installed to permit the flow of air, fuel or vacuum in one direction only.

CHOKE: A device, usually a moveable valve, placed in the intake path of a carburetor to restrict the flow of air.

CIRCUIT: Any unbroken path through which an electrical current can flow. Also used to describe fuel flow in some instances.

CIRCUIT BREAKER: A switch which protects an electrical circuit from overload by opening the circuit when the current flow exceeds a predetermined level. Some circuit breakers must be reset manually, while most reset automatically.

COIL (IGNITION): A transformer in the ignition circuit which steps up the voltage provided to the spark plugs.

COMBINATION MANIFOLD: An assembly which includes both the intake and exhaust manifolds in one casting.

COMBINATION VALVE: A device used in some fuel systems that routes fuel vapors to a charcoal storage canister instead of venting them into the atmosphere. The valve relieves fuel tank pressure and allows fresh air into the tank as the fuel level drops to prevent a vapor lock situation.

COMPRESSION RATIO: The comparison of the total volume of the cylinder and combustion chamber with the piston at BDC and the piston at TDC.

CONDENSER: 1. An electrical device which acts to store an electrical charge, preventing voltage surges. 2. A radiator-like device in the air conditioning system in which refrigerant gas condenses into a liquid, giving off heat.

CONDUCTOR: Any material through which an electrical current can be transmitted easily.

CONTINUITY: Continuous or complete circuit. Can be checked with an ohmmeter.

COUNTERSHAFT: An intermediate shaft which is rotated by a mainshaft and transmits, in turn, that rotation to a working part.

CRANKCASE: The lower part of an engine in which the crankshaft and related parts operate.

CRANKSHAFT: The main driving shaft of an engine which receives reciprocating motion from the pistons and converts it to rotary motion.

CYLINDER: In an engine, the round hole in the engine block in which the piston(s) ride.

CYLINDER BLOCK: The main structural member of an engine in which is found the cylinders, crankshaft and other principal parts.

CYLINDER HEAD: The detachable portion of the engine, usually fastened to the top of the cylinder block and containing all or most of the combustion chambers. On overhead valve engines, it contains the valves and their operating parts. On overhead cam engines, it contains the camshaft as well.

DEAD CENTER: The extreme top or bottom of the piston stroke.

DETONATION: An unwanted explosion of the air/fuel mixture in the combustion chamber caused by excess heat and compression, advanced timing, or an overly lean mixture. Also referred to as "ping".

DIAPHRAGM: A thin, flexible wall separating two cavities, such as in a vacuum advance unit.

DIESELING: A condition in which hot spots in the combustion chamber cause the engine to run on after the key is turned off.

DIFFERENTIAL: A geared assembly which allows the transmission of motion between drive axles, giving one axle the ability to turn faster than the other.

DIODE: An electrical device that will allow current to flow in one direction only.

DISC BRAKE: A hydraulic braking assembly consisting of a brake disc, or rotor, mounted on an axle, and a caliper assembly containing, usually two brake pads which are activated by hydraulic pressure. The pads are forced against the sides of the disc, creating friction which slows the vehicle.

DISTRIBUTOR: A mechanically driven device on an engine which is responsible for electrically firing the spark plug at a predetermined point of the piston stroke.

DOWEL PIN: A pin, inserted in mating holes in two different parts allowing those parts to maintain a fixed relationship.

DRUM BRAKE: A braking system which consists of two brake shoes and one or two wheel cylinders, mounted on a fixed backing plate, and a brake drum, mounted on an axle, which revolves around the assembly.

DWELL: The rate, measured in degrees of shaft rotation, at which an electrical circuit cycles on and off.

ELECTRONIC CONTROL UNIT (ECU): Ignition module, module, amplifier or igniter. See Module for definition.

ELECTRONIC IGNITION: A system in which the timing and firing of the spark plugs is controlled by an electronic control unit, usually called a module. These systems have no points or condenser.

END-PLAY: The measured amount of axial movement in a shaft.

ENGINE: A device that converts heat into mechanical energy.

EXHAUST MANIFOLD: A set of cast passages or pipes which conduct exhaust gases from the engine.

FEELER GAUGE: A blade, usually metal, or precisely predetermined thickness, used to measure the clearance between two parts.

FIRING ORDER: The order in which combustion occurs in the cylinders of an engine. Also the order in which spark is distributed to the plugs by the distributor.

FLOODING: The presence of too much fuel in the intake manifold and combustion chamber which prevents the air/fuel mixture from firing, thereby causing a no-start situation.

FLYWHEEL: A disc shaped part bolted to the rear end of the crankshaft. Around the outer perimeter is affixed the ring gear. The starter drive engages the ring gear, turning the flywheel, which rotates the crankshaft, imparting the initial starting motion to the engine.

FOOT POUND (ft. lbs. or sometimes, ft.lb.): The amount of energy or work needed to raise an item weighing one pound, a distance of one foot.

FUSE: A protective device in a circuit which prevents circuit overload by breaking the circuit when a specific amperage is present. The device is constructed around a strip or wire of a lower amperage rating than the circuit it is designed to protect. When an amperage higher than that stamped on the fuse is present in the circuit, the strip or wire melts, opening the circuit.

GEAR RATIO: The ratio between the number of teeth on meshing gears.

GENERATOR: A device which converts mechanical energy into electrical energy.

HEAT RANGE: The measure of a spark plug's ability to dissipate heat from its firing end. The higher the heat range, the hotter the plug fires.

HUB: The center part of a wheel or gear.

HYDROCARBON (HC): Any chemical compound made up of hydrogen and carbon. A major pollutant formed by the engine as a byproduct of combustion.

HYDROMETER: An instrument used to measure the specific gravity of a solution.

INCH POUND (inch lbs.; sometimes in.lb. or in. lbs.): One twelfth of a foot pound.

INDUCTION: A means of transferring electrical energy in the form of a magnetic field. Principle used in the ignition coil to increase voltage.

INJECTOR: A device which receives metered fuel under relatively low pressure and is activated to inject the fuel into the engine under relatively high pressure at a predetermined time.

INPUT SHAFT: The shaft to which torque is applied, usually carrying the driving gear or gears.

INTAKE MANIFOLD: A casting of passages or pipes used to conduct air or a fuel/air mixture to the cylinders.

JOURNAL: The bearing surface within which a shaft operates.

KEY: A small block usually fitted in a notch between a shaft and a hub to prevent slippage of the two parts.

MANIFOLD: A casting of passages or set of pipes which connect the cylinders to an inlet or outlet source.

MANIFOLD VACUUM: Low pressure in an engine intake manifold formed just below the throttle plates. Manifold vacuum is highest at idle and drops under acceleration.

MASTER CYLINDER: The primary fluid pressurizing device in a hydraulic system. In automotive use, it is found in brake and hydraulic clutch systems and is pedal activated, either directly or, in a power brake system, through the power booster.

MODULE: Electronic control unit, amplifier or igniter of solid state or integrated design which controls the current flow in the ignition primary circuit based on input from the pick-up coil. When the module opens the primary circuit, high secondary voltage is induced in the coil.

NEEDLE BEARING: A bearing which consists of a number (usually a large number) of long, thin rollers.

OHM: (Ω) The unit used to measure the resistance of conductor-to-electrical flow. One ohm is the amount of resistance that limits current flow to one ampere in a circuit with one volt of pressure.

OHMMETER: An instrument used for measuring the resistance, in ohms, in an electrical circuit.

OUTPUT SHAFT: The shaft which transmits torque from a device, such as a transmission.

OVERDRIVE: A gear assembly which produces more shaft revolutions than that transmitted to it.

OVERHEAD CAMSHAFT (OHC): An engine configuration in which the camshaft is mounted on top of the cylinder head and operates the valve either directly or by means of rocker arms.

OVERHEAD VALVE (OHV): An engine configuration in which all of the valves are located in the cylinder head and the camshaft is located in the cylinder block. The camshaft operates the valves via lifters and pushrods.

OXIDES OF NITROGEN (NOx): Chemical compounds of nitrogen produced as a byproduct of combustion. They combine with hydrocarbons to produce smog.

OXYGEN SENSOR: Use with the feedback system to sense the presence of oxygen in the exhaust gas and signal the computer which can reference the voltage signal to an air/fuel ratio.

PINION: The smaller of two meshing gears.

PISTON RING: An open-ended ring with fits into a groove on the outer diameter of the piston. Its chief function is to form a seal between the piston and cylinder wall. Most automotive pistons have three rings: two for compression sealing; one for oil sealing.

PRELOAD: A predetermined load placed on a bearing during assembly or by adjustment.

PRIMARY CIRCUIT: the low voltage side of the ignition system which consists of the ignition switch, ballast resistor or resistance wire, bypass, coil, electronic control unit and pick-up coil as well as the connecting wires and harnesses.

PRESS FIT: The mating of two parts under pressure, due to the inner diameter of one being smaller than the outer diameter of the other, or vice versa; an interference fit.

RACE: The surface on the inner or outer ring of a bearing on which the balls, needles or rollers move.

REGULATOR: A device which maintains the amperage and/or voltage levels of a circuit at predetermined values.

RELAY: A switch which automatically opens and/or closes a circuit.

RESISTANCE: The opposition to the flow of current through a circuit or electrical device, and is measured in ohms. Resistance is equal to the voltage divided by the amperage.

RESISTOR: A device, usually made of wire, which offers a preset amount of resistance in an electrical circuit.

RING GEAR: The name given to a ring-shaped gear attached to a differential case, or affixed to a flywheel or as part of a planetary gear set.

ROLLER BEARING: A bearing made up of hardened inner and outer races between which hardened steel rollers move.

ROTOR: 1. The disc-shaped part of a disc brake assembly, upon which the brake pads bear; also called, brake disc. 2. The device mounted atop the distributor shaft, which passes current to the distributor cap tower contacts.

SECONDARY CIRCUIT: The high voltage side of the ignition system, usually above 20,000 volts. The secondary includes the ignition coil, coil wire, distributor cap and rotor, spark plug wires and spark plugs.

SENDING UNIT: A mechanical, electrical, hydraulic or electro-magnetic device which transmits information to a gauge.

SENSOR: Any device designed to measure engine operating conditions or ambient pressures and temperatures. Usually electronic in nature and designed to send a voltage signal to an on-board computer, some sensors may operate as a simple on/off switch or they may provide a variable voltage signal (like a potentiometer) as conditions or measured parameters change.

SHIM: Spacers of precise, predetermined thickness used between parts to establish a proper working relationship.

SLAVE CYLINDER: In automotive use, a device in the hydraulic clutch system which is activated by hydraulic force, disengaging the clutch.

SOLENOID: A coil used to produce a magnetic field, the effect of which is to produce work.

SPARK PLUG: A device screwed into the combustion chamber of a spark ignition engine. The basic construction is a conductive core inside of a ceramic insulator, mounted in an outer conductive base. An electrical charge from the spark plug wire travels along the conductive core and jumps a preset air gap to a grounding point or points at the end of the conductive base. The resultant spark ignites the fuel/air mixture in the combustion chamber.

SPLINES: Ridges machined or cast onto the outer diameter of a shaft or inner diameter of a bore to enable parts to mate without rotation.

TACHOMETER: A device used to measure the rotary speed of an engine, shaft, gear, etc., usually in rotations per minute.

THERMOSTAT: A valve, located in the cooling system of an engine, which is closed when cold and opens gradually in response to engine heating, controlling the temperature of the coolant and rate of coolant flow.

TOP DEAD CENTER (TDC): The point at which the piston reaches the top of its travel on the compression stroke.

TORQUE: The twisting force applied to an object.

TORQUE CONVERTER: A turbine used to transmit power from a driving member to a driven member via hydraulic action, providing changes in drive ratio and torque. In automotive use, it links the driveplate at the rear of the engine to the automatic transmission.

TRANSDUCER: A device used to change a force into an electrical signal.

TRANSISTOR: A semi-conductor component which can be actuated by a small voltage to perform an electrical switching function.

TUNE-UP: A regular maintenance function, usually associated with the replacement and adjustment of parts and components in the electrical and fuel systems of a vehicle for the purpose of attaining optimum performance.

TURBOCHARGER: An exhaust driven pump which compresses intake air and forces it into the combustion chambers at higher than atmospheric pressures. The increased air pressure allows more fuel to be burned and results in increased horsepower being produced.

VACUUM ADVANCE: A device which advances the ignition timing in response to increased engine vacuum.

VACUUM GAUGE: An instrument used to measure the presence of vacuum in a chamber.

VALVE: A device which control the pressure, direction of flow or rate of flow of a liquid or gas.

VALVE CLEARANCE: The measured gap between the end of the valve stem and the rocker arm, cam lobe or follower that activates the valve.

VISCOSITY: The rating of a liquid's internal resistance to flow.

VOLTMETER: An instrument used for measuring electrical force in units called volts. Voltmeters are always connected parallel with the circuit being tested.

WHEEL CYLINDER: Found in the automotive drum brake assembly, it is a device, actuated by hydraulic pressure, which, through internal pistons, pushes the brake shoes outward against the drums.

MASTER
INDEX

Total Car Care, continued

Eclipse 1990-98
PART NO. 8415/50400
Pick-Ups and Montero 1983-95
PART NO. 8666/50500

NISSAN
Datsun 210/1200 1973-81
PART NO. 52300
Datsun 200SX/510/610/710/
810/Maxima 1973-84
PART NO. 52302
Nissan Maxima 1985-92
PART NO. 8261/52450
Maxima 1993-98
PART NO. 52452
Pick-Ups and Pathfinder 1970-88
PART NO. 8585/52500
Pick-Ups and Pathfinder 1989-95
PART NO. 8145/52502
Sentra/Pulsar/NX 1982-96
PART NO. 8263/52700

Stanza/200SX/240SX 1982-92
PART NO. 8262/52750
240SX/Altima 1993-98
PART NO. 52752
Datsun/Nissan Z and ZX 1970-88
PART NO. 8846/52800

RENAULT
Coupes/Sedans/Wagons 1975-85
PART NO. 58300

SATURN
Coupes/Sedans/Wagons 1991-98
PART NO. 8419/62300

SUBARU
Coupes/Sedan/Wagons 1970-84
PART NO. 8790/64300
Coupes/Sedans/Wagons 1985-96
PART NO. 8259/64302

SUZUKI
Samurai/Sidekick/Tracker 1986-98
PART NO. 66500

TOYOTA
Camry 1983-96
PART NO. 8265/68200
Celica/Supra 1971-85
PART NO. 68250
Celica 1986-93
PART NO. 8413/68252
Celica 1994-98
PART NO. 68254
Corolla 1970-87
PART NO. 8586/68300
Corolla 1988-97
PART NO. 8414/68302
Cressida/Corona/Crown/MkII 1970-82
PART NO. 68350
Cressida/Van 1983-90
PART NO. 68352
Pick-ups/Land Cruiser/4Runner 1970-88
PART NO. 8578/68600
Pick-ups/Land Cruiser/4Runner 1989-98
PART NO. 8163/68602

Previa 1991-97
PART NO. 68640
Tercel 1984-94
PART NO. 8595/68700

VOLKSWAGEN
Air-Cooled 1949-69
PART NO. 70200
Air-Cooled 1970-81
PART NO. 70202
Front Wheel Drive 1974-89
PART NO. 8663/70400
Golf/Jetta/Cabriolet 1990-93
PART NO. 8429/70402

VOLVO
Coupes/Sedans/Wagons 1970-89
PART NO. 8786/72300
Coupes/Sedans/Wagons 1990-98
PART NO. 8428/72302

General Interest / Recreational Books

We offer specialty books on a variety of topics including Motorcycles, ATVs, Snowmobiles and automotive subjects like Detailing or Body Repair. Each book from our General Interest line offers a blend of our famous Do-It-Yourself procedures and photography with additional information on enjoying automotive, marine and recreational products. Learn more about the vehicles you use and enjoy while keeping them in top running shape.

ATV Handbook
PART NO. 9123
Auto Detailing
PART NO. 8394
Auto Body Repair
PART NO. 7898

Briggs & Stratton Vertical Crankshaft Engine
PART NO. 61-1-2
Briggs & Stratton Horizontal Crankshaft Engine
PART NO. 61-0-4
Briggs & Stratton Overhead Valve (OHV) Engine
PART NO. 61-2-0
Easy Car Care
PART NO. 8042

Motorcycle Handbook
PART NO. 9099
Snowmobile Handbook
PART NO. 9124
Small Engine Repair (Up to 20 Hp)
PART NO. 8325

Total Service Series

These innovative books offer repair, maintenance and service procedures for automotive related systems. They cover today's complex vehicles in a user-friendly format, which places even the most difficult automotive topic well within the reach of every Do-It-Yourselfer. Each title covers a specific subject from Brakes and Engine Rebuilding to Fuel Injection Systems, Automatic Transmissions and even Engine Trouble Codes.

Automatic Transmissions/Transaxles
Diagnosis and Repair
PART NO. 8944
Brake System Diagnosis and Repair
PART NO. 8945
Chevrolet Engine Overhaul Manual
PART NO. 8794

Engine Code Manual
PART NO. 8851
Ford Engine Overhaul Manual
PART NO. 8793
Fuel Injection Diagnosis and Repair
PART NO. 8946

Collector's Hard-Cover Manuals

Chilton's Collector's Editions are perfect for enthusiasts of vintage or rare cars. These hard-cover manuals contain repair and maintenance information for all major systems that might not be available elsewhere. Included are repair and overhaul procedures using thousands of illustrations. These manuals offer a range of coverage from as far back as 1940 and as recent as 1997, so you don't need an antique car or truck to be a collector.

Auto Repair Manual 1993-97
PART NO. 7919
Auto Repair Manual 1988-92
PART NO. 7906
Auto Repair Manual 1980-87
PART NO. 7670
Auto Repair Manual 1972-79
PART NO. 6914
Auto Repair Manual 1964-71
PART NO. 5974

Auto Repair Manual 1954-63
PART NO. 5652
Auto Repair Manual 1940-53
PART NO. 5631
Import Car Repair Manual 1993-97
PART NO. 7920
Import Car Repair Manual 1988-92
PART NO.7907
Import Car Repair Manual 1980-87
PART NO. 7672

Truck and Van Repair Manual 1993-97
PART NO. 7921
Truck and Van Repair Manual 1991-95
PART NO. 7911
Truck and Van Repair Manual 1986-90
PART NO. 7902
Truck and Van Repair Manual 1979-86
PART NO. 7655
Truck and Van Repair Manual 1971-78
PART NO. 7012

3P2VerB